NEIL MACCORMICK

Neil MacCormick (1941–2009) was one of the twentieth century's most important legal philosophers and one of Scotland's most influential public intellectuals. This book tells the story of his political and philosophical life, from his intensely political childhood as the son of 'King John', one of the founders of the Scottish National Party, through to his involvement in Scottish politics – especially as the author of SNP's constitutional policy – and his role as a Member of the European Parliament, helping to draft the European Constitution. With special attention to MacCormick's character, this book offers a reading of his entire oeuvre, covering his contributions to theories of legal and moral reasoning, institutional legal theory, nationalism, post-sovereignty, subsidiarity, and constitutional pluralism in Europe. This book reads MacCormick as a highly creative thinker who excelled in the art of constructing inclusive middles and thereby developed his own distinctive approach to politics and philosophy.

MAKSYMILIAN DEL MAR is Professor of Legal Theory and Legal Humanities at the School of Law, Queen Mary University of London.

NEIL MACCORMICK

A Life in Politics, Philosophy, and Law

MAKSYMILIAN DEL MAR
Queen Mary University of London

CAMBRIDGE
UNIVERSITY PRESS

CAMBRIDGE
UNIVERSITY PRESS

Shaftesbury Road, Cambridge CB2 8EA, United Kingdom

One Liberty Plaza, 20th Floor, New York, NY 10006, USA

477 Williamstown Road, Port Melbourne, VIC 3207, Australia

314–321, 3rd Floor, Plot 3, Splendor Forum, Jasola District Centre, New Delhi – 110025, India

103 Penang Road, #05–06/07, Visioncrest Commercial, Singapore 238467

Cambridge University Press is part of Cambridge University Press & Assessment, a department of the University of Cambridge.

We share the University's mission to contribute to society through the pursuit of education, learning and research at the highest international levels of excellence.

www.cambridge.org
Information on this title: www.cambridge.org/9781009609883

DOI: 10.1017/9781009609937

When citing this work, please include a reference to the DOI 10.1017/9781009609937

First published 2025
First paperback edition 2025

Cover image: Neil MacCormick, Edinburgh 2016, detail of bust by Kenny Hunter. Photo by Olga Tyukova.

A catalogue record for this publication is available from the British Library

Library of Congress Cataloging-in-Publication data
Names: Del Mar, Maksymilian, 1979– author.
Title: Neil MacCormick : a life in politics, philosophy, and law / Maksymilian del Mar, Queen Mary University of London.
Description: Cambridge, United Kingdom ; New York, NY : Cambridge University Press, 2025. | Includes bibliographical references and index.
Identifiers: LCCN 2024057545 | ISBN 9781009609913 (hardback) | ISBN 9781009609883 (paperback) | ISBN 9781009609937 (ebook)
Subjects: LCSH: MacCormick, Neil – Political and social views. | Law – Scotland – Philosophy. | Law – Political aspects – Scotland. | Law – Philosophy. | Law – Moral and ethical aspects. | Philosophers – Scotland – Biography.
Classification: LCC KDC318 .D45 2025 | DDC 328.4092 [B]–dc23/eng/20241203
LC record available at https://lccn.loc.gov/2024057545

ISBN 978-1-009-60991-3 Hardback
ISBN 978-1-009-60988-3 Paperback

For Alexandra

It is with good reason, says Sancho to the squire with the great nose, that I pretend to have a judgment in wine: this is a quality hereditary in our family. Two of my kinsmen were once called to give their opinion of a hogshead, which was supposed to be excellent, being old and of a good vintage. One of them tastes it; considers it; and after mature reflection pronounces the wine to be good, were it not for a small taste of leather, which he perceived in it. The other, after using the same precautions, gives also his verdict in favour of the wine; but with the reserve of a taste of iron, which he could easily distinguish. You cannot imagine how much they were both ridiculed for their judgment. But who laughed in the end? On emptying the hogshead, there was found at the bottom, an old key with a leathern thong tied to it.

David Hume, *Of the Standard of Taste*, 1757

Another finds himself urged by need to borrow money. He well knows that he will not be able to repay it but sees also that nothing will be lent him unless he promises firmly to repay it within a determinate time. He would like to make such a promise, but he still has enough conscience to ask himself: is it not forbidden and contrary to duty to help oneself out of need in such a way? Supposing that he still decided to do so, his maxim of action would go as follows: when I believe myself to be in need of money I shall borrow money and promise to repay it, even though I know that this will never happen. Now this principle of self-love or personal advantage is perhaps quite consistent with my whole future welfare, but the question now is whether it is right. I therefore turn the demand of self-love into a universal law and put the question as follows: how would it be if my maxim became a universal law?

Immanuel Kant, *Groundwork of the Metaphysics of Morals*, 1785

CONTENTS

ACKNOWLEDGEMENTS

When one writes a book as long as I have been writing this one, one acquires many debts – too many to acknowledge. Nevertheless, there are several people, as well as several institutions, who I would like to thank. Without them and their support, this book would never have been written.

Firstly: Flora MacCormick. Flora not only allowed me access to MacCormick's papers after his death; she was also unfailingly supportive without ever putting me under the slightest pressure. Flora once said to me, in a moment – one of many – in which I struggled with this project: 'Neil would have wanted you to enjoy it'. Indeed, it was only once I found a way to enjoy it that the book became writeable. Flora has welcomed me into her home for so many years and trusted me often with the most precious of archival material. The faith and trust that Flora has bestowed upon me has been one of the most important sources of inspiration for me in writing this book. Thank you, Flora.

I had two supervisors in Edinburgh: MacCormick and Zenon Bańkowski. Zenon has been a father to me, as he was to so many of his PhD students. He is the first to express anxiety, as befits a true Pole, but his writing is fearlessly creative and self-inquisitive, and through that, and his teaching, as well as in countless conversations and in everyday moments, he has shown me what it might mean to live as a philosopher. Without Zenon's counsel and support, this book would never have been written. Dziękuję kochany.

It was William Twining who, in his endlessly energetic way, suggested the possibility of a book on MacCormick to me, all the way back in 2007. It was also William who, often when I had been neglecting this project for too long, got back in touch, to see how things were going and to express never-ending enthusiasm for the idea. Bursting with insight and brimming with curiosity and playfulness, but also determined and practical minded, William has been the most wonderful of companions to this project. He, too, is a father of sorts to it. Thank you, William.

Neil Walker, who succeeded MacCormick in the Regius Chair in Edinburgh, has become, ever since I got to know him soon after his appointment in 2008, a most supportive and kind friend. Neil patiently and generously listened to and read various attempts over the years at framing the project. He also read the entire manuscript and gave invaluable encouragement and feedback. Thank you, Neil.

Within my home institution, at the School of Law at Queen Mary University of London, I have been blessed to have both deans and colleagues who, from the outset of this project, were hugely supportive and expressed interest in it. Again, I cannot mention everyone, but I would like to thank: Roger Cotterrell and Michael Lobban, who were present when I first arrived at Queen Mary, and who encouraged me early on, and have continued to listen to me with great patience about MacCormick over the years; Kenneth Armstrong, also an early colleague who later left for Cambridge and who encouraged me at just the right time; Lizzie Barmes, who was a very supportive Director of Research in the later stages of this project, again encouraging me when the going got tough; and my various collaborators in the Centre for Law and Society in a Global Context, including Tanzil Chowdhury, Sionaidh Douglas-Scott, Noam Gur, Eva Nanopoulos, and Isobel Roele. Colleagues in the School of History at Queen Mary have also been very supportive, and I thank in particular: Andrew Fitzmaurice, Miri Rubin, Quentin Skinner (together with Susan James), Gareth Stedman-Jones, and Georgios Varouxakis.

There are so many colleagues and friends who have been enormously important to me, especially in relation to this project. Many have shared memories of MacCormick with me and sometimes also their correspondence with him. Many have simply expressed a kind interest in the project and supported me with words of encouragement. I cannot list everyone, but I warmly thank: Amalia Amaya, Fernando Atria, Karen Barr (MacCormick's first wife), Joxerramon Bengoetxea, Stefano Bertea, Jes Bjarup, Stephen Bogle, Alexander Broadie, John Cairns, James Chalmers, Emilios Christodoulidis, Sharon Cowan, Rowan Cruft, Keith Culver, Adam Czarnota, Julie Dickson, Robin Downie, Owen Dudley Edwards, Antony Duff, Paul du Plessis, David Edward, Pavlos Eleftheriadis, Lindsay Farmer, Joshua Getzler, Michael Giudice, Peter Goodrich, Randy Gordon, Jaap Hage, Andrew Halpin, Duncan Hamilton, Conrado Hubner Mendes, Caroline Humfress, Lorna Hutson, Chloe Kennedy, Colin Kidd, Martin Krygier, Nicola Lacey, Massimo La Torre, Cormac Mac Amhlaigh, Hector MacQueen, Gerry Maher, Roger Mason, Emmanuel Melissaris, Claudio Michelon, James Mitchell, Oche Onazi, Haris Psarras, Joseph Raz, Elspeth

Reid, Kenneth Reid, Nicole Roughan, Burkhard Schafer, Frederick Schauer, Drew Scott, Jo Shaw, Niamh Nic Shuibhne, Richard Sparks, David Sugarman, Sanne Taekema, Brian Tamanaha, Stephen Tierney, Christopher Tomlins, Scott Veitch, Vittorio Villa, Kevin Walton, and Gordon Wilson.

Several institutions invited and hosted me to give talks on MacCormick, and I am very grateful to the organisers and audiences on these occasions. These included the Institute for Advanced Studies in the Humanities and the School of Law in Edinburgh in 2011; Osgoode Hall School of Law in Toronto in 2013; the Legal Biography Project at the London School of Economics in 2014; the Centre for European Legal Studies at the University of Cambridge in 2014; the Legal Philosophy Forum at the Faculty of Laws, University College London, in 2014; the School of Law at the National University of Singapore in 2015; the Edinburgh Legal Theory Research Group and the Centre for Law and Society, both in Edinburgh Law School, in 2015; the Institute of Scottish Historical Research at the University of St Andrews in 2015; the UK IVR (the United Kingdom branch of the International Society for Legal and Social Philosophy), online in September 2022, for the Inaugural Lecture named in honour of MacCormick; the Faculty of Law at the University of Helsinki in 2024; and Edinburgh Law School in June 2024.

I have also received vital financial support for this project, especially from the Leverhulme Trust (2013–14) and the British Academy (2020–21), who each funded research fellowships and without which I would never have been able to do the research that forms the basis of this book. The Royal Society of Edinburgh also funded a research stay during a crucial period, early in the project, at the Institute for Advanced Studies in the Humanities (May–June 2011), where I had the immense pleasure of meeting the-then director Susan Manning, whose work remains an inspiration. My home institution, Queen Mary University of London, also provided a number of crucial periods of sabbatical leave and some extra research time. For the last few years, I have been a visiting scholar at Edinburgh Law School, and this has also enabled much-needed access to resources, especially a quiet place to read and write (special thanks to the Research Office Team, especially Shauna Thompson and Stephanie Lewis). The staff of various libraries and archives have helped hugely, including in the libraries of the Universities of Glasgow and Edinburgh (special thanks to Graeme Eddie), as well as at Balliol College, Oxford, and the Oxford Union archives in Oxford, and the National Library of Scotland. I am also grateful to Ms Amanda Green, Librarian at the High School of Glasgow.

Finally, but of course also firstly, I thank my wife, Alexandra Braun, and my son, Tristan Del Mar. Tristan has changed and brightened my life in endless ways, including via the countless hours we spent reading together. As partners often do, Alexandra has suffered the most through this project's most intense stages, but she never faltered in her support and love, even when, as was frequent, I'd lost faith or connection with the world beyond the book. It was Alexandra who spurred me on to finish writing this book, when I had almost given up hope that I could do it. She deserves the greatest credit for this book coming to completion, and I dedicate the book to her.

Introduction

Reading with Character

What is it to read another person well? This book is an extended meditation on this question, and an essay – in the old sense of that word of an attempt – at reading another. The question of how to read another person is itself tied up with a broader question: how ought we to relate to each other? At its deepest, then, this book concerns the ethics of relation, including as exemplified by the challenge of reading.

It is possible that this question – of the particular ethics of reading, the broader ethics of relation – arose as the guiding animus of this project because of how, as I have come to think, it mattered to the person I read in this book: Neil MacCormick. There are certain terms, and associated themes, in MacCormick's philosophical as much as his political vocabulary, that appear again and again: respect, decency, civility, inclusiveness, and considerateness.

MacCormick is deeply sensitive to relations going badly: to relations of domination and exploitation, and breaches of trust, but also to more prosaic forms of relational injustice, such as disappointing another or letting each other down, e.g., not taking one's children to the beach after promising to do so. MacCormick's sensitivity to relational injustice thus ranges very widely: from intergovernmental relations or the relations between governments and their citizens, all the way through to everyday, interpersonal relations, where persons deliberate together or simply live with each other.

In fact, this relational sensitivity goes yet further, in ways that connect closely to MacCormick's various roles: as a teacher vis-à-vis students, as a colleague in a college, a faculty, or a university, as a member of a political party, as a philosopher in relation to other disciplines, as a scholar in relation to those in practice, as a member of an Anglo-American community of philosophy vis-à-vis continental European traditions, and much else besides. Everywhere one looks, and in ways that MacCormick sometimes explicitly reflects on throughout his work, the good of relations matters.

Indeed, this sensitivity to relational injustice, and the importance of good relations, is so acute and so deep running in MacCormick that it also colours the tenor or style of his thought and expression: MacCormick, one could say, in the very concepts he employs and how he expresses them, as well as in his methods, adopts and promotes attitudes that aim to bring persons together into peaceful, though not homogenous, relations. Concepts such as a post-sovereign commonwealth governed and animated by subsidiarity, or the Smithian Categorical Imperative, or social democracy, or 'Scotland in Europe', or civic or liberal nationalism, or indeed whole bodies of theory like the institutional theory of law, are all expressions of this relational sensitivity.

MacCormick's concern, throughout, is to not only criticise failures of relational justice; it is also, more positively, to construct inter-subjective spaces where difference can be maintained, and respected – for that, too, is part of the ethics of relation – but where persons can still be engaged together in a common enterprise. His conceptual poetics is one of peace, moderation, and reconciliation: it is about keeping relations going.

This relational sensitivity, as MacCormick practices it, extends to how one sees oneself and one's role in a community, including as a philosopher: does one see oneself, and philosophy, as epistemically superior and thus legitimately in charge of a community, or does one instead see oneself, and philosophy, as but a particular kind of participant – no more, but also no less, than a stone in an arch – aiming to maintain good relations in communal life? MacCormick is very much in the latter category: he creates – in his politics and in his philosophy, and thus in his political actions as well as in his philosophical theories – differential unities, complex middle spaces, and mechanisms for balanced, non-dominating, respect-preserving, decent, caring, and considerate relations.

Of course, this relational sensitivity, this critique of relational injustice and this practice of constructive differential unity, results in a particular approach to power and authority, and consequently, in a certain way of theorising law. It permeates not only MacCormick's approach to the most general questions of jurisprudence, but also to his readings of particular cases, and his concern with the detailed, messy, practice of legal reasoning (indeed, it is part of why he pays so much attention to so many cases, thereby seeking to balance theory and practice). It also colours his involvement in politics, including how he configures and situates the relations between Scotland and England, and the United Kingdom (UK) and the European Union (EU), but also how he himself acts in relation to others in various communities he is part of, from the Scottish National Party through to his life as an academic, both in his beloved University of Edinburgh, as well as in broader communities, such as the International Association for Legal and Social Philosophy.

Given the breadth and depth of MacCormick's involvement in both politics and philosophy, including his particular interests in the law, balancing all these aspects, and giving each of them their due, quickly becomes very complex. It is my challenge, in this book, to bring them together, and to balance them, and in so doing, to tell a story about how I have read MacCormick. The concept and approach I draw on, in telling this story, is 'character', i.e., what I do in this book is read MacCormick with character.

Character is a somewhat cumbersome term, and one also burdened by reliance on it in biographies of another age, which may strike us today as outdated and overtly moralistic, celebrating some great person – typically a white, privileged male – as a hero or a saint. Of course, that is not my aim. Instead, I am drawing on a notion of character as itself relational, i.e., as helping me track, as I read MacCormick, both in his politics and in his philosophy, his manner or style of relating with others.

The 'character', then, that I have in mind, as I 'read with character', is very much a relational one (in many ways, this mirrors the very substance of MacCormick's thought, i.e., as above, his relational sensitivity). As a methodological principle, character – understood as the manner or style of relating with others – allows me, or so I hope, to avoid certain ways of reading the work of another that strike me as inadequate, while also striving to balance a number of considerations that strike me as important.

One of the pitfalls I seek to avoid is reading another with a view to summarising their beliefs, properly reconstructed, and supported, as one evaluates this, by reference to a certain set of arguments. The reading I have attempted does not wish to iron out the difficulties of philosophising – those hesitations, roads taken and then abandoned, inconsistencies, all those confusions and anomalies; I want to embrace those difficulties, and thus help illuminate the complexity of another's thought. Even more so than this, I want to look beneath the surface of the text – though often precisely by paying attention to, rather than ignoring, its surface forms of expression – and try to understand its animating concerns, its passions, its struggles and attitudes.

The concept of character I employ, then, is partly an attempt to read without (or at least with less) summary, and thus also without forcing the thought of another into any particular label (e.g., that of a positivist, or a nationalist). Again, this is in keeping with how I have come to read MacCormick: rather than fixing himself into a certain identity, which was then to be defended against all incomers, MacCormick often found a way of being that related dynamically with others, including being willing to transform himself in the process. Yes, MacCormick was Scottish, and proudly so; yes, he was a philosopher; yes, he was a Scottish nationalist, of a kind; but in all these, and other identities, he was reflexively inclusive, seeking to occupy a space in the middle, the difficult and unsettling middle, and thereby enable respectful and considerate relations, whether that be between Scotland and England, or positivist and natural law traditions, or analytical and sociological approaches to law.

Equally, the concept of character I employ seeks to balance, for instance, the sense in which a person is both a self-conscious and deliberate agent and someone caught up in forces larger than themselves. My claim in this book is not that MacCormick strategically employs and instrumentally projects, a kind of character in order to achieve certain ends. In fact, there are plenty of moments, in MacCormick's own corpus, where he thinks of himself in certain ways (e.g., sometimes, as a positivist) that are at odds with how I read him (e.g., as someone who was never quite a positivist, but instead worked to relate and reconcile positivist and natural law intuitions). MacCormick was not a fully self-conscious, strategic actor; he was, like all of us, uncertain and fragmented in his awareness of the broader forces that were shaping him and others around him, which often only become visible (and even then, only partly) in hindsight. He was caught up in languages and images, institutions and communities, that were larger than him, and that carried him, to an extent involuntarily, in various directions.

Thus, the concept of character I employ seeks to be sensitive to the sense in which we are never quite in control of our own lives, even while we seek to guide it and shape it. In other words, MacCormick's character – i.e., his manner or style of relating with others – is not always found explicitly in his own writings and reflections; just as often, and even more so, it is found in his actions, in his modes of expression, in the attitudes he displays or performs. Character, in that sense, is less strategic or deliberate, and less determined or structured, as it is lived, precisely in this middle space – that difficult to capture, balanced space between agency and structure.

At stake, too, in the concept of character I use, or in the method of reading with character, is another kind of balancing act: balancing the political and the philosophical. My claim in this book is certainly not that, for instance, MacCormick's politics determines his philosophy; nor is it the other way round. I am interested, instead, in maintaining the tension, or if you like, tense collaboration, between the two: sometimes MacCormick dwells more intensely in one world, and sometimes in the other; sometimes he relates them closely together and sometimes he tries to keep them well apart; sometimes he borrows something from one and moves it over to the other, thereby dissolving any boundaries between them, while at other times he sees them as competing with one another, as if he must choose between doing one or the other. Thus, his experiences in politics – in his childhood, for example – do not determine his philosophy; instead, his philosophical education and practice allows him to reflect on and qualify his experiences in various ways. Equally, though, one cannot say that his philosophy operates in some vacuum outside his political interests and concerns. The relationship is complex – it is a relational complexity in its own right – and it is precisely this complexity that interests me, and that I try to hang on to with the concept of character.

Of course, it is one thing to try to hang on to complexity, and another to write a (I hope!) coherent book. The challenge, then, was to find a way of writing a book, and telling a story, and thus aiming at some level of coherence and unity, while not summarising MacCormick as if he was but a set of propositions, a wrinkle-free and easily portable or usable set of philosophical theses and political beliefs. Thus, when I try to read with character, I try to pay attention to the particular circumstances in which relations occur: if character, as I think of it, is the manner or style with which one relates with others, then one needs to understand the circumstances of any particular relational occasion or set of occasions. There may be echoes across those circumstances – again, I am after a certain style or manner of relating with others, and this implies some continuity and consistency – but I try to remain aware, throughout, that this can never be pushed so far as to suggest that a person has one character, for their whole life, which determines all they do. Instead, my point is to try to track, to describe, to consider both continuities and discontinuities, echoes and anomalies, in and across the circumstances in which MacCormick relates with others.

Whether the concept of 'character', and the method of 'reading with character', that I use in this book, is robust or clear enough, to hold all this, is another matter. Again, this book is an essay – an attempt – at reading another, and one that I am conscious is but a very partial and necessarily incomplete reading. Character, as I am trying to use it, is not meant to flatten, summarise, or fix MacCormick into one box; it is, in a way, an attempt to offer a portrait of MacCormick himself as a kind of differential unity – relating with others, in a certain manner or style, but in many different circumstances and with particular inflexions and intonations, which are always to an extent in dynamic friction with each other. It is an attempt to pay my respects to the complexity of MacCormick as a philosopher and a political actor, and indeed to philosophy and politics more generally and the complex roles they play in culture.

Knowing MacCormick

There is another kind of relation, and thus also another character, that is at stake in this book. And that is my own relation with MacCormick, and thus also my character as a reader and writer. There is always such a relation, between the author and the subject they write about, but it is even more complicated in this instance because I knew MacCormick. Thus, this is a book about MacCormick, but it is not ultimately his character that is on the line; it is the character of my reading and writing. This is a reading, and a book written, from a certain perspective, from a certain set of experiences, coloured by a certain set of emotions, including those I felt and still feel towards MacCormick. It is thus appropriate – and I hope not indulgent – to say a few words about how I knew him.

Before I met him, and even before I read him, I heard his name mentioned in a lecture – as an undergraduate student in the early 2000s, studying jurisprudence as part of a law degree at the University of Queensland in Brisbane, Australia. At that time, MacCormick was largely presented to me as a disciple of the great English legal philosopher, H. L. A. Hart, with whom he had, so I was told, studied in Oxford, and whose work he amended and refined. Thus, at that time, I had heard of him and duly read his philosophy as but a series of modest footnotes to Hart's analytical legal positivism. I do not think I even realised at that time that MacCormick was Scottish; certainly, this was not something identified as relevant in jurisprudential classes.

Not too long after my first encounter with MacCormick's work, an opportunity arose to invite him to give a lecture to an organisation I was then running – the Australian Legal Philosophy Students Association. As luck would have it, in 2004, MacCormick was visiting Sydney, and his hosts there – in particular, Martin Krygier and Adam Czarnota – were generously open to MacCormick taking in a brief detour to Brisbane. To my astonishment, MacCormick came, together with his wife, Flora, and delivered a lecture – in a Scottish accent! – on whether law was a system of rules (which was duly published in 2005). At the dinner after the lecture, I had the honour and pleasure – truly a pleasure, as anyone who knew MacCormick will attest – of sitting next to him, undoubtedly pestering him with my over-enthusiasm for legal philosophy. I also had the pleasure, then, of meeting Flora, and already then, even if dimly, realising how important she was to his life. In due course, and after encouragement from MacCormick, I applied, and was accepted, for a doctorate in legal philosophy at the University of Edinburgh, MacCormick's academic home.

During those years – from 2006 to 2009 – I read his work again (although, as was typical of Edinburgh, it was never expected that one would focus, and I also did not focus, on interpreting MacCormick's oeuvre or even writing on the same problems as he had worked on). As luck would have it, I was present at just the right time to be privileged enough to be able to help act as a proofreader for two texts MacCormick was then working on: the second edition of his H. L. A. Hart book, published in 2008, and, a little later, the manuscript of his final book, *Practical Reason in Law and Morality*, also published in 2008.

2007 was also the year in which MacCormick had just published what he considered, at the time, to be his magnum opus, *Institutions of Law* (2007). I also read this work, and was again fortunate in co-organising, with my other supervisor and long-time friend of MacCormick's, Zenon Bańkowski, a conference on that book. That conference resulted in an edited collection (*Law as Institutional Normative Order*, 2009), which included many of MacCormick's friends and colleagues responding to this statement of his general jurisprudence. By this time, in 2007, I had become a more thorough reader of MacCormick's work, taking in also *Questioning Sovereignty* (1999) and *Rhetoric and the Rule of Law* (2005).

In truth, however, although by the end of 2007 I had read much more of his work, I was still deeply influenced by the view that MacCormick was a Hartian positivist – an Oxford-trained analytical philosopher who defended positivism (according to some, not especially successfully) against its various attacks, especially those of Ronald Dworkin, and whose own contribution was to extend Hart's view of the nature of law to a theory of legal reasoning and a theory of transnational legal authority (whether in the form of constitutional pluralism in the UK or the post-sovereign order of the EU).

At this point, I had come to appreciate a little better the Scottish context in which MacCormick lived and worked; I, too, after all, was studying in Scotland. Nevertheless, I did not reflect or investigate deeply what this might mean. I did not think geographically or historically about jurisprudence – I was too deeply embedded in the debates of contemporary Anglo–American jurisprudence, which largely operated without any reflexivity about the political geography of legal philosophy.

Furthermore, it was still mainly MacCormick's more recent work – his quartet of books from 1999 to 2008 – that I had digested. I did, slowly, begin, at that time, to read some of the earlier work – especially his *Legal Reasoning and Legal Theory* (1978) – but even when I did so, I still read this with the same kind of historiographical lens, i.e., with MacCormick as a disciple of Hartian positivism and with a strong identity as an Oxford analytical philosopher.

It was at this time, in late 2007, soon after the above-mentioned conference on *Institutions of Law*, that I first met William Twining – a long-time colleague and friend of MacCormick's. Amongst numerous hats, Twining was then editing and actively commissioning for a series of books called the *Jurists in Profile* series. It was Twining, intellectually enterprising as always, who first floated the idea of a book on MacCormick in the series and I, being both naïve and ambitious to a fault, with no sense of what I was taking on, said that I would love to do it. As it began, then, the idea was that I would offer a sympathetically critical overview or summary of MacCormick's main contributions to jurisprudence, much like, I was told, MacCormick himself did in his 1981 book on Hart. Naturally, even the slightest hint of a parallel flattered my vanity.

All these plans, and much else, was put on hold and placed into the cruellest of perspectives in the first quarter of 2008. On the day after his first official day of his retirement – 1 February 2008 – MacCormick had felt unwell. After a series of tests and diagnoses, he was told he had an incurable cancer, and did not have long to live (indeed, he was initially told three months). It was some time before this news reached all of us in the Edinburgh community, including me and my fellow PhD students. I had some inkling then, but only an inkling, of the outpouring of sympathy that came from so many quarters, not only from colleagues in philosophy, but also from his friends and acquaintances in politics, both in Scotland but also more widely in Europe and beyond.

MacCormick did not entirely stop working after his diagnosis, and, although I saw him less than many of his colleagues and friends at the time, I recall with great pleasure, though accompanied by great sadness, meetings with him, both about my doctoral research as well as about his final book, which he was then trying to finish. In one meeting, I struck up the courage to mention to him I was thinking about writing a book about him: he must have exercised great self-control not to dismiss it out of hand.

MacCormick died on 5 April 2009. He had, in the end, nine months after his diagnosis. Having had so many plans for his retirement, especially with a view to finally – after an intense five years in the European Parliament and then back in academia – enjoying a quieter life with his wife, Flora, he had in the end so little. His death was an enormous loss to so many, in and beyond his family, in both philosophy and politics. For me also, his death meant the loss of a mentor I was only beginning to know, since those few days in Australia in 2005. I missed him a great deal, as I still very much do.

Meanwhile, in 2009, I had defended my thesis and also left Edinburgh. In the years that followed, I returned to read MacCormick – not consistently, as I was often distracted by other projects, but then at certain times, again, very intensively, often thanks to funding breaks (from the Leverhulme Trust and the British Academy). Slowly, little by little, I realised how little I knew about MacCormick: I learnt more about his childhood in Glasgow and his remarkable political family; I learnt more about his teachers, especially in Glasgow, and his early passions already then, and continuously thereafter, for the thinkers of the Scottish Enlightenment; I learnt more about his involvement, often behind the scenes, in the SNP and in Scottish politics more generally; I learnt more about the constitutional, legal, and cultural history of Scotland; I learnt more about the contexts and communities in which MacCormick participated, including the student debating societies in Glasgow and Oxford, and the universities he taught at (Dundee, Oxford, and Edinburgh), as well as the various political and other community associations, organisations, inquiries, and committees he was part of, and the philosophical communities he was engaged in.

As I did this, thereby reading him now for over twenty years, I looked for ways in which I could read him more carefully, more slowly than I was often prone to reading him. Could I read MacCormick without rushing to agree or disagree with him? Could I read him without hurrying to put a label on his jurisprudence? What really might it mean that he was a Scottish philosopher, or a Glaswegian-trained philosopher, as well as an Oxford-trained one? How could MacCormick be so local, but so cosmopolitan at the same time? How could I connect – if I should connect at all – the political and the philosophical in his work? How, in short, could I and should I read him? And what did all this say about me as a reader and why did this matter? This book is an attempt at wrestling with these questions, and thereby, by reading the character of another, to reflect on my own character, especially as a reader.

In many ways, the emotions I felt, and still feel, as a result of having had the immeasurable privilege of knowing MacCormick are the worst possible ingredients for writing a book. For a long time, the only book I found myself writing was a homage – a monument, in celebration of his life and work. If I was not writing a homage, then, as a reaction to that, I would move too far in the other direction, critiquing and caricaturing, or simply ignoring what was before me. It took me a long time to find a degree of both intimacy and distance that I could live with. I hope this book shows how immensely fortunate I feel to have known MacCormick, and how passionate I am about the value of his thought, but also that it is disciplined enough not to descend into hagiography.

The Structure of This Book

As Chapter 1 of this book describes, MacCormick was born into a very political family. His father, John, and his mother, Margaret, were both, in different ways, deeply involved in Scottish politics. John MacCormick, also known as 'King John', won many headlines in the Scottish press in the 1930s, 1940s, and 1950s: he was, for instance, one of the founders of the Glasgow University Nationalist Student Association (GUSNA), which he established while a law student in Glasgow, and he went on to play a leading role in creating first the National Party of Scotland (NPS, in 1928), and then the Scottish National Party (SNP, in 1934). Following a split with the SNP in 1942, he established the Scottish Constitutional Convention, and, a few years later, the Scottish Covenant (1949–51), a cross-party political movement for home rule in Scotland, which attracted 2,000,000 signatures. He was also Rector of the University of Glasgow (1950–53), a key player in the taking (1950) and then eventual return (1951) of the Stone of Destiny, and the petitioner in the famous case of *MacCormick* v *Lord Advocate* (1953). Margaret MacCormick, meanwhile, though she did not win any headlines, was the rock on which the family was built, running a busy political household, with four children, including herself doing vital communal work, as a social worker, in some of Glasgow's poorest areas. It is into this family that MacCormick was born in 1941, experiencing the above highly emotionally charged political events as a boy of between 8 and 12.

MacCormick was thus born into one of the familial crucibles of Scottish mid century nationalist politics. Nevertheless, he is not easily classifiable as a nationalist, at least if one understands by that the pursuit of independence for Scotland in the form of a sovereign state. In fact, one way to approach MacCormick, the politician, is to trace how, over the course of many years, he confronted his own political inheritance, and how, philosophically, he examined his own commitment to nationalism. Philosophy, then, was never far away from the politics. Was nationalism philosophically credible? This was an important – indeed deeply personal and existential – question for MacCormick, and one that I begin to reflect on in Chapter 1, and then focus on in Chapter 7.

Philosophy and politics were also interwoven in other ways, earlier in MacCormick's life: as Chapters 2–4 explore, MacCormick was simultaneously a student – studying philosophy and literature in Glasgow (1959–63) and then law in Oxford (1963–65) – while, at the same time, being very active in student politics. Echoing his father, MacCormick became President of GUSNA, and was a leading member of the remarkable generation of debaters at the University of Glasgow, which included many debaters that became his personal, life-long friends, e.g., Donald Dewar and John Smith, both such prominent figures in Scottish and British political life. He wrote and edited numerous student publications in Glasgow and, in Oxford, he became both the Librarian and then President of the Oxford Union. In all this, or so I argue, he related with others in a certain manner or style: he participated in certain ways in the various political communities he was part of, thereby developing and negotiating his character. Indeed, his time as a debater, as well as an editor and contributor to student publications, was crucial for him, shaping and informing his subsequent philosophical interests, especially in the ethics and politics of practical reason.

As Chapter 3, in particular, illustrates, while participating actively in student politics, MacCormick was being formed as a philosopher. Here, too, character plays a role, for MacCormick found his own way of relating with his teachers or his predecessors, i.e., the philosophers from the past that he reads and wrestles with. His teachers here included W. D. Lamont, a moral philosopher whose particular approach to moral philosophy built bridges with the practice of law, as well as others, such as Robin Downie and David Raphael, all of whom, as was customary then in Glasgow, were devoted both to reflecting on the methods and aims of moral philosophy, as well as to interpreting the moral philosophers of the Enlightenment. This last point is important: much of the debate in Glasgow at the time revolved around the relationship between Kant and the Scots, such as Hume and Smith. Thus, the education that MacCormick received in Glasgow was very much an education in Scottish moral philosophy. Showing what this meant is the aim of Chapter 3.

Thus, when MacCormick arrived in Oxford, in 1963, he did not come as an empty slate, to be written on by Oxford analytical jurisprudence, and especially by H. L. A. Hart. Rather, he came as an already highly educated Glaswegian moral philosopher, interested, for instance, in the logic of moral reasoning and interested, too, in the relationship between law and morality. MacCormick's legal studies at Balliol College, Oxford, are the topic of Chapter 4, and here too we confront MacCormick's relations with his teachers, including Alan Watson, Donald Harris, and R. M. Hare (the last of these, though not formally a teacher of MacCormick's, was nevertheless, through his writings, an important influence on MacCormick). At the same time, we see MacCormick active in Oxford student politics, especially with respect to race relations, e.g., MacCormick is the Librarian at the time of Malcolm X's famous speech to the Oxford Union in 1964. We also see MacCormick relating with others in particular ways when touring America in the summer of 1965 (with, amongst others, Chris Patten, the future Governor of Hong Kong), courtesy of a Balliol Pathfinder scholarship. Here, we read, with character, MacCormick's American diary, showing how he wrestled with the difficult and delicate racial politics of mid 1960s America.

Upon graduating from Oxford in 1965, MacCormick took up his first teaching job in Dundee Law School, which at the time was radically changing its legal pedagogy under the leadership of Ian Willock. Chapter 5 considers these two years in Dundee, and thus MacCormick's early formation as a teacher, going on to focus on his time, from 1967 to 1972, as a College tutor in law in Balliol College, Oxford. In those years, MacCormick cut his legal philosophical teeth in the justly famous jurisprudential discussions that were then held with, inter alia, Hart, Ronald Dworkin, Joseph Raz, John Finnis, and numerous others.

These 'legal philosophical teeth', however, were not cut in isolation from the politics of the period: in fact, MacCormick's relations with Hart need to be set in the context of the various debates over student discipline and university authority, including academic authority, of the mid-to-late 1960s. Hart played a crucial role in this time in Oxford, authoring the famous Hart Report in 1969, while MacCormick, who was of course much less senior, also had several crucial roles, both within Balliol as, for instance, the Head of its Disciplinary Rules Committee, as well as at the University, as one of its Pro-Proctors. Chapter 5 thus tackles MacCormick's relationship with Hart, but within the context of the heady days of student unrest in the mid-to-late 1960s.

In 1972, at the age of thirty-one, MacCormick was chosen as the University of Edinburgh's Regius Professor of Public Law and the Law of

Nature and Nations. He was to stay in this role for the next thirty-six years, before retiring in 2008. In those thirty-six years, MacCormick once again combined a rich philosophical life with an astoundingly busy political one. Having become a member of the SNP in the wake of Winnie Ewing's famous by-election victory in 1967, once in Edinburgh, MacCormick threw himself, with remarkable energy, into either supporting other SNP candidates – such as his brother, Iain, who was one of the MPs elected in the two 1974 elections – or into SNP committee work, especially its Constitutional Policy Committee. This included fighting to win the 1979 referendum on home rule, as well as standing as an SNP candidate in no less than five Westminster elections (none of them successfully).

MacCormick's involvement in Scottish and British politics, however, was by no means confined to activity within the SNP. MacCormick had a complex relationship with the SNP. He contributed to it enormously – whether that be through drafting the SNP's Draft Constitution for a Future Independent Scotland or advising its leadership on the constitutional relations of Scotland with the UK and Europe. But he was also sometimes very publicly critical of the party, as when, for instance, in the 1980s, it refused to be part of the Claim of Right. Further, all alongside this, MacCormick developed his own political philosophy.

Chapters 6 and 7 tell this story of MacCormick's contribution to politics in Scotland and to political philosophy. Chapter 6 focuses more on MacCormick's conceptualisation of obligations and rights, the relationship between law, liberalism, and justice, as well as his construction of a social democratic vision. We see MacCormick working as a jurist concerned with the practice of good government, i.e., one that protects civil liberties, but also one that is not too powerful, and thus diffused and decentralised. This has many concrete manifestations, including MacCormick's contribution to the Edinburgh University Settlement.

Chapter 7, in turn, as noted above, focuses on MacCormick's theorisation of nationalism and constitutional change, as well as his involvement in Scottish nationalist politics. Throughout, I pay particular attention, reading with character, to the kind of concepts MacCormick crafts in his political philosophy, but also to the kind of political interventions he makes, whether that be within the SNP or within Scottish politics in general. I seek, then, to place side by side concepts such as 'civic' or 'liberal nationalism', with, for instance, MacCormick's interventions aimed at bringing the '79 Group back into the SNP fold or his participation in the Claim of Right. I also seek to shed some light on the way in which he campaigned as part of his candidature for the Westminster Parliament.

MacCormick's active interest in, and theorisation of, Scottish nationalist politics and constitutional change cannot be read in isolation from an equally active interest in Europe. This is the topic of Chapter 8. MacCormick backed Europe as a political theatre for Scotland before many others did – for instance, unlike the SNP, he campaigned for 'Yes' in the 1975 referendum on Britain staying within the European Community. From the early 1980s, he embraced SNP's policy on 'Scotland in Europe'. But at the same time, he, along with colleagues in Edinburgh and beyond, theorised the *sui generis* quality of the European Community and then the EU. He developed, as he did so, complex concepts such as 'the post-sovereign commonwealth' governed by 'subsidiarity', as well as theories of what democracy might mean in Europe. I examine these philosophical theories alongside MacCormick's contributions as a Member of the European Parliament (from 1999 to 2004) and Alternate Member of the Convention on the Future of Europe. As in other contexts, but perhaps especially here, politics and philosophy really cannot be disentangled, but neither do they collapse into each other: instead, we find MacCormick both drafting constitutions (whether for Scotland or the EU) while at the same time digging deeply into the meaning of constitutionalism for persons.

MacCormick's contributions to political philosophy, in the form of conceptions of nationalism, rights, social democracy, as well as constitutional change, both in Scotland and Europe, were profound. But there were also two other areas of philosophical work with which he was deeply engaged: the institutional theory of law and the practicality of reason, including reasoning in both law and morality. I examine these two bodies of theory in Chapters 9 and 10. In doing so, I seek, once more, to read MacCormick, the philosopher, with character.

In Chapter 9, I explore the institutional theory of law as a relational act – indeed, as many relational acts over the course of the four decades that MacCormick develops it. This includes understanding the substance of the institutional theory of law as relational, e.g., with MacCormick tracing the emergence of norms and values from interactions between persons over time (such as in queues or in communicating with language). And it also includes tracing the sense in which the institutional theory of law allowed MacCormick to mediate between and connect various bodies of theory, disciplines, or domains of practice, such as philosophy of law and sociology of law.

Similarly so with practical reason in Chapter 10: I extract the themes, again in development for a long time and across many texts, that pick out the sense in which MacCormick's theorisation of practical reason is relational. This includes discussing MacCormick's meta-ethical theory, or his account of the ontology or epistemology of value: a theory that I call 'perspectivalism about value'. It also involves considering his two-step conceptualisation of legal reasoning: first, the construction of an inter-subjective space in the form of universalisation; and second, the process of deliberation and decision within that space, in particular by reference to the three tests (consistency, coherence, and consequences) as well as the attitude one could, and should, take to any decision made via this procedure. All these aspects of his theory of practical reason can, I argue, be read as negotiations and expressions of his character: in particular, all involve a basic commitment to keeping relations going, not allowing them to devolve into relations of domination.

My reading of these two highly complex bodies of philosophical thought includes, in the case of both chapters, showing how MacCormick's own ideas developed in conversation with, and often precisely in order to begin and strengthen relations with, scholars both in the Anglo–American tradition of legal philosophy as well as on the European continent. Indeed, one of the striking features of MacCormick's philosophical career is just how richly he related to both traditions, e.g., writing an important book on Hart, while also co-authoring with Ota Weinberger, or translating Robert Alexy, or participating in the circle of Chaïm Perelman, or indeed leading the Bielefelder Kreis, a group of largely European jurists who, over two decades, jointly inquired into the comparative study of interpreting statutes and reasoning with precedent. Finally, it is a further critical feature of the reading I do in these two chapters to show how MacCormick was often in dialogue – again from his student days – with the philosophers of the Enlightenment, and especially Stair, Hume, Smith, and Kant.

This brief tour through the chapters of this book might alone give the reader a sense of how difficult it is to situate MacCormick, both within the historiography of Scottish and British politics, as well as in the historiography of jurisprudence. This is because, as already alluded to earlier, MacCormick is not easily classifiable as either a straightforward nationalist or unionist, or positivist or natural lawyer, or Humean or Kantian, or liberal or socialist – or indeed any number of other oppositions. In fact, what the process of reading with character allows me to do – or at least what I try to do, by reading with character – is to show how MacCormick's process of constructing concepts, and at the same time the very substance of those concepts, is often oriented to acknowledging what he sees as the strength in traditionally opposing views, combining them into complex wholes.

MacCormick's philosophy is often relational in the sense that it creates complex in-between spaces, such as spaces between nationalism and unionism, or between positivism and natural law, or between Hume and Kant, or between liberalism and socialism, which are not easy to capture, but which are highly generative (certainly, but not only, for him) and in which MacCormick thinks and works, as a philosopher, as well as a politician. Thus, the process of reading character is designed, in many ways, to avoid flattening the historiography to such an extent that we see only rivalries between opposing philosophical views or political ideologies: if we do that, we will not see MacCormick at all, for he operates precisely in the difficult spaces between such oppositions.

A Note on Sources

A major part of this project has involved archiving MacCormick's papers. Some of them – in particular, those relating to his work as a Member of the European Parliament (1999–2004) – were already catalogued and archived at the University of Edinburgh Library Archives. To this were added numerous boxes, to which I was given access by Flora MacCormick. These are not professionally catalogued, but descriptions of the items deposited are available. All references to sources other than those available in the public domain (such as letters by and to MacCormick, his various personal notes, some SNP policy documents, drafts of papers and texts of speeches, as well as Edinburgh University papers) are available in the University of Edinburgh Library Archives. Occasionally, I have also consulted other archives, such as the University of Glasgow Library Archives (e.g., for letters by MacCormick to Lamont) and archives relating to the Glasgow University Union and the Oxford University Union, as well as the Balliol College Archives.

This project has also been supported by a website, hosted by Queen Mary University of London: www.qmul.ac.uk/law/maccormick/. This website contains a timeline, a bibliography, as well as some further audio-visual materials (e.g., select recordings of MacCormick's interviews and talks). MacCormick often recorded his own talks, going on to write them up and work on them afterwards, so these recordings are very valuable, as they show earlier versions of later publications. They are also moving – at least I find them so – as opportunities to listen to his voice. Indeed, if I had more world enough and time, I would have made more than I do in this book of MacCormick's qualities as a speaker and broadcaster; all too often we forget that the philosophers we read and study had bodies, voices, and a particular kind of physical presence. MacCormick's presence, as many will attest, was of infectious joy – an ability to start a party in an empty room, as some have said about him – as well as, in seminars, of incredible diligence. As again many have told me, and as I too witnessed on many occasions, MacCormick often wrote copious notes in seminars, even when the subject was something he had heard countless times. This, too, counts as a kind of physical presence, and one that is difficult to record in a book that reads his work.

When citing MacCormick's works in this book, I refer to the year of publication and a short version of the title. For the major books, I use abbreviations (LRLT, for *Legal Reasoning and Legal Theory*; HLA for *H. L. A. Hart*; LRSD, for *Legal Right and Social Democracy*; ITL for *The Institutional Theory of Law*; QS, for *Questioning Sovereignty*; RRL, for *Rhetoric and the Rule of Law*; IL, for *Institutions of Law*; PRLM, for *Practical Reason in Law and Morality*). Alongside the usual 'General Bibliography', I have included a Bibliography of MacCormick's published works. A project for the future would be to collect and publish MacCormick's many unpublished speeches and talks, amongst which are many gems.

1

Scottish Home Rule

A Political Childhood in Glasgow

To what extent are we, if at all, determined by our experiences of childhood, of home, of the relations with our family, especially our parents or guardians? There is no easy answer to this question, but it is important to ask it, especially with respect to Neil MacCormick. Born on 27 May 1941 in Glasgow into a family that was very self-consciously political as well as Scottish, MacCormick became aware, from early on, of his own deep roots in Scotland and in its politics.

That MacCormick himself was alive to the question of the power of one's childhood experiences and influences can be gleaned from how he reflected on the lives of his close friends in those years, e.g., Donald Dewar and John Smith. Writing about Dewar, for instance, MacCormick noted that 'probably no one ever completely sheds the sympathies of their younger years'.[1] MacCormick both observed Dewar in action as a debater in the Glasgow University Union and sparred with him on matters concerning home rule. Dewar, who was at one time chairman of the University Labour Club in Glasgow – precisely the time that MacCormick was President of the Glasgow University Scottish Nationalist Association (GUSNA) – 'developed his own stance on the social democratic wing of the Labour Party'.[2] It is those arguments – those 'sympathies' of one's younger ears – that were still in evidence later, for instance, when Dewar wrote a chapter for MacCormick's 1970 collection on *The Scottish Debate*, and later still, when Dewar became the inaugural Scottish First Minister in 1999. According to MacCormick, Dewar's home rule sympathies were 'an almost hereditary commitment, and certainly went back to his own boyhood', with his grandfather being a member of the Scottish Home Rule Association (SHRA) and his aunt, 'the formidable Aunt Elanor Dewar', who was also an informal aunt to the MacCormick children, working in the 1940s and 1950s, alongside MacCormick's father and mother,

[1] MacCormick, 'Enduring Foundations' (2004), 144.

[2] Ibid., 143.

under the umbrella of the Scottish Convention, for the cause of a Scottish Parliament.[3]

On the other hand, whereas such sympathies may stay with one, and be to some extent unshakeable, conversions to a view very different from one's youthful beliefs were still always possible. As MacCormick saw it, this was the case with John Smith. Like the Dewar family, the Smith family were close to the MacCormicks: for instance, Archie Smith, John's father, was, for a time, a friend of John MacCormick, and together they were members of the student Labour Party at the University of Glasgow.[4] Smith himself, said MacCormick, was from early on and then 'for a long time highly sceptical about Scottish home rule'.[5] Nevertheless, Smith later converted and became genuinely committed to 'supporting a form of Scottish Home Rule'.[6] Tragically, Smith, who was then the Leader of the Labour Party, died in 1994, just when he was on the cusp of becoming the Prime Minister of the United Kingdom, with Labour edging closer to a political victory, and one which they eventually achieved in 1997, but under the leadership of Tony Blair.

I mention these childhood friendships here not only to convey how alive the question of the influence of one's 'hereditary commitments' and 'youthful sympathies' was for MacCormick but also to give an immediate flavour of the highly political childhood and home that MacCormick grew up in. Glasgow, in the 1940s and 1950s, was a hotbed of political creativity and of a growing Scottish self-consciousness, including, very significantly, burgeoning literary and historical self-awareness. At the very heart of this was MacCormick's family, including MacCormick's family home in Kelvingrove, and in particular his father, John MacCormick. Indeed, I shall be spending most of this chapter following John MacCormick's remarkable political initiatives, which captured the public imagination and, in doing so, brought the issue of Scottish identity and self-government to the fore. This is vital to do for, as we shall see, MacCormick often saw himself as, in some ways, continuing the work begun by his father. Certainly, MacCormick took almost every opportunity he could to keep the memory of his father alive, sometimes taking this to extraordinary lengths. To give just one example, when asked by the *Scottish Review*, in 1999, to name 'The Greatest Scot of the 20th Century and the Greatest Scot in History',

[3] MacCormick, 'Review of *John Smith*' (2006), 144.
[4] MacCormick, 'John Smith' (1994), 5–6.
[5] Ibid., 7.
[6] MacCormick, 'Review of *John Smith*' (2006), 144.

he mentioned, as might be expected, Adam Smith and his *An Inquiry into the Nature and Causes of the Wealth of Nations*, but to this he added his father, highlighting in particular his father's memoir of 'the story of the national movement in Scotland', *The Flag in the Wind* (1955).[7]

Here, then, right at the outset of this chapter, we encounter something delicate and difficult: how to understand MacCormick's relations with his father. The matter is complex, and my aim is to illuminate that complexity, rather than reduce it to any one view of it. On the one hand, there is no doubt, as the above example alone illustrates, that MacCormick was enormously proud of his father. As we shall see, there are many aspects of his father's arguments and beliefs that MacCormick took on, to some extent, as his own. One could argue that this at times clouded MacCormick's own judgement or that it somehow 'determined' his politics, which, in turn, 'determined' his philosophy. That is not the view I endorse here, while nevertheless acknowledging the enormous influence of John MacCormick, the father, on his son. For, on the other hand, it is clear that MacCormick reflected carefully on his own inheritance: in fact, in some ways, the story of his life might be told as one of adopting, and always negotiating, his own reasoned response to the political world he grew up in and then contributed to. In that respect, one could argue that the very problem that animated so much of his philosophical work – e.g., whether reason was practical – was an existential one for MacCormick: could someone who had inherited such an emotionally powerful political orientation come to terms with that reasonably and thus adopt his own attitude to it? Could one remain loyal and faithful to the memory of one's father while nevertheless becoming a man of one's own?

If all this feels like skewing the story too much in the direction of the relationship between a father and a son, to the exclusion of all other relations, then that feeling is worth listening to. Indeed, for all its explicit and visible importance, and although it is what MacCormick himself wrote most about, including in his unpublished memoirs, the relationship with his father was certainly not the only important, and perhaps not even the most important, relationship of his childhood. The relationship that, although somewhat occluded by the very public life of his father, was arguably even more crucial, especially for the development of MacCormick's character, was his relationship with his mother.

Margaret MacCormick, born Margaret Isobel Miller, was a social worker, dedicated to improving the lives of the people trying to survive in

[7] MacCormick, 'Untitled', *Scottish Review* (1999), 62–4.

Glasgow's poorest areas. As we shall see, and as MacCormick described her, hers was an ethos of fundamental and unshakeable respect for others. Unlike, arguably, her husband and MacCormick's father, who was an orator, a public performer, someone keen to be in the political limelight, rubbing shoulders with luminaries, Margaret MacCormick worked quietly, behind the scenes, holding the family together, steering it often through turbulent times – turbulent, in part, because of her husband's initiatives – while at the same time spending her time amongst the most marginalised and invisible members of the community.

There is, in Margaret MacCormick, an inclusiveness, a considerateness, and a deep respect for others, which runs equally deep, if not deeper – or so I wish to argue – in MacCormick's character. As George Reid put it, Margaret MacCormick 'left her children with a commitment to an inclusive society and Neil, in particular, with a lifetime inability to see ill in anybody'.[8] Maintaining alive the memory of MacCormick's father, especially given his early death at the age of fifty seven in 1961, was certainly traumatic for MacCormick, and this trauma left its mark. However, although undoubtedly important, it was not his father's sensibilities – nor his arguments or beliefs – that are of deepest significance to understanding MacCormick's character. It was, instead, Margaret MacCormick who gave nourishment to MacCormick's soul at its most resonant and deep running.

I therefore begin this chapter with Margaret MacCormick, even if only briefly, given the relative lack of information about her life, as well as the wider MacCormick family, before turning to John MacCormick, the context of the 1920s and 1930s in which he first became involved in Scottish nationalist politics, and the three events in which his father was deeply involved and that were particularly formative for MacCormick's political childhood: first, the establishment of the Scottish Convention in 1942, and later, the Scottish Covenant and its two-year campaign in 1949–51 for a plebiscite for home rule; second, the taking of the Stone of Destiny from London in the Christmas of 1950; and third, the case of *MacCormick* v *Lord Advocate* in 1953. This is hardly a full history of family life and the extraordinary political hub that was MacCormick's family home in the 1940s and 1950s – that is a story that still awaits telling. But telling it, even partially, is crucial for a study of MacCormick's character.

[8] George Reid, 'Tribute', online memorial website following MacCormick's death in 2009 (the website is no longer working).

Margaret MacCormick and Family Life

If John MacCormick was the MacCormick's family most publicly visible face, the heart of its home – its most private face – was undoubtedly Margaret MacCormick. Born in 1909 as Margaret Isobel Miller, she came from a family whose roots were in Fife and Lanarkshire, and who were, as MacCormick recalled, 'Lowland and Scotch-spoken … with some Ulster-Scots flavouring'.[9] They were accomplished and well educated, 'medical people and merchants', and they had built their own flats in Townhead (in Glasgow), which stretched back several generations.[10] When MacCormick was a boy, after returning from July holidays in Mull or Tayvallich, he would often spend a month running 'wild' in his maternal grandmother's home in Bothwell.[11]

It is worth pausing to observe here that whereas MacCormick traced his mother's heritage to Lowland Scotland, he traced his father's to its Highlands. That side of the family, MacCormick said, was 'intensely Highland, from Mull, Iona, and Glenurquhart, Gaelic-speaking, song-composing, pipe-playing bards and (in case of Great-Uncle John) Gaelic novel writing'.[12] Later, in Chapter 2, when we meet MacCormick in Glasgow High School, we shall see how important the musical culture as well as the Gaelic tongue were to MacCormick, and what a crucial role in that respect was played by his great uncle Neil and his brother Dugald.

The dual Lowland–Highland heritage is significant, too, for, as we shall see, MacCormick was an artist in combining what others might see as opposites – a conceptual maker of blended, in-between spaces. Indeed, at times, he remarked explicitly on the importance of the two strands of Scottish culture working together, respecting each other, and learning from one another, with this being, for instance, a major reason why he thought Walter Scott such a pivotal figure in Scottish history; Scott was, MacCormick thought, a writer of peace and reconciliation, skilfully weaving together these two strands of Scottish culture.[13] The fact that MacCormick admired Scott, precisely for his capacity to relate what might otherwise be opposed, is not incidental to understanding MacCormick's character: after all, Scott was also a passionate national unionist,[14] writing

[9] MacCormick, 'Being Scottish' (2002), 153–4.
[10] Ibid.
[11] Ibid.
[12] Ibid., 153.
[13] See MacCormick, 'The Memory of Sir Walter Scott' (1997).
[14] See, e.g., McLean, 'Understanding the Union' (2000), 123–5; generally, Kidd, *Union and Unionisms* (2008).

to intertwine, while still differentiating, not only Lowland and Highland Scottish culture but also Scotland and England.

Margaret MacCormick was, as MacCormick described her, 'a formidably clever woman'.[15] This was illustrated, for instance, by her completing, at the University of Glasgow, a combined degree of an MA and BSc a whole year sooner, then taking the extra year to take the then-new course in social administration, but also by the delight she took in wordplay and how quick she was on her feet. MacCormick recalled, for instance, once asking her, when one of his own children had a child: 'Well, Mum, what does it feel like to be a great grandmother?' Quick as a flash, she replied: 'I have always been a great grandmother'. 'Verbal quickness and a love of words', MacCormick recalled, 'were very much part of her', as was her wide reading in history and current affairs.[16] As we shall see in Chapter 2, MacCormick inherited and himself relished in the delights of language, along with the joys of wit and repartee.

After graduating, Margaret MacCormick was employed by the City of Glasgow Society for Social Service, working as a social worker 'in the Calton district of Glasgow's desperately poor city centre and inner east end'.[17] This was in the 1930s and 1940s, which were difficult times, to say the least. As MacCormick put it, 'she did a great deal of good in these pre-Beveridge days, trying to alleviate circumstances of dire poverty among those who came to the Society seeking assistance'.[18] Later, in 1954, after her children had started school – in addition to Neil, there was Iain, Marion, and Elspeth – she returned to the City of Glasgow Society, working this time in 'large municipal estates in Knightswood and Garscadden', before moving to 'the Guild of Aid, a charity based in the Gorbals area of Glasgow'.[19] In due course, in 1968, Margaret MacCormick became the Warden of the Guild and remained in that position until retiring in 1974 at the age of sixty five.[20] During her tenure, she provided clothing for those who didn't have them, day nurseries, as well as 'fresh air fortnights' in the countryside for women from deprived areas of the city.[21]

It may seem, from the above account, as if Margaret MacCormick was not active in politics. Such a view is only tenable if one understands

[15] MacCormick, 'Nationalist Memories I' (2008/9), 8.
[16] Ibid.
[17] Ibid.
[18] Ibid.
[19] Ibid.
[20] Ibid.
[21] Reid, 'Tribute' (2009).

politics in a very narrow sense as relating to front-line party manoeuvring. In fact, she was often involved, but typically behind the scenes, supporting John MacCormick's various initiatives, including when he was National Secretary of the National Party of Scotland (NPS) in the early 1930s before its merger with the Scottish Party (SP) to form the Scottish National Party (SNP) in 1934. Later, in the 1940s, and still in the early 1950s, she assisted with John MacCormick's Convention movement, and in particular, the Covenant in 1949–51, 'nearly wrecking her eyesight with the job of manual transcribing names and addresses from the signed petition onto index cards'.[22] This was an important task, given the many accusations made by Convention opponents of fraud in the number of names and addresses that were being claimed as having signed the Covenant. It was this sort of task that Margaret MacCormick would regularly perform, again quietly, unacknowledged, except by those immediately around her.

But Margaret MacCormick's politics lay deeper still. For MacCormick, it was crucial to see that her nationalism, such as it was, came from her experience as a social worker. What she saw, MacCormick said, was 'the need for an absolute renewal of Scotland through self-government'.[23] The basis of her political sensibility was equality and respect for persons. As MacCormick articulated it, remembering her in the memoirs he dictated towards the end of his own life:

> Her philosophy throughout was that people were to be treated with absolute respect no matter how unfortunate their circumstances. Above all, the problem of poverty was simply that people had not enough money and the task of social work was to help them either to find ways of making effective economies or to find them some small packet of financial assistance beyond the rules of the welfare state. I think she did much good and brought a lot of unobtrusive relief to many people.[24]

Margaret MacCormick was, in the words of Robert Burns, which she herself regularly quoted, 'contended wi' little and cantie wi' mair' – contented with little and joyous with more.[25] Indeed, she often had to be, given the tight budget with which she had to run the household, especially after John MacCormick lost his job, following his involvement in the *MacCormick* v *Lord Advocate* case in 1953, and during which, in order to alleviate his pain from kidney stones, he took to drink, dying a few years later in 1961.

[22] MacCormick, 'Nationalist Memories I', 2008/9, 9.
[23] Ibid., 8.
[24] Ibid.
[25] Ibid., 9.

None of this is to suggest that the MacCormick home was not a happy one: indeed, much to the contrary, Margaret MacCormick 'loved a party and kept a hospitable house'.[26] By all accounts, this was a riotous, perpetually busy, perpetually sociable home. In addition to the four MacCormick children, there were two cousins – Donald and Alastair – who were frequently there, having lost their father, John MacCormick's brother, and, 'especially during the holidays', MacCormick recalled, 'we functioned to a large extent as a family of six siblings'.[27] The home was also often visited by three unmarried aunts and one widowed – a not infrequent phenomenon in many families across Europe, and beyond, following the Second World War.

To this one can add the uncles, including the great uncles mentioned above, as well as an endless stream of visitors, connected either to the Convention and Covenant, or to Glasgow University. In truth, these two groups were often difficult to tell apart, and impossibly so during 1950–53, when John MacCormick served as Rector of the University of Glasgow. These years, MacCormick recalled, 'brought much happiness and many friendships', and they continued when MacCormick, and his siblings were studying, with frequent visitors from the 'Glasgow Union boys', such as Smith and Dewar, but also Derry Irvine and Menzies Campbell, amongst many others. As MacCormick further recalled:

> Home was both a political base with phone often ringing, and a place of hospitality both to political friends and associates and to the extended family. So there was always surrounding talk and often a buzz of excitement about whatever was current in the news and whatever the Covenanters were currently agitating about – the closure of Clyde piers, or of West Lothian shale oil, for example. If you were a small boy or young teenager interested in political affairs, simply assuming the role of an unobtrusive listener gave a great political education in a very particular kind of politics.[28]

I will return to this political apprenticeship, but it is worth emphasising, once again, that throughout all this it was Margaret MacCormick who held the family together, amidst all this rather chaotic sociability and political discussion: she was, MacCormick said, 'a tower of strength to us all', creating a space 'in which, for all his [i.e., John MacCormick's] huge

[26] MacCormick, 'Nationalist Memories I' (2008/9), 9.

[27] Ibid., 2. MacCormick's first name was Donald, but because the family was often joined by his cousin, also Donald, he was known by his second name, Neil, which stuck.

[28] MacCormick, 'Introduction', *The Flag in the Wind* (2008), xiii.

workload between his legal practice and his politics, my father remained a very engaged dad to his children'.[29]

In addition to her intelligence, her social work and thus her sensitivity to equality and respect for all persons, her responsibility, but also the joy she took in life and in the company of others, including her delight in wordplay and repartee, there was yet one more connection that MacCormick had to his mother. Speaking in 2003, in a lecture on 'Europe's Future, Scotland's Future', MacCormick recalled what he also dubbed 'one of my earliest non-memories':

> My mother on several occasions told me that, after she took me home from the hospital where I had been born, she one evening took me out to the front garden in Stepps, just to the east of Glasgow where my family then resided. She held me up so that she and I could see the scarlet glow to the west of Clydebank in flames after the dreadful blitz there. That is clearly the world into which I was born, a world of catastrophic war. This is the world which we Europeans have spent the last half-century and more, escaping, burying and putting behind us.[30]

And, MacCormick continued, it was thus in Europe that Scotland's future lay – in a future of peace, built on the co-operation and mutual goodwill evidenced by the European Union. Peace was indeed a fundamental value for MacCormick – a fundamental orientation of his politics and his philosophy. Peace was fragile, and this needed constant reminders, especially for generations that did not have the experience that those like MacCormick did, who was conscious that, being born on 27 May 1941, he was 'born in the depths of wartime'.[31] And it was peace – the active, generative pursuit of peace – which manifested itself in his mother's running of the household, but also in her community-building abilities, helping others to help themselves out of the difficulties they faced, held up by egalitarianism, decency, and respect for persons, that ran so deep in MacCormick's character.

In the quote above, MacCormick spoke of his mother holding him outside the house at Stepps. This was, indeed, where the MacCormick family lived before moving, in 1943, to 2 Park Quadrant – a large, double top flat home in Glasgow park district overlooking Kelvingrove Park. This was quite a change – and an unaffordable one for the MacCormick's in any other time outside war (the flat was perched on quite an exposed hill and

29 Ibid., x–xi.

30 MacCormick, 'Europe's Future, Scotland's Future' (2003), 2–3.

31 MacCormick, 'Nationalist Memoirs II' (2008/9), 1.

was thus vulnerable to bombing). From the flat you could, MacCormick recalled, see 'Scotland in miniature'.[32] The view, especially for a boy of considerable imagination, like MacCormick, was quite something:

> From on high there [2 Park Quadrant], one enjoyed spectacular views over the Campsie Fells and Kilpatrick Hills, past Dungoyne to the Highland peaks of Perthshire and Argyll. There was an impressive cityscape looking over Kelvingrove and Maryhill, and also a view to the dark and crane-fettered splendours of the Clyde docks and shipyards, still at the peak of their production. But the real glory of the view was its majestic centrepiece – Gilbert Scott's spectacularly neo-Gothic Glasgow University, with grand turrets surmounted by a fretwork stone steeple on the centre tower (the steeple was actually made to a later design). For me in childhood, the University, seen in profile rather than full face, seemed like a fairy castle.[33]

It was at this University – this fairy castle – where both his mother and father had studied. Even more poignantly, it was also to this magical place that, in 1950, when MacCormick was nine, his father had been elected to serve as Rector. As MacCormick remembered it: 'One day, in 1950, driving over University Avenue towards Whiteinch Park to sail a model yacht he had built for us, my father remarked that he might later that year be elected Rector of the University. Without quite knowing what he meant by this, I was profoundly impressed'.[34] No wonder this nine-year old was 'profoundly impressed': his father was about to become a magician in a fairy castle, and one he could see from the windows of his own home!

Family life, for MacCormick, was, then, full of legend and mystery, intense political discussion and intrigue, immensely sociable, and a place generally of buzz and activity. I will be turning, below, to how this was especially so with respect to three events that loomed large in MacCormick's childhood, but it is worth adding here, that for all the everyday hustle and bustle, there were also plenty of periods of carefree play, enjoyed, invariably, in the Scottish landscape.

As was mentioned above, John MacCormick, despite his commitments, was not an absent dad. For instance, he built, as MacCormick recalled, kites and boats for his children – indeed, once, when flying a kite, 'bringing down the telephone wires as a consequence of over-zealousness'.[35]

32 MacCormick, 'Introduction' *Flag in the Wind* (2008), xi.
33 MacCormick, 'Doubts about the Supreme Court' (2004), 238.
34 MacCormick, 'John MacCormick Memoirs' (2008/9), 3; 'Doubts about the Supreme Court' (2004), 238.
35 MacCormick, 'Introduction' *Flag in the Wind* (2008), xi.

John MacCormick also made 'balsa-wood gliders and taught us how to make more elaborate planes from kits', and with these, along with various 'toy soldiers and spring-cannons that could fire wire nails at lead soldiers without danger to boyish eyes or limbs', he, together with his siblings and cousins 'had terrific games'.[36] 'Above all', MacCormick remembered the boats, for instance: 'three beautifully made model yachts devised and built by Dad, and rowing boats that we rented along with the holiday house when we were in Mull or Tayvallich, and in which we learned to be safe boat people and to be self-reliant in the rough waters of Loch Sween or Lochan na Lathaic'.[37]

In addition to those Lochs, the family went on picnics also to Loch Lomond, Loch Lubnaig, or Inverkip on summer weekends. And, for the summer holidays, there were frequent visits to Bunessan in Mull, to Killin in Perthshire, and, to the family favourite, Tayvallich in mid-Argyll.[38] This is important to record, for, as we shall see in later chapters, MacCormick was to return often, with deep emotion, to his childhood memories, and thus to his immersion, as a boy, in the Scottish landscape, and indeed also to his family's roots, especially his father's in Mull and Iona. This included on occasions when he was visiting the area as a parliamentary candidate, for Argyll and Bute, in the Westminster elections. Thus, in 1992, in a letter ahead of a visit to the Mull and Iona Annual Gathering, he wrote:

> The MacCormicks are an ancient Mull family associated with the MacLaines of Lochbuie (hence our family motto 'Biadh is Deoch do MacCarmaig').[39] My great great great grandfather Dugald settled in Iona in about 1792, and many of his descendants are still there; but my great great grandfather John came back to the Ross of Mull around 1838, and in due course became Free Church schoolmaster. His youngest son Neil, my great grandfather, worked in the quarries at the building of Skerryvore and Dubh Heartach, and eventually became manager of the Mull granite quarries. His wife, Annabella MacLachlan, was descended from the armourers of the MacLachlans of Strathlachlan, one of whom was Aide de Camp to Prince

[36] Ibid.

[37] Ibid.

[38] Ibid.

[39] This literally means 'food and drink for MacCormick', but was a colloquial way of saying 'MacCormick is welcome here'. The motto is carved into a stone lintel over the doorway entering Moy Castle. It is there because it commemorates the support, in the 1550s, of the McDonnell Earl of Antrim guards – twelve armed men who all happened to have the surname 'McCormick' – who helped chieftain Maclaine of Lochbuie to recapture Moy Castle from his cousin McLean of Duart. See www.familytreedna.com/groups/mc-cormick/about/background; last accessed 18 January 2024.

> Charles at Culloden; through her, I have many relations in Mid-Argyll. My grandfather Donal was a ship's captain from Robertson's of Glasgow, and his wife Mario. MacDonald (from Glenurquhart via Campbeltown, descendent of a Jacobite family) was the first Queen's nurse in the Ross of Mull. My father John, alias 'King John' was brought up in the Stepps outside Glasgow.[40]

MacCormick was an SNP candidate in five Westminster elections, all five unsuccessful, which was less a testament to his own political abilities, and more the result of contesting seats he was unlikely to win. Even if, in the above, he stood something to gain politically from his family history, it would be unfair to suggest that this was posturing for political gain. For MacCormick, such personal genealogies mattered, as did his connection – again, deeply and genuinely felt – for Scotland and its lands. This was commented on often by those who knew him, e.g., George Reid, writing a tribute after MacCormick's death, emphasised how MacCormick 'was always conscious of his family's Highland roots', and how this often manifested itself, for example, in his piping: 'he would appear in bunnet and kilt, radiating bonhomie'.[41] We shall encounter MacCormick's piping on numerous occasions to come in this book. Again, for MacCormick, this was no mere entertainment: it was full of joy, certainly, but this emerged from the depths of an awareness that he was part of a rich and personal Scottish tradition.[42]

Indeed, it has often been observed by his family members, that MacCormick held such genealogies, amongst many other threads of Scottish history, in his 'prodigious memory', as was noted by his cousin, Donald, who wrote a letter to his Aunt, when he was seventeen and Neil was fifteen, saying that 'It looks as if we have a budding eccentric professor in the family!'.[43] Stories of MacCormick's intellectual promise are rife in MacCormick family folklore – from him being able to solve complex maths puzzles (e.g., at 3, answering his father's question correctly as to how much 2.5 and 2.5 made) to his winning all the family word games – although, it

40 MacCormick, 'Letter to Mr Mackenzie', 21 October 1991.

41 George Reid, 'Tribute', online memorial website following MacCormick's death in 2009 (the website is no longer working).

42 Religion, which is such a vital thread in the history of Scottish politics, was less a factor in the case of the MacCormick family: 'We were an essentially Presbyterian family', MacCormick said, 'but we were not sharply aware of it, for we were far removed from any kind of Orangeism, and were brought up in a free-thinking way outside of the dour dominion of the Kirk': MacCormick, 'Being Scottish' (2002), 154. That MacCormick was nevertheless very aware of the religious dimension of Scottish political history can be gleaned from, for instance, his unpublished lecture on 'The Kirk and Sovereignty'.

43 Email from Donald MacCormick 19 April 2009, 2.

should be added, these are usually quickly followed by an equal number, if not many more, of stories concerning his 'uneasy relationship with the external world'. As his cousin Donald put it, 'As a young boy, he seemed to attract skelfs [i.e., splinters] much as a magnet attracts iron filings' – something that was echoed in later life, when 'any motor car driven by Neil fell some way short of poetry in motion'.[44]

This combination, both of intellectual play and pleasure – of genuine delight taken in language, for instance, but also in exploring it with others – accompanied by 'an uneasy relationship with the external world', never left MacCormick. As Owen Dudley Edwards remarked,[45] MacCormick had 'a kind of brilliant childishness' about him – the child never quite disappeared. This joyous innocence, alongside a capacity to be genuinely and generously surprised, which, again, was not strategic but which came naturally to him, was infectious, and was a large part of what made him such enjoyable company.

John MacCormick

Before turning to the three events that were such a striking feature of MacCormick's political childhood, it is important to place these in the context of how John MacCormick has often been viewed by historians of Scottish politics. This is important to do because, as we shall see, the judgement of John MacCormick by historians has not been kind, and if accepted wholescale, can lead to a narrowing of the historiography of Scottish politics that obscures the relationship between MacCormick and his father, and in particular what his father's legacy meant for him.

The words that one frequently encounters, reading about John MacCormick, are 'flawed', 'failure', 'weakness', 'shallowness', 'opportunism', 'vanity', and 'naivete'. Thus, for instance, Tom Devine, in his highly influential and widely acclaimed history of *The Scottish Nation 1707–2000* (2006), acknowledges the efforts made by John MacCormick in the 1940s and 1950s, saying that 'on the face of it, [John] MacCormick's Scottish Convention was much more successful' than the SNP at the time.[46] 'However', he soon adds: '…as a vehicle for delivering Home Rule it proved a failure. Self-government could be achieved only through the ballot box,

[44] Ibid., 1.
[45] Private communication to the author.
[46] Devine, *The Scottish Nation 1707–2000* (2006), 566.

by voters backing candidates prepared to advocate self-government. The Covenant movement was avowedly non-partisan and apolitical'.[47]

According to Devine, matters were made worse – for the possibility of Scottish Home Rule – when John MacCormick decided, in 1945, to join the Liberal Party and stand, as a Liberal candidate, both in 1945 as well as in a by-election in Paisley in 1947. This was viewed with considerable suspicion – to say the least – by the governing Labour Party: 'This', concludes Devine, 'was most certainly not the way to convince the Labour Government of the need for constitutional change'.[48] Within a short time, Devine added, 'The Covenant was ignored and the movement soon fell apart into political irrelevance', making 'little impact on the general elections of 1950 and 1951'.[49]

This historical judgement – that the movement established and led by John MacCormick was ultimately a 'failure',[50] for it made little inroads into party politics, and largely because of John MacCormick's own actions, and thus the quality of his leadership – is the dominant historiographical view. Thus, for instance, Paula Somerville, in her wonderfully insightful account of the history of the SNP from 1947 to 1967, does acknowledge the great public interest in the Convention and the Covenant, but describes it, once again, as a 'failure'.[51] As Somerville puts it:

> The Scottish Convention had been hugely successful in grabbing the headlines and gaining widespread support. It had organised some of the most representative assemblies of Scottish society and had helped mount the largest petition ever raised in Scotland. It spurred on investigations by both Government and Opposition which would later take the shape of the Catto Committee and the Balfour Commission. But in terms of fundamentals, the Convention ultimately failed. Its primary aim was to attain a Scottish parliament with adequate controls over Scottish domestic matters and this it failed to achieve. Given the weight of support the Convention and the Covenant campaign experienced, the question begs why did it fail?[52]

47 Ibid., 567.
48 Ibid.
49 Ibid.
50 See also Levitt, 'Britain, the Scottish Covenant Movement and Devolution, 1946–60' (1998), who argues that 'The Movement's failure was its inability to translate a deeply held cultural distinctiveness to the level of political awareness and significance' (35). According to Levitt, the movement was held in suspicion, and 'regarded as encouraging parochial thought and the Jacobite tradition, a desire for self-expression whatever the cost to public order' (51) – a view that is at odds with John MacCormick's own characterisation of it.
51 Somerville, *Through the Maelstrom* (2013), 38.
52 Ibid.

Somerville's answer to that question is that it was caused by a mixture of naïve and impractical political leadership. The leader was, of course, John MacCormick, so once more we have a harsh historical judgement made of him personally. 'One critical factor was the Convention's refusal to play the parliamentary cards and contest elections', argues Somerville,[53] echoing the dominant view that the Convention failed because it did not make inroads into party politics. The Government could, and did, ignore the Convention, simply because it was not an electoral threat and had no 'political strategy'.[54] The Convention's 'refusal' to 'take up the ballot weapon … proved its fundamental weakness'.[55] Again, it did not help that John MacCormick stood, in his personal capacity, as a Liberal candidate. Further, he made some mistakes, such as seeking the support, while on a tour of America in 1950 to raise awareness of the Scottish cause, of a 'controversial individual' – a certain Colonel R. R. McCormick, 'editor of the *Chicago Tribune* and a well-known republican', and someone who was characterised, by the press back home, as 'a hater of Britain and friend of Franco'.[56] Ultimately, Somerville concludes, the Convention's 'failure to devise an electoral strategy and the ineptitude of its leadership' showed it was 'a gimmick organisation' and, once 'the novelty wore off', the Convention soon petered out, dying not with a bang, but with a whimper.[57]

Richard Finlay's account, in his detailed history of the origins of the SNP from 1918 to 1945, also points to John MacCormick's many personal flaws. While noting John MacCormick's youthful energy and organisational abilities, including his oratical skills, all of which were important especially early on in the 1920s and 1930s, enabling some consensus, often simply because of a lack of awareness or less entrenchment in old disagreements,[58] the running theme of Finlay's history are the 'weaknesses' in John MacCormick's 'political ability': ignoring voices within his own party,[59] misreading the opposition,[60] acting in an 'unprincipled' manner, with 'underhand manoeuvrings' and displaying 'an arrogant tendency to treat [in this case] the NPS as if it were his own private organisation'.[61]

[53] Ibid.
[54] Ibid., 39.
[55] Ibid.
[56] Ibid., 42, quoting the press at the time.
[57] Ibid., 47.
[58] Finlay, *Independent and Free* (1994), e.g., 77, 88.
[59] Ibid., 104.
[60] Ibid., 105.
[61] Ibid., 108.

John MacCormick, Finlay argues, was 'shallow' in his politics; he was 'not an ideological politician';[62] he was an able 'Machiavellian';[63] he was an 'opportunist' who 'consistently wavered in his political commitments';[64] 'becoming increasingly bitter' over the years with ever-more personal clashes;[65] ignoring 'legitimate arguments about strategy and policy', often simplifying 'disputes into ones revolving around personalities rather than politics';[66] an 'eternal optimist',[67] if not romantic, and, on the whole, someone who was just too much in love with his own vision for Scotland and his own place in it.

There is an air of paradox about this judgement, including its harshness. Why should one understand 'success' or 'failure' here as a matter of electoral results, in the short-term, as evidenced by official changes in policy by the Government of the time? Is politics necessarily a game of such short-term gains made in officialdom? It is not that the above judgements do not acknowledge the ways in which the Convention and the Covenant – as we shall see further in a moment – made astonishing contributions to the general public's self-consciousness, and thus to the rising self-awareness of the community as a political one, with a possible future worth hoping for. This is acknowledged, but it is then quickly dismissed as something of but temporary and minor significance, with its politics judged to be, as we have seen, a failure.

At stake here, then, is a certain understanding of politics, and the relationship between, on the one hand, official, party politics, electoral success, and government policy, and, on the other, public opinion, popular culture, and collective self-awareness. Further, at stake is a question of time: of the short-term versus the long-term. At what point can one be confident about making a historical judgement as to the significance of some political initiative? Must we, when we exercise such judgement, evaluate political initiatives from the perspective of whether they led to immediate results, where the notion of a result itself is said to be nothing less than electoral success or a change in government policy? Does public opinion, public sentiment, and public imagination really matter so little? Just how much of a gap do we want to insist on between culture and politics?

62 Ibid., 110.
63 Ibid., 111.
64 Ibid.
65 Ibid.
66 Ibid., 134.
67 Ibid., 137.

These questions are important for understanding the relationship between MacCormick and his father, including how MacCormick himself related to his father's legacy. After all, confronting such a legacy was no passive matter: it required the son to consider how to interpret and characterise his father. Who was his father? What was he really trying to do? Was it, and if so, why was it, important for Scotland and its future? We shall see that these questions animated MacCormick throughout his life.

To raise these questions is not to ignore or not acknowledge, as insightful, many of the judgements made by the historians above. Further, Finlay is surely right to argue that a history of this period cannot rely too much on John MacCormick's own account of the 'National Movement in Scotland': *The Flag in the Wind*, first published in 1955 (and reissued in 2008, with an introduction by MacCormick). A number of historians of mid twentieth century Scottish politics have made this point: the early historiography of the nationalist movement was too reliant on John MacCormick's 'self-justificatory version' of this history, a version that 'should no longer be viewed as anything other than flawed and highly partial'.[68] Indeed, it is quite possible that John MacCormick did not do himself a favour in writing his memoir: much of it does reveal that many of his initiatives were based on enlisting the support of the Scottish upper-classes – the Establishment figures, Dukes and Ladies – with whom John MacCormick was keen to be associated and with whom he built personal relationships, often without knowledge or endorsement by the party membership.

Acknowledging this to be so, it may nevertheless be helpful to place John MacCormick, and his views, in a broader context – one in which what is at stake is less an evaluation of his own role in party politics, and more an inquiry into how we might think about politics and its relation to culture. Could it be that, perhaps especially in the period in which John MacCormick was operating, nationalist politics, including as John MacCormick saw it, was inseparable from generating collective political self-consciousness and public opinion, public sentiment, and the social imagination? Was politics really reducible to electoral success, or some other measure of immediate gain, or was it potentially something more encompassing, something more principled, or even moral? Can we, further, stretch the historical frame so as to include a richer sense of political time – a more expansive, more geological, time, which recognises that the

[68] See Mitchell, 'History of the SNP' (2015), reviewing Somerville, *Through the Maelstrom* (2013); see also Somerville, *Through the Maelstrom* (2013), 114; and Finlay, '"For or Against"' (1992), 184.

political identity of a community needs to percolate slowly, necessarily gradually, and is often not visible in momentary results of party politics, but only within a long view, which intimately intertwines politics and culture?

Some political historians have indeed grappled with this possibility – as indeed have many of the above already mentioned historians, at least in part, when they have spoken of John MacCormick's coalition-building, organisational skills, or moderate, cross-party approach.[69] Thus, for instance, Malcolm Petrie, in a collection on SNP leaders, certainly acknowledges the 'ambiguous position' that John MacCormick holds 'within the pantheon of SNP leaders', including the assessments of him as 'a flawed figure': '…a political pioneer who lacked the discipline to see his myriad schemes through to completion; a gifted orator and campaigner, who, though dedicated to the cause of Scottish self-government, squandered his gifts; and individualist and romantic unable to submit to the constraints of party politics; even, perhaps, a shallow politician, guilty of opportunism and naivete'.[70]

Petrie sees all this, and does recognise these various 'weakness', but, he suggests, perhaps this 'ostensibly erratic career can be seen as a rational response to the political climate within which he worked'.[71] Yes, Petrie says, John MacCormick had many 'flaws': 'He was elitist, uncomfortable in the demotic world of mass politics; he was dismissive of those who challenged his authority; he could spectacularly misjudge his ability to convince others'.[72] However, as Petrie then adds: John MacCormick 'kept the Scottish question alive … he got Scotland talking about its own purpose and destiny'.[73] Yes, John MacCormick had – as we shall see further in a moment – a 'fondness for the more theatrical aspects of student politics',[74] but can this sense of 'political theatre' be so easily dismissed? John MacCormick had no commitments to 'doctrinal purity' – he was, instead, 'a practical politician, skilled at garnering publicity',[75] more like an 'impartial broker' whose 'objective was to find enough common ground to allow' for certain political initiatives, whether these be the formation of a political party, or the pursuit of cross-party movements, such as the Convention and the

[69] See, e.g., Finlay, *Independent and Free* (1994), 157–8.
[70] Petrie, 'John MacCormick' (2016), 44.
[71] Ibid., 45.
[72] Ibid., 62.
[73] Ibid.
[74] Ibid., 50.
[75] Ibid., 46.

Covenant.[76] Yes, his 'leadership rested upon an outmoded combination of personal influence and public spectacle',[77] with alliances especially with high-profile establishment figures (celebrities and 'influencers' in today's language), but this can also be understood as conveying a certain kind of respect for popular, public opinion.

Perhaps most importantly, and especially with his historically resonant Convention and Covenant, including its incredible success in bringing together such a range of different people – many of whom were otherwise not actively engaged in politics, certainly not in party politics from which they were very much alienated – John MacCormick 'bequeathed a rhetoric and a battery of tactics that could be redeployed in more propitious circumstances', and, from this perspective, can be characterised 'as one of the most significant figures in the political history of twentieth century Scotland'.[78] Petrie's choice of words here is not his alone: others, too, have spoken of John MacCormick as a 'most significant figure in the Scottish nationalist cause',[79] saying that 'by experience and temperament [he] was a coalitionist' and that this 'strategy of coalitionism … was against the temper of the times and party interests at the national level'.[80] There is a sense, in these views, that John MacCormick was operating out of time, or even ahead of his time. There was just no space for John MacCormick's kind of politics, at least at the time at which he made them.

It is here, precisely, that we reach the question of MacCormick's, the son's, judgement of his father's legacy. A number of observers have noticed how key to the development of MacCormick's own political voice was the way in which he came to terms with his father. Recalling an event in 2008 – in what may well have been MacCormick's final public appearance – Miller, Rodger, and Dudley-Edwards comment that MacCormick spoke up 'in vindication of his father, so often accused of having wasted Scottish chances'.[81] They may be overstating the case when they say that it is 'clear that John MacCormick was a colder man than his son, weaker in intellect, more limited in horizons, and proud of himself where Neil was proud of his father', but they are close to the mark when they add that 'No father has been better defended by his son … and none has been more eloquently hymned in love', as they say he is

[76] Ibid., 48–9.
[77] Ibid., 53.
[78] Ibid., 63.
[79] Dyer, 'A Nationalist in the Churchillian Sense' (2003), 307.
[80] Ibid., 306.
[81] Miller, Rodger, and Dudley Edwards, *Tartan Pimps* (2010), 263.

in MacCormick's 2008 introduction to his father's *Flag in the Wind*.[82] More generally, they add, 'Few sons have the greatness to show where Father knew best despite Father's failure to realise or indeed witness it, or to show how in one of the greatest intra-party battles of his own political life [a battle over the leadership of the SNP and its direction] both he and his opponents were right'.[83]

Here, indeed, we see how there was an enormous amount at stake for MacCormick, personally, in confronting and interpreting his father's legacy: one can characterise this as an inescapable burden, but it is not in that spirit that MacCormick approached it; instead, his was an upbeat, relentlessly optimistic, undoubtedly partial and biased (as he was the first to admit), but still a very selective and very particular judgement, of what was most valuable, for Scotland, about his father's political sensibilities and actions. To better appreciate this, however, we need to delve into the granular specifics, the concrete circumstances, of Scottish nationalist politics from the 1920s through to the 1940s and 1950s.

The 1920s and 1930s: New Political Energies

The roots of many of the initiatives John MacCormick was to undertake in the 1940s and 1950s lie in student politics at the University of Glasgow in the 1920s and what emerged from them in the 1930s. Indeed, it is remarkable what political energy, with implications for the whole of Scotland and the United Kingdom, emanated from student political activity in this one Scottish university. No doubt, such a judgement can be exaggerated, but Finlay is surely close to the mark when he notes how influential in this period of the 1920s were the 'pragmatic young men from the Glasgow University Nationalist Association led by the charismatic and able John MacCormick'; they were 'new to the scene', and wanted 'to do something positive'; they 'brought a freshness of approach and a sense of urgency to the nationalist cause, which had long been lacking'.[84] Thus, even if only necessarily briefly, in order to reveal the threads that come to compose the making of the Convention in 1942, and the Covenant in 1949–51, as well as the taking of the Stone of Destiny in 1950, and ultimately the *MacCormick* v *Lord Advocate* case in 1953, we need to track back into the 1920s and 1930s.

[82] Ibid., 264.
[83] Ibid., 265.
[84] Finlay, *Independent and Free* (1994), 72.

John MacCormick matriculated at the University of Glasgow in 1923, pursuing the-then common Scottish degree of a Masters in Arts and a Bachelor in Laws, and further combining his studies, as his financial situation demanded, with an apprenticeship in a law office in the city.[85] On one evening during his studies, in the mid 1920s, John MacCormick was invited, by a friend, to come along and watch one of the Glasgow Union's famous mock parliamentary debates. These were traditionally packed, and a seat was difficult to get, but, as it happens, there were some seats that were free in the Labour benches. The Speaker of the House, as was routine, kept inviting members of the audience to speak, should they so wish, and, being nudged in the ribs and dared by his friend, John MacCormick, much to his own surprise, found himself standing up and speaking. It was a momentous three minutes of his life, at least in his own telling, for after it, he was approached by the President of the University Labour Club and asked if he wanted to become their Treasurer, a job he duly accepted.[86] Matters move fast in student politics.

Indeed, matters moved remarkably fast. Not long after, in 1927, over cups of tea in a café in Sauchiehall Street, John MacCormick, along with a few friends (James Valentine and Fergus Rodger), decided to constitute themselves as the 'Glasgow University Scottish Nationalist Association' (GUSNA), recording this self-constitution on the back of an envelope in the café.[87] Such were the modest beginnings of a largely student-driven revival of the nationalist movement in Scotland – again, at least in John MacCormick's telling. GUSNA's membership card at the time had two simple aims: 'To foster and maintain Scottish nationalism by (1) securing self-government for Scotland and (2) advancing the ideals of Scottish culture within and without the University'.[88]

Soon enough, GUSNA held its own in the mock Parliamentary debates in the Union – as we shall see later, this crucible of political debate was to prove crucial for MacCormick, as well as for a whole generation of Scottish politicians (Dewar, Smith, Campbell, and many others down the years). On one such occasion, in a debate over Scottish nationalism, when John MacCormick was making one of his innumerable speeches for Scottish self-government, a heckler called out: would Scotland become a kingdom and, if so, would you John, be our king? The moniker stuck, and from

85 MacCormick, *The Flag in the Wind* (2008), 12.
86 Ibid., 13.
87 Ibid., 18.
88 Ibid., 19.

that moment on, John MacCormick was known as 'King John'.[89] And, indeed, it was also on that same occasion, at least in John MacCormick's memory, that someone also 'suggested that an immediate raiding party should be formed so that the Stone of Destiny might be recovered from Westminster for the Coronation ceremony'.[90] The seed of that idea had been sown, and it would soon return, as we shall see.

In the meantime, however, it is important to briefly note how matters proceeded, again at breakneck speed, from this moment in 1927, through to the formation of the Scottish Convention in 1942 and then subsequently the Covenant in 1949. In 1927, a Convention had been organised by the SHRA, which had been established in 1886, but was rather dormant for many years before its revival in 1918. Having already made contact with the leaders of the SHRA, John MacCormick and his fellow GUSNA students were invited to this Convention. Following that Convention, a meeting was held with 'delegates from the Scots National League, the Scottish National Movement, the Scottish Home Rule Association' and GUSNA, which, in due course, and after numerous further discussions, formed, on 23 June 1928, the NPS.[91]

The NPS suffered from internal squabbles, and given the range of political views it had brought together, was inherently unstable, but there were moments of unity. One such moment was the 1928 Rectorial election at the University of Glasgow. As a newly formed student association, GUSNA was able to propose a candidate, which they duly did: Cunninghame Graham. Though widely expected to be an easy win for Stanley Baldwin, the incumbent Prime Minister, it was, in the end, a close contest between him and Graham, with Baldwin winning only by sixty-six votes. From one perspective, such moments may seem trivial and ineffectual – after all, not only did this one concern an election for a symbolic office in one university, but, in addition, that election was lost; however from another perspective, they were important in galvanising people, raising hopes, enlisting growing sentiment, and ever-enlarging the audience for Scottish nationalist political theatre. Indeed, as we shall see, their symbolic significance was to echo in times to come.

In the meantime, John MacCormick threw himself, with remarkable energy, into the NPS. That he genuinely and fervently believed in it can be

89 Ibid.

90 Ibid.

91 Ibid, 22; see also the detailed account in Finlay, *Independent and Free* (1994), chapters 2 and 3.

gleaned from a remarkable letter, addressed to his then-future wife, Miss Margaret Isobel Miller, in 1928:

> May I presume, Margaret, that there is no need to bore you with all the facts and figures which show that under English Government, Scotland's industry, agriculture and social development are almost entirely neglected? I shall proceed throughout on the hypothesis that you believe self-government to be a worthy object and have doubts only over how it should be achieved, or its urgency.[92]

Other parties, John MacCormick continued, were unlikely to take up this cause, at least not properly so. The NPS was the 'only medium through which Scotland can a) gain self-government and b) rebuild her social, economic, and cultural life'.[93] 'I believe', John MacCormick argued – and in its tone one can certainly feel his youthful fervour – 'that it is only by the sudden uprising of some tremendous human sentiment (such as patriotism) that we can ever rid ourselves of the degradation of poverty and wasted life that is our shame today' – an argument that may well have appealed to Margaret and her egalitarian sensibilities.[94] 'I want', John MacCormick continued, 'to make Scotland as near a Utopia as is humanly possible'.[95]

There was, then, no shortage of ambition or romantic vision, in John MacCormick at this time – a time when, it must be remembered, he was twenty four. John MacCormick duly stood for election in 1929, as a NPS candidate, putting 'Scotland First', and quoting Nehemiah: 'Ye see the distress that we are in, how Jerusalem lieth waste, and the gates thereof are burned with fire: come, and let us build up the walls of Jerusalem, that we be no more a reproach'.[96] His candidature was unsuccessful, but he was hardly deterred. In 1930, he launched the first of so-called 'Covenants', with this one reading:

> We, the undersigned, holding a high ideal of our nation's destiny, believe in the urgent necessity of Self government for Scotland. In the faith that a regenerated Scotland will take a pleading place among the nations of the world in all peaceful progress, we solemnly pledge ourselves to do everything in our power to restore the independent national status of Scotland. We bind ourselves to act on our belief that the mandate of a majority of Scottish citizens is sufficient authority for setting up an Independent Parliament in Scotland.[97]

92 MacCormick, 'Why a National Party', Appendix to *The Flag in the Wind*, 2008, 220.
93 Ibid.
94 Ibid., 222.
95 Ibid., 224.
96 MacCormick, *The Flag in the Wind* (2008), see insert, just after page 130.
97 Hanham, *Scottish Nationalism* (1969), 158.

These were busy and heady days, filled with public meetings, but also private discussions, which were to become enormously significant in the years to come. Thus, for instance, as recounted by John MacCormick, at the end of an NPS public meeting in Inverness in the autumn of 1929, John MacCormick asked for volunteers to step forward who may be willing to form a local, Inverness-based, NPS branch. Two such volunteers did indeed step forward: Neil Gunn and Duncan MacNeill.[98] In due course, these two figures – one of whom, Gunn, went on to become one of Scotland's most important twentieth century novelists, and the other, MacNeill, a solicitor, who went on to write influential histories of the Scottish Constitution[99] – established a local NPS branch with 500 members.[100] More significant, perhaps, than the branch, were the late night discussions that John MacCormick had with them, often in Gunn's house (known as 'Larachan') in Inverness. This house, John MacCormick recalled, had become 'our unofficial headquarters' in which the discussants delved, in particular, into the particularities of Scottish political – especially constitutional – history.[101]

Soon enough, such discussions found their way into the public arena. There were, again, numerous manifestations of this, such as John MacCormick organising a Bannockburn Day celebration in 1930.[102] But they also included more legally based arguments. Thus, after the passing of the *Local Government Act* of 1930, John MacCormick wrote, in the *Scots Independent*, raising the argument that the Act may well be in 'contravention of the Treaty of Union entered into in 1707, and we find that there is no court or tribunal which can test the validity of that Act'.[103] He then added:

> We find that we are bound to accept whatever law England cares to force upon us in spite of the safeguard or bargain, and we have therefore decided once and for all without any ambiguity that there is only one authority to which we are appealing, to set our independent Parliament in Scotland, and that is the authority of the Scottish people. I find it very strange and amusing when I am asked to propose what to do if England will not give us self-government. We are not concerned whether England will give us it or not. England has nothing to do with it. It is for us to make up our

98 MacCormick, *The Flag in the Wind* (2008), 45.
99 MacNeill, *The Scottish Constitution* (1943); and *The Scottish Realm* (1947).
100 MacCormick, *The Flag in the Wind* (2008), 45.
101 Ibid., 45–6.
102 Finlay, 'Declaration of Arbroath' (2020), 319.
103 MacCormick, 'Special Supplement', *Scots Independent*, July 1930, 5: quoted in Finlay, 'Declaration of Arbroath' (2020), 319–20.

> minds whether we want it, and if we want it we are going to have it, and in this Covenant we declare our belief and bind ourselves to act on it that the authority of a majority of Scottish citizens is sufficient for setting up an independent Scottish Parliament.[104]

This was in July 1930, but just a few months earlier, in March 1930, John MacCormick expressed a similar sentiment:

> Our history in Scotland since the Union seems to be a record of local but ineffective protests against insults from the English parliament. Time and again we have seen the Treaty of Union that 'safeguard' of our national rights being wantonly ignored by the predominant partner: time and again we have declared that no proud nation can tolerate such national humiliation, but time and time again for all our vain protests, we have accepted breach of trust as a fait accompli.[105]

In these, and other such statements made at the time, John MacCormick was raising a question that was to become one of the central pillars of debates over Scottish nationalism: the prospects for a constitutional history of the United Kingdom that recognised Scottish rights, that respected its particular constitutional tradition, and that did not treat the 1707 Union as a mere 'scrap of paper' (the very title of John MacCormick's article quoted above).

As we shall see, much was to be added, over the years, to this appeal, not only by John MacCormick himself, but a whole generation of Scottish constitutional historians, including MacNeill, but then, later, many others, including J. D. B. Mitchell,[106] H. J. Paton,[107] and of course, from the 1970s on, Neil MacCormick himself. What is important to notice at this point is that re-telling the history – renewing historical self-consciousness and awareness, with collective passion, amongst the people – was vital to the Scottish nationalist movement. No doubt the roots of this rejuvenation lie earlier, for instance in the work of the great, but neglected, Scottish historian, Agnes Mure Mackenzie, whose many historical books – on Robert Bruce, King of Scots, but also on the rise and fall of the Stewarts, on Queen Mary Queen of Scotland, as well as an influential school textbook and collection of important documents from Scottish history – reached a wide audience in the 1930s and early 1940s. But there is also no doubt that they

[104] Ibid.

[105] MacCormick, '"The Scrap of Paper": Should We Accept the Local Government Act', *Scots Independent*, March 1930, 54; quoted in Finlay, *Scottish Nationalism* (2022), 96.

[106] Mitchell, *Constitutional Law* (1964).

[107] Paton, *The Claim of Scotland* (1968).

were given a boost by John MacCormick's public interventions, including his arguments for a proper recognition of the 1707 Treaty of Union. After all, John MacCormick was not only a politician: he was a trained lawyer, soon to have his own practice as a Glasgow solicitor.

In the 1930s, further discussions would lead to the creation of yet another political party: the SNP in 1934. Back in 1932, the SP had been founded, led by Alexander McEwan, along with others such as the Duke of Montrose and Andrew Dewar Gibb (who later became the Regius Professor of Scots Law at Glasgow). This party was ostensibly oriented towards a more 'moderate' direction, aiming less for outright independence – they were said to be especially concerned with maintaining a voice and role in the British Empire – than for some version of self-government, for instance, in the form of a Scottish parliament. Opposed to this were certain members of the NPS that took a more forthright or 'fundamentalist' view, many of whom had been affiliated in some way with the Scottish National League (SNL). The SNL, it should be added, had been formed in 1920, and 'advocated a go it alone strategy, which was free from any British connections', and which was especially 'hostile' to and 'highly critical of' the British Empire.[108] On the way the SNL saw it, 'the Scottish nation was little more than an English colony and was being treated as such'; much like Ireland, with whom the SNL identified the Scottish case, Scotland was an 'oppressed nation', and it was thus time to tear Scotland away from the British Empire.[109]

The NPS, as it had been formed in 1928, was composed, in part, of many of these members of the SNL. For John MacCormick, who was attracted to a moderate position, which, he judged, along with many others, had more of a chance to be taken up by the majority of people in Scotland, this posed a dilemma. Still riding, perhaps, on the back of a this-time successful Rectorial campaign in Glasgow in 1931 (which saw the Nationalist candidate, Compton Mackenzie, elected), and having had numerous discussions with members of the newly formed SP, in 1933, John MacCormick took his chance and voted for an expulsion of the hardliners – the former members of the SNL – in the NPS. The resolutions were carried, and this mass expulsion opened the door to the formation of the newly moderate, but also larger, SNP, which was a merger of the NPS and the SP. This was achieved, officially, on 20 April 1934.

108 Finlay, '"For or Against"' (1992), 188; and for a detailed history, see Finlay, *Independent and Free* (1994), chapter 2.

109 See Finlay, 'For or Against' (1992), 188.

The early SNP was hardly an electoral success, and the discussions and disagreements over its future did not end with the expulsion of the SNL members in 1933. Matters came to a head over the issue of conscription in the early years of the Second World War. A key figure, who was personally involved in this issue at the time, was Douglas Young, a Greek scholar, tall and with a magnificent beard, and a commanding public presence. As described by Pentland:

> At an Aberdeen May Day meeting in 1939, Young had answered a heckler by asserting a legal and constitutional rather than a moral point: that it was ultra vires for the Westminster Parliament to impose conscription for foreign service on Scottish subjects. Young evidently tested this point on the legal expert and nationalist Andrew Dewar Gibb, whom Young had met at the party conference of 1939 and who attempted to burst his bubble with a statement of the Diceyan orthodoxy that 'Parliament can do anything'. Undeterred, Young went on to restate this approach and in November 1940 three nationalists came before Glasgow Sheriff Court and justified their failure to register on the grounds that the military service act did not apply to Scotland, because it breached the Treaty of Union.[110]

This was an important moment, but it was, as we have seen, not the first time that the Treaty of Union had been appealed to. This time, though, the stakes were personally very high, and the cases that tested this argument were also the first occasions in which the Treaty of Union was judicially discussed.

Young lost his case, with the Court not being sympathetic to his arguments against Westminster Parliamentary sovereignty, but in losing the case, and indeed being for a time imprisoned, he won many followers. In fact, he became a kind of radical hero, echoing other old-style radicals, who had used 'courtrooms and legal reporting as a soapbox for their views', stretching back to 'the state trials of the 1790s'.[111] As Pentland observed, 'From his dramatization of trial and imprisonment, through his use of constitutionalist languages, to the elaborate and choregraphed procession that marked his release, Young tapped into a long and rich radical tradition'.[112] Young further capitalised on this in numerous publications, making the constitutional arguments, which might have otherwise failed to capture the public imagination, personally dramatic.[113] As we shall see, this is not the only time that a constitutional argument,

[110] Pentland, 'Douglas Young' (2016), 153.
[111] Ibid., 155.
[112] Ibid.
[113] See Young, *Free-Minded Scot* (1942).

argued for in a courtroom, was to take on dramatic – if not tragic – personal consequences.

These wartime issues of conscription were to play their crucial part in the formation of the Scottish Convention. For, in 1942, at the SNP Annual Conference, a showdown emerged between Young, who, resisting conscription as he was, pushed a hard-line, 'fundamentalist' argument, for the separation of Scotland from the British Empire, as against the-then incumbent, William Power, an elderly journalist, a moderate, a gradualist, and very much John MacCormick's man.[114] On what has been described as a 'stiflingly hot June day', and amidst 'an ill-tempered debate',[115] John MacCormick argued passionately for Power but was defeated by thirty-three votes to twenty nine. According to Andrew Marr, the vote was in reality against the style of John MacCormick's leadership, which Marr describes as 'autocratic',[116] but either way, Power's defeat, and Young's victory, although achieved by the slimmest of margins, had very significant consequences.[117] For, in the wake of Young's victory, John MacCormick resigned his position in the SNP, and walked out, going across the road, to the Rutland Hotel, and, together with a good number of followers, who also resigned from the SNP that afternoon, formed a new cross-party initiative: the Scottish Convention.

Convention and Covenant

Established in June 1942, the Scottish Convention grew rapidly – indeed, a great deal more rapidly than the SNP, the membership of which stalled or even shrunk. Finlay notes that within a year, in 1943, the Convention had 1,000 members, already then more than the SNP,[118] and this grew steadily, especially immediately post-war: towards the end of 1945, the membership was 3,691, and then 4,733 in 1946.[119] Equally, the finances improved, reaching a surplus in 1946, assisted not only by membership but also by

[114] See also Finlay's account in Finlay, *Independent and Free* (1994), chapter 6.

[115] Marr, *The Battle for Scotland* (2013), 93.

[116] Ibid., 94; Marr also added that John MacCormick had 'organisational genius and energy': 94.

[117] Incidentally, in 1972, after Neil MacCormick got his Regius Chair in Edinburgh, Douglas Young wrote to him – on 22 July 1972 – and congratulated him warmly on it, and added 'You would be conveniently placed to function in a Scottish parliament', advising MacCormick to 'associate yourself with the Edinburgh city Labour folk, who have usually been favourable to self-government'.

[118] Finlay, *Independent and Free* (1994), 231.

[119] Somerville, *Through the Maelstrom* (2013), 29; Mitchell, *Strategies for Self-Government* (1996), 85.

raffles and bazaar schemes.[120] Although the Convention was a non-party or cross-party movement, with membership open to members of all political parties, it did maintain a link to party politics, and was certainly 'being noticed in the parliamentary arena'.[121] Scottish MPs sometimes pledged their support, and the Convention would sometimes also send delegations to London to give those MPs 'ammunition' in home rule debates in the Commons.[122]

Conventions were hardly a new political form in Scotland. Even if we just restrict ourselves to the immediate past, following the revival of the SHRA in 1918, there were calls for a Scottish National Convention in 1919. Thus, for instance, Roland Muirhead, who was largely responsible for the revival of the SHRA, called for a 'National Convention in order to consider what steps should be taken to the early establishment of a parliament in Scotland'.[123] Calls for such a Convention would be renewed throughout the 1920s, and, as we have seen above, there were Convention meetings, even if only a relatively small scale, in 1927, in which John MacCormick and his fellow students participated.

Thus, John MacCormick's efforts in the early 1940s were hardly new. Indeed, all through the 1930s John MacCormick had made various calls for such 'an all-party Scottish Convention', e.g., in 1932, when he 'made approaches to prominent Home Rulers and the SP with the aim of drumming up support for the idea'.[124] In the 1930s, the idea did not get off the ground. Members of the NPS at the time, and later, the SNP, did not warm to it, preferring to stay within the bounds of party politics, though we have also seen how MacCormick tried to steer the various parties he was involved in into more moderate waters, where something more like a general, popular, if not wholly non-party, movement for home rule could garner support.

Having split from the SNP for good in 1942, John MacCormick was arguably liberated from the constraints of party politics, and threw himself with remarkable energy into the Convention. I shall return in a moment to the Convention's rise, and its culmination in the Covenant of 1949–51, in which MacCormick, at the ages of eight to ten, was very much involved, collecting signatures and sitting in on the Convention's public meetings.

[120] Ibid.
[121] Ibid.
[122] Somerville, *Through the Maelstrom* (2013), 29.
[123] Quoted in Finlay, *Independent and Free* (1994), 3.
[124] Finlay, *Independent and Free* (1994), 100.

However, it is important to pause here, for a moment, to consider just how John MacCormick pitched this Convention. As we shall see, at stake in John MacCormick's articulation of the principles of the Convention was precisely the prospect for a long-term, morally resonant, non-party, democratic politics – something that MacCormick, the son, was to pick up on later.

An important and understudied source in this respect is not John MacCormick's memoir of the time, but instead, a thirty-five-page pamphlet entitled *The Scottish Convention: An Experiment in Democracy* published in Glasgow in 1943. Prefaced by William Power, who hails John MacCormick as descending from the 'original "Scots" of Argyll', describing him as a 'practical genius' whose 'words are winged with beauty',[125] the text is a remarkable political testament, setting out a vision not only for Scotland, but also of what politics could be.

John MacCormick's 'Scottish Convention' begins, tellingly, with a particular view of Scotland's history, including its legal and constitutional history. Scotland, he says, 'lays claim to being the oldest of all the European nations', with the 1320 Declaration of Arbroath cited as 'set[ting] forth', for 'the first time in Europe's history' 'the claim of a people to be itself'.[126] Scotland continued to be 'completely independent' until the Union of the Crowns in 1603.[127] Within that period, from 1320 to 1603, Scotland flourished, both in terms of trade as well as various other areas of policy, such as education. Perhaps most significant was its unique legal system, which 'was her own and expressed her own spirit', and which differed 'wildly from that of England, not only in particular matters but in the fundamentals of its jurisprudence': whereas 'in England law defended property', 'in Scotland law defended the person'.[128] Accordingly, the Scottish people 'were masters in the art of personal relationship', with a particular commitment to 'freedom', which was 'more real to them than almost anything else'.[129]

For John MacCormick, the Union of Crowns in 1603 was a disaster for Scotland: 'the departure of James to England at once shattered the unity of the Scottish constitution', and the 'anomaly' of operating a Legislature with an Executive so far away, and now 'animated by entirely different and often completely hostile policies', had 'tragic implications'.[130] The

125 Power, 'Foreword' to John MacCormick, *The Scottish Convention* (1943), 3–5.
126 MacCormick, *The Scottish Convention* (1943), 8.
127 Ibid., 9.
128 Ibid.
129 Ibid., 10.
130 Ibid., 11.

Union of 1707 was an attempt at solving the problems raised by this anomaly operating for over 100 years, but this was far from a helpful solution: 'No solemn engagement', John MacCormick said, 'has ever been so haphazard in its compromises, so lacking in self-consistency or so completely impractical in its proposals'.[131] It was not that some kind of union was a bad idea in itself: something needed to change, as the split between the executive and the legislative powers was unworkable, but the scheme was made too hastily, and under it, 'Scotland as an active nation was wiped out', unable to 'become an articulate partner in the new joint enterprise' of the Empire.[132] What happened since, in the 235 or so years from 1707, was that some administration had evolved, via the Scottish Office, but in a way that only furthered the 'anomaly', once again failing to achieve the requisite balance, in Scotland, between the various branches of government.[133]

All this was, said John MacCormick, a 'tragedy', which was now, during wartime, slowly coming to be recognised, not only because the war illuminated the problematic 'social and economic conditions in modern Scotland', which would need to be addressed urgently post-war, but also because the war was bringing about 'a sudden change in the mood of the people', with everyone showing a 'new willingness to work together to avert the disaster they foresaw might overtake their country after the victorious conclusion of the war'.[134] It was in these circumstances – 'in that atmosphere' – that 'Scottish Convention was formed'.[135] The very name 'Scottish Convention' was chosen because 'the word Convention signifies the act of a people coming together in unity of purpose' – a kind of answer, both in its unity and as an 'experiment', 'of the democratic state to the Fascist and totalitarian ideal'.[136] As John MacCormick set out somewhat more programmatically in the last page of his pamphlet, the Convention had three aims:

> (a) To provide a medium through which such matters as the better housing of our people, education and health, the redistribution and planning of our industries, and the full employment of all our resources may be discussed in a non-party atmosphere so that measures upon

[131] Ibid.

[132] Ibid., 12.

[133] See MacCormick, *The Scottish Convention* (1943), 12. The language of 'anomaly' is one that MacCormick himself later used, e.g., 'The English Constitution, the British State, and the Scottish Anomaly' (1998).

[134] MacCormick, *The Scottish Convention* (1943), 15.

[135] Ibid.

[136] Ibid., 44.

which there is substantial national agreement may be discovered and pressed forward;

(b) To find the best means of adjusting our political and economic life to the great changes which are bound to follow the War;

(c) To secure Self-Government for Scotland in federation with England and the other parts of the British Isles so that she may play a fuller and more responsible part in the affairs of the British Isles and Commonwealth and exercise her own influence in the social and economic developments which are inevitable in the world of tomorrow.[137]

It is significant, in light of MacCormick's later thought, that the aim of the Convention was clearly the pursuit of self-government within the Union: if this was nationalism, as it surely was, it was a participatory, inclusive, unionist nationalism.[138] Even if it was critical of the 1707 Union, it nevertheless did not wish to undermine it wholly. Indeed, the Convention was explicitly against the 'extreme view' that Scotland 'should sever all but the flimsiest ties with England', becoming 'again an independent kingdom or republic'.[139] As John MacCormick puts it:

> The advocates of this idea [of independence] forget that the Scottish people, even if they did not actively welcome the original Union in 1707, have at least acquiesced in it ever since. Scotland and England have thus between them created joint responsibilities in the modern world which they cannot separately discharge. They have in the same manner acquired common interests which cannot easily be disentangled. Scotland would inevitably be the loser in any severance which tacitly implied that she had always been an unwilling partner and that the assets and liabilities of the partnership should be taken over by England.[140]

John MacCormick went on, just a few pages later, to assert that 'good relations ... now exist between the English and the Scots', but these good relations rest not on 'the fact that England governs Scotland', but instead 'depend upon a proper understanding of their common interests and a proper mutual appreciation of differing qualities of character and temperament'.[141] Self-government is vital, said John MacCormick, but this must

[137] Ibid.

[138] See also Torrance, *'Standing up for Scotland'* (2020); Kidd, *Union and Unionisms* (2008). I will be returning to this question of the middle ground between unionism and nationalism in chapter 7.

[139] MacCormick, *The Scottish Convention* (1943), 22.

[140] Ibid.

[141] Ibid., 30.

not be taken so far, for instance in the name of 'national freedom', so as to turn Scotland 'inward upon herself' such that she 'wrap[s] herself up in contemplation of her own perfection'; rather, John MacCormick said, what is needed is that Scotland 'become an active agent in the processes of world change and progress'.[142] To do this, Scotland needs to understand the need for global co-operation: yes, Scotland was a nation – a proud and ancient nation – but this must not be pushed so far as to render Scotland incapable of being a partner in a network of relationships. None of this, however, will happen immediately:

> It is true ... that national freedom must be reconciled with international co-operation; that the old conception of sovereignty must give way to a new acceptance of world-wide loyalties. But such developments will not take place all at once. They will be evolved from natural groupings and from existing relationships. The establishment of a federal system within Great Britain and its possible growth to include the other members of the British Commonwealth of Nations, might well be one of the starting points for the new working out of international relations.[143]

As significant as this is already – for the articulation of a unionist-like nationalism – as well as prescient in light of what comes later, e.g., MacCormick's vision of Scotland's participation in Europe conceived of as a 'post-sovereign commonwealth', including his life-long call for Scotland to be part of various unions, John MacCormick's vision, however, did not stop there.

More conventionally, the text contained some particular policy proposals, e.g., for 'reform of the land law and system of land tenure', or various changes to housing, agriculture, transport, education, and health services,[144] a critique of the attempts at administrative devolution through the Scottish Office,[145] as well as an account of the powers a future Parliament would have,[146] something which the Convention would return to later in the publication of its 'Blueprint for Scotland' (1948).[147] But what makes John MacCormick's text most remarkable is the breadth and depth of its horizons. In articulating these broader and deeper horizons, John MacCormick reached into philosophical references, e.g., to John MacMurray's *Freedom in the Modern World* (1932) and even to Aristotle.

[142] Ibid., 31.
[143] Ibid.
[144] Ibid., 17.
[145] Ibid., 22–4.
[146] Ibid., 25–6.
[147] Included as Appendix One to John MacCormick, *The Flag in the Wind* (2008).

To confront Scotland as a nation was to 'develop something in the nature of a collective consciousness and character' – some kind of distinctive 'new statement of our attitude to life'.[148] In other words, what was needed was reflection on what was meant by 'politics'. And this meant precisely reaching into the philosophical depths.

What was 'the true purpose of all political activity'? Here, John MacCormick did not hold back from the 'fundamental' questions that needed to be asked:

> Are politics concerned merely with the best means of organising communities so that they may continue just to exist in their own right as complexes of human life? Are all our human problems economic in their nature and will they be solved when everyone has enough to eat and drink and wear and adequate shelter over his head? Are there any permanent values in the universe and if so have these values any relation to human activity? Has man a sense of spiritual reality and does he feel a need, however inarticulate he may be, for relating all his striving to some moral purpose?[149]

Yes, John MacCormick answered: there was more to politics than it being a 'system of organisation'; the 'dead hand' of 'efficiency' was not enough – that was not where the real spirit of politics lay.[150] There was more to the value of communal life than the pursuit of economic efficiency:

> Unless we believe that it is in itself a good thing that men should live in social intercourse with one another, then it would be unlikely that we should be concerned about the community at all. So long as I myself had all I wanted in the way of wealth and security I should have no urge to help my neighbour to a similar satiety. It is because we believe for one reason or another that the happiness and prosperity of the whole community is a desirable goal that we take an interest in any kind of politics. We somehow feel that our own individual life cannot be as fully and as rich as it might be in a community in which others live in abject poverty or in ugly and squalid surroundings. That is why we are prepared to sacrifice our leisure and often indeed our own personal security in political effort which may have an immediate economic end in view. It is, however, our belief in the 'worth-whileness' of the life of community which gives that effort any real meaning.[151]

Politics has a moral life – it is ultimately animated by a vision of the moral good of the members of the community, including the importance of a

[148] MacCormick, *The Scottish Convention* (1943), 33.
[149] Ibid., 34.
[150] Ibid., 35.
[151] Ibid.

good life for all. Here, at this moment, John MacCormick was at one with the vision – not articulated in such high-flying words, but certainly lived in action – by his wife, MacCormick's mother, Margaret Miller. Here, too, we see the seed, if not the foundation, of MacCormick's, the son's, orientation towards an inclusive, egalitarian, moderate, and gradualist politics, which was driven not by any one political aim, but more by a moral commitment to decency, considerateness, and respect for persons.

I say 'in this moment' above, because there are other aspects of John MacCormick's statement that do not echo, neither in his wife's views or sentiments, nor indeed in his son's. For John MacCormick's vision also contains a paean to the 'personalities' of 'very great men', like 'Jesus' or 'Socrates', who are 'so real, so richly alive, that' they 'radiate an influence all round' them.[152] If only we could discover, John MacCormick said, what 'makes up this quality of personality', then we could somehow steer ourselves into striving 'towards a complete expression of personality'.[153] 'The truly great man', he added, 'is in the deepest sense truly free', for 'he has escaped from those inner compulsions which enslave the rest of us', such as 'the bonds of prejudice, of custom, and of fear'.[154] John MacCormick did temper this hymn to the freedom of great men, liberated from their societies, by arguing that such freedom of personality was only possible within a community – 'He can only express his personality in his relations with other persons' and 'its highest expression will be in the quality of these relations' – an important qualification, but still one that placed, on the pedestal, the great man, the patriot, the responsible citizen, who was truly free and who showed us all what it meant to be free.[155] One has a sense, as a reader, that John MacCormick was, in part, talking about himself, at least in aspiration. He, too, wanted to be a great man.

I have spent some time setting out John MacCormick's 'philosophy' not only because there are, as we shall see, echoes – albeit selective echoes – of his views in those of MacCormick, but also because he was willing to go there: for all the talk of 'great men', and thus the elitist and establishment aspects of his views, there was, in John MacCormick, a genuine search for what was most important about life, both for individuals and communities. Further, this search included a deeper vision of politics, and what it meant, than simply the pursuit of electoral success, or even

[152] Ibid., 37.
[153] Ibid.
[154] Ibid., 38.
[155] Ibid., 38–9.

achieving certain efficient results in policy terms. Politics was a matter of morality – of finding 'a unity of moral purpose'.[156] Politics was, in the end, not far from moral philosophy itself. As John MacCormick put it, towards the end of this remarkable document:

> It [the unity of purpose, for instance as articulated in the Convention] will try to give politics a new meaning, so that the word will come to convey in the sphere of men's relations with one another something of the same significance as the word 'philosophy' does in the realm of knowledge – a synthesis of all our activities, of our art and our literature and our music, of our planning and our striving, of our toil and of our leisure; in other words, an understanding in the fullest sense, of the whole business of living together as communities of live men and women.[157]

It is this deeply morally resonant vision of politics, at one with a vision of philosophy, that MacCormick, the son, would have heard, at the impressionable age of eight to ten, and beyond, John MacCormick, his father, articulate, whether around the dinner table, in the discussions that were frequently had at 2 Park Quadrant, or on the rostrum at the many public meetings of the Convention in the years after 1943.

It is important here to give just a brief sense of the buzz of activity in those years leading up to and then culminating in the Covenant of 1949–51. Thus, for instance, in early 1947, the Convention sent out invitations to a very wide spectrum of public associations in Scotland – 'every local authority, every Church of Scotland presbytery, every trade union, chamber of commerce and trade association, and a variety of other bodies as well'[158] – inviting them to 'Scottish National Assembly' (the 'Assembly') to be held in Glasgow on 22 March 1947. The SNP was also invited, but declined to participate, though, in the end, a number of SNP members, including senior ones (such as Douglas Young), did attend and speak at the Assembly, albeit not in their official capacity. In the end, there were no less than 600 delegates from all stripes of Scottish public life. This event was described by *The Scotsman* at the time as 'perhaps the most widely representative [meeting] ever held to discuss Scottish affairs'.[159] John MacCormick, who presided over the entire proceedings, opened it in ringing tones:

> This is the first time in the history of Scotland that such a gathering has been brought together. We are, in fact, today a Convention of the Estates

156 Ibid., 42.
157 Ibid.
158 Hanham, *Scottish Nationalism* (1969), 170.
159 Somerville, *Through the Maelstrom* (2013), 31.

> of Scotland. This meeting is representative of the people of this country. There are here today representatives of no less than 60 Burghs, including the great cities of Aberdeen and Glasgow, as well as County Councils, Co-operative Societies, Trade Unions, Political Parties, the Church, and every organ of public opinion. We are gathered to consider the needs of our own country. There is ample precedent for the holding of such an Assembly. In the year 1689, for example, there was convened a Meeting of the Estates of Scotland without the authority of any King or Government. That body offered the throne of Scotland to King William and Queen Mary. It is interesting to remember the terms of their opening Resolution: 'We come together for the most serious consideration of the best means for attaining the ends before us as our ancestors in the like cases have usually done'. Today I suggest that we are met, in a similar spirit, to vindicate our ancient rights and liberties and to prove to the world that there is still life and heart in Scotland. I should like to say this, that we are here today not to find out how far we differ but in how much we agree.[160]

This opening was duly met, as the report from the proceedings indicate, with 'applause'. The object of the Assembly was to discuss and vote on three resolutions. The text of the second resolution was as follows:

> This Assembly, representative of all shades of opinion in Scotland, is convinced that a substantial majority of the Scottish people favours a large measure of Scottish Self-Government, and therefore resolves to request that the Government should forthwith introduce in Parliament a Bill to give effect to the Scottish Self-Government proposals set forth in the Declaration by a representative Committee of Scotsmen under the Chairmanship of Mr William Leonard MP, a copy of which is attached to this agenda.[161]

This Resolution was passed by a very large majority. As the Resolution envisaged, a thirty-five-person Committee, which naturally included John MacCormick, was then empowered by the Assembly delegates to form a new constitutional plan for Scotland. This Committee convened soon after the Assembly, on 7 June 1947, and just three months later published a document, 'Blueprint for Scotland' (published in blueprint), which set out a vision for the competencies of a new Scottish parliament. Published as Appendix One to John MacCormick's memoir, 'Blueprint' is a remarkable document, and all the more so for being so prescient – as MacCormick himself observed later on numerous occasions – in foreshadowing the

160 Scottish National Assembly, *Report of Proceedings* (22 March 1947), 9.

161 Ibid., 31; this was directly linked to what was known as the wartime Leonard Declaration, which had also argued for a Scottish parliament: see Mitchell, *Strategies for Self-Government* (1996), 86–7.

eventual *Scotland Act* 1998, e.g., by only listing explicitly the reserved matters, rather than those devolved, thereby also leaving room for the Scottish Parliament to grow and expand in scope.

There was, in Scotland at the time, genuine enthusiasm for the Convention and its 'Blueprint'. As Somerville described it, the Convention 'demonstrated the appetite which existed for non-partisan nationalism from an overwhelming and varied body of opinion in Scotland'.[162] It also, as she adds, 'produced widespread, and on the whole positive, publicity for the Home Rule movement when it was reported extensively in the Scottish press and recorded by the BBC in Scotland, an extract being broadcast the evening the Assembly convened'.[163] It clearly did capture the public's imagination and sentiment.

The official response, from the Government, was much less enthusiastic. The-then Secretary of State for Scotland, Arthur Woodburn, serving in Clement Attlee's post-war Labour government, replied dismissively to the 'Blueprint'. In reaction to that, John MacCormick decided to convene a second Assembly on 20 March 1948. The second Assembly agreed that 'a plebiscite or petition was needed to demonstrate the widespread support that existed amongst voters for a Scottish parliament',[164] and this was duly carried out, albeit on a small scale, with the Government refusing to consider holding an official plebiscite for the whole of Scotland. This, in turn, prompted a meeting of the Assembly Committee, held in April 1949, which decided to 'launch a Scottish Covenant scheme which they hoped would demonstrate beyond all reasonable doubt the widespread desire felt in Scotland for a Scottish parliament'.[165] This Covenant, echoing previous efforts, such as that mentioned above in 1930, but this time wearing its moderate and gradualist vision on its sleeve more explicitly, pledged as follows:

> We, the people of Scotland who subscribe this Engagement, declare our belief that reform in the constitution of our country is necessary to secure good government in accordance with our Scottish traditions and to promote the spiritual and economic welfare of our nation.
>
> We affirm that the desire for such reform is both deep and widespread throughout the whole community, transcending political differences and sectional interests, and we undertake to continue united in purpose for its achievement.

162 Somerville, *Through the Maelstrom* (2013), 32.
163 Ibid.
164 Ibid., 35.
165 Ibid.

> With that end in view we solemnly enter into this covenant whereby we pledge ourselves, in all loyalty to the Crown and within the framework of the United Kingdom, to do everything in our power to secure for Scotland a Parliament with adequate legislative authority in Scottish affairs.[166]

Empowered with these words, the Convention organised a third Assembly, on 29 October 1949, at the Church of Scotland's Assembly Hall, in order to begin collecting signatures in support of the Covenant. This was, on all accounts, a grand occasion, with the Duke of Montrose signing the Covenant first, followed by John MacCormick, again gaining very considerable interest from the public and the press. Indeed, the Covenant was remarkably popular, collecting 50,000 signatures by the end of the first week, and going on, in the space of two years, and thus by 1951, to collect around two million signatures – a 'staggering two-thirds of the voting population' at the time.[167] As Somerville puts it, 'It was an extraordinary endorsement for the Home Rule camp and, crucially, provided the Convention and the Assembly Committee with the evidence they needed to show St Andrew's House the popular support felt in Scotland for a firm measure of Home Rule'.[168]

In 1949, when the Covenant was launched, MacCormick was eight. He may have been too young to attend the first Assembly in 1947, but he was very likely present at this spectacular and grand third Assembly on 29 October 1949, witnessing his father speaking in front of a very large crowd, and undoubtedly feeling a complex mix of emotions, including pride and a sense that something genuinely important was being done for Scotland, not only by his father but by an enthused and broad spectrum of the community. Certainly, his father saw that day as 'one of the great occasions in the long history of our nation … a turning point in the life of our people from which there will never be any going back',[169] and one can only imagine that this passionate atmosphere filled the MacCormick household at this time. Indeed, the whole family, MacCormick included, was very active in assisting with collecting signatures for the Covenant over the period of 1949–51. MacCormick recalled, in his memoires, how 'perpetually busy' his father was, 'regularly being interviewed on the phone and photographed for and quoted in the daily papers', adding that 'we children knew a fair amount about the Scottish Covenant and the

166 Ibid., 36.
167 Ibid., 37.
168 Ibid.
169 MacCormick, *The Flag in the Wind* (2008), 130.

seemingly irresistible tide of opinion it was building up towards the re-establishment of a Scottish Parliament'.[170]

This passionate sociability, this expression of democratic energy, this collective self-consciousness and sentiment, which were clearly present on a large scale in Glasgow, and beyond, at the time, were concentrated – like nectar – in the MacCormick household. Again, they must have been powerfully affective experiences for a young boy of eight to ten. Arguably, though, they went beyond the kind of emotional experiences one might have at that age, for during this time, MacCormick would have been exposed to beliefs, arguments, ideas, dispositions, and attitudes – such as those we saw his father articulate above – and though, of course, we cannot expect him to have understood them all, given his age, it is surely more than possible that they informed his worldview. None of this is to say that MacCormick adopted his father's notions wholescale – in fact, he very much did not. However, there are echoes in his later views, of some of his father's passions and orientations, such as gradualism, a commitment to democracy, an interest in Scotland's legal and constitutional history, a sensitivity to historical wrongs and the importance of certain documents, and, perhaps most importantly, a sense of the intertwinement, at a certain moral depth, between the political and the philosophical.

The Convention and the Covenant clearly remained in MacCormick's memory. He returned to it in many speeches down the years, e.g., on 16 January 1999, on the occasion of the 71st anniversary of the SNP, he spoke of 'the Covenant strategy' and how it 'raised to national consciousness two million Scots, who were willing indeed to sign up, but most of whom were not then ready to abandon traditional party loyalty and vote SNP'.[171]

Beyond MacCormick himself, the Convention has also been actively invoked, as a precursor, in crucial moments, such as in the 1980s, with similar Conventions Assemblies, and plebiscites then held, leading to the Claim of Right. Indeed, the story of the Convention's many public meetings and speeches has been retold on numerous occasions, e.g., recently, in 2019, writing in *The Nation* with a double feature on the Convention and the Covenant, Hamish McPherson said, straightforwardly, that 'The Scottish Covenant was an important development in the long-running battle to win the Parliament, as it made home rule a live issue, which

170 MacCormick, 'John MacCormick Memoir' (2008/9), 3.

171 MacCormick, 'Speech on the 71st Anniversary of the SNP' (16 January 1999), 2.

people discussed'.[172] As we shall see, this democratic, cross-party, collective political energy was to bubble up to the surface in MacCormick's political and philosophical life on numerous occasions.

The Stone of Destiny

'This is the BBC Home Service: Here is the news on Christmas Day 1950. The Stone of Destiny has been removed from Westminster Abbey. It is thought that this may have been the work of the Scottish nationalists'.[173] If the Convention and the Covenant had captured some of the public's imagination, then the events of Christmas 1950 pulled at the heartstrings, and recalled, in the most theatrical way, the indignities of the past. Neal Ascherson, who remembers that, in 1951, when he was nineteen and serving in Singapore on military service, he took with him 'a copy of the Scottish Covenant … the petition for a Scottish parliament, launched by John MacCormick', wanting to show it to 'far-flung colonial Scots',[174] also said, this time about the 1950 event:

> The Christmas break-in at the Abbey electrified people in Scotland, because it was cheeky and patriotic and put right an old wrong – but also because the Stone had prompted an authentically Scottish act. No grave committee in Edinburgh had recommended this, no body composed by the Kirk and the Faculty of Advocates and the other institutions preserved by the Union. A bunch of twenty-year-old nobodies, shabby law students and a young woman in a tweed skirt, had asked nobody's leave. They had asserted, in effect, that the Union's articles did not stand at the end of every road. Beyond it, above it, there survived some residual Scottish right to change an aspect of the relationship between Scotland and England.[175]

It is important that Ascherson links the Stone to the 1707 Union, while also characterising the act of taking it as an act of the people, stemming from something deeper than any document could symbolise. The Stone of Destiny, also known as the Stone of Scone, had been woven into the Scottish imaginary for some time, most recently in the form of stories told to children by their parents and teachers. Indeed, MacCormick himself remembered that:

[172] McPherson, 'Back in the Day: The Lessons We Can Learn from "King John"'(17 December 2019) and 'Back in the Day: "King John" and the Scots' Covenant' (24 December 2019), *The Nation*.

[173] MacCormick, 'Nationalist Memoirs I' (2008/9), 1.

[174] Ascherson, *Stone Voices* (2002), 232.

[175] Ibid., 19.

> We [the children in the MacCormick household] had been brought up on the story how Edward I seized it [the Stone] from Scone in his conquest of Scotland in 1296. He took the most sacred symbol of the Scottish nation, the stone on which we crowned our kings. He had iron rings bolted into it. He had poles stuck through the rings and carried it in ostentatious triumph through Scotland to show the Scots who was their master. And he took it to London.[176]

As Ascherson put it, 'what mattered about the Stone was precisely its absence: the fact that it had been carted off by an English king in an act of plunder which was also intended to be a symbolic act of conquest'.[177] Effectively, the Stone did not just symbolise the 1296 moment: its absence was filled by many other stories, tumbling on top of that one. Rising against King Edward, and his pretension to be 'legitimate Lord of Scotland', were William Wallace and Andrew Murray, who, raising an army against him, 'drove his troops out after their great victory at Stirling Bridge'.[178] In the end, Wallace was defeated and caught and 'given the hideous torture and execution provided for "traitors" in English law then and for long after'.[179] The 'struggle' continued with King Robert, and his eventual triumph at Bannockburn in 1314, and finally the Treaty of Northampton in 1328, but still the Stone remained in London, and that Treaty was, as well as the Scots in generally were, thus 'dishonoured'.[180]

Arguably, stones have always had a place in the Scottish psyche, and thus also in its story-telling, in its history-spinning; but amongst all those stones, it was the Stone of Destiny that stood out as the talisman: the one that, in Ascherson's words, 'became, in the modern period, an indispensable foundation stone for the reconstruction of a Scottish national – and eventually political – identity'.[181]

The story of what happened in the Christmas of 1950 has been told many times before; it can be heard still today often in the streets of Edinburgh, especially near Edinburgh Castle, being retold in a myriad of languages to visitors. The idea of taking the Stone was sown, as we saw earlier in this chapter, in the 1920s when students in Glasgow joked about taking it so that John MacCormick – King John – could sit on it in the new Kingdom of Scotland. And, indeed, John MacCormick presided, as if a monarch – he was, after

176 MacCormick, 'The Stone of Destiny: Symbol and Reality' (1996), 1.
177 Ascherson, *Stone Voices* (2002), 23.
178 MacCormick, 'The Stone of Destiny: Symbol and Reality' (1996), 1.
179 Ibid.
180 Ibid.
181 Ascherson, *Stone Voices* (2002), 23.

all, the Rector of the University of Glasgow (which was close enough!), over the whole affair, funding the group of students who did the taking, and then hiding the Stone and leading the negotiations for its eventual return.

The four students who took the Stone – one of which was Ian Hamilton, later to become Queen's Counsel, then a law student who John MacCormick knew well and who was soon to be involved, with him, in the *MacCormick* v *Lord Advocate* case in 1953[182] – broke into Westminster Abbey on a wet, dark night, and managed, after many adventures, to drive it back to Scotland. A year later, after protracted negotiations – and especially, according to MacCormick, given the ill-health of King George VI who was known to be anxious about the Stone[183] – it was returned, albeit once again with historical poignancy, for it was left in Arbroath Abbey.[184]

Within the MacCormick household, back on Christmas Day in 1950, the atmosphere was charged with great emotion. One has to imagine the family already somewhat exhilarated, though undoubtedly also tired, this being in the middle of the Covenant's signature-collecting and soon after the election of John MacCormick to the Rectorship in Glasgow. Amongst them sits a nine-year old boy with an imagination for adventure, right there in the eye of the storm. As MacCormick recalled it, in the unpublished memoirs he recorded when ill, the news came through at one o'clock. His mother was in the kitchen making soup, along with other final preparations for Christmas dinner. Gathered together, in anticipation of the feast, was the extended MacCormick family, including MacCormick's siblings – Marion, Elspeth, and Iain – MacCormick's cousins, Donald and Alastair, as well as four aunts, two uncles, and a maternal grandmother.

Moments before the news, John MacCormick had received a call, and invited the whole family to come and listen. 'John, I'm making the soup. This is Christmas day, we don't have to listen to the wireless news today'. But John MacCormick insisted: 'Margaret, the news is just coming on. I think you should come and listen to it'. The news, when heard by all, resulted in 'prolonged cheering'. The mood was one of jubilation: there was, MacCormick recounts, 'high enthusiasm for and speculation about

182 See Hamilton, *The Taking of the Stone of Destiny* (1991); and *A Touch of Treason* (1990).

183 MacCormick, 'John MacCormick Memoir' (2008/9), 4.

184 Though not, it seems, without retaining a fragment. Recently released Scottish government documents apparently show that MacCormick was given a fragment of the Stone from his father and that, in 2008, when he knew he was dying, he gave that fragment to Alex Salmond, then the first minister of Scotland. See 'Missing Stone of Destiny Chip found in SNP Cupboard', 8 January 2024, BBC. See www.bbc.co.uk/news/uk-scotland-67911483; last accessed 18 January 2024.

the daring raid on the Abbey of Westminster and retrieval of this ancient symbol both of Scottish identity and of a long-past English attempt to extinguish that identity'.[185] For all the cheering and celebrating, however, and as told to him later by his mother, the news also came with apprehension, causing not a little anxiety. John MacCormick himself remained steadfastly jubilant: 'Well, Margaret, is this not the most wonderful news?', he asked. 'No, it is not', Margaret MacCormick replied. 'I know who did it and I know that you are in it up to your neck. You have four children under twelve and who is going to look after them if you go to jail?' John MacCormick was a little put off and indeed astounded that she clearly knew more than he realised: 'How can you possibly know who did it?', he asked. 'It is that Ian Hamilton, and you have been secret talks with him for weeks. It is obvious. How did you know what was going to be on the news?'[186] The reader can draw their own inferences as to how this scene sheds light on the relationship between John and Margaret MacCormick.

Looking back, in these memoirs, at what happened in that Christmas of 1950, MacCormick is understandably charmed by his father's risk-taking. His father did, indeed, have a lot to lose, but then it was important to keep in mind, MacCormick added, 'the sacrifice he was willing to make', including in this situation, 'when an opportunity for a grand symbolic gesture came his way'.[187] One needed to situate the taking of the Stone of Destiny in the context of the Covenant: by supporting the students in their daring raid, John MacCormick was able to convey to the Scottish public that the Stone was 'a kind of symbol of Scotland's captivity in a Union that the Covenant contended was in deep need of radical amendment in favour of Scottish Home Rule'.[188] In fact, MacCormick went as far as to suggest that no real offence was committed in the Stone's taking, for it would only have been classified as a special statutory offence after the enactment of the *Theft Act* 1968.[189] Composing his memoirs, as he was here in 2008, MacCormick undoubtedly found himself living through the excitement of this period. He recalled, for instance, the many discussions of the negotiations in the ensuing year:

> As it happened, the internal layout of my parental home at 2 Park Quadrant, created a situation ideal for confidential and even conspiratorial

185 MacCormick, 'Nationalist Memoirs I' (2008/9), 1.
186 Ibid., 1–2.
187 Ibid., 2–3.
188 Ibid., 4.
189 Ibid., 6.

> conversations involving several different parties in different rooms, each of which could be accessed via an intricate arrangement of connecting doors and corridors, so that different people in different rooms need at no point in a visit realise that anyone else was visiting in a different room (it was, as I said, a large flat – running to fourteen rooms on two internal storeys). At the climax of the negotiations, in what must have been early April or perhaps late March 1951, there were present representatives of the receivers and the custodians, the Scotsman journalist Wilfred Taylor,[190] and Sir John Cameron, all in separate rooms and none able to (or subsequently exposed to having to) confirm or deny the presence of any others.[191]

This time must, indeed, have been a thrill and a delight for a boy of nine and then ten, observing hushed, late-night discussions. On another occasion in which he recalled these discussions, MacCormick remembered a particular night:

> I remember clearly, with the vividness attaching to my recollections of a nine year old allowed out of bed very late to witness great things, the night that Neil Gunn and various other stalwarts, among them Robert Gray and William Whyte (deeply involved also in the Stone of Destiny affair, thought that was not a fact known to me then), sat talking late into the night as I sat half hidden at the edge of the circle watching and listening. I remember more of the mood and the passion than the words of those present, a mood expressed with a strangely sombre vitality by Gunn, quite the most striking person in the room with his curly grey hair, gaunt features, hollow eyes. As impressionable as I was, I felt myself in the presence of greatness and of great events in that meeting.[192]

That kind of emotion is not one that one shakes off easily, if ever: it stays, simmering, as a constant, even if not foregrounded, hum of affective memory.

Even more so than that, the Stone's absence remained firmly in MacCormick's mind years later, for he took active steps to have it returned. For instance, in November 1990, when MacCormick was SNP parliamentary candidate for Argyll and Bute, and honorary President of the SNP constituency there, he 'wrote to Secretary of State [for Scotland] Ian Lang, suggesting that the 1150th anniversary of the uniting of the Picts and Scots under Kenneth MacAlpin [dated to 843 or 844 AD] would give a good moment to celebrate the oldest monarchy in Europe, and to return

190 See Taylor, *Scot Free* (1954).

191 MacCormick, 'Nationalist Memoirs I' (2008/9), 5.

192 MacCormick, 'Neil Gunn and Nationalism' (2013), 40; originally published in *Chapman* (1991–92).

the Stone'.[193] He 'proposed to him that the Government take steps to restore the Stone of Destiny to safekeeping in Scotland – with provision for its use for coronations at Westminster when required'.[194] This attempt had no immediate effect, with the Secretary replying that 'the government did not see fit to re-open the question of the proper location of the Stone', but it was only a little later, in 1995, that the decision was reversed, and the Stone was 'solemnly conveyed over the Tweed bridge between Cornhill and Coldstream to eventual safe-keeping in Edinburgh'.[195]

Like many others, MacCormick had mixed feelings on that day – a wet St Andrews Day in 1996 – when the Stone was returned. Enthusiasm was qualified, with most Scots clearly feeling that this was an attempt by the struggling Tories to gain some political capital in Scotland. As MacCormick put it, 'At the time the Conservative Government of John Major was fighting a rearguard action against the flowing tide of opinion in favour of Scottish Home Rule… Its aim was to show the high esteem in which Scotland stood within an unreformed incorporating Union'.[196] All this was, for him, as for many Scots, 'too little, too late, however'.[197] Speaking in 1996, a week before the Stone was returned, he was even more robust: 'They [the Tories] want to show that they are the patriotic party, that Scotland is a full member of the Union, well respected and entitled to her own ancient laws, institutions, and symbols. I don't think it will work. It's a high risk strategy, with pictures on the TV of English soldiers handing over the Stone at Coldream Bridge to Scottish soldiers'.[198] If anything, the act's dubious attempt to acquire political capital was likely to backfire, adding only fuel to the movement for home rule. And so it would prove to be.

One might try and explain away MacCormick's emotion by saying that it was inevitable, given the involvement of his father in the whole affair. Of course, that personal dimension cannot be denied. But we must also be careful not to take it too far. MacCormick's passionate memory of the taking of the Stone, and his fight for its return, cannot be attributed simply to the continuing of his father's project. After all, like other Scots, he was immersed in its historical connotations – in the powerful stories about the past that touched something deep-running in him and others. There was,

193 MacCormick, 'The Stone of Destiny: Symbol and Reality' (1996), 2.
194 MacCormick, 'Nationalist Memoirs I' (2008/9), 6–7.
195 Ibid., 7.
196 Ibid.
197 Ibid.
198 MacCormick, 'The Stone of Destiny: Symbol and Reality' (1996), 2.

undoubtedly, an experience of disrespect, if not dishonour, that was tied to the memory of the Stone. Further, this was itself inseparable from the genuine love that MacCormick, along again with his fellow Scots, had for the Scottish landscape, including its stones.[199]

None of these emotions can be easily dismissed. Indeed, it is telling that, in October 2008, when MacCormick was dying with cancer, and given, in his home, a private preview of the Hollywood film, *Stone of Destiny* (2008), with the Director also being present, he said: 'Of course I love my father very much', but 'I won't be saying, "Oh, here's a film about my dad and there's the Stone in it as well." More the other way round'.[200] For MacCormick, there was something more universally significant in a story that was nevertheless also highly personal: this was a matter of respect, which was not diluted or weakened by being wrapped up in emotion or in myth-making.

MacCormick v *Lord Advocate*

It was one thing to draw on ancient stones and mythical histories as part of political theatre, but it was another to use law and the courtroom to generate collective self-consciousness. Or was it? The strategy was not new: as we saw, above, Douglas Young used the courtroom to great political effect, echoing past acts of courtroom rebellion, though in his case, one might argue, there really was no choice. Further, Young was a classicist and not a lawyer, and he relied heavily on the advice of those who were legally trained. It was something else entirely, one might think, for a trained lawyer, with his own legal practice, to take on a case for the main purpose of communicating a political message, especially if, on legal grounds, the case itself was weak. Could law, should it, be deployed as a symbol in a political fight for self-government?

The question took on direct, personal proportions for John MacCormick in 1953. King George VI died in February 1952. Shortly afterwards, his daughter, Elizabeth, was proclaimed 'Queen Elizabeth II'. MacCormick recalled the day the proclamation was made. He was at school, and he rushed home to tell his mother about the new Queen, 'Elizabeth II'. Margaret MacCormick stopped him in his tracks: 'She is no such thing. We have had no previous Queen Elizabeth, and there has been no Elizabeth Queen of the United Kingdom. Elizabeth Tudor was Queen

[199] See generally Ascherson, *Stone Voices* (2002).

[200] 'Premier brings Stone of Destiny Home to dying son of "King John"', *The Scotsman*, Scotland on Sunday (5 October 2008). For more about the film, see Porter (2010).

of England only'. When he returned to school the next day, MacCormick says, he 'found that some other boys had been similarly informed by their parents'.[201] As the news spread throughout Scotland, matters escalated: post-boxes with the offending numerals being demolished in Edinburgh, including one with explosives.

The numeral stuck in the throat of many. As we have seen above, the Scots – not just a small group of nationalists, but many Scots, including those who had just signed up to the Covenant, which were two-thirds of the electorate – were steeped in a rebirth of historical awareness. History mattered: it was a carrier of attitudes. History was no matter of dry facts, of one event after another: it was a form of passionate, collective self-expression. In the case of the Queen's numeral, at stake was basic respect for the Scots and their ancient kingdom. As John MacCormick put it, 'The assumption in the minds of most Scots was that the numeral could only convey and was deliberately intended by her advisers to convey, that Great Britain was really England continuing and that the Union with Scotland had merely been an annexation of the smaller realm'.[202]

As we have seen above, this was not a new frustration. Certainly, for John MacCormick, this was a matter that had been brewing since the days he was a law student in the 1920s, required to read and expound what had become the traditional English constitutional position. As he recalled in his memoir:

> My own interest [in the numeral] was largely from a legal and constitutional view. Even as a law student in Glasgow University studying constitutional law and history I had resented and suspected Dicey's famous doctrine of the sovereignty of Parliament, which, of course, we were taught to regard as sacrosanct. Throughout the writings of all the English constitutional lawyers, and particularly those of Professor Dicey, there runs the arrogant assumption that the history of the Kingdom of England has been continuous from the Norman Conquest until the present day. The Treaty of Union which on 1st May 1707 created, under certain unalterable conditions, the entirely new Kingdom of Great Britain, is represented as being of no more consequence, and no more binding on subsequent Parliaments than any prior act of the English Parliament.[203]

As if poking around in a fresh wound, Dicey had famously compared the status of the Act of Union – the Act passed by the English Parliament to make effective, in English law, the Treaty of Union (the Scottish Parliament was also passing a similar Act in Scotland) – to the *Dentists Act* 1878; none

[201] MacCormick, 'John MacCormick Memoir' (2008/9), 4.
[202] John MacCormick, *The Flag in the Wind* (2008), 187.
[203] Ibid., 188.

was more important than the other.[204] The sovereignty of Parliament was unlimited and untrammelled. Dicey's view can hardly be seen in that simplistic light, e.g., his later *Thoughts on the Union between England and Scotland* (1920), co-authored with Scottish historian, Robert Rait, and some time Principal of the University of Glasgow, somewhat softened and qualified his position, indicating that his view as to the unlimited sovereignty of Westminster was probably more informed by his defence of the Union with Ireland.[205] Nevertheless, it remained an incredibly influential source of constitutional doctrine. Indeed, it had been picked up with enthusiasm by certain Scots, such as Walter Fraser, lecturer in constitutional law in Glasgow, whose *An Outline of Constitutional Law* (1938, then again in 1948) was an influential textbook of the time.

For John MacCormick, however, along with his fellow late-night discussants of Scottish history, such as Gunn and MacNeill, amongst many others, this Dicyean orthodoxy was both bad constitutional history as well as a symbol of disrespect. Even if it was accepted legal doctrine, in both England and Scotland, the sheer confidence in which it was articulated, as if it could never be doubted, as if it was an article of faith, was like a slap in the face for Scotland. It ignored so many centuries of the Scottish past.

The constitutional history of England and Scotland, insisted John MacCormick, was simply very different: in England, 'the law was the law of conquest. The king, having imposed himself on the people, could do no wrong'.[206] In Scotland, however, 'the country had never been conquered, even by the Romans'. It was not the king who could do no wrong in Scotland, but instead, the 'Community of Scotland', or the 'Community of the Realm',[207] e.g., Scotland had the law of desuetude, which meant that if a statute was not obeyed by the community, then it was no longer binding. The Parliament of Scotland, then, 'had always been subject to the ultimate sanction of community assent', and insofar as it thus 'had no sovereign powers itself', it followed that it could not 'by the Act of Union convey sovereign powers to its successor. The Parliament of Scotland could not by any conceivable rule of law create a new institution with powers wider than its own'.[208] Thus, the new Parliament – the Parliament of Great Britain – could not 'enjoy any greater powers than the Parliament of Scotland'; this

204 Dicey, *Introduction to the Study of the Law of the Constitution* [1885] (1959), 445.
205 See also Walters, *Dicey* (2022).
206 MacCormick, *The Flag in the Wind* (2008), 189.
207 See Barrow, *Robert Bruce* (1965).
208 MacCormick, *The Flag in the Wind* (2008), 189–90.

new Parliament was, 'in any case … limited by the "entrenched" clauses in the Treaty which had created it'.[209]

Again, it bears repeating that these arguments were not provoked for the first time when Queen Elizabeth styled herself as Elizabeth II. They had been woven into the fabric of nationalist constitutional debate in Scotland from the 1920s on – certainly in the case of John MacCormick. When, then, the *Royal Style and Titles Act* 1953 was passed, the temptation to use it as an occasion to challenge the Dicyean orthodoxy must have been overwhelming.

Still, John MacCormick hesitated. As mentioned above, he was a lawyer, and it is a well-known duty of lawyers that they do not take on hopeless cases: to do that is a sign of disrespect for both the law and the legal system, in particular the courts. But was this a hopeless case? John MacCormick found himself thinking first one way, then another. He discussed the matter with his fellow partners of the law firm he helped established in Glasgow: Stewarts Nicol MacCormick and Co. They, however, did not hesitate: the case was hopeless, he should not take it on. Indeed, it was made clear to John MacCormick that if he did, the loss of reputation to the firm would be too great, and he would have to resign his position. For John MacCormick, however, the momentum of history was simply too great: such an opportunity only came around once in a lifetime, and it had been building for the last twenty-five years.

Accordingly, together with Ian Hamilton and John Bayne, John MacCormick petitioned the Court of Session 'to pronounce an order prohibiting Her Majesty's ministers from describing' the Queen as Queen Elizabeth II.[210] As it transpired, there were two hearings: first, in the Spring of 1953, before the Outer House where Lord Guthrie gave judgement. And then, in the summer, before the Inner House, with Lord President Cooper presiding, sitting with Lords Carmont and Russell. On both occasions, the courtroom was packed, and there was 'immense public interest'.[211] To some extent, already, the political gamble had worked: as with the Convention and the Covenant, the Rectorship, and the taking of the Stone of Destiny, so with the 1953 case, the issue of Scottish identity, including its constitutional past and future, was firmly in the public eye. It was discussed in the popular press as well as around dinner tables in Scottish homes – indeed, none more so of course than the MacCormick household

209 Ibid., 190.
210 Ibid.
211 Ibid., 192.

itself. As MacCormick recalled, with the timing of the appeal in the summer, first the hearing and then the judgement 'cast[] a bit of a pall over the annual family holiday at Tayvallich in Argyll'.[212]

The first instance of judgement by Lord Guthrie in the Spring could not have been worse. It was, in John MacCormick's own words, 'as complete a defeat as I could possibly have feared'; there was 'not one word of comfort in his findings'.[213] Indeed, for anyone trained in the law, reading the judgement is like being in one's worst possible professional nightmare: the 'petitioners' propositions in law are unsound and indeed extravagant'; it is 'incompetent for the petitioners to crave the Court to interfere with the execution of the will of Parliament'; 'This petition appears to have been brought under misconceptions as to the respective functions under the constitution of the Legislature and the judiciary, as to the legal rights of the petitioners and as to the matters which can be competently brought before the Court'.[214] There could hardly sharper words said by a judge to a practising lawyer. The one consolation for the petitioners – but a very significant one – was that the judgement was of some length, allowing them to appeal to the Inner House. Interestingly, too, Lord Guthrie had expressly said that he did 'not feel called upon to express my opinion on the petitioners' submissions as to the historical inaccuracy of the proposed enumeration'.[215] As we shall see, Lord President Cooper, in the Inner House, as a committed historian in addition to being a jurist, did feel so called upon.[216]

The argument before the Inner House was heard on 10 July 1953, with judgement delivered on 30 July. Unsurprisingly, given how much was at stake, on the day of the hearing, John MacCormick was in quite a state:

212 MacCormick, 'John MacCormick Memoir' (2008/9), 5.

213 MacCormick, *The Flag in the Wind* (2008), 192.

214 *MacCormick* v *Lord Advocate* (1953) SC 396, at 403, per Lord Guthrie.

215 Ibid., at 404–5, per Lord Guthrie.

216 Lord Cooper is a fascinating character in this story. See MacQueen, 'Public Law, Private Law, and National Identity' (2013), who notes that earlier, during the Second World War Cooper had 'given judgements supporting the Diceyean view of the status of the Union Agreement, but since then, he had been much involved in the travails of the History of Parliament project, as chairman of its Scottish Committee from 1948 to 1955. In 1951 the scheme became one for the history of the Westminster Parliament only, and it had been decided not to accept any break in that account at 1707': 192. This experience, says MacQueen, must have informed Cooper's view in 1953. The story is complicated too by numerous relationships, e.g., between Cooper and Andrew Dewar Gibb. About the latter, see Farmer, 'Under the Shadow of Parliamentary House' (2001); and for more on Cooper as a historian, see MacQueen, 'Legal Nationalism' (2005). MacQueen's forthcoming history of Scottish legal nationalism will undoubtedly shed more light on the figures of this period.

> I must admit that when the day came for the hearing I was in a state of acute depression and nervousness. Many of our best friends had thought it unwise to pursue the matter to such lengths and advice had not been wanting to the effect that we should just make fools of ourselves in the Inner House. I had practised law for more than twenty years, but only as a solicitor, and I was unaccustomed even to speaking in the lower Courts. Now I was to advance a thesis which had been dear to my mind from student days but which might seem in the cold light of other people's reason to be merely a wild bee in my bonnet.[217]

Indeed, when it came to speaking on the day, though John MacCormick was to open the argument, in light of the former's nerves, John Bayne spoke first. When his turn finally came, John MacCormick spoke for over two hours, eventually overcoming his nervousness, and engaging in what was, by all accounts, an intense conversation, if not cross-examination, especially as conducted by Lord President Cooper. 'I found myself', John MacCormick recalled, 'at long last proclaiming in public in the Supreme Court of Scotland [sic] the disagreement with Dicey which long ago as a student I had longed to express to my mentors'.[218] In light of this being a book about Neil MacCormick, it is difficult to underestimate this moment: here, at the age of twelve, was a son observing his father, in Scotland's highest court, taking on the English orthodox view of constitutional doctrine.

At the conclusion of the hearing, there was considerable euphoria, with matching expectations: the court appeared to have taken the petitioners seriously. Might there not even be hope for victory? Much of this came crashing down when the judgement was delivered on 30 July. The petitioners did, indeed, not have title to sue. In what MacCormick was later (in *Legal Reasoning and Legal Theory*, 1978) to classify as an argument from consequences, Lord President Cooper said: 'I cannot see how we could admit the title and interest of the present petitioners to raise the point in issue before the Court of Session without conceding a similar right to almost any opponent of almost any political action to which public opposition had arisen'.[219] Even if, Lord Cooper added, Scottish law did have an action called the *actio popularis*, 'in which any member of the public may be entitled as such to vindicate certain forms of public right', this 'device has never been extended to a case such as this'.[220]

217 MacCormick, *The Flag in the Wind* (2008), 194.

218 Ibid., 195.

219 *MacCormick* v *Lord Advocate* (1953) SC 396, at 413, per Lord Cooper.

220 Ibid.

As Lord Russell put it, 'the petition ... is entirely misconceived',[221] echoing the tone of Lord Guthrie in the Inner House. Even if the Lord President's tone was softer – for instance, he went out of his way 'to place it on record that the petitioners expressly disclaimed any attempt to criticise Her Majesty or any disloyalty to her, their action being based upon considerations of which the present issue is merely symbolical',[222] it remained the case that for the great majority of the legal profession in Scotland, the case was indeed a hopeless one. The courts were simply not the proper forum for political resistance of the kind championed by John MacCormick – and he, as an experienced solicitor, should have known better. He was using, as not only the judges, but also many of his fellow practitioners, saw it, the law as a means towards a political end.

Professionally, for John MacCormick, this was a step too far. Soon after, he lost his partnership in his own law firm. Further, he tried, but failed, to subsequently qualify as an advocate (he needed dispensation for but one minor exam, but although this could have been granted by discretion, it was not). He remained unemployed, with his wife, Margaret, having to go back to work to support the family. He used the time to write his memoir, *The Flag in the Wind* (1955), but the affair of the case had largely sapped his energy, and took the wind out of his sails. Even the Convention appeared to run out of steam. The pain in his kidneys worsened, and he took to drink to alleviate the pain, sinking into a deep depression. In 1961, at the age of fifty seven, he died.

The professional and personal price paid by John MacCormick for the case was high – as high as it gets. And yet, both in the emotions of the moment, and in the longer arc of Scottish politics in the twentieth century, the case was and remains of considerable importance. It has been variously described by subsequent commentators as a 'turning point',[223] as 'nationalist unionism's intellectual high point',[224] as an event that 'marked the emergence of Scottish nationalism as a political force',[225] and as a resource seized upon by subsequent generations of nationalists in Scotland,[226] becoming a

[221] Ibid., at 414, per Lord Russell.
[222] Ibid., at 413–14, per Lord Cooper.
[223] Kidd, *Union and Unionisms* (2008), 116; see also Kidd, *From Jacobitism to the SNP* (2013), 37.
[224] McLean, 'Understanding the Union' (2020), 118.
[225] Tierney, 'Scotland in the Union' (2023), 431.
[226] Page, 'The Scottish Constitution' (2020); including legal nationalists, see Smith, 'The Union of 1707 as Fundamental Law' (1957).

kind of icon of 'a full-throated endorsement of popular sovereignty as the Scottish tradition'.[227]

As Gavin Little noted in a wonderful chapter on the case, *MacCormick v Lord Advocate* has been 'taught, since the mid 1950s, to generations of Scots law students as the pre-eminent Scottish case on constitutional law',[228] appearing also in influential textbooks on Scottish constitutional law, e.g., Mitchell's important text, *Constitutional Law*, in 1968. Figures such as Donald Dewar, Gordon Wilson, David Steel, Menzies Campbell, and Jim Wallace, 'all studied the case at school'.[229] The case has also featured in parliamentary debates.[230] Although the legal significance of the case has been questioned,[231] it remains very much alive. For instance, in May 2021, in a questionnaire run by *Scottish Legal News*, it was voted third in the history of the greatest Court of Session cases.[232]

Placing the case in a broader political context, one can surely say that the fact that it had been a court case truly mattered: the Court was not a political body, at least not in the conventional sense of a political party or an association or organisation actively and directly involved in ideological battles. Ironically, perhaps, it only added to the case's significance that it was lost: the court was clearly not biased in favour of the petitioners. If anything, as we have seen, it went out of its way to criticise them for bringing the case in the first place. Anything said by the court thus needed to be treated with respect: this was a source that could be cited, safely, by all sides in the debate. The case thus resonated in Scottish public opinion, in Scottish political self-consciousness, whether that be in parliamentary debates, or at times – difficult times, such as the 1980s – when something iconic had to be appealed to that spoke to the distinctiveness of a Scottish constitutional tradition.

[227] Jackson, *The Case for Scottish Independence* (2020), 136.

[228] Little, 'A Flag in the Wind' (2014), 43.

[229] Ibid.

[230] See ibid., referring to January 1998; see also the discussion in the House of Lords on 22 June 1999. See https://api.parliament.uk/historic-hansard/lords/1999/jun/22/membership-of-house-of-lords-scottish (last accessed on 16 September 2024).

[231] See, e.g., Tomkins, 'The Constitutional Law' (2004); Munro, *Studies in Constitutional Law* (2005), 137–42; and Tierney, 'Scotland in the Union' (2023); for doubts, too, about the uses of the case in histories of an allegedly distinctive Scottish constitutional tradition of 'popular sovereignty', see, e.g., Kidd, 'Sovereignty and the Scottish Constitution' (2004); and McHarg, 'The Declaration of Arbroath and Scots Law' (2020).

[232] See '*Donoghue v Stevenson* named greatest Session case' (5 May 2021). See www.scottishlegal.com/article/donoghue-v-stevenson-named-greatest-session-case (last accessed 16 September 2024).

So what was it, then, that was said that was so significant? The key passage comes about halfway through Lord President Cooper's judgement in which, effectively, he repeats, and thus endorses, John MacCormick's long-held view that Dicyean orthodoxy as to the unlimited sovereignty of Westminster Parliament was untenable, at least in the context of Scottish constitutional history:

> The principle of the unlimited sovereignty of Parliament is a distinctively English principle which has no counterpart in Scottish constitutional law. It derives its origin from Coke and Blackstone, and was widely popularised during the nineteenth century by Bagehot and Dicey, the latter having stated the doctrine in its classic form in his Law of the Constitution. Considering that the Union legislation extinguished the Parliaments of Scotland and England and replaced them by a new Parliament, I have difficulty in seeing why it should have been supposed that the new Parliament of Great Britain must inherit all the peculiar characteristics of the English Parliament but none of the Scottish Parliament, as if all that happened in 1707 was that Scottish representatives were admitted to the Parliament of England. That is not what was done.[233]

It is these words that have echoed down the years since they were written and delivered in the summer of 1953. Although not strictly necessary to decide the case – and thus falling within what the lawyers call 'obiter' – the statement was no less significant for that. In fact, if anything, it was all the more powerful politically for being said over and above what needed to be said. Did that not mean it was thus truly and passionately held? And, indeed, the words above are not without passion: 'That is not what was done', Lord Cooper pronounces, with some confidence. This confidence was also on show in other passages in the judgement, such as when Lord Cooper characterised Lord Guthrie's formulations of Dicyean orthodoxy as 'extreme', and 'not now supported', either by Dicey's own later statements made in the above-cited booklet with Rait, or indeed by later editions of various constitutional law textbooks.[234] Also significant was that, although Lord Cooper did agree that the petitioners did not have standing to sue, for their complaint regarded 'public right', he expressly said that 'I reserve my opinion with regard to the provisions relating expressly to this Court and to the laws "which concern private right: which are administered here"'.[235] This opened to the door to potential future claims,

[233] *MacCormick* v *Lord Advocate* (1953) SC 396, at 411, per Lord Cooper.
[234] See ibid., at 412, per Lord Cooper.
[235] Ibid.

legitimating such grounds for argument where they had arguably not been so legitimated previously.

There is no doubt that, for MacCormick, the son, his father's case remained imprinted in his memory, and was a matter of great pride. Indeed, MacCormick extrapolated on the significance of the case, as he saw it, on numerous occasions over the course of the half-century after 1953.[236] He did so not only in academic circles, but also in the popular press. For instance, in 1994, writing in *The Scotsman* under the title of 'Rights of a Sovereign Nation', MacCormick recalled his father speaking for two hours in the courtroom, arguing 'that traditional doctrines of parliamentary sovereignty belonged to English law and history alone', with the doctrine in Scotland being that 'the King and parliament are under law, not over it', while Lord Cooper 'listened closely and critically, interrupting, cross-questioning, pursuing every point to its logical conclusion'. And MacCormick added: 'I am rather proud to be the son of one who helped have this eminently [Scottish] civilised doctrine restored to its proper place in our constitutional law'.[237] Indeed, for some time, especially in the 1970s, MacCormick contemplated writing a book on 'the status of the Articles of Union of 1707 as the historically first Constitution of the United Kingdom', which, he acknowledged, was all very much a 'retrospective musing' on the *MacCormick* v *Lord Advocate* case.[238]

The memory of the case never left MacCormick. In 2008, when dictating his memoirs, MacCormick spent the bulk of them re-playing the memories of his father's arguments in 1953. At the time, planned reforms of the Judicial Committee of the House of Lords were coming to a head, with the Supreme Court of the UK about to be established (as it happened in 2009), following the *Constitutional Reform Act* 2005. Drawing on some 'doubts' he had already articulated in late 2003,[239] MacCormick mused, once more, that there might yet be legal significance in what he referred to as 'the Cooper doctrine':

> What remains an open possibility … is that the Court of Session itself, backed by a substantial body of opinion among Scots lawyers and the broader legally interested elements of civil society in Scotland, might

236 See MacCormick, 'Does the UK' (1978); 'Scottish Anomaly' (1998); and 'Doubts about the Supreme Court' (2004).

237 MacCormick, 'Rights of a Sovereign Nation' (1994), 6.

238 See MacCormick, Letter to Secretary of Law Society, Diane Finlay (10 November 1976).

239 Published as MacCormick, 'Doubts about the Supreme Court' (2004).

> favour carrying forward the Cooper doctrine that there is scope, even in a unitary state (now indeed a unitary-but-devolved state), for a distinctive Scottish interpretation of the fundamentals of that state's constitution. Even if in the end the Court [of Session] were to decide that the jurisdiction of the [UK] Supreme Court ought to be accepted, it would be more than interesting to see elaborated the grounds for such a holding. Is Scots law no more than a fragmentary system of private and criminal law now largely assimilated by the English common law and Westminster statute law? Or is it a complete system of private and public law capable of giving its own account of the fundamental law of the United Kingdom and the dovetailing of Scots law and the residual Scottish state into that larger entity? Can Scots law generate a distinct conception of the United Kingdom constitution, or was the Union really a take-over masquerading as a merger – an 'incorporating Union' in the strongest possible sense of the term?[240]

MacCormick did not accept his father's arguments wholescale – amongst them, he thought the most persuasive was the idea of the Treaty as fundamental law, the originally first constitution of a new state, even if vague and incomplete, at least the beginnings of one.[241] He always acknowledged that even this was not a view held by most, e.g., in a 2008 entry on 'Treaty of Union' in *The New Oxford Companion to Law* he noted that 'there had been controversy whether or not it [the Treaty] had continuing effect as "fundamental law"', but he nevertheless reiterated its importance, even if theoretical (for it had not been tested in legal practice), of 'guarantees concerning the law and the courts and the system of local government in Scotland as well as that concerning the Church of Scotland'.[242] He realised, of course, that for him, the case resonated personally, unlike for others, and that the matter should be debated and contested: but, even if for him, it arguably resulted in the loss of his father at too young an age, at no point did MacCormick suggest it was a foolhardy act, something to be embarrassed about. It was wise not to overstate the legal significance of the case: but could its political meaning – for generations of Scots – really be dismissed so easily? Were law and politics really that far apart? Was there really no role for law to play in the adoption of attitudes of respect, this time as between ancient nations?

240 MacCormick, 'John MacCormick Memoir' (2008/9), 17; 'Doubts about the Supreme Court' (2004), 250.

241 MacCormick, 'Doubts about the Supreme Court' (2004), 241–2.

242 MacCormick, 'Treaty of Union' (2008), 1192; recently, see also Douglas-Scott, *Union and Disunion* (2023), chapter 1, who is likewise cautious about this claim, while noting that it does help to show that the principle of unlimited Westminster sovereignty, and thus the Dicyean orthodoxy, is doubtful.

Filial Tributes

As intimated at the outset of this chapter, there is no easy answer to the question as to whether one's childhood experiences, including the powerful emotional memories and allegiances one may have to one's parents, determines what comes later in one's life. What I have tried to show is that the emotion matters, certainly, and that there are plenty of continuities as between the beliefs, arguments, and sensibilities between MacCormick, the son, and both of his parents.

I have suggested, above, that it was MacCormick's mother, Margaret MacCormick, who perhaps influenced him most deeply: care and respect for others came to her so naturally, and was expressed by her without spectacle in daily life, that, if anything did, this must have impressed itself upon MacCormick's character in a most powerful way. But there is also no doubt that, throughout his life, MacCormick kept returning to the memory of his father, characterising and re-characterising him and the importance of his legacy in numerous ways. 'Struggle' is too strong a word for this lifelong interpretative memory, for MacCormick remained enormously and unshakeably proud of his father. But it is also true that in the course of these reflections, MacCormick came to adopt his own beliefs, arguments, and sensibilities, and perhaps most importantly, his own ways of relating with others.

In 1999, speaking on the occasion of the 71st anniversary of the SNP, MacCormick said:

> Naturally, I look back on my father with special love and regard. He was quite a remarkable orator and a brave and gallant man, carrying the torch under a burden of incurably painful illness. He was often obstinate, and sometimes wrong, but also sometimes right in his judgements. Along with other men and women of 1928 [the date of the formation of the NPS] he stands as a true architect of our own future, one of our great leaders of the lost generations who never saw their country free. I am proud to be his son.[243]

For the son, MacCormick, the father, John MacCormick, did not have to be perfect to be dearly loved. But it is also clear that, when he came to characterise his father, he chose to emphasise those aspects of his character that he found most attractive – something that undoubtedly tells us more about MacCormick than it does about his father. Thus, for instance, he said: 'my father's deepest commitments were always to Scotland – the people, the history, the philosophy and poetry, the land and landscape'.[244] His

[243] MacCormick, 'Speech on the 71st Anniversary of the SNP' (16 January 1999), 3.
[244] MacCormick, 'Introduction' to *The Flag in the Wind* (2008), xi.

father had been, he said further, 'the master of compromise in committee and a pursuer of the practical rather than the ideal, a gradualist rather than a fundamentalist in his approach to Scottish self-government'.[245] This was in 2008, but in 1974 the judgement was similar: his father was not, MacCormick said, 'in politics of his own aggrandisements ... but in pursuit of an end', about which he had 'irrepressible optimism'.[246] This end was self-government for Scotland in the form of its own parliament, or, put less concretely, the democratic flourishing of Scotland, the gradual ripening of its own self-awakening as a political community. And he then quoted the final words of his father's memoir, as his was often to do:

> Flags as well as straws show the way the wind is blowing. Movements of the spirit, springing from the most deeply rooted sentiments of the people, can never be denied their goal. There is no doubt in my mind that long before the end of this century the Parliament of Scotland will once more be opened with ancient pomp and ceremony and that in this new age the representatives of her people will make her a valued partner in the British Commonwealth and an ideal ground for experiments in human progress. The promise implicit in her long history will yet be fulfilled.[247]

And so it transpired to be: what intense emotion must have been present for MacCormick, the son, on 1 July 1999, when the Scottish Parliament was indeed inaugurated in the sunny streets of Edinburgh. Whatever the judgement one may have about John MacCormick, the son was to go on to carry, until the end of his own life, the genuine passions, virtues, and hopes that he interpreted his father as having. The son was not the father, but the father did help to make the son.

[245] Ibid., xii.
[246] MacCormick, 'A Filial Look' (1974), 13.
[247] MacCormick, *The Flag in the Wind* (2008), 198.

2

A Land of Many Tongues

Language, Self, and Community

There is, in MacCormick's oeuvre, a deep-running love for language, both oral and written, and a fascination with its world-making and normative powers. Language, in turn, as MacCormick both experiences and later theorises it, is deeply social: it is rooted in places and cultures, and it is entangled in interactive and communal dynamics. Language's magical powers are social through and through. It is in large part thanks to language that social realities are constructed, and it is via language that we can generate emotion, compete and collaborate, and create insights that we can share and contest. In that sense, as we shall see, for MacCormick, language and its powers – its promise and its dangers – are entangled with the ethics and politics of conversation and debate.

For all the talk of what language can do, however, it is important to emphasise, again, the love for language that is ever-present in MacCormick: alongside serious respect for language, and a recognition that a change in terminology can either open up or close the potential for peace and reconciliation, there is also a genuine pleasure, even cheek and playfulness, which MacCormick takes in the pliability and plasticity of language, as well as in the interactive and communal joys it affords.

To some extent, as we have just seen in Chapter 1, this rich experience of language, including its charms and capacities, was present already in MacCormick's childhood. It was present, for instance, in how he understood his father's legacy. His father, MacCormick writes in his memoires, was, in private, 'a man of poetry and romance', and in public, 'a spectacularly good platform orator'.[1] Similarly, it was present in the memories he had of his mother and her wit and repartee. Further, his childhood home incubated a love for a variety of languages – and, indeed, for the importance of linguistic diversity – with Gaelic and Scots both being present, alongside English, in various ways, within his extended family and amongst his friends. We have seen too, in Chapter 1, how MacCormick's home

[1] MacCormick, 'Introduction', *The Flag in the Wind* (2008), 2.

was a meeting place for passionate, often late-into-the-night, discussions, including between writers and politicians. MacCormick was thus exposed, early on, to both the oral and written delights of language. Although he himself was often said to be naturally shy, he too, as many who heard him will attest, was an outstanding oral speaker, often delivering complex philosophical talks with meagre notes, and indeed often thinking through oral performance (his writing typically came after, as a kind of editing of, the oral performance).

Although MacCormick did, indeed, become an experienced and confident speaker, he nevertheless never embraced the identity of being a 'great orator' and, in this sense, was very unlike his father. Instead, he is better thought of – if this is not too idealistic a picture – as a good-humoured, even if on occasion still sharply tongued, participant-guardian of communal discussion and debate. Experiences of MacCormick's participation in discussion, whether in small seminar rooms or in large public halls, is consistently of someone who combined well timed, insightful humour with serious recognition of the vital significance of the norms of mutual respect and contestation; and someone who was committed to hearing all sides of a question, making sure all parties and their views are represented and considered. As we shall see in later chapters, the importance MacCormick gave to such norms of discussion and debate are pervasive in his scholarly work, both in the form in which he edited publications on controversial topics, as well as in his more abstract treatment of the practicality of reason. Indeed, one might well argue that, for MacCormick, the practicality of reason resides precisely in the attitudes of mutual respect and considerateness that are enshrined in the norms of communal debate, i.e., in short, in the practice of the democratic intellect. Once again, we see that the experience of language, oral and written, is here inseparable from the broader stakes of the ethics and politics of interactive and communal relations.

Picking up on the entwined themes of language and sociality, the aim of this chapter is twofold: first, to portray the early life of MacCormick's love, fascination with, and exploration of language, especially as these are on display in his own writing and editing as a student in Glasgow; and second, to provide a sense of the nature and scale of his participation in communal debate in the Glasgow Student Union ('the Union') – a place that MacCormick described as his 'spiritual home'.[2]

Throughout, I trace the importance of both these features as informing MacCormick's character. There is, on the one hand, sheer joy in the

[2] MacCormick, 'Glasgow Style' (1965), 10.

energies of language and what it can make possible, which reappears, later in MacCormick's philosophical writing, for instance in his view of law as institutional fact, and his frequent resort to the conventions of language as analogous to law's dynamic existence and knowability. And there is, on the other hand, a related and equally pervasive sense of respect for others, of considerateness, inclusiveness, and the possibility of peace and friendship across difference, including the ingenious arts of reconciliation and synthesis. Both these features very much colour the manner and style in which MacCormick engages and relates with others, and thus, both are fundamental to his character.

The Joys of Language

Scottish Letters

Before turning to MacCormick's own writing, it will help to situate in a little more detail the passion for language and literature, including its connection to politics, in MacCormick's household. As was mentioned briefly in Chapter 1, MacCormick's father, John MacCormick, was not only a student politician, a lawyer, and the founder of the Scottish National Party; he was also a writer[3] and one deeply moved by the thought and letters of the Scottish tradition. He was also keenly aware that any nationalist movement in Scotland was one that had to involve an intimate collaboration between politics and culture. Put another way, the revival of Scottish political consciousness, its self-awareness as a nation in need of a democratic renewal, was entangled with the cultural rebirth of Scottish literature and art. The origins of Scottish nationalist politics in the 1920s, which as we have seen were pioneered in many respects by John MacCormick and his fellow students in Glasgow, were from the outset characterised by a close partnership between politicians and writers, and, more generally, between politics and culture.

A good example of this, alluded to briefly in Chapter 1, is the friendship and collaboration between John MacCormick and Neil Gunn. After meeting in 1929, at one of the public meetings John MacCormick organised

[3] John MacCormick's words were once described by William Power as being 'winged with beauty; they will fly far, and bear vital truths to many people when language less clear and graceful would repel': Power, 'Foreword' (1943), 5. The history of 'winged words' is long, as Power would have known: in the ancient Greek, the metaphor came from describing words as feathered arrows, flying 'straight to the comprehension of the listener': Thomson, 'Winged Words' (1936), 1.

on behalf of the NPS, Gunn soon became involved in supporting John MacCormick, for instance, offering administrative support for his bid for a parliamentary seat in 1931. Gunn lived in Inverness then, and because he was in the Civil Service, was only able to support John MacCormick anonymously. Serving as his behind-the-scenes publicist, Gunn threw himself into the organisation of the campaign. Although John MacCormick did not win the seat (he came third with over 4,000 votes), he was supported by a number of writers, including not only Gunn, but also Cunninghame Graham, Compton Mackenzie, and George Blake. That was significant, but it was also not the first time that John MacCormick had collaborated with Graham and Mackenzie: both had been supported by the Glasgow University Scottish Nationalist Association (GUSNA) as candidates in the elections to the role of Rector at Glasgow University (once again, literature and politics were never far away in Scotland).

As for Gunn, he had already written of the challenges facing Scotland in his first novel, *The Grey Coast* (1926), which had depicted the 'dying economy and culture of the Northlands',[4] and went on to write such classics as *Morning Tide* (1931), *Butcher's Broom* (1934, about the Clearances), *Highland River* (1937), and most famously *The Silver Darlings* (1941), which won him acclaim and which enabled him to make the transition to full time writing. In the years in which he resided in Inverness (1926–37), Gunn, his wife, and their home ('Larachan'), played host to many meetings and late night discussions about Scotland, literature, and culture. As Dairmid Gunn notes, Larachan 'was the spiritual home of the Scottish National Party in the Highlands',[5] and the discussions there, which ranged widely, were an important incubator of Scottish political thought. As John MacCormick once reminisced:

> Neil Gunn's house in Inverness, Larachan it was called, became our unofficial headquarters and no matter how late our return from distant parts we would find him [Gunn] waiting for us, eager for our report and ready to sit up talking with us till all hours… Our talks ranged over the whole field of Nationalism and far beyond. We used to remark that as soon as the clock struck four in the morning we would find ourselves discussing the most abstract problems of the human soul and its relationship to God.[6]

The roots of Scottish nationalist political thought, then, at least as John MacCormick recounts the story, are not reducible to the pursuit of quick

[4] See Gunn, 'Neil M. Gunn' (2013).
[5] Ibid., 36.
[6] Quoted in MacCormick, 'Neil Gunn and Nationalism' (2013) [1991–92], 41.

immediate electoral success, but lie instead more deeply and at different temporal scales – in late night and early morning discussions of the soul, which looked far into the horizon.

As we saw in Chapter 1, MacCormick recalled visits by Gunn as part of the various discussions in the family home about the Covenant or the Stone of Destiny. In the years after, MacCormick, the son, was to maintain his father's contact with Gunn. For instance, when taking on the task of editing *Ossian*, the Gaelic-language magazine of Glasgow University's Highland Students' Society (one of his many editorial roles, and to which I return below), MacCormick managed to secure an essay from Gunn – a piece, as MacCormick described it, that was 'characteristically allusive' and concerned 'the reseeding of common grazings in the Outer Hebrides, with an obvious but not overdone symbolism about a still-to-be-hoped-for revitalisation of the life of our rural (and also urban) communities'.[7]

Further, taking a Masters in Arts in Glasgow from 1960 to 1963 – initially taking classes in Classics, Philosophy and Literature, but after the first year focusing on the latter two – MacCormick later recalled that he wrote an essay on Gunn (as well as Lewis Grassic Gibbon)[8] drawing on the-then just published *The Scottish Tradition in Literature* by Kurt Wittig.[9] Although MacCormick's own essay is lost, we may glean a little of what interested in him in Gunn via Wittig's own characterisation of him.

Wittig says of Gunn that he is 'so far [in 1958] the only Scottish novelist whose work in some measure embodies all the ideals of the Scots

[7] MacCormick, 'Neil Gunn and Nationalism' (2013) [1991–92], 40.

[8] Gibbon was the pen name of James Leslie Mitchell (1901–35), whose trilogy, *A Scots Quair*, comprising *Sunset Song* (1932), *Cloud Howe* (1933), and *Grey Granite* (1934), is a classic of Scottish literature. Wittig (1978) [1958] emphasises Gibbon's play with language, not only in its experimentation with Scots, but also in it employing 'traces of Gaelic sentence structure': 333. It is significant, too, that the trilogy 'deals [first] with the breakdown of the crofting system after the artificial boom of the war; the second with the disintegration of small-town society, which it represents as a consequence of lack of understanding and co-operation between the crofters and the working classes; and the third ... with the fermentation in the city and the resultant upsurge of socialism and communism': 330.

[9] MacCormick, 'Neil Gunn and Nationalism' (2013) [1991–92], 40. Wittig's book positions Scottish literature as part 'of our European heritage', and although entangled in Europe in all kinds of ways, it also 'grows out the life of the community' in Scotland (3), which results in its having its own 'moral, aesthetic and intellectual values' (4). Its beginning, alone, with John Barbour's *The Bruce*, must have stirred the passions of those who saw links between the history of Scottish literature and contemporary politics. For example, Wittig argues that 'Barbour's *Bruce* is, in some respects, a handbook of leadership, and it is severely practical' (27) – indeed, almost a guide for a community at any moment, including in the political present, eager to fight for its freedom.

Renaissance'.[10] Gunn's writing, he adds, 'is full of such wonderfully poetic impression of the outside world', to such an extent that the things in that world take on lives of their own: 'the object is no longer a dead thing but a living creation: the thing itself is alive'; Wittig calls this Gunn's 'animism', which conveys the deep connections between poetic language and the land.[11] In fact, according to Wittig, 'Gunn's animism has a conscious Gaelic undertone', which is 'apparent in the rhythms, sentence-structure and idioms of the dialogue' and, 'though less obviously, in the narrative'; 'Gaelic', says Wittig, is for Gunn 'the unique expression of the working his people's mind'.[12] This poetic intensity is not sentimental – instead, it holds a kind of magic, inventive, imaginative power; it is a carrier of 'traditional lore and wisdom', compromised of 'imaginative comparisons', of proverbs, satirical versus, songs, witty sayings, and divinations – a kind of 'pagan animism'[13] that is full of the spirit of the people, their joys and sufferings, and their land. Significantly, Wittig ends his book with Gunn, saying that Gunn's 'strength, his vision, his style come from his people, from the Scottish tradition, from the Gaelic, but he applies them to the crucial questions of our time'; this, he adds is 'Scottish literature', yes, it is 'national, yet knows no national limitations'.[14]

All this must have resonated deeply with MacCormick; it certainly comes through in his own political speeches, his later political acts (such as defending linguistic diversity in the European Parliament), and, as we shall see in a moment, his various student publishing initiatives, especially in support of Gaelic. MacCormick recalls all of Gunn's novels being available on the shelves at home.[15] One imagines these shelves heaving with many other novels, histories, and collections of poetry: Scottish politics always had a parallel life in the literary imagination. No doubt there were many influences here – Gibbon, as mentioned above – among them, but Gunn does appear to hold a special place. Gunn's voice may not be the loudest; it may not be the most politically direct, and in any event, the themes he addresses, the depths he reaches, are difficult to limit to any nationalist message. Gunn's voice, for all its Scottishness, is a quiet, gentle, humane voice, concerned for the plight of people living in poverty, sensitive to the particularity of individuals and their dreams of a better life,

[10] Wittig, *The Scottish Tradition* (1978) [1958], 333.
[11] Ibid., 334.
[12] Ibid., 335.
[13] Ibid.
[14] Ibid., 339.
[15] MacCormick, 'Neil Gunn and Nationalism' (2013) [1991–92], 40.

and full of love for the environment and its animals. It certainly resonated politically, also for MacCormick, but perhaps more in the form of a vision of what a country could be. As MacCormick put it himself, writing in 1991, 'Gunn's writing remains a key part in my conception of Scotland and of a civilised response to our sense of our own country and its reasonable rights alongside those of others'.[16]

More particularly, the link, very present in Gunn, between Scottish politics and the culture of the Highlands, especially the period of the Clearances, was also crucial for MacCormick, both early and late in his life. Gunn had written movingly of 'our own Gaelic folk music and dances' which 'deeply affect me',[17] and it is important that, as we have seen in Chapter 1, MacCormick was very much aware of the Highland roots of his father's side of the family. MacCormick knew, for instance, of the Gaelic speaking and Gaelic novel writing of his Great Uncle John MacCormick. For MacCormick, Gaelic was one of the strands of continuity tying his own identity to that of his family:

> My own father used to be set on his grandmother's knee in a humble house in Mull and asked, 'Co that hu (Who are you)?'; 'Cha n'eil f hios agam (I don't know)'; 'Is tu Iain Mac Dhomhnuill 'ic Neill 'ic Iain 'ic Dhugail … (You are John, son of Donald, son of Neil, son of John, son of Dugald…)' – and so on went the genealogy, up to thirty-three generations, no doubt some of them fictitious. I have inherited a similar conception of having a familial past and (as it were) of a hope for a familial future.[18]

Another source of Highlands' culture, its language, and the sounds of its stories, was the education in music that MacCormick received from his uncles in Glasgow. MacCormick writes movingly about this in his unpublished memoirs. When he entered his first year of senior school, at the age of eleven (in 1952), in the High School of Glasgow, MacCormick decided he would become a piper and join the Cadets' pipe band at the School.[19] He initially approached his Aunt Annie, who promptly brought out three manuscript books of chanter tunes composed by MacCormick's grandfather, Captain Donald MacCormick, who composed the music while 'engaged throughout most of the Great War on extremely boring boom defence duties at Scapa Flow'.[20] MacCormick duly learnt some of these

[16] Ibid., 41.
[17] Gunn, 'Neil M. Gunn' (2013), 3.
[18] MacCormick, 'Nation and Nationalism' (1979), 102.
[19] MacCormick, 'Ross of Mull Memoirs' (2008/9), 1.
[20] Ibid.

tunes, e.g., 'the Lads that will return no More', which was a tune played at the dedication of the Glasgow cenotaph, adding that 'I think I am the only living piper who can play it'.[21] But his piping really picked up when, one day after school, he decided to visit his Great Uncle Neil, who lived just around the corner from the High School. Uncle Neil lived with younger brother, Dugald. The two of them were too old to play – they were in their eighties – but they were both passionate and experienced musicians, with Uncle Neil on the bagpipes and Dugald on the fiddle, both embodying deep musical knowledge that doubled as a store of stories in Gaelic.

From that day on, MacCormick would regularly go to his Great Uncles to learn to play. His Uncle Neil taught him by 'singing over the tunes to me, and pointing to my fingers when making mistakes', while 'Dugald would listen and comment, often from the perspective of tunes as he remembered them played in the Ross of Mull in his young days'.[22] MacCormick thus learnt how to pipe as if he was in the Ross of Mull in the 1870s and 1880s. These were clearly memorable afternoons, accompanied by 'massive high tea with bacon and egg', and leaving MacCormick with both pride and excitement: 'I still remember', MacCormick recalled, 'the thrill of going home up the hill quite late' one Friday 'to give my parents a rendering of a real tune'.[23]

His uncles were present in MacCormick's life in various ways – for instance, arranging 'highland games' when on holiday at Fidden, where 'we putted the stone and raced on the beach and long jumped into the deep white sand',[24] or in Fionnphort Bay, or in Erraid, where MacCormick learnt of the relation between the Torran rocks there and the ideas employed by Robert Louis Stevenson in *Kidnapped*.[25] MacCormick was clearly moved by this landscape, not only because it was fun and adventurous for a boy, but also because of its aesthetics: he recalled, for instance, 'the redness of the red granite seen from Fionnphort pier', which he said were 'better than any man-made monument'.[26] Here, we see a mix of music, literature, as well as joy and adventure, and in both natural as well as in social settings, as when the chanter would be played, and the members of the family would get up to dance a Scotch reel.[27] Piping, fiddling,

[21] Ibid., 2.
[22] Ibid., 3.
[23] Ibid.
[24] Ibid., 4.
[25] Ibid., 5.
[26] Ibid., 6.
[27] Ibid., 7.

literature, dance – all this flowed in the veins of the MacCormick family. Later, in 1956, when MacCormick was fourteen, Great Uncle Dugald lived his last years with the MacCormick's in their family home in Glasgow, which, as MacCormick described it, 'gave me an ever-present audience for my piping and chanter-playing', and an opportunity also to practice speaking in Gaelic.[28]

Gaelic, and the Highlands – its sounds, its words, its dancing – were all very present in MacCormick's upbringing, and clearly shaped his imaginary. This was not, however, to the exclusion of either English or Scots; Scots, in particular, and especially via MacCormick's mother and her Lowlands' family, was certainly present and was charged with its own joys and magic. His mother's people, as we saw in Chapter 1, were from Fife and Lanarkshire, 'with some Ulster-Scots flavouring'; 'medical people and merchants', living in flats in Townhead that they had built themselves.[29] Thus, MacCormick had the twin cultures of the Lowlands and the Highlands both entangled and intertwined in his own family history. As we will soon see, all this comes together in his own writing from the days he began writing, already in the High School of Glasgow.

Student Writer

MacCormick was a frighteningly brilliant pupil. As his Principal recalled, upon his graduation in 1959, MacCormick had been Dux (the student with top academic marks) in all of his years at the school.[30] He won scholarships and prizes in pretty much every subject, from English composition to Latin and Greek, as well as Public Speaking and History. Again, the roll call of his achievements is overwhelming: excelling not only academically, but also in sports (he was in the first XV Rugby team and in the second XI in Cricket, and a member of the Mudhook Regatta – sailing was to go on to be an important source of physical relaxation for him later), as well as in other extracurricular activities at the school, e.g., in the Theatre Society, in the Literary and Debating Society, and in the junior corps (where he rose to become the Company Sergeant Major), as well as in music (serving as the Pipe Major and playing a solo in the Highland Club Competition). His literary and debating skills were, unsurprisingly, especially highlighted by the Principal: he showed, it was said, 'fluency, method, and humour' in his

28 Ibid., 10.

29 MacCormick, 'Being Scottish' (2002), 153–4.

30 Principal's report, 'Donald Niall MacCormick', *Glasgow High School* (1959), 46.

public speaking, displaying 'a personality that is both forceful and loveable', while his writing evoked 'maturity, range, and wit', and was accompanied by his editing the student school newspaper, *The Pleb*.[31]

MacCormick's published writing, first in the magazine of the High School of Glasgow, and then, while he was a university student, in the *Glasgow University Magazine* (*GUM*), spans many different kinds of genres: there is poetry, drama, and criticism, and the tone varies from comic to tragic. For all this variety, and taken as a whole, the dozen or so pieces published, exhibit certain consistent features: there is much wordplay (e.g., 'a lass'/'alas') and evident joy taken in the ambiguities and complexities of language; there is a good deal of play, too, with certain traditional and especially English literary forms, often offering a comic meta-commentary on them, including the Shakespearean sonnet, the Chaucerian tale, and poems by other canonical English writers (including Edward Spenser, Samuel Coleridge, and T. S. Eliot); there is much self-aware reflection on the very process of writing; there is both a use of, as well as a defence of the beauty of, the Scots tongue, including its musicality; and there is a deliberate echo, sometimes only by a subtle allusion, of Scotland's past, especially to the Highland Clearances.

The following piece, which is MacCormick's first known published poem, was written when MacCormick was in his third year in Glasgow High School and demonstrates not only a good ear for Scots, but also self-ironic conception of Scottish life:

The Midge

Frae Highland glen tae lowland valley
There's no one safe agin your sally;
Although y're sma', you bite right brawly,
Ye midge sae black,
And out o' doors we daurna dally
Lest you attack.

And after sunset, in the gloamin',
We daurna for a walk go roamin';
Ye'll come to us like pigeons homin'
And mak your prey,
A' rushing up like flood-tide foamin',
Tae join the fray.

Frae Everest tae Alpine ridges,
Frae Golden Gate tae Sydney's bridges,

31 Ibid.

Within the Universe's edges,
West, South or East,
There's nought sae fierce as Scotland's midges
'Mang man or beast.[32]

Burns-like in its sympathetic and cheeky attention to a seemingly minor and marginalised, if not detested, animal, MacCormick takes on, in this poem, an aspect of Scotland that is well-known but hardly a matter of pride. Without wishing to read too much into it, one could say that the poem shows MacCormick's lack of defensiveness about Scotland, and thus his ability to not to take it, or himself, too seriously. One could be proud of Scotland, but playfully and self-critically so. But even if we ignore such more vaunted attitudes and stay on the surface of the language of the poem, we see how much rhythm there is, how good an ear MacCormick had for the dynamics of Scots, and how much pleasure is taken in spinning and twisting the words and their sounds.

As mentioned above, MacCormick continued to write while studying at the University of Glasgow. The principal outlet for his writing was *GUM*, to which he contributed from 1959 to 1962. In this, as in much else that concerned student life in Glasgow, the MacCormick family were over-represented: his brothers and cousins were involved in *GUM* in various ways, e.g., with his cousin, Donald, serving as the *GUM* editor in 1961–62. MacCormick himself assisted with layout, publicity, and sales, as well as contributing many pieces, including the most of anyone in 1961–62.

As with his writing in high school, there is considerable comic self-consciousness in these early pieces, which one could easily brush away as typical of undergraduate writing. Although they could be read this way, in light of MacCormick's lifelong fascination with language and what it can do – what realities we can construct through the conventional use of language (an interest he shared with many eighteenth-century Scottish thinkers, especially David Hume) – one cannot but notice just how pre-occupied many of the pieces are with the magic and richness of language.

For instance, writing under the pseudonym of 'Crockmace' (it was common in *GUM* to publish under pseudonyms, which were unveiled at the end of the year), one of MacCormick's first stories was about a character, George, who drives his wife crazy by becoming obsessed with finding the right word for a particular object. George cannot get to sleep, mulling over what to call the thing that goes on top of a bottle, thinking it might be a cork, a stopper, a cap, and being unsatisfied with all of those options,

[32] *High School of Glasgow Magazine* (1955–56), 142–3.

finally exclaiming, over breakfast, to his non-plussed wife, and spilling coffee all over her to boot, that it must be a 'screw cap!'.[33] The story may seem to be harmless fun, and in some ways it is, but it also speaks to MacCormick's sensitivity to how things are named – indeed, to a self-conscious obsession with naming and the significance of linguistic labels.

The following year, in 1960–61, MacCormick returned to the character of George, this time not writing in the first person, but instead as a narrator observing George, situating him as an anxious and awkward Scot in a music record shop in London, looking, to no avail, for Scottish dance music records. Indeed, a number of MacCormick's pieces convey a keen sensitivity to the cultural relations between Scotland and England, including some very serious – if not downright grumpy – condemnations of the preference of some Scots for English over Scottish literature and drama. A good example of this is a piece published in 1961–62 that offered a double review of two theatre performances – one of 'West Side Story', performed at the King's Theatre, and another of 'The Gentle Shepherd', a play in Lowland Scots, performed at the Citizens' Theatre. In the case of the first performance, MacCormick observes, the theatre was packed, 'the music blaring and alien-sounding, the social background far from familiar'.[34] In the case of the second, where 'the setting was Scottish, the language Lowland Scots, and the social background of a certain relevance to modern Scotland', was 'sparsely' filled.[35] MacCormick does not mince his words, giving full vent to his 'cultural despair',[36] contrasting the 'pleasant poetry' and 'the very best tradition of Scottish folk-singing' in 'The Gentle Shepherd' with the supposed 'hits' of 'West Side Story' that were 'spewed into the plastic bucket of modern musical comedy'.[37] MacCormick's tone here is indignant and unrelentingly critical of the audience and their tastes, but it is also not resigned or forlorn – indeed, in parts the piece sounds like a call to arms: 'For too long now we have been a nation built upon shifting sands, with no sure basis on which to rest. We must look within our own past to find the seeds we can sow for our future; it seems clear that we are failing miserably to do this'.[38] MacCormick is conscious, too, in this piece, that he may be accused of 'parochialism', but counters this potential objection forcefully, drawing

[33] MacCormick, 'Untitled', as Crockmace, *GUM* (1959–60), 173–4.
[34] MacCormick, 'West Side Story', *GUM* (1961–62), 317.
[35] Ibid.
[36] Ibid.
[37] Ibid., 318.
[38] Ibid.

upon the work of William Power (from an essay on 'Scottish Literature') and arguing that 'the provincial attitude is the one which regards Scots literature as a mere branch and feeder of English literature'.[39]

The mix of tones across these pieces is instructive: on the one hand, MacCormick is clearly more than willing to be self-critical, even self-mocking (as in 'The Midge' poem, or in the character of George and his doomed hunt for Scottish dance records in London); on the other hand, he passionately defends the uniqueness and dignity of Scottish culture, calling for respect where he finds it lacking or missing (as in the tendency to see Scots literature as a branch of the English).

Other pieces, too, can be read as prescient previews of sensibilities that mature later, as in the sensitivity MacCormick displays to peace and reconciliation, and the associated criticisms he makes of either violence or frivolous indiscipline. The latter theme, for instance, is on display in MacCormick's account of the behaviour of students at Rectorial elections, which were notoriously riotous occasions (not only in Glasgow, but all over Scotland).[40] In this piece, 'The Road to Bute Hall',[41] MacCormick manages to combine humour with unflinching criticism of his peers, making the latter much more palatable as a result of the former – a hallmark, perhaps, of his later interventions as a figure with some authority. Noting the many incidents that occurred on the occasion of some of these Rectorial elections (e.g., those of Edmund Burke or Ignacy Jan Paderewski, but also that of his father in 1951), such as the 'Commando-style crossing of the Hall by means of a rope slung from one balcony to another', which also involved 'a duck' and 'incessant rain of flour, vegetables, eggs, toilet rolls and streamers',[42] MacCormick manages to entertain, while at the same time observing, in a quick change of tone, that 'There is no servility in civilised behaviour, but only disgrace in the abysmal conduct of the past few Rectorials'.[43] This was not to be the first time that MacCormick stood up for responsibility and civility, albeit less paternalistically than playfully and fraternally.

Some of these pieces, then, were not only experimental inquiries into the pleasures and politics of language and its forms and genres, but also moments when MacCormick cut his teeth as a leader amongst his peers, capable of critiquing his audience, when needed, without alienating

39 Ibid., 319.
40 See, e.g., Macdonald, '"To Form Citizens"' (2009).
41 MacCormick, 'The Road to Bute Hall', *GUM* (1960–61), 12–13.
42 Ibid., 12.
43 Ibid., 13.

them – quite the diplomatic challenge, and one in which he appeared to excel. Another good example, which is difficult to resist including, of this comic and diplomatic art of criticism, was a poem entitled 'Mainly About People or Cursus Honorum', where MacCormick commented, not without cheek, on the debating styles and temperaments of some of his peers, including Donald Dewar:

> Donald Dewar is the first
> Of all the Union people.
> The chaps with rotten eyesight curst
> Imagine he's the Union steeple.
> Some members find this rather acid
> But all his friends will say,
> He makes the effort to be placid
> Every Scottish Quarter Day.[44]

As all who knew him – then and later – could readily attest, MacCormick could be irresistibly funny, while being, at the same time, insightful, including sometimes critically insightful precisely via humour. This was, again, an important aspect of his character, i.e., his manner and style of relating with others. Whether diffusing a difficult and tense situation, or communicating something otherwise unpleasant, including putting someone who was overreaching in their place, MacCormick was able to employ humour in ways that created conditions for peace, or for safe passage of much-needed criticism. This was a delicate art, balancing critique, in the name of certain values – such as responsibility and civility – with not alienating those it was critiquing, offering them a route back into the community.

That this sensitivity to the value of peace, and the abhorrence of violence or incivility, was present even in this early creative writing is evident from a number of the pieces, including one of his last and longest, a drama in three acts entitled 'West Coast Story'.[45] Writing under yet another pseudonym – each one of which had its own stylistic personality – MacCormick tells the story of a feud between 'the Barbarous MacPherson and the Savage MacTavish', in 'a suitably indeterminate place in the west Highlands',[46] which is both initially exacerbated and finally resolved through a love between the son of one and the daughter of the other. Once again, MacCormick shows his ability not to take himself too seriously,

[44] MacCormick, 'Mainly about People or Cursus Honorum', *GUM* (1961–62), 353.
[45] MacCormick, 'West Coast Story', *GUM* (1961–62), 251–5.
[46] Ibid., 251.

describing the story as 'a hideously sentimental one of love triumphant over adversity',[47] i.e., he conveys an ability to be both inside the story (as a narrator) and outside it (as a meta-commentator).

The story involves an ingenious plot by the two lovers to escape and stage a fight between the two fathers, such that they are confronted by someone pretending to be a Glasgow policeman, 'carrying a smoking revolver', and admonishing the two fathers for their violence, only to offer the fathers a way out: they will not be prosecuted if they consent to the son marrying the daughter. MacCormick ends the story, with a final overtly moralising verse:

> Now these two are victorious
> The battle's off it's glorious
> You'll see no more o' us
> A wedding is much better than
> A battle for either clan.[48]

Of course, one can easily over-read the significance of pieces like this, over-determining them by what comes later. Nevertheless, even with this proviso, there is scope for reading this story as one in which MacCormick deploys his linguistic and conceptual ingenuity – his ability to craft and create possibilities with language – in the name of peace and reconciliation.

MacCormick's early literary exploits were not confined to writing. As mentioned above, he also took on other tasks, editing numerous publications, including *The Pleb* while still at high school, and then *Ossian, the Glasgow Guardian* (the *Guardian*), and the *Glasgow University Handbook* (the *Handbook*) while at the University of Glasgow. Although they could themselves be very self-critical about the quality of their publications, the students in Glasgow were clearly enormously productive, with publications including those three mentioned above, as well as *GUM* (which was the oldest of the lot), various departmental magazines (such as *Surgo* and the *Alchemist*), and other experiments, such as *Ygorra*. Experimental literary culture was evidently well and truly alive at the University of Glasgow.

The *Handbook* contained descriptions of the above-mentioned publications and their aims, e.g., writing as the editor of *GUM*, MacCormick's cousin, Donald MacCormick, asked for submissions that displayed a 'remarkable perception of human nature', advising students not to 'immediately … rush into emotional short stories', but instead to describe, 'with

[47] Ibid.
[48] Ibid., 255.

insight and accuracy, such aspects of their new environment as seem striking, or ridiculous, or pathetic', and also inviting them to come and discuss their stories 'till all hours of the night'.[49] Where *GUM* was set on being a literary magazine, the *Guardian* presented itself as the university's student newspaper, 'stimulating discussion and communicating news', and thus offering a forum 'for informed comment, criticism, and a wide range of interests'.[50]

The *Handbook*, in turn, which MacCormick edited in 1961, offered incoming students an introduction to the history of the Glasgow University Union, as well as overviews of the various activities, especially the university's political clubs. A key aspect of the *Handbook* was an explanation of the opportunities for and format of Union debating (a topic to which I will return shortly). The relevant summaries, in particular of the policies of the various political clubs, were accompanied by photos of those who were running them, as well as brief quotes associated with them, e.g., MacCormick, when he was President of GUSNA (in 1961), had, amongst the quotes associated with him, one from Dr Johnson: 'He was so generally civil that no man thanked him for it'.[51]

All this may seem like just superficial undergraduate fun, but it was much more than that. It conveyed a strong sense of a reflective community, one in which individuals took on responsibilities, and which gave scope for the expression of both idiosyncratic personality as well as collective visions. The students at the University of Glasgow were surrounded by regular publications in which they either appeared themselves, voicing concerns or contributing their literary experiments, or in which they found their own contributions scrutinised and evaluated. Once again, this was a tight-knit, emotional, and epistemic community, which was involved in mutual description and evaluation, and which was clearly dedicated to its own improvement, both of the individuals within it, as well as to itself as a community. Again, it mattered that this was a community that left room both for literary innovation as well as mutual criticism. For all its training in political acumen and debate – as we shall see in a moment – the University Glasgow was clearly also, at the same time, a crucible for literary self-consciousness, albeit always with close links to politics. Indeed, it opened the possibility of understanding language as a kind of magic communal and political glue – as something directly involved in the making of political communities.

49 Donald MacCormick, '*GUM*', *Handbook* (1961), 100.

50 Iain MacFarlane, 'The Guardian', *Handbook* (1961), 102.

51 Anonymous, 'GUSNA', *Handbook* (1961), 149.

Student Editor

In addition to contributing to student publications as a writer, MacCormick was also busy as an editor. In 1960, he became the editor of the *Guardian* – his first volume as editor was 29 April 1960 and his last that of 9 December 1960. Within this period, he regularly produced an eight-page publication, culminating in ten issues over the course of the year (with a break during the summer months). In the issue of 9 December, at the end of his term, the new incoming editors indicated just what 'a considerable debt of gratitude' the University owed to MacCormick (along with Donald Dewar, who was the editor immediately prior to MacCormick). The two of them, it seems, had revitalised the *Guardian*, putting it once again on a stable financial footing (finding advertisers, etc.), with the newspaper finally reporting a good circulation and even a profit.

Typically for MacCormick, while he was the *Guardian* editor, he made an appeal to 'all clubs to write to the *Guardian*, so it can be more representative', and so that the newspaper can 'reflect the whole fullness' of the life of the University.[52] Also typically, MacCormick attributed the success of the *Guardian* to the previous editor, Dewar, while also clearly taking pride in new developments, such as the *Guardian* having a regular cartoonist and Art editor.[53] The incoming editors, wondering what to give him as a token of thanks, thought of 'a plasticine Stone of Destiny that he [MacCormick] can steal whenever he wants to'.[54] In a subsequent issue, on 10 February 1961, a cartoon of MacCormick appeared, where once again he was thanked and described as the editor 'who produced more Guardians than any other Editor', also noting that MacCormick continued to serve, behind the scenes, as a 'consultant in matter of policy'.[55]

Meanwhile, having only just recently passed on the editorial mantle of the *Guardian*, MacCormick took on the task of producing the *Handbook* in 1961, as well as, perhaps most significantly, editing *Ossian* (with Donald T. MacDonald). This was an incredible load to take on while studying – and indeed excelling in the study of – philosophy and literature (MacCormick graduated with a First, winning a Snell Exhibition to Oxford).

52 MacCormick, 'Editorial', *The Guardian* (19 April 1960), 4.

53 MacCormick, 'Last Will and Testament', *The Guardian* (9 December 1960), 4.

54 'Editorial', *The Guardian* (9 December 1960), 6.

55 *The Guardian* (10 February 1961), 2.

Ossian had recently been revived – indeed, MacCormick had reported its reappearance in the *Guardian* on 14 October 1960.[56] The issue that revived it, in 1960, incidentally, contained a piece by MacCormick's father, entitled 'But we shall be free', which discussed the important place of the 'Gaelic inheritance' in Scottish history and its future. For MacCormick, then, editing the *Ossian* was particularly meaningful. Indeed, this is all the more so when one realises that MacCormick's *Ossian*, which was published in the autumn of 1961 (there is no more specific date), contained perhaps the last publication of his father, which MacCormick had commissioned from him, before he died on 13 October 1961. The poem, entitled 'Ossian's Address to the Sun' is almost overwhelmingly poignant, describing the rise of the 'might Sun, in the splendour of thy majesty … the Giver of dawn … the mighty Lord of Day', only to end with the following verses:

> Mine eyes grow dim, my hand scarce clasps the lyre,
> My trembling song grows faint with rising tears;
> Life ebbs away, as wanes the evening fire,
> And I am called to pay the toll of years;
> No more shall I behold they face, oh, Sun,
> No more the night's grim fears
> Be banished with the coming of the dawn –
> My soul goes forth into the dim unknown,
> Eternal night.
> Rejoice in lasting youth, though mighty Sun,
> For age is wan and grey,
> Like the pale glamour of the misty moon
> That mocks the light of day.
> Smile yet on other men though I must go,
> Alone and sadly down the hidden way,
> No more to sing thy might, no more to know
> The kindly gleam of thy first morning ray,
> The coming of the dawn.[57]

It is difficult not to be moved by this, the last known poem, of MacCormick's father, which John MacCormick wrote when he clearly knew he was at the end of his life.

In addition to containing this poem, this issue of *Ossian* also included, as noted above, a piece by Neil Gunn, entitled 'By Pastures Green', in which, among other things, Gunn had expressed his regret that An Comunn Gaidhealach – the Association promoting Scottish Gaelic language and

56 *The Guardian* (14 October 1960), 5.

57 John MacCormick, 'Ossian's Address to the Sun', *Ossian* (1961), 10.

culture – had not joined forces with the SNP, for the flourishing of Gaelic culture was not separate, as John MacCormick had also written, from the flourishing of Scotland generally. This issue also contained, again illustrating the personal resonance this had for MacCormick, a piece by his Great Uncle, Captain Dugald MacCormick, entitled 'Na Gaidheil agus a Gaidhlig'.

Significantly, too, there was a piece by MacCormick's lifelong friend, Allan Macartney, with whom, in 1961, MacCormick established the Federation of Student Nationalists, which brought together the various nationalist student associations, and which still survives, now known under the name 'SNP Students'. This Federation undertook, in a meeting in Dundee on 9 and 10 February 1962 to, among other things, publish a monthly student magazine, which was to be called 'Daisy!', meaning 'awake' in Gaelic. Once again, support for the preservation and flourishing of Gaelic language and culture was not separate from, but instead an integral part of, Scottish nationalist political thought. Tellingly, in his contribution, Macartney writes of how 'the decline in Gaelic … is merely one aspect of a national decline which, with the advent of the Anglicising mass medium of TV, has reached a catastrophic rate', critiquing the isolation of the Celtic people as merely '70,000 people in the North West', and instead, seeing 'the Celtic question as a whole', which 'can lead us [all Scots] to see a new awareness of ourselves'.[58]

This view is very much reinforced by the editorial penned by MacCormick and MacDonald. This piece, though short, is important for the light it sheds on MacCormick's attitude to language. MacCormick and MacDonald tie language to the practice of culture and a way of life: the manner in which persons, communicating together, make their community, including their habits, their emotions, and their relations with each other:

> But if what we are speaking of is the business of seeing that the language [Gaelic] remains a living means of communication between people and the medium of a vital culture, then it [the project of preserving Gaelic] is of great worth. There is a real value in our language for itself, as what we have made for ourself [sic], the means of personal contact which we have developed for our use over the ages. The loss of it would be disastrous, enduring and irreparable. More than that, we would lose in its wake things of even greater value. A culture not sophisticated or stately, but therefore with its roots more firmly than most in the ordinary people, one of unique beauty, would be lost with it. The way of life … would not linger long after it.[59]

[58] Macartney, 'The Celtic Peoples', *Ossian* (1961), 30.

[59] MacCormick and MacDonald, 'Editorial', *Ossian* (1961), 4.

The articulation of warnings against the loss of the Gaelic tongue is combined with a call to action: enough of 'procrastination and recrimination', they write; for the sake of 'self-respect', we must be 'responsible' and 'save … ourselves'.[60] Being 'concern[ed] alone is not enough'; instead, what is needed is 'well directed and concerted action', informed by a change of attitude, which sees the problem of Gaelic 'in relation to the general problems of Scotland, for they are substantially the same'.[61] To fight, practically, for the preservation of Gaelic, is to resist and fight against 'our national loss of faith in ourselves'.[62]

Language, here, is no mere efficient means of communication: it is something that is inherently important, culturally, politically, socially, and morally. It is part of the way in which a culture survives and a community makes itself. This respect for the 'magic' of language – its capacity to constitute social realities – was, as mentioned earlier, to be a recurring theme in MacCormick's philosophy. It is sometimes thought that the roots of this approach to the world-making capacity of language were J. L. Austin's speech act theory, which became so important for Oxford philosophers (and the so-called language turn in analytical philosophy). Undoubtedly, this was important for MacCormick too – he was reading Austin at this time, while studying in Glasgow – but the roots of MacCormick's approach to language lay arguably more deeply, precisely in the fragile but powerful role of language in Scottish culture and in the place of Scotland in the world. MacCormick's ties to language were not only, or even mainly, conceptual: they were deeply emotional, deeply personal, and deeply social.

Towards the end of his life, in his last book, *Practical Reason in Law and Morality* (2008), MacCormick returned once again to language, drawing on the new science of DNA to speak of 'the human genome as a book', while connecting it to religious traditions (religions of the book, for whom the word lies at the beginning) and of what is written 'in the hearts of human beings'.[63] The idea here was not of a written code, which one then had to subsequently conform to, but instead something deeper: the conventional use of language – 'the power of speech', which 'is one of the irreducibly social powers of the human mind' (following Thomas Reid and Ludwig Wittgenstein)[64] – involving 'common adherence to the common

[60] Ibid.
[61] Ibid., 5.
[62] Ibid.
[63] MacCormick, PRLM (2008), 27–8.
[64] Ibid., 28.

norms of grammar and the like that structure our speech' and that 'must include a norm favouring truthfulness and sincerity over falsehood and cheating'.[65]

MacCormick's conception of language is rich enough to encompass the values of sincerity and truth, as inhering in its use, but also extends to seeing language as deeply set within the very life – the everyday life – of a community. Languages are, as MacCormick insists, 'highly normative', but this is a normativity that resides in the norm-using practices of ordinary persons – not in the say-so of a norm-giver, or someone clad with institutional authority.[66] This, in turn, is a clue to MacCormick's conception of law, at least in the later version of the institutional theory, of law as institutional normative order – an order that is set within us as primarily norm-users (rather than norm-givers). But this, to reiterate, was a conception of law based on an emotionally filtered understanding of language that, for MacCormick, was deeply social and, at once, deeply personal and Scottish.

Communal Debate

A Family Affair

Just as important, for MacCormick, as the joys of language, and its significance for the flourishing of a community, and its individuals, was the practice of debate – and especially the oral performance and oral interaction of committed individuals over issues of controversy. Further, as we have seen with language, so with debate: MacCormick's experience of this was set within a familial tradition, strongly present already in his father's life, and then continuing with his brother (Iain) and cousin (Donald). Indeed, 'the MacCormick clan' as they were sometimes called, were known to be a force to be reckoned with in the Union debating circles of the late 1950s and early 1960s. Very significantly, too, the personal connections for MacCormick extended beyond his family: many of the debaters, including those in rival political clubs, became MacCormick's friends, some life-long, such as John Smith and Donald Dewar.

Not only, then, was Glasgow University debating an incubator of MacCormick's skills as a speaker, as a debater, as someone with a keen eye for political controversy, with extensive political knowledge, and someone deeply sensitive to the norms of debating, including respecting the right of

65 Ibid.
66 Ibid., 29.

everyone to be heard, but it also – precisely through participation in the activity of debating – formed his character, i.e., as a person who related with others in a particular manner or style. This was a manner or style that did not shy away from criticism when it was due and extended to holding one's ground and arguing for what one found valuable and important, but it was also, at the same time, a manner or style that was always one step removed, avoiding dogmatism and fanaticism, capable of diffusing tension when it went too far, with one eye firmly on the quality of relations between persons involved in discoursing together, and thus mindful of the importance of peace amidst disagreement and of being respectful, considerate, and inclusive.

One can see this as a process of safeguarding the morality of politics, or one can see it as an enriched, normative conception of the political, which was not merely a matter of a winner-takes-all war of positions represented, say, by political parties, but was instead a matter, ultimately, of the flourishing of a community, including its capacity for including multiple voices, for disagreeing respectfully, and for living peacefully together. Glasgow University debating was, then, not only an apprenticeship in the arts of public speech or a course in the issues then affecting Scottish and British politics, but also an experience of the value of democracy in action, which was incredibly formative for MacCormick's character and which shaped his deepest philosophical intuitions (for instance, about the nature of reason).

It is important to see how far Glasgow University debating, and more broadly the Glasgow Student Union, reached into both the history of Scottish nationalist politics as well as into MacCormick's family history. Although debating, as part of rhetorical and dialectical pedagogy, can be traced back much further in the history of Glasgow and other Scottish universities, the modern era of university debating arguably begins in Glasgow with the establishment of the Glasgow University Dialectical Society (the Dialectical Society) in 1861. This was followed soon after with the establishment of the Glasgow University Union in 1885 (the Union). These, alongside other changes in the structure of Scottish universities, Glasgow included, such as the elevation of the Rector to the chair of the University Court (in the 1858 *Universities (Scotland) Act*), or in the establishment and recognition of Students' Representative Councils by 1886, all suggest, as Catriona Macdonald argued, that in Scotland, there was a close relationship between 'studentship and citizenship'[67] – a recognition of universities as civic spaces, and, indeed, given the heterogeneous nature of the 'social composition of the Scottish student body', ones that

[67] Macdonald, '"To Form Citizens"' (2009), 401.

were infused with a much more egalitarian and 'meritocratic ethos' (than, for instance, their English counterparts).[68] Students in Scottish universities, it seems, were, already from the nineteenth century, very politically involved and politically self-conscious as well as politically organised. One manifestation of this, at the time of MacCormick's studies there, is the debating culture in Glasgow.

The aim of the university's Dialectical Society was to promote and enable discussion of literary, philosophical, and political subjects, particularly via the form of a debate based on the Westminster Parliament, and thus involving a number of political parties debating a motion put forward by one of those parties (which constituted the government for that purpose). These debates would traditionally last twelve hours – from 1 pm to 1 am. The times for speeches were strictly controlled: eight minutes for the mover and seconder, fifteen minutes for the leaders opening and closing the debates, and eight minutes for all other members. Between five and six of such debates were held annually, though, in addition to these, others were at times introduced, including inter-university competitions, special debates in honour of particular guests to the university, and preparatory, private debates organised by the various clubs. One's studies in Glasgow could literally be filled with debating and preparing to debate.

Over the years, motions would naturally pick up on the most controversial of issues in contemporary Scottish and British politics. An especially striking example in this context is the motion for the Union's third political debate in 1929 (held on 1 February), which had been proposed by the Nationalists. The motion involved the submission of a 'Draft Constitution of Scotland', which included, amongst its articles, the following provisions:

Article I: Scotland is a sovereign nation and all authority therein is vested in the Scottish people.
Article II: The authority of the Scottish People shall be exercised through the Estates of Parliament as by the constitution established and through their representative King George V, and his lawful successors.
Article III: All citizens of Scotland shall have equal rights and every citizen shall have the right to free education.

In the government of the Nationalists, the Minister without Portfolio was none other than John MacCormick, who had already graduated in 1928 (hence, presumably, the reason for not having a portfolio), but clearly returned to participate in the debate. As we already know, having initially

[68] Ibid., 385.

joined the Labour Club, John MacCormick had left it in 1927 to form GUSNA, which, in turn, played a crucial part in the merger of various previously existing associations to constitute the NPS in April 1928, and, later, the merger of the NPS and the SP to form the SNP in 1934. As we saw in Chapter 1, this cascade of political communities owed a great deal to the energy and enthusiasm of the students at Glasgow University, as, arguably, were the ideas that were no doubt created, contested, and refined in the Union debates. The 1929 debate was just one example among many: at least one debate per year since the creation of GUSNA was held on a motion proposed by it and therefore dealing directly with Scottish nationalist politics.

A further important context, alluded to earlier but worth repeating, was the election of the Rector. Andrew Marr has called the election of the Rector of the University of Glasgow a kind of 'barometer' of Scottish politics.[69] Others, too, have pointed to the crucial role played by the debates surrounding the Rectorial candidates, and in particular the arguments of GUSNA representatives.[70] The Rector is directly chosen by the students for a period of three years and is tasked with communicating student concerns to the university's senior management. But, in Glasgow, the elected Rector took on much greater symbolic importance, indicating a direction in which not only Glaswegian, but perhaps also broader Scottish politics, was heading. For MacCormick, this was especially meaningful because, as we already know, the Rector elected in 1950 was none other than his father, John MacCormick, who had won a close contest with Sir David Maxwell Fyfe and Rev. Dr George MacLeod.

By the early 1960s, when MacCormick was studying, Rectorial elections were eagerly discussed by student nationalists – whether celebrating past successes, such as not only that of John MacCormick's, but also Compton Mackenzie's in 1931–34 (or the near win of Cunninghame Graham in 1928), or plotting the next campaign (in 1962, that of Dr Robert McIntyre, who was in the end defeated by the President of the African National Congress and Nobel Peace Prize winner, Albert Lutuli).

Undoubtedly, too, MacCormick had heard his father speak about the importance of the Rectorial position. Writing about the Rectorship in 1959 (in the student *Handbook*, which he had himself previously edited), John MacCormick took a long view of this position, tracing it back to the sixteenth century, and arguing that the change introduced in 1858 and 1889,

[69] Marr, *The Battle for Scotland* (2013), 63.

[70] See, e.g., Mitchell, *Strategies for Self-Government* (1996); Finlay, *Independent and Free* (1994); Somerville, *Through the Maelstrom* (2013).

resulting in the Rector serving as the President of the University Court, shows that 'in a real sense, the Scottish Universities were self-governing institutions in which the students no less than the professoriate played a conspicuous part'.[71] For John MacCormick, then, at stake in Rectorial elections were the values of self-governance and democracy.

Prime Minister

It is against this background that we need to view MacCormick's own participation in the Union debates. It must have, for instance, been very special for MacCormick to serve, as he did in the Second Union debate in 1961, as the Prime Minister in a Scottish Nationalist Government, which had proposed, as its motion for debate, the resolution 'To establish a separate Parliament for Scotland; and as the Government of Scotland, to join the Common Market regardless of British and Commonwealth Ties'. This was, again typically, an all-MacCormick affair, with his brother, Iain, serving as The Master of All the Queen's Horses and all the Queen's Men, and his cousin, Donald, as Humpty Dumpty (these last two were positions as part of what was called 'The Lunatic Fringe' in this imaginary parliament).

As reported in *GUM*, in November 1961, the performance of the Scottish Nationalist Government, 'particularly in the closing stages of the evening when their benches were packed to overflowing, was first class', though, the report then adds, 'they must learn … to be quicker-witted and funnier-minded in answering written queries at Question Time'.[72] MacCormick himself is singled-out in the following way: 'The Prime Minister, Neil MacCormick, made a good speech, perhaps his best yet on Home Rule, but he failed badly in not paying enough attention to the Common Market'.[73] MacCormick clearly learned his lesson for he did, as we shall see, pay very much attention to the Common Market (or, later, the European Union). There is some frivolity, no doubt, in such remarks, but the same reporter goes on to say, in a very different tone:

> But the last reflection which the debate prompts is the seriousness with which people came forward to discuss the affairs of their own country and its relation to Europe; and that it is a good thing they should do so. It seems good that there is one club whose business is to make people take thought, at least once in the year, for the significance of Scotland. It was cheering to

[71] John MacCormick, *Glasgow University Handbook* (1959), 127.
[72] *GUM* (November 1961) 73(2), 80.
[73] Ibid., 81.

> see people from both sides show such awareness of identity and concern for the better things of nationality.[74]

This, indeed, is typical of the reports of these debates: their mix of good-humoured criticism (e.g., Iain MacCormick, in the same debate, is reported to have 'started in the old style, but ended in a diatribe of dubious relevance'),[75] with more serious observations on the very content of the motion or the quality of the debate. Incidentally, this also indicates just how early MacCormick had been reflecting on Europe as a political theatre for Scotland.

MacCormick is discussed in many of these debating reports, written by his peers: early on, in his first year (1959–60) he wins the most promising speaker prize, though even then he by no means escapes criticism, e.g., he, along with others, 'will improve when they learn to vary the pace and tone of their delivery';[76] and, later, in 1961, in the Fifth Union Debate, the report observes that 'The debate was opened with the swirl of the kilt and skirl of Niall MacCormick's voice', but continues to say that 'His tune, though well played, was not as deep and as stirring as might have been expected when a fiery Highlander discusses his native health's perilous position'.[77] In all this, MacCormick must have been testing and fine-tuning, negotiating and wrestling with, the tone and attitudes of Scottish nationalism.

MacCormick picks up numerous prizes in his debating career, including outstanding individual in the famous Observer debating tournament, and has numerous leading roles, such as Clerk of the House, the Secretary and President of GUSNA, as well as serving on the management committee of the Union (alongside, for instance, Dewar, Smith, and Campbell). It is also clear that he is much appreciated as a presence in the debates by his peers, and for a variety of reasons: for example, in the Fourth Union Debate on 12 January 1962 (which is reported as being the birthday of Edmund Burke), MacCormick is said to have made 'an amusing speech', which, 'at this stage in the debate … came as a godsend',[78] though, on another occasion, what is praised is how 'sincere' and 'emotional' he was (this was on a motion 'to place all local authority schools under the direct control of the Ministry of Education and the Scottish Office and provide state scholarship for 75% of public school places'),[79] and yet on

[74] Ibid.
[75] Ibid.
[76] *GUM* (December 1959), 213.
[77] *GUM* (March 1961), 278.
[78] *GUM* (January 1962), 73(4).
[79] *GUM* (1962), 73(5).

another that he was 'witty, lucid and (need I say it?) logical', being 'the first of many to introduce the question of morality to the debate, and who better?'.[80] Sometimes MacCormick is praised for his 'brilliance', making 'the most outstanding speech of the opening round if not the Debate';[81] sometimes, if not his humour, then it is his musical talents that are appreciated: in 1961, after the First Queen Margaret debate, it is his 'accordion' that enlivens the party, resulting in 'a greater unanimity of melody than is usual at that time on that sort of night'.[82]

As the reports run down the years, MacCormick moves from being the most promising speaker, to one of its 'elder statesmen',[83] such that, on the occasion of his final speech, with a motion 'on the promulgation of enforced economic rents in council houses and the repeal of the Trades Dispute Act', MacCormick, 'opening for his club', is described as 'holding the attention of the house from the beginning to the end with a characteristically witty speech punctuated by the quick caustic asides to his protagonists'.[84] The report goes on to note that the 'tremendous applause to Neil' at the end of the debate 'is a measure of his tremendous popularity in this university'.[85] As his peers discover he has been selected for the Snell Exhibition to Oxford, they write, not without some cheek:

> Exactly what Oxford University have done to merit the invasion of Neil MacCormick is not yet known. But what will happen to the Scots Nats when their voluble mouthpiece deserts them in the most unpatriotic manner? Who will step into the large void created by the dissention and desertion of Neil? … At the moment there is nobody with the same qualities and capabilities…[86]

This, it should be noted, is not the judgement of a fellow student nationalist, but instead a fellow debater, and a fellow member of the student political community.

A Political Apprenticeship

For MacCormick, all this must have been quite the training, not only in the arts of speech, but also in the nuances of Scottish and British politics – an

80 *Guardian* (25 January 1963), 2.
81 *GUM* (1961), 73(2), 82.
82 Ibid., 55.
83 *Guardian* (23 November 1962), 2.
84 *Guardian* (8 March 1963), 2.
85 Ibid., 2.
86 *GUM* (8 March 1962), 4.

apprenticeship in political knowledge. The content of the motions gives a sense of the range of subject-matter that debaters were immersed in, the diversity being secured precisely by there being six political clubs, each with the right to propose one motion a year. These motions ranged from the above-noted Nationalist ones, to others, such as 'That this House regrets the Reformation' (the motion for a special invitation debate in 1960, and in which John MacCormick himself participated as a special guest)[87] or:

- 'This House recognises the FLN government in Algeria'
- 'This House advocates economic aid for Cuba'
- 'This House calls for the abolition of fee-paying schools and for the regionalisation of Education'
- 'This House proposes a tax on advertising, institutes a capital gains tax of 50%, and makes income tax 10 in a pound'
- 'This House resolves that Burns was a Bum'
- 'This House resolves that a belief in Democracy is a submission to Vulgarity'
- 'This House endorses the pay pause, will not underwrite losses in the coal industry, will allow the import of foreign coal, and will refuse housing subsidies'; and
- 'This House prefers the Celtic Twilight to the Greater European Dawn'.

This variety – stretched out along the political spectrum and extending even to international politics – gives a flavour of the kind of political experience this was.

This is not to say that the students themselves always, or even often, thought the standard of 'political knowledge', as they put it, was sufficiently high. It bears emphasis, at the risk of repetition, just how critical these debate reports often are: this was a community whose members disciplined and cajoled each other into improvement. It was less a mode of individual performance, though this did matter, and more a matter of collective training in political knowledge. Indeed, the self-critique often extended to more general discussions of the quality of the entire enterprise.

Thus, for example, John Smith, who, in the *Handbook*, spoke of 'the peculiarly important role which debating plays in Glasgow' – which he attributed, no doubt with a wink, to 'the disputatious mentality found in the West of Scotland, an addiction to argument and a love of demagoguery in an atmosphere conditioned by a healthy radicalism and bounded by

[87] 'Debate Report', *GUM* (29 April 1960), 4.

weighty common sense' – and in which he sang the praises of past speakers, such as 'Robert Horne, Walter Elliott, Jimmy Maxton', and Hector McNeill'[88] – did not hesitate, initially under a pseudonym, to raise concerns about the standard of debates. Yes, he said: 'Glasgow University tends to prize itself on an interest in politics. Certainly, a University where political clubs reach the size they do and command such a large share of undergraduate life is to be preferred to the almost complete indifference to politics which exists in other Universities…'.[89] But: 'We might think we had a good forum for the discussion of politics. Certainly the opportunity exists but too often it is grossly misused. Most debaters have learned [sic] how to speak but they have simply nothing to say. The result is that the level of political discussion is extremely low'.[90]

Responding to this in a letter to the Editor, James McMeekin and Gordon Hunter wrote:

> …it is true that the political consciousness of the so-called political groups leaves a good deal to be desired … [But] Debating requires something more than political knowledge. Our best informed political thinkers have far from universally been our best debaters… For our own part, we freely concede the need for increased intellectual activity on the part of the political clubs; but we feel compelled to call in question the equation of political with dialectic banality and the inference that better politics will necessarily mean better debating.[91]

Which, in turn, triggered Smith, this time writing under his real name, to reply:

> Of course, better politics does not necessarily mean better debating. Union debates must be more than a series of intellectual theses – as if this was a serious danger. [But] I cannot understand why better politics should mean worse debating. We should attempt to make Union debates a forum for political ideas as well as entertainment… The great strength of Glasgow has been the alliance between politics and debating. It is rather pointless to train people to speak when they have nothing to say.[92]

This debate is illustrative of the highly self-reflexive nature of the Union's debating community. Both sides, in fact, show commitment to

88 *Handbook* (1961), 135.
89 'Debates' *GUM* (1961), 270.
90 Ibid.
91 McMeekin and Hunter, 'Letter', *GUM* (1961), 303–4.
92 Smith, 'Letter', *GUM* (1961), 304.

improvement in the quality of 'political knowledge', or of 'having something to say', amongst its members, with the disagreement seeming to be about just where to place the emphasis: on the quality of the dialectics or on the quality of the content. But what is interesting is not who is more correct, but the very fact that there is a discussion of this kind, and in quite passionate terms. There is serious commitment to maintaining, and indeed potentially improving, the high standards of the Union and its proud tradition of political debating. Clearly, the participants in this community did not just see this as an apprenticeship in debating skills: they were concerned about the intellectual seriousness of the enterprise, and about the prospects of these debates being genuine fora for the development of political thought.

MacCormick, too, participated in these debates, and he did so in both aspects, i.e., with concern about the quality of the dialectics, as well as about the seriousness of the content. Reflecting on the year's debating, in 1963, he wrote about how the 'debates have suffered grievously from motions which failed to spark off fierce debate', it often seeming 'that the gap between right and left was more formal than real'.[93] That is important, for it shows how crucial he thought it was to have a genuine, robust, albeit respectful debate. To enable that, however, one needed some distance between the speakers, thereby making room for genuine dissensus, but with all this still occurring in a space where everyone was committed and where everyone listened to others speak. The point was to make room for opposing and alternative voices, but still within a community of respect for persons.

At other times, MacCormick focused on style: he spoke of some speakers being 'smooth' and 'keen',[94] of how funny some of them were, of how they were well prepared and well informed but failed to 'produce sufficient dramatic tension to reach the top flight of Union speaking'.[95] But, amongst all the stylistic comments, what shone through, repeatedly, was MacCormick's call, echoing in this sense that of John Smith, for speakers to develop 'more serious political interests'.[96] For MacCormick, Glasgow University debating was fun, and that was important, but the pleasure of it sat alongside the seriousness of it: it was both a pleasant and a serious collective exploration of political possibilities and what was at stake in them.

93 MacCormick, *Guardian* (8 March 1963), 2.
94 MacCormick, 'Sixth Union Debate', *GUM* (1962), 263.
95 Ibid., 264.
96 MacCormick, *Guardian* (8 March 1963), 2.

Perhaps most evocatively of all, however, he compared the style of debating in Glasgow with that in Oxford (where, as we shall see in more detail later, he also participated in the Oxford Union, serving for a year as its President). Oxford had 'a wide profusion of drama, literature, debating, sport and like', and its debating society was 'a comfortable – almost stately – club situated in its own quiet garden in the heart of the University … characterised by an overwhelming graciousness'.[97] But what Glasgow lost in elegance, it gained, he said, 'in vitality'.[98] In Glasgow, the 'partisanship of the House … gives it its distinctive character', it being 'a crucial fact that a Government brings forward a Bill and an Opposition opposes it', with 'the six political clubs … firmly arranged in the geometric absurdity of the two-sided hexagon'.[99] Importantly, 'everyone is committed one way or the other'[100] – also importantly, speakers are curtailed in the length of their speech (which was unlike Oxford where the chair had discretion to give extra time to a particularly brilliant speech).

In Glasgow, MacCormick said, there is a 'contentious atmosphere, such that 'when the House is packed and smoky', with the 'gallery crowding in over the speakers', then the 'stage is perfectly set for debating of unparalleled vigor'.[101] The 'relation between speaker and audience provokes wit and eloquence, and the competitive urgency keeps up a devasting exchange of invective'.[102] Such is the atmosphere, and format, that the twelve hours of debating is genuine 'good fun'.[103]

By contrast, debating in Oxford was 'a far cry from that partisan fog of argument'.[104] Here, instead: 'The main part of the debate consists of six 'paper' speeches, those delivered by the principal speakers whose names are listed on the order paper. Two of these are usually given by distinguished guests who lend glamour to the proceedings, and, to be truthful, attract a large part of the audience'.[105]

The Oxford house is 'cold and dispassionate', but this does not mean that to speak in it is not a valuable experience. In fact, quite the contrary: 'As you stand', says MacCormick, 'dry-mouthed at the dispatch box

97 MacCormick, 'Glasgow Style' (1965), 10.
98 Ibid.
99 Ibid.
100 Ibid.
101 Ibid.
102 Ibid.
103 Ibid.
104 Ibid.
105 Ibid.

surrounded by a slur of faces the hall appears gigantic in size',[106] and you need to not only confront your fear, but also make sure you are well prepared – well enough to be able to deliver the speech with 'apparent spontaneity and wit'.[107] The Oxford debate, said MacCormick, was 'impressive' and 'fascinating', but, for him, it is Glasgow and its debating that were his 'spiritual home'.[108] That is telling: where Oxford was more about the brilliance of the individual performance, with all eyes on how such an individual can deal with the pressure of so much attention, Glasgow was much more sociable and more about a robust, but still respectful, exchange of views in a community. In any event, MacCormick added, typically, 'I am glad to have had both experiences'.[109]

The debating in Glasgow was, for MacCormick, hugely formative. One can traces its legacies in numerous ways. One of these legacies is his style of speaking and writing – his written pieces, such as his book reviews, often dipped into the art of (humorous, but still sharp) invective he picked up in Glasgow. MacCormick clearly took great pleasure in such 'refutational rhetoric', as this aspect of rhetoric has been called.[110] For instance, MacCormick's university diaries from those years include hastily scribbled down examples of effective invectives, e.g., 'Unfortunately, he has been treading on such soft ground that in laying his ear to the ground he has assumed the position most characteristic of an ostrich. Accordingly, he suffers from precisely the same restriction of vision as his feathered friend'.[111] Again, such an ability – to humorously defeat a rival argument – is not to be dismissed as trivial, for such turns of phrase, such interventions, often prove to be vital, especially in large political debates.

Another legacy was of course a substantive continuity with the positions and arguments MacCormick argued as a member of GUSNA, proposing motions on nationalist themes, trying out which arguments worked and which didn't, being involved in Rectorial campaigns, running plebiscites on home rule, setting up the Federation of Student Nationalists, and making arguments in favour of preserving Gaelic and Scots. Although we no longer have the speeches he gave on those occasions, it can hardly be doubted that this aspect of the political apprenticeship of Glasgow debating prepared him well for his later political involvement.

106 Ibid.
107 Ibid.
108 Ibid.
109 Ibid.
110 Eden, *Rhetorical Renaissance* (2022), chapter 2.
111 MacCormick, 'Glasgow University Diary', (1960–61), (unnumbered page note).

But the influence of Glaswegian debating culture ran more deeply than this and fed into the larger, philosophical themes MacCormick would later go on to tackle, e.g., the practicality of reason, the ethics of argument, the rhetorical or argumentative quality of legal reasoning, and the value of democracy. Even more deeply, it ran into his character: his manner or style of relating with others, i.e., encouraging and facilitating debate and discussion, but respectfully, considerately, and inclusively.

Glasgow's debating culture provided a real theatre, a genuine practice, in which these ideals could be experienced, albeit on a much smaller, granular scale. Once one knows about the extent of MacCormick's involvement in it, it is difficult not to see it echoing in MacCormick's seemingly most abstract treatment of philosophical questions, such as the practical reach of reason. As we shall see later, in more detail, there is in MacCormick's treatment of these questions always a vein of pragmatism and sociability, of the treasured value of civility, and of a commitment to the good of the community and its peace as overriding any fanatical defence of a dogmatic truth. There was, in MacCormick, a genuine and deep commitment to making multiple voices heard, to retaining spaces for the respectful exchange of opposing and alternative views: in a sense, this was precisely where the practicality of reason resided. Practical reason was democratic reason. Again, it is difficult not to connect this to what MacCormick experienced – both as a participant as well as, in his writings, as an observer – of Glasgow debating culture.

One powerful echo of this, worth mentioning here, is MacCormick's very first editorial project, which he, tellingly, entitled *The Scottish Debate* (1970). The title itself suggests MacCormick was not interested in advocating for a nationalist cause. He could have, but did not, bring together voices of a common mind all arguing for some versions of independence or at least greater devolution. Instead, what he wanted, and what he created, was a genuine debate, including voices across the political spectrum, all the while inquiring as to whether there was any potential for 'common ground'.[112] Thus, he commissioned pieces from Donald Dewar, laying out the Labour position; from David Steel, the Liberal; from Esmond Wright, the Conservative; and from his brother, Iain, the Nationalist. This was MacCormick's first major foray into academic publishing and it set the tone for his life-long contribution: a tone that enabled respectful dissensus rather than fanatical confrontation, and one that looked, pragmatically

[112] MacCormick, 'Introduction', *The Scottish Debate* (1970), 3.

and patiently, for novel and creative ways to unite rather than separate, while still retaining difference.

Another echo, more intimate than the above, is embodied in the many long-lasting friendships MacCormick nurtured from his time at the University of Glasgow – friendships that ran, importantly, across the political spectrum. Sometimes, of course, these were friendships formed with those he shared much in common politically, such as Allan Macartney – a friendship that began with their joint passion for the Gaelic language and Scottish nationalist politics, and which developed into joint interests in the good of Europe (with both serving in the European Parliament) and in a belief in the possibility of European democracy. Macartney, MacCormick said, 'was a living embodiment of the nationalism that is tolerant, inclusive, and universalistic in outlook and commitment. For him, the fundamental principle in politics was that of self-determination for individuals and for peoples'.[113] Writing about Macartney after his death, MacCormick described him as 'one of my best friends, my political conscience who kept me from retreating completely into academic life'.[114] He showed him, MacCormick said, by living it, a politics that was not about 'self-aggrandisement'.[115]

In other cases, MacCormick developed friendships across political differences. Perhaps the most outstanding example was with John Smith. To recall, the Smith and MacCormick families had had a connection before – with Archie Smith (John Smith's father) and John MacCormick being students together, and with the latter leaving Labour to form the SNP – and this connection was renewed and strengthened in their friendship. At that time, while they were students, Smith was often over at the MacCormick's house, and MacCormick recalled a scene of passionate debate between Smith and his father:

> John was one of a crowd in for a ceilidh ... and he fell into an argument with my father, then very ill with his last illness, in the kitchen. They were two of the most eloquent people I knew, and in their Highland backgrounds and orientations to the world have come to seem to me more and more similar as I have looked back at them. The one had set his cap at an apparently unreachable ideal, and failed in the attempt. The other was embarked on a career, guided by a realism and commitment that went back to an old disagreement. You have got to have power said John Smith. He gave his life to that view. It is the saddest of ironies that a flaw of physical constitution

113 MacCormick, 'Allan Macartney' (1998), 1.
114 Ibid.
115 Ibid.

> deprived him of the opportunity that he had done all else to earn, and had practically earned in the end.[116]

MacCormick, in this respect, was unlike Smith: not only did their politics differ (Smith, for example, was 'for a long time highly sceptical of Home Rule'),[117] but so did their attitude to the political life – MacCormick, unlike Smith, was not after power (even a power to do good, as he knew Smith pursued (MacCormick said of Smith that he believed 'that one had to acquire real power to do extensive good').[118] He preferred to dwell, instead, behind the scenes, or on the border of party politics, always with one foot outside the factions and disputes of the day. This is not to say MacCormick did not stand up for his beliefs and call for recognition and respect for Scotland when he thought it was missing, but it is to say that he was always inclined to see a larger horizon, to have, in his words, a more universalistic outlook – to see beyond the vagaries of any current disagreement to the very conduct of debate and to the values at stake in it. Perhaps this is why he was drawn to philosophy, despite all the many links that his philosophy always had to the practice of politics, especially the politics of Scotland. MacCormick was not unaware of this: speaking again of Smith, he said that Smith was primarily 'the practitioner, the pragmatist, the operator, even' and not a 'political theorist or philosopher'.[119]

Neither, however, the political differences, nor professional habitus, got in the way of friendship and one they continued, this time as families with children, when MacCormick took up his post in Edinburgh in 1972, with the two families living a block away from each other.[120] It was with genuine emotion that MacCormick piped Smith to his grave in 1994. As an article in *The Jerusalem Post* recorded at the time: 'The ceremony [of Smith's burial] ended in a walled burial plot overlooking the sea with two haunting laments played on bagpipes by family friend, Neil MacCormick, a professor of law at Edinburgh University: "A Man's a Man for a' That" and a Gaelic tune, "Caolmuile", known as the Hymn of St Columbia of Iona'.[121]

In addition to Smith, the other friendship, again mentioned briefly in Chapter 1, that MacCormick formed in Labour circles was with Donald Dewar. This friendship too, as with Smith, had deep-set familial

116 MacCormick, 'John Smith' (1994), 8.
117 Ibid., 7.
118 Ibid.
119 Ibid., 8.
120 Ibid., 6.
121 Anonymous, 'John Smith Buried on Remote Scottish Island', *The Jerusalem Post* (22 May 1994), 3.

connections. To recall, Aunt Eleanor Dewar was an informal aunt to the MacCormick children and was a particularly close friend of Margaret MacCormick. Further, Aunt Eleonor had participated in the Scottish Covenant campaign, as well as, even earlier, in the NPS and then subsequently the SNP. Despite the various inevitable political adaptations, there ran, in Dewar's political outlook, a nationalism of kind, even if with a small 'n',[122] and it is no accident that there are echoes, if not continuities, between the Covenant Association of Dewar's boyhood and its *A Blueprint for Scotland* (1948) and the *Scotland Act* 1998.[123] MacCormick did not just share an informal aunt with Dewar: they shared a love of language (MacCormick calls Dewar 'crabbit and carnaptious', adding that these were 'two words of which he much approved')[124] and they shared a commitment, despite all other political disagreements, to Scottish democracy: '"There shall be a Scottish Parliament" was a phrase famously well-liked by Donald Dewar. It is a liking many of his compatriots share and will go on sharing'.[125] It was certainly a phrased liked by MacCormick.

Public Reason

It may be helpful to step back for a moment from the details of all these Union activities and friendships to see just what was it about them that resonated so deeply in MacCormick's character. We can get a sense of that by recalling the importance John Stuart Mill, in *On Liberty* – one of the books that MacCormick indicated was most influential for him in his Glasgow days[126] – placed on the free contestation of truths. For Mill:

> There is the greatest difference between presuming an opinion to be true because, with every opportunity for contesting it, it has not been refuted, and assuming its truth for the purpose of not permitting its refutation. Complete liberty of contradicting and disproving our opinion is the very condition which justifies us in assuming its truth for purposes of action; and no other terms can a being with human faculties have any rational assurance of being right.[127]

122 MacCormick, 'Enduring Foundations' (2005), 142.
123 Ibid., 144.
124 Ibid., 141.
125 Ibid., 145.
126 In his *5 Questions* interview, MacCormick noted that 'Mill's essay *On Liberty* exercised great influence on my thinking both philosophically and in politics': 'Sir Neil MacCormick' (2007), 172.
127 Mill, *On Liberty* [1859] (1985), 79.

Key to the practicality of reason here is the opportunity for respectful dissensus – for testing a belief rigorously via creating opportunities for a variety of opposing and alternative views to be heard about it. Mill sings beautifully in favour of 'living truth' rather than 'dead dogma',[128] i.e., a truth that can be apprehended emotionally,[129] but also a truth that is the outcome of a process of discussion and controversy: 'Truth, in the great practical concerns of life, is so much a question of the reconciling and combining of opposites that very few have minds sufficiently capacious and impartial to make the adjustment with an approach to correctness, and it has to be made by the rough process of a struggle between combatants fighting under hostile banners'.[130] For truth, as reconciliation after struggle, to have a chance meant, for Mill: '…giving merited honour to everyone, whatever opinion he may hold, who has calmness to see and honesty to state what his opponents and their opinions really are, exaggerating nothing to their discredit, keeping nothing back which tells, or can be supposed to tell, in their favour'.[131]

Such, Mill added, was 'the real morality of public discussion'.[132] And such indeed was the morality that MacCormick espoused in both his political life and in his philosophical work. Both his politics and his philosophy convey a character deeply committed to the democracy of reason: to it being the nature of reason to make opportunities for all to be heard, to test opinions and intuitions in communal contexts, to avoid the self-aggrandisement of infallibility, and to search for common ground amongst a genuine and free struggle of views.

This sounds very high-minded and abstract but if we relate it to the practice of parliamentary politics in Glasgow University debating then we can see how it can be experienced at a smaller, perhaps more achievable scale. This is especially so if, as suggested above, we see Glasgow debating as a complete package, involving not only in the practice of debating, but also the accompanying culture of self-reflexiveness (in the form of many publications, written and edited by many hands, for generations) and willingness to criticise each other and the practice as a whole.

There is, indeed, a long history of public reason understood in this way, as linked to parliamentary politics,[133] but also to debating clubs and

128 Ibid., 97.
129 Ibid., 102.
130 Ibid., 100.
131 Ibid., 118.
132 Ibid.
133 See, e.g., Palonen, *Parliamentary Thinking* (2019).

associations. This is a tradition which creates opportunities for invention in the midst of dialectical play, and which sees value in maintaining tension, as well as 'irony, duplicity, and ambivalence' in discussion.[134] There is, in this tradition, a celebration of conversations that do not necessarily reach a resolution, and of knowledge that is seen to be inherently controversial, where little, if anything, 'is ever beyond contention'.[135] This is a world in which multiple claims are always juxtaposed, set in circumstances where what matters is the civil and decorous, but still rigorous and robust (and often amusingly so), exchange of views and experiences, and where argument is always multiple and 'aimed at judgement but predicated less on the immutability of truth than on the possibility of human concord'.[136]

Thus, the very form of the Glasgow debates, modelled as they were and are on the Westminster Parliament, matters: the above rhetorical values are, as a number of scholars have observed, 'embedded in British parliamentary practices ... since the Renaissance'.[137] The carriers of this rhetorical Renaissance were, arguably, the clubs and associations of talk and speech in the eighteenth century, such as the Select Society of Edinburgh (established in 1745) and, later, the Speculative Society of Edinburgh (established in 1764), as well as the early debating societies, such as those in Ireland (the earliest student debating society is said to be the College Historical Society in Dublin, founded in part by Edmund Burke, in 1747).[138]

Set against this history, it is, surely, no accident that Mill founded the London Debating Society in 1825.[139] The commitment to free and robust debate could not be achieved through abstract encomia in its favour: practical action was required. The forms, the procedures, the practical realities, are crucial – a point also made forcefully by Kari Palonen, who argues for an understanding of 'parliamentary thinking' as creating a 'form of politics' that 'introduces the chance to think otherwise',[140] to think *pro* and *contra*, where politics is understood to be the 'contingent and controversial activity *par excellence*', a kind of institutionalisation of 'contingency and controversy'.[141] It is telling that Palonen emphasises 'respect' as

134 Sloane, 'Rhetorical Education' (1993), 174.
135 Mendelson, *Many Sides* (2002), 277–8.
136 Sloane, 'Rhetorical Education' (1993), 166.
137 Happala, *Political Rhetoric* (2016), 6–7.
138 Ibid., 30–1.
139 Ibid., 36–7.
140 Palonen, *Parliamentary Thinking* (2019), 2.
141 Ibid., 4.

central to parliamentary thinking – 'a civilised acceptance of the existence of opposing standpoints', as he defines it.[142] 'Parliament', he adds, 'provides a model for a politics that operates with distances in time, space, person and language in order to create conditions for respect and civil conduct'.[143] Arguably, parliament – as practised, lived, and experienced by students in the Glasgow Union – also provides a model for what it means to philosophise and be a philosopher amidst the vagaries of common life. This experience included mutual respect, certainly, but it also included joy, the pleasure taken in the company of others, the pleasure of interactive deliberation, the possibility of friendship beyond political differences, and thus a companionship of democratic argument. We shall see just how much all this was to echo in many of MacCormick's actions and writings.

For now, I end this chapter with a message MacCormick gave to new law students in a welcome address to them in 1977. He said: '…there is … [no] fanaticism worse than the fanaticism of a closed mind… No one's opinion is sacrosanct, not free from the need to be tested and set in competition against opposing opinions. An opinion not tempered in the heat of fair argument is rarely worth holding, and never known to be'.[144]

This did not mean, of course, that anything goes – commitment to democratic reason did not result in 'mindless relativism which holds that any opinion is as good as any other'.[145] Rather, it was a commitment to not leaving any opinion unheard. Reason, ultimately, was a form of listening to others – a manner or style of relating with others. Reason, its practicality, was inseparable from character.

142 Ibid., 9.

143 Ibid.

144 MacCormick, 'Welcoming Address to New Students in the University of Edinburgh' (1977), 5.

145 Ibid.

3

A Democratic Intellect

The Making of a Glaswegian Moral Philosopher

As we saw in Chapter 2, during his student days in Glasgow from 1959 to 1963, MacCormick was busy as a member of the University of Glasgow Union, participating in a wide range of activities, including university publishing and debating. This, however, is only half the story, for he was of course also studying for his Master of Arts, initially taking classes principally in Classics, he soon switched to focus on Philosophy and, to a lesser extent, Literature. As he himself put it, 'philosophy took a grip of me in my second year'.[1] He duly completed these studies, with First Class Honours, and won a Snell Exhibition to study Law at Balliol College, Oxford. MacCormick's time in Oxford will occupy us in Chapters 4 and 5. In this chapter, I turn to MacCormick's apprenticeship in Glaswegian moral philosophy and to his relations with his philosophy teachers in Glasgow.

Philosophy and Democracy in Scotland

When MacCormick recalled his studies in Glasgow, he often mentioned the publication of George Davie's highly influential, *The Democratic Intellect: Scotland and Her Universities in the Nineteenth Century* (1961). The publication of this book, MacCormick said, was, 'for those who were students in the Scottish Universities' in the 1960s, 'a momentous event'.[2] Davie had offered a defence of not only the importance of philosophy to university education, but also, more specifically, a spirited account of the

[1] MacCormick, 'Sir Neil MacCormick' (2007), 171.

[2] MacCormick, 'Idea of Liberty' (1984). MacCormick often emphasised Davie when speaking about education, e.g., on receipt of an honorary Doctor of Laws at Queen's University in Kingston, Ontario, on 1 June 1996, MacCormick spoke of Davie's 'insistence on the need for a relentless intellectualism in regard to the pursuit of learning and of practical affairs, a willingness to pursue and to test our principles wherever they lead. At the same time, the approach has been in spirit a democratic one, opening education and access to learning and to the progressions to whoever has the interest and ability to pursue them': MacCormick, Speech at Queen's University (1 June 1996), 1.

pedagogical tradition, which Davie argued was unique, in Scottish universities, which had integrated philosophical education into all university degrees.[3] This tradition, Davie argued, was slowly eradicated by English-led interventions into university reform in the nineteenth century.

Davie's book clearly touched a nerve, inspiring a generation to reflect on what was lost in Scotland and what was unique about the Scottish approach to philosophy and its education.[4] When MacCormick wrote an obituary of Archie Turnbull, the Secretary of Edinburgh University Press from 1953 to 1987 – a figure that MacCormick was to get to know well when he served on the advisory board of the Press, advising, for example, on the publication of Stair's *Institutions of the Laws of Scotland* and Walter Scott's novels – he said, of Davie's book:

> Here is a book that became, for two, or maybe three, generations of Scots intellectuals and academics, the manifesto of our cultural inheritance, a book that remains iconic... We learned from this [i.e., the history that Davie recounted] that we were to be democratic, open to every talent from everywhere, but it was talent we were to care about, that is, the philosophically informed intellect and its cultivation.[5]

This sentiment has been echoed by others – Lindsay Paterson, for example, reflecting on the contribution of Davie has said that Davie was: '...one of the handful of academic writers who have shaped how Scotland came to see itself during a journey from fairly contented immersion in the British Union to the acquisition of a newly democratic political authority with the creation of the Scottish parliament'.[6]

The re-establishment of the Scottish Parliament is further ahead in our story, but the crucial connection, which MacCormick encountered via Davie when he was himself a philosophy student, is indeed between philosophy and democracy, with both having been presented as especially important to Scotland. Where England, for instance, had its 'social elite of classical scholars and a barely educated populace', such an attitude to educational policy was 'utterly alien to the intellectual democracy of Protestant Scotland'.[7]

[3] See Paterson, 'George Davie' (2015).

[4] It also inspired a generation of historians of Scottish philosophy: see, e.g., Graham, *Scottish Philosophy* (2022), chapter 1; see also Jackson, *The Case for Scottish Independence* (2020), chapter 2.

[5] MacCormick, 'Turnbull Obituary' (2003), 25.

[6] Paterson, 'George Davie' (2015), 236.

[7] Ibid., 238.

Davie's argument, it must be said, was not narrowly focused on technical issues of changes in education policy in the nineteenth century. Such a focus, one might have thought, was not very likely to get hearts or minds racing. Although it did not neglect those details, the book framed itself around a narrative of much broader significance: the increasing anglicisation of Scotland, the loss of its political identity, and the loss, too, of its European influence (so present, for instance, in the humanist period, with George Buchanan and John Mair as glittering stars on a European scale).

As Davie put it in his foreword, 'this study attempts to break new ground on a subject of interest from the general educational point of view, as well as from the point of view of Scotland's cultural contribution to the world'.[8] A good deal was thus at stake. Education was one of the pillars that continued the distinctive tradition and culture of Scotland after the Union of 1707: education, Davie said, along with religion and law, constituted 'the distinctive code regulating the Scottish way of life'.[9] Writing the history of education in Scotland, then, was essential, for without it we might be 'unable to see anything in Scottish history but an uninterrupted, irreversible trend towards conformity with England'.[10]

What Davie argued was crucial to see in this history – this resolutely Scottish history – was 'the genuinely democratic character' of Scottish universities, where 'every effort was made' to 'neutralise the inequalities of scholastic and family backgrounds'.[11] All evidence, Davie argued, pointed to the success of this 'programme of democratic intellectuality',[12] before, that is, it was killed off by English reforms. The Scottish 'national ideal of the democratic intellect'[13] was demonstrated, for instance, in the role that philosophy played in the curriculum as well as how it was taught, i.e., how the teachers who taught it related with the students who were learning it. Thus, in the curriculum, not only was philosophy taught early in any course one took, whether that be exact sciences, mathematics, or humanities, but also in the links made, within the philosophy curriculum, between, say, metaphysics and mathematics, or between logic and moral philosophy.[14]

In the context of the method of teaching, the Scots introduced what were called 'meetings in committee', where one of the Professors engaged

8 Davie, *The Democratic Intellect* [1961] (2010), vii.
9 Ibid., xi.
10 Ibid., xiv.
11 Ibid., xvii.
12 Ibid.
13 Ibid., xix.
14 See ibid., 11–14.

with them 'more on a level, and, in the course of questioning them round the class on the subjects of the lecture, might himself become involved in argument'.[15] Further, in these 'meetings in committee', the 'emphasis was less on questions of detail than on topics connected with what one might call the common sense of subjects, and with their relation to life in general'.[16] Such 'meetings in committee', then, gave opportunities for pausing and suspending the usual hierarchies and distances between professors and students, constituting 'a middle term or bridge between the formal work of the University and the informal work of the students' societies'.[17] Significantly, too, these 'meetings in committee' were by no means confined to philosophy classes: John Millar, for instance, the Professor of Law in Glasgow, also employed such teaching methods, thereby both relating law to other subjects as well as subjecting it to what was as close as one could get to a public debate in a university environment.[18]

Whether one agrees with these historical claims or not, it is undoubtedly the case that they made an enormous impact on MacCormick, who, in part in light of Davie, saw the centrality of philosophy – including making it accessible to all students – as part and parcel of the democratic revival of Scotland. Scots were traditionally, and could again, be educated into reflexivity, debate, and mutual respect, precisely via philosophy. Philosophical education could be practically meaningful, i.e., it could be directly connected to the avoidance of 'disciplinary narrowness'.[19]

Philosophical pedagogy could, in other words, be an education in the very practice of democracy, which required its citizens to make room for controversy, while also learning the norms of debate. Indeed, one could argue that a large part of the point of philosophy was not so much exposure to different ways of seeing the world, although this too could be valuable, but more training in the ability to respectfully disagree, and thus the ability to participate in the art of conversation between persons who might otherwise have very different intuitions about the good life or matters of controversy. This included conversations between students and professors, and thus the possibility of the ripening of non-hierarchical relations of friendship, at least at some point in the future if not during the course of the degree.

15 Ibid., 14.
16 Ibid., 15.
17 Ibid., 15–16.
18 Ibid., 22–4.
19 MacCormick, 'Archie Turnbull' (2003), 25.

All this was to have a profound impact on MacCormick. It is, for instance, not an accident that when MacCormick was invited to give his Presidential Address to the Society of Public Teachers of Law, in Edinburgh in 1984, he entitled it 'The Democratic Intellect and the Law'. Here, too, MacCormick stressed that part of the value of philosophical education was to 'avoid fallacious and factitious oppositions of view as between schools of thought which actually have different foci of theoretical attention'.[20] Philosophy embraced controversy and debate, but not of a fruitless, scholastic kind. What philosophy could offer to legal education was 'a range of questions, not a set of cut and dried answers' – questions 'which ought to remain open and alive for every law teacher, law student and indeed legal practitioner'.[21] Indeed, and again in light of Davie's account, one could see 'the development and exposition of legal doctrine' as 'expressions of positions in practical philosophy'.[22] Accordingly, MacCormick argued, 'law can only be a rational discipline in so far as it is informed by a practical philosophy'.[23] 'Lawyers', MacCormick insisted, 'are above all else practical reasoners',[24] and what philosophy offered was training precisely in practical reason.

The term 'practical' is fundamental here and offers a guide to what may be argued to be a unique flavour of Scottish philosophy and, perhaps especially, moral philosophy in Glasgow. While being mindful of the difficulties of making generalisations about any national tradition, historians of Scottish philosophy have articulated a distinct 'ambition' of Scottish philosophy. Gordon Graham, for instance, has argued that it has been the ambition of Scottish philosophy 'to speak in a culturally significant voice beyond the classroom'.[25] Such a 'culturally significant voice' combined two aspects: first, a commitment to practicality, i.e., to engaging with the concrete details of everyday life and its history (already a legacy of the Scottish Enlightenment, with its passionate interests in the history of society and its customs and manners); and second, a commitment to ethics and morality: 'Scottish philosophy', Graham said, 'itself is, even in its metaphysical aspects, primarily and characteristically ethical in its method and its point of view'.[26]

[20] MacCormick, 'The Democratic Intellect and the Law' (1985), 173.
[21] Ibid., 180.
[22] Ibid., 181.
[23] Ibid.
[24] Ibid., 180.
[25] Graham, 'Scottish Philosophy after the Enlightenment' (2015), 16.
[26] Ibid.

The Scots, Graham argued elsewhere, were 'moral scientists': figures such as Francis Hutcheson and David Hume, for example, did not just argue that naturalism was a better method for studying morals because 'it would put knowledge of human nature on a more solid foundation, but because it promised thereby to make philosophy better at producing good citizens', e.g., citizens that did not fall prey to 'the gross dangers of superstition and enthusiasm'.[27] Even the most abstract and abstruse reflections on method or metaphysics were moral through and through, though in a particular way: the point was to make a contribution to the improvement of lives on the ground, and, at the same time, to carve out a particular communal role, and value, for philosophy.

Philosophy in Scotland, then, was often entangled with urgent, practical questions, concerning the free exercise of conscience, the prospects of democracy, the plight of the poor and thus the need for welfare and the just distribution of goods, and the social, economic, and cultural conditions of justice. And, if one looks beyond Scotland, one could argue that, through various channels – including, significantly, through the Snell Exhibition to Balliol College, Oxford, which included a long line of Scottish philosophers, from Adam Smith in the eighteenth century, through to the twentieth century, with H. J. Paton, John MacMurray, T. D. Campbell, and of course, MacCormick – Scottish philosophy had a distinctive impact on English philosophy.[28]

In fact, one of the key contributions that Scottish philosophy was to make to British philosophy in the nineteenth and twentieth centuries – and one I will be returning to in later chapters – was the attention the Scots gave to German philosophy, especially interpreting and indeed translating Immanuel Kant and G. W. Hegel. One of the reasons for this may well be that Kant was understood, as he himself said, to have been spurred on by the provocations of Scottish philosophers, including both Hume and Smith. This desire and need to respond, perhaps especially to Hume, was shared by Scots, such as Thomas Reid, as well as the Scottish Kantians. Hegel was brought in, or so it has been argued, to 'overcome Kant's subjective presuppositions',[29] though it may be argued that both Kant and Hegel, in different ways, with their combined attention to self-realisation, autonomy, and freedom, were music to Scottish ears, with their political

[27] Graham, 'The Integrity of Scottish Philosophy' (2015), 310.

[28] MacCormick also liked to point out that John Snell, after whom the exhibitions in Balliol were named, was a pupil of Stair: see MacCormick, 'Rational Discipline' (1981).

[29] Boucher, 'Scottish Contribution' (2015), 155.

sensitivities to their own idiosyncratic, if not precarious, position in the British union.

The important point, for present purposes, is that Kant's philosophy, as dominant in Scottish philosophy as it has been for a long time[30] – including when MacCormick was a student in Glasgow – was given a particular twist, precisely in keeping with the practically minded Scottish attitude to the role of moral philosophy in public affairs and to the prospects for the democratic flourishing of Scotland. This is visible biographically: for instance, Paton, one of the most important twentieth century Scottish interpreters of Kant, and author of *Kant's Metaphysic of Experience* (1936), *The Categorical Imperative* (1947), and translator of Kant's *Grundlegung zur Metaphysik der Sitten* (1785, translated as *The Moral Law* in 1947), was also the author of *The Claim of Scotland* (1968).[31] But, in addition, and as we shall see more in a moment, it is also visible both methodologically and substantively in the work of Kantian-inspired Scottish philosophers. For now, the key point is that, for the Scots, Kant was part of a commitment to the practicality of reason; this was philosophy, but it wasn't philosophy that looks with superior disdain on common life – instead, it was philosophy as a humble servant of common life and its practicalities. Ultimately, one could perhaps argue, it was a peculiarly Scottish combination of Hume and Kant.[32]

MacCormick's Teachers in Glasgow

All this comes to play a vitally important role in MacCormick's philosophical education. His philosophy lecturers and tutors are steeped in this tradition of practical philosophy, including Scottish Kantianism. As MacCormick pointed out on numerous occasions, his studies in philosophy in Glasgow were 'particularly focused on the neo-Kantian ideas of W. D. Lamont'.[33] I will be turning to Lamont in a moment, but it is important to emphasise that even when MacCormick encountered criticism of Kant from other teachers – for instance, W. D. Maclagan, who was heavily influenced by W. D. Ross – this retained a strong connection to Kant, e.g., Ross, who incidentally had also studied at Balliol College, Oxford, wrote

30 See also Burns, 'Scottish Kantians' (2009).

31 See also Guyer, 'The Scottish Reception of Kant' (2015).

32 Of course, this is but one take – one partial glimpse – of the complexity of the Scottish tradition of philosophy: see, e.g., the work of Alexander Broadie. MacCormick was also interested in this broader tradition, corresponding with Broadie about it.

33 MacCormick, 'Sir Neil MacCormick' (2007), 172.

sensitively about Kant (writing a well-regarded introduction to Kantian ethics in 1954), and Maclagan's work, too, had strains of Kant.[34] Maclagan had become Professor of Moral Philosophy in Glasgow in 1946 and was still lecturing and tutoring when MacCormick was a student: according to Robin Downie,[35] he would have lectured MacCormick in his Ordinary Class lectures in the first year and then tutored him in his final year of senior honours. In addition to inspiring a lifelong interest in logic and reasoning, Maclagan also encouraged MacCormick to pursue a career at the Bar, where MacCormick's affinity for logic, alongside his debating prowess, would have the opportunity to shine.[36]

Robin Downie and Respect for Persons

Apart from Lamont, other influential teachers in philosophy at Glasgow for MacCormick were Robin Downie, David Raphael, and H. J. N. Horsburgh.[37] Downie is a good example of the Scottish Kantian or neo-Kantian trend: himself influenced by Lamont, Downie tutored MacCormick in his junior honours' year. Having been a Glasgow graduate in Philosophy and English, and, after National Service during the Second World War, where he worked as a Russian Linguist, Downie studied philosophy in Oxford before being appointed Lecturer in Glasgow in 1959 (the first year of MacCormick's degree). In 1964 Downie published *Government Action and Morality*, the title of which already signifies its practical and applied orientation, and this was followed up, in 1969, with Elizabeth Telfer, by *Respect for Persons*.

In this book, Downie and Telfer – inspired, as they acknowledge in their preface, by two works that were clearly central in the philosophy community in Glasgow in the 1960s: Kant's *Groundwork of the Metaphysics of Morals* and Mill's *On Liberty* – argued that 'the ordinary rules and judgements of social morality presuppose respect for persons as their ultimate ground'.[38] To respect persons 'is to value them as persons',[39] which involved respecting them as practical reasoners, i.e., possessing two abilities: first, to be 'self-determining' and second, to be 'self-legislating', and

[34] See, e.g., Ross, *Kant's Ethical Theory* (1954); and Maclagan, 'Respect for Persons' (1960).

[35] Private correspondence (on file with the author).

[36] Interview with Karen Barr.

[37] MacCormick, 'Sir Neil MacCormick' (2007), 172.

[38] Downie and Telfer, *Respect for Persons* (1969), 9.

[39] Ibid., 18.

thus capable of formulating and following rules,[40] though they added that this was entirely compatible with the equally important ability to 'feel and express a wide range of emotions', and thus 'to cultivate and sustain complex emotions'.[41] Respect for persons, they argued, was 'an attitude – a way of regarding persons', which in turn always gives 'rise to certain characteristic principles of action – ways of treating persons'.[42]

Although *A Respect for Persons* was published after MacCormick had left Glasgow, the ideas that found their way into it were clearly being worked out and discussed during the years MacCormick was studying there, e.g., Maclagan, in his earlier article on 'Respect for Persons as a Moral Principle' (1960), had spoken of it as a 'reflective, "principled" … version of … active sympathy',[43] which also features in Downie and Tefler's book, though with an important difference. Maclagan emphasises, much more than they do, the emotional content of this attitude, speaking of the significance of 'the warmth of attitude', or 'the subjective, emotional quality of the attitude', which disappears somewhat from the more 'moralised' and 'abstract' concept of 'respect for persons'.[44] These issues, especially as to the balance between emotion and reason, were to accompany MacCormick throughout his theorisation of the practicality of reason – indeed, they were to feature most prominently in his last book, *Practical Reason in Law and Morality* (2008), where MacCormick made a point of combining the sentimental and rational dimensions of practical reason.

Respect for Persons was clearly a work that influenced MacCormick considerably, for he referred to it throughout his career.[45] Indeed, in his Stevenson Lecture in Citizenship (a lecture series intended to educate the public on citizenship rights), delivered in Glasgow on 18 June 1994,[46] MacCormick returned to this notion of 'respect for persons' when making a philosophical case for the value of nationalism. Highlighting both Lamont and Downie as important presences in his philosophical formation in Glasgow, MacCormick stressed Downie's work on respect for persons as leaving a special mark on him.[47] For instance, MacCormick drew

[40] Ibid., 21.
[41] Ibid., 23.
[42] Ibid., 37.
[43] Maclagan, 'Respect for Persons' (1960), 216.
[44] Ibid., 216–17.
[45] For example, MacCormick, 'What Place for Nationalism' (1994); 'Reply to Mr Tur' (1983); 'What Is Wrong with Deceit?' (1983).
[46] Published as MacCormick, 'What Place for Nationalism' (1994).
[47] MacCormick, 'What Place for Nationalism' (1994), 95.

on that work to argue for nationalism as a value precisely because it was part of a respect for persons – but persons understood in a richer sense than just 'rational moral agents'.[48] Persons were also 'sensual' and had 'desires, friendships, pleasures or pains'.[49] Furthermore, these 'flesh and blood humans' belonged to 'particular familial, social, and historical context[s]'.[50]

Thus, to respect persons must involve taking into account 'human sense and sentiment', and thus 'the subjective importance for' particular persons 'of the interests and values at stake'.[51] A strict Kantian – or indeed Rawlsian – analysis missed the importance of these 'contextual individuals',[52] but if one does extend one's understanding of individuals in this way, then one can 'insist on respect for persons as implying respect for contextual individuals',[53] including, very significantly, those for whom 'attachment to a culture as a historically evolved social reality, particularly attached to a particular place' was important.[54] In that sense, nationalism – a kind of liberal nationalism – was of value, though contingently so, for it depended on whether there were persons for whom their contexts mattered in this way.

We will encounter, in due course, more of MacCormick's reflections on nationalism, but the above is an illustration of just how his training in Glaswegian moral philosophy continued to echo for him down the decades. An argument could also be made, and I will be returning to this point too later, that the attitude and principle of respect for persons was part of what motivated MacCormick's highlighting of the 'hermeneutic point of view' as Hart's most important contribution to jurisprudence. Although traditionally understood as a methodological principle, one can also see it, simultaneously, as a moral one, based precisely on the need for respecting persons.

Downie himself went on to write books in the philosophy of education, social work, and medicine – again, all these are indicative of just how practically minded Glaswegian moral philosophy was. He had, too, a more immediate effect on MacCormick's future: having tutored him, and although recognising his philosophical talent, he discouraged MacCormick from further postgraduate studies in philosophy (which he said MacCormick had been keen on) and instead urged him to study law, encouraging him

48 Ibid., 83.
49 Ibid.
50 Ibid.
51 Ibid., 84.
52 Ibid.
53 Ibid., 86.
54 Ibid.

to 'think of law as a good supplement to his work at Glasgow and a possible career as a barrister or in politics'.[55] Coming from his junior year tutor, where the classes in philosophy were small (about a dozen students in each class) and where one submitted weekly essays (in the Oxford style) – thereby forming a close bond with tutors – this advice must have been highly persuasive for MacCormick.

There were other influences, too, in Glasgow, though they too had a connection to this overall interest in reason as a practical art of respect for persons. The Professor of Logic at the time was C. A. Campbell, who was an idealist and enthusiastic teacher of F. H. Bradley and Bradley's scepticism about metaphysical knowledge. MacCormick sometimes recalled that one of the 'interests that stayed with me from my philosophical education in Glasgow was an interest in issues of logic and informal reasoning',[56] and Campbell would have played a role in sparking that interest. Interestingly, Campbell also sometimes deployed the language of 'self-realisation',[57] which was picked by Downie and Telfer, and which was also used by MacCormick in his work on contextual persons, mentioned above.[58]

Horsburgh, in turn, tutored MacCormick in emotivism and also had an interest in practical reason – writing, for instance, a paper on prudence in the 1960s.[59] Significantly, especially in light of the importance that MacCormick later placed on 'consequential' (forward-looking) reasoning in adjudication, Horsburgh, in this piece, argued for a conception of prudence as 'one that involves distinctively human powers of rational foresight and self-control, and that can be expected to protect the agent, either in the relatively distant future or over a protracted period that may date from the action's performance, from a considerable misfortune or disaster of a kind that might overtake any agent'.[60] Once more, the rational agent was aware of the consequences of their actions both for themselves, but also for the wider community.

David Raphael and the British Moralists

Finally, there was David Raphael, who was to be a lifelong connection for MacCormick. Raphael had written a DPhil at Oxford on the British

55 Downie (private correspondence, on file with the author).
56 MacCormick, 'Sir Neil MacCormick' (2007), 176.
57 See Campbell, 'Moral Intuition and the Principle of Self-Realisation' (1948).
58 See MacCormick, 'What Place for Nationalism' (1994), 95.
59 See Horsburgh, 'Prudence' (1962).
60 Ibid., 66.

Moralists and was appointed to the philosophy faculty in Glasgow in the early 1950s (he left Glasgow in 1970). Raphael's interests overlapped very considerably with what came to be also MacCormick's. Most significantly, Raphael published widely on the British Moralists, especially Smith – serving, later, as editor of the Glasgow editions of the Works of Adam Smith, including Smith's *Lectures on Jurisprudence* – and this was very important to MacCormick, who not only taught this material later in his class with John Cairns in Edinburgh on 'Legal Thought in the Eighteenth Century', but who, as we shall see, also read and wrote on Smith, Hume, and other Scottish eighteenth century thinkers throughout his philosophical life.

Raphael's first book, *The Moral Sense*, published in 1947, was concerned with 'the epistemology of morals', focusing on the question: 'When I judge that I ought to do a certain action, do I make this judgement on the basis of knowing, or of feeling, or of sensing something?'.[61] Raphael reviewed the work of four philosophers – Hutcheson, Hume, Price, and Reid – finding arguments for a moral sense unpersuasive. Particularly noteworthy in the present context is Raphael's criticism of Hume. Raphael was deeply appreciative of Hume's philosophical subtlety – he thought Hume's *Treatise of Human Nature* to be the greatest work of philosophy in English – but, in this early work, he was not convinced that Hume had established that reason did not play a significant role in the epistemology of morals. MacCormick's 1978 book, *Legal Reasoning and Legal Theory*, was to be similarly keen to respond to Hume's scepticism about practical reason, while still retaining respect for Hume's view as to the limits of reason – a typically difficult balancing act.

The rub of Raphael's argument against Hume was that he was mistaken, most probably as a result of Hutcheson's influence, in overdoing the analogy between ethics and aesthetics. According to Raphael, it is not that emotion and feeling play no role in moral epistemology – it is just that their exercise presupposes a moral judgement. Here, he argued, one had to make a distinction between two kinds of emotions in moral life: first, emotions related to a judgement that someone is morally good; and second, emotions related to a certain attraction we experience towards virtuous persons. Although the first are 'moral emotions', e.g., involving 'approval or esteem or admiring respect', they 'presuppose a judgement', whereas the latter (such as love), 'do not presuppose moral

[61] Raphael, *Moral Sense* (1947), 1.

judgements in the same way as do the emotions felt towards moral goodness and badness'.[62]

Thus, for Raphael, there was a 'grain of truth' in the analogy between ethics and aesthetics, but only in the limited sense that attractions to virtue were similar to attractions to beauty.[63] But there was more to moral epistemology than attraction to virtue: there was also judgement of goodness or badness, and this did not rely on emotion, and in any event, the role that virtue played in our moral lives could not be exhausted by the emotional experience of attraction to virtue (instead, what was needed was a theory of obligation). As we shall see, this attack on Hume by Raphael – and thus the scepticism about Hume's non-cognitive approach to moral knowledge – was to play an important role in MacCormick's lifelong engagement with practical reason.[64]

Raphael's interests overlapped with MacCormick's in yet other ways. Raphael was clearly interested in legal philosophy and also in drawing on law as part of his work in moral philosophy. He reviewed Hart's writings on causation in law, and on law, liberty, and morality, as well as other work, more directly on legal reasoning, such as Chaïm Perelman's *The Idea of Justice and the Problem of Argument* (1963). In 1956, for example, in a paper on 'the consequences of actions', Raphael endorsed an approach to the study of consequences that was 'practical', with its 'business' being 'to inquire into the uses of language and to make recommendations',[65] which is what he did via a close study of the language used in the law of negligence. This is already telling, but what is even more significant is Raphael's attitude to language: for Raphael, we could ascertain and sharpen the meaning of concepts by analysing their use in ordinary language use, including in practical contexts such as law. Lawyers, for instance, had to 'draw a line somewhere',[66] and this was a better guide to the meaning of concepts than 'wandering in the labyrinth of a metaphysical minotaur'.[67]

This was not an isolated argument of Raphael's: many of his papers in this period show extensive engagement with ordinary language

[62] Ibid., 81.
[63] Ibid., 82.
[64] See also MacCormick, 'Children's Rights' (1976), 311, where MacCormick drew on Raphael's 1975 address to the Aristotelian Society, 'The Standard of Morals' as part of an argument that 'respect for persons is both a fundamental and an ultimate moral principle'.
[65] Raphael, 'The Consequences of Actions' (1956), 106.
[66] Ibid., 114.
[67] Ibid., 116.

philosophy, especially Austin's theory of performatives and thus what one could do with language.[68] MacCormick, then, via Raphael was exposed early on to Austin's theory, which, also significantly, Raphael had connected to Hume: 'Like Professor Austin', Raphael said, 'Hume shows [in the *Treatise*] that promising is a special sort of linguistic performance, but Hume adds that in our ordinary use of the word "promise" we often think it describes a special sort of non-linguistic performance, a mental act'.[69] The interest in the practical world-making capacities of language, in Hume and beyond, with its consequences for philosophical method and attitude (e.g., the respect it pays to ordinary language use), were also to prove crucial for MacCormick. Again, it is important to underline that these were interests and attitudes that were already present in MacCormick's Glaswegian philosophical education, and thus very much prior to MacCormick's Oxford days.[70] With respect to ordinary language philosophy, in addition to Austin, he also read Wittgenstein, but it is interesting that he notes that his writing 'never attracted' him.[71]

It is also clear, from MacCormick's subsequent correspondence with Raphael, that MacCormick continued to debate these issues with Raphael in later years. For example, MacCormick's letters contain his response to Raphael's criticisms of the way he treated consequential reasoning in *Legal Reasoning and Legal Theory*, with Raphael insisting there was a difference between practical consequences and legal implications,[72] as well as to many exchanges on how to interpret Smith, e.g., in relation to MacCormick's reliance theory of promising, which MacCormick thought was already present in Smith, but which Raphael thought was better expressed in Kames.[73]

Finally, it is worth noting that Raphael's interests, including his lecturing in Glasgow, extended to political philosophy. Published, later, as *Problems of Political Philosophy* (1970), Raphael tackled a range of issues that were to become important for MacCormick later, including the relations between sovereignty, power, liberty, and authority, and on democracy and justice. Amongst these, the chapter on sovereignty, power, and

68 See, e.g., Raphael, 'Linguistic Performances and Descriptive Meaning' (1956).

69 Ibid., 517.

70 MacCormick not only read Austin's work on performatives in Glasgow – he also read his *Sense and Sensibilia*, which he reported as finding 'extremely challenging': 'Sir Neil MacCormick' (2007), 172.

71 MacCormick, 'Sir Neil MacCormick' (2007), 172.

72 MacCormick, 'Letter to Raphael' (3 December 1980).

73 MacCormick, 'Letter to Raphael' (9 March 1977).

authority,[74] argues, inter alia, that 'State sovereignty' must be understood as 'legal sovereignty', which was distinct from 'political sovereignty', i.e., the realm of power.[75] Raphael also raises the question whether 'the concept of sovereign authority' is even needed and suggests that there may be circumstances in which it is not helpful, e.g., 'a Quaker's meeting, or of any association or community based on love, or friendship, or mutual respect'.[76] Although only suggestive, if we accept the possibility that this book gives us at least a flavour of Raphael's lectures in Glasgow, then we can see that, just as MacCormick was exposed to these ideas in the political debates over Scotland's relations with England, so he was also exposed to them in the realm of philosophy, already in his Glasgow days.

W. D. Lamont

The influence that Downie and Raphael, along with Maclagan, Campbell, and Horsburgh, had on MacCormick were all significant, but of all of his teachers in Glasgow, it is arguably Lamont who played the most important role in MacCormick's philosophical formation, in his subsequent work in legal philosophy, but also more generally in MacCormick's attitudes to the relations between law, philosophy, and politics.

Lamont is a neglected figure, especially amongst legal philosophy circles,[77] though there is evidence he was read, and even admired, by earlier generations, e.g., Hart himself speaks very highly of his *The Principles of Moral Judgement* (1949), saying it was a 'most original and valuable analysis of the concept of justice, and of the related concepts of right, duty, interest, and responsibility',[78] and referring also, in his *The Concept of Law* (1961) to Lamont's *The Value Judgement* (1955), which was concerned with the relationship between economics and moral philosophy.[79] According to Downie, 'Lamont had a highly original mind which out of step' with various strands of philosophical tastes around him, such as emotivism in the 1940s and 1950s.[80] But, in addition, in Downie's view,

[74] Raphael, *Problems of Political Philosophy* (1970), chapter 3.

[75] Ibid., 55.

[76] Ibid., 75.

[77] I have attempted to argue for his significance in another context: see Del Mar, 'Learning from W. D. Lamont' (2014).

[78] Hart, 'Philosophy of Law and Jurisprudence in Britain' (1953), 357.

[79] Hart refers to this book as work 'on the place of moral considerations in the interpretation of law': *The Concept of Law* (2012) [1961], 303.

[80] Private correspondence (on file with the author).

Lamont 'looked forward to ways of doing moral philosophy which had not yet arrived'.[81]

Indeed, it is in Lamont's attitudes to the role and value of moral philosophy, and how it could be done, that a large part of his influence on MacCormick lies. This influence is not confined, however, to beliefs or arguments: it is submerged in something that lies deeper, i.e., in MacCormick's character. To see this, however, it is not enough – though it is still important to – engage with Lamont's writings. In other words, although it matters what arguments Lamont raised, for example with respect to the methodology of moral philosophy, the place of law in relation to the science of ethics, or what beliefs he held about authority, what also matters, or matters even more, is the manner and style with which Lamont and MacCormick related to each other. This is a relation that, of course, changes over time. Where, initially and to some extent till the end, Lamont was an authority for MacCormick – he was, formally speaking, his teacher, and thus, again formally, in a position of superiority, including epistemic authority, over MacCormick – this aspect of the relation is negotiated over time, maturing into a more equal friendship.

Lamont had been a Glasgow graduate himself (winning the Edward Caird medal, as indeed MacCormick did), and, again like MacCormick, studied at Balliol College, Oxford, obtaining a DPhil there (in 1930) under the supervision of John Macmurray (himself so admired by MacCormick's father), on the philosophy of T. H. Green. Lamont taught in Glasgow in two stints: pre-war and post-war. In 1939, with the outbreak of the Second World War, he served in the Clyde River Patrol and as a Naval Intelligence Liaison Officer (1939–42), becoming, when his war service ended, Professor of Philosophy at the University of Cairo from 1942 to 1946, and then Principal of Makerere College, Uganda, from 1946 to 1949. It was in 1949 that he returned to lecture in Glasgow, as Senior Lecturer and then Reader in Moral Philosophy, teaching there until 1968, and then continuing to be active during his retirement, until his death in 1982.

Importantly, for it constituted a crucial part of their relationship, Lamont, though not born in Scotland (he was born in Canada in 1901), was the son of Scottish parents (one of whom was a Church of Scotland Minister) and had a deep love and passion for Scottish history, especially the history of Islay, where he traced his ancestors ('Clan Lamont', as he called them in his letters and papers). In fact, Lamont published several

[81] Ibid.

important studies relating to the history of Islay.[82] Thus, during the initial period in which MacCormick and Lamont knew each other, from 1959 to 1963, Lamont was actively engaged – in addition to his philosophical work – in the writing of Scottish local history. There is evident pride and excitement on the pages of Lamont's historical work: he is proud of and fascinated by his family's Islay past, though also by the beauty of its natural and artificial landscape. This love of Highland nature and culture is something he shared with MacCormick and that must have created an important, and emotional, bond between them – even if, of course, at this stage, the relationship was only one of undergraduate student and teacher.

What is also visible from Lamont's writings on the history of Islay is the attention he gives to the history of its laws and customs, whether they be the complicated and technical procedures of land tenure, or the various areas of law that the Islay Charter addressed, including criminal, family, and succession law. This, as we shall see in more detail in a moment, was no passing interest for Lamont. His 1946 book, *The Principles of Moral Judgement* (PMJ), incorporated law as part of the 'data' for ethics understood as 'one of the mental and social sciences' with a focus on 'moral ideas',[83] and his final work, published in 1981, to which MacCormick contributed in various ways, was dedicated to examining the relationship between law and morality – indeed, the title, *Law and the Moral Order* (LMO), was one suggested by MacCormick. There is a story – amusing and moving in equal measure – that accompanies the use of law in PMJ, the first book: the examples of cases deployed in that book are all taken from one volume of the *All England Reports*, this being the only collection of reports that Lamont had access to during his period, mid-war, in Cairo. Lamont, thus, had a long-standing interest in law, which was theoretical as well as historical, and encompassed both Scotland and England. This was, and it is important to underline this, an interest that came not from the quarters of either the legal profession or of a professor of law, but precisely from someone who was interested and wrote about moral philosophy and social history, especially Scottish history.

I shall turn to Lamont's work in moral philosophy, and the place of law in it, in a moment, but it is important to add another element to the

[82] Including a paper on medieval land tenures in Islay in the first issue of *Scottish Studies* in 1957; a paper on the Islay Charter 1408 in 1960; a book offering an overview of Islay's history from 500 to 1726 in 1966; and a book on Islay's beautiful ancient and medieval carved stones in 1972.

[83] Lamont, PMJ (1946), 1.

relationship between Lamont and MacCormick: the political. Where, with some differences, Lamont and MacCormick shared an interest in Highland history and culture, and in the relationship between law, custom, and morality, there is some evidence that they did not see eye to eye about the way in which one might make a political contribution. We do not have evidence of any correspondence between Lamont and MacCormick early on in their relationship, but later letters, in the 1970s, do shed some light. It would not be surprising to learn, if we had evidence of it, that Lamont had advised MacCormick to study, though as a trained moral philosopher, law in Oxford. After all, as noted above, for Lamont, law was part of the data for moral science: studying law, then, did not mean discontinuing his studies in moral philosophy – it meant extending them. But when it came to politics, Lamont, it seems, was clear that pursuing a more active political career would be nothing but an interruption – an unhelpful distraction from the work of the moral scientist. For Lamont, MacCormick's future was a scholar, albeit a very practically grounded one.

In a letter from MacCormick to Lamont on 19 April 1979 – a significant date, for it was soon after the debacle of the 1 March 1979 Referendum on the Scotland Act 1978 (a debacle because although 51.6% had answered 'yes', the level of participation did not meet the threshold of 40%) – MacCormick thanks Lamont for advice 'about politics and the academic life'. MacCormick's reply manages to both agree and disagree with Lamont. On the one hand, MacCormick says that 'What you say matches entirely what has been my own growing conviction as to the role I should try to play in future', meaning less of an active political role and a more academic one. Further, MacCormick confesses that he 'found it a great strain to carry out the duties of being SNP candidate for Edinburgh North', even if he did not expect to be elected. On the other hand, though, he says:

> ...one has at least a prima facie duty (in my view), a duty not to abstain from political activity even when it is disagreeable. It concerns me that politics is so readily dismissible as a 'dirty game' [perhaps a phrase used by Lamont?] or such. If everyone stands back and leaves it to more or less unscrupulous power seekers or party hacks, such attitudes become self-confirming. Not that I necessarily escape these epithets myself. But if I could satisfy myself that I had objectively good grounds for withdrawal, coincident with my affective inclination, I should be delighted.[84]

[84] MacCormick, Letter to Lamont (19 April 1979), 2–3 (Lamont Archive at the University of Glasgow).

The tone of the letter is interesting: it suggests much greater confidence in meeting the advice of his past teacher on his own terms. While acknowledging Lamont's advice, and noting even his agreement with it, MacCormick nevertheless expresses, and justifies, his reservations: if he could 'withdraw', he would, but … the call of duty, the call for keeping politics civil, for raising standards of political debate, makes it impossible to accept the advice wholescale and 'withdraw', entirely, from politics. By this stage, in 1979, Lamont is not a figure of authority for MacCormick in the sense that he automatically takes the advice of a superior, someone who knows better. Indeed, MacCormick had by this time developed a more complex and subtle relationship to authority, and one that is ultimately filtered by reason: he takes seriously the advice of his former teacher, but he articulates, with reasons, his own position. He does so with qualifications and softeners, including both the use of conditionals and subjunctives, as well as self-disparagement, but he does nevertheless offer a principled reason for doubting that advice and holding his own ground.

Lamont's advice on politics might have been, in part, informed by his lack of enthusiasm about the SNP, and here we see another possible moment of tension between MacCormick and Lamont. Although he may never have articulated this to MacCormick directly, Lamont appears not to have had an especially positive view of the SNP: he wrote, for instance, in a letter to Malcolm Rifkind, a conservative politician who served in Thatcher and Major governments, around the time of the devolution debates in the House of Commons, that not only was he against devolution, 'on the basis that only an Anglo-Scottish effort can place limits on the executive', but also that the SNP, which he described as 'a breakaway from the Glasgow University Labour Club and led by a law student, John MacCormick', was 'an emperor with no clothes' and had been 'from the outset, 'more an anti-English than a constructively pro-Scottish movement, attracting a curious amalgam of personalities'.[85] No wonder Lamont was not enthusiastic about MacCormick throwing in his talents with the SNP.

This one-off statement, in a letter to a conservative politician who was no ally of the SNP, must not be taken as representative of Lamont's evaluation of Scottish nationalism. In fact, his position was much more nuanced, as is visible, for example, from his 1935 paper, 'Nationalism and the International Ideal'. This paper is significant for how much it prefigures about MacCormick's own writings about nationalism, especially the

[85] Lamont, 'Letter to Rifkind' (9 December 1976; Lamont Archive at the University of Glasgow).

potential place of Scotland in Europe. It must be emphasised that Lamont is writing in the mid 1930s, when nationalism is fast becoming a charged political issue, to say the least. He does not, however, simply dismiss the arguments of 'national movements' 'at the present day'; rather, he repositions them, arguing that, properly understood, they are 'assertions' rather than 'denials' 'of those moral principles on which a healthy internationalist sentiment must be founded'.[86] Nationalism and internationalism are not opposed: instead, Lamont argues, they are 'complementary expressions of the one social ideal – the ideal of an international democracy'.[87] Lamont's strategy is to divorce nationalism from the 'nation-state': the latter, he says, does not have to 'be accepted as a permanent factor in social organisation'; political theory and practical politics need not and should not 'take for granted the existence of national sovereign states'.[88] We can recognise that there are nations – in the sense of 'a people, inhabiting a certain tract of the earth's surface, with generally common sentiments and habits of thinking, though possibly of mixed race',[89] while leaving open the possibility that 'the nation-state should disappear in favour of some more inclusive form of political organisation'.[90]

There is no direct evidence that MacCormick read this piece, but given the closeness of their relationship, with Lamont teaching MacCormick, and then the two of them corresponding for many years after, it is difficult to resist the possibility that, even if the piece was not read by MacCormick, the substance of its arguments was discussed between them. There is a similar hope and optimism in Lamont's voice in this piece, as there is in MacCormick's later writings on the possibilities of a post-sovereign commonwealth of nations, but not, necessarily, nation-states. There is the same emphasis on inclusiveness and democracy, precisely in a larger political theatre. There are even similarities in phrasing: 'it is my view that the days of the nation-state are numbered', says Lamont, which is echoed in MacCormick's later writings. The nation-state is not valuable in itself, insists Lamont: it is only as valuable when, and to the extent, it conserves and enriches the interests of individuals living within it,[91] i.e., if it really does make a 'contribution … towards human welfare',[92] which it

86 Lamont, 'Nationalism and the International Ideal' (1935), 290.
87 Ibid.
88 Ibid., 289.
89 Ibid.
90 Ibid., 294.
91 Ibid., 295.
92 Ibid., 299.

may not. In fact, Lamont uses quite strong – quite passionate – language in his criticism of the view of those who tie together nationalism and the nation-state: 'So far as any form of nationalism maintains, or implies, that the national life lacks an essential attribute if it lacks the powers of a sovereign state, then that form of nationalism, I am prepared to say, exhibits a retrograde mentality'.[93] This is, indeed, strong language, and not language that MacCormick ever used, but it is also clear that MacCormick thought, like Lamont, that there was no conceptual, no necessary, overlap between nationalism and the notion of a sovereign state. It is also clear that, again like Lamont, MacCormick looked for bigger political platforms within which to locate nationalism. In his paper, Lamont looks to the level of 'supra-national', such as the League of Nations.[94] It may be, he says, that, as international trade expands, as 'non-political relations become more extensive and intimate', that 'the appropriate seat of authority' also 'expands'.[95] Somewhat apologetically, he adds: 'I am only arguing that, in the interest of national, local, and ultimately, of individual development, certain powers, now exercised by nation-states in their severality, should be pooled and centralised in a more universal authority, because it is no longer possible for those powers to remain so localised, and efficiently serve the purposes of humanity'.[96]

MacCormick, in due course, was to look for his own preferred solution to questions concerning the appropriate place of authority – he preferred, as we shall see later, not to centralise authority, but instead to decentralise and diffuse it, via the principle of subsidiarity. He never deployed the term 'universal authority', though, to be fair to Lamont, his insistence on this term may be to do with the worries and anxieties of seeing nation-state-based-authority being expressed in particular ways at this time, especially in Nazi Germany (indeed, as we shall see later, Lamont eschews 'universal authorities'). But, in other respects, MacCormick's later work echoed the sentiments and the tone, the creativity and optimism, of this 1935 piece by Lamont. There is no inherent moral value of the sovereign state, and no conceptual connection between nationalism and the nation-state: in fact, the time may well have come, Lamont was saying, for transcending state sovereignty, and for inquiring into the possibility of a 'more inclusive

93 Ibid., 291.
94 Ibid., 299.
95 Ibid.
96 Ibid., 295.

form of political organisation'.[97] MacCormick may not have agreed with Lamont's call, in this paper, for pooling and centralising authority, but he did agree that we should be open about political possibilities, not be hampered by apparent conceptual necessities, and look for ways of enhancing democracy in transnational and global contexts, while not sacrificing what was valuable about nationalism. That this argument, by Lamont, was made with reference to ways of envisaging authority, and practicing it creatively, is important – it constitutes yet another way in which authority, and its links to reason and democracy, were part of the relationship between Lamont and MacCormick.

That MacCormick retained, and on occasion recalled, Lamont's work is visible throughout MacCormick's oeuvre. There are numerous examples of this: when writing about Locke and Stair, for example, in 1979, MacCormick recalled that it was Lamont who 'drew his attention' to the possibility of whether 'during their [Locke and Stair's] common period of exile they ever met and discussed' matters,[98] given just how much in common they had as to how 'rightful political superiority of one over another' was dependent on 'voluntary consent of the subject',[99] such as, interestingly, the consent expressed in 'oaths in Highland society'.[100] Certainly, it was from Lamont, MacCormick said, that he 'learned of Stair's hitherto neglected qualities as a moral and political philosopher'.[101] Lamont was also an early advocate of the interest theory of rights (chapter 3 of PMJ), which, as we shall see later, MacCormick championed in his own work on rights.

Following the publication of *Law and the Moral Order* in 1981, MacCormick often cited Lamont as having penned 'the best recent statement of the Kantian case on autonomy as a condition of morality'.[102] For MacCormick, Lamont had shed a beacon on the relations between 'the moral order and the positive law', showing how, for all their 'superficial diversity', they could be united by a conception of practical rationality.[103] This possibility was conveyed to MacCormick, via Lamont and his book (the drafts of which MacCormick was reading in the late 1970s), at precisely the moment when he was writing his own book on Hart (published, like

97 Ibid., 294.
98 MacCormick, 'Locke and Stair' (1979), 388.
99 Ibid., 395.
100 Ibid., 401.
101 MacCormick, 'Rational Discipline' (1981), 146.
102 MacCormick, 'A Moralistic Case' (1985), 12; 'Universalisation' (1987), 97.
103 See MacCormick, 'W. D. Lamont' (1982).

Lamont's, in 1981), which famously, in MacCormick's own words, made Hart out to be more of a natural lawyer than he himself thought he was.

Lamont on Authority

It is instructive, for an understanding of MacCormick's character, to look more deeply at Lamont's PMJ, especially his take on authority in the book. PMJ sets out to make both a methodological and a substantive contribution to moral philosophy. Methodologically, the book argues for ethics as a science (or, as he also puts it, 'the science of moral ideas'). What is instructive about this methodological approach is how inclusive it is: how much it stretches the domain of ethics, but also how it relates it to other disciplines, from which it might otherwise seem to be separate. Thus, for Lamont, seeing ethics as a science means that one can and ought to engage with 'psychology, economics, jurisprudence' and 'one might even add physiology', for all are 'concerned in some sense with human conduct or behaviour'.[104] This is not to say ethics does not have its own distinctive subject matter – ethics studies, says Lamont, 'the supreme, or ultimate principles of right and wrong in human conduct'[105] – but this reference to 'supreme' or 'ultimate' principles does not mean that the moral philosopher deals in timeless, ideal abstractions. Quite the contrary, the practice of moral philosophy for Lamont is a practical and grounded art, involving careful attention to the standards of judgement that actually guide our notions of moral right and wrong. For Lamont, this means that moral philosophy ought to learn from best practice in the sciences, and thus also employ the tools of 'observation, hypothesis, deduction from hypothesis, verification with or without the aid of experiment, and statement of "established" theory'.[106]

As disciplined as moral science must be, it is 'not a study of a mathematical type' – 'its field of inquiry is much more complex'.[107] It studies the rough ground of the value judgements that persons make in practice – value judgements that may sometimes be incompletely articulated or indeed not articulated at all, but for which evidence can still be found. Very significantly, the evidence that Lamont engages with in this book – the 'data' he gathers for moral science and thus the practice

[104] Lamont, PMJ (1946), 2.
[105] Ibid.
[106] Ibid., 15.
[107] Ibid., 18.

of value judgement – is taken from 'the examination of systems of social institutions, laws, and customs which have had a more or less continuous development over a considerable period of time'.[108] Ethics, he says, has much to learn from a careful investigation of these systems. In the case of law, for instance: 'Systems of law are slowly built up through men's reactions to and judgements upon concrete situations in life; and, in so far as they can be said to offer a clue to moral ideas at all, it is obvious that they will be of special value as affording insight into the common moral consciousness'.[109]

It is very telling, in the present context, that Lamont not only ties law to ethics, seeing law as a valuable domain of data for moral science, but also that he positions law, alongside custom, within a slowly evolving 'common moral consciousness'. His inspiration for this, also tellingly, is a particular reading of Kant, and especially his *Groundwork of the Metaphysics of Morals*. Kant may be a surprising choice for a book on moral science, but, when one places Lamont's move in the context of the Scottish tradition of engaging with Kant's work, the choice becomes much more understandable. According to Lamont, when Kant opens his book 'with a series of propositions about the goodwill, its absolute value, the merely relative value of other things such as natural talents, gifts of fortune, etc', what he is doing is offering them as 'the most important moral convictions of "the plain man"'.[110] Having said that, Lamont added, what is missing from Kant is 'appropriate evidence' of the ideas 'in fact … entertained by men in general'.[111] Indeed, we may well doubt that the propositions with which Kant opens 'do really represent what ordinary men think' – what is lacking in Kant is 'a technique for the collection and analysis of actual moral judgements'.[112]

It is vital to see just how Lamont relates to Kant – an authority figure, of course, for him, as for many generations of Glaswegian moral philosophers. Lamont makes his own Kant: he reorients Kant's thought in a particular way. He does so by grounding Kant – by turning Kant into a kind of Scottish moral philosopher, and thus a thinker much closer to the practices of ordinary persons whose moral experience is fallible, conventional, and resides in the practices they are part of. Lamont adds, in a footnote, that

108 Ibid., 27.
109 Ibid.
110 Ibid., 21.
111 Ibid.
112 Ibid., 21–2.

he does not himself 'accept the extreme "rationalist" interpretation sometimes placed upon' Kant's philosophy, including the *Groundwork*.[113] For instance, he takes it as very important that Kant 'made his students attend his Anthropology lectures before those on ethics'.[114] He then adds:

> The principal point of my criticism here is this: Kant is clear that, although experience is necessary for the practical application of moral principles, the principles themselves – the very conception of obligation itself – come from reason. Now one may admit this contention – as I do – and yet hold that, for the moral philosopher to know what those principles are, a prior empirical investigation is necessary, an empirical inquiry into the sort of judgements which men actually make, as a preliminary to the analysis which will reveal the principles on which those judgements are based.[115]

It is instructive that Lamont looks for, and articulates, a way to combine fact and reason, and thus also to connect Kant to the naturalism of the Scottish tradition. One can draw on both in one's vision of ethics as a science, in one's practice of moral philosophy. Reason, on this view, is resolutely practical, both in the sense that it resides in particular practices, but also, when it is manifested in the practice of philosophy, it is something that must ground itself in concrete, everyday practices. We shall see, in later chapters, how grappling with these supposed oppositions – between metaphysics and science, or between fact and reason, or indeed Kant and the Scots (especially Hume), between the ideal and the actual, between positivism and natural law, between is and ought, and between the transcendent and the everyday – is key to MacCormick's own work, and how, to some extent like Lamont, MacCormick looks for and finds his own way of articulating a middle path between such apparent oppositions.

For Lamont, then, law is a key domain of practice from which the moral scientists glean their data, and he accordingly goes, in his book, to study that data, whether that be as expressed in the writings of jurists (e.g., he draws on Gloag and Henderson's *Introduction to the Law of Scotland*, amongst other works) or in the judgements of judges in case law, or indeed in customary practices. None of this means that we need to 'suppose that legal and moral right and wrong entirely coincide', for there are 'many moral issues of which the law courts take no cognizance; and legal and moral duties frequently conflict'.[116] The point is instead one of method: for the purposes of moral

113 Ibid., fn. 1, 22.
114 Ibid.
115 Ibid.
116 Ibid., 28.

science, we approach law and morality as 'intersecting circles', neither being reducible to the other, but both overlapping in various ways.[117] Again, this is important: for Lamont, there is moral data present in the law, which means we can take as evidence of 'common moral consciousness'. But that does not mean we reduce law to morality, or morality to law. There can be a complex, overlapping relation without reduction of difference. 'Intersecting circles', 'overlapping relations': this was the conceptual poetics of Lamont, though equally, later, of MacCormick.

This approach to the method of moral science, but also to the relationship between law and morality, suggests, for Lamont, a particular strategy for reading case law. This, in turn, is closely related to how Lamont understands authority. Put another way, the methodological issues being confronted by Lamont here – for instance, the relationship between fact and reason, or between law and morality – are intertwined with his attitude to authority. Does the mere existence of a certain fact mean that it has the authority to bind us in some moral way? But if not, then does that mean that 'mere facts', so to speak, are without any normativity? Again, what Lamont does with his 'intersecting circles' or 'overlapping relations' is to offer a middle way, a way to combine both fact and reason, which also leads to an interesting attitude to authority.

When we read cases, Lamont suggests, we must of course pay attention to the actual language used by courts, including 'the use of particular, published rules'.[118] But, at the same time, crucially, when we examine how judges reason with rules, we see that they also 'look beyond existing rules to general principles'.[119] As he puts it:

> It can be shown that the interpretation and application of existing law assumes that existing rules and principles are complementary, in the sense that the interpretation of rules always or generally requires looking beyond the rules to the principles which they are supposed to express. The importance of this point is that, if it is true, then legal authority will have been shown to be regarded, not as a final standard of rightness, but as subordinate to some standard not identical with the will of the authority.[120]

The point is fundamental – also for understanding MacCormick's later work. Law cannot rest solely on an understanding of its authority as pure will. Law's normativity is not reducible to mere fact in the form of

117 Ibid.
118 Ibid., 52.
119 Ibid., 53.
120 Ibid., 54.

a will imposed by one to another. But this does not mean that we cannot approach law as fact, to a degree. Nor does it mean that law, as fact, has no normativity. It means, instead, that we need to be open to the possibility of values infusing facts in a particular way, e.g., for the rules, as published, to be imbued with principles, against the light of which the rules make moral sense. As Lamont puts it, in a way which is arguably echoed by MacCormick later in his *Legal Reasoning and Legal Theory* (1978):

> It seems that, in all but the most simple cases, the particular direction which is given to the application of a rule depends upon one's retaining a grasp of the principle to be embodied, using it as a kind of mental compass. In only slightly complicated cases this use of principles is so implicit that it will ordinarily pass unnoticed; but when the complications increase it becomes explicit.[121]

Talk of explicit rules coexisting with implicit principles is but one way of squaring the circle of relations between fact and reason, or law and morality, of order and autonomy; what is important, more than any particular way of talking or expressing the point, is that Lamont is sensitive to the need for relating them. Where does this need come from?

Part of the answer, I think, lies precisely in one's attitude to authority, as this is expressed in one's relations with others. In this sense, chapter 2 of PMJ, entitled 'Customary Morality and the Principle of Authority' is crucial to the argument. On the one hand, Lamont does want to recognise that there are aspects of our normative lives that show how we rather unreflectively either follow the commands of others (for instance, as children, obeying our parents) or conform to the norms of a community, some of which (as in certain religious communities) may be understood to be the will of a supreme lawgiver. But, Lamont insists, moral life is not reducible to a life of rule-following or norm-conforming to the will of rule-or-norm-givers. To take this view of moral life would be to approach it as an 'authoritarian', i.e., to argue that 'right and wrong are determined by the will of some authority'.[122]

But, looked at more closely, there are no such practices: moral life is never reducible to an authoritarian order. Even children, for instance, will not obey an authority figure when it conflicts with some principle of 'fairness', which they develop early on.[123] The will of an authority, for children,

[121] Ibid.

[122] Ibid., 43.

[123] Here, Lamont draws on the work of Piaget. See Lamont, PMJ (1946), 45–7. It may be, too, that there is an echo here of Hume's positioning of sociability and politics in the family

is always to some extent subject to judgements of fairness. Similarly with customary contexts: drawing, here, on work in anthropology and sociology, Lamont argues that, in fact, peoples in these communities 'exhibit the same principle of flexibility and development as characterises our modern systems'.[124] Something else, in addition to customary authority, is at work in these communities: a sense of 'responsibility', which imbues the interpretation and development of customary rules:[125]

> It appears that customary morality, which is most conspicuous in early forms of society, is not, as has so often been suggested, a rigid conformity to rules quite uninfluenced by any sense of some good to be realised by this conformity, or any sense of principles in the light of which these rules and the authorities prescribing them are evaluated. Customary morality, though laying great stress on precedent and traditional observance, is relatively flexible; and its rules tend, over a period, to adjust themselves to the ends and principles which they serve.[126]

In both the context of children and customary practices, then, Lamont's point is 'that, at the basis of respect for particular rules and authorities, there lies some implicit or explicit reference to certain principles which the rules and authorities are supposed to express and apply'.[127] Even when it may not be entirely explicit, subsisting as it were in relatively unreflective practices, there is always an underlying judgement, either in the form of a moral compass guiding the action of persons (some sense of fairness, perhaps, or responsibility), or, sometimes, in the form of a critical, reflective judgement pointing to some newly discovered limit of a rule or an authority, and thus a change in the explicit rules.

For Lamont, there is always, at bottom, a relation: the base, as it were, is never wholly hierarchical, with a figure of authority determining order from above. Put another way, order is always in some sense normative, though the normative, too, requires order – again, neither is reducible to the other. One can acknowledge, as Lamont does, that there are

first; the politics of a state are to some extent the outgrowth of the politics of a family. This has implications not only for how one understands politics, but also for mental life: as Annette Baier argues, for Hume, 'it is the perceived relations and associations between persons that provide the models of Humean mental relationships, and his idea-associates can be "kin"': *A Progress of Sentiments* (1991), 29. Incidentally, MacCormick is one of those thanked in Baier's acknowledgements to that book as helping her 'to see the influence of Hume's law studies': ix.

[124] Lamont, PMJ (1946), 48.

[125] Ibid., 48–9.

[126] Ibid., 59.

[127] Ibid., 49.

periods in the development of either individuals or communities, where the experience of normative order is more heteronomous, i.e., something hierarchical and imposed from above, but there is always potential for autonomy (for critical reflection on inherited practices), and this becomes more so as occasions for reflection arise over time, including as we grow, as persons, from children with less autonomy and reflection, to adults with more autonomy and more reflection. Put another way, morality is always grounded in practices, but these practices are never reducible to explicit commands: there is always a normativity implicit in them. This is also why the authoritarian approach is insufficient, but without this meaning that there is no space for authority. Rather: '…our respect for authority depends upon the sense (however obscure) of some good to be realised and of certain principles to be embodied in human behaviour by the instrumentality of this authority; and that, hence, we cannot treat the principle of authority as itself the ultimate standard of right and wrong'.[128]

If one places this thought, as I suggest we do, in a geographical and political context, and thus, for our present purposes, in Scotland, we can see this also as an expression of a kind of nationalism: of a plea for respect in a political environment that can all too easily become the will of a dominant figure – England, and its sovereign Parliament – imposing itself on a less powerful, more vulnerable community. Even if that is not so present in Lamont's own writing, it certainly is so in MacCormick's: one had to look, methodologically, for relations between law and morality, between fact and value, between positivism and natural law, and one had to look for relating normativity and order, authority and judgement, heteronomy and autonomy, because if one did not, there was always a risk of the undue domination of one party (or indeed one philosophical community) over another.

But more deeply too, and thus as an expression of character: to articulate an authoritarian theory – one that reduced law to non-normative fact, and thus thought of law as the command of a sovereign – was to ignore the ultimate base of non-hierarchical relations between persons, and thus of mutual respect and recognition. Theories of law, including methods for studying law, were not separable from the manner or style with which one related with others. This did not mean one had to be unrealistic and not recognise that there was a need for authority – for explicit rules, for the making of decisions, and thus also for some

[128] Ibid., 60.

institutional hierarchy – but it did mean never allowing that authority to become authoritarian, to allow it to become a meaningless order where the will of a superior dominated the lives of others. This 'post-positivism', as MacCormick was to call it later, was simultaneously a theory of law and an existential question of how one related with others – a matter, precisely, of character.

Lamont on Law and Morality

When, later in life, in what was an extended and active retirement, Lamont worked on and published his last book – *Law and the Moral Order* (1981; LMO) – he returned to the question of how law and morals relate to each other. As I have suggested above, the issue of this relation was part of Lamont's reflection on the methods of moral philosophy as well as, crucially, on how to read Kant. For it was via a particular kind of reading of Kant, and Kantian practical reason, that Lamont was to build bridges between law and morals, and thereby offer his own distinctive take on how to do moral philosophy. This is no mere methodological project: it is an existential one, as with all methodological issues. The question was always what kind of moral philosopher ought I to be? What is the point and value of moral philosophy? How is it – and thus how am I, as a moral philosopher – related to the world of common life – the grounded, practical, everyday life of persons?

Although it takes us somewhat beyond MacCormick's studies in Glasgow, it is important to look briefly at how Lamont answered this question in his last book – not only because MacCormick commented on drafts of this book, but also because he was, at the same time as he was commenting on it and thus reflecting, once again, on Lamont's understanding of Kant and practical reason, and the relations between law and morality, writing his own book on *Hart* (1981), which itself followed hot on the heels of his *Legal Reasoning and Legal Theory* (1978). This period, as we shall see in more detail in later chapters, of the late 1970s and early 1980s, was a crucial one for MacCormick: it constituted his return, following a lengthy stint in Oxford jurisprudence, to Scottish moral philosophy. The differences, in that respect, between the 1978 book, and his 1981 book, are important: MacCormick, in this transition, was finding again his own philosophical feet, having been steeped in Oxford jurisprudence and in particular Hart's version, defending it against unexpected newcomers, especially Ronald Dworkin. Renewing relations with Lamont, over his last book, was arguably an important part of this process.

This re-engagement with Lamont over his last book was also, one imagines, an emotional one. Lamont published it in 1981 and died in 1982. When MacCormick wrote an obituary of Lamont, he stressed the 'friendship' that both Lamont and his wife, Ann Christie, had extended to him, along with others, while he was a student.[129] Lamont would have known this was his last work, and it is interesting that he chose this theme, which after all also lay at the heart of his relationship with MacCormick: precisely the relations between law and morals, or jurisprudence and ethics, mediated by a particular reading of Kant on the practicality of reason.

That MacCormick realised what was at stake is also visible from his obituary. He said, of Lamont's 'last book' that 'though published in his eighty-first year', it 'was a beautifully clear and concise statement of a Kantian vision of principles of legality and practical rationality as unifying the moral order and the positive law for all their diversity'.[130] It was also obvious that MacCormick recognised the links between this book and what he had learnt as a student from Lamont: this last book, he said, 'distilled something of the spirit of his earlier books', as well as serving as a 'tangible reminder', for 'his students at Glasgow', of 'his extraordinary vividness and lucidity as a teacher, and of the imaginative sympathy which he brought to his restatement of Kantian philosophy'.[131] Again, all these issues were entangled, but also brought to life in a personal way for MacCormick: how to read Kant (especially as a Scot), whether and how reason was practical, what was the relationship between law and morals, and how to be a (moral) philosopher. MacCormick, it must be emphasised, was not a distant interlocutor here for Lamont: as Lamont himself acknowledges, MacCormick, along with Richard Tur, 'read the whole script in two successive drafts and advised on general presentation and inclusion of legal material', so much so, Lamont added, that 'it might with some justification be said that this is about as near to being a joint work as it could be while remaining under the name of a single author'.[132]

That the very aims, and the role, of moral philosophy was at stake for Lamont in this book is clear from its first sentence: 'The main purpose of this book', Lamont wrote, 'is to strengthen moral philosophy's links with the living world, so that ordinary thoughtful men and women may find in this philosophical analysis an aid to their understanding of the

[129] MacCormick, 'W. D. Lamont' (1982); see also 'What Place for Nationalism' (1994), 95.
[130] Ibid.
[131] Ibid.
[132] Lamont, LMO (1981), xxvi.

moral order'.[133] This is no moral philosophy that seeks to stand outside or above, in superiority to common, ordinary life. Further, this is not Lamont going out on a limb, offering an unfamiliar approach to moral philosophy; instead, he sees himself as part of a tradition in 'British moral philosophy' – of Smith, Hume, Bentham, Mill, Sidgwick, and Green – who combined their philosophical work with 'wide public interests'.[134] Moral philosophy for these thinkers, and Lamont included, was no 'retreat from reality';[135] rather, it was a reflective engagement with the 'moral order', which Lamont defined in the following way:

> This is not a realm inhabited by some spiritual elite. It is the workaday world covering family, economic, political, cultural, and religious associations, the world in which people try to decide what things are good and bad, what pattern of life it would be sensible and honourable to pursue, how far individuals are responsible for the quality of life in their society, and how far personal and political standards of behaviour can be identical.[136]

As with the earlier work, PMJ, so here in LMO, such reflection on the moral order was best enabled by engagement with jurisprudence. For Lamont, once again indicating the relevance of the question of the relations of law and morals to the role and value of moral philosophy:

> The essential concepts are the same in law and morals, and an acquaintance with the systematic exposition of these concepts in judicial practice and legal theory is essential for a sound understanding of the moral order. It may be safely asserted that a study associating jurisprudence with ethics provides the only standpoint from which we can assess what is living and what is dead in twentieth century ethics.[137]

Interestingly, then, the relationship between law and morals, and, by association, jurisprudence and ethics, was not one in which ethics evaluated how well, say, law reflected morals. This was not ethics sitting in judgement on jurisprudence; this was not a matter of a moral philosopher setting out an ideal morality against which the moral quality of the law was to be tested. Rather, ethics itself could be challenged and tested by jurisprudence; morality was, to an extent, dependent on law, for law gave life to moral ideas. Further, ethics could be assisted by jurisprudence: as

133 Ibid., vii.
134 Ibid.
135 Ibid.
136 Ibid., viii.
137 Ibid., ix.

Lamont says later in the book, he is not writing as a 'lawyer', but as a 'moral philosopher enlisting jurisprudence in the service of ethics'.[138] The relationship was mutual and dialogical – both were vulnerable to each other, and none was more dominant than or superior to the other. This was the vision of a true 'partnership' or 'friendship': an equal and mutual respectful relationship.

That in constituting the relationship between ethics and jurisprudence, and law and morality, Lamont also had one eye on his personal relationship with MacCormick – a moral philosopher relating to 'a thoroughly professional jurist'[139] – is especially explicit in the Appendix to the book, entitled 'On the Necessary Connexion between Law and Morality'.[140] Here, Lamont engages directly with MacCormick's work, significantly prefacing that engagement by showing how his (i.e., Lamont's) position differed from that of Hart's, and thus also how MacCormick's position could be closer to Lamont's than to Hart's.

From the outset, as was characteristic, Lamont tries to first sympathetically understand the position of the jurisprude who argues that there is no necessary connection between law and morality. 'The lawyer', says Lamont, 'is tempted to insist on the distinction' between law and morality 'in ways which obscure the relationship'.[141] The lawyer here is protecting a value: clarity, for instance, about what the law demands of us, given its coerciveness in a system of law backed up by the state, that is not obscured or made impractical by a moral test. But insistence on this value, out of proportion to much else, can distort our understanding of the relationship between law and morals, which in fact is much more intimate than this suggests.

All this, for Lamont, is evident in Hart. As Lamont sees it, Hart's answer to the relationship between law and morality 'would seem to be something like this':

> There is such a relationship [between law and morality] because of the nature of man – a roughly natural equality to help or harm, a natural desire to continue existing and to have a share in the same means of survival. No system of law can be an effective ('good') system which does not meet these natural requirements, distributing opportunities in a just, equitable manner. But the fact that a system of law is effective only so far as it meets natural demands, and that it can meet the demands of members of a group only by paying regard to principles of justice so far as they are embodied in

[138] Ibid., 79.
[139] Ibid., 112.
[140] Ibid., 110–13.
[141] Ibid., 110.

> the social consensus, does not mean that there is a necessary relationship between the concept of law and the concept of morality. Such a necessary relationship would mean that law by definition would include a reference to morality. It would mean that no rule could be accepted as a rule of law if it could truly be described as unjust. This would be contrary to all experience and common sense.[142]

Lamont goes so far as to acknowledge Hart's position as 'true' – but 'it is not', he adds, 'the whole truth'.[143] A vital part of the relationship between law and morality – indeed, where law and morality are necessarily connected – consists in that which lies 'between the judicial process and personal moral judgement',[144] i.e., in the practice of practical reason, which is precisely something that Hart neglects (having but one chapter on the theme in *The Concept of Law* – chapter 7), leaving a gap or hole in his theory, and which, again most significantly, MacCormick in *Legal Reasoning and Legal Theory* attempts to address. For Lamont, then, MacCormick, unlike Hart, turns to that aspect of the relationship of law and morality that shows just how close they are – indeed, how they operate in many ways on the same plane, precisely the plane of practical reason.

Courts and individuals alike must make judgements about practical matters. As they do so, they employ the same basic technique, characteristic of practical reason, namely 'treating like cases alike and unlike cases differently'.[145] If Hart had given more attention to the practice of judgement, to the exercise of practical reason, in his jurisprudence, then he would have seen a much closer – indeed, necessary – connection between jurisprudence and ethics, and, equally, between law and morality. MacCormick did pay such attention, which is also why MacCormick's jurisprudence has the potential, unlike Hart's, to show how law and morality are necessarily connected. And, again, that is also why the relation between MacCormick and Lamont was, according to Lamont, closer, more intimate, than the relation between MacCormick and Hart – at least potentially so.

I say 'potentially' because there is a snag. According to Lamont, on the one hand, MacCormick was on the right track. MacCormick's discussion of the constraint of formal justice on legal reasoning – precisely treating like cases alike by requiring the judge to 'universalise' the grounds of their

142 Ibid., 111.
143 Ibid., 112.
144 Ibid.
145 Ibid.

judgement – overlaps with the best account we have of what moral judgement entails, i.e., Kant's account of practical reason. The requirement of universalisation is of course the requirement that Kant insists upon in the *Groundwork* – the book that was so central in the thought of Glaswegian moral philosophers, Lamont included. In that work, Kant is showing the workings of judgement in common moral consciousness – in the lives of ordinary persons, not that of judges or legal officials. Thus, argues Lamont, what MacCormick's recognition of the role of universalisation in legal reasoning shows is that there is a necessary connection between law and morality, precisely at the level of the practice of judgement or practical reason.

On the other hand, and this is the snag, for all his use of the requirement of universalisation, MacCormick's account falters when 'he thinks that Kant's ethics fails to "make sense in the real world" because of the complete autonomy ascribed to the will as pure practical reason'.[146] Put bluntly, according to Lamont, MacCormick has not really understood Kant. Not that this is a difficult mistake to make: there are plenty of passages in Kant where 'practical reason is set in sheer opposition to our desiring nature'.[147] But this is not, says Lamont, the only way to interpret Kant: there is more to Kant than this, and we cannot let those passages stand for the whole. We can approach Kant more sympathetically, i.e., reading him as 'elucidating the moral thinking of ordinary people',[148] not completely autonomous beings exercising some pure will. Sure, there is an 'early rationalism' in Kant, which obscures the real significance of his insights into practical reason, but then one must read Kant in light of his mature position. Summarising his own take in chapter 8 of LMO, Lamont articulates Kant's mature insights as follows:

> The clue to the practical relevance is in his [Kant's] conception of a 'maxim'. Beginning with a down-to-earth desire for some end in certain circumstances and requiring certain means for its realisation, a person will make explicit the maxim he proposes to follow – I shall pursue this end x by these means y in these circumstances z. The moral question arises when he asks whether he could universalise the maxim, affirming the right or duty of every person everywhere to pursue such an end by such means in such circumstances. Could he will that in this instance all like cases should be treated alike? This is analogous to the issue placed before a judge. The moral agent (like the judge), having been bred in the ethos of a certain

146 Ibid., 113.
147 Ibid.
148 Ibid.

> society, and now faced by an issue directly involved with day-to-day values, employs the same test of universalizability as that applied by the judge to any rule proposed to him as the basis of a decision.[149]

Thus, Kant's moral agent – and, by analogy, the judge in a court – is not some 'rational will' taking 'decisions uninfluenced by mundane values and traditional norms', i.e., some abstract autonomous being entirely separated from conditions of heteronomy. Rather, the Kantian moral agent is autonomous only in the sense that he or she has 'the capacity to take responsibility for a final decision, those values and norms having been taken into account'.[150] The exercise of practical reason by ordinary persons, as much as by judges, is a grounded, practical, down-to-earth exercise, beginning with the materials ready to hand in the culture, tradition, system, or institution of which they are part, made by a person full of feeling and desire, but moral only insofar as it is not determined by inclinations or thoughtless desire, but instead by the reflective test of universalisation.[151]

Lamont's discussion here is brief, suggestive, and allusive – he packs a good deal into a four-page appendix. But what matters more is where Lamont looks for an answer and also where he positions MacCormick, especially vis-à-vis Hart. Lamont does not think that we need to oppose reason from ordinary, down-to-earth, practice of judgement, whether moral or legal. It is not that, on one side, we have an ideal rational process and, on the other, an agent who might often fail in real conditions to exercise it. We do not have ideal rationality on one side and, say, the practical, real-world evaluation of consequences (so as to decide between equally appealing alternatives) on the other. The practical, the grounded, the down-to-earth, is already built in to Kant's understanding of the process of practical reason, properly understood.

Put another way, this is no abstract Kant living in the clouds – this is a Scottish Kant, grounded in the tradition of Scottish, especially Glaswegian, moral philosophy, which is firmly embedded in reflection amidst common life and common moral consciousness. The (Scottish) Kantian agent is situated, by virtue of the material, concrete maxim that is being universalised, in their concrete, desire-filled, emotion-filled circumstances,

149 Ibid.

150 Ibid.

151 For a similar reading see Paton, *The Categorical Imperative* (1947), e.g., chapters 4 and 14, where he also stresses the role of material maxims as the starting point for practical reason as well as making room for the role of feeling. For Kant, practical reasoning is not necessarily a process bereft of feeling; instead, what is important is that it is not dominated by feeling or inclination alone.

and what this agent does is discipline their own desires, inclinations, emotions, and dispositions so as to test them against the constraint of formal justice: would I want, the Kantian agent asks, everyone to act in this way all the time? Analogously: would I, as a judge, want all future courts to decide on these grounds? The practicality of this process is not outside it – it is, again, a built-in-feature. As Lamont puts it in his chapter 8, the test of universalisation is 'one of practicability', albeit in a social context: could society really function if such-and-such a maxim was acted upon, or such-and-such grounds were to constitute the basis of a legal decision? Without asking these questions, any decision made would not emanate from reason, but this is not reason unanchored by or divorced from real-world circumstances; quite the contrary. Again, for Kant, properly understood, practical reason is, certainly, reason, but it is also precisely, practical.

In his chapter 8, Lamont adds another insight that is worth mentioning here, for it ties back to the above-mentioned principle of respect for persons. As Lamont sees it, the exercise of practical reason in Kant is an exercise that involves, as Kant himself says, respect for the form of law as law. This may seem very abstract, but the point is what it tries to exclude: it tries to exclude, from the exercise of practical reason by the agent, acting solely in contemplation of one's own ends, using other persons as means to those ends. If one fails to universalise, then one fails to step back from one's own inclinations and dispositions, which are most likely to be self-serving and other-ignoring. The test of universalisation is a self-disciplining measure, certainly, but one made in the name of acting as a responsible, other-regarding member of society. If I acted in this way, we ask ourselves by virtue of the categorical imperative, what would this mean for a society of persons who all acted in this way? By focusing on the form of law as law – testing the maxims of our actions by universalising them – we demonstrate respect for persons.

There is, thus, an ethics to understanding the moral order as a 'system of normative rules', i.e., 'a system of universals'.[152] As Lamont also puts it: 'respect for the pure form of normative or juridical law has its source in respect for persons universally'.[153] There is something deeply ethically valuable about the form of law – in the sense of this test of universalisation, which characterises practical reason. This net, this order, of rules – this moral order, or, as he also calls it, this 'normative order'[154] – is a kind of condition of us

[152] Lamont, LMO (1981), 64.
[153] Ibid.
[154] Ibid., 41.

exercising moral and legal judgement, i.e., practical reason, for it helps us to act reflectively, respecting persons rather than using them for our own ends.

This link, between the notion of a normative order, including it being made up of rules that have been universalised, and respect for persons was something MacCormick returned to often in his own writing, e.g., in his argument for the 'ethics of legalism'[155] or in his many works on practical reason as the key to jurisprudence. Writing, for instance, about the state of 'Contemporary Legal Philosophy' in 1983, MacCormick argued that it was an 'essential task of legal philosophy' to 'elucidate the nature and working of practical reason'.[156] Enlisting Lamont's LMO as part of this tradition – of a jurisprudence led by an inquiry into practical reason – MacCormick recalled precisely the connection Lamont made between 'respect for the form of law as foundational for reasonable judgement' and the idea that law was 'concerned to give concrete embodiment to practical requirements of respect for persons'.[157] And he added: 'Once the discussion is cast in terms of the place of law within a general view of practical reason, it ceases to make any serious sense to suppose that there is a choice to be made between being a positivist or natural lawyer'.[158] Practical reason, in the way Lamont had theorised it, was part of what allowed MacCormick to transcend – or at least desire to transcend – the debate between positivism and natural law, relating, rather than separating, law and morality, ethics and jurisprudence.

As mentioned above, MacCormick was deeply involved in the making of Lamont's LMO. He commented on various drafts and corresponded with Lamont – his old teacher – now in the twilight of his life. This engagement had, or so I have been suggesting, a deep impact: from the earliest time as a student in Glasgow, being apprenticed into the Glaswegian tradition of moral philosophy, through to the crucial period of the late 1970s and early 1980s when, as we shall see, MacCormick was finding his own voice after being steeped in Oxford and Hartian jurisprudence, all the way to the final book, which MacCormick wrote when he himself was dying, when he returned to the question of practical reason and to how to interpret Kant.[159]

155 See MacCormick, 'The Ethics of Legalism' (1993).

156 MacCormick, 'Contemporary Legal Philosophy' (1983), 1.

157 Ibid., 8.

158 Ibid.

159 Arguably unlike Lamont, though, MacCormick's approach was not to defend a certain interpretation of Kant, but instead to find a middle space between Kant and Hume, or Kant and Smith – the substantive position may, in the end, be similar, but it is a hallmark of MacCormick's approach that he was inclusive in this way.

The issue of practical reason – of when, how, reason was practical, in the contexts of both law and morality – was not an isolated, stand-alone problem for MacCormick (nor, indeed, for Lamont). The very practicality of reason was what related whole domains that might otherwise be seen as separate, such as law and morality, or jurisprudence and ethics, but also, crucially, what might relate real, living persons, such as MacCormick and Lamont, in mutually respectful and mutually generative friendships and partnerships. This was the legacy of the formation of MacCormick's character in the democratic-intellectual tradition of Scottish philosophy and especially Glaswegian moral philosophy.

4

A Scot in Oxford

Law and Politics in England and America

When MacCormick arrived in Oxford, in September 1963, he came as a Glaswegian moral philosopher and as someone steeped in Scottish politics, history, and culture. He had been, as we have seen, a keen and skilled debater, a writer of poetry and prose, an editor of student newspapers and handbooks in Scots, Gaelic, and English, and a bagpipe player. He had also been an organiser of student politics, whether that be via the Glasgow University Student Nationalist Association or broader initiatives, such as the Federal Association of Student Nationalists. Of course, as we have also seen, prior even to that, as a young boy, he had a political apprenticeship in the very heart of Scottish nationalist politics, being submerged in the exhilarating atmosphere of the Convention and Covenant, the taking of the Stone of Destiny, and the *MacCormick* v *Lord Advocate* case. He had followed, as only a young boy can, his father's political, literary, and historical passions, hearing his father speak and debate with others, reading his father's writing, and, finally, seeing his father's health deteriorate until his death in 1961. He had also been exposed, if less publicly, then also arguably more powerfully, to his mother's egalitarianism and deep-set respect and care for others. None of this meant that his Scottishness was narrow-minded, inward-looking, or defensive: quite the contrary, as both his friendships across the political spectrum and his writings of his university days illustrate, MacCormick's Scottishness was often self-ironic, if not self-critical, and keen to connect to, relate with, and include others.

Thus, arriving as he did in Oxford at the age of twenty two, MacCormick had already a richly developed character, with its own dispositions, tastes, and styles. Nevertheless, the encounter with Oxford was to challenge and change him profoundly. This is all the more so because he experienced Oxford both as a student – studying law from 1963 to 1965 – and then as a tutor – teaching law from 1967 to 1972 – both in Balliol College. Further, these were, as we shall see in both this chapter and Chapter 5, tumultuous and exciting years to be in Oxford. This was the case politically, with the debates, for instance, around rights and race, the emergence of the British

New Left and welfare politics, and the student protests of the late 1960s. And it was also the case philosophically, with passionate debates, following hot on the heels of Wittgenstein and Austin, about, in particular, the nature of language and its relation to practice, as well as the methodology of philosophy and its relations to the social sciences, including anthropology. In the realm of jurisprudence, certainly, the 1960s were a watershed in England, with Hart's *The Concept of Law* appearing in 1961, with the beginnings of the debate between Hart and his (to many surprising) American successor, Ronald Dworkin, and generally with the rise of an extraordinary generation of legal philosophers, including MacCormick's peers, such as Joseph Raz and John Finnis. For a twenty-two-year old bursting with political and philosophical energy, Oxford must have in many ways seemed like the epicentre of both a political and a philosophical revolution.

There is no doubt that Oxford exposed MacCormick to much that was, then, new for him. However, and especially in light of the preceding chapters, this attention to what was new in Oxford needs to be combined with awareness of the continuities between Oxford and his Glasgow years. There may well have revolutions in Oxford, but MacCormick did not encounter them as a blank slate. MacCormick, like any twenty-something-year old, may well have been open to influence, to being charmed and to being persuaded, and to acquiring new philosophical likes and dislikes, but it is also the case that he both sought out Glaswegian echoes in Oxford – he continued, for example his interests in debating in the Oxford Union – and that he did not hide, but on the contrary relished and was proud of, his Scottish identity. Further, although MacCormick immersed himself in both his periods in Oxford in English law (albeit alongside Roman law), this was mainly with a view to returning to Scotland, whether that be initially as an advocate in the Scottish courts or, later, as an academic. It is no accident that in between the two Oxford stints, MacCormick was teaching law in Scotland. Indeed, his two years in Dundee (1965–67), at what was then Queen's College, St Andrews, were also important in his development (a point I shall return to in Chapter 5). MacCormick, then, brought Scotland with him to Oxford, and this is just as significant as the way in which he took Oxford with him when, in 1972, at the still-remarkably young age of thirty one, he returned to Scotland to take up the Regius Chair of Public Law and the Law of Nature and Nations at the University of Edinburgh.

The aim of this chapter is to shed some light on MacCormick's first period in Oxford, i.e., the two years, 1963–65 he was studying law and participating in the activities of the Oxford Union. In both cases, MacCormick's moral philosophical interests were never far away, and indeed in many ways, they were strengthened, especially by the presence, in Balliol, of R. M. Hare, who MacCormick had already begun reading in Glasgow. MacCormick, one might argue, brought a Glaswegian moral philosophical attitude and ethos with him to the study of law and participation in Oxford student politics. At the same time, he acquired new interests – especially in English and Roman law – and was exposed to the fervent political issues of the time, especially over civil rights and racial tensions in both England and America. This, as we shall see towards the end of this chapter, was all the more so as he travelled the length and breadth of America in the summer of 1965, courtesy of a Coolidge Pathfinder scholarship.

Balliol College

Tradition has it that Balliol College is named after John Balliol (or John de Balliol), who, following a dispute with the powerful Bishop of Durham, Walter Kirkham, in the mid thirteenth century, was induced, as part of the resolution of that dispute, to establish a house in Oxford, covering the accommodation and modest costs of some sixteen poor scholars. Balliol's wife, Dervorguilla of Galloway, played a large – if not larger than Balliol himself – role in the College's foundation, writing an important letter in 1282 that came to constitute the first constitution of the College, setting out, for instance, the daily life of the scholars and the powers and responsibilities of its administrators.[1]

For a Scot, of course, the name 'Balliol' will have other connotations: John Balliol was the King of Scots from 1292 to 1296, only to be deposed, when he was in exile in France, and replaced by Robert Bruce.[2] John Balliol, King of Scots, was the son of John Balliol, the founder of Balliol College, though it was through his mother, Dervorguilla, that the son had a claim to the Scottish crown. Be that as it may, the very name of the College would, for a Scot, resound with the late thirteenth and early fourteenth century Scottish Wars of Independence. Add to that the long history of Snell Exhibitioners, holders of a prestigious scholarship at Balliol, who were always graduates of Glasgow University, and you have a College that might feel like a little bit of Scotland in Oxford.

Certainly, MacCormick felt sufficiently at ease, as a Scot, to don the kilt on special occasions as well as to pipe – often and it seems to some acclaim.

[1] Jones, *Balliol College* (2005), 5–6.
[2] The story is told vividly in Barrow, *Robert Bruce* (1965).

When he arrived back in Balliol, in 1967, he piped on the occasion of the opening of a new joint graduate institute of Balliol and St Anne's. 'Rarely', it is reported, can the tune he played, 'The Bonnie Hoose o' Airlie', 'have made so profound an impression on an audience', especially given it was 'played in the small and reverberating dining hall of Holywell Manor'.[3] The piping continued, for when he was leaving, the Balliol Record reported that 'during his four years as a Fellow he and his bagpipes have become an indispensable asset to the College'.[4] Not always, though, it must be added was the piping appreciated. Writing in early 1964 in *Isis*, an Oxford student newspaper, a 'Doctor Fell', under the title 'Too Much Haggis', wrote, not without a hint of cheek:

> Dr Fell is alarmed by the growth of Scottish nationalism in Oxford, illustrated by noisy junketings at the Royal Oxford Hotel and elsewhere on Burns Night. One returning reveller was seen in Merton Street divesting himself of coat, kilt and shoes, which he proceeded to throw over the Corpus gatespikes. Only then did he discover that an excessive ballast of haggis prevented him from following them, and he was forced to roam the streets dressed only in ceremonial pocket and tartan stockings. Scarcely less offensive is the behaviour of Neil MacCormick, the up-and-coming Union speaker, who disturbs the peace of Cherwell Edge Covent by playing his bagpipes in the Parks while his friends stand around criticising his fingering in Scots accents.[5]

Apart from the Scottish connections, Balliol also had another reputation that must have appealed to MacCormick. Although excelling academically – Balliol, in the 1960s was consistently the, or one of the, top academic Colleges – this academic prowess was not achieved at the cost of any loss in public engagement or political influence. Quite the contrary: Balliol was known to be a College where academia was intertwined with politics, with many of its graduates, though also tutors, playing important roles in the British government, from Prime Ministers to economic advisers in the Treasury. When, in October 1964, the beginning of MacCormick's second year at Balliol, Harold Wilson and Labour won power after thirteen years of Conservative rule, several Balliol tutors joined Wilson as advisors, including Thomas Balogh and Paul Streeten. As Martin Kettle, a student in those years, wrote, in the 1960s 'Balliol certainly had an extremely political reputation' – a reputation that derived, in part, from

[3] *Balliol Annual Record* (1967), 13.
[4] Ibid., 8.
[5] Doctor Fell, 'Too Much Haggis', *Isis* (8 February 1964), 6.

Balliol figures such as Edward Heath (Prime Minister) and Roy Jenkins (Chancellor of the Exchequer and Home Secretary under Wilson, and later President of the European Commission) – but also, more locally, from the presence of Christopher Hill, an influential Marxist historian, who was Master of the College from 1965 to 1978.[6]

Politics and public engagement were, then, never far from the College; in fact, they were a central part of its identity. This was, as we shall see, an identity that MacCormick embraced, though in his own way. Indeed, initially, in March 1963, when filling out his 'Application for Admission to Balliol College', MacCormick enrolled in the Philosophy, Politics, and Economics degree – a well known route into British politics. It was only in November 1963 that he switched to law. Being a law student, however, did nothing to dampen his political engagement, whether that be through the choice of moot topics and guests in his involvement in Balliol's Younger Society (the College's law society) when he was a student, or, later, in his various roles, both in College and at the University, related to student protests and student discipline. Throughout the period of the second half of the 1960s, and into the early 1970s, MacCormick combined attention to legal developments – publishing on particular law reforms or other legal events of note in Scotland and England[7] – with attention to matters of political controversy, including of course Scottish politics, which culminated in his editing of *The Scottish Debate* in 1970. These publications were complimented by others more explicitly in jurisprudence, such as papers on stare decisis,[8] reviews of books on legal reasoning and justice,[9] and, in due course, more advanced work, in debate with Joseph Raz on promising.[10] All this was to come later, but it serves as a reminder of how attention to issues in legal theory or legal scholarship were entangled with current, political events and controversies.

There are, indeed, several important points to emphasise, first as to what MacCormick brought with him when arriving in Balliol, and second, as to what Balliol offered MacCormick. In terms of what he brought with him, as has been noted above, MacCormick arrived already with some experience, and well defined interests, in philosophy, especially Glaswegian moral philosophy. He also came with both experience and

[6] See Kettle, 'It Was Right to Rebel', *Balliol Annual Record* (2009), 20.

[7] MacCormick, 'Misrepresentation Act' (1967); 'Seabathing' (1967).

[8] MacCormick, 'Stare Decisis' (1966).

[9] MacCormick, 'Review of Legal Systems' (1966); 'Review of Human Law' (1966).

[10] MacCormick, 'Voluntary Powers and Normative Obligations' (1972).

knowledge of Scottish politics and a deep love of Scottish culture. Finally, more personally, having already acquired a four-year degree, and thus being older than other undergraduate students, he came with his partner, Karen Barr.[11] Balliol, in many ways, was a welcome home for someone of MacCormick's background and interests: there were many Scottish connections and there was a lively relation between academic excellence and public service. The fact that he was older also offered opportunities: it meant that he was more likely, as indeed he did, to take on certain leadership positions vis-à-vis his peers (in College as well as beyond in the University) and also to take a more mature distance from some of the more undergraduate aspects of student politics in this period.

These points need to be remembered, for they colour MacCormick's legal studies in Oxford. There are many evocative illustrations of this. MacCormick, it must be recalled, was no stranger to law: as we know from Chapter 1, his father had been a lawyer and MacCormick was very sensitive to the historiography of British constitutionalism. When he arrived at Balliol in 1963, the Master was Sir David Lindsay Keir, who was not only a lawyer, but also someone interested in constitutional history. Further, Keir was a Scot. However, as MacCormick recalled in his 1997 British Academy Lecture on 'The English Constitution', in Keir's *Constitutional History of Britain 1485–1937*, 'the Act of Union [of 1707] merits a couple of two-line throwaway comments relating to the balance of power among Queen Anne's Ministers'.[12] This puzzled MacCormick for, he said, 'Yet Keir was a Scotsman' and 'proud of it', so his 'taking the common law perspective was by no means genetically or ethnically determined'.[13]

That MacCormick approached his legal studies always with one eye on Scotland and British constitutional politics can also be gleaned from his choice of guest for the annual dinner of Balliol's Younger Society. This was Balliol's undergraduate law society and it was the duty of its President – which MacCormick became in his second year in Oxford, 1964–65 – to 'organise the annual dinner for all past and present members of the College connected with law, and to find a suitably distinguished Balliol lawyer for the address to the gathered company'.[14] MacCormick's choice was Lord

11 MacCormick met Karen Barr in Glasgow in 1959, when she was a student in Iain, MacCormick's brother's, class. They married in 1965 and had three daughters: Janet was born on 21 August 1966; Morag, born on 24 February 1969; and Sheena, born on 9 September 1971.

12 MacCormick, 'The English Constitution' (1998) [1997], 140.

13 Ibid.

14 MacCormick, 'Special Conception' (2001), 4–5.

Kilbrandon, then at the Court of Session, but in the coming years the commissioner in charge of the Royal Commission on the Constitution (which reported in 1973). MacCormick did not hide his own motivation for the choice of speaker: he chose Lord Kilbrandon 'with all due consciousness of my own roots and of my then intention to enter practice at the Scots Bar after leaving Oxford',[15] but also because of a very personal connection, with Kilbrandon having supported his father in the Convention and Covenant of the 1940s and 1950s. As the Younger Society report for 1964 recorded: 'Seventy-five past and present members of the Society came to the annual Younger Dinner in December and heard a Scottish president, D. N. MacCormick, and a Scottish guest of honour, Lord Kilbrandon, make some deft shots at anyone who discounted the lessons that Scots Law could teach English lawyer'.[16] MacCormick's relationship with Kilbrandon, it should be added, 'ripened into a friendship of mutual respect and admiration', so much so that, when Kilbrandon was running the above-mentioned Royal Commission, MacCormick, after he gave evidence to it, had the 'very great pleasure' of a 'lunch that was held in Blackie House in Lady Stairs Close in the Kilbrandon flat'.[17]

Equally important, for MacCormick, as Balliol's Scottish connections, were its connections to politics and public service, and perhaps especially to the right-of-centre politics of the Labour party. This, too, very much coloured MacCormick's engagement with law in Oxford. One has to see this both at the level of MacCormick's personal experience as well as in light of what was happening politically in Britain at the time. Personally, as mentioned above, MacCormick was older than many of his peers at Balliol. Reflecting on 1968 – a topic I will return to in Chapter 5 – MacCormick said that rather than there being a gap between 'disaffected youth … and their venerable seniors', there was, it seemed to him at the time, 'actually quite a gap between people of my own age, born just before or during the war of 1939–45 and those born after it'.[18] For those in his generation, 'life had been largely an experience of melioration of conditions following on the grim years of war and post-war

15 Ibid. MacCormick never entered the Scots Bar, but he did qualify in the English Bar, being called to the Inner Temple in 1970.

16 *Balliol Annual Record* (1964), 22.

17 See MacCormick, 'Special Conception' (2001). See also MacCormick's glowing, but still in places critical, review of Kilbrandon's *Other People's Law*: 'Review' (1967); it is significant that, in that review, MacCormick admired and praised Kilbrandon's book in particular for going 'to the roots of important social problems': 79.

18 MacCormick, '1968 and All That', *Balliol Annual Record* (2009), 14.

and rationing'.[19] MacCormick's self-identification with a generation that had experienced both the war and post-war poverty, while also experiencing a sense of progress, even if that had been slow, is important. It is so not only because of MacCormick's sensitivity to the experience of violence and the value of peace (between nations, but also between philosophies and persons), but also because of his sensitivity, which he inherited from his mother, to the dire experience of poverty and the value of welfare, of social protection, for the most vulnerable in society.

I will be returning to these themes – for instance, to MacCormick's social democratic sensibility – but what is important, for now, is that Balliol, Oxford, and Britain more generally, in the post-war politics of the 1950s and 1960s, had witnessed extensive social changes that brought to light the need for welfare provision. There is no simple way to summarise these changes, but they included 'rapid social mobility', 'more extensive consumerism', an 'altering of class structure of British society' and the 'ushering in of a new managerial and technical class',[20] all of which affected 'the structure of the state and the nature of law in a number of ways'.[21] The state became much more active, but also at once more bureaucratic, 'involved in wholescale planning and intervention in the mechanisms of the market', with a 'snowballing mass of social legislation' that regulated 'previously private realms such as economy and family'.[22] This is, of course, the complex history of the rise of the post-war British welfare state, with the state being not 'a locus of discipline and power as in the Austinian mould but rather a provider, a manager, and a non-authoritarian resolver of social problems'.[23] There was, here, a tendency to see progress in a 'socially upwardly mobile working class'[24] – a 'dynamic post-war modernisation',[25] which also came with an understanding (philosophically inspired by the utilitarianism of Bentham and Mill) of law serving social justice, of law being infused with progressive purposes and administered by courts armed with the discretion to deliver them. Again, there is a consciousness of progress and modernisation – thereby also a sense of optimism and hope, including in law as a vehicle of social justice – albeit underwritten by the historical memory of poverty, vulnerability, and war.

19 Ibid.
20 Edgeworth, 'Hart' (1989), 278.
21 Ibid., 283.
22 Ibid.
23 Ibid., 285.
24 Ibid., 286.
25 Ibid., 289.

Of course, MacCormick comes to this as part of a generation younger than the one who had served in the war – including Hart himself – but there remains a connection between MacCormick's generation and the one that was teaching him in those years in Oxford in the mid 1960s. As we shall see in subsequent chapters, this connection was an important part of Hart's influence on MacCormick – in many ways, it was Hart's politics (both his social democratic views as well as his university politics), perhaps more than his jurisprudence, that appealed to MacCormick (or, to put it another way, MacCormick read Hart's jurisprudence through these political orientations). But this post-war British political context did not just colour MacCormick's relationship to Hart. It also coloured his legal studies in other ways.

A clear example of this is MacCormick's relationship with his law tutors. There were two such tutors in Balliol: Theodore (Theo) Tylor and Donald Harris. It was the second of these who illustrates the connection between law and welfare politics, but it is also important to say a brief word about the first, for he too clearly influenced MacCormick in an important way.

As colourfully described by Anthony Kenny (later Master of Balliol) 'Tylor was an awesome figure, a chess grandmaster with a gravity of seniority which was only enhanced by his blindness'.[26] Tylor was officially 'Tutor in Jurisprudence' at Balliol from 1927 to 1967. Tylor's obituary in the *Oxford Magazine* noted that 'he had lived for his College', teaching generation after generation of law students in Balliol and becoming 'one of the most celebrated of Oxford Law dons'.[27] His approach to teaching law was described as 'essentially concrete and practical', with 'the lawyer's main task' being 'to try to ensure that justice was done between the parties to a case'; he was, it is said further, 'a case lawyer' with a special interest in tort and contract.[28] The Younger Society, Balliol's undergraduate law society, was his project – and he is said to have 'great gifts as a host, loved good company, talk and stories, and like to keep his friendships, which were many, in repair'.[29] As MacCormick's principal law tutor, one could argue that one can see his legacy in the facility with which MacCormick discusses, in his works on legal reasoning, multiple cases, with great sensitivity to the policy considerations at play in them. Indeed, when, in

[26] Kenny, *A Life in Oxford* (1997), 5.

[27] D. L. K. [the author is listed under initials], 'T. H. Tylor 1900–1968', *Oxford Magazine* (7 February 1969), 167.

[28] Ibid.

[29] Ibid.

1967, MacCormick returned to Oxford, it was his old tutor, Tylor, who he replaced, going on to campaign, with Hill and Harris, that the law library would be renamed 'The Tylor Library' in his honour.[30]

Donald Harris and Normative Legal Sociology

Harris, like Tylor, had a life-long association with Balliol. He had been a Balliol graduate (1953) and joined Balliol as a tutor in law in 1956. When MacCormick arrived, in 1963, Harris was thirty five and was in the second year of his role as Senior Tutor at Balliol.[31] Significantly, in light of later events, among Harris's other roles in the College was a period, in 1968, when he drafted governance reforms for Balliol, breaking up 'a small number of large College committees' and replacing 'them with a larger number of small, specialised ones', with places for students on the Disciplinary Committee and the Domestic Committee.[32] But more immediately in 1963, for MacCormick, Harris was both his Senior Tutor as well as his tutor in tort law. In accordance with Oxford's tutorial system, MacCormick wrote many essays on tort law for Harris – one of which, penned on 9 May 1964, is an answer to the question 'Examine the Duty of Care Concept in the Tort of Negligence with Reference to careless Misstatement', and in which MacCormick discusses the relation between considerations of policy and what he calls 'the logical structure' of the judgement.[33]

But the real influence of Harris is more visible later. As we shall see in particular in Chapter 9, that influence can be traced to MacCormick's positioning of the institutional theory of law – for instance, in his Inaugural Lecture in Edinburgh in 1973 – between analytical jurisprudence and sociology of law, and to the many times thereafter where he sought to build bridges between the two disciplines. Another example is MacCormick's piece on 'Rights and Discretion' (published in 1989), which MacCormick first delivered as a presentation in the 1987 W. G. Hart workshop, co-organised by Harris and Keith Hawkins, on 'Discretion in Legal Contexts: Socio-Legal Perspectives'.

But it can also be traced, perhaps more directly, to his work on the aims and purposes of private law, including specifically tort law. For example,

[30] See the Theodore Tylor dossier at the Balliol Archives.
[31] Kenny, *A Life in Oxford* (1997), 68.
[32] Ibid., 94. Harris was also the Estates bursar at Balliol.
[33] MacCormick, 'Examine the Duty of Care Concept in the Tort of Negligence with Reference to careless Misstatement' (9 May 1964), Edinburgh University Archives.

in his 1978 paper on the 'Obligation of Reparation', delivered as a talk to the Aristotelian Society in March 1978, MacCormick cites an early conference paper by Harris on 'The Law of Torts and the Welfare State' (1963: the year of MacCormick's arrival in Oxford), and specifically thanks Harris 'for the stimulation of my interest, over many years, in the subject matter' of the paper.[34] What matters here is less any particular technical account of tort law doctrine, and more the attitude with which one might approach tort law, i.e., that even the most technical of doctrinal issues had to be approached with a sense of law's 'moral worth'.[35]

It is important to note that in this piece MacCormick seeks to articulate a sense of the moral worth of the obligation of reparation that is not reducible to any cost-benefit analysis. MacCormick's approach to law's aims and purposes, though grounded and practically minded, was never reducible to any account of its efficiency. A large part of this stems from MacCormick's Glaswegian education in moral philosophy and, in particular, its mantra of respect for persons, and indeed this plays a crucial role in his account of the moral worth of the obligation of reparation. But a part, too, comes from the manner in which, again grounded and empirical though it was, Harris and others in the early days of British socio-legal studies in the 1960s, were concerned with the basic justice and fairness of law. Indeed, the very point of empirical work was that it could help us better see the unfairness or injustice of existing legal rules and procedures, as they affected ordinary persons on the ground. As Max Travers put it in his account of 'Sociology of Law in Britain' (2001):

> Socio-legal research in Britain is mainly concerned with influencing or serving government policy in the provision of legal services. It first developed in the 1960s as a political movement concerned with fairness and justice. Many of the first studies were, for example, concerned with demonstrating unmet legal need, and securing government funding to address this. Researchers were also interested in identifying differential treatment in the legal process. There were also more radical studies advocating law reform, so that new rights were created, or injustices removed.[36]

If this was legal sociology, it was less descriptive (as in Hart's unfortunate phrase), and more normative. For sociologists of law, this meant designing empirical methods in partnership with reflection on morality

[34] MacCormick 'The Obligation of Reparation' (1978), fn. 13, 198.

[35] Ibid., 188.

[36] Travers, 'Sociology of Law in Britain' (2001), 27, and the work cited therein, including by Michael Zander, Brian Abel-Smith, and Robert Stevens.

and justice, including law's relationship to ethics and politics. There was throughout this – certainly in the late 1960s and more intensively in the early 1970s – close attention paid to the rights of persons and whether law was enhancing and protecting them or standing in the way of their realisation. Harris, who had a collaborative approach to legal research,[37] and was thus an ideal first Director of Oxford's Centre for Socio-Legal Studies (established in 1972),[38] was invested precisely in this rights-driven empirical investigation of law-in-action, e.g., through what became his *Compensation and Support for Illness and Injury* (1984), where, as Linda Mulcahy, the current CSLS Director, put it he 'drew attention to the roles of government agencies, local authorities, employers and informal organisations in providing such services as social security, criminal injuries compensation, sick pay and private insurance' and which, she added, 'helped to establish the reputation of the CSLS'.[39] Again, if this was legal sociology, it was rights-based legal sociology, which was always sensitive to the point of view of law's recipient, the ordinary person on the street. Arguably, all this was music to MacCormick's ears, with his Scottish practically oriented moral philosophy background and his commitment to respect for persons, and his growing interest in legal rights and social democracy.

Harris's influence on MacCormick is unlikely to have been restricted to MacCormick's interest in private law, or even to a moral, rights-based approach to law and its everyday workings. It is interesting, for instance, that Keith Hawkins, in his retrospective about Harris in a collection in his honour – tellingly titled *The Human Face of Law* (1997) – emphasises Harris's 'optimism', adding that this was 'one of the first things you notice about Donald Harris'.[40] This optimism extended – as it did for MacCormick – to a belief in the value of law: that law could, if designed well, be a 'mechanism for the attainment of social order', including changing society for the better.[41] Even if this optimism was to suffer somewhat in the face of his empirical findings,[42] Harris, in the mid-to-late

[37] See Mulcahy, 'Remembering Donald Harris' (2020); Travers, 'Sociology of Law in Britain' (2001), 29.

[38] Initially, Harris was the Associate Director, but given how busy the Director, Oliver Ross McGregor, was, Harris was effectively the de facto Director, becoming the formal Director in 1975: see Hawkins, 'Prologue' to *The Human Face of Law* (1997), 13.

[39] Mulcahy, 'Remembering Donald Harris' (2020), 10.

[40] Hawkins, 'Prologue' *The Human Face of Law* (1997), 1.

[41] Ibid.

[42] Ibid.

1960s, was animated by the normative promise of law, which only seemed more urgently needed in those days of growing law-reform proposals.[43]

Again, it is important to emphasise, in light of MacCormick's later interests, that Harris approached law as a social and normative phenomenon: as something that had the potential, through its technicalities, to achieve a more just and fairer society. But it is also in his manner or style of relating with others that Harris must have had an influence on MacCormick. In this respect one must mention Harris's ability to encourage and facilitate collaborative research between economists, sociologists, and lawyers,[44] taking '"parity of esteem" between social scientists and lawyers very seriously',[45] and leading through sheer hard work, example, and humour, and thus with a 'gentle touch'.[46]

MacCormick's commitment to justice and fairness, and the capacity of law to deliver it, which he had in common with Harris, was by no means merely abstract or confined to questions about legal or jurisprudential methodology. In fact, they were most concrete and included an active interest in one of the thorniest topics and biggest challenges facing Oxford colleges in the 1960s: admissions. There may well have been upward social mobility for the working classes in 1950s and 1960s Britain, but sometimes, if not often, this was not exactly visible in the profile of students in Oxford. Balliol, with its high Eton count, was no exception. The tensions, as Keith Thomas explains, were present already in the 1950s, when the distinction between 'scholars' and 'commoners' came under strain, as exhibited in the conflict between, on the one side, 'the head and the older tutors, who tended to favour the claims of old members' sons and who liked having about the college good-looking sportsmen and people of, as they put it, 'character' and, on the other side, 'the younger tutors, who were more exclusively interested in academic potential and suspicious of anything which looked like nepotism or social injustice'.[47] Despite some changes, for instance combining entrance and scholarship exams in 1962, the numbers of state school boys in the mid 1960s was low: 45% in 1964 and 41% in 1965.[48]

When he returned to Balliol, in 1967, MacCormick soon became involved in – if not, in fact, leading – discussions in January 1968 about

43 Ibid., 5.
44 Ibid., 3–5.
45 Ibid., 11.
46 Ibid., 14.
47 Thomas, 'College Life' (1994), 193.
48 Ibid., 194–5.

the 'experiment of running a three week summer school for schoolboys from smaller state schools in each of the years 1969, 1970, and 1971'.[49] Writing, in the *Oxford Magazine*, a report on the first cohort, and lamenting that 'it remains true that a disproportionately large number of our undergraduates comes from a disproportionately small range of schools', MacCormick characterised the motivation for the scheme as follows:

> The College believed that something really useful might be done by bringing such boys into residence here for a short period and exposing them to intensive study of academic subjects in circumstances as near as possible to the ordinary conditions of undergraduate life. At least it seemed worthwhile to find out whether a college such as Balliol *can* do any real good in this field.[50]

In the result, MacCormick reported that the 1969 'experiment' was 'on the whole extremely successful', with twenty-nine boys from small state schools in Leicestershire, Monmouthshire, and Northumberland, participating. This was a major logistical exercise, which also involved co-ordinating the Master, ten fellows of the College, and twelve graduate and undergraduate students, to give up their time for three weeks in the summer, teaching courses in literature, social studies, and the sciences, and arranging excursions, such as a trip to various theatres and sports facilities. It also included securing support from the Local Education Authority. MacCormick's enthusiasm for, indeed pride taken in, the scheme, is visible when he says, though in a typically modest tone:

> And when we claim some success for the course, our claim adds up only to this: the novel experience of working with dons and students inside a university may help to awaken schoolboys to a sense of the long-term values and objectives towards which their school education may lead. That is an awakening which boys who have the advantages of a professional middle class home, or of attending large and famous schools, do not need. Our role can be no more than complementary to the schools', but it might be an extremely useful component.[51]

MacCormick's passion for social democracy – which I will return to in later chapters – is very present in such understated expressions, which were accompanied, again typically, by the practical details of the scheme. The passion was there, but it was toned down in the writing and it was by

49 MacCormick, 'The Balliol Experiment' (1969), 44.
50 Ibid., original emphasis, 44.
51 Ibid., 45.

no means hot air: indeed, it was exhibited mainly in the sheer hard work put in to make such schemes as this one a success (not incidentally, precisely the kind of hard work, behind the scenes, that was characteristic of MacCormick's mother).

Turning back the clock to MacCormick's time as a student, his two years were packed with study, though by no means only study. As we shall see in Chapter 5, MacCormick was already then engaged in student politics in Oxford, but he was also interested in much else besides. After all, when answering a question, in 1963, on his application form, about what were his interests outside academic work, MacCormick's long list was: 'Sailing, Rugby, Debating, Politics, Pipe Music, Student Journalism, Painting, Committee of Management of Glasgow University Union March 1961 – March 1963'.[52] How many of these interests he pursued in Oxford is not known, but it is clear that however much he did, this did not stand in the way of achieving a first class degree[53] or numerous academic prizes, e.g., the Balliol College Register has him winning the Ernest Walker Prize, the Younger Prize, the Jenkyns Prize, and being chosen as both a Paton Student and a Coolidge Pathfinder.[54] He took the full range of courses that students studying in law Oxford then took, including – as recorded in his Oxford diary from 1964 to 1965 – land law, torts, contract, administrative law, Roman law, and international law. This was supplemented by the moots organised by the Younger Society, which included topics such as bigamy, trade disputes and intimidation, as well as themes taken from Roman law.

Alan Watson and Roman Law

The presence of Roman law deserves a special mention. As MacCormick recorded on a number of occasions, in addition to Donald Harris and Theo Tylor, his other important law tutor in his Oxford student days was Alan Watson. Watson was not at Balliol, but rather at Oriel College, but since

52 As Peter Mackay observed, in response to an obituary of MacCormick, he was a 'considerable rugby player. While still a student at Glasgow he was a member of the High School Former Pupils rugby team that won the Scottish Club Championship in 1962': *Times* (9 April 2009), 65.

53 One of his examiners was Guenter Treitel. Chris Patten once recalled, that MacCormick's first was obtained despite MacCormick sleeping in and missing the first half hour or hour of his first exam – something, Patten added, that 'MacCormick was especially proud of': Royal Society of Edinburgh MacCormick lecture (17 June 2011), see www.youtube.com/watch?v=dK2zNvPQLJk (last accessed on 17 September 2024).

54 Balliol College Register (1956), 315.

Balliol did not have an expert in Roman law, so MacCormick was sent to study with Watson. As he himself described it, MacCormick was a 'suitable pupil' for Watson,[55] given that Watson, like MacCormick, was a Glasgow graduate (Watson, at the time, was pursuing a DPhil under David Daube). The connection with Watson developed into 'a deep and valued friendship', later enabled by the two being 'close colleagues in Edinburgh, from 1972 to 1979'.[56] In due course, Watson commissioned a translation by MacCormick of Book 1 of Justinian's *Digest*.[57] It is telling that when MacCormick came to reflect on that task, in 2001, he focused on the meaning of the term 'iurisprudentia', or jurisprudence, explaining why he chose to understand and translate it as 'practical wisdom as directed to ius – in short, iuris-prudentia'.[58] As he added:

> The claim is indeed being made that law as a life's study is more than a science, it belongs as much to praxis as to techne. In particular, we might want to suggest, learning in law that rested content with a listing or recitation or even full grasp of rules ... would not amount to iurisprudentia... It is these rules, principles and implicit values brought into the concrete setting, weighed and balanced and finally applied to yield an answer to a concrete question of right, that amounts to iurisprudentia.[59]

For all its technicalities – and MacCormick never shied away from those – law, and its theoretical study, was a practical art, an art concerned with how we ought to live, an art very much of practical wisdom, and an art that resonated with MacCormick's formation as a Glaswegian moral philosopher.

Roman law certainly helped MacCormick fine-tune his sensitivity to legal technicalities. One further connection that is worth mentioning here, which provided for MacCormick a more personal relationship with Roman law (though also the civilian aspects of Scots law), was a life-long friendship with Alan Rodger (who, in due course, became a judge of the Court of Session, the Court of Appeal, and finally the Supreme Court of the UK). The MacCormick and Rodger families had a connection dating back to when John MacCormick and Fergus Rodger had left the Labour Party and together established the Glasgow University Scottish Nationalist Association.[60] Rodger overlapped with MacCormick for a couple of years

[55] MacCormick, 'Iurisprudentia' (2001), 79.
[56] Ibid.
[57] MacCormick, 'The Digest of Justinian: Book One' (1985).
[58] MacCormick, 'Iurisprudentia' (2001), 81.
[59] Ibid.
[60] John MacCormick, *The Flag in the Wind* (2008), 18.

at the University of Glasgow (he arrived in 1961) and was also involved in Glasgow Union debating.[61] Rodger and MacCormick were then colleagues in Oxford, with Rodger arriving in Oxford in 1967 to study for a doctorate in Roman law under David Daube and becoming (albeit briefly) a Junior Research Fellow in Balliol in 1969.

Rodger and MacCormick had very different political orientations – for instance, Rodger had little patience for Scottish nationalism, including legal nationalism – but despite this, as so often with MacCormick's friendships, they formed a close bond. MacCormick and Rodger clearly discussed points of law together, and some of these discussions, including disagreements, found their way into print, e.g., the debate over third party rights in contract.[62] Watson, and his teaching of Roman law, was an important presence for both Rodger and MacCormick (Watson moved to Glasgow in 1965, where, in 1964, Rodger had just started his legal studies). MacCormick's legal studies in Oxford were thus certainly not confined to English law – in fact, he did a lot of Roman law,[63] and this was only enhanced by the friendships MacCormick formed, both with Rodger and with Watson. Indeed, MacCormick's interest in and knowledge of Roman law is attested not only by his translation of the first book of the *Digest*, but also in a number of publications where MacCormick tackles as yet unsolved 'riddles' of Roman law.[64]

Richard Hare and Moral Reasoning

Part of what is interesting about MacCormick's attitude to law – supported and enhanced, as I am suggesting, by his tutors, such as Harris and Watson – was that attention to technical detail was not at odds with attention to practicalities and questions of ethics and justice. Indeed, the two needed each other – just as Lamont had shown him, ethics needs the practical, technical details of law, and law needs the reflexivity and sensitivities of ethics. There was one other figure at Balliol in whom this combination of attention to both technicality and practicality was visible. That figure was Richard Hare.

61 MacQueen, 'Alan Rodger' (2013), 364.

62 Rodger, 'Molino, Stair' (1969); MacCormick, 'Ius Quaesitum Tertio' (1970).

63 MacCormick, 'Sir Neil MacCormick' (2007), 172. Later, as a tutor in Oxford, MacCormick examined in Roman Law for Law Moderations. To this should be added his exposure to Comparative Law via Bernard Rudden, Tony Honoré, and Otto Kahn-Freund.

64 See, e.g., MacCormick's 'Iudex Qui Litem Suam Fecit' (1977), which is a tribute to Ben Beinart, the founder and long-time editor of *Acta Juridica*.

MacCormick first read Hare in Glasgow in the early 1960s. His Glasgow diaries (in 1960–61) list Hare's *The Language of Morals* (first published in 1952) as one of the books he is reading, this being a book that clearly remained important for him, for it is also listed (with emphasis on Chapter 5 of that book) as a key source for MacCormick's research, in the late 1960s and early 1970s, on 'Law and Logic'.[65] Later, reflecting on his studies in Glasgow and Oxford, MacCormick recalled that Hare's moral philosophy 'connected well with my Kantian interests' in Glasgow[66] and he notes explicitly that when he went to Oxford he 'made contact' with Hare.[67] This 'contact' does not appear to have been especially personal. As Ved Mehta points out, vividly describing his own visit to Hare's house, Hare and his wife did host well-known reading parties for the most able undergraduate philosophers at Oxford,[68] but it seems unlikely MacCormick ever attended these. There was no particular personal connection that MacCormick would have shared with Hare – although it is difficult to resist mentioning that Hare's wife, Catherine Verney, who Hare married in 1937, traced her ancestry back to Robert Bruce, King of Scotland, and Hare was proud that his children were 'more than a quarter Scottish'.[69]

Despite there being no evidence of a personal friendship between them, there is no doubt that Hare's work on the logic of moral language was a frequent resource for MacCormick. This included *The Language of Morals* (1952), *Freedom and Reason* (1963 – the year MacCormick arrived in Oxford), as well as the later *Moral Thinking* (1981). I will be returning to the details of MacCormick's view of practical reason in Chapter 10, but it is important to briefly mention Hare's views and attitudes, for they were important for MacCormick. Again, even though MacCormick was not actively studying philosophy in Oxford, Hare's presence in Balliol (up to 1966), and MacCormick's continuing interest in logic and its connections

[65] See undated notes on Balliol notepaper, Edinburgh University Archives. The full list is: 'Levi, *Introduction to Legal Reasoning*; Jensen, *The Nature of Legal Argument*; Wasserstrom, *The Judicial Decision*; Hodgson, *Consequences of Utilitarianism*; Guest and Simpson in the *Oxford Essays in Jurisprudence*; Cross on *Precedent*; Castberg, *Problems of Legal Philosophy*; Hart, *Concept of Law*; Frank, *Law and the Modern Mind*; Stone, *Legal System and Lawyer's Reasoning*; Hare, *Freedom and Reason*; Cohen and Nagel, *Introduction to Logic*; Kelsen, *The Pure Theory of Law*; Popper, *British Philosophy*, and *The Logic of Science*; Austin, *Lectures*; Klug; Murphy, *Law, Logic in Ethics*; Toulmin, *The Uses of Argument*; and Wisdom, "Gods"'.

[66] MacCormick, 'Sir Neil MacCormick' (2007), 172.

[67] MacCormick, 'My Philosophy of Law' (1998), 141.

[68] Mehta, *Fly and the Fly-Bottle* (1962), 47.

[69] Hare, 'A Philosophical Autobiography' (2002), 293.

to moral and legal reasoning, both strongly suggest that Hare's work was an important part of his two periods in Oxford.

Hare was part of a generation of Oxford philosophers who fought in the Second World War. He had fought, for instance, in the Battle for Singapore (January to February 1942), which the Allies lost, and he was captured and spent most of the rest of the war in prison. As he recalled it later, when reflecting on this period of his life and its links to his philosophy, he said:

> My desire to be a philosopher had been increased by my experiences in the fighting and before. I have already mentioned the feeling of guilt engendered by the gulf between rich and poor in the world; India is a good place in which to observe this. I had assuaged any remaining feelings of guilt at killing people by saying to myself that I was not fighting for my King and country but on a more universal principle, for India, whose conquest by the Japanese would have been a calamity for its people, as was the Japanese conquest of China.[70]

This reflection offers a little summary of Hare's moral philosophy, though it is also interesting that Hare links his reasoning here, as he perhaps did not so much in his other work, to the emotions he felt at the time (with feelings of guilt triggering and informing the process of moral reasoning). Hare insisted that one could find morality in the exercise of reason, which for him meant acting on a principle that was universalizable. This was a principle that one, as it were, prescribed for oneself, such that one's conduct was guided by it. A principle was universal not in the sense that it was general – generality was something properly contrasted with specificity – but in the sense that it would apply to anyone in the same or similar situation. Acting on a universal principle did not, however, mean acting solely out of duty, in ignorance of the consequences of one's actions. Rather, attention to consequences could be included in the process of universalising the principle upon which one acted: in the above example, I can kill if, by doing so, I help save a people from the calamity of a conquest by a particularly evil foreign power.

Morals, then, for Hare, were a matter of reason – of practical reason prescribing for itself universalizable principles upon which to act. This 'prescriptivism', as he also called it, thus did without positing metaphysical strange objects, so-called 'moral realities' that one could intuit or 'moral truths' that one could describe. Morality was not a realm of realities or truths, but instead a much more grounded and practical process of rationally constructing and acting on principles, learning over time to become a skilled practical reasoner. This had its connection to the logical

[70] Ibid., 281.

positivists, especially A. J. Ayer, in that it avoided asserting the existence of strange metaphysical objects. But it went beyond them in looking for evidence of morals solely in, say, the expression of emotions. Instead, it took inspiration from work being done in Europe (especially by Alf Ross, Jorgen Jorgensen, and significantly with respect to MacCormick, Ota Weinberger) on the logic of imperatives (including legal language)[71] as well as, ultimately, from Kant's insistence on the practicality of reason.

Both of these inspirations – an imperative logic and Kant on practical reason – were already, and became even more so, crucial interests for MacCormick. There are several important observations to make about this approach to moral philosophy, for they help avoid misunderstandings – ones that Hare himself had to confront throughout his career. To avoid positing moral realities or moral truths did not mean that one was a moral sceptic or a moral relativist. Those pushing for moral objectivity could characterise positions such as Hare's in those ways, but this was misleading. For Hare, to pursue moral objectivity – again, by positing moral realities or moral truths – was to ignore something crucial and something that, once again, he had experienced when fighting in Asia: cultural diversity. As he put it himself:

> We only took two Japanese prisoners during the entire Malayan campaign. On being released, they went back to their regiments, saluted their commanding officer, and committed hara kiri to expunge the disgrace of being taken prisoner. This and many other illustrations of cultural diversity made me stop believing in a universal objective moral standard known by intuition without reasoning, such as is posited by Sir David Ross.[72]

Hare's wartime experiences had sensitised him too much to cultural diversity, which, for him, could not be divided easily, if at all, from moral reasoning. This diversity, one could say, offered a different kind of approach to moral realities or moral truths: they were linked closely to cultural practices. This did not demean them or make them any less moral, for there was no absolute morality that somehow stood above culture. Further, morality was not static: one developed, as a person living in a culture, learning to make distinctions, discerning consequences, and therefore crafting principles that made sense in the world one was in. Indeed, as Hare said in his *The Language of Morals*, to observe his students was to see that what they were doing was testing the 'set of principles' they had inherited from their

[71] Ibid., 289.
[72] Ibid., 281.

elders and making them their own: a painful process, but one which every generation had to do for themselves.[73]

Thus, to posit moral realities or moral truths that one could discern with, say, a moral sense, was to ignore both cultural differences as well as the history of morals (especially in the sense of a person's development over their life-time). For MacCormick, as we shall see, this was important, for it meant that it was possible, indeed desirable, to craft an approach to morals that was not authoritarian, but was rather democratic in spirit, acknowledging differences between persons, while still proposing (and thus finding some place for authority) a practical procedure for making decisions rationally. Again, as Hare insisted, to do this was still to do moral philosophy, but this was a politically sensitive, grounded, practical, real-world, and democratic approach to morals.

Hare had begun to articulate this approach in writing a thesis for the T. H. Green Moral Philosophy Prize in 1950 in Oxford, which was on the subject of 'Practical Reason'.[74] His thesis there was to culminate in *The Language of Morals* (1952), which, as noted above, MacCormick read while he was studying philosophy in Glasgow. Part of Hare's direct source for this book were the lectures of H. J. Paton on Kant in Oxford – published as *The Categorical Imperative* (1947), which MacCormick also read in Glasgow – and another part were a series of little-known essays on practical reason and Kant by Reginald Jackson published in the 1940s.[75]

The language of 'imperatives', in Kant but also in other writings on practical reason at the time, could be misleading: the idea, as Hare had to say many times, was not 'to represent moral statements or judgements as meaning the same as simple imperatives'.[76] Hare's theory was neither an emotivism, nor an imperativism, but, instead:

> ...a form of rationalism which, all the same, borrows important insights from these theories. It borrows from emotivism the negative idea that moral judgements are not essentially statements of moral facts, and from imperativism a positive idea about what they might be instead, namely, prescriptions. For there are other kinds of prescription besides imperatives; moral judgements might belong in the genus prescriptions, but not in the species of it called simple imperatives.[77]

[73] See Hare, *The Language of Morals* (1952), section 4.7.

[74] Hare, 'A Philosophical Autobiography' (2002), 285.

[75] See, e.g., Jackson, 'Practical Reason' (1942). This series of articles by Jackson appears to have been influential on work on practical reason in the 1950s and 1960s.

[76] Hare, 'A Philosophical Autobiography' (2002), 289.

[77] Ibid.

This is important, also for MacCormick, for otherwise, the language of 'imperatives' could be understood as a kind of command-based theory of morals (and possibly also, by extension, law). What distinguished moral imperatives from simple ones was precisely that they were principles, and of a particular sort: universalizable principles. When one acted morally one acted – and in order to act morally one had to act – under the guidance of universalizable principles. Significantly, this was less a process of imposing on others how they ought to act, and more a matter of disciplining oneself so that one acted in a way that respected others, precisely testing one's inclinations to act in a certain way by universalising them (again, one asked oneself: 'what if everyone acted on this maxim all the time?'). One acted morally when one tested and justified one's actions by principles that enabled one to respect persons and the values of living together. This was miles away from any sort of hierarchical, top-down imposition of commands, or any other authoritarian establishment of moral order; it was, instead, a matter of exercising one's conscience reasonably, i.e., with a view to respecting others and social life.

There was one final misunderstanding that was important to clarify. To be interested, as Hare was – and MacCormick too – in the logic of moral language, including in consistency amongst the moral statements one made and in an overall coherence amongst the principles one acted on, was not an exercise of abstract reason divorced from the realities one lived in. Quite the contrary: the whole point, as noted above, of avoiding positing moral realities and moral truths was to make room for a more real-world, practical, and grounded, moral orientation that made room for moral learning. Conscience, one could say, was like a muscle, which one trained in real-world conditions, i.e., precisely by exercising one's practical reason and thus testing one's inclinations and dispositions through constructing and acting on universalizable principles.

This was also crucial for Hare, whose approach to moral philosophy was in this respect profoundly practical. Hare was, for instance, fascinated by the philosophy of education – he had four children and the question of how to educate them morally was very important to him[78] – but he was also not one to shy away from the most difficult and challenging questions of his time. There are many examples of this, such as the lectures he delivered in Germany in 1955 on 'the duties of citizens whose government is acting

[78] Hare, *The Language of Morals* (1952), 75–6.

immorally'[79] and the final chapter of *Freedom and Reason*, where he tested his theory by applying it to racism. Hare was also active on numerous public bodies, writing on issues ranging from apartheid and bioethics, and it is no surprise that when the Society of Applied Philosophy was formed, he became its first President.[80] Hare's insistence, then, on clarity and lucidity, on consistency and coherence, in moral language, including attention to its 'logic', was not at odds with practical ethics: for Hare, that clarity was a condition of doing moral philosophy well. Moral philosophy could be both logical and practical at the same time. Indeed, this uniting of apparent opposites was said by many to be characteristic of Hare: as Price noted, many admired Hare not because of any 'doctrine' he held, but because of how he practised the 'discipline' of moral philosophy, in particular how he managed to unite 'apparent opposites: freedom and reason, tradition and rationalism, eclecticism and rigour'.[81]

All this was, as we shall see in more detail in later chapters, crucial for MacCormick. Not only did MacCormick practice a philosophical art devoted to blending opposites, crafting delicate spaces for thought in between rival views, but he was also fascinated by the prospect of reason being practical, and with how this was key to moral, political, and legal philosophy, including the relations between them (indeed, one way in which reason was practical was precisely because it created such inclusive spaces of differentiated unity).

More immediately, in the late 1960s, when MacCormick returned to Oxford, be began writing a book on the 'logic of legal reasoning'. The 1968 *Balliol Annual Record*, in its introduction to MacCormick as the new incoming Tutor in Jurisprudence, says that he is 'working on the logic of legal reasoning'[82] and, when he was leaving in 1972, MacCormick's sabbatical report notes that he has 200 pages of a manuscript on legal reasoning.[83] Of course, the impetus for this work was multifaceted: an important

79 Hare, 'A Philosophical Autobiography' (2002), 292; and see Hare, 'Ethics and Politics', *Listener* (1955).

80 Price, 'R. M. Hare' (2004), 136.

81 Ibid., 118.

82 *Balliol Annual Record* (1968), 12.

83 MacCormick says that he spent his 1972 Hilary and Trinity Terms 'working in the Bodleian Law Library and in College', but that he was unable to complete the book on legal reasoning 'chiefly because of the burden of preparing during the summer a course of lectures to be delivered in my present job', i.e., the Chair of Public Law in Edinburgh; he also, quite typically, 'sought and obtained permission to undertake teaching in Land Law' at Balliol 'to ease teaching difficulties consequent on my departure'; see the MacCormick dossier in Balliol (15 November 1972).

role, as we shall see in Chapter 5, was played by his two years teaching in Dundee (1965–67). Upon his return to Balliol, MacCormick continued what he had started in Dundee, namely his intensive reading of works on 'Law and Logic', and the manuscript that he had written in 1972 was to become – after a stint as Dean of the School of Law at Edinburgh – one of his most famous and influential works, *Legal Reasoning and Legal Theory* (1978). Though there were multiple strands that informed this work – including, as we shall in later chapters, his engagement with Hart, as well as the echo, for MacCormick, of the Scottish institutional writers on the principled coherence of Scots law[84] – a part must surely be attributed to the influence of Hare's approach to moral philosophy and his commitment to both the logic and practicality of moral language and the grounded and gradual exercise of practical reason.

Oxford Union President

MacCormick's time in Oxford was not only a time in which he was immersed in the study and teaching of English and Roman Law, and its technicalities, but also a time in which he was steeped in both local and not-so-local politics. This included student discipline in Balliol and Oxford (which I will consider in Chapter 5), and it included the more global context of protest and unrest, especially with respect to race and civil rights, in America.

Indeed, the global, and in particular American, context is important to keep in mind. Soon after MacCormick arrived in Oxford, John F. Kennedy was assassinated (on 22 November 1963). However, though of course momentous, this was not an isolated incident, but instead part of a broader history of civil rights struggle in America as well as struggles for independence and liberation worldwide. If we look a little further back, in June 1960 Congo had gained its independence, along with nearly twenty African nations. The year 1961 saw horrific events in France, including the killing of around two hundred Algerians (Algeria was to finally gain independence from France in 1964). In America, following protests and sit-ins in 1962 (alongside the Cuban Missile Crisis, in October 1962), the civil rights movement gained momentum with important protests in Birmingham, Alabama in April 1963, and an equally important March for freedom in Washington in August 1963, where Martin Luther King

[84] MacCormick, 'Stare Decisis' (1966), and 'Principles of Law' (1974).

addressed over a quarter of a million people. These protests and marches, and King's speech, were televised, and, like others in Britain, Oxford students were 'gripped by the drama of "the freedom marches and the brutality of Alabama's police … and the individual acts of black bravery on public buses and at school entrances"'.[85] A little earlier, in June 1963, Kennedy had proposed a Bill on civil rights in his *Report to the American People on Civil Rights*. The Bill stalled in the autumn of 1963 and it was only after the assassination that Lyndon Johnson, Kennedy's successor, was able to get the Bill moving again. The Bill was finally passed in the summer of 1964, but not before a whole string of events, including arguably a more combative stance from leaders of the movement. That stance included, significantly, for present purposes, Malcolm X, who also began his travels to Africa, seeking a more global presence.

Meanwhile, in the UK, the rise in immigration in the 1950s began to lead to conflict, with both anti-immigration riots as well as anti-racist political activity. Oxford itself had changed rapidly: 'between 1955 and 1965, Oxford had the fourth fastest-growing immigrant community in the country'.[86] This, in due course, led to a housing crisis, with many property owners in Oxford being reluctant to rent their properties to black students. Even if Oxford was not at the centre of these struggles,[87] there were still an important and growing political consciousness, especially amongst students, in Oxford. One important student body that was established in Oxford in the late 1950s, and only gained momentum through the 1960s, was JACARI: the Joint Action Committee Against Racial Intolerance. In 1959, this club had over 2000 members and was the biggest university club in Oxford.[88] Its membership was boosted in part by a change in the 'type of student at Oxford by the late 1950s', which now included 'increasing numbers of black and Asian students' – a change precipitated not only by a general increase in immigration, but also because of expanded provisions of Commonwealth scholarships and changes in Oxford admissions policies.[89]

85 Tuck, citing remarks of an Oxford student, *The Night Malcom X* (2014), 107.

86 Tuck, *The Night Malcom X* (2014), 70.

87 A better claim for that can be made for Smethwick, which was visited by Malcolm X in 1965 just days before his assassination, where an especially racist campaign in the elections of 1964 ('If you want a nigger neighbour vote Labour' was one slogan of the time: see Ambar, *Malcolm X* (2016), 23) had been endorsed, or at least not disavowed, by Conservative party candidate Peter Griffiths (who went on to win his seat). On Smethwick, and its resonances in Oxford, see also a special issue of *Isis* on the city and its events (21 November 1964).

88 Tuck, *The Night Malcom X* (2014), 101.

89 Ibid., 102.

JACARI kept a close eye on world-wide developments, including apartheid in South Africa, as well as the civil rights movement in America. JACARI was well-organised, and thanks to their efforts 'Oxford witnessed' – in 1964 – 'the most widely publicised student anti-apartheid demonstrations in the UK'.[90] There were clashes between these organisers and protesters – including Eric Abrahams and Tariq Ali – and the Proctors (those responsible for the University discipline in Oxford), throughout 1964, culminating in six of those students being charged with 'disorderly demonstrations and disobedience and for bringing the university's name into disrepute'.[91] Abraham's case, in particular, made headlines – it became, as Tuck puts it, 'a cause celebre in the city and in the press'.[92] Already then (in October 1964) the University tried to calm the atmosphere by conducting a review – the Williams Committee – into the power of the Proctors, though little was changed at the time.

Race was of course not the only political issue of these years – there were also crucial debates at Oxford around gender, as to whether all colleges should admit women,[93] and whether women could be admitted into the Oxford Union (they were in 1963), and there were broader changes in British politics, with the Wilson Labour government beating the Conservatives in the 1964 elections – but a good case can be made that race was especially important political issue in Oxford at that time. As mentioned above, race was a key issue in the 1964 British elections, and it is no accident that Britain followed America, in 1965, passing its first *Race Relations Act*. Again, the question of civil rights was, throughout this period, both intensively local and global at the same time: domestic crises were, simultaneously, international ones, and debates over civil rights (as well as rights more generally) took on both a local and a global tinge.[94]

In Oxford, all this was to find an especially telling apogee: the Oxford Union Debate held on 3 December 1964.[95] Martin Luther King had just won the Nobel Peace Prize (in October 1964) and Johnson was re-elected, beating Arizona Senator Barry Goldwater. The air was thick with pro- and anti-racial rhetoric. In an earlier speech, in the summer of 1964, to

[90] Ibid., 117.
[91] Ibid., 122.
[92] Ibid., 123.
[93] In 1964 in Oxford women formed only 16 per cent of the student population: see Ambar, *Malcolm X* (2016), 16.
[94] See Dudziak, *Cold War Civil Rights* (2000).
[95] For helpful accounts of this episode see Tuck, *The Night Malcom X* (2014); and Ambar, *Malcolm X* (2016).

the Republican National Convention, Goldwater had uttered the phrase: 'Extremism in the house of liberty is no vice. Moderation in the pursuit of justice is no virtue'. And it was this phrase that was chosen as the motion for the Oxford Union debate.[96]

The person responsible for this choice, as well as for the choice of speakers, was the President of the Oxford Union. Presidents of the Oxford Union were chosen for one term (roughly three months) and for the autumn term (known as Michaelmas in Oxford) the President was none other than the student who had been disciplined by the Proctors for the JACARI-led anti-apartheid protests, Eric Abrahams. By tradition, as Abrahams was speaking, there was another chair that evening for the debate, and this student too was one of the six previously disciplined: Tariq Ali. Abrahams's choice of speaker was Malcolm X, and the speech that he delivered that night, on 3 December 1964, was to be his final speech before an international audience (he was, as noted above, assassinated in February 1965). Interestingly, amongst the other speakers was Hugh MacDiarmid, the poet and Scottish nationalist (also speaking for the motion, and thus in favour of extremism and against moderation), though undoubtedly it was Malcolm X who was the star of the show. Indeed, his visit caused a stir not only in Oxford – where the *Oxford Mail*'s headline was 'Black Muslim in Oxford'[97] – but also in Britain, thanks to the BBC's coverage of the debate.

I have spent some time setting out the context of this occasion because it is directly relevant to understanding MacCormick's political experience in Oxford, especially as a student. The Oxford Union had two prestigious student positions, which were highly sought-after by politically active students: the post of Librarian of the Union and the post of President. Quite often, the Librarian of the previous term became the President of the next one. MacCormick was the Librarian in Michaelmas 1964–65 and he duly became President in Hilary 1964–65 (Ali was to become President in Trinity 1964–65). Indeed, it is at the beginning of this debate, on 3 December 1964 (the final debate of the term) – which can still be heard online[98] – that MacCormick gives his report as Librarian and is then recorded as having been successful in the Presidential elections for the following term.[99]

96 Tuck, *The Night Malcom X* (2014), 100.

97 Ambar, *Malcolm X* (2016), 11.

98 See www.youtube.com/watch?v=fhAmObHbjuc&t=296s (last accessed 19 January 2024).

99 Although it is not entirely clear from the recording, it appears that MacCormick beat Mr Roderick Floud, Nuffield, and that he did so by 214 votes to 455.

It is also in this debate that the report of the term includes notice that at the immediately preceding debate (there were usually between six and eight debates per term), on Thursday 26 November 1964, MacCormick had risen and moved the motion 'that deterrence and not reform is the most important aspect of criminal punishment', with one of the speakers including MacCormick's friend from Glasgow, John Smith. That choice of motion is itself significant, for it was one of Hart's central interests at the time, with a debate occurring between Hart and Barbara Wootton on the aims of criminal punishment.[100]

It is moving to hear, again at the beginning of this debate, MacCormick's voice: it is the earliest known recording we have of him speaking (in that moment, MacCormick was twenty-three years old). He does not seem overawed by the occasion: indeed, following his report of the books purchased for the Union library (ranging from *Quantum Theory of Solids* to *Studies of Some Problems in the History of England*), MacCormick quips that 'We've also received one presentation, the President's [i.e., Abrahams'] Autobiography: Not So Much a Way of Life, More a Program', which is greeted with a long laugh.

MacCormick, it seems, was a popular figure in the Union. Not only did he win the Presidency by a comfortable margin, but he clearly had a reputation as someone who, like many Union Presidents before and after him, would go on to have a successful political career. As Michael Beloff – who was Librarian in Hillary 1961–62, and then President in Michaelmas 1962–63, and later a well-known barrister – put it, after MacCormick's death, 'none of his [i.e., MacCormick's] Oxford Union contemporaries would have guessed that he would choose to excel in esoteric academic legal philosophy. We all had him marked down as the first Prime Minister of an independent Scotland'.[101]

MacCormick did not speak in the debate on 3 December 1964, and its details need not concern us, although the arguments for and against violence and moderation were certainly important for MacCormick – his own voice always in favour of the latter and against the former. What is significant for present purposes are two observations: first, that MacCormick was exposed to, indeed steeped in, the various struggles of student politics in Oxford in the period, including in questions over race and gender, and the role of rights with respect to those questions; and second, that he clearly had political ambitions, as well as considerable political skills, rising to become the President of the Oxford Union.

[100] Lacey, *Hart* (2004), 266–7.

[101] Beloff, *The Times* (11 April 2009), 84.

We have seen, in Chapter 2, how MacCormick himself contrasted debating in the Unions of Oxford and Glasgow. But it is important to emphasise, alongside those differences in the style and etiquette of debating, that the Oxford Union was – and still is – an especially visible political institution in Britain (in ways that Glasgow has never been, even if unjustly so). The Oxford Union, established in 1823, is regularly described as 'the most prestigious student debating organisation in the world, regularly welcoming heads of state and stars of screen'.[102] It has sometimes been called 'a kind of children's House of Commons', resembling 'a gentlemen's club complete with reading rooms, writing room and bar, and across the garden, Europe's largest purpose-built debating chamber'.[103] Speakers get dressed up, with Union officers in white tie and speakers in black tie, referring to each other as 'honourable member', and the walls are 'lined with busts of former Prime Minister who had been union men'.[104]

Unlike the Glasgow Union Parliament, with six political clubs sitting around in an octagonal shape, the Oxford Union debate is structured adversarially, with speakers sometimes preparing one side but then having to deliver the opposite to replace someone who dropped out. There is, as a result, more an emphasis on performance and thus on displaying a particular kind of political skill – more charm, arguably, than policy. Those who succeeded – often by way of 'carefully timed jokes, calculated lowerings of voice, and ad hominem jibes',[105] all of which are audible in the recording of 3 December 1964 – could be confident they would not only survive, but possibly flourish, in Westminster politics. Indeed, it was well established that 'once you had ascended the Union, Downing Street felt within your grasp',[106] and it is thus no accident that many politically ambitious Oxford students make it their primary aim to win the Presidency of the Union.

The Union President is, indeed, a figure of considerable importance for the Union. As Christopher Hollis expressed it, in his 1965 history of the Oxford Union, 'the orderliness, vigor, amusement and general health of the Union's debates depend so much on the President of the day'.[107] The

102 Tuck, *The Night Malcom* X (2014), 1.

103 Kuper, '"A Nursery of the Commons": How the Oxford Union Created Today's Ruling Political Class', *The Guardian* (19 April 2022), see www.theguardian.com/news/2022/apr/19/oxford-union-created-ruling-political-class-boris-johnson-michael-gove-theresa-may-rees-mogg (last accessed 17 September 2024).

104 Kuper, 'A Nursery of the Commons', *The Guardian* (2022).

105 Ibid.

106 Ibid.

107 Hollis, *The Oxford Union* (1965), 219.

President's role is delicate, and it is easy to get it wrong (something Hollis, having been a President himself, describes evocatively and clearly with practical insight):

> ...quite frankly plenty of Presidents do fail. One, anxious not to get the reputation of a prig and a kill-joy, allows too much rope to the buffoons who are trying to rag off the debate. Another, anxious not to be thought a tyrant, does not call the interrupters to order as soon as he should. Other Presidents make the opposite mistake – show too crudely from the first that Henry V is no longer Prince Hal and come down too abruptly, whether in committee or in debate, on those who had the previous term been their equals, and in muttered comments complain that the new young President is giving himself airs. Those who care to attend a debate at all wish the motion to be debated. They may welcome a little light relief and a modicum of horseplay but it very soon becomes tiresome, and the ordinary Member of the House wishes to see in the chair a President who has the courage and the tact to keep order and to preserve them from the intolerable tedium of the persistent interrupter or the professional buffoon. He despises the President who has not the wit or the courage to perform his task. Yet the President's task – that of holding the balance, of being firm without being pompous or tyrannical – of carrying the House with him without appearing to curry to it – is not an easy one.[108]

Being a President, then, offers intense training in the exercise of diplomatic and charismatic authority, with Presidents having to subtly balance many interests and values, as well as relate with a wide range of personalities, the features of which are only exaggerated by the young age of its members. Presidents also need to exercise political wisdom in choice of motions and choice of guest speakers, being responsive to the issues of the day, but also demonstrating leadership and adding their own personal flavour to the debates.

Motions for debate range from the more to less serious, e.g., 'The House prefers the Beatles to Beethoven'; 'The House believes that Southern Rhodesia should not be permitted independence until there is majority rule'; 'The House urges sanctions against South Africa'; and 'The House supports Arab interference with Israeli trade'.[109] Some of the motions also tackled local, university issues, potentially mixed in with larger ones, such as the motion on 6 June 1963, which debated 'That the State and University authorities should have no part in the enforcement of individual adult morality'.[110]

[108] Ibid., 221.

[109] Tuck, *The Night Malcom X* (2014), 114.

[110] Hollis, *The Oxford Union* (1965), 226.

The life of a Union President, then, is not only very busy (the President, in the mid 1960s, had a 'private office, messengers, private telephone and the like'),[111] but one that involves managing all the vagaries and passions of student political life, including confronting motions of protest.[112] From what we know, MacCormick was able to hold his own in such a demanding environment. Certainly, as we shall see in Chapter 5, upon his return to Oxford as tutor, he was entrusted with various positions of authority, where he had to exercise similar political acumen in tense relations between students and university teachers and administrators.

MacCormick built his reputation at the Union bit by bit. He did so primarily as a debater, which is unsurprising, given his experience in Glasgow. MacCormick's maiden speech was a spectacular success. Speaking against the motion 'That the British Police System is unworthy of the confidence of this House' (which was passed by 291 votes to 227), he is described as showing 'every sign of an independent and highly critical mind'.[113] Then, in a prophecy that was to come true, Edward Mortimer, the reporter (and future Chief of Staff to Kofi Annan at the United Nations), added: 'An ex-President of the Glasgow Union, he gave us a tantalising glimpse of what debating can and ought to be. On this form he should soon be President of the Oxford Union, too, if he stoops to seek the post'.[114] Tony Hart, writing a report of the debate for *The Oxford Magazine* didn't prophesise, but also praised MacCormick, saying that he deserved his applause, describing him as follows: 'A debater of some experience Mr MacCormick is ruthless with slipshod arguments in his opponents and an expert in the reductio ad absurdum'.[115]

The maiden speech was thus a success, but some subsequent performances less so, e.g., in a debate on the motion 'That the British Commonwealth has no significant part to play in world affairs', which was lost by 152 votes to 248, and in which Tariq Ali, in his first performance, is described as 'the Pakistani Tarig-Ali', MacCormick, along with a few others (including

[111] Ibid., 228.

[112] For instance, 'against the punishment of undergraduates, both male and female, who have been found guilty of sexual offences', or 'against a Proctorial censorship' of articles in student magazines: see Hollis, *The Oxford Union* (1965), 229.

[113] Mortimer, *Isis* (30 October 1963), 25. Mortimer was also, like MacCormick and Patten, one of the holders of the Coolidge Pathfinder Scholarship.

[114] Ibid.

[115] Hart, *Oxford Magazine* (31 October 1963), 50. We see again, as we saw with debating in Glasgow, that MacCormick's grasp of refutational rhetoric, including its humour, was a large part of his charismatic authority.

Abrahams), is only 'marginally excepted' from what is said to be an 'abysmal' floor debate.[116] Later still, in a debate on the motion 'That this House is ashamed of the British Empire', MacCormick is said to be 'still impressive but not so incisively clear as when he spoke on the police'.[117]

At times, MacCormick scores highly with his peers for witty repartee, e.g., in a debate on the motion 'That the British Government should subordinate its national decisions to those of the United Nations', which was passed by 274 votes to 200, MacCormick is reported as saying, in response to Maurice Mendelssohn who had said 'that nationalism was a father-substitute and we must walk on our emotional feet': 'That makes internationalism either a grandfather substitute or emotional stilts'.[118] Another such example, again with a Scottish flavour, was on the occasion of a debate on a motion that 'This House deplores the influence of African Nationalism on World Politics', which was defeated by 314 votes to 145. There, Michael Harloe, reporting on the floor debate, said:

> Wassim Sajjad (Wadham) made an interesting but irrelevant speech on the perils of nationalism and then we were treated to the spectacle of Dick Condon caressing his lapels and looking remarkably like Long John Baldry, who spoke up bravely for '1000 years of history'. When he inquired, 'What did we do when William the Conqueror came over?' he was informed by Neil MacCormick that, 'We Scots didn't take any notice'.[119]

Points and fans were thus won, sometimes more by witty repartee on the floor, than by performance as a speaker. Having said that, MacCormick certainly impressed on occasion as speaker as well. In a debate on the motion 'That this House would not fight for West Berlin', the reporter says this of MacCormick:

> Speaking without notes, the kilted Mr Neil MacCormick (Balliol) quickly took command of his audience with a solid opening. There was a very real sense in which you could not fight for West Berlin. He had his audience roaring with delight as he portrayed the international situation as a young lady awaiting her would-be seducer. A mutual accommodation was necessary. It was his eloquent discussion of how this accommodation might come (Rapacki, disengagement etc.) that held Mr Scott Thompson (Balliol) following him, to remark amiably that the Glaswegian had made half his speech for him.[120]

116 Mortimer, *Isis* (6 November 1963), 28.
117 *Isis* (27 November 1963), 8.
118 Mortimer, *Isis* (20 November 1963), 25.
119 Michael Harloe, 'Floor Debate', *Isis* (14 November 1964), 6.
120 GVJP (the author uses only this abbreviation), *Oxford Magazine* (5 February 1964), 184.

By the time of the elections for Union President, MacCormick had only been active in the Union for four terms. Indeed, an account of the elections published in *Isis* (on 28 November 1964) indicated that 'it will be interesting to see how he fares in the light of his four terms only in the Union'.[121] As the anonymous author of this report indicates, MacCormick was Balliol's candidate and 'the latest in the long line of hopefuls sponsored by effortless Balliol', which was an important voting bloc in the Union elections (others included 'the feminist vote, the political, religious and racial votes').[122] These particular elections were said to 'probably be of unprecedented interest'.[123] The two candidates for the Presidency were to 'fight' it out in a debate the night before. MacCormick's opponent, Roderick Floud, was a postgraduate student at Nuffield – a status that perhaps did not aid him, for the report indicated that this 'contributes to an unfortunate impression of aloofness and contempt for undergraduate politics'.[124] The report added that his 'debating style is dry, unbending and a trifle acid; his interests entirely serious. He has a reputation for painstaking administration and a Wilsonian capacity for factual administration'.[125] The report then turned to summarise MacCormick:

> By contrast, Neil MacCormack [sic] (Balliol), Librarian, is matey almost to a fault, a man almost without personal enemies. A sometime Officer of the Glasgow University Union, he is in his final year for a degree in Law. He is an experienced and quick debater with a strong line in lewd jokes. As Chairman of the Consultative Committee he might claim credit for the success of the membership drive, although he candidly admits that the Committee was not the decisive factor.[126]

In the event, as mentioned earlier in this chapter, MacCormick won the contest comfortably. Writing later, in 1965, about the previous year, Chris Sheridan noted that the choice between the two was 'far from difficult': 'Neil by then', i.e., since becoming Librarian the previous term, 'had become a great friend, apart from being fairly and squarely on the left-hand side of the fence' whereas 'Roderick, on the other hand, had begun to display, to an alarming degree, just those pro-Establishment feelings we were all against'.[127]

121 *Isis* (28 November 1964), 7.
122 Ibid.
123 Ibid.
124 Ibid.
125 Ibid.
126 Ibid.
127 Sheridan, *Isis* (13 October 1965), 14.

MacCormick is reported to have 'introduced his card' – meaning his term card of debates as President – by saying: 'I want a Union where as many members as possible can be attracted to come and speak, rather than be lectured to'.[128] According to Meakin, previewing the debates on this occasion, this 'isn't really what he got', perhaps submitting too easily to requests for 'a typical string of technical "debates" – NATO, Incomes Policy, Comprehensive Schools, Public Ownership', which offered only opportunities for the 'Union cloque' to 'have a go at each other over some hoary topic they've thrashed out twenty times before'.[129]

It is significant that MacCormick attempted to be inclusive in his choice of topics, though it also appears to be true that the term was thought to be a mellow and low-key one, at least following the previous term's excitement over the visit of Malcolm X. Indeed, it was in this term that the students heard the news that Malcolm X had been assassinated. A special joint meeting of JACARI and the Union was held, still under MacCormick's Presidency, on 6 March 1965, with James Baldwin speaking. Baldwin's remarks were printed in *Isis*. On that occasion, he said:

> Malcolm and I did not agree. He was a Black Moslem leader and then he was a Black Nationalist, and I have never been either. Yet he knew some of the same things because we were produced by the same circumstances; we are in revolt in different ways against the same conditions; we knew the same streets, knew some of the people, had in common beneath our public differences the knowledge that we were menaced, and our families were menaced, by the same indefinite forces. And these forces are precisely what make it so hard to read the evidence.[130]

MacCormick continued to debate after his term as President, and he is noted, in particular, to have delivered speeches on two occasions in May 1965: one on the motion 'That Blanket Welfare Benefits from the State are

[128] Chris Meakin, *Isis* (23 January 1965), 6.

[129] Ibid. In due course, the debates under MacCormick's Presidency were indeed reported to be: 'That the time has come to dissolve NATO', which was defeated by 185–197 (*Isis*, 6 February 1965, 10); 'That this House would have nothing to do with an Incomes Policy', in which Enoch Powell amongst others spoke (*Isis*, 13 February 1965, 12); 'That Christianity is the religion of revolution', which was won by 221 to 116 votes (*Isis*, 20 February 1965, 11); 'That this House believes that all schools could be comprehensive and State-run', in which Alasdair MacIntyre was said to give a brilliant speech (*Isis*, 27 February 1965, report by Mary Kaldor, 8); and 'That this House believes in a Conservative Philosophy', which was defeated 283 to 381 votes (*Isis*, 13 March 1965).

[130] James Baldwin, *Isis* (6 March 1965), 26. It is possible that this was held instead of the President's Debate, which would otherwise have been held on 4 March 1964, out of respect for Malcolm X.

irrelevant in an Affluent Society'[131] and another on the motion 'That this House would not fight for Queen and Country', in which he is said to have argued, not untypically, that 'Britons should fight for the principle that a country should order her own affairs as she thought fit'.[132]

MacCormick's graduation in 1965 did not prevent him from subsequent appearances in Union debates. There is one such occasion, though a few years later, that deserves special mention. Following a visit to the Union by the Queen in the week prior to 10 May 1968 (on the motion 'That personal freedom in Britain is being dangerously eroded') – the first time a monarch had visited the Union and heard the debates – the following week (i.e., the week ending 17 May 1968) the Union debated the motion 'That this House would like to see Scotland take her place between Saudia Arabia and Senegal in the United Nations'.[133] The motion had been proposed by Johnny Grimond, Balliol, a future writer for the *Economist* and whose father was a MP for Orkney and Shetland and Leader of the Liberal Party, who argued that, in addition to 'neglect of Scottish interests by Whitehall, notably from the fishing industry', Scottish representation at the UN was justified by 'self-determination for a people that was beginning to demand it'.[134] Opposing the motion was John Gray, who 'cited examples from Eire to show that national independence did not necessarily mean that either liberalism or efficiency were advanced' as well as Howard Rogers who 'defended the record of the Wilson government in Scotland and said that real progress was being made'.[135]

In favour of the motion were MacCormick himself as well as Winnie Ewing, who had just recently, in 1967, won a famous by-election contest for the SNP. MacCormick's performance is recorded in the following way:

> Speaking third and in favour, Neil MacCormick, Balliol ex-President, raised the standard considerably. He asked whether we did not think that if James had made Edinburgh the capital England would not now be trying to reassert itself. Indulging in some genuine debating – too infrequent in Union paper speeches – he knocked holes in those arguments of the opposition that he had been able to discover and left the House considerably more enlivened than he found it.[136]

131 *Isis* (5 May 1965), 6.
132 Leofranc Holford-Strevens, *Isis* (26 May 1965), 22.
133 *Oxford Magazine* (17 May 1968), 322–3.
134 Ibid., 322.
135 Ibid.
136 Ibid.

MacCormick was followed by Mrs Ewing, who is said to have 'deployed a battery of arguments with great force and charm and a welcome measure of wit'.[137] Her strategy was different to MacCormick's: 'Why, she asked, did the opposition speakers who had all accepted the principle of devolution to some degree, not take their principle to its logical conclusion of complete independence?'.[138] Scotland, she added, 'had been very patient; but at the end of 260 years England still exploited her'.[139] It was, the reporter summed up, 'a very good speech which got the reception it deserved'.[140] Indeed, in the result, the motion was carried by 169 to 93, with 'the nationalist success' being said to be 'on the strength of the arguments we heard, deserved'.[141] It is fascinating that the arguments for and against Scottish nationalism and independence that were, in due time, to get a much wider airing, were being tested this early on, in the Oxford Union, where MacCormick was by then one of its stars emeritus.

Race and Civil Rights in America

Before leaving this chapter, it will be instructive to look at the diary MacCormick kept of a trip to America he made in the summer of 1965. From Monday 19 July to Saturday 4 September 1965, MacCormick travelled – courtesy of Balliol's Coolidge Pathfinder scholarship, which he received, in that year, along with a number of other recent Balliol graduates, including Chris Patten, the future Governor of Hong Kong[142] – all around America, from Boston to Washington, and including Ann Arbor, Chicago, Utah, San Francisco, Las Vegas, Denver, Dallas, and Atlanta.

It was a whirlwind trip – not only fast-paced, often spending only one day per city, but also often otherworldly in its proportions, e.g., lunching at the Petroleum Club in Texas, after travelling there in a private plane, and then later taking a helicopter to the nearest airport.[143] The routes were well

137 Ibid.

138 Ibid., 323.

139 Ibid.

140 Ibid.

141 Ibid.

142 Patten famously said, on the occasion of his Royal Society of Edinburgh MacCormick lecture (17 June 2011), that when MacCormick arrived in Balliol, 'he took the College and Oxford by storm, not just because he played the bagpipes', but also because he had a 'genius for making friends' and 'the ability to discuss and debate rigorously, but without rancour': see www.youtube.com/watch?v=dK2zNvPQLJk (last accessed on 17 September 2024).

143 MacCormick, *College Pathfinder Report* (1965), 27. The report is available in the MacCormick Dossier in the Balliol College Archives.

trodden – MacCormick refers to 'the Pathfinder legend'[144] – with Balliol alumni and Balliol-established networks all over America. MacCormick met with Rhodes Scholars as well as with both prominent business and political contacts, including farmers on large ranches, newspaper editors, lawyers, and doctors. He went to the cinema (e.g., he reflects on the political satire in *Dr Strangelove*), he visited art galleries and national parks, he went to spectacles (from jazz to cabaret), and he did a great deal of dining and whiskey-drinking in old-fashioned, male-dominated, privileged clubs. 'Fun' is a word that appears often, and the diary is pockmarked with light-hearted moments and jokes – a reminder of just how much joy such convivial occasions gave MacCormick.

However, the diary is not only or even mainly light-hearted. It reveals a twenty-four-year old MacCormick confronting certain political realities in mid sixties America, filtering them to an extent through his knowledge of politics in England and Scotland, and reflecting, often with remarkable and disarming honesty, on his reactions and observations. This includes directly experiencing aspects of what he had already been exposed to, indirectly, in the debates of the Oxford Union: the politics of America, and especially its racial tensions. Indeed, although the trip is only two months long, one can trace, in the report, a change in tone and self-scrutiny, from a sense of distant amusement at the beginning to something much more serious, if not anxious and certainly more self-reflective, in its later stages.

Early on in the trip, on 21 July, in Boston, MacCormick, watching TV before dinner, finds it 'strange and quite amusing to see a hearty, out-of-door advertisement for Marlborough cigarettes somewhat ineptly juxtaposed to a film of US troops in Vietnam', but this is quickly forgotten over a 'very cheerful dinner' where, he says, 'I fear that in the later stage of coffee and brandy, I became rather boring on the topic of Scottish Nationalism – a conversational pitfall into which I too readily fall'.[145] Perhaps the most striking of the early, more cheerful, tone is his report on a visit to Letchworth State Park, which, as MacCormick says, was, until the early nineteenth century, 'all Indian Territory'. Here, he says, that 'for the first time, I fully realised how very primitive Red Indian culture was' and adds that it is 'small wonder that they are now so thin in numbers'.[146] He recalls the 'Red Indian' as a 'figure of fiction' from his childhood

[144] Ibid., 1.
[145] Ibid., 2.
[146] Ibid., 3.

reading and says that 'it will be very interesting to find out a little more of the facts'.[147] This comment is made in the same paragraph as when MacCormick reports wondering whether he should 'feign a cramp' by the pool, for there a 'large number of exceedingly curvaceous, prettily-tanned, and whistle-equipped life-guards'.[148] Just a few days later, when setting off to Chicago, he is 'bent on seeing the Civil Rights demonstrations', but expresses some surprise, when visiting a district of Chicago, that there are 'no obvious signs of segregation', adding that 'we saw a couple of baseball games with black and white people playing together'.[149] Still in Chicago, he expresses 'a real disappointment that we arrived too late to see any of the Civil Rights demonstrations'.[150]

The tone, however, soon changes and MacCormick begins to reflect critically on his own initial reactions. In the midst of a storm, near New Ulm, in Minnesota, reflecting on 'how understandable is the fear of storms and thunder and lightning among primitive peoples' he 'realised, 'once in the thick of it', 'that I, as a civilised man, had been a bit patronising towards primitives, or that I was more primitive than I had conceded'.[151] By the time he visits two Indian Reservations in the North of Minnesota – in particular the Red Lake Reservation – he finds himself at odds with his initial reaction, questioning the easy opposition he had made between superior, comfortable civilisation and a primitive way of life:

> We heard a pleasant anecdote of an Indian boy who was being treated by a local Mental Health worker. She asked if he lived on the reservation; he said he did not and that he lived down by the river near Walker. When she asked how his family had come to be by there, he told her that they had been driving by, had seen an attractive spot, and simply decided to live there. So, there they built a house and there they stayed. The amusing thing, in a way, is that the psychologist found this puzzling and funnily primitive. Like much else of what I saw of the Indian-way-of-life, it struck me as a pretty civilised attitude to life. Likewise their indifference to progress.[152]

Amusement still appears in this account of 'a pleasant anecdote', but MacCormick begins to distance himself from taking up that stance himself. He sees around him more sadness. Indeed, it is especially striking to

[147] Ibid.
[148] Ibid.
[149] Ibid., 5.
[150] Ibid., 7.
[151] Ibid.
[152] Ibid., 8.

see MacCormick reflecting on the plight of the Indians by analogy to what happened to Highlanders during the Clearances:

> Much of what happened to the Indians appears to me analogous to what happened to the Highlands in Scotland after the '45 and during the Clearances. Much the same blend of fear, ignorance and intolerance on the part of a more (technologically) advanced culture towards a more backward civilisation seems to have taken its toll in both cases, though the fate of the Indian seems to have been much the worse. It is perhaps a pity … that the Americans did not follow a similar imaginative course to that of William Pitt, when he recruited specifically Highland Regiments to fight in the Seven Years War (the French and Indian War) barely a decade after the 1745 Rising, thus making it possible for the Highland culture to fit into and grow with that of the rest of Britain – but perhaps this is nonsense.[153]

The confidence and lightness of the diary in its earlier pages is, if not entirely gone, then at least undergoing some serious self-scrutiny. He finds his own presence, for instance, in the Reservation, 'intolerably rude'.[154] Later, when in an airport in Idaho, he encounters 'a group of Indian forest fire fighters', of the 'Blackfoot Nation'.[155] He hears what has now become 'the same story' that 'apart from a few ventures such as this, the Indians in Idaho are by and large in the same kind of inert condition as elsewhere'.[156] This time, however, MacCormick does not accept this framing and characterisation:

> It is at least clear that the Indian culture of today is totally at variance with the characteristically 'Renaissance' attitude of modern America – individualistic, and having a firm belief in the manifest value of progress. It does occur to me, bearing in mind some of my Highland friends, that there is a quality of indolence which is intensively civilised, though also intensely annoying to those possessed of a faith in the value of moving mountains. I wish it had been possible – perhaps I should say that I wish I had the energy and aptitude for making it possible – to make social contact with some of the Indians.[157]

It is interesting that MacCormick's increasingly sceptical and self-critical observations are enabled by how he relates the experience of the 'Indians' he encounters to the experiences of the Highlanders. He works his way towards a more self-critical attitude via his own personal experience,

153 Ibid.
154 Ibid., 9.
155 Ibid., 14.
156 Ibid.
157 Ibid.

which he begins to universalise. This is not only a matter of recalling his 'Highland friends', but also the history of his ancestors: in Ontario, Oregon, for instance, he meets the family relations of one of his fellow Pathfinder scholars, whose mother turns out to be distantly related to MacCormick's grandmother, with 'both of them … born and brought up in Glenurquhart in Invernesshire'.[158] MacCormick recalls that 'in the time of the Clearances, in the 1880s, my grandmother's family was evicted and left for Canada, but got no further than Campbelltown in Argyll', and he finds himself 'amazed at the fortitude they', i.e., those who successfully migrated to America, 'must have shown in carving out a living'.[159] Here, and not for the first time in his diary MacCormick is balancing a growing sympathy for the plight of the Indians (and also, as we shall see, the Black communities) with an attempt to understand, again sympathetically, the attitudes of white Americans with which he increasingly disagrees. He draws on his knowledge – including his personal awareness of his family's history – of Highland peoples to do both: to reflect critically on his initial response to the 'Indian primitive way of life' and the alleged laziness, inertness, and indolence of the Indians, as well as to distance himself, albeit still sympathetically, with understanding, from the attitudes of white Americans.

By mid-August, be finds himself saying that 'The American ethos appears to be too much involved with the old frontier idea of individualism: Everyman's ideal is a house of his own, some land of his own, and a car of his own'.[160] He expresses a 'dislike' to 'the overindulgence of the young, in which present American affluence has resulted'.[161] He finds the 'detached, cynical, uncommitted attitude to life of Evelyn Waugh's people'[162] very much at odds with his own temperament. There is, in the Report, an expression of growing impatience with the highly privileged, white, distant, amused, and self-congratulatory mentality, and a growing sense of the need for a more serious, responsible, and self-critical attitude to Western 'civilisation and progress'.

And yet, this is only ever taken so far: MacCormick clearly feels the difficulty of spending time – a time that, at another level, he very much enjoys – with his privileged, white hosts, even those with views that are far removed from his own political sensibilities. This reaches a certain

158 Ibid.
159 Ibid.
160 Ibid., 17.
161 Ibid., 18.
162 Ibid., 16.

apogee when he meets 'Hanmer Cobbs', the Editor of a local newspaper in Greensboro. Mr Cobbs' 'faults were glaring' – for instance, entering the town's restaurant, Mr Cobbs introduces the Balliol Pathfinders as 'they aren't Civil Rights Workers', which has the consequence that 'the air grew warmer' in the restaurant.[163] He visits the 'Cobbs farm and plantation, and the country retreat', and sees the 'amazingly paternalistic attitude (by no means unfriendly) of Mr Cobbs to his black servants'.[164] But, although he disagrees with how Mr Cobbs lives and with his political outlook, he clearly struggles to square his more cognitive judgement with a more affectionate relation to the human being he is spending time with:

> My initial impression of Cobbs had been of a vast, coarse man but, as the day wore on, I was growing more and more to appreciate and like him. He was very friendly and his gruffness was all due to defensiveness about his way of life. We were, in truth, in the awkward situation of being faced with the kindness of a wholly-likeable man whose view of life was, to us, in most ways quite unacceptable. I do not know how to understand such a situation.[165]

This exercise in sympathy, even (or especially) with the views of those he disagrees with, was to become, if it was not already well established, a central feature of MacCormick's character. MacCormick tries hard to understand where the attitudes that he disagrees with come from – what could explain the strength of feeling, for instance, among White Americans in the South. He has no doubt that 'the Whites were in the wrong', but he tries nevertheless to see their point of view:

> The white people are clearly faced with the break-up of their present culture and with the loss of some of their privileges and comforts – obtained as they are at the expense of the black people. It is easy to sympathise with people faced with such a change and appalled at the ending of a known way of life. But, even while sympathising, I still felt that it was better that the change be made. Southerners everywhere were very kind to us, and Southern charm and hospitality lived up to its reputation, and this charm and kindliness was a fine thing and one which I should be sorry to think of passing. But, if their price is the rigidly-divided society, and the unequal distribution of comforts (everywhere plain in the South), I do not see how one could justify keeping the present structure of society.[166]

163 Ibid., 30.
164 Ibid., 31.
165 Ibid.
166 Ibid., 30.

Typically, MacCormick spends more time critically reflecting on his own processes of judgement, including his own initial affective dispositions – he speaks frankly, for instance, of how, when 'in the South … I was ashamed to find how glad I was not to be involved on the Civil Rights side'.[167] He judges, certainly, and he holds his ground – he repeats that he finds the arguments of the Whites 'wrong', and that the situation should change – but he combines this with sympathy for all sides, especially those he disagrees with. Perhaps, as he himself notes, this sympathy came easily, given how generously he was being hosted by White Southerners, and how much he genuinely enjoyed being in their company, but his frankness, then, in this diary, is all the more illuminating: he does not spare his own blushes, and he is honest about his own conflicting emotions, preferring to lay bare the emotional complexity rather than pontificate about being more superior and more enlightened.

There are a wide variety of political sensibilities – very much recognisable in light of his later writings – that MacCormick expresses in this Pathfinder diary. He expresses support, for instance, for a 'more gradual approach' to political change,[168] and he is impressed with 'the tremendous concern' he sees in America 'for education and a far greater involvement, at a far lower administrative level, in politics here than at home'.[169] Although he does not believe in America's confidence in 'progress', he does think there is a lot to learn from the practice of local democracy in American cities, e.g., with involvement in 'school boards'.[170] Interestingly, what he sees 'confirms my opinion that more devolution is needed at home', and he adds, after meeting with the President of the First National Bank in Marshall, Minnesota, which is a 'single unit bank specifically located in Marshall', and thus exercising 'greater local business autonomy': 'Being prejudiced against concentrations of power and responsibility and overcentralisation of government and business, I hope that financially this arrangement is as beneficial as socially it ought to be'.[171]

It is well to remember that this is MacCormick at twenty-four years of age, expressing attitudes that were to become of immense importance in his political and legal theorising in future years and indeed throughout his life. At this point, in 1965, he was still set on a career as a lawyer – one

[167] Ibid.
[168] Ibid.
[169] Ibid., 9.
[170] Ibid.
[171] Ibid.

of the persons he meets, a local dressmaker, Madame Smith, 'assured me that I would be a good lawyer'[172] – but it is interesting that, perhaps partly as a result of the encounters and experiences he has in this trip in America, he comes to see ever-increasing value in political involvement, especially in local politics. An illuminating example of this comes from a conversation with 'Max', a farmer in Billings, Montana:

> At one stage, Max asked us whether we, as educated people, felt a 'duty' to go into politics. We all recoiled from such a suggestion as evidence of arrogance, probably because to British ears it sounds rather like 'have you a duty to become an MP?' which it would be rather arrogant to answer in the affirmative. But, it became clear in further conversations that he was thinking rather in terms of local politics: e.g., school boards, state politics, etc. It is interesting – to me – to think that this misunderstanding could occur. We hardly think of local politics as 'politics' at all. Further evidence, in my view, of the greater health of local institutions in America than at home. Probably it would be better if people DID feel a duty to take a real part in such politics.[173]

MacCormick would go on to take such a duty very seriously, standing to become an MP on five occasions, and being involved in many local institutions, some more obviously political than others, but always with an approach to politics that was more about enabling local democracy (at various levels) than enforcing party ideology. It is interesting to see that these attitudes and dispositions, which were to play such a large role in his life to come, were already being articulated by a reflective twenty-four-year-old on a very privileged Balliol tour of America.

172 Ibid., 10.
173 Ibid., 12; original emphasis.

5

'Taking It to Hart'

Protest, Authority, and the Morality of Law

In English-speaking jurisprudence classes, from England to Australia, if MacCormick is mentioned at all, he is presented as a Hartian – a follower or disciple of H. L. A. Hart, and ultimately a positivist in the Hartian tradition. Given Hart's standing in the history of British twentieth-century jurisprudence, to do this is by no means meant to be derogatory or to somehow sideline MacCormick; quite the contrary, by being associated with Hart, MacCormick is being presented as a part of what was taken to be the most important and most insightful revival of legal philosophy after a period characterised as stagnation.[1] Nevertheless, framed in this way, MacCormick is largely understood to be a figure who, at best, qualified or made relatively minor adjustments to a picture largely determined by Hart himself. Further, for many, although MacCormick had made a valiant attempt at defending Hart from various criticisms, especially those of Ronald Dworkin (Hart's own preference as successor to his Chair in Oxford upon his early retirement), he was only, at best, partially successful. In short, there is a tendency to see MacCormick as but a footnote to Hartian jurisprudence.

It should be said at the outset that there is no doubt about the importance of Hart as a figure, not only in Oxford or more broadly Anglo-American jurisprudence, but also specifically for MacCormick. Duly acknowledging this, Hart certainly features as an important interlocutor for MacCormick in this book. However, neither the historiography of legal philosophy in the twentieth century, nor the task of reading MacCormick himself, are well served by overemphasising Hart's significance and influence.

There is also a further problem. The historiography of legal philosophy often focuses on debates in general jurisprudence, and typically between legal positivism and natural law, or, to a lesser extent, legal positivism and realism. As a consequence, Hart's work is itself often treated very narrowly, focusing almost entirely on *The Concept of Law* (1961), to the

[1] But see Hart's own more generous take in 'Philosophy of Law' (1953).

detriment of not only his other contributions in legal philosophy (especially to the philosophy of private law, criminal law, and public law), but also to his broader role in public debates of the age, including over the limits of state authority and the administration of discipline in universities.

The narrowing of the historical frame, both by overemphasising Hart but also by (ironically) limiting Hart's contributions, has particularly deleterious consequences for appreciating MacCormick. It has been the burden of the previous chapters to show just how much MacCormick was bringing with him to his encounter with Oxford jurisprudence. MacCormick was not arriving in Oxford as a blank slate to be written upon by either Hart or Hartian positivism. He came, instead, as a young man steeped in and exposed to a range of political issues, especially in Scotland, but also extending to student politics and civil rights issues in England and America, and as a young philosopher schooled in the sensibilities and methods of Glaswegian moral philosophy.

There are indeed two issues here, though they overlap. One is how to understand MacCormick's relationship with Hart. Another is how to understand MacCormick's relationship with positivism. I shall suggest, in this chapter, that while it is certainly helpful to pay attention to MacCormick's relationship with Hart, this relationship has to be understood much more broadly: not as confined solely to any debate between legal positivism and natural law, and thus by no means exclusively to Hart's *Concept of Law*, but rather also on, if not more so in relation to, Hart's politics, including both his approach to the state and its authority, as well as to Hart's engagement with the very concrete problems of proctorial and academic authority in Oxford amidst student unrest and protest in the mid-to-late 1960s. These aspects of Hart's politics were of particular importance for MacCormick, and it is in many ways through them that MacCormick gravitated to Hart. It is also through Hart as a deft political actor, as set against the background of MacCormick's own formation in Glaswegian moral philosophy, that MacCormick reads Hart's general jurisprudence, coming, eventually, in his 1981 book on Hart, to offer a much more strongly normative picture of Hart than Hart himself expressed.

MacCormick's Hart, then, was always coloured by the sensibilities of a Glaswegian moral philosopher, albeit a cautious one – one who avoided imposing any positing of moral truths or moral realities, being thereby mindful of the importance of respecting the diversity of moral orientations, while still being morally responsible. In this respect, approaching MacCormick via a dominant frame of a debate between legal positivism and natural law is distinctly unhelpful. It is also unhelpful, or so I have come to think, to ask whether MacCormick was a positivist: the label of positivism here is simply misleading and a distraction from understanding what really mattered to MacCormick.

To see all this, however, we need to proceed more slowly, with more attention to what was happening on the ground, in practice, including at Oxford, in the late 1960s and early 1970s. We need to see, in particular, how MacCormick's experience of Hart, and Oxford, was filtered through the debates over authority exercised in universities in this period. Throughout, we shall see how firmly MacCormick always had his eye on the moral value of law, and on how and why it matters to officials and citizens. MacCormick was able to do this theoretically in a similar manner to the way in which he himself lived authority, and thus related with others, i.e., by rationally justifying any exercise of authority, and thus acting out of respect for other persons.

Dundee

Before turning to Hart and Oxford, however, it is important to acknowledge the significance of the time MacCormick spent in between his periods in Oxford – first as a student from 1963 to 1965, and then as a Tutor in Jurisprudence and Frankfurter Fellow in Oxford from 1967 to 1972. The two years in between were spent in Queen's College, Dundee, then a division of the University of St. Andrews. The lectureship post in Dundee was MacCormick's first academic job and one which he took, as he himself put it, as a 'means to an end': 'At that time', MacCormick said reflecting back on this period sometime later, 'my intention was to return to Scotland and enter into legal practice in Edinburgh'.[2] Part of the reason for this was personal: as MacCormick explained, 'I initially took up an academic position with the aim of paying my way through qualification as a Scottish advocate, since after six years of study I wanted to get married and to have an income sufficient for that'.[3] But part of it must also be attributed to a genuine interest in legal doctrine and legal practice, including in Scotland.

[2] MacCormick, 'Sir Neil MacCormick' (2007), 172.

[3] Ibid., 171. MacCormick got married in 1965 and with a young daughter in tow (born on 21 August 1966), he was undoubtedly feeling the pressure of acquiring gainful employment. Karen Barr, MacCormick's wife at the time, recalls not finding it easy in Oxford. As she put it: 'I did not feel included in academic circles' and 'Oxford was not set up for a family – very much for bachelors with no family responsibilities' (interview with Karen Barr). This was, unfortunately, the common experience for many partners of Oxford dons.

Indeed, as we shall see in a moment, MacCormick's first publications in this period clearly indicate how intensively he was studying Scots law and how fascinated he was by its technical and practical problems. This interest in Scots law, however, was never in isolation, either from his interest in and knowledge of English and Roman law, nor from his Glaswegian moral philosophical sensibility.

The significance of MacCormick's time in Dundee is not, however, confined to MacCormick's deepening of his knowledge of legal doctrine and legal practice. In addition, MacCormick's return to Scotland coincided with a return, albeit a modest one for now, to Scottish politics. I will be focusing on MacCormick's relationship with the SNP in later chapters, but it is important to note here that it was while in Dundee that MacCormick 'made contact with the SNP in Perth and voted in a municipal election for the SNP candidate', further supporting his 'brother Iain in his newly started venture as Parliamentary Party Candidate for Argyll', and going in addition 'up to Oban to speak at a crowded SNP meeting backing also George Leslie, who recently put up a hugely encouraging result in the Glasgow Pollock by-election of 1966'.[4] This renewed connection with the SNP was only to get more intense after the famous by-election win of Winnie Ewing in 1967. The return to Scotland, then, renewed what was in any event never dormant in MacCormick, i.e., the interest in and passion for Scottish politics, though it did focus it somewhat on the fate and promise of the SNP.

But Dundee's significance for MacCormick went further still. 1965 was an exciting time to be joining Dundee Law School.[5] The years from 1960 to 1965 had seen immense changes – indeed, as Robin White calls them, a series of 'revolutions'.[6] This included the introduction of a full time LLB degree, without the need for prior studies or experience in practice. Accompanying this was emphasis on the importance of both jurisprudence and English law in the curriculum – indeed, it was recognised early in the 1960s that jurisprudence was 'to be a vital subject in the Faculty'[7] and early plans were made to recruit for a Chair in Jurisprudence. Further, after much wrangling, Honours were finally permitted in a law degree, thus turning the LLB into a four-year degree, now with advanced courses in law. Jurisprudence was to be a real star in this new degree: compulsory

[4] MacCormick, 'Campaigns and Gradualism Memoirs' (2008/9), 1.

[5] For an overview, on which the following relies, see White, *Dundee Law* (2018).

[6] Ibid., chapter 6.

[7] Ibid., 307.

courses in jurisprudence featured in the first three of those four years. English law, too, featured prominently, with courses on contract, torts, and criminal law, especially in the fourth year.

In due course, the first Chair in Jurisprudence was recruited. Initially offered to Alan Watson (who declined), the first holder was Ian Willock. Willock started in 1965, at the age of thirty five, and it is likely that it was Willock, who also immediately took on the deanship, who recruited MacCormick (possibly via the advice of Watson). Willock had written a PhD in Glasgow on the history of the jury in Scotland and his interests in jurisprudence were broad. As White characterises it, Willock was 'never closely tied to any school of Jurisprudence' and he treated the subject 'as a device to explore a wide range of topical legal issues', with jurisprudential courses under his leadership tackling such topics as 'criminal responsibility, industrial relations and race relations (the latter two very unusual for their time)'.[8] Importantly, too, it is clear from his later writings that for Willock, it was vital that legal scholars found ways of collaborating with sociologists. His contribution, to the first issue of the *British Journal of Law and Society* (in 1974) was tellingly entitled '*Getting on with Sociologists*'.[9] In this piece he sets out to 'confront more squarely the difficulties inherent in the relationship of lawyers and sociologists in the hope of facilitating the increasing degree of contact between them'[10] – an aim that MacCormick himself emulated, as we shall see later, in his institutional theory of law, and that was also very much in keeping with MacCormick's inclusive, relation-generating character.

[8] Ibid., 322. This breadth is in part reflected in the questions asked in the 1967 jurisprudence exam, which one suspects MacCormick too had a hand in crafting. The questions include more (to contemporary eyes) familiar ones, such as one on Hart ('The command theory seems breath-taking in its simplicity, and quite inadequate'), and another on Austin ('"The state" is usually synonymous with "the sovereign", the individual or body bearing the supreme power' (Austin). Is this an adequate definition of the state?'), but also less familiar questions, such as: '"A continually more efficacious social engineering". Discuss the limitations and implications of this approach to law'; questions on *Marbury* v *Madison* and on the First Amendment in American constitutional law; and two questions picking up on the European and international context of law respectively, 'In what ways may the European Human Rights Convention be expected to affect the rights of Englishmen?' and 'Can any sensible meaning be given to the phrase "the rule of law" in either a national or an international context?' (University of St Andrews Examination, Jurisprudence – General Course, 7 June 1967).

[9] Willock, 'Getting On' (1974). Incidentally, this same issue includes a short note by MacCormick on 'Privacy' (1974), illustrating what might be termed a Willockian approach to a pressing social issue.

[10] Ibid., 3.

Willock not only approached the research and teaching of jurisprudence as closely related to practical, social problems of the age, but was also personally involved in local reform and politics, including serving on the Stewart Committee on Alternatives to Prosecutions and setting up the Dundee Legal Advice Centre and the Scottish Legal Action Group.[11] It is, then, very significant, that it was Willock who recruited MacCormick and who had asked MacCormick, as MacCormick himself said, 'to prepare a course of lectures on logic and legal reasoning'[12] as well as to teach courses in English law.[13] This was important for MacCormick, not only because it encouraged him to pursue his already-strong interests in the relationship between moral reasoning and logic and the practice of law, but also because it further strengthened MacCormick's attitude to law as something that could be, and should be studied from the perspective of how it could be of moral value to individuals and communities.

It is likely, too, that Willock influenced MacCormick's attitudes as a teacher. The Dundee Law School was small (at that stage, no more than sixty students per year), which facilitated close links between staff and students. Willock was known for organising student trips to Loch Tay as well as for his willingness to engage students in debate in class. MacCormick likewise was to acquire, even in the short space of two years, a reputation as a popular and approachable teacher. As White reflects, drawing on personal experience:

> It is worth recalling his [MacCormick's] popularity among students… His style of lecturing was distinctive, involving 2½ × 5 record cards with notes about the relevant cases thereupon, removed one by one from the left side pocket of a hairy tweed jacket for exposition, then transferred to the right side pocket (except when dropped on the floor). He readily appeared at student parties, and in 1967, fulfilled a promise to play his bagpipes on the top of the Dundee Law on a Sunday morning, though requiring to be 'dragged from his pit' to do so.[14]

Once again, MacCormick's trusty bagpipes were to single him out in the memories of students and staff alike. Indeed, the Dundee community – being rather small – was not only significant for its friendly relations

[11] White, *Dundee Law* (2018), 323. There is now more acknowledgement of Willock's leading role in the development of Scottish legal scholarship and teaching: see Keane and Robson (eds.), *The Ian Willock Collection* (2023).

[12] MacCormick, 'Sir Neil MacCormick' (2007), 172.

[13] White, *Dundee Law* (2018), 326. It is also Willock and MacCormick who together started a weekly Jurisprudence Discussion Group in 1965: see Peter Robson's remarks in the 'Introduction' to *The Ian Willock Collection* (2023), 2.

[14] Ibid. See also White, 'Recollection', *The Scots Times* (4 August 2009).

between students and staff, but also for the collegiate and convivial atmosphere amongst staff, which included, in White's words, 'the most friendly Gordon Cowie, the most clubbable Jim Robertson, the most amicable Jim Ryan, the most entertaining J. W. R. Gray, the most earnest Ian Willock, and the most stimulating Neil MacCormick'.[15] The conviviality – the joy in each other's company – was crucially important to the scholarly and pedagogical vibrancy of Dundee in this period, and together with its generative mix of approaches and disciplines, again largely thanks to Willock, this period in Dundee was undoubtedly highly significant in MacCormick's development, just as much, if not more so, than the later experience tutoring in Oxford.

In addition, MacCormick's time in Dundee was also marked by his first publications – indeed, his piece on the rights of the public to access the seashore[16] – itself a very practically oriented topic – was the first to have been published by a member of staff in post in Dundee.[17] It was also marked by his having taught the first generation of full time LLB students in Dundee, amongst whom, significantly, was Zenon Bańkowski, MacCormick's subsequent close friend and interlocutor in Edinburgh, who graduated with the first-ever First in Law in 1969 (as part of a Joint Honours Law and Philosophy degree).

Although I cannot dwell on it here, it is worth underlining MacCormick's approach to law in his first-ever publications, while still teaching in Dundee. These included a piece, in the *Juridical Review* (1966), on the then-recent statement that the House of Lords would 'no longer apply the strict rule of *stare decisis* to its own decisions'.[18] For MacCormick who, importantly, embraced the idea that 'the law may be governed by more rational principles than mere ancestor worship',[19] this was most 'welcome', but it did mean that more reflection was needed on the kinds of standards that were to guide judges in this brave new world of legal reasoning. MacCormick's analysis, though brief, is already marked with features that were to be his hallmark in work on legal reasoning in the years to come: it is full of examples of cases, from both English and Scottish legal systems; and it is informed by a broader history of theorising legal reasoning, again both in England (especially via Bentham and Austin) and in Scotland (especially via Stair).

15 Ibid., 327.
16 MacCormick, 'Seabathing' (1967).
17 White, *Dundee Law* (2018), 326.
18 MacCormick, 'Stare Decisis' (1966), 197.
19 Ibid.

Furthermore, MacCormick's approach in this piece is sensitive to the multiple factors that affect, and in his view also ought to affect, the practice of justification in the courts, including: first, showing that a justification does not directly conflict with existing authority (via the technique of distinguishing or indeed overruling a precedent); second, that it is desirable, including in terms and thus via consideration of 'hypothetical consequences';[20] and third, that it offer, via analogy (both with cases and statutes) 'warrant' for the proposed justification, especially when it ventures beyond current law. The room MacCormick made in this piece for policy considerations playing an important and legitimate role in legal reasoning, informed, as he puts it, by 'the modern approach to sociological jurisprudence (in a wide sense)',[21] all the while still making a case for a kind of practical reason in the practice of 'the courts in a democratic welfare state',[22] is, again, in light of later work, typical of his approach. This is an approach that not only drew on MacCormick's training in moral philosophy in Glasgow, but also received further encouragement and impetus from his teaching and his colleagues in Dundee, especially Willock.

The two early pieces in the *Scots Law Times* – one, as mentioned above, on the public right of accessing the seashore and the other on the *Misrepresentation Act* of 1967 – both demonstrate MacCormick's thinking as a future Scottish advocate, tracing the potential impact of English law on Scotland.[23] It is important, however, that even though MacCormick approached English statutes and cases from a Scottish perspective, he did not do so with any legal nationalist defensiveness: on the contrary, he thought, for instance, that the *Misrepresentation Act* might bring benefits to Scottish contract law, if only to remind the Scots of their older tradition, which had since been Anglicised. Thus, he noted, with some relish, that 'Not for the time, we may observe the irony of English law seeking, as pastures new, fields once happily grazed by Scots'.[24] MacCormick's legal art here, as elsewhere, involved asserting a Scottish identity, with awareness of its distinctive history, but always with an openness to improving Scots law, no matter where the influence may come from.

[20] Ibid., 211.
[21] Ibid., 207.
[22] Ibid., 208.
[23] MacCormick, 'Misrepresentation Act' (1967); 'Seabathing' (1967).
[24] MacCormick, 'Misrepresentation Act' (1967), 192.

'1968 and All That': A Crisis of Authority?

Student Unrest in Oxford and Beyond

Leaving Dundee, and arriving back in Oxford, MacCormick entered a cauldron of unrest, protest, and fervent discussions over the scope and limits of authority in universities. Although, in 1967, and in the years to come, this would become ever more intense, issues around student discipline and the authority of the Proctors in Oxford started much earlier. It is clear, for instance, that trouble with Proctors and questions being asked about Proctorial authority were already prominent in the early to mid 1960s. Joint Action Committee Against Racial Intolerance had begun organising protests against apartheid in South Africa in 1963, and as noted in Chapter 4, by 1964, six of the students who participated in one such protest had been 'gated' by the Proctors. Students had been voicing concerns with the Proctors in February 1964, with one editorial – in *Isis* on 22 February 1964 – simply asserting: 'Proctors go Home'. The tone of that editorial suggests that already then the concerns raised had been articulated many times before:

> Oxford Proctors have done it again. Just when we were beginning to have humanitarian doubts that perhaps they really are people after all, they have come out with a piece of dictatorial interference in the lives of students that ranks with the classic examples of the bans on lecture reviews, carrying banners, and parking cars in the centre of Oxford.[25]

Bans had indeed been issued on the kinds of information that could be included on political leaflets. By the time the six students had been punished by the Proctors, pieces in student publications questioning Proctorial authority were coming quick and fast. An especially telling example is a piece co-authored by the six students in *Isis* on 10 October 1964:

> When you matriculate you officially become a member of Oxford University; you offer up your soul to the safe keeping of the Proctors for the duration. And in a way you have been done. You aren't given time to read the small print. Henceforth you can't park a car in the centre of Oxford... your car must display a green lamp... Your bedtime is now midnight and you can be fined for being abroad in the wee hours (hence the tradition in the Union of recording the hour of adjournment as '11.55 Proctorial Time'). You can't leave Oxford without permission... You can, you can't, you must... A whole more such rules are hidden away in those

[25] Peter Gillman, 'Editorial', *Isis* (22 February 1964), 5.

> dusty Statutes – many fossilised in their original Latin; many are quaint, most are redundant and all want thoroughly revising.[26]

The complaint about the secrecy or non-transparency of the rules was one of a number of protests against the violation of 'natural justice'. This was extended to the process via which students were brought before the Proctors and the way they exercised their power:

> Imagine a court of law in which the accused is brought before the judge without previously being told what he is accused of; where he is not permitted a legal representative; where the judge informs the accused of the charge and then decides on a verdict and punishment; where there is no effective course of appeal – and you have the blueprint of the most primitive judicial system in the civilised world. Yet that is how the Proctors work.[27]

Right from early on, then, in 1964, criticism of Proctorial authority was linked to issues with the publicity of rules as well as the fairness of the procedure for adjudicating student discipline. Given the entanglement, in these criticisms, of questions raised about the legitimacy of proctorial authority on the one hand, and law and legal procedure, on the other, it is no surprise that they attracted the attention of politically and philosophically minded law students and dons. Richard Buxton, one of the members of Oxford's jurisprudence discussion group in which (from 1967) MacCormick also participated, and a future judge, wrote in 1964 that proctorial authority and the way it is exercised:

> ...runs counter to some of the principles most highly regarded in the university's government. This is a democratic university, yet the Proctors seem to be answerable to no-one. College autonomy, particularly with regard to matters touching undergraduates, is thought to be important, yet the Proctors are an exclusively university institution... Granted the need for some disciplinary measures it is nonetheless important that they should be justly and rationally administered, and on this score the proctorial system scarcely gives grounds for much enthusiasm.[28]

Buxton characterised proctorial authority as an 'informal autocracy' and called for numerous procedural changes, including splitting the various powers exercised by the Proctors, so that 'the decision as to guilt and penalty should be taken by someone other than the principal witness for the prosecution', adding: 'It cannot be satisfactory for such wide

26 Eric Abrahams, Tariq Ali, Nick Fogg, Gerry Fowler, Chris Meakin, Bob Smyth, 'The Proctors', *Isis*, 10 October 1964, 9.

27 Ibid.

28 Buxton, 'The Proctors', *Oxford Magazine* (4 February 1965), 188.

discretionary powers to be exercised by two individuals' (there being two Senior Proctors, along with four Junior or Pro-Proctors).[29] These were not isolated complaints: student magazines regularly carried editorials or articles stating, e.g., that 'The Proctors have acted with their usual flair for tactlessness and heavy-handing stupidity'.[30] These only increased from the mid 1960s on.

Although Oxford had its own particular disciplinary system, and although its College structure placed it, along with Cambridge, somewhat in its own category, the troubles and student protests at Oxford were of course but one of many occurring in universities at the time. 1964 had seen well-publicised protests in Berkeley, where in October 1964 a student had also been arrested, and in similar circumstances concerning the freedom of speech, also in relation to racial tensions and anti-racism protests. One can, of course, trace some causes of protest in Oxford to changes in the numbers of students and their backgrounds, and to the concerns raised by students as to the relevance of an outdated and overly narrow curriculum,[31] with some of those concerns taken seriously by academics and senior administrators and resulting in numerous reviews (in Oxford and beyond).[32] For instance, the Franks Commission, in 1964–65, was a major self-examination of the Oxford system, though it came out very much in favour of it and took little notice of student complaints (despite the Student Representative Council (SRC) having given 'some well-presented evidence' to it).[33]

The changes in admissions and numbers of students from a variety of backgrounds also had an impact on relations between junior and senior members, both in Colleges, where the increasing gap was felt,[34] as well as, even more strongly, at the level of the university, where there was, in truth, very little communication. But changes in Oxford alone do not give anywhere near a complete account of the causes of student unrest from the mid 1960s on. As Keith Thomas articulated it:

[29] Ibid.

[30] Angus Hone, 'Editorial', *Isis* (25 May 1965).

[31] For example, the debate about teaching Latin in the late 1950s and early 1960s is telling in this respect, but institutionally so was the debate over the establishment of the Student Representative Council (SRC) in 1961.

[32] See Harris, 'The Arts and Social Sciences' (1994), 225–9. See also Kidd, *Twilight of the Dons* (forthcoming), and especially chapter 8 on the strange role of All Souls College, Oxford, in these various debates (strange because they were the one College without undergraduate students).

[33] Harrison, 'Government and Administration' (1994), 704.

[34] See generally, Thomas, 'College Life' (1994).

> The reasons for this change lie in the social history of the period. Growing prosperity had made young people an important consumer group. An international youth culture had developed, based on popular music and distinctive styles of clothing. It was disseminated by the mass media and intensified by the invention of the contraceptive pill. In Oxford, the passing of the national service generation, the arrival of television sets in the JCR's and the increase in the proportion of undergraduates from state schools, all helped to make junior members responsible to these wider changes. They felt a new affinity with students in other universities.[35]

The Oxford-based changes went along with broader changes, and each reinforced the other. Indeed, as Robert Gildea and James Mark point out, in their introduction to a study of the 1968 generation in Europe, the 'late 1960s and early 1970s marked a moment of political and cultural radicalism during which the authority of governments, institutions and ways of thought were challenged across Europe'.[36] The students participating in protests at university did not see themselves as protesting only against procedural irregularities in the administration of student discipline. Authority itself seemed very much on the line. Many student activists 'saw themselves as part of a common anti-authoritarian revolt for greater democracy, inspired by anti-imperialist politics globally'.[37]

The broad range of targets of criticism by students is borne out in Oxford's student magazines of the late 1960s. What we see in these student publications is a mixture of protest against society in general – and in particular its hierarchies and divisions between classes, races, and genders – along with protest against Proctorial and, to a little lesser extent, academic authority in the university. There was, in short, a general revolt, in particular by the young, and in Britain, Europe, and America especially, against tired old social structures and authorities, including, but by no means necessarily focused on, the kinds of structures and authorities that affected students most immediately in their university environment. One could argue that the protests against university discipline were but a microcosm, an intensely felt microcosm, of a much broader distrust of and dissatisfaction with authority and the organisation of society. But this, of course, made this microcosm all the more significant.

It is important to get just a sense of the tone of the student voice in this period, for it will allow us to see the delicate nature of the task facing university Dons and administrators (including MacCormick and Hart).

35 Ibid., 204.

36 Gildea and Mark, 'Introduction' *Europe's 1968* (2013), 1.

37 Ibid.

Writing in May 1968, Peter Adamson, the then-editor of *Isis* and a future philosopher, wrote, in an editorial piece entitled 'Academic Democracy':

> One of the most important things which the senior members of this university will have to decide soon is whether the university exists for dons alone or for both dons and undergraduates alike. If the answer, as seems fairly necessary from a brief glance at the composition of Oxford, should be the latter option, it must be vital to allow the other element of the partnership – the students – to voice their suggestions in some orderly way; indeed, if senior members refuse to face this problem, the peaceful workings of the university could be seriously undermined.[38]

The references to potential violence were common. Indeed, student publications show the students engaged in a debate as to how far protest could be taken and when, if ever, violence was justified. Thus, for example, Christopher Hitchens (Balliol), a Committee Member of the more radical Oxford Revolutionary Socialist Students Federation, put the position of his group as follows: 'Peacefully if we may; violently if we must', and called for a range of reforms, including abolishing examinations and short-circuiting 'the artificial distinctions between students and society'.[39] Others, though, such as Michael Burton (a past captain of Eton, President of Balliol JCR, and now Chairman of the Student Council), took a more subtle view, declaring 'I am not a canvas-cleaning radical' and that 'I have an innate feeling everyone is reasonable. Let's give them [the University administrators] a chance to show they are'.[40] There were thus a range of views, but even then, the scope of the student protests, and the general tension in the air, was very palpable.

This scope extended beyond dissatisfaction with the disciplinary system and into the details of academic content and manner of teaching at Oxford. Thus, for example, in a spread on 'Students: Democracy or Anarchy', Gareth Stedman Jones, a future influential historian, including biographer of Marx, certainly advocated for changes to the disciplinary system – arguing that the 'private lives and … public political lives' of the students 'should only be subject, like that of other citizens, to the constraints of the civil courts' – but he also added that the student movement would not 'properly be called revolutionary' if students did not 'open up liberated zones of critical knowledge in the dead body of institutional learning'.[41] Writing a little later, in 1969, but indicative of the

[38] Adamson, 'Academic Democracy', *Isis* (8 May 1968), 1.
[39] Hitchens, *Isis* (9 October 1968), 11.
[40] Burton, *Isis* (9 October 1968), 11.
[41] Stedman Jones, *Isis* (29 May 1968), 18.

kind of critique being made in the late 1960s of the curriculum at Oxford, G. G. Amyot, said that 'we', i.e., student socialists, 'did not want to force students to follow a rigid syllabus which will prescribe Marx and exclude Mill', but 'we do want to give students a choice, so that they may study, for example, Hegel instead of Hume' – this was, he added, 'the only way in which students can really regain the keen interest in intellectual endeavour' that the university should in any event be supporting.[42]

Once again, for many of these students, there was little distinction to be made between the university and society as a whole: both needed radical reform. Speaking in the name of the socialist student voice, Victor Bulmer-Thomas, Paul Cartledge, and John Lean argued that 'the university is part of the fabric of British society', and that the 'university does not only function as a purely academic institution', but instead 'propogate[s] and perpetuate[s] the ideology of the ruling class', taking for granted 'the presupposition[s] of western capitalist society'.[43] And, they added, as again was quite typical of the period, the 'direct action' they had taken, such as the 'Whit-Monday occupation in 1968', was 'triumphantly successful' and would be undertaken again, depending 'partly on what reforms the Hart Committee advocates and the speed with which they are put into effect'.[44]

And, indeed, as this first reference to the Hart Committee suggests, Hart was soon thrust straight into the eye of the storm of these student protests and complaints. On 13 May 1968, Hart was appointed, by the Hebdomadal Council, to lead the Committee on Relations with Junior Members. This Committee soon became known as the 'Hart Committee', and its subsequent report, 'the Hart Report'. Hart certainly had his work cut out for him, but it is also important to note that his appointment appeared to be acceptable both to the Dons and administrators as well as, on the whole, to the students.

From the outset, Hart showed that he was willing to take student protests and complaints seriously. Initially, the committee was to 'consider … what arrangements and channels are desirable for consultation between the University and Junior Members on faculty and other university matters affecting them, and the machinery for considering proposals and suggestions emanating from Junior Members'.[45] Significantly, and in a move that the students appreciated, Hart sought 'clarification' of the

42 Amyot, *Oxford Magazine* (7 March 1969), 229.
43 Bulmer-Thomas, Cartledge, and Lean, *Oxford Magazine* (14 March 1969), 243.
44 Ibid., 244.
45 *Hart Committee Report* (1969), 7.

committee's terms of reference so that the committee was able to also consider and address changes in the 'present disciplinary arrangements' – an extra power which was duly granted.[46] Hart not only made sure that the Committee had the powers it needed to address student concerns, but he also took the task very seriously, working for an entire year, meeting on fifty-five occasions, consulting widely with both students and staff, and, in May 1969, writing a large portion, and then editing the remainder, of the 203-page report.

To be appreciated, Hart's stance and the manner – as we shall see in a moment – in which he wrote about and then sought to address student concerns, needs to be put in the context of other staff reactions at the time. Initially, the University, in answer to the Junior Members' Petition to the Hebdomadal Council in early 1968, which called for 'recognition' of the student voice, e.g., via official acknowledgement of a body representing junior members, had responded by saying that 'because the life of junior members is still mainly organised around the college and the tutorial system, there exist plentiful channels and opportunities for undergraduate opinion to be made known to senior members'.[47] Such a 'body', the University said, was 'not necessary' and 'not desirable'.[48] In answer to calls, in the same petition, for changes in the disciplinary system – especially for avoiding the Proctors acting as 'policeman, prosecutor, judge, and jury',[49] the University had answered that 'the existing disciplinary system was fully reviewed as recently as 1965', and that the calls for 'natural justice' in disciplinary proceedings were misplaced, for the system was 'perfectly defensible as a system of justice simpliciter', and in any event, the cases 'where the Proctors are themselves witnesses very rarely arise'.[50]

From the perspective of the students, this was dispiriting enough, but the University's stance was, if anything, made further insulting by a steady stream of opinion from certain dons, such as J. R. Lucas, who argued that by 'not organising undergraduates into constituencies and communities, we leave them much freer to make their own individual choices', calling for 'the demands of Student Power' to 'be resisted' and arguing that 'the present Oxford system is better than any alternative suggests'.[51] There were paternalistic (to say the least) analyses, by Dons, of 'the psychology

[46] Ibid., 8–9.
[47] *Oxford Magazine* (15 March 1968), 267.
[48] Ibid.
[49] Ibid.
[50] Ibid., 269.
[51] J. R. Lucas, 'The Tutorial System', *Oxford Magazine* (22 November 1968), 83–5.

of the British Leftwing student today', which characterised such a figure, named 'Leftie', as having the 'strong tendency to dramatise the importance both of his own political actions and of all that is happening in the world at large'.[52] This 'Leftie', it was added, 'employs an ill-understood, pseudo-intellectual Marxist jargon', had an 'evident desire to control the universities',[53] and was very much a symbol of 'a vast and general decline in standards of decency'.[54] For this kind of student, 'Permanent happiness needs permanent revolution, permanent rebellion, permanent protest'; it was a 'totally negative outlook on life', and one that did not provide 'a positive solution to the undoubted problems of advanced industrial society'.[55] There appeared, in the pages of these university publications, an enormous and yawning gulf between many of the Dons and the attitudes of the university administration on the one hand, and, on the other, the voice of the students, especially on the radical side.

We have already seen that Hart did not take the approach of the above Dons, and thus sought to reduce, rather than increase, the gap between staff and students. Nevertheless, Hart was also aware there were limits to how far he could go and, indeed, how far, in his own view, he should go, i.e., there were limits to student protests and complaints, especially about academic authority. We thus need to look in more detail at his response.

MacCormick and Discipline in Balliol

Before turning to the details of Hart's response, however, it is important to pause here and ask: how, if at all, is all this relevant to MacCormick? First of all, MacCormick himself was very much in the thick of these debates. He had already been exposed to them when he himself was a student in the mid 1960s, especially as President of the Oxford Union in what was already then a volatile time. Upon his return to Oxford, in 1967, he was to take on a number of positions of authority at Balliol, such as serving as Camerarius, i.e., the Fellow responsible for sorting out accommodation allocation – a position of considerable power, especially given the difficulties surrounding accommodation in Oxford at the time – as well as Assistant Tutor for Admissions. Most significantly, he served as Chair of a 'committee appointed to revise the College's disciplinary code and

52 Raymond Kershaw, *Oxford Magazine* (24 January 1960), 132.
53 Ibid.
54 Ibid., 133.
55 Ibid., 134.

procedure.[56] Even more relevantly, albeit just after the Hart Committee reported, he was the College's candidate for, and duly served as, Pro-Proctor (one of the four Junior Proctors to the two Senior ones) in 1969–70. Further, when he left Oxford, in 1972, he was about to become 'Dean of Balliol'[57] – again, a position of considerable authority, dealing with the then-very-delicate matters of student discipline.

Just as in Oxford generally, so in Balliol – if not more so – tempers were high. MacCormick's positions of authority in Balliol were precisely at the peak of student radicalism there. As Martin Kettle, who was Balliol's JCR President in 1969–70 and future *Guardian* journalist, reflected later, there was much happening: there was 'the campaign against the Proctor's ban on political leafleting in 1968; the occupation of the Clarendon building in 1970 over the issue of student files, and the very large campaign against Margaret Thatcher's plan to restrict the funding of student unions in 1971'.[58] Of course, these were University-wide issues, but, within Balliol, 'an intimate and self-regarding environment … where everyone knows everyone else', such 'campaigns' were not only 'political', but could also 'rapidly turn personal'.[59]

Reports vary as to just how large the more radical student movement was at Balliol, with some arguing that it 'would be a mistake to claim that all Balliol was in a ferment over the new cultural revolution'.[60] It is also possible that in 1969 the alleged radicalism was especially noticeable given that the JCR President immediately before Kettle was Michael Burton, who 'adopted a constitutional approach to achieving change'.[61] On the other hand, it was Burton, as representative of JCR Presidents across the University, who had led the above-mentioned petition, which itself led to the formation of the Hart Committee.

Either way, there is no doubt that under Kettle relations became 'more strained',[62] and resolutions of the JCR included motions of no confidence in the-then Dean (March and May 1970), as well as, a little later, in November 1970, motions: that 'High Table be abolished', which was passed; that 'Balliol refrained from electing a Proctor unless Junior

56 MacCormick, '1968 and All That' (2009), 13.

57 Ibid.

58 Kettle, 'It Was Right to Rebel', *Balliol Annual Record* (2009), 19.

59 Ibid.

60 Moynihan, 'The Events of '68: A Social, Not a Political, Phenomenon', *Balliol Annual Record*, 31.

61 Ibid., 32.

62 Ibid.

Members are given full voting rights', which was rejected; and that 'students are given full control over their own discipline', which was passed.[63] As Jones noted, in his history of Balliol, in the years 1968–72, 'the JCR Committee pressed the Governing Body hard'.[64] Jones added:

> It was a difficult time, during which the patience of the representatives of the senior and junior parts of the College was often tested to its limits, but fragile civility was generally maintained. Complete breakdown of relations did, sadly, happen twice – when personal attacks were made on the Dean and Chaplain [in 1970], and when the College was mortified by the misbehaviour of its students on the occasion of a visit by Sir Edward Heath, then Prime Minister [on 21/22 June 1971].[65]

It was only 'from 1972 onward', with the changes introduced in 1970–71 'agreed and notionally in place' that 'confrontations and disagreements became more and more infrequent'.[66] These changes, to recall, were precisely the ones that MacCormick had introduced as Chair of the disciplinary committee – changes that, as Thomas noted, included not only greater student involvement and representation in disciplinary procedure, but also changes in nomenclature, referring no longer to 'gentlemen admitted to College', but instead to 'men' and 'students', describing the JCR as 'the Balliol Students' Club'.[67] This signalled a kind of political recognition of the undergraduate voice, and an inclusion of undergraduates as part of a broader 'worldwide student community'.[68] One could say that these were changes that reflected a new respect for undergraduate students; a new recognition of their standing as members of the community.

It is important, at the cost of repetition, to underscore MacCormick's role in the introduction of these changes at Balliol. The Balliol archives reveal that MacCormick certainly played a significant, if not leading, part in the undoubtedly difficult negotiations over the form and content of these disciplinary rules, at least from 1968 onwards. MacCormick is recorded as a member of the Joint SCR/JCR Disciplinary Committee from at least 3 December 1968, and he then becomes the Chair, drafting the relevant documents – including the new draft disciplinary rules – in the crucial year of 1971, and continuing through to at least early 1972. The changes

63 Ibid., 33.
64 Jones, *Balliol College* (2005), 303.
65 Ibid., 303–4.
66 Ibid., 304.
67 Thomas, 'College Life' (1994), 205.
68 Ibid., 204.

to the rules reveal the close attention paid to the rights of the accused, including rights of appeal, confidentiality, and a right to be informed, in writing, well advance, of any intention to prosecute. MacCormick was thus involved in drafting, if not being the lead drafter, of a set of detailed and highly contested procedures, and it is a testament to him that he steered these negotiations sufficiently well to have the rules approved (as they were, ultimately, first by a JCR general meeting on 30 November 1972, and by the governing body on 11 December 1972).[69]

As we shall see in a moment, Hart's take, in this period, on these issues and both the need for change and the manner and style of those changes, were to prove important for MacCormick, not only because he was himself dealing with similar issues at a College level, but also because they were entangled with certain philosophical questions – about law's authority, the rule of law, the rights of the accused – that MacCormick, along of course with others in Oxford, was reflecting on. Although MacCormick's way of dealing with these issues, including the way he, too, sought to balance the needs of the students and the staff, was not in the public eye in the way that Hart's was, we can gain a sense of his approach from MacCormick's own reflections, many years later, about these years, and from stories told about him at that time.

For MacCormick, the roots of unrest and conflict in this period had as much to do with legitimate concerns about disciplinary procedure as they did with what was a generational gap. There was, MacCormick said, a real difference between the generation born in the 1940s and 1950s who were 'in haste to get on with real life', especially 'after years lost at war or in barracks', and thus 'never had time to get involved in the politics of university organisation and governance', and the new generation of 'English students who in a kind of reciprocal way felt that their status as adults was challenged, indeed it was denied by the concept of the undergraduate *in statu pupilari*'.[70]

The gap that MacCormick saw, then, was not between the junior members and the senior members of the University, but instead between 'people of my own age, born just before or during the war of 1939–1944 and those born after it – subsequently dubbed the "baby boomers"'.[71] The later missed the kind of experience that the former had, which was that 'life had been largely an experience of the amelioration of conditions following on the

[69] Balliol Archives of the Joint SCR/JCR Disciplinary Committee (1968–72).

[70] MacCormick, '1968 and All That' (2009), 13.

[71] Ibid., 14.

grim years of war and post-war and rationing', with 'the relative liberalism of our way of life' contrasting 'favourably with the USA of the McCarthy years and the troubled conditions of countries like France and Italy'.[72] As a result, MacCormick himself, identifying with this earlier generation, had 'found it difficult to take on board the degree of what seemed radicalised resentment of the world ... that was experienced by our immediate juniors'.[73]

Amidst these real divisions, MacCormick sought to articulate a middle path. He agreed that 'in substance ... real change was at hand', and that with regard to discipline in College and the University the time was 'ripe for a measure of re-thinking', but this could not be at the cost of 'civility'.[74] This was, indeed, crucial to his approach. For MacCormick, it was vital to emphasise that one could maintain civility while 'contesting great political questions'.[75] Once again, for MacCormick, debate on such questions, as well as on the issues of more local changes in disciplinary procedure at University, certainly ought to be held, voices listened to, and changes made, but not to the point of disrupting teaching and thus not via violent or repressive protest. A sense of the manner and style of MacCormick's interventions at this time can be gleaned from a reflection by Andrew Graham, Master of Balliol from 2001 to 2011, who, when he heard that MacCormick was unwell in 2008, wrote a letter that contained the following memory:

> I am not sure if you know this, but, as far as I am concerned, you are a core part of what makes Balliol a significant college. When I first arrived, I was immediately deeply impressed by your powerful and perceptive interventions in the discussions at College Meeting. You always seemed to know more, and to have thought more, than most others about what was going on. On top of this came a specific event. It was in the midst of the student turmoil and you, at least as I recall, chaired a seminar in Lecture Room XXIII with many of Balliol's brightest and most difficult students gathered in the room. The topic was when, if ever, it was justified to disrupt the teaching and research of a university. The debate went to the core of the issue. The audience were, at least to start with, not particularly sympathetic. They were more interested in end points than in the particularities of the argument. You, however, were scrupulously fair but, equally, not willing to give an inch on principles that you felt had to be defended. It was, for me, a defining moment. I already liked and admired Balliol, but, from then on, I knew it stood for something of deep and lasting significance.[76]

72 Ibid.
73 Ibid.
74 Ibid., 14–15.
75 Ibid., 14.
76 Graham, 'Letter to Neil MacCormick' (4 November 2008).

One of MacCormick's guides in this delicate task of both addressing student concerns and defending, in a principled manner, the aims and values of university education, was, in addition to Hart to whom I shall return in a moment, the-then Master of Balliol, Christopher Hill. Hill had been a student at Balliol, and then a Fellow and a Tutor in Modern History for many years. He was – and this is significant in MacCormick's case – an expert in English constitutional history, specialising in the constitutional crises of the seventeenth century, where he took a broadly Marxist approach, paying special attention to the voices of protest from below. An example of his work, which is indicative, too, of his approach to what was happening in Oxford at the time, is *The World Turned Upside Down* (1972), which seeks to recover, and treats with utmost seriousness and respect, the constitutional creativity of voices from below, thus avoiding the elite bias of so much of English constitutional history.

Hill became the Master of Balliol in 1965 (remaining so until 1978), and it is typical of his approach that soon after being appointed he deprived himself of the power 'to obstruct the wishes of the Fellows in elections', transferring various prerogatives of the Master to College Committees, and creating the office of Vice-Master.[77] A number of Balliol figures have written on Hill's approach to authority,[78] noting how he 'steered between agitated dons and passionate student radicals', on one hand 'wryly enjoying the Marxist reference when they painted "Eggheads of the world unite!" on the walls of Balliol, under his study window', while at the same time finding constructive ways to channel student dissatisfaction, for example by increasing student representation on College committees.[79] Clearly, for MacCormick, Hill was an important exemplar at the time – a model for how to relate with both students and Dons in this delicate period. It is instructive to see just what MacCormick appreciated in Hill:

> Christopher Hill became for me, then and thereafter, a principal mentor and guide in the exercise of academic authority. He led by example not precept. He treated people with universal courtesy, even under acute disagreement, and he largely succeeded in keeping not just the peace but the conditions of mutual cordiality across deep disagreements about substantive issues and about reasonable ways to pursue issues of substance. We had our moments of tension no doubt. But we remained a cohesive and

[77] See Jones, *Balliol College* (2005), 294.

[78] See also Pennington, 'Christopher Hill' (2005).

[79] Corfield, 'Christopher Hill: Marxist History and Balliol College', *Balliol Annual Record* (2009), 39.

> coherent academic society. It has come as no real surprise that so many of the firebrands of the that time have become respected figures commenting on affairs in a decidedly Hill-like way.[80]

MacCormick clearly gravitated to Hill for how he lived his position of authority, and thus the manner or style with which he related to others. There was, as the above quote indicates, a 'Hill-like way' of dealing with conflict and even 'acute disagreement' – a way that depended on courtesy, cordiality, civility, and respect.

The Hart Report

Hill mattered to MacCormick, but there is no doubt that a, if not the, crucial figure that modelled academic – and perhaps more generally philosophical – authority for MacCormick in Oxford was Hart. So, to return to the question posed earlier: just how did Hart negotiate student needs and concerns with those of the Dons and administrators at this time, and why was the manner or style with which Hart did so important for what attracted MacCormick to Hart?

A piece in *Isis*, on 9 October 1968, gives a good flavour of the manner or style with which Hart related with the students. Entitled 'The Hart Attack', it is an interview with Hart, conducted by Philip Maxwell, and was clearly intended by Hart as an invitation to students to engage with the inquiry. The interviewer does not pull his punches: 'Would your terms allow you to recommend, say, that undergraduates be included with voting powers on to faculty committees?'. 'Yes', replies Hart, 'we could recommend this if we thought it the appropriate machinery'. Ok, then, well 'What did you think of last term's sit in at the Clarendon?'. Hart's response was typical of his approach:

> I don't know how big a group is prepared to do sit-ins and this kind of thing. Not many, I should think. Their stock tactic is to seek confrontation with the authorities on an issue which looks plausible to a much wider group. It was used at the Clarendon with success. Some undergraduates genuinely interested in constitutional reform have submitted detailed recommendations on specific topics and channels of representation, and this is immensely valuable. I sharply distinguish between these people and the extremist militants – who regard us as liberal fuddy-duddies. So far, no evidence has been submitted to my committee by these militants. I should love some.[81]

80 MacCormick, '1968 and All That' (2009), 15.
81 Maxwell, 'The Hart Attack', *Isis* (9 October 1968), 9.

There is an undoubted paternalism in the tone of this reply, but it is also one that seeks to acknowledge the efforts of the majority of the students, while still inviting the 'extreme militants' to the table. But what did Hart think of the arguments being made by the militants? Here, again, Hart found a way of both acknowledging the arguments being made, even agreeing with them to an extent, but limiting their relevance for the purposes of the inquiry he was leading:

> They [the militants] are out to change society, using universities as a jumping-off point. They are, or think of themselves as, guerrillas in the field of culture. This is a very different thing from the others. I don't want the University sacrificed for some 'visionary view' of society. But don't think I'm not in favour of social reform. I agree with the militants that society is hell, in many respects – materialism, deadened factory life, the failure of the organs of representative government to reflect people's aspirations – these are all disastrous. But I don't agree to destroying something very precious, liberal university education, from which the real hope of social reform comes, and replacing this by the militants' series of perpetual discussion groups or shout-ins or what-nots.[82]

Hart here plants one of his feet firmly on the side of the students, even the militants. He shares, along with them, a reformist zeal, acknowledging that 'society is hell'. But he also places one foot, just as firmly, outside that view, placing a limit around the arguments being made, bracketing out the university as a zone that has distinctive aims and distinctive values. Alongside this is Hart's ability to create distance, not only by attempting to genuinely understand the roots of the views of the students, and thus characterising them from afar, but also by articulating how he believes the students are likely to see him, e.g., as a 'liberal fuddy-duddy'.

The approach is a mixture of intimacy and distance, of inclusion and exclusion – a mode of pragmatic accommodation, which combines acknowledgement and even identification to an extent with some clear differences. When asked, for instance, whether he was involved in protests in his own undergraduate days, Hart reports that he was – though also expresses surprise as to whether the students 'really want to hear about it', given it was 'forty years ago'. He did 'protest against the Proctors, of course, but not', he adds, 'against authority in general'. What concerned the students then, said Hart, was 'individual liberty', the 'private life, sexual tastes and literature' – 'we didn't worry much about changing society'. Perhaps this 'was a frivolous, aesthetic period with a serious undertone',

[82] Ibid.

but in any event, it was not the kind of 'organised', 'militant', 'guerrilla'-like approach of (some) current students. This, he insists, has its limits: the university is not society writ large. Even if it is true that 'society is hell', we need a more disciplined, focus inquiry as to the aims and values of university education.[83]

At this point, Hart reiterated his invitation to the students, asking them a series of questions (relating in particular to the modes of participation of junior members in both academic and disciplinary decision-making), and calling for them to express their views to him. This was a sincere invitation and, in the result, over 200 students did submit evidence. Hart made sure that the Report included the names of these students, as well as the various associations and bodies that submitted views. Thus, despite the graffiti around the University saying 'Don't take it to Hart' – it is clear that many did precisely that, some as individuals and some via more formal channels, with more expressing their views less directly in student magazines.

The Report itself continued this difficult balancing exercise, oscillating between recognition and acknowledgement of student needs and concerns on the one hand, and, on the other, giving Dons and administrators their due, introducing changes that increased student participation but also limiting them carefully, once again creating an atmosphere in which views were listened to, even sympathetically so, but were also circumscribed and put in their place.

Significantly, for present purposes, Hart's approach was often characterised as a 'rational one': Mercurius, for instance, whose humorous commentary on Oxford were widely read at the time, said, undoubtedly with no little irony but also in ways that did capture a grain of truth, that he found himself 'truly … almost in love with' Hart's 'Socratic rationality'.[84] There seemed to be general consensus that the document was not 'revolutionary', but instead 'peaceful' and 'progressive – but barely'; it was a 'breakthrough' for Oxford, but 'outside Oxford, it breaks little new ground'; 'within a controlled framework, students are invited to participate', especially in the 'setting up of disciplinary regulations'.[85]

Of course, there were complaints, for instance from John Prebble, the President of the SRC in 1969, that the Report 'has not proved to be the daringly progressive document we hoped; not a canon, but a squib, and a

83 Ibid.

84 Quoted by Harrison, 'Government and Administration' (1994), 706.

85 Marshal Jordan Breger, 'Plugging the Dike', *Oxford Magazine* (30 May 1969), 323.

rather damp, slightly patchy squib at that', which was not entirely in touch with the present political situation in English universities'.[86] But there was also acknowledgement that, 'in all probability … moderate students in Oxford' will accept Hart's recommendations, if they are implemented, and also some recognition that Hart was up against 'a lot of old men', and had to put 'sugar on the pill' of reform, so that there had been some genuine progress made thanks to Hart.[87] Even those students critiquing the Report said that 'perhaps if taken as a very tentative first step … Hart could be quickly gulped down', especially as there was a 'moderately delightful sauce … provided by the proposed destruction of the monolithic force of Proctordom'.[88] Throughout, both then and in later years, when the Report has been judged, what appeared to be emphasised is Hart's pragmatism, his very practical and even 'optimistic rationalism',[89] with both Alan Ryan and Tony Honoré arguing that the Report 'did much to bring students peacefully into the governance of Oxford'.[90]

Hart's particular exercise of practical rationality, of a principled approach to the value and authority of a university and its teachers, all the while mixed in with an ability to nevertheless relate, listen, and sympathise, to an extent, with the students, is present throughout the Report. Thus, for example, although it was 'quite wrong to approach questions of academic authority with the assumptions that a university either is or should be a microcosm of society at large',[91] students did make a 'powerful' case that 'those who have the authority to decide academic matters which are of vital concern to any generation of students, such as the syllabus and methods of teaching and examination or assessment, should be under an obligation to explain their exercise of their authority to students and to modify their practice in the face of cogent criticism'.[92] Authority was needed, but it had to be reasonable and responsive to criticism. Indeed, this was precisely the kind of authority that was the hallmark of the university: 'authority divorced from such readiness to give reasons to those over whom it is exercised and to attend to their arguments is a foreign

86 Prebble, 'Hart Report', *Oxford Magazine* (6 June 1969), 341.

87 Phillip Hodson, 'Heart to Hart, The Hart Report: A Critique', *Isis* (14 May 1969), 4.

88 Ibid.

89 Lacey, *Hart* (2004), 287.

90 Honoré, 'Hart' (1994), 317. In Jennifer Hart's *Ask Me No More* (1998), Alan Ryan is quoted as saying that Herbert Hart 'wasn't frightened by the young', even if he found them 'harder to understand' as he got older: 225.

91 *Hart Committee Report* (1969), 22.

92 Ibid., 24.

element in a university whose whole educational policy is designed to foster critical and rational discussion'.[93]

What the University needed to avoid – and what had been emerging, especially in light of a gap 'in age and experience between teacher and taught' in recent years – were 'dogmatic forms of authority which do not listen to the student'.[94] 'For this generation', the Report continued, 'new forms of authority must be provided, if authority is to be acceptable at all'.[95] Articulating such a new form of authority did not mean all agreeing on a substantive vision of what a 'single community of scholars' ought to be like, and that was because there were likely to be very 'diverse conceptions' of what a community was and what it needed. What was important was that there were no great divides between 'Them' and 'Us', i.e., the students and the teachers, for such divides produced 'a howling wilderness where no academic purposes can prosper'.[96] Although academic authority had to be protected, this could not be done in such a fashion as to make this authority remote and incapable of critique and reform. As the Report articulated it (with fascinating echoes of an approach to authority that was clearly different to that articulated later by Joseph Raz):

> So far as authority in educational matters was concerned, the teacher was regarded by the students, [at an earlier time, when 'gentlemen' talked to 'gentlemen'], to an extent no longer possible, much as a doctor is regarded by most patients – as an expert practising a science, in the exercise of which a student could have no views of value and about which it would be idle and even dangerous for the expert to consult him. Social changes have eroded these older bases of academic solidarity and it is necessary to replace them by sharing responsibilities where inequalities of knowledge, experience, and continuity are not important factors, and by providing channels for critical discussion and argument where they are.[97]

This search for a 'new form of authority' was clearly a delicate task, but there is no doubt that this is the conceptual and political space that the Report attempted to carve out. Practically speaking, this meant both protecting academic authority from the more radical critiques of the university, while at the same time bringing academic authority down to earth.

In terms of the former, Hart's famous 'Appendix' on 'Student Radicalism in Oxford' was crucial, for it argued that a university was not

93 Ibid.
94 Ibid., 25.
95 Ibid.
96 Ibid., 26.
97 Ibid., 26–7.

the appropriate outlet or platform for more general 'political, economic, and social revolution',[98] even if, otherwise, such reform was much needed and its 'horror of contemporary forms of society' were well founded, given 'the condition of the world's poor ... racial intolerance ... extremes of inequality ... spread of materialism ... impoverishment of human life in advanced industrial societies ... monotonous labour and ... artificial divisions between social classes'.[99] The university was not the place for realising 'direct democracy'; forms of 'radicalism', which critique academic authority as 'hypocrisy' were mistaken.[100] Hart made sure he set out the arguments of the radical critique carefully, quoting from student publications – and in this he went far beyond many, if not most, other Dons at the time. But he also put his foot down: these arguments were flawed when applied to the university; the university was simply not the place for them – the anger, legitimate as it may be, was misplaced if and when targeting academic authority.

However, for Hart, for all the value he placed in academic authority, such authority was also not impervious to critique and change. 'There should be no brute assertion', the Report argued, 'of a monopoly of wisdom on the part of teachers when it comes to deciding matters of academic policy'.[101] The previously stated position of the University in response to the student petition, i.e., as above, that informal channels between junior and senior members, as they already existed, were enough for the student voice to be heard, were wrong. Here, too, the Report did not mince its words: 'We think that it is not too harsh to say of this view that it is an illusion'.[102] Although such informal channels are 'immensely valuable features of Oxford life ... they do not serve as effective organs of communication and debate and (what is more important) of mutual explanation at university level'.[103] It was certainly the case that the exercise of academic authority was 'dependent on experience, accumulated knowledge, and organisation' – anyone who denied this 'ignore[d] the complexity of the truth'[104] – but this did not mean that the kind of authority that was exercised by university teachers was something to be imposed on high, from an unreachable heaven, with any criticism of it stifled by

98 Ibid., 157.
99 Ibid.
100 Ibid., 159.
101 Ibid., 28.
102 Ibid., 29.
103 Ibid.
104 Ibid., 23.

being whispered in informal relations. Instead, such criticism deserved to see the full light of day, albeit in properly circumscribed form, such as on a series of consultative commissions. What was important was that room was made both for the exercise of academic authority, but in a defeasible way: in a way that was always subject to genuine contestation, debate, and the justification of any such exercise through reason. No one, again, had a 'monopoly of wisdom'.

The Report deserves serious study as an exercise in applied political theory: again, what was at stake in it was the concept and practice of authority. Among the Report's many virtues, for instance, is an important critique of 'disciplinary authority', as this was exercised at the time through the Proctors. Although there were some good features of the system – for instance, the Proctors were 'themselves young enough to be accessible to Junior Members and to understand and even to be influenced by their attitudes'[105] – the system was also deeply flawed, for it concentrated power too much in one office. The Proctors exercised legislative, judicial, and police powers and operated 'in blaze of secrecy';[106] such concentration of powers and lack of transparency simply did not 'conform with commonly recognised standards of justice'.[107]

One of the Report's major recommendations, accordingly, was that the legislative, 'rule-making power' of the Proctors 'should be entrusted to a mixed body of which one-half should be Junior Members',[108] and further, that the basis of disciplinary authority in the university should be narrowed from a much too broad power prohibiting 'conduct likely to bring the name of the University or any of its members into disrepute',[109] to the more limited one of 'conduct likely to disrupt teaching or study or research or the administration of the University' and likely to 'damage or deface any property of the University'.[110] The Report added that 'beyond this indispensable minimum almost everything is open to debate', with the 'proper scope of university discipline' to be subject to debate and contestation and justification for any position taken.[111] The Report was at pains to state that when it came to the bounds of university discipline, 'the most diverse views can be held', and so it was vital that 'those who

[105] Ibid., 41.
[106] Ibid.
[107] Ibid., 42.
[108] Ibid., 43–4.
[109] Ibid., 52.
[110] Ibid., 44–5.
[111] Ibid., 45.

are most immediately affected by them', i.e., decisions as to 'the extent of disciplinary rules', should 'share in the decision', and it proposed detailed procedural rules for how the student voice should be included, including make it 'easy' for students to participate, and for the deliberations of the rule-making body to be 'relatively public and accessible'.[112] This, along with changes to the hearings system of Proctorial authority, was thus designed to thwart the concentration of power, and to respect diversity of views on questions of the morality of student life, subjecting any decisions taken to as much contestation and debate as possible.

In great practical detail, and accompanied by principled argument, the Report thus articulated what might be thought of as a typical Hartian attitude, or a typical Hartian political sensibility: mindful always of the possibility of rational disagreement, especially as to matters of morality, but mindful, too, of the need for decision-making, Hart looked for and articulated concepts (authority) as well as practical procedures (committee structures, disciplinary hearings, etc.) that balanced the need for order, including in the distinct environment of the university, with contestation, avoiding the concentration of power, and of top-down commands from some distant, unreachable height, and making room, within limits, for democratic participation. This could be called 'liberalism', as indeed it was by many, though it was liberalism of a particular kind – as Dworkin, speaking at Hart's funeral put it:

> He [Hart] was a liberal of temperament not doctrine. He despaired of finding any great truth about human nature or natural rights or economic psychology that could generate concrete theories of law and justice. He built his liberalism on virtues not abstract principles, on the virtues of sympathy, attention and decency, on tolerance and a good lawyer's passion for fair procedure. He believed in reason, and exemplified it, but more in the way of Hume than of Kant, as an engine not of transcendental thought but of practical accommodation. He thought the best we could do in politics was to turn away from abstract systems or theologies, which draw on subterranean and divisive emotions, and take up instead familiar, day-to-day methods of reasoning, particularly reasoning about matters of fact within agreed procedures for good argument. These methods are much more likely to produce liberal tolerance, he thought, not just by marginalising ideology, but also because day-to-day, procedure-grounded, cooperative reasoning itself bring people together if anything can.[113]

[112] Ibid., 47.

[113] Dworkin, quoted in Hart, *Ask Me No More* (1998), 214. It is interesting that Dworkin mentions the importance of Hume to Hart. To my knowledge, this link between Hart and Hume has been neglected.

But whether one calls it 'liberalism' or not, there was no doubt that it was highly significant for MacCormick, tapping into, as well as strengthening and informing, features that were already sympathetic to it in MacCormick's character: of a sensitivity to the value of peace, of responsible, moderate, accommodating, respectful pragmatism, of the need to protect disagreement and the diverse views of persons, of finding structures in which voices could be heard while allowing for decisions still to be made, of avoiding the concentration and centralisation of power, of creating an ethos of reason-giving amongst those who make decisions, and of making sure there are no great gaps between 'Us' and 'Them', but instead an inclusive space for both order and change, for a defeasible, contestable order.

It is this attitude – this orientation towards how to relate with others, and how persons generally can relate with each other – that so attracted MacCormick to Hart, and that, much more than any position in general jurisprudence, was to be where Hart influenced MacCormick the most. It was precisely this attitude that MacCormick experienced – not just understood in some abstract manner, but really experienced, especially as he too found himself in positions of academic and disciplinary authority in the College and in the University – that endeared MacCormick to Hart and that also shaped MacCormick's own character.

Hart, the Critical Moralist

Hart and his Circle

MacCormick's engagement with Hart's jurisprudence begins in earnest in 1963, when MacCormick arrives as a student in Oxford, though it is very likely that MacCormick had already begun, most likely via Lamont, reading Hart in Glasgow. In the years 1963–65, MacCormick attended Hart's lectures on 'Rights and Duties' as well as on 'Problems in Kelsen's General Theory'[114] and carefully read *The Concept of Law*, which had been published two years earlier in 1961.

MacCormick kept his notes from Hart's lectures.[115] According to MacCormick, lecturing 'never gave him [Hart] pleasure'; instead, he 'most at ease in more intimate scholarly discussion and in postgraduate

[114] MacCormick, 'Sir Neil MacCormick' (2007), 172; the Kelsen course appears to have been taught in 1963: see Simpson, *Reflections* (2011), 113.

[115] They are available in MacCormick's University of Edinburgh Archive.

supervision'.[116] Nevertheless, MacCormick added, the lectures 'were at their best brilliant and fascinating'.[117] A little of the flavour of these lectures can be found in Raz's description of them:

> For several years running he [Hart] packed North School as I have never seen it since with students, colleagues and visitors eager to hear his lectures on Rights and Duties. Tall, handsome and animated, his imposing figure and agitated immersion in his topics were captivating. Watching him continuously shuffling from distance to reading glasses, wiping them each time with a long white handkerchief, mislaying them and rediscovering their whereabouts, matched in fascination the long and complex arguments, elegantly presented, and greatly taxing the ability of the audience to follow their drift. In the lectures he examined and criticised all the current accounts of rights and duties, and developed his own views.[118]

When MacCormick returned to Oxford, in 1967, he renewed his relation to Hart. Here, it is important to remember that this relation was always multifaceted, and certainly in this period of the late 1960s and early 1970s combined three strands: first, as we have seen, issues surrounding student discipline and authority;[119] second, through Hart's interests in social democracy and the limits of the state, including the importance of rights (an engagement to which I shall return in Chapter 6); and third, through Hart's general jurisprudence. We separate these strands at our peril, and indeed my argument is that it is especially through the first two, and thus Hart's politics, that MacCormick relates especially closely to Hart, with the third thus being filtered through those two.

Of course, the engagement with Hart's jurisprudence has itself many aspects, including conversations with others in Hart's circle. Returning to the fold in 1967, MacCormick's encounter with Hartian jurisprudence was thus mediated by his relations with other scholars, especially his peers. As Lacey notes, 'in the mid-1960s', and then only increasing in momentum and activity in the late 1960s and early 1970s, Hart was surrounded by 'talented graduate students' and young scholars, such as Joseph Raz, Peter Hacker, David Richards, John Finnis, and Lee Irish.[120] Many of these

116 MacCormick, 'H. L. A. Hart', *The Guardian* (23 December 1992), 6.

117 Ibid.

118 Raz, in Hart, *Ask Me No More* (1998), 217.

119 This possibly extended to other aspects of student politics, as MacCormick reports working with Hart on 'certain matters concerning the Oxford Union Society, of which he [Hart] was a Trustee and I was for a period Acting Senior Treasurer': MacCormick, 'Sir Neil MacCormick' (2007), 173.

120 Lacey, *Hart* (2004), 272.

graduate students and young scholars became important interlocutors for MacCormick. Amongst them, Raz and Finnis stand out.

Raz had arrived in 1965, a year after meeting Hart in Jerusalem when Hart delivered the 1964 Lionel Cohen lectures and during the course of which, as Raz reported it, he 'demolished Lady Wootton's proposals for the reform of the criminal law, displaying his unique ability to bring the most rigorous philosophical analysis to bear practical fruits for legal reform'.[121] Raz was to be an important philosophical companion for MacCormick, the two sharing an interest in practical reason, and often engaging in philosophical debate – in the late 1960s and early 1970s,[122] but also thereafter. They did not have a close friendship, but they did correspond often together, sharing their various publications with each other.

Finnis, too, was an important interlocutor for MacCormick. Finnis's work on natural law, culminating in his 1981 book, *Natural Law and Natural Rights*, of which MacCormick had seen earlier drafts, had a profound effect on MacCormick. As with Raz, this was not a close friendship, but Finnis did visit Edinburgh on numerous occasions (including as an external examiner in Jurisprudence) and corresponded with MacCormick. Further, along with Finnis and Buxton, MacCormick 'took on responsibility for a postgraduate seminar' on the Bachelor of Civil Law degree, reading and discussing 'some selected texts in jurisprudence'.[123] MacCormick reports that 'Hart regularly attended' these seminars, 'as in due course did Raz and Dworkin'.[124]

Dworkin had arrived in Oxford in 1969, replacing Hart in the Chair of Jurisprudence – a 'surprising appointment' to MacCormick and to others.[125] The tradition that Hart had started of a jurisprudence discussion group continued, with the above-mentioned participating, as well as 'Gareth Evans, Brian Simpson, David Bentley, Philip Lewis, Jean Floud' and occasional visitors, such as 'Adam Podgorecki, Philippe Nonet, Philip Selznick and Harry Frankfurt'.[126] This group met, as MacCormick reported it, 'on Wednesday evenings in University College, originally in

121 Raz, in Hart, *Ask Me No More* (1998), 216. As we saw in Chapter 3, it was also these proposals that MacCormick suggested as a topic for debate at the Oxford Union, inviting his friend, John Smith, to join that debate.

122 See MacCormick, 'Review of Raz' (1971), and 'Voluntary Obligations' (1972).

123 MacCormick, 'Sir Neil MacCormick' (2007), 173.

124 Ibid.; Raz joined in 1968 and Dworkin in 1969: see MacCormick, 'Preface' to Japanese translation of *Hart* (1996), 2.

125 MacCormick, 'Sir Neil MacCormick' (2007), 173.

126 Ibid.

Hart's rooms' and then in those of Finnis, 'and held informal discussion of legal-philosophical themes, starting from an informal presentation of a theme chosen by the discussion leader of the evening'.[127]

Thus, although Hart had officially retired from his Chair in 1968 – an announcement made during the Hart Committee inquiry, and one about which 'most of his colleagues were baffled', given he could have continued in the Chair till 1974[128] – the tradition that Hart inspired very much continued and if anything increased in fervour and enthusiasm by his students and the next generation of scholars. It is clear that, like others, MacCormick came to admire Hart in discussion: he remembers that he 'fell much under the spell of his charm and brilliance in discussion and conversation'[129] and that he appreciated Hart's 'quickness of mind in debate … and the profundity of his thought'.[130] Again, though, it is important to emphasise here that this was not a one-to-one relationship with Hart, but a social enterprise, with Hart a leading voice, no doubt, but with MacCormick forming many other important relationships too.

The Range of MacCormick's Interests

MacCormick's engagement with Hart is very much present in his publications from the late 1960s and through the 1970s. It is an important part, for instance, of the position taken in *Legal Reasoning and Legal Theory* (1978), as well as in pieces on rights and in reviews of Dworkin's works. One could argue that this long decade of the 1970s culminates in the publication of MacCormick's book on Hart in 1981. This book is undoubtedly important, and I will turn to it in a moment. However, in order to understand in what ways it was significant, it is vital to place it into a broader context of MacCormick's interests in the 1970s.

In particular, what is crucial to emphasise is the range of MacCormick's interests, especially in questions of normativity and value, both in morals and in politics. This is significant because, as I have been suggesting, MacCormick's connection with Hart was by no means dominated by debates over general jurisprudence; quite the contrary, it was dominated, if by anything, by politics, both in theory and practice, whether that be the politics of authority or the politics of social democracy and the responsible

127 MacCormick, 'Preface' to Japanese translation of *Hart* (1996), 2.
128 Lacey, *Hart* (2004), 289.
129 MacCormick, 'Review of Lacey' (2005), 433.
130 MacCormick, 'Preface' to Japanese translation of *Hart* (1996), 2.

state, both of which were crucial issues for Scottish politics. Even when it comes to MacCormick's take on general jurisprudence, this too was filtered, and needs to be read via, MacCormick's deep-running knowledge of and commitment to Glaswegian moral philosophy. MacCormick's engagement with Hartian jurisprudence, then, is very much coloured by MacCormick's normative interests – in morals and politics, in theory and practice – and it is these that really drive MacCormick's interpretation and criticism of Hart's general jurisprudence.

As an indication of these more normative interests – and thus also the way in which MacCormick was consistently approaching issues in legal philosophy as a Glaswegian moral philosopher and as a Scottish political philosopher – it will help to identify just a few important themes from a number of publications that led up to the book on Hart in 1981. This is by no means to cover this period in this perfunctory way, for I shall be returning to these in more detail in subsequent chapters: it is instead to acknowledge the breadth and depth of MacCormick's interests, especially his normative interests, which then very much inform his interpretation and critique of Hart. Though the listing of publication titles is tedious, and for this, I apologise to the reader, doing so will also help illuminate the sheer range of MacCormick's work in this period, and thus also indicate that engagement with Hart, though important, was but one aspect of MacCormick's work in those years. Doing this, further, will help us shed light on MacCormick's reading of Hart.

One could organise MacCormick's publications from 1966 to 1981 into five broad themes. The first involved work on the conceptual structure, but also simultaneously the moral and political value, of different types of law or areas of law, including obligation, power, liberty, right, and (as he articulated it in his Inaugural Lecture in Edinburgh) the trifecta of institutive, consequential, and terminative rules. MacCormick's concern here was often to show that there was a particular and distinct moral value of a certain rule or set of rules worth preserving (such as 'the obligation of reparation'), or to argue for the importance to the practice of the responsible state, of respect for rights, liberties, and equality. Relevant publications here included 'Delegated Legislation and Civil Liberty' (1970), 'Voluntary Obligations and Normative Powers' (1972), 'Legal Obligation and the Imperative Fallacy' (1973), 'Law as Institutional Fact' (1973), 'Children's Rights: A Test Case for Theories of Rights' (1976), 'Rights in Legislation' (1977), 'Civil Liberties and the Law' (1977), 'The Obligation of Reparation' (1978), 'Privacy and Obscenity' (1978), and 'Law, Obligation, and Consent: Reflections on Stair and Locke' (1979). I will be returning to this work in

Chapter 6, with a particular focus on how MacCormick squared the circle of rights, liberties, and equality in his account of social democracy.

The second theme concerned theorising the practice of legal reasoning, but with a special focus on the crucial role, as MacCormick saw it, of values and principles as 'underpinning reasons' (the term comes from LRLT [1978]), and the construction and relation of these values and principles (e.g., by way of consistency, coherence, and consequences) as non-deductive but still rational elements in the justification of legal decisions. This line of work was steeped in the Glaswegian tradition of theorising the logic and practice of moral reasoning, which MacCormick applied to legal reasoning. Here, relevant publications included: 'Can Stare Decisis be Abolished?' (1966), 'Principles of Law' (1974), 'Formal Justice and the Form of Legal Arguments' (1976), 'The Motivation of Judgement in the Common Law' (1978), *Legal Reasoning and Legal Theory* (1978), 'The Coherence of a Case and the Reasonableness of Doubt' (1981), 'The Artificial Reason and Judgement of Law' (1981), and 'The Rational Discipline of Law' (1981). I will be returning to these publications in Chapter 10.

The focus of the third theme was British, and especially Scottish, constitutional history and theory, which extended both to analyses of relevant concepts, such as authority, sovereignty, and nationalism, but also to more immediate matters of practical concern in Scottish politics, such as the 1975 Referendum on the European Community, the *Scotland Act* 1978, the 1979 Independence Referendum, and various policy matters of importance to the SNP (especially since, in this period, MacCormick became an SNP candidate for the Westminster Parliament). Relevant publications here include: *The Scottish Debate* (1970), 'Review of *Constitutional and Administrative Law* by SA de Smith' (1972), 'Review of *The Scottish Political System*, Kellas' (1973), 'The Rise of Scottish Nationalism: A Case of Too Little, Too Late?' (1974), 'A Filial Look at Home Rule's Founding Father' (1974), 'Independence and Federalism After the Referendum' (1975), 'We Need a New Politics' (1975), 'The Mandate Question' (1976), 'Two-Stranded Support for Legislative Devolution' (1976), 'Does the United Kingdom have a Constitution? Reflections on *MacCormick* v. *Lord Advocate*' (1978), 'Nation and Nationalism' (1979), and 'Constitutional Points' (1979). These publications, and others on nationalism and constitutionalism, will be the subject of Chapter 7 and, to an extent (especially in terms of Scotland's place in Europe), Chapter 8.

The fourth theme of MacCormick's work in this period can be characterised as relating to the methodology of practical philosophy, and including the relative merits and limits of positivism and natural law traditions, the possibility for a third type of legal theory (the 'institutional theory') that combined aspects of both these traditions, the need for a theory that did not prioritise or reduce law to coercion, command, and the imperative, and the prospects for greater collaboration between analytical, normative, and sociological threads of jurisprudential inquiry. Here, too, belongs MacCormick's engagement with Lamont and his approach to moral philosophy, which was especially intense in the late 1970s, as well as to his reading, commenting, discussing, and reviewing of Finnis's *Natural Law and Natural Rights*, a book that had been commissioned by Hart already in 1966,[131] and that MacCormick held in high regard, along with other re-imaginings of the natural law tradition.[132] This re-imagining was important for MacCormick, not only because he took his duties as a holder of a Chair in the 'Law of Nature and Nations' seriously, but also because (as per the fifth strand below) of his renewed interest in the philosophy of the Scottish Enlightenment. A further aspect of this interest was another duty that MacCormick took seriously: his role as a teacher of jurisprudence and thus what a course in jurisprudence ought to focus on. Relevant publications here include: 'Review of *Human Law and Human Justice*, Stone' (1966), 'Review of *The Concept of a Legal System*, Raz' (1971), 'Law as Institutional Fact' (1973), 'Justice According to Rawls' (1973), 'Jurisprudence in the Law Course' (1974), 'Justice: An Un-Original Position' (1976), 'Challenging Sociological Definitions' (1977), 'Dworkin as Pre-Benthamite' (1978), 'Review of *Natural Law and Natural Rights*, Finnis' (1980), 'Natural Law Reconsidered' (1981), and 'Law, Morality, and Positivism' (1981).

As mentioned above, the fifth and final strand related to a growing interest – always present and arising from studies in Glasgow but reignited upon MacCormick's return to Edinburgh in 1972 – in Scottish intellectual history, and in particular the moral, legal, and political thought of the Scottish Enlightenment. This interest, of course, informed the others – indeed, it was increasingly through the work of Stair, Smith, and Hume that MacCormick reflected on the above themes and problems, finding in these writings stylistic, substantive, and methodological resources that were to be a continuous source of nourishment for him. Relevant publications here include: 'Can Stare Decisis be Abolished?' (1966), 'Ius Quaesitum Tertio: Stair v. Dunedin' (1970), 'Law as Institutional Fact' (1973), 'Review of Smith, *Lectures on Jurisprudence*' (1978), 'Law, Obligation and Consent:

131 See Lacey, *Hart* (2004), 273.

132 See, e.g., Duff, 'Legal Obligation' (1980).

Reflections on Stair and Locke' (1979), 'Stair as Analytical Jurist' (1981), 'Adam Smith on Law' (1981), and 'The Rational Discipline of Law' (1981). I will be returning to these Scottish thinkers later, for they inform a good deal of MacCormick's philosophical work in the decades to come.[133]

Reading Hart

It is against this extraordinarily rich background that we need to consider MacCormick's reading of Hart in the 1981 book. Seen against this light, it is perhaps not surprising that what emerges from MacCormick's reading is a very normative Hart: a Hart that is a moral critic and reformer, a leading voice in social democratic politics, and, at least in potential, much closer than Hart himself thought, to traditions of theorising law that foreground and pay special attention to its moral and political value. MacCormick's Hart is a critical moralist who employs a method (the hermeneutic point of view) for studying law that renders law of much greater service (than previous methods, especially that of Austin's and Bentham's, but also some natural lawyers, on a certain understanding of these) to ordinary citizens and the way in which law can be morally and politically valuable to their lives.

What MacCormick does, effectively, is to raise Hart's method to moral and political significance: from the perspective of a Glaswegian moral philosopher, as well as a British constitutional theorist, Hart now appears as someone whose jurisprudence can be characterised as respecting persons (and the autonomy of their conscience, and thus, in a society, the diversity of their views and the contingencies of their particular loyalties and commitments), thereby avoiding the assumption of a political formation (especially a state) that exercises concentrated, central, and unlimited power, and that is but an effective means of imposing commands and

[133] It is interesting to note here that MacCormick in the late 1970s, early 1980s, was considering numerous possibilities for books – including one on 'Scottish Home Rule' (Letter to David Martin, Basil Blackwell Publishers, 6 May 1981). In his correspondence with Edward Arnold, the publishers of his book on Hart, he said: 'In some ways I do think that to write something on Smith would be more exciting from my point of view than to write something on Hart', but in the end he decided, writing on the latter would be 'easier', especially given his 'existing knowledge' of Hart (Letter to Susan Loden, Edward Arnold, 19 January 1979). I would argue that writing a book about Hart was crucial for MacCormick: it is what allowed him to articulate his own take on Hart, and thus move forward as a legal philosopher in his own right. But, of course, part of that meant returning to, and embracing more thoroughly, the arguments of the thinkers of the Scottish Enlightenment. In that respect, it is also telling that throughout his book on Hart, MacCormick referred to Hart numerous times as Humean, or as closer to Hume than to Kant, e.g., HLA (1981), 26; and fn. 27, 165.

imperatives on an oppressed population. It is, in other words, Hart's moral and political sensitivities, filtered as these were through MacCormick's personal experience of Hart in Oxford, that appeal most to MacCormick and that inform his reading of Hart's jurisprudence.

That this is the way in which MacCormick reads Hart – which also means, for MacCormick, not only creating his own Hart, but also allowing himself to develop his own philosophical voice, his own unique approach to jurisprudence – is evident from the first pages of *H. L. A. Hart* (1981).

MacCormick begins by emphasising the significance of certain practical attitudes, casting theory precisely as something that informs or constructs practical attitudes that are of moral importance. Jurisprudence is no unhinged speculation far above the mess of everyday affairs; quite the contrary: 'Juristic theories are available to, and to tend to become part of the intellectual equipment of, those who have particular practical concerns in the law. Jurists contribute to practical debates, practitioners contribute to jurisprudence. The law in its practical working reflects practical men's understanding of law'.[134]

Jurisprudence may pursue 'understanding for its own sake',[135] but it is still always steeped in practice, while practice itself is always in need of theory. Hart's theory, too, MacCormick argues, needs to be seen in light of the practices he was part of and to which he sought to contribute to; indeed, what is crucial is to understand in what manner or style Hart did that – what attitudes, in other words, he sought to construct as a distinctive mode of participating in practice. Once again, to do theory was to reflectively build attitudes to, and within, a practice. MacCormick thus foregrounds Hart's years as a barrister – where he practiced the art of 'manipulation of words to practical ends'[136] – and which very much inform his jurisprudence: Hart's juristic writings, MacCormick says, are 'clearly recognisable as the work of an English lawyer'.[137] Hart's Britishness is evident, too, in the influence upon him of 'British tradition of liberal utilitarianism and legal positivism' deriving from Hobbes, Hume, Bentham, Mill, and Austin.[138]

But what is just as, if not more, important, is Hart's lived experience, both of the Second World War and thus of 'Fascism and Nazism and their

[134] MacCormick, HLA (1981), 1.
[135] Ibid., 2.
[136] Ibid.
[137] Ibid., 3.
[138] Ibid., 6.

British copies',[139] as well as of the enormous changes 'in the moral climate' from 1955 to 1970 in the UK.[140] As we shall see in more detail in Chapter 6, at stake in these years, as MacCormick sees it, was liberty as well as social welfare: of the protection of individual freedom of action from an overly moralised state on the one hand, to, on the other hand, a growing recognition of not just the 'existence' of liberty, but also its 'value' to individuals, and thus a commitment to equalising opportunities for the enjoyment of that liberty for all citizens.[141] For Hart, as indeed for MacCormick too, properly conceived, liberalism was not in opposition to social welfare: 'the liberalising and the welfare equalising trends of modern legislation and modern state practice are fully compatible each with another'.[142] Their compatibility was signalled in a particular practical attitude – precisely an attitude crafted by Hart as a critical moralist – namely: social democratic liberalism.

For MacCormick, Hart 'has been one of the most important and influential contributors of the post-war period to the liberal / social democratic way of thought and action'[143] – something he fought for and exhibited in his many writings on criminal law and punishment, as of course very publicly in the debate with Lord Devlin, but which was something that really permeated all of his philosophy, and thus his reflective and critical engagement in practice. For Hart, as MacCormick read him, theory was never far from practice: Hart was always building bridges, 'directly across from linguistic philosophy to practical law', and reconciling, for instance, 'scientific and commonsense modes of thought'.[144] Both in the style and structure of his work, then, as well as in the substance of his arguments, no matter how abstract, Hart, for MacCormick, was a critical moralist and, more precisely, a liberal social democrat.

All this was well and good, but the trouble was that, according to MacCormick, Hart did not always own up to his primary identity as a critical moralist – he hid a bit under the covers of 'legal positivism', a label that was in any event not helpful in reading him.[145] As MacCormick urged us: we must avoid such labels and instead 'We must look to that work in itself and examine what it really says'.[146] And, when he engaged in this

139 Ibid., 11.
140 Ibid., 8.
141 Ibid., 9.
142 Ibid.
143 Ibid., 10.
144 Ibid., 18.
145 Ibid., 162.
146 Ibid.

examination, MacCormick found that Hart's jurisprudence, in light of his primary identity as a critical moralist – in his case, a maker of liberal social democratic attitudes – was in fact properly read as a contribution to a moral philosophy of law. Hart's main concern was to develop a method for studying law (the hermeneutic point of view) that preserved the capacity of both theorists and, potentially, citizens, for critiquing law morally, but also – if only Hart had emphasised this more – of recognising the moral experience of law by persons.

Thus, Hart's reasons for drawing a line between law and morality where he did – his insistence on the social sources of law, his locating it in the conventional internal point of view of officials alongside general conformity by the population – were moral reasons. Law should not be assumed to be morally conclusive. To do that would be effectively to undermine the practice of critical morality: it would encroach upon the capacity to criticise law morally and thus our capacity to reform it. The reason for Hart's adherence to what we might call 'the positivist thesis of the conceptual differentiation of law and morals is itself a moral reason'; the point of the theory was 'to make sure that it is always open to the theorist and the ordinary person to retain a critical moral stance in the face of the law which is'.[147] Hart's jurisprudence, in that sense, was an answer to the 'demands' of his 'critical moral philosophy: Hartian 'positivism', properly understood, was the attitude to law of a liberal social democrat. It was a resolutely moral theory of law.

But, as precisely such a theory, Hart's version of it, at least in *The Concept of Law*, did not go nearly as far as it ought. The logic of the theory, MacCormick thought, committed it to more than Hart thought it did. The relations between law and morality were, indeed, even closer than Hart articulated them. To see this, MacCormick said, one needs to go back to Hart's writings on criminal law and his deep-felt recognition of the suffering of persons when faced with state-imposed punishment. That this was deeply felt could not be missed by anyone who read Hart's lectures on *Law, Liberty, and Morality*, especially the moving passages on the burdens placed on persons who could not be free in their choice of sexuality. What Hart saw in these burdens was that alongside a legal judgement – for instance, that an act of homosexuality was to be criminally punished – was moral condemnation. After all, Hart attacked Devlin for assuming that it was law's role to enforce some alleged conventional social morality (the

[147] Ibid., 25.

position of 'legal moralism'). But this argument in itself yielded another insight: that law was morally loaded. MacCormick put it this way:

> Hence it seems simply inconceivable that appeals to law – even iniquitous law – can ever shed their moral load. That is and has to be one of the messages emanating from a hermeneutic study like Hart's of laws as special social rules. Hence it seems inconceivable that it will ever be thought other than virtuous, albeit at a modest point on the scale of virtue, for a person to be 'law-abiding' – even when the law by which he or she abides contains much of evil. By the same token, the law breaker however conscientious will be stigmatised by the legal officials as a moral wrongdoer and a moral danger.[148]

If one paid, in other words, attention to the moral experience of law's subjects – especially to those subjected to criminal punishment – one could more clearly recognise how law 'is always a morally loaded as well as morally relevant institution'.[149] Indeed, this is what a properly hermeneutic approach to the study of law prescribed: as MacCormick put it in his 'Law, Morality, and Positivism' – a lecture delivered in London on 10 November 1980, and thus around the time he was writing the Hart book – the hermeneutic point of view required that we 'put ourselves by sympathetic imagination in the shoes of insiders to the practice in order to account for matters otherwise inexplicable'.[150] Although this may have been primarily the perspective of officials for Hart, it need not be restricted in this way: sympathetic imagination could extend also to citizens, as it clearly did in Hart's writings on criminal law and policy.

But if one did look at the practice of officials, then this too was revealing of the way law was morally loaded and morally relevant. Law, like morality, required the giving of reasons – it was essentially a practice of justification, as was evident especially in the judgements of courts. As such, it belonged, again with morality, 'within the domain of practical reasoning'.[151] Thus, when one examined the practice of legal reasoning, one could see, once again, another aspect of how law was always morally loaded and morally relevant, for law, like morality, involved invoking standards – values and principles – that justified imposing certain rules and judging the behaviour of others in accordance with them.

As MacCormick put in his above-mentioned lecture, 'those who exercise power and discretion within a legal system must always at least

[148] Ibid., 161.
[149] Ibid.
[150] MacCormick, 'Law, Morality, and Positivism' (1981), 135.
[151] MacCormick, HLA (1981), 161.

purport to be acting on the basis of seriously held and seriously considered values'.[152] When one examined the practice of courts, though legislators too, the acts of these officials were always made, in some way, in the name of something morally valuable: legislators did not call their legislation unjust, but instead sought to justify it, and judges too, in their application of rules to particular cases, crafted their meaning and application by reference to principles, or what MacCormick had called, in *Legal Reasoning and Legal Theory* (1978), 'underpinning reasons'.[153]

Thus, whether seen from the perspective of the experience of subjects – especially in criminal contexts – or from the perspective of examining the reason-giving practices of legal officials – what was clear was that there really were conceptual links between law and morality. Hart was right that the very existence of law did not mean it was morally conclusive, but he missed that there were other conceptual links between law and morality. If only he had embraced his primary identity as a critical moralist, he would have acknowledged this. Hart's 'positivism', then, read properly, and supplemented by the above further acknowledgements of the conceptual relations between law and morality, was a moral theory; its 'descriptive sociology' was always in the service of the construction of practical attitudes that were of moral value in a community.

MacCormick's take on Hart can be read alongside other, more normatively inflected, readings of positivism – especially the ethical positivism of Tom Campbell and that of Will Waluchow, the latter being especially important to rapprochements, both personal and philosophical, between Hart and Dworkin.[154] It is perhaps no accident that it was in 1980 that MacCormick examined Waluchow's thesis in Oxford, on 'Adjudication and Judicial Discretion'.[155] Waluchow's articulation of inclusive legal positivism did much to bridge divides between Dworkinians and Hartians – a position that was very much in this spirit of MacCormick's own reading of Hart.[156]

Campbell, in turn, was well-known to MacCormick already from his student days – MacCormick records, for example, a dinner with

152 MacCormick, 'Law, Morality, and Positivism' (1981), 144.

153 Indeed, the appendix to LRLT (1978) was where MacCormick first sought to extend the significance of his work on the importance of values and principles in legal reasoning to a more general jurisprudence: the Hart book was in some ways an elaboration of this appendix.

154 See Lacey, *Hart* (2004), 334–5.

155 See MacCormick, Letter to Hart (27 May 1980).

156 See Waluchow, *Inclusive Legal Positivism* (1994).

Campbell in 1964 in Oxford in his student diary for that year, and there is no doubt that they continued to discuss and correspond together on mutual interests, including the work of Adam Smith.[157] It is thus possible that MacCormick's reading of Hart emerged from conversations they had together. Certainly, Campbell's later articulation of 'ethical positivism'[158] has much in common with MacCormick's views.[159] But, seen in light of MacCormick's formation as a Glaswegian moral philosopher, and thus as a participatory critical moralist in his own right, this reading of Hart was hardly a surprise: it was precisely the kind of reading one would think that a Scottish-trained moralist would provide.

As we have seen, this was not only because of the liberal social democratic outlook that appealed to MacCormick, but also because of the very much related pragmatic, accommodating, and moderate approach to authority, which shone through Hart's delicate management of student protest in the late 1960s. Thus, Hart's critique of Bentham and Austin's imperative theory of law – the idea that law was a command, backed up by a sanction, issued by a superior to inferiors – was most persuasive to MacCormick, not only, and not mainly, because it did not fit the diversity of legal phenomena and thus did not make analytical sense, but also, if not more so, because that was an unhelpful, indeed destructive, attitude to take towards authority, and thus an unhelpful way of relating with others.

For law to make moral sense to persons it could not be a top-down command: at least we should not assume that law had to take the form of such centralised and concentrated power. Law could not be the mere arbitrary will of someone superior: it mattered more to people and played a more morally and politically significant role in their lives than this assumed. It was the job of the jurisprude to protect that. MacCormick fulfilled that role not only in his most abstract jurisprudential analyses, including reflections on the method of jurisprudence (precisely the importance of the hermeneutic point of view), but also, as we shall see, in his constitutional theorising: there was a pluralising, person-respecting, non-dominating, anti-authoritarian, freedom-preserving, aspect of Hart's jurisprudence that was vital also for theorising the place of Scotland in the United Kingdom.

It was in these ways – with enormous sensitivity to the wrongs of domination, to the dangers of disrespecting persons – that MacCormick read

157 MacCormick read and admired Campbell's 1971 book, *Adam Smith's Science of Morals.*

158 See Campbell, *The Legal Theory of Ethical Positivism* (1996).

159 See, e.g., MacCormick, 'The Ethics of Legalism' (1989).

Hart. Hart, of course, did have a role to play in this reading – though one mediated less by his general jurisprudential works, and more by how MacCormick observed and experienced Hart's role in the debates over discipline and authority in Oxford in the late 1960s – but what one ultimately sees in MacCormick's reading of Hart is less Hart and more MacCormick. In that sense, the 1981 book was a vital one in MacCormick's oeuvre – perhaps the most vital for MacCormick to write. In writing it, he found the courage to articulate his own voice, which was a kind of recovery of his roots in Glaswegian moral philosophy, and which he went on to develop in distinctive ways in the philosophical work of the next few decades.

6

A Jurist in Search of Good Government

Law, Liberty, and Justice

The long decade of the 1970s, from the late 1960s to the early 1980s, was a remarkably creative one for MacCormick. Teaching and writing intensively in Oxford in the late 1960s, he returned to Scotland, in 1972, taking up the Chair of Public Law, and the Law of Nature and Nations, at the age of thirty one, at the University of Edinburgh. Although immediately thrust into the role of the Dean of the Law School in Edinburgh, from 1973 to 1976, he kept up his research interests, and when the administrative duties loosened in the late 1970s and early 1980s, he published three books: *Legal Reasoning and Legal Theory* (1978), *H. L. A. Hart* (1981), and *Legal Right and Social Democracy* (1982). This was supplemented by an increasing number of invited lectures and papers, as well as many new academic friendships and collaborative projects, especially with scholars in continental Europe.

MacCormick's philosophical interests in this period were many and included: an interest in the analytical structure and moral value of legal forms, especially rights, but extending also to normative powers and obligations; an interest in civil liberties, and in particular the critique of encroachments by executive power into such liberties; and third, an interest in equality, fairness, and distributive justice – in social welfare in general – and its compatibility with the legal protection of right and liberty. All three might be grouped as attempts to forge a sense of responsible, moderate, left-of-centre government – in short, good government, as MacCormick saw it – and it is in this way that this chapter treats them.

The range of these philosophical interests matched and related in dynamic ways to the politics of the period. In fact, as his wife at the time, Karen Barr, put it, there was a 'sense' that 'while he [MacCormick] was in Oxford that he was missing out on all that was happening in Scotland'.[1] Certainly, the late 1960s and early 1970s were a source of enormous excitement and optimism for anyone with nationalist sentiments in Scotland. Winnie Ewing's famous

[1] Karen Barr (interview).

and electrifying 1967 by-election win in Hamilton – often called the beginning of 'modern Scottish politics'[2] – fuelled the membership of the SNP, which grew from 2,000 in 1960 to 70,000 in 1969 (including MacCormick himself in 1967), and provided a platform upon which the SNP sought to build. The atmosphere was undoubtedly given a boost, as a result of the *Continental Shelf (Jurisdiction Order)* in October 1968, with Scotland gaining jurisdiction over oil.[3]

As we saw in Chapter 5, when MacCormick went to Dundee in 1965, he contacted the SNP branch in Perth and assisted SNP candidates running in the 1966 general election.[4] Gordon Wilson, who was to become SNP leader in 1979, noted that MacCormick was very much 'involved in those years in the 1960s', particularly in the late 1960s and early 1970s, for instance by 'helping his brother [Iain MacCormick], who had become a SNP candidate in 1971'.[5] There was, in the late 1960s, following the by-election victory, sudden and electrifying interest in Scottish nationalism – indeed, Wilson recalls that MacCormick had been approached to speak in London about it in 1967, but could not and asked Wilson to go in his place. This was one of the rare occasions in which MacCormick did not accept an invitation, for, as Roger Knox observed, 'such was the energy and dedication of the man' that 'I never knew Neil refuse an invitation to speak at an SNP meeting, whether during the surge in the 60s, the wave of SNP expansion in the 70s, or much later during his tenure as one of our MEPs'.[6]

Although the 1970 General Election saw the SNP win only one Westminster seat (Donald Stewart becoming an MP for the Islands and Highlands) – which some viewed as a disappointment after the party had picked up 107 council seats in the 1968 local elections in Scotland – it was also the first such seat won in a general election (rather than a by-election), and it saw the SNP achieve 11 per cent of the vote in Scotland. Another famous SNP by-election win, this time by Margo McDonald, in the Glasgow Govan by-election of 1973 (once considered a safe Labour seat, just like Hamilton), created electoral momentum, which culminated in seven seats and 21.9% of the vote in the February 1974 election

[2] Hassan, 'The Making of the Modern SNP' (2009), 1.

[3] MacCormick subsequently became involved in some of the legal debates surrounding Scottish title: see Harvie, *Scotland and Nationalism* (2004), 136.

[4] Karen Barr (interview) recalls MacCormick himself being approached to run in 1965, but MacCormick apparently declined this.

[5] Wilson (interview).

[6] Knox, Online tribute website after MacCormick's death (2009; website no longer working).

and then, following a hung Parliament, in the rerun in October 1974, a remarkable eleven seats and 30.4% of the vote (in which, importantly, the SNP had contested all seventy-one Scottish seats for the first time). It was in the 1974 elections that MacCormick's brother, Iain, became an MP – a moment of great pride for the family, with MacCormick in particular feeling that his father would have been proud of the electoral success of his brother. Indeed, as recalled by Owen Dudley Edwards, it was as part of the 1974 campaign that MacCormick himself was approached, by the-then leader, Billy Wolfe, to stand for South Angus, but declined, and Andrew Walsh was duly voted in.[7]

But the excitement of those years – the late 1960s and early 1970s – was not confined solely to the electoral potential of the SNP; it also very much concerned basic questions of the British constitution, both in theory and history. Indeed, it was in response to the flurry of discussion on constitutional change in the late 1960s – with the Conservative Prime Minister, Ted Heath, having 'committed his party to a Scottish parliament … in his "Declaration of Perth" of 1968', and with the Wilson Labour government appointing a Royal Commission on the Constitution to look into devolution[8] that MacCormick edited his important and still-read collection on *The Scottish Debate* (1970). This Royal Commission was first led by Lord Crowther, but after his death, came under the devolution-sympathetic, but still union-oriented, leadership of Lord Kilbrandon. As we saw in Chapter 4, MacCormick came to know Kilbrandon, having invited him to give the 1964–65 Annual Younger Society Lecture in Balliol. In due course, MacCormick gave (private) evidence to the Commission, which, when it reported in 1973, subsequently recommended the re-institution of a Scottish Parliament. As Mitchell put it, the Kilbrandon Commission 'helped thrust the constitution to the fore of Scottish politics to the SNP's advantage'.[9]

As we will see in more detail in Chapter 7, MacCormick was from this moment on prominent and active in the SNP and, more broadly, in Scottish politics and debates over constitutional change. This did not mean he always saw eye to eye with the SNP – in fact, there were many important instances when MacCormick went his own way, even publicly critiquing the SNP stance. As Wilson indicated, there was a 'need for someone to be able to be constructively critical of the party' and 'MacCormick was

[7] Dudley Edwards (interview).

[8] See Duclos, 'The 1970s' (2017), 3.

[9] Mitchell, 'From Breakthrough to Mainstream' (2009), 33.

one of those'.[10] This constructive criticism had a wide range, including, for instance, supporting staying in Europe in the June 1975 Referendum (with the UK having entered the-then European Economic Community in 1973); criticising the Party's stance on the so-called 'mandate question' in 1976; and, later, participating, when the SNP did not, in the Claim of Right in the 1980s.

Characteristically, though, MacCormick combined this constructive criticism with being very much active in the party. He contested no less than five Westminster elections – in 1979 (for Edinburgh North), 1983, 1987 (both for Edinburgh Pentlands), and, later, 1992 and 1997 (for Argyll and Bute). More important, though, for these were largely unlikely seats for MacCormick to win, was MacCormick's involvement in policymaking behind the scenes as well as his role in keeping the party responsible, moderate, and left-of-centre, via carefully timed interventions and resolutions, throughout the 1970s and the 1980s. Chapter 7 will chart MacCormick's contribution to the constitutional policy of the party – something that began in the mid 1970s, when MacCormick was the principal drafter of 'A Constitution for a Future Independent Scotland' in 1976 – but MacCormick was also active in other SNP committees, especially the Committee on the Structure of Government (in the late 1970s), and as a member of the SNP's National Executive from 1978 to 1981 (and then again in years to come).

The very scale of MacCormick's political involvement – sometimes in the public eye, with contributions in the media, but often behind the scenes, especially within the SNP – suggests that we need to track the relationship between his philosophical interest and political participation. Indeed, what is of interest in this chapter is how both the philosophy and the politics reflect, but also affect, MacCormick's character, i.e., how both MacCormick's philosophical analysis and his politics (within the party, but also more broadly) convey the manner or style with which he related with others. There is no doubt that the two were intimately connected: MacCormick's intensive philosophical interest in legal rights, civil liberties, and social welfare need to be seen against the backdrop of increasing centralisation of executive power in Westminster, especially following Margaret Thatcher's landslide victory in the 1979 elections. Just as they were for many others, the provocations of this increasingly authoritarian regime were crucial to MacCormick as a constitutional theorist. But

[10] Wilson (interview).

also in the other direction: the political events themselves were noticed, debated, and responded to against a backdrop of philosophical discussion, precisely around the basis and scope of authority, the concept of rights, and the role and limits of a state. Once again, as so often in MacCormick's case, politics and philosophy are distinct but inseparable.

MacCormick's contributions, including the most abstract and analytical of these, need to be seen in this light and thus as part of MacCormick's search for the principles of good government, of the just state, but also as part of his own more existential search for being a responsible jurist. This, in turn, was very much connected to the SNP's search for good government within its own ranks – to being, that is, a credible, stable, and dependable party that acted in Scotland's best interests (and not just its own short-term electoral gains). MacCormick was very much at the forefront of meeting these challenges, both as a philosopher-jurist and as a constitutional and nationalist thinker.

In approaching MacCormick's contribution, especially to this politically informed philosophical analysis of rights, liberties, and welfare, but also to the philosophically informed political participation in the SNP, it will be helpful to set it briefly in two contexts, both of which show as well as affect MacCormick's character. The first concerns his role in the SNP, especially with respect to the debate over its ideological platform. The second related one concerns other sources of inspiration for his social democratic stance.

The SNP in Crisis

The SNP's electoral victory in 1974 was certainly a high-water mark, but the speed of the success was also, arguably, a curse in disguise. As Mitchell has observed, following the 1974 elections, 'there were significant differences over strategy, policy, and personalities in the group of eleven [MPs]; there was a tension between the MPs and the party's National Executive Committee (NEC) in Scotland; and there was a larger tension within the party that spanned both its MPs and NEC hardliners who supported independence and those willing to accept a measure short of independence, at least as a "stepping stone"'.[11] The tensions within the party, however, were not solely about constitutional policy, including, as was becoming ever more important, the policy over Europe (an issue to which I return later). They also concerned the very identity of the party: was it, in fact, a party, or more a movement? This was, in turn, related to the vexed issue of whether

[11] Mitchell, The *Scottish Question* (2014), 180.

the party had an ideology (was it on the left or the right of the political spectrum?) or whether it sought to rise above ideological differences, making it more of a cross-party movement for constitutional change. Debates over these tensions were intense in the 1970s,[12] though they also had a much longer history, e.g., they are very much echoed in the split that occurred, as we saw in Chapter 1, between the SNP and John MacCormick's cross-party Convention of the 1940s and 1950s.

Indeed, it may be possible to trace a social democratic ethos much further back into the 1930s and 1940s, though perhaps especially post-Second World War in the 1950s, with the early leaders of the SNP, as argued by Maxwell, being of 'Presbyterian heritage', which 'gave them a strong sense of the fundamental equality of all men and women, as well as a robust ethic of social responsibility'.[13] Thus, for example, Robert McIntyre, who was leader of the SNP from 1947 to 1956 (and then SNP President from 1956 to 1980), and the Convenor of the Constitutional Committee at the time (1976) when MacCormick helped draft a 'Constitution for a Future Independent Scotland', had already sought to 'steer a middle path, as he saw it, between the excesses of socialism on the one hand and the excesses of capitalism on the other'.[14] McIntyre had consistently stressed the importance of the rights of the individual, which he claimed were 'being squeezed by both the forces of impersonal capitalism and big government'.[15]

Rather than placing the emphasis on any particular ideology, what McIntyre emphasised was the need for local democracy, and thus the diffusion of economic power, so as to maximise 'democratic control of the economic structure of the state'.[16] Indeed, for McIntyre, the very concept of 'ideology' was too rigid and not pragmatic enough: 'Beware of ideologies', he argued, for they 'produce a scheme, a system, a faith', such that those caught in them 'get stuck with the system of thought rather with the original ideal and you have an ideology for its own sake'.[17] Social

[12] See Hassan, *The Modern SNP* (2009); Jackson, *The Case for Scottish Independence* (2020), chapter 2; Finlay, *Scottish Nationalism* (2022), chapter 5. The debate included books edited or written at the time, such as Gavin Kennedy, *The Radical Approach* (1976) or Tony Carty and Alexander McCall Smith, *Power and Manoeuvrability* (1978), as well as, importantly, journals and periodicals such as the *Scottish International Review* and *Question*. More broadly, this was against a background of intense debate inspired, for instance, by the important work of Tom Nairn and Michael Hechter.

[13] Maxwell, 'Social Justice' (2009), 120–1.

[14] Finlay, *Scottish Nationalism* (2022), 187.

[15] Ibid.

[16] McIntyre, quoted in Finlay, *Scottish Nationalism* (2022), 188.

[17] Ibid., 189.

democracy, as McIntyre saw it, was not so much an ideology as it was an exercise precisely in this middling art, this pragmatic accommodation in the name of the democratic flourishing of Scotland. McIntyre's flexible pragmatism, his commitment to local democracy and diffusion of power, and his insistence on the rights of individuals, were all to be of considerable importance for MacCormick.[18]

Looking further into the 1960s, one could also argue that a commitment to a kind of social democratic platform within the SNP gained momentum in that decade, especially via the figure of Billy Wolfe, who became party leader in 1969 (and remained in post until 1979). Wolfe had already campaigned as a social democrat in his unsuccessful, but still strong, performance in the 1962 West-Lothian by-election.[19] Certainly, under Wolfe, the SNP did move further in this direction in the late 1960s and early 1970s, aided considerably by Wolfe's reorganisation of the party into specialist policy committees all working to create a 'vision of what an independent Scotland would look like'.[20] Indeed, at the time of the 1974 electoral campaign, the party had proclaimed itself as a Social Democratic Party (SDP), even considering renaming itself as the SNP (Social Democrats) in the 1975 Annual Conference.[21] Nevertheless, even here, 'social democracy' had a quite specific resonance, less ideological, and more 'signifying moderation and a judicial distance from the conventional ideological polarities that dominated British public life'.[22] Throughout, there was an attempt to rise above traditional party divisions, and appeal to something that transcended the usual run-of-the-mill party politics, e.g., by invoking 'Scottish humanitarian traditions'[23] and by emphasising 'participatory and decentralist commitments'.[24] That, in turn, needs to be placed alongside an often passionate commitment – as articulated by George Reid, one of the 1974 SNP MPs – to 'social justice', and to 'the creation of a compassionate, caring, egalitarian Scots society', which required 'control of our own affairs by Scots, for Scots, in Scotland'.[25]

All this would suggest a seemingly inevitable rise of a kind of social democratic platform for the SNP, albeit one that was always at one remove

[18] For more on McIntyre, see Douglas, *At the Helm* (1996).
[19] Lynch, 'From Social Democracy' (2009), 627.
[20] Ibid., 629; see also Wolfe, *Scotland Lives* (1973); and Wilson, *The SNP* (2009).
[21] Lynch, 'From Social Democracy' (2009), 624.
[22] Jackson, *The Case for Scottish Independence* (2020), 91.
[23] Wolfe, quoted in Jackson, *The Case for Scottish Independence* (2020), 92.
[24] Jackson, *The Case for Scottish Independence* (2020), 94.
[25] Reid, quoted in Jackson, *The Case for Scottish Independence* (2020), 94.

from anything resolutely ideological and was always more about signalling the need for greater autonomy and democracy in Scotland. However, the 1974 electoral success threw a spanner in the works. Many felt that the SNP victory in 1974 was a victory for traditional, fundamentalist nationalism, which sought to focus on achieving independence, and not get distracted by questions over economic and social policy. On the other hand, there were those, in the SNP National Executive especially, who were not only gradualists on constitutional policy – supporting devolution as a stepping stone, and possibly never reaching independence – but who were also 'left-wingers'.[26] Of course, these 'left-wingers' themselves came in various shapes and varieties, including more radical socialist views as well as those who saw themselves more on the right-wing of the Labour party (such as the social democrats).

For many observers, writing the history of the SNP during this time, these ideological disagreements were important, and the lack of consensus, direction, and policy discipline within the party on this score is one reason why the party's fortunes collapsed so quickly and dramatically in the late 1970s.[27] For others, the debates of this time were necessary, growing-birth pains, for a party that was maturing, but also more broadly, for a society – Scotland – that was reflecting on the distinctiveness of its traditions, e.g., the 'social contract in which the citizen could rely on the state from the cradle to the grave to secure his or her best socio-economic interests',[28] or a 'Social consensus that was somehow able to bridge the gap between social classes',[29] as well as figuring out how to position itself in the future, especially with a view to maximising its chances for gaining more autonomy from Westminster. The story is thus a complex one, and one which I cannot tell in detail here,[30] but what is of direct relevance is that following the somewhat shambolic, soul-searching five years within the party following 1974, matters came to a head in 1979 and immediately thereafter.

After much wrangling in Westminster, and broadly in line with the recommendations of the 1973 Kilbrandon Report, the Labour Government, led at that point by James Callaghan (Prime Minister from 1976 to 1979), proposed, in 1977, and then passed, in 1978, the Scotland Act 1978. The

[26] Duclos, 'The 1970s' (2017), 11.

[27] Ibid.

[28] Finlay, *Scottish Nationalism* (2022), 180.

[29] Ibid., 175.

[30] But see Mitchell, *Scottish Question* (2014); Lynch, 'From Social Democracy'; Finlay, *Scottish Nationalism* (2022), chapter 5; Jackson, *The Case for Scottish Independence* (2020), chapter 4.

Act, if it had come into force, would have resulted in the establishment of a 'Scottish Assembly'. Governed by a Scottish Executive, with a 'First Secretary', the Assembly would have had powers to pass 'Measures' (rather than 'Acts'), and elections to it would have followed the 'first-past-the-post' system. Like much else, the Act was highly contested and debated within Scotland, and its technicalities required considerable translation and explanation – a task that MacCormick, characteristically, undertook, writing a manuscript on the Act, though one which he never published.[31] The Act required that, for it to come into force, a 'post-legislative referendum' would need to be held. However, a late procedural amendment in Westminster secured the further condition that any majority win had to be by 40 per cent of Scotland's registered electorate. In the result, in March 1979, although 51.6% (1,230,937 people) of those who voted were in favour of the Act, the total number who participated in the referendum represented only 32.9% of the registered electorate as a whole. Thus, the referendum was lost, and with it the possibility of a return to a Scottish Parliament.

The 1979 referendum was a bruising loss, but matters were to get worse in May that year. In the general election of 1979, the SNP fell to just two seats and 17.3 per cent of the vote, and, sweeping into power came Margaret Thatcher and her Conservatives. Thatcher had already made it clear, when she became leader of the Conservatives in 1975, that she was, to put it mildly, uninterested in devolution, and did not want to have any dealings with the SNP. Indeed, there was a 'growing perception, which intensified over the course of the 1980s, that 'Conservatives had no respect for the distinctive nature of Scottish politics'.[32] This was so on the matter of constitutional change, but also, and again increasingly in the decade after 1979, with respect to economic policy and the role of the state. Thatcher was ruthlessly intent on pursuing an ideological program of free market, Hayekian-inspired economic policies,[33] and this, combined with

[31] But see MacCormick, 'Constitutional Points' (1979), which offers a short summary of what the book would have contained: although the Act fell short of 'a far more extensive form of self-government' than MacCormick embraced, his own 'strong conviction' (48) was to argue for it, seeing its longer-term potential for something more 'experimentally democratic' (67).

[32] Mitchell, 'From National Identity to Nationalism' (2000), 160.

[33] Hayek's role in this story is complex and deserves further attention. For instance, as Malcolm Petrie has shown, 'Scottish nationalism espousal of an intensely individualist stance during the post-war decades remains underappreciated'; immediately post-War, for instance, the SNP's newspaper, *Scots Independent*, 'could be found employing lengthy quotations from Hayek's *Road to Serfdom* in its editorial column': Petrie, 'Anti-Socialism, Liberalism, Individualism' (2018), 214.

her neglect of Scottish needs and interests, and her steadfast commitment to centralised Westminster power, made her, again to put it mildly, deeply unpopular in Scotland. In due course, as Geoffrey Barrow was often said to have articulated it, Thatcher was to become 'the greatest Scottish nationalist', for it was in reaction to, if not revolt against, her and her policies that not only Scottish nationalism, but also generally left-wing thought, including social democracy, got its biggest boost and continuous source of stimulation.

More immediately, however, the twin results of the referendum and the elections in 1979 created what can only be described as a deep existential crisis within the SNP. It did not take long for cracks to appear. Already on 31 May 1979, barely a few weeks after the election, the SNP '79 Group was formed. Many felt that the reason for the SNP's electoral demise had been 'failing to adopt a more clearly working class profile'.[34] Independence, it was thought, could not be achieved with the help of the middle classes alone.[35]

Looking back on it now, the '79 Group certainly brought together a 'formidable array' of political 'talent', including Stephen Maxwell, Andrew Currie, Margo MacDonald, Owen Dudley Edwards, Jack Brand, Gavin Kennedy, Roseanna Cunningham, Alex Salmond, Kenny MacAskill, and, from 1980, Jim Sillars (who joined the SNP after the short-lived attempt to set up a Scottish Labour Party).[36] The intense debate within the Group, but also the broader debate triggered by it, informed as this was too by commentary on Scottish and British politics from the New Left – especially by Tom Nairn – generated new political ideas, especially in the form a more radical, socialist, republican, and overall more aggressive nationalism, though one which was also different to Labour, i.e., precisely a 'much less centralised and bureaucratic model of socialism'.[37]

The rise of the '79 Group needs to be seen in the context of the emotion of 1979 – the sense of loss and disillusionment, as well as anger and angst, of 'catastrophic electoral and psychological defeat'.[38] It is not an accident that alongside the '79 Group, a further splintering occurred with the establishment of Sion Nan Gaidheal (SNG), a 'fundamentalist movement believing in militant direct action'.[39] These were heady

[34] Jackson, *The Case for Scottish Independence* (2020), reporting Neal Ascherson's view, 105.
[35] Ibid., 105.
[36] Ibid., 106.
[37] Ibid.
[38] Mitchell, 'Factions, Tendencies' (1990), 54.
[39] Ibid.

days, ripe for making sweeping, controversial statements, e.g., the SNP Annual Conference in 1979 passed a resolution, by large majority, that it would 'not engage any more dealings in assembles, devolution or meaningful talks'.[40]

Even if this was a time in which necessary debates and soul-searching occurred, there is no doubt that it was also a moment of immense existential danger for the SNP: following the defeats of 1979, it was all too easy for the party to fragment into a wilderness of instances. Post 1979, splintering attempts kept surfacing, e.g., the formation of the SDP in 1981 (which attracted MacCormick's brother, Iain, who had lost his seat in 1979)[41] and, in 1982, the formation of the Campaign for Nationalism.[42]

What was MacCormick's role in this crucial time? As observed above, MacCormick had been a member of the SNP National Executive since 1978. According to Wilson, who became leader in 1979, MacCormick played a crucial role in keeping the party together, enabling it to steer a cautious, but still optimistic, and importantly moderate, peaceful, and responsible path, amidst all the emotional disarray and ideological disagreement. Following 1979, Wilson said, with 'everyone demoralised', with a loss of 'faith in democracy', 'a feeling that the "yes" vote had been manipulated by Westminster', with groups splintering and emotions being high between them (Wilson spoke of 'hatred'), with the SNP membership falling and SNP finances dwindling, there was an urgent need for stability, for peace-making, and for new ideas capable of maintaining interest in Scottish nationalism and uniting the party.[43] The years from 1979 to 1983 were, then, utterly crucial.

Here, MacCormick was one of a number of figures – alongside Wilson of course himself – who, through well timed and carefully crafted motions and resolutions at the party's Annual Conference or at National Executive meetings, was able to manage dissent and disagreement, and renew belief in constitutional change in Scotland. An important bridging role was played by the SNP policy on Europe (with a number of figures in the '79 Group also being pro-Europe, such as Sillars, Salmond, and MacAskill'),[44] but equally important, too, was a commitment to a non-fundamentalist, gradualist, and legal means for constitutional change – both topics I shall return to in later chapters.

40 Ibid., 52.
41 See 'From SNP to SDP,' *The Guardian* (2 May 1981).
42 Mitchell, *Scottish Question* (2014), 231.
43 Wilson (interview).
44 Michell, Bennie, Johns, *The Scottish National Party* (2012), 32.

All this often required bursts of creativity, to get the party membership to think through new options – one example being MacCormick's proposal for a bill on a multi-option referendum, which Wilson used in the early 1980s as an idea to be debated.[45] Another, as we shall see in Chapter 7, was a return to older strategies, such as the Constitutional Convention movement of the early 1980s (culminating in the Claim of Right). Sometimes, too, it involved standing up for certain values that one argued were non-negotiable: a good example of such an act by MacCormick was moving a motion, which was seconded by Jim Fairlie, that the SNG be banned – a motion defeated at the time, but one which signalled MacCormick's commitment to a peaceful, responsible party.[46] This was one of many motions that MacCormick lost (another was a motion supporting the SNP's participation in the Constitutional Convention of the 1980s; yet another his speaking up for monarchy, as a lone voice in the 1977 SNP Conference), and which he probably realised he would lose, but which he nevertheless moved, not being afraid to stand up for principles that he thought were crucial to the survival of the party.

But perhaps the most significant intervention by MacCormick came at a more personal level, designed to avoid splintering and mend tensions and emotions. The 'long drawn out saga' of the '79 Group, with members of it being initially expelled in 1982, returned to a NEC special meeting in Larbert on 30 April 1983.[47] Wilson describes this moment with clarity:

> The Appeals Committee had spent around 40 hours in considering the case, some of it with the appellants represented by counsel. It found for the National Executive. Prof. Neil MacCormick had come up with an amendment that sought to mitigate the sentence. My first thought was to disallow it, but, after consideration, it seemed to be a possible solution, especially since the NEC majority had fractured. To me, there were three issues. Was the NEC's decision approved in principle? Had the democratic authority of the Party been maintained? What should be the sentence – expulsion or suspension? On the main issue, the Council voted to uphold the expulsions and the procedures by 157 to 138… On the question of sentence, it agreed to Neil MacCormick's motion to commute the expulsions to suspension, but only provided that each suspended member wrote to the Secretary accepting the position and requesting the lifting of the suspension… The formula was accepted by an overwhelming

45 Wilson (interview).

46 Wilson, *The SNP* (2009), 205.

47 Ibid., 217.

> majority and the sense of the relief amongst the delegates allowed me to turn the feeling to positive advantage by calling forcefully for unity in contesting the General Election.[48]

This contribution by MacCormick speaks volumes and illustrates his character, within a very concrete political context, at work. MacCormick deployed considerable creativity in finding a way to appease both sides, allowing the charge against the '79 Group to stand, thus appealing to the National Executive, while giving the members of that Group a chance to come back into the fold, precisely by commuting the sentence to a conditional suspension. This intervention is in many ways typical MacCormick: it found a way of relating with others that did not necessarily iron out disagreement – indeed, to the contrary, it preserved difference – but that nevertheless created the conditions for peace and unity to emerge. As we shall see, the same kind of creative strategy of generating blended spaces, or differentiated unities, was employed by MacCormick at various levels – from the social democratic stance that steered a middle path between socialism and liberalism, through to the most abstract philosophical positions, such as an institutionalism that merged insights from positivism, natural law, and realism.

Thanks to interventions like the 1983 commuting of the sentence for the '79 Group, which John Swinney picked out as perhaps MacCormick's 'greatest',[49] the SNP turned a corner with the 1983 general election.[50] Although the electoral results were still nothing to write home about, basically maintaining its level from 1979 with two seats, the party had survived, and was about to become more professionalised, disciplined, and more organised in the 1980s. Under Wilson's gradualist, non-fundamental, social democratic, and pro-European leadership (from 1979 to 1990), and thanks in no small measure to Thatcher's growing unpopularity in Scotland, the party, along with Scottish nationalism, slowly gained momentum, which was to culminate in the successes of the 1990s and beyond in the 2000s. Certainly, with respect to its social and economic policy, the party officially and much more confidently adopted a social democratic stance in 1987.[51] It had, in part thanks to

[48] Ibid., 216–17.

[49] Swinney, Eulogy at MacCormick's Funeral Ceremony, 17 April 2009.

[50] Not everyone agreed, certainly not at the time, that this was MacCormick's best contribution: in fact, as MacCormick reported later – in MacCormick, 'The Tories Raised the Stakes' (*The Scotsman*, 18 Friday 1988, 17) – 'One of my most respected friends told me that in moving that motion I had done my greatest disservice'.

[51] Hassan, 'The Modern SNP' (2009), 4; see also Lynch, 'From Social Democracy' (2009).

interventions like MacCormick's, survived, even if bruised and battered, and began, from the mid 1980s on, to stabilise and operate with more professionalism and confidence.

Liberalism, Positivism, and Social Justice

The challenges faced by the SNP – seeking, as MacCormick saw it, to make itself a credible, responsible, moderate party – was one political theatre in which MacCormick acted, negotiating his role, and making his character. But MacCormick the political actor was just one side of MacCormick's contribution: the other was philosophical. MacCormick did not just seek to steer the SNP safely through the years of disappointment, disillusion, and dissent – he also sought to articulate, in substance and detail, a philosophy of good government, including the role of law in it, in and for these years. Some of the triggers of this search for good government came, as we have just seen, from attempts to keep the SNP afloat and viable, and some came, as we shall see in due course, from provocations of evermore centralised, evermore authoritarian executive power in Westminster government, especially under Thatcher.

But there were also inspirations, and other interlocutors, here, which informed MacCormick's philosophical writing in the 1970s and 1980s, as seen most clearly in his collection on *Legal Right and Social Democracy* (1982). In this book, and the largely previously published papers that constituted it, MacCormick articulated a philosophy for the times – one that could be usable by the SNP, but one that also rose above party politics and engaged with broader philosophical themes. He worked hard to confront contemporary political controversies and the broader issues that were at stake in them. For MacCormick, these broader issues fell broadly under the canopy of the role and value of law in the practice of good government. This, however, was also a personal issue, a matter of character, for it involved carving out a role for himself as a jurist in a polity, as a moral philosopher interested in and knowledgeable about the law. MacCormick's character, then, was at work not only in the political interventions he made – as we have seen above, to moments of crisis within the SNP, or as we shall see, to SNP policy, for instance on the structure of government – but it was also at work in his philosophy.

Here, it is important to note a number of sources and inspirations, in particular for his sensitivities to the fate of citizens and persons under the law, including the protection of their interests and liberties, as well as the safeguarding of their welfare, and thus the need for protection for the most vulnerable in society. These sources included: MacCormick's mother, Margaret MacCormick, who had been, as we saw in Chapter 1, a social worker in Glasgow, and who instilled in MacCormick a sense of duty, as well as respect, towards those in need; his training in Glaswegian moral philosophy, which, for instance via Lamont,[52] but also reaching back to eighteenth-century Scottish Enlightenment thinkers, was oriented towards the practice of philosophy with a social conscience, operating within the details of practical, ordinary life, and keen on contributing to its improvement; and his exposure to Hart's social democratic ethos, including his approach to philosophy precisely as anti-authoritarian art of clarifying the terms of public debate.

This last source is worth dwelling on for a moment. It is telling, as mentioned already in Chapter 5, that when writing about Hart, MacCormick often emphasised his contribution as a social democrat, concerned both with protecting civil liberties and thus using philosophical resources to combat the imposition of a particular morality by the state (for instance, in the form of criminal laws), as well as with crafting a limited role for the caring, welfare state (visible, for instance, in Hart moving away from Mill's classical liberal anti-paternalistic position, as well as, more personally, in Hart's friendship with Douglas Jay and the right-wing of the Labour party).[53] MacCormick's reading of Hart, as someone who was a social reformer and critical moralist with a deep-set passion for social justice,[54] was a crucially important intellectual context for MacCormick's

[52] Including Lamont's interest in T. H. Green. Green is an interesting figure in his context, for he has often been thought of as someone who helped provide the philosophical foundations of the welfare state, showing how it was both possible and desirable to move beyond classical laissez-faire liberalism to a kind of 'collectivism': see Lamont, *Introduction to Green's Moral Philosophy* 1934); and Melvyn Richter, *The Politics of Conscience* (1964), which was, incidentally, reviewed during MacCormick's time in Oxford as a student, by Gareth Stedman Jones, *Isis* (10 October 1964), 33. Green was Whyte's Professor of Moral Philosophy in Oxford and also an important figure in Balliol College, Oxford, hence another link with MacCormick. Indeed, there is a broader story to tell here about the British Idealists, who often included Scots, sometimes based in Oxford, and indeed often in Balliol. These figures included: T. H. Green (1836–1882), Edward Craig (1835–1908), William Wallace (1843–1897), F. H. Bradley (1846–1924), Bernard Bosanquet (1848–1923), Richard Burdon Haldane (1850–1928), Henry Jones (1852–1922), David G. Ritchie (1856–1903), Robin G. Collingwood (1889–1943) and Michael Joseph Oakeshott (1901–1990). For a discussion, see, e.g., Fergusson, 'Scottish Idealism' (2013).

[53] See Jay, *Socialism* (1963).

[54] Which is arguably what attracted Hart to Bentham in the first place: see Jennifer Hart's *Ask Me No More* (1998). As mentioned in Chapter 5, Hart's influence has been diminished by emphasising his contribution to general jurisprudence; he was also, if not more, a passionate moral reformer of law.

work on legal rights, civil liberties, and social welfare in the long 1970s. This was in many ways continuous with MacCormick's pre-Hart, Scottish sensibilities, but it was also a factor in its own right, informing the original, creative work MacCormick engaged in during this period, crafting new conceptions of legal rights, and more broadly, philosophising law as something potentially of great value to social democratic societies.

Although it lies outside the scope of this book, this approach to Hart – again, as primarily a social democrat, a reformer, a critical moralist – may also be placed in a larger intellectual context that could allow for a different reading of 'liberalism' and 'positivism'. Both are easy targets, and quickly became so in late twentieth and early twenty-first-century critical legal theory, but their much more complex histories are also just as often ignored.[55] If, however, one considers, even briefly, the practice of liberalism towards the end of the nineteenth century, and one is also prepared to include the small 't' theorising that occurred in the context of such associations as 'the Young Liberals, regular gatherings within the framework of the National Liberal Club, or even the Settlement Movement', then one can see how connected liberalism was to concrete and progressive engagement with social reform.[56]

To this one can add the need for a more nuanced history of 'positivism', which can be widely understood as 'the application of scientific methods to social questions' (as indeed in Auguste Comte and Herbert Spencer), and which was thus always subservient to a value-oriented program of moral improvement and the social conditions that enable it.[57] What was important to positivism, from this perspective, was not accepting, on face value, arguments in the context of social reform debates, made on the basis of some allegedly consensual and conventional morality, without empirical proof[58] – a point that is very much echoed in Hart's work, for example in his 'Social Solidarity' paper and in general in his critique of Devlin's legal moralism.[59] From this perspective, as Herbert Samuel had put it, 'The trunk of the tree of Liberalism is rooted in the soil of ethics',[60] which itself is to be supported by disciplined, empirical research, i.e., positivism. Neither liberalism nor positivism, set in this light, are a-moral or anti-reformist programmes: on the contrary, they are properly

55 But see, recently, Moyn, *Liberalism against Itself* (2023).
56 Freeden, *The New Liberalism* (1978), 4–5.
57 Ibid., 7–8.
58 Ibid., 9.
59 Hart, 'Social Solidarity' (1967); Hart, *Law, Liberty, and Morality* (1963).
60 Freeden, *The New Liberalism* (1978), 11–12.

understood, certainly in their time, as critical sensibilities and as means towards reformist and ethical ends.

Similarly, neither liberalism nor positivism, when historicised in this way, need to be seen to be at odds with a commitment to ethics that balances individualism with communitarianism. If one sees both liberalism and positivism as embedded in projects of moral improvement and social reform – including in religious ones, which certainly informed 'the moral fervour of English social reform'[61] – then one can see that neither was committed to individualism as opposed to the good of the community. The complexity, but also change over time, in the thought of J. S. Mill is a good example here: rather than being a straightforward advocate of individualism, Mill is better thought of as a champion of 'socially rooted individuality as the main attribute of human welfare',[62] and can thus be read, especially in his later work, as a socialist.[63] This would, in turn, support MacCormick's gravitation to Mill in his early years – not because of an enthusiasm for rampant individualism, but instead, in MacCormick's case, because of a sensitivity to the ethics of communal debate.

These are, of course, contested histories, and there are many genealogies one can tell,[64] but the important point here is that we need to be careful about labels like 'liberalism' and 'positivism', including, in the present context, as these are associated with Hart and his jurisprudence. Hart's 'liberalism' and Hart's 'positivism' are better understood – though a full case for this would need to be made elsewhere – as part of a program of progressive, socially conscious, morally infused reform. They were very far from being the kind of stolid, conservative, a-political, a-moral, abstract, impractical philosophies that they are sometimes associated with today. This, in turn, very much informed their jurisprudence, including Hart's.

[61] Ibid., 15.

[62] Ibid., 23.

[63] As indeed he has been recently: McCabe, *Mill, Socialist* (2021); Phillips, *The Liberalism Trap* (2023); Ghosh, 'Mill before Liberalism' (2024).

[64] If we take just the history of legal positivism, see Natasha Wheatley's remarkable account of Hans Kelsen's positivism as a response to other kinds of political challenges in the Hapsburg Empire: *The Life and Death of States* (2023). To this, we would need to add a history of science and aesthetics – a more broadly cultural account of the epistemological transformations of the nineteenth and twentieth centuries, which were crucial in the making of positivisms of all kinds, including legal. The point being made here is that one large part of the history of at least British legal positivism is the pursuit of a progressive, radical, and even, to an extent, communitarian social program. Ignoring these histories results in a greatly impoverished understanding of these complex labels, which hold and carry more nuance, including contrary forces, than we tend to think.

And this, also, informed MacCormick's relation to Hart and more broadly to liberal and positivist traditions. MacCormick was an optimist, certainly, and also a self-proclaimed believer in law ('I believe in law', he said straightforwardly),[65] but this was a belief rooted in the promise of law as being of moral value to the ordinary citizen, protecting that citizen's interests and liberties against the risks of an over-centralised and authoritarian state, while at the same time making that liberty meaningful and valuable by creating conditions of fairness and equality of opportunity.

Thus, the jurisprudence developed by MacCormick, in part in dialogue with Hart, was a jurisprudence in search of good government, i.e., as MacCormick saw it, a social democratic state. For all its generality – for instance, its general claims as to the nature of legal rights – and for all its disciplined pursuit of analytical clarity, this was very much a practically situated and practically oriented jurisprudence that was formed in the political contexts in which both Hart and MacCormick were participant-observers. If MacCormick must be labelled as 'liberal' or 'positivist' – or, worse still, an 'analytical liberal positivist' – then we should at least historicise these labels and recover their progressive, committed, value-oriented, reform-minded, and socially aware meanings.

To these observations – made, I am very conscious, swiftly and impressionistically – we should add something that was, from the 1970s onwards, of increasing importance and interest to MacCormick: the tradition of Scottish philosophical thought, especially in the Enlightenment. There are many links to make here. One of them is with the New Liberalism tradition I mentioned above. As Finlay has observed, the 'ideas of New Liberalism were very strong in Scotland before the First World War' and 'these passed into the post-war Labour Party, where then subsequently made their way into the early SNP', e.g., through associations such as the Young Scots Society.[66] McIntyre, who was mentioned above as a proponent of a non-ideological social democracy, but also a champion of individual rights – and who 'advocated for the creation of a Scottish Bill of Rights' – 'had been a member of the Labour Party in his student days', and was thus also a conduit for these deep-running ideas of a new, reformed, socially conscious, welfare-oriented liberalism.[67] As Chris Harvie has shown, these ideas reach back into the nineteenth century,

[65] MacCormick, 'My Philosophy of Law' (1998), 1.
[66] Finlay, *Scottish Nationalism* (2022), 189.
[67] Ibid.

where there is a Scottish side to the story of social democracy under the guise of liberalism.[68]

The Scottish angle, however, can be pursued even further back. As Dennis Rasmussen has shown, the 'liberalism' of the Scottish Enlightenment, especially in the figures of David Hume and Adam Smith, was a 'realistic, moderate, flexible and contextually sensitive' one.[69] Theirs was a liberalism that was:

> … grounded in experience and empirical observation instead of transcendent or a priori first principles; it addressed practical human concerns rather than aiming to satisfy abstract standards of right derived from God, Nature, or Reason; it was flexible in its application and attentive to the importance of historical and cultural context; and it favoured gradual, piecemeal reform over the pursuit of perfection or the imposition of strict requirements for legitimacy.[70]

In Rasmussen's terms, this was 'a pragmatic Enlightenment', and one which the Scots were at the forefront of. Morality for these thinkers, such as for Hume, was 'an eminently practical phenomenon, embedded in human concerns, rather than based on any kind of sacred, mysterious, or otherworldly authority',[71] and one furthermore that one accessed less by any 'perfect rationality' and more by way of 'generalised sentiment', from the construction of 'the common point of view', which was not detached, but which sought consensus amongst pluralism.[72] For both Hume and Smith, 'moral standards arise as people coordinate their sentiments and behaviour in response to others'[73] – an approach at odds, once more, with any kind of transcendent appeal to untrammelled authority. As Rasmussen expressed it elegantly:

> Far from adopting a hegemonic form of moral and political universalism, they emphasised the importance of context in the formulation of moral standards and adopted a flexible, nonfoundationalist form of liberalism. Far from having a blind faith in reason, they continually stressed the limits

[68] See Harvie, *The Lights of Liberalism*, London, 1976. It would be instructive to trace the historical links here between Scottish nineteenth-century liberalism and the British Idealists, and also beyond to, for instance, John Macmurray, who as we saw, was an influence on John MacCormick, but also, more profoundly within British twentieth-century politics, on Blair's New Labour.

[69] Rasmussen, *The Pragmatic Enlightenment* (2014), 1.

[70] Ibid., 2.

[71] Ibid., 30.

[72] Ibid., 34.

[73] Ibid., 48–9.

> and fallibility of human understanding and advocated a cautious reformism in politics. And far from promoting atomistic individualism, they saw people as inherently social and sought a healthier and more reliable way to unite them than the traditional bonds of blood, religion, and nationalism, which they found above all in commerce.[74]

There is, thus, a self-critical modesty in this approach to moral and political philosophy. By no means sitting back and defending the status quo – indeed, on the contrary, there was a large-scale passion for improvement[75] – this was an approach that was nevertheless mindful of the deeply social character of moral life, as well as the deeply social (competitive and collaborative) character of reason, and of the dangers involved in neglecting the slowly acquired stability of social conventions, for instance by expecting too much from a certain narrow version of rationality. Perhaps it is this 'pragmatic', social, and self-critical Enlightenment where we need to search for the roots of a grounded, limited, reform-minded 'liberalism' and 'positivism'. Certainly, for MacCormick, this long-running tradition, from the Scots of the eighteenth century to his training in moral philosophy in Glasgow, resonated deeply and informed his own philosophical approach, from proposing a revised form of nationalism to theories of rights and other legal phenomena.

The Middle Space: 'Social Democracy'

We can identify three steps in MacCormick's search for good government and the role of law in it. The first, which I consider in this section, is the carving out of a middle space between what MacCormick saw as extremes, and in which he could work out, with analytical sharpness but also delicate balancing of values, how to deal with certain political controversies and practical difficulties. As has already been observed, this was often a move that MacCormick would make in his philosophy (as well as in his political action): acknowledging and seeking to learn from diametrically opposed positions, MacCormick looked for a language and a conceptual space that

[74] Ibid., 4.

[75] Of course, 'improvement' is a loaded term, and (as MacCormick was well aware) much destruction and havoc were caused in the name of 'social improvement', including in Scotland. None of what is said above is meant to uncritically idealise Enlightenment thought; the point, instead, is to point to potentially deeper roots of nineteenth- and twentieth-century liberalism and positivism, and to problematise certain caricatured associations with the Scottish Enlightenment.

enabled him to combine and reconcile aspects of both positions. His articulation of a social democratic position needs to be seen in this light: as precisely carving out a middle path and a middle space in which he could then more delicately confront practical issues. For MacCormick, as we shall see in a moment, this meant showing that the pursuit of social welfare, and thus ameliorating inequality, was not incompatible with the rule of law. Good government did not mean, as the Hayekians thought, giving up on the protection of social welfare; but nor did it mean, as the Marxists thought, giving up on law.

Once this space was carved out, the next step involved examining just how law might protect the values at stake. In truth, MacCormick also pursued this investigation separately to the question of good government and the place of law in it, but it helps, or so I argue, to see it in the context of this broader project. Here, as we shall see in the next section, MacCormick worked to identify the interests, needs, and expectations of human beings in relations with each other, going on to show how legal forms could be understood (sometimes via analytical reconstruction) as protecting these interests, needs, and expectations, and thus as making sense in light of the related underlying values. In this context, the role of the responsible jurist – the practically oriented, but at the same time analytically skilled, moral philosopher turning their attention to law – was to analyse law, and its forms, with a view to illuminating the links between legal forms and values, especially as the latter was experienced by ordinary persons in their relations with each other.

Finally, the third step, with which I will end this chapter, flips this round: yes, law plays, or could play, a role in good government in helping to protect certain interests, needs, and expectations, but there was also a limit as to how far a government could go in using law to protect them. There were limits to the law's imposition of morals. This was especially so in the case of a government seeking to maximise what it saw as economic efficiency, utility, and progress. Here, law had another value, i.e., it was morally relevant and significant in another way: it was a means of limiting government, thwarting attempts by those exercising executive power to extend that power too far, thereby exercising it in an authoritarian way. This involved thinking not about law's role in the constraint of government, but it also meant thinking more broadly about the overall structure of government: how it could be decentralised, devolved, and thus made more democratic.

One way to see the point of these steps is that they sought to make the value of freedom real: to protect civil liberties, but also to enable persons to have more autonomy over the decisions that affect their lives. For this to happen, law had to be compatible with and supportive of democracy. Of course, this also meant limiting and holding accountable other domains of the exercise of power, such as judicial: here, the theory of legal reasoning mattered normatively, endeavouring to make sure that any decisions made were defeasible, and disciplining the giving of reasons for those decisions via various values, such as consistency, coherence, and testing-by-consequences. The aim was to make law principled, not arbitrary, but never so principled as to be irreversible or unchangeable, as if its legal status guaranteed its moral one.

So how did MacCormick carve out the above-mentioned middle space, demonstrating that the pursuit of social welfare was compatible with the rule of law? MacCormick's name for this middle space was 'social democracy'. He acknowledged that, at the time of publishing his 1982 collection, this was also the name of a new political party: the SDP – the party, incidentally, that, as mentioned above, had recently attracted the defection of his brother, Iain, from the SNP.[76] But, he said, though the name is the same, he was 'not a member of that party' and, in addition, 'would contest its sole proprietorship in the concept "social democracy"'.[77] He then set out his understanding of the concept in the following way:

> 1. That social justice cannot be realised through free market institutions premised on the classical rights of liberal individualism as protected by the classical liberals' minimal state;
> 2. That it is therefore necessary for state (and other collective) agencies to take an active role in economic affairs with a view to securing fair shares and fair opportunities for all citizens;
> 3. That the civil rights and liberties proclaimed by classical liberalism are, however, of fundamental importance to human beings, as moral persons, and ought to be qualified only so far as necessary to the securing of fair shares and fair opportunities; and
> 4. Because of the importance of classical rights and liberties, and because these require recognition of private property, no proposal for a completely collectivised or state socialist reorganisation of, or revolution in, post-liberal societies is either acceptable or desirable.[78]

By his own description, this somewhat schematic account is designed to sit halfway between 'Whig and Marxist' views, which are, he added, 'for

[76] See also Williams, *Politics Is for the People* (1981), which MacCormick cites as a platform articulated from within the SDP: LRSD (1982), 1.

[77] MacCormick, LRSD (1982), v.

[78] Ibid., 1.

me thesis and antithesis', it being his 'aim' to 'achieve an acceptable synthesis' of them.[79] Fighting off, in other words, 'a new polarisation in politics, between an increasingly Hayekian right, and an increasingly Marxist left', was an urgent task.[80]

Creating this 'morally and intellectually defensible' 'middle way' begins, MacCormick argued, by acknowledging that 'there is some truth in both the Whig thesis and the Marxist antithesis'.[81] The truth in Marxism consists in seeing that the Hayekian, Whig position 'gives undue priority to securing liberty in a certain sense of the term, "negative liberty"', i.e., 'the liberty to do whatever one is not legally required not to do'.[82] Blindly pursuing the protection of this liberty, including by law, is a mistake: as MacCormick put it, 'advocacy of this stern regime of liberty under minimal law and equality before minimal law commonly ignores the morally unacceptable consequences of grave economic disparities'.[83] It follows that 'freedom from the law's coercion is an instrumental not an ultimate good' and, in that sense, the 'socialist critique of the Whig position' is an accurate diagnosis of its ills.[84]

However, as accurate as the critique of the Whig position is, the remedy provided by the Marxist position is also ill-conceived. This, in turn, shows the germ of truth on the Hayekian, Whig side. It is true that, as the Marxists claim, 'equal liberty before formally universal laws is no guarantee of a universal opportunity for access to the good life', but it does not follow 'that formal legal liberty is not a valuable form of freedom at all'.[85] It matters to individuals that they exercise their 'capacity to make and follow out individual and joint plans of life without arbitrary impediment set by other persons'.[86] But the exercise of this capacity is possible only in the form of 'governance under pre-announced laws mainly negative or prohibitive in tenor'.[87] The protection of this liberty may seem formal, but it is no less valuable for that, even if the good it identifies, as above, is an instrumental, not an ultimate good.

[79] Ibid., 8.
[80] Ibid.
[81] Ibid., 8–9.
[82] Ibid., 9.
[83] Ibid., 10.
[84] Ibid.
[85] Ibid.
[86] Ibid., 12.
[87] Ibid.

But is it really possible, MacCormick asks rhetorically, to pursue social justice via law and still possess 'the admitted good of governance under universally applicable laws?'.[88] Yes, it is, he answers: 'There is nothing non-universal about a law which ascribes to every adult citizen a right to enjoy an annual minimum income of £3,000, and to obtain this or that balance from the appropriate authorities of the state in the event that he/she can provide that reasonable personal efforts have failed to procure an income so large'.[89]

Of course, to show that something is possible is one thing; to show it is desirable, is another. To argue that it was, MacCormick drew briefly on Finnis's arguments, as representative, of 'the old natural lawyers' insight that the stock of material goods available for human use and exploitation is in principle a common stock of mankind'.[90] Material goods do not cease to be common stock through the enterprise and labour of particular individuals, for the very value of such enterprise and labour is really only possible in the context of communities. If those who appropriate, for private possession, elements from this common stock, go on to call upon the community for protection (e.g., via enforceable law) of their possession, then it equally falls upon these persons not to 'exclude other more needy people from any share in the goods they have appropriated'.[91] At bottom, there is community, and the needs of its members, such that the fruits of any private appropriation protected – significantly, by the community – ought to be, in part, shared by those who are most vulnerable. In summarising his overall position – the middle space he has carved out – MacCormick writes:

> My contention is that legal right and civil liberty indeed matter, and matter for the Kantian reasons our new Whigs give, for they are indeed essential conditions of respect for persons. But I deny that the protection of civil liberty adequately justifies the inequalities of fortune which a merely libertarian legal order facilitates. I assert a debt of justice owed by the haves to the have-nots, a debt payable by redistribution of assets to the latter to secure to them adequate worth for their legal liberties. But there are practical limits on such distribution, bounded by the moral imperative against schemes productive of tyranny.[92]

Characteristically balancing what he saw as partial truths, MacCormick articulated his own delicate, middling position between extremes. In so

[88] Ibid., 13.
[89] Ibid.
[90] Ibid., 14.
[91] Ibid.
[92] Ibid., 15.

doing, he recognised of course that much will depend on the details of any particular controversy or practical difficulty: careful judgement will need to be exercised to see just where to draw the line, e.g., with respect to taxation and thus redistribution, or with respect to the limits of governments using law to pursue their ends. Indeed, engaging in that painstaking exercise of circumstantial judgement is precisely what he does, e.g., in his response to particular cases decided by the courts or through participation in the law reform process. Exercising careful, circumstantial judgement in this way is one of the tasks for a responsible jurist. But, first, space needs to be created for the exercise of this judgement. That is precisely what MacCormick attempts in crafting the above 'social democratic' position, and thus recognising and balancing, the value of formal liberty, but at the same time, the value of material equality, with law playing a crucial role in protecting both.

It may be possible to relate MacCormick's preservation of the ongoing process of judgement, enabled by the crafting of this middle space, to his response to the theory of justice that was published in the early 1970s, John Rawls's *A Theory of Justice* (1971), and which quickly became, over the course of that decade, the dominant work of political theory. MacCormick engaged with Rawls's book on a number of occasions – reviewing it in 1973,[93] then returning to it again in 1976,[94] before turning to it once more for his 1982 collection.[95]

Without developing this engagement in detail, it is telling that, in the 1982 version, MacCormick presents Rawls's method, of constructing the hypothetical social contract via forming a society behind a 'veil of ignorance', as problematic if it assumes that it can generate principles of a just society, rather than simply being a procedure for testing the tenability of such principles. As MacCormick sees it, the imaginary exercise behind the veil of ignorance requires that we characterise, which inevitably we will do in a selective and imperfect way, the knowledge of those doing the imagining (informed by our knowledge of the natural and social sciences),[96] which, in turn, will affect what and how they will imagine. All this presupposes certain values that the procedure cannot itself yield, e.g., impartiality, or that 'people are ordinarily the best judges of their own interests and ought always to be treated as such'.[97] For MacCormick, if

93 MacCormick, 'Justice According to Rawls' (1973).
94 MacCormick, 'Justice: An Un-Original Position' (1976).
95 MacCormick, LRSD (1982), chapter 5.
96 Ibid., 93.
97 Ibid., 92.

Rawls's method is understood as generating principles of a just society, it risks 'concealing'[98] what would otherwise be points of contention (precisely those characterisations and presuppositions). But it can be read in another way, precisely:

> ... as a convenient method for testing the implications of adhering to certain factual views about the essential nature of human beings as social animals and to certain broad principles of formal and procedural justice, together with the ideal that human societies should be such that all their members would be able willingly to consent to their organisation as free and rational moral agents.[99]

What matters to MacCormick here is that we do not rest content, somehow thinking that we have reached, through a certain method, a perfect account of a perfectly just society. As he puts it: 'I do not believe in final blueprints, but rather in a permanent effort to articulate the principles by which one conceives oneself to be acting, and in a permanent disposition to criticise them in the light of what results from putting them into effect, and to amend principles and practice in the light of the critique of their effects'.[100]

This relentless, never-ending, self-critique, but at the same time pursuit, despite awareness of the inevitable limitations, the imperfect knowledge, the contestable presuppositions, of one's sense of justice, is what attracts MacCormick to Rawls, or at least to his reading of Rawls. What MacCormick wants, in other words, is not a method that allows us to rest on our laurels, satisfied that we have somehow solved the problems of moral and political theory. Such a method is a mirage, a dangerous illusion. But that does not mean that we can do nothing, as if demoralised and immobilised by the impossibility of perfection. We simply have to give up on the idea of 'final blueprints' and safeguard, instead, spaces where we continue to exercise cautious, difficult judgement, contesting and balancing values (in other words, exercising 'practical reason') – spaces, precisely, like that of 'social democracy'.

Law's Imperfect Justice

What did MacCormick see as the role of the jurist – the moral philosopher with interest in and knowledge of the law – in a social democratic state?

[98] Ibid., 94.
[99] Ibid., 95.
[100] Ibid., 96.

A large part of it was precisely the duty to judge – which for MacCormick meant to justify, in accordance with certain standards of justification – under conditions of imperfect knowledge and with awareness of the inevitability of one's limitations (as above, no 'final blueprints', just the continuous and always defeasible task to keep judging). As we shall see in more detail in the next section, one aspect of the value of law – understood as a regime of formal justice – was that it enabled persons to live in an order that at least sought to limit excesses of power. But another aspect was more substantive: the need for a government that at least sought to protect the goods of persons, for instance by protecting their rights and enforcing obligations.

Thus, the job of a jurist was, as MacCormick saw it, and as he practised it over this period of the long 1970s (though also beyond), to search for the moral 'foundations', or 'grounds', or simply moral justifications for certain areas of law or certain specific legal instruments. This did not necessarily mean defending the status quo, but it did mean looking hard for the moral import or moral value of existing legal rules in case this was obscure or was about to be sacrificed (for instance, in a project of law reform) in the name of some other value, e.g., economic efficiency. The jurist, working as a kind of moral philosopher, had to be creative, including drawing on his or her analytical skills, and noticing nuanced distinctions that others may miss.

The point, throughout, was not to show that law, as it was, was perfectly just; quite the contrary: it was a matter of attempting, with awareness of one's limits and one's fallibility, and thus mindful also of the inevitable controversy surrounding any moral justification, to articulate the moral underpinnings of particular laws or areas of the law, precisely so that they could be evaluated and, where needed, reformed. This, incidentally, was not only the job of the jurist, but also the basis of political obligation – as MacCormick put it when discussing Stair and Locke:

> The point of having positive law as he [Stair] saw it is precisely that human imperfection makes achievement of a perfect order of justice impossible among mere humans. We have to do the best we can in the knowledge that we cannot secure the ideal. That necessitates a choice for each of us between on the one hand demanding full satisfaction of our own conception of ideal justice, the consequence of which is descent or perhaps reversion into some kind of anarchy, and on the other hand acquiescing in arrangements which inevitably fall short of our own ideal… That is precisely the choice we have. The mere fact that a legal order secures only a partial or imperfect protection of the rights we conceive people to have does not justify us in attempting to bring down the whole edifice.[101]

[101] MacCormick, 'Stair and Locke' (1979), 408; later included as chapter 4 of LRSD (1982).

The inevitability of imperfection did not justify either revolution or giving up on the job of seeking moral justification and moral improvement of the law. Indeed, the above stance – for both citizen and jurist alike – was only possible in circumstances where the system was 'animated by some conception of rights and some genuine effort to secure in practice the announced conception of rights'.[102] The system, to be owed respect, needed to be attempting to secure the rights of persons.[103] And this meant, once again, the jurist springing into action, articulating the moral justifications for positive law, seeking to safeguard the role and value of law in good government. Imperfection, and the existence of moral controversy, did not make the task of morally reconstructing law hopeless or unnecessary: quite the opposite, it is precisely what made it crucial and urgent.

The task of the jurist, conceived of in this way, is certainly an ambitious one. For instance, it is holistic – it reaches across areas of the law, combining them into an overall mission to, once again, investigate and protect the role and value of law in good government. Issues of private justice, for example – of the kind of justice protected by private law – were entangled with issues of social justice, i.e., with matters of equality, fairness, and welfare, as well as with other kinds of justice, such as formal justice or corrective justice. To be ambitious in this way, of course, did risk taking on too much and being accused of incoherence. Indeed, in answer to one such reading, made by Richard Tur,[104] of the 1982 collection, MacCormick noted that he was aware of the dangers, but still defended precisely this kind of holistic approach:

> I am grateful that in his critique Tur does not separate the discussion of 'private law' points from the rest of the discussion. Among the reasons why I included these essays in the book is precisely because I don't think one should shunt questions of the justification of private rights and obligations into a siding separated from the main line of inquiry in legal and political philosophy. Our view of social justice has to be a whole view of the rights against fellow-citizens and the rights against the state which are held by all citizens. Too little attention is paid to so-called 'private law' matters in most current legal and political philosophy. Too little is done to compare the principles at stake in this with those at stake in other fields. I may indeed have failed (although I do not think I have failed) to establish a coherent line of argument connecting issues of public law, of criminal responsibility and of civil liability. But I am certain that the task is one worth undertaking.[105]

[102] Ibid.
[103] Ibid., 409.
[104] See Tur, 'Taking Rights Left' (1983).
[105] MacCormick, 'Reply to Mr Tur' (1983), 207–8.

It is thus precisely this holistic, analytical, but at the same time normative, task that MacCormick undertakes in a series of papers and chapters in the long 1970s, culminating in the 1982 collection, and then continuing in a variety of ways – indeed, all the way to the 2007 book, *Institutions of Law*, which was similarly holistic and similarly concerned with identifying the distinctive, but still related into one whole, moral grounds, foundations, or justifications of particular areas of law and legal instruments. As we shall see later, to call this an 'institutional theory' was, among other echoes, to allude to the Scottish tradition of institutional jurists, i.e., as MacCormick saw it, philosophers, such as Stair, who combined analytical skill and moral inquiry so as to reconstruct law as a rational, principled, but still always imperfect, overall scheme of justice.

Voluntary Obligations

A vital part of this juristic enterprise for MacCormick was arguing that the goods that law protected, or sought to protect, were in existence prior to any rules of law or, in some circumstances, conventional social practices (this did not mean that MacCormick could not also acknowledge, as indeed he did, that law, as a conventional order, possessed its own kinds of value). An early example of this is MacCormick's debate with Raz over 'Voluntary Obligations and Normative Powers' (1972). Here, MacCormick confronted a view – which he attributed, for instance, to Bentham, Hart, and Raz – that 'contractual' or 'voluntary' obligations 'presuppose the existence of power-conferring rules'.[106] On this view, it was only because 'certain rules exist in virtue of which persons may by performing certain actions place themselves under obligations to perform further acts specified by themselves'[107] that such obligations were generated. There was no other source of such obligations. If one had to justify the existence of obligations generated through such power-conferring rules, then one could say that 'the answer to that should be in terms of the general expediency of providing "facilities" (Professor Hart's term) of this sort'.[108] The same kind of move could be made at a higher level of generality with respect to promising: thus, one could argue, as MacCormick took John Searle to argue (in his *Speech Acts*, 1969), that promises generated obligations only because there was a prior rule-defined social practice, according to which

[106] MacCormick, 'Voluntary Obligations and Normative Powers' (1972), 60.
[107] Ibid.
[108] Ibid.

the utterance of certain words counted as an obligation-generating promise. The practice, as a whole, had no other moral justification – at best, it could be justified on grounds of utility.[109]

For MacCormick, however, as 'very neat and tidy' as such an account was, it was 'quite unconvincing', and this was not only because it was 'quite unnecessary in the explanation of promising and of the obligation to keep promises to invoke the concept of a power-conferring rule enshrined in a social practice',[110] but also because – and this is what is of most importance at present – it obscured, rather than illuminated, the moral ground of voluntary obligations (including of the social practice of promising and the legal doctrines of contract law).

The above view had things the wrong way round: it was not the prior existence of any rule, or associated social practice, that explained the normativity of promising, but rather, there was a moral reason that explained and justified the existence of the rules (e.g., of contract law) and the practice of promising. What was this moral reason – this moral ground? Here, MacCormick, as was characteristic of him, turned to examples of what we may call 'relational justice' (not MacCormick's term) – a sense of what persons owed to each other, as they experienced this in everyday life. In this case, this meant a sense of reliance: what 'promises do' and 'are calculated to do' is 'induce their addressees to rely upon future performance by the promisor'.[111] MacCormick was careful to distinguish this from merely creating an expectation: when we rely on another person, we do not merely expect them to behave in a certain way, but we 'base' our conduct on what promised, 'as when a host takes trouble and expense in preparing a dinner for an expected guest, or when a man deliberately refrains from catching a train because he believes his neighbour will give him a lift to work'.[112]

What is evident in MacCormick's proposal of reliance being at the moral ground of the practice of promising, and thus also voluntary obligations, such as those imposed by contract law, is his enormous sensitivity to the wrong of letting down another, of disappointing another person, and thus of failing in one's responsibility of respecting them as persons.[113] Rather

[109] Ibid., 60–1.
[110] Ibid., 61.
[111] Ibid., 64.
[112] Ibid.
[113] MacCormick's interest in a reliance theory of promising appears already in his 1970 paper on third-party rights in contract: see 'Ius Quaesitum' (1970), 239–40; later, it is reinforced by his reading of Smith's lectures: see MacCormick, 'Adam Smith' (1981).

than focusing solely on any duties generated by rules, and thus on the perspective solely of the first person agent, MacCormick placed normative emphasis on the relationship between persons, and in particular on the second person point of view, i.e., precisely the reliance placed by one person on the words or actions of the other. He dramatised this in an example that is worth setting out in full, as it is illustrative of MacCormick's approach:

> Suppose that Jones has been swimming from a beach at the foot of a cliff on a stormy day. He has failed to notice the speed with which the tide is rising, and is now in such a position that a desperate dash along the beach will perhaps enable him to reach the path up to safety before he is cut off by the tide. Macdonald happens just then to be strolling along the cliff top carrying a few hundred feet of stout climbing rope. He spots Jones's predicament and lowers the rope down the cliff-face to him. Jones sees what he is doing and waits for the rope to reach himself, thus losing time so that he can no longer conceivably reach the path before the tide comes in. He then starts to climb the rope.[114]

MacCormick's work, even at its most analytical, is always replete with such mini-dramas – easily accessible examples, which resemble, for instance, the mini-narratives that can be found on the pages of Adam Smith's *Theory of Moral Sentiments*. In this example, what MacCormick is inviting us to experience, as readers, is precisely the bond created by the actions of the two persons, Jones and Macdonald. This is a moral bond – or, put another way, the morality of the situation is created by the relational acts of the two parties – which MacCormick further elaborates on in the following way:

> From the moment at which it ceased to be possible for Jones to reach safety by running, because he had waited for Macdonald's rope to reach him, as Macdonald intended he should or knew he would, we can surely say that it would be wrong for Macdonald to abandon the enterprise, drop the rope, and go away – it would be wrong even if he could do equal good, save another person, even two other persons, by going and rescuing them from some other predicament. Jones has acted in a way which is now irrevocable, and which will be greatly detrimental to him unless Macdonald holds on to the rope till Jones has climbed up. Jones so acted because Macdonald intended him to take it that Macdonald intended him so to act (or knew that he would). Macdonald therefore has an obligation to hold on to the rope till Jones reaches the top.[115]

It is this moral, relational, experience, that grounds the obligation that Macdonald has. Notice that at no time did we need to 'suppose that he

[114] MacCormick, 'Voluntary Obligations and Normative Powers' (1972), 67.
[115] Ibid., 67–8.

[Macdonald] belongs to a society which recognises some practice or institution according to which persons have a power, by throwing ropes over cliffs, and such like acts, to incur obligations'.[116] Not only is this unnecessary, attempts to explain voluntary obligations in this way simply do not reach far enough into the morality of situations such as this. The quality of justification provided by the rule-first explanation is inadequate – it ends up resting on the utility of the practice. But this fails to see the depth of the obligation that, in the above scenario, Macdonald has to Jones. There is, as MacCormick sees it, a deep-running wrong that Macdonald would commit by letting go of the rope (and, say, attempting to save two other persons): that would be the wrong of 'disappointing people whom we have wilfully inducted to take action on the faith of assurances of ours about present facts or future facts'.[117] Of course, this situation, this illumination of the moral bond created between these persons, did not explain or justify all aspects of contract law – there were many particular difficulties that the law needed to confront (such as 'whether or not a promise was genuinely made, or genuinely "taken up" by the promisee', and many others)[118] – but this did not detract from the basic point: that the good, which the law was based on, and in the light of which it could be said to be morally significant and justifiable, was the protection of this moral experience of reliance.

The Obligation of Reparation

The above early, 1972, paper, was by no means the only occasion on which MacCormick found moral significance in temporally extended relational experiences – in the normative bonds created by persons as a result of actions or words said in interactions between them – which he then deployed in the juristic task of justifying the existence of certain legal rules. In another paper delivered to the Aristotelian Society (as the 1972 had been), this time in 1978, MacCormick confronted what the Scots termed the 'obligation of reparation', which MacCormick applied '(by a slight extension of that usage)' to 'any such case of a person's being bound to make good another's harm on the ground of his responsibility for it'.[119] At stake this time was not the moral justification of contract law, but instead tort or delict, and in particular the moral distinctions between

116 Ibid., 68.
117 Ibid., 73.
118 Ibid., 75.
119 MacCormick, 'The Obligation of Reparation' (1978), 175.

compensation of victims of torts or delicts and the punishment of criminal offenders.

This, it should be added, was in the context of the *Royal Commission on Civil Liability and Compensation for Personal Injury*, known as the Pearson Commission, which had begun in 1973, and which reported in December 1978, and before which MacCormick had given evidence. Speaking in March 1978, MacCormick sought, as a jurist, to articulate the moral grounds of this area of the law. It was in the service of this task that he deployed an example – once again, an easily accessible example, though in this case also one that is likely to have been the result of a personal experience:

> … suppose for example that a University teacher has promised to take his children to the beach one afternoon, but before setting off he is visited by a student in a condition of apparently suicidal depression; that he gives himself over to helping the student for the rest of the day by talking over his problems, and thus fails to keep his promise to his children.[120]

In analysing this situation morally, one could say, if one approached the situation in a temporally restricted way, focusing only on the moment of choice and thus solely on whether the decision-maker was at fault, that the University teacher in question made the right choice – saving the student, or at least attempting to, and thus rightfully breaking the promise to his children. On this approach, that is all there is to it: the University teacher was faced with a choice between two options, and, given the seriousness and possible repercussions (loss of life) to the student, he did the right thing. He was thus not to blame for breaking the promise to his children.

That, however, is not how MacCormick analysed the situation. Yes, MacCormick acknowledged, the University teacher did the right thing by choosing to spend the day with the distressed student. In that limited sense, he is not to blame for not taking his children to the beach. However, and this is crucial, this choice did not end the normativity of the relation between the University teacher and his children: that relationship, and its obligations, continued, and survived the choice the University teacher rightfully made. As MacCormick saw it, the University teacher 'now owes it to his children as soon as possible to make good their disappointment by taking them to the seaside'.[121] In other words, the lack of blame or fault, such as in the above scenario, does not exhaust or dispel the obligation

[120] Ibid., 176.
[121] Ibid., 175.

already incurred: this remains, and thus the University teacher still 'has an "obligation of reparation" even though he did not do the wrong thing in failing to keep the promise'.[122] The duty, not to disappoint others, survived and reached into the future of the relationship.

Why did this matter to the task of morally justifying tort or delict? Many attempts at an explanation or justification of this area of the law rested on attributing some blame or fault to the wrongdoer. However, there were many instances in which we might want to say – as indeed in the above situation – that the wrongdoer was really not to blame or at fault for acting as she did, but still owed a duty of a kind. In another example that MacCormick uses in the paper, a father, who is rushing to visit his wife in hospital, where she is giving birth to their first child, crashes into his neighbour's parked car. Although deliberately less clear than the first example, there is still a sense, or so MacCormick argues, in which we would say that the father is understandably not at fault.

Of course, the law here, partly in response to such cases, legislates an 'objective test' for fault, it being irrelevant whether the father subjectively was not able, in his circumstances, to take sufficient care – what mattered was whether a reasonable person in his place would have done. For MacCormick, however, such attempts at objectifying fault ultimately 'obscure[d] the moral justification of the law'.[123] They did so because they placed all the focus on the duties of the alleged wrongdoer; they focused, to the detriment of the moral justification of the law, solely on the 'harm-causer'. 'But', asked MacCormick, 'what about the sufferer of the harm?'.[124] Following the example of the father crashing into the neighbour's car, MacCormick's analysis continued: 'Would we not say that people who park their cars on well-lit roadsides are entitled to expect that others will avoid banging into them? Does that not point towards a rather different sort of justifying principle, concerning the right of individuals to be secured form certain kinds of harm which others may inflict on them?'[125]

As he had done in the context of voluntary obligations, so here in the context of obligations of reparation: the normative emphasis need not, and indeed should not, be placed solely on the wrongdoer or the harm-causer, but rather seen in the light of a relationship between persons, which extends over time, and survives even the absence of any fault. The

[122] Ibid.
[123] Ibid., 184.
[124] Ibid., 179.
[125] Ibid.

important 'good' that is brought into view, as a result of this more relational and temporally extended moral analysis, is a certain 'right to reasonable security'.[126] The focus on the wrongdoer, and their 'objective duty', alone, has, MacCormick argued, 'led us to conceive of awards of damages in negligence cases as some kind of "sanction" for wrongful conduct', but in this light, 'the law cannot but seem arbitrary and unjust, because the "sanction" is in no way proportioned to the degree of fault involved, and is sometimes applied in the total absence of any kind of moral blameworthiness whatsoever'.[127]

Thus, if we were engaged in the juristic task of 'justification of this branch of the law' – as indeed the Pearson Commission was at the time – then 'it is evident that we must start from the right, not from the duty which lawyers put at the centre of the map but which is itself unintelligible'.[128] This, in turn, not only made the law more morally intelligible, making clear its moral value where it was otherwise obscure, but it also helped to bring into view the stakes of law reform in this area, including the relations between this area of private justice and questions of distributive, or social, justice.[129] Further, and as mentioned above, seeing matters this way helped us to avoid conflating the distinctive moral grounds of private law and criminal law: what we were doing when enforcing a duty to compensate a victim (for instance, of a car accident) was not sanctioning the wrongdoer, but instead 'securing pecuniary reparation for the infringement of a right', with the 'coercion' in question simply making sure that the reparation is made.[130]

In the above two examples, we see MacCormick, the jurist – the moral philosopher with an interest in, and knowledge of, the law – at work. A vital aspect of this task, as MacCormick saw it, was avoiding an explanation and justification of the law as but a utility-based series of rather arbitrary and coercively backed duties, imposed from the top by a legislator onto the life of citizens. By no means did this mean that one had to go to the other extreme and argue that the legal order as it existed was as good as it could be, i.e., that it was morally perfect, and thus had to be obeyed because it was the very embodiment of perfect justice. Instead, one worked, as a jurist, in the difficult middle space: law's justice was always imperfect, but it had to aim for it. It was the job of the jurist to draw on her analytical skills and moral experiences to try to safeguard the moral

[126] Ibid., 181.
[127] Ibid., 184–5.
[128] Ibid., 185.
[129] Ibid., 187–8.
[130] Ibid., 192.

intelligibility of the law – to show what kinds of goods it was seeking to secure. To present law as but a species of command, imposed by a superior onto an inferior, was to fail in this task of being a responsible jurist. Hence also MacCormick's consistent critique of what he called 'the imperative fallacy'[131] and other attempts at understanding law via coercion.

For a Scot, this had another connotation, of course – explaining or justifying law in that way meant reducing law's legitimacy to the effective domination of a power over a population (e.g., the Westminster parliament over the whole of the UK) – and this could not be. Law had to be more deeply set in the lives of ordinary persons and their moral experiences, even if, as often happened, it also failed to protect them. Once again, the task of a jurist was to stand up for the possibility – even if not actuality – of law being principled, and thus morally intelligible, albeit always defeasibly so.

Conceptualising Rights

We have already seen how, in the above example, MacCormick turned a duty on its head: the obligation of reparation was justified not by some duty owed by an objectified wrongdoer, but instead by the importance of securing rights to persons. And, indeed, throughout this period of the long 1970s, MacCormick was highly animated by, and interested in, the question of legal rights: what they were and how they could be justified; how they could be made morally intelligible; and what was their relationship with duties.

Rights, as has been mentioned above, were not a new topic for MacCormick in the 1970s. MacCormick had already been exposed to the importance of a philosophy of rights in the work of his teacher in Glasgow, Lamont, who early on had formulated an interest-based theory of rights that took seriously, for instance, the rights of animals.[132] He had also, as we have seen, sat in Hart's lectures on 'Rights and Duties' in the mid 1960s, conscientiously writing out, and keeping for years to come, his own notes on them. As MacCormick's notes reveal, Hart's starting point in these lectures was to argue – in answer to the first question he posed to the students, namely 'What is the source of all the trouble about rights and duties?' – that the 'factual language of law (legislatures, courts etc.)

[131] See MacCormick, 'Legal Obligation and the Imperative Fallacy' (1973). I return to this paper in Chapter 9.

[132] See Lamont, *Principles of Moral Judgement* (1947), chapter 3.

scarcely ever uses them'.[133] It was, instead, 'theorists' who 'use them to refer to situations in a legal framework'; it was 'theorists who pick out duties and rights from law-created situations'; 'hence', Hart concluded, all the 'disagreements'.[134]

Further, according to Hart, the 'notion of legal rights is a comparatively new one' – it wasn't there in Plato or Aristotle, and Maine was right that the Romans did not have a concept of rights, for the Romans 'saw law not as protection of individual [sic], but as prescribing ways to behave in a particular situation'.[135] But if we did have to speak of 'rights', Hart continued, then we ought to conceptualise 'the individual with a right' as being 'in a special legal position – he can determine whether the corresponding duty continues; he can waive or enforce it at his own choice. The law is put at his disposal to use if he wants'.[136] MacCormick's notes continue on to record Hart's views of the views of previous theorists on rights, including Hohfeld and Bentham, tracing also various confusions and troubles in particular cases.

Hart's insistence, in these lectures, that rights were 'scarcely used' in legal language, and his defence of the will or choice theory rights,[137] were clearly triggers for MacCormick.[138] As he put in his 1977 paper on 'Rights in Legislation', in his lectures, Hart had stated 'the view that "right" is a term used in discourse about the law, used for making statements about individual's position as seen in terms of the law, rather than a term used in the law itself'.[139] For MacCormick, not only as a Glaswegian moral philosopher,

133 MacCormick, *Hart's Lectures on Rights and Duties*, Edinburgh University Archives, 1. The lectures are likely to have been delivered in the 1964–65 year (during which Hart also gave lectures on Kelsen). Robert Summers also attended both lecture series: Summers, 'H. L. A. Hart's "The Concept of Law"' (1995), 596.

134 Ibid.

135 Ibid., 2.

136 Ibid.

137 In the lectures, Hart it seems preferred to speak of 'choice' rather than 'will', as in eighteenth and nineteenth century will theories, indicating that much depended on 'the meaning of "will"': see MacCormick, *Hart's Lectures on Rights and Duties*, Edinburgh University Archives, 17. Incidentally, Hart's lectures covered also other theories of rights, such as 'Expectation', 'Predictive' (here, Holmes featured), and 'Reductive' (here Kelsen was mentioned) Theories of Rights: see MacCormick, *Hart's Lectures on Rights and Duties*, Edinburgh University Archives, 19–27.

138 In terms of definitions, MacCormick noted, as a sideline, in his lecture notes, that Hart's definition of 'interest', as 'whatever is required for a man's happiness', 'can be extended': MacCormick, *Hart's Lectures on Rights and Duties*, Edinburgh University Archives, 18; he also ticked 'good', when Hart had employed 'good or happiness' in the next sentence; already, then, it seems, in the mid 1960s, MacCormick was attracted to the interest theory, but one understood as protecting the goods of individuals.

139 MacCormick, 'Rights in Legislation' (1977), 190.

but also as a Scottish jurist, self-consciously used to prioritising rights rather than (as, arguably, in the English tradition) remedies, this was an anathema: not only did it ignore the language of the law, and its frequent recourse to 'rights', but also, even more importantly, it failed to make the law morally intelligible – it did not convey the moral significance of the law as much as it could, especially to a wide range of persons, i.e., beyond those that could exercise the power to waive the duties of others.

It is very telling, in that respect, that, writing in 1975, in a paper first delivered in Cambridge, that MacCormick chose to 'test' theories of rights by considering the rights of children. For the will theory, as expounded for instance by Hart, rights 'presuppose duties as their correlative', and duties, in turn, 'exist when there exist legal or social rules … in virtue of which individuals in certain circumstances are required to act or abstain from acting in certain ways'.[140] Where, in those rules that impose duties, 'the performance by a duty bearer of the required act (or abstention) is to be conditional on some other person's choice', then we can properly speak of a right.[141] Thus, as MacCormick put it, for the will theorist, 'a legal or moral right is equivalent to a legal or moral power of waiver or enforcement of duties'.[142] Evidently, however, children (though also incapacitated persons, and one could add animals too) were not able to exercise such a power: 'A baby cannot in fact, cannot in morals, and cannot in law relieve his or her parents of their duty towards him or her in those matters'.[143]

In response to these criticisms, the typical tactic of the will theorist is to argue that 'it is sufficient if either B or some other person C acting on B's behalf has the relevant powers over A's duty in respect of B'; but, for MacCormick, this was not a good answer, for 'there seems to be no reason whatever to suppose that the child or anyone acting on the child's behalf should be permitted or empowered to wave the parental duty or in any sense to acquiesce in its non-performance'.[144] Yes, the law did contain certain remedial or enforcement powers in which public authorities, for instance, could remove a neglected child from their parents, so as to secure their care, but this was hardly the foundation of the right:

> To regard such powers as constitutive of rights (as the will theory does), is to foreclose the possibility of justifying them on the ground that they do

[140] MacCormick, 'Children's Rights' (1976), 306.
[141] Ibid.
[142] Ibid., 307.
[143] Ibid.
[144] Ibid.

> protect rights which might otherwise be insecure, and thus in my submission to confuse the substantive right with ancillary remedies provisions. It is unduly anglo-centric to erect the brocard *ubi remedium ibi ius* into an analytical truth.[145]

Putting the enforcement or remedial provisions first, or making them somehow constitutive of the very existence of rights, was to get things the wrong way round. Instead, it was because children had the right that there were provisions in place imposing duties on parents and, if parents fell short, on public authorities. As MacCormick summarised it, 'So far from its being the case that the remedial provision is constitutive of the right, the fact is rather that recognition of the right justifies the imposition of the remedial provision… *Ubi ius, ibi remedium*'.[146] This allowed us to 'recognise the moral importance and the significance' of this right, and other moral rights, and it also offered us 'a clear conception of legal right', which can then be understood as attempting, however imperfectly, to embody the moral right.[147]

This, of course, still leaves unanswered the question: what is a moral and a legal right? What is it that it is seeking to protect? Here, MacCormick found himself wrestling with the language of the 'interest' theory, which spoke, precisely, in terms of 'needs, interest, or desires' of individuals, with the protection of these not being subservient to 'ulterior advantages', as articulated by a utility-based theory.[148] The emphasis on protecting individuals, as against the pursuit of utility, was vital, but the language was not entirely satisfactory: indeed, MacCormick said, it was 'the characteristic failing' of the interest theory that it spoke of '"want-regarding" categories such as needs, interests, and desires'.[149] Instead, MacCormick argued, it is better to think of 'goods' that rights secure to individuals. Summarising his neo-interest theory of rights, MacCormick argued they were better conceptualised in the following way:

> … to ascribe to all members of a class C a right to treatment T is to presuppose that T is a good of such importance that it would be wrong to deny it or withhold it from any member of C. That as for moral rights: as for legal rights I should say this: when a right to T is conferred by law on all members of C, the law is envisaged as advancing the interests of each and every member of C on the supposition that T is a good for every member of C,

145 Ibid., 308.
146 Ibid., 309.
147 Ibid.
148 Ibid., 310.
149 Ibid., 311.

> and the law has the effect of making it legally wrongful to withhold T from any member of C.[150]

We might call this the 'good theory of rights'. For MacCormick, it was an expression of a broader commitment – which we have already encountered in previous chapters – of respect for persons, i.e., that 'sentient beings ought to be respected as ends in themselves'.[151] This 'belief in respect for persons', MacCormick argued, in this defence of children's rights, 'is both a fundamental and an ultimate moral principle'.[152] As he saw it, it was the job of the jurist to account for the moral foundation of law and its forms – in this case, legal rights – and thus to make it morally intelligible. In light of the principle of 'respect for persons', doing that meant casting the net as widely as possible, and thus not merely making the law intelligible morally to those who could exercise the power or capacity to choose, but also precisely to those who could not.

Writing in 1977, in a collection of papers in honour of Hart, MacCormick chose to focus precisely on the inadequacies of Hart's theory of rights. Here, MacCormick reiterated his observation that the law contained many examples of rights language, where, significantly, the law first imposed rights and then, as a secondary and contingent matter, and one which occurred later in time, imposed duties on persons as part of the enforcement of that right, e.g., this was so in the case of children having a 'right to the whole of the intestate estate' where an 'intestate is survived by children'.[153] Such rules were best conceived as having 'as their specific aim the protection or advancement of individual interests or goods'.[154] Similarly so with other kinds of examples, such as the right not to be enslaved: Hart's attempt to conceive of these as 'unwaivable immunities' conveyed the 'implausibility of the theory, for by saying that the right-holder, in this case, could not exercise a power (to waive away his own right), the will theorist was effectively saying that when it came to especially important rights, like the right not to be enslaved, these were not even properly called rights (for the right holder had no power to choose to impose them or waive them).[155] This had an air of 'paradox'[156] and was, again, obscuring

150 Ibid.
151 Ibid.
152 Ibid.
153 MacCormick, 'Rights in Legislation' (1977), 190, citing s. 2(1) of the *Succession (Scotland) Act* 1964.
154 Ibid., 192.
155 Ibid., 194–6.
156 Ibid., 196.

the moral importance of such moral rights potentially enshrined in law (via, e.g., a constitutional Bill of Rights): the point was not the existence of a power by an individual, but the protection of a good, which outweighed other arguments of utility. This is not to say that in many cases where there were rights, there could not often be good grounds for giving individuals the power to waive their enforcement, but this was something conditional on or secondary to the prior – both normatively and temporally prior – existence of the right.[157]

For MacCormick, to analyse rights in this way was no dry analytical exercise; the analysis mattered, yes, but it was always in the service of making the law morally intelligible. Part of this meant clarifying how it worked – e.g., temporally, with duties coming after rights – thereby making the law more intelligible practically, and this too was of moral value, but part of it was conveying the importance of the protection of some good, and thus, for instance, when put in the form of legislation, the legislature communicating 'to the judiciary … the intended aim and object of the measure'.[158] But a large part was also about illuminating and protecting the moral importance of law and its role in the practice of good government.

The Link to Jurisprudential Methodology

A similar concern to make the law morally intelligible to persons, especially to ordinary citizens, but also to those often neglected by juristic theories (of the time), such as children,[159] or third parties in the context of contract law,[160] was present throughout MacCormick's work on rights (as well as obligations) in the long 1970s. It also connected to other growing interests of his, e.g., to Adam Smith's defence of natural rights in his *Lectures on Jurisprudence*,[161] but also, importantly, to his amendments to Hart's jurisprudence and thus the carving out of his own role as a philosopher. It is worth dwelling on this point, and thus connecting the above substantive views of obligations and rights to issues in jurisprudential methodology.

The kinds of examples a philosopher offers are often telling, not only because, via their description of experiences that were normatively

157 Ibid., 207–8.

158 Ibid., 206. For more on MacCormick on rights, see also MacCormick, 'Stair' (1990).

159 See, later, also MacCormick, 'A Special Conception' (2001). Ruth Adler, a PhD student of MacCormick's, was also an important inspiration here.

160 See MacCormick, 'Ius Quaesitum' (1970).

161 See MacCormick, 'Adam Smith' (1981).

evocative for the philosopher, they may indicate the philosopher's substantive normative theory, but also because they give us an insight into what that philosopher thought might be the very point and aim of philosophy. We saw in the above examples how sensitive MacCormick was to what we might call 'relational justice': his examples often showed him being painfully aware of the potential or reality of 'disappointing' others, including others who were in position of vulnerability, such as children. We see, in MacCormick's corpus, these kinds of examples occurring often, e.g., in his book on Hart, MacCormick speaks of 'the crucial value of considerateness to others', giving the following examples:

> To fail to turn up at the right time for a meal someone has taken trouble to get ready at that time is to show an inconsiderateness which is not excusable except when attributable to genuinely unforeseeable and unplanned diversions – as distinct from wilful pursuit of mere diversions! To fail without warning to carry out one's particular allotted tasks shows at least inconsiderateness to one's workmates and perhaps imperils the well working of an enterprise on whose success yet some others depend.[162]

These examples – which are so central to MacCormick's theorisation of rights and obligations, and to illuminating the moral importance of legal forms – are equally central to how MacCormick thinks of the very role and value of philosophy. This comes through, for instance, in how MacCormick reads Hart, from emphasising Hart's early work on natural rights,[163] to highlighting where Hart employs a tone of deep moral commitment (as when Hart speaks of the importance of the freedom to sexual orientation),[164] but also in how MacCormick amends and extends Hart's jurisprudential methodology.

In chapters 3, 5, and 12 of his 1981 book on Hart, MacCormick returns, again and again, to the possibility of a morally more-committed Hart. One aspect of this is noticing that Hart's hermeneutic approach needs more refinement: the internal point of view can be broken down into a 'cognitive' and a 'volitional' aspect. The cognitive refers to one's knowledge of the standards in a community, while the volitional to the extra endorsement of those standards. The full internal point of view has both cognitive and volitional aspect: that is, ideally, the citizens' knowledge of and commitment to the community's standards. Other perspectives were possible too, of course, so there was an extreme external perspective (which

162 MacCormick, HLA (1981), 53.
163 Hart, 'Are There Any Natural Rights?' (1955).
164 See MacCormick, HLA (1981), 49.

had neither the cognitive, nor the volitional) and the non-extreme external (which had the cognitive, but not the volitional). But the important point here is that part of what a theorist did, in attempting to understand a community's standards, is pay attention to the internal point of view, including the volitional – and thus also the desire-based, feeling-infused – commitments of those participating in it.

To do this methodologically as a theorist was to do what MacCormick was doing in other ways when theorising obligations and rights: to respect persons, to be considerate to others, to put philosophical talents (such as analytical rigour) in the service of both seeing and seeking to protect the goods of individuals. The point, throughout, was to practice philosophy as considerateness: to be serious about one's duties to others, to be mindful of their needs, interests, desires, and expectations, but to go even further, to exercise as much sensitivity as possible to the worlds of others – as we shall see, this is also the basis of MacCormick's endorsement of nationalism (precisely as a contingently valuable means of respecting persons). Here, the substantive analyses of rights and obligations are very much at one with methodological commitments, with both being the expression of MacCormick's character, i.e., the manner or style with which he related with others.

This link between conceptions of rights and jurisprudential methodology offers an opportunity to make one more clarification. The figure who, during this period of the 1970s, electrified discussions of rights, and indeed tied them, very explicitly, to questions of jurisprudentially methodology, was of course, Ronald Dworkin. MacCormick's relationship with Dworkin is complex and deserves its own extensive treatment. One crude way of putting it would be to argue that, taken by surprise, as many others were, by Dworkin's appointment, after Hart's early retirement, in 1969 to Hart's chair, and in light of Dworkin's extensive attack on Hartian jurisprudence, MacCormick was at first highly critical of Dworkin, perhaps precisely out of loyalty to Hart. This was a loyalty that, one could argue, was more personal than philosophical, given how otherwise MacCormick was willing to depart from Hart's views, or to extend them in directions that Hart did not himself endorse. Later, in this crude story, MacCormick came to realise that his differences with Dworkin were in fact fewer than he had first imagined.[165]

However, although there may be some truth to this story, on the whole, it obscures something more important, i.e., an attitude to theorising, and

[165] See, e.g., MacCormick, 'MacCormick on MacCormick' (2008).

thus to the role and value of philosophy, which did mark a difference between MacCormick and Dworkin. There was, in Dworkin's work, an extraordinary confidence in the importance of philosophy, including its practical importance. This came through not only via particular arguments or devices, such as 'the right answer thesis' or the figure of Hercules, but also, as MacCormick saw it, in how Dworkin wanted to 'unify' the 'expository' and the 'censorial' side of jurisprudence.[166] MacCormick's attitude, by contrast, was marked more by a modesty, including epistemic humility, about the role of philosophy and what it could achieve.

In an extended essay on Dworkin's *Taking Rights Seriously* (1977), entitled 'Dworkin as a Pre-Benthamite' (hence the reference to Bentham's language of censorial and expository jurisprudence), MacCormick acknowledges the advantages of a 'constructive' model over a 'natural' one to morality, politics, and law. Thus, whereas the natural model finds an objectively existing order of values, independent of our judgement, the constructive model is to be preferred for 'what it amounts to is an insistence on rationality in practical affairs'.[167] It is better, as MacCormick sees it, to think of ourselves as making values as a community as we go along, rather than just finding them, for this enhances our sense of 'responsibility'.[168] However, Dworkin, according to MacCormick, does not stop here – he wants more. He wants a constructive model that can yield 'the right answer' – a position that is 'self evidently or even evidently the best for everyone'.[169] In calling for the kind of 'unity' that he calls for between 'law, politics, and morality', a 'unity in substance, not only in method',[170] Dworkin, MacCormick says, evinces 'a desire to have it both ways'.[171] But this, MacCormick argues, cannot be: Dworkin 'cannot in my judgement make the switch to the "constructive model" and at the same time assert that unity in substance and method', especially in the form of there being in a hard case 'a single uniquely right answer'.[172]

Perhaps in pursuing too ambitious a role for philosophy – in seeking to insert jurisprudence, especially in the form of a theory that justifies the coercive power of the state, into the very practice of law – Dworkin goes, in MacCormick's eyes, too far. The details of MacCormick's theory of legal

166 MacCormick, 'Dworkin as Pre-Benthamite' (1978), 586.
167 Ibid., 587.
168 Ibid.
169 Ibid., 588.
170 Ibid., 589.
171 Ibid., 588.
172 Ibid., 589.

reasoning will be a matter for Chapter 10, but the important point for now is a different one. MacCormick wants to hang on, in a way that he understands Dworkin to be giving up, to a 'gap between the description of law and the framing of critical principles against which to test the quality of actual laws'.[173] This is not at odds, though it is somewhat in tension, with his role as a jurist: as above, MacCormick was heavily invested in the role of analysing law from the perspective of a moral philosopher, keen on articulating law's moral importance and making it morally intelligible to as wide a range of persons as possible. But there was, for MacCormick, an important difference between this and Dworkin's methodological stance. For MacCormick, Dworkin's ambition – again, evident in the figure of Hercules and in the right answer thesis – was to seek to go beyond the inevitable limits of any one way that one may articulate a vision of the good life.

There was, for MacCormick, value in retaining self-constraint, precisely as a philosopher: to say, in other words, that there were limits to how far one could illuminate the morals at stake, no matter how hard one tried. On the one hand, one was under a duty to 'find the way or ways in which we are to live, and that can only be found in terms of what we find by experience acceptable to us'; in doing this, 'one is offering to others for their adoption a certain form of life which for oneself one finds more acceptable than available alternatives'.[174] But – and this is a crucial 'but' – to expect more from this, to claim that somehow the way one has crafted or constructed was really better than any other – was to go too far. 'It is', MacCormick said, 'a delusion to suppose that that which we find to be the best is the best there is for any human being'.[175] 'None of us', he added, can elevate ourselves 'to a position above others as self evidently or even evidently the best for everyone'.[176]

Whether this is a good reading of what Dworkin was trying to do is not the central question here.[177] The point for present purposes is to see what attitude MacCormick was expressing – precisely in this deep matter of the value of one's philosophising. To attempt to sell one's philosophical wares too expensively – to portray them as being essential, vital, crucial to a community, so much so that it was the best form of life for them, better than any other – was to go too far in promoting one's self-importance. It

173 Ibid., 587.
174 Ibid., 588.
175 Ibid.
176 Ibid.
177 See, e.g., Dworkin's reply to MacCormick: Dworkin, 'A Reply' (1984), 278–81.

was precisely to fall short of the principle by which MacCormick sought to live: to show respect for persons, to be considerate. It was to overstretch, to impose oneself too much. It was to seek to master, rather than to serve, others. Hence the importance of holding back: of adopting, as a method, the hermeneutic (non-extreme external) point of view, of clinging on to a 'gap' between describing and evaluating law.

One could even argue (though I would not) there was something self-contradictory about this stance – being, on the one hand, such a clearly morally committed jurist and, on the other, insisting on the importance of such a 'gap' between description and evaluation. But, for MacCormick, the deeper truth here was a relational one – it was a matter of character: one had to show theoretical self-restraint, to acknowledge the inevitability of the limits of one's philosophising, while nevertheless trying as hard as one could to articulate 'the truth' as one saw it. This was relationally vital, for it meant not imposing one's own views too much on others: it was, in short, a matter of respecting others, of being considerate to persons. It is interesting that, in the context of jurisprudential methodology, MacCormick's character – his manner or style of relating with others – found its expression in an extension of Hart, pushing him further into a more morally committed philosophy, and, at the same time, in a contraction of Dworkin, pulling him back from over-claiming the significance of the moral insights of any one philosophical effort. Philosophy could be of value, but only if it served others, rather than dominating them. This was a balancing act, a really difficult and never-ending exercise – in a way, that was the very challenge of living a philosophical life, of being a philosopher.

Constraining and Diffusing Power

As much as it was the job of a jurist, as MacCormick saw it, to seek to protect the moral import of law, making clear the links – always imperfect, always fragile – between legal forms and the goods of persons, it was also the jurist's job to make sure that the state did not go too far, and could always be held accountable, in its pursuit of various aims and goals. Here, the jurist was concerned with the role and value of law in the practice of good government in another way, i.e., the protection of civil liberties via formal justice, but also with the enhancement of democracy via the structures of government. It is thus important that, in completing this chapter, we take note of MacCormick's theorisation of the possibility and importance of law serving the function of constraining and decentralising power – a theme of general importance for MacCormick, not only in the long 1970s, but throughout, and certainly in later decades.

Civil Liberties

MacCormick's sensitivity to the dangers of over-centralised and over-concentrated executive power was of course evident in his arguments for nationalism and constitutionalism, as we shall see in Chapter 7. But it was also evident in even the shortest of his contributions in this period. Thus, for example, in a short note in the *Law Quarterly Review* in 1970, MacCormick tackled two recent decisions in the House of Lords, both of which related to ministerial regulations and each of which had civil liberty at stake. In the first, *McEldowney* v *Forde*,[178] the issue was the validity of a Northern Ireland regulation that proscribed 'Republican Clubs' and other similar organisations. Here, the challenge to the legislation's validity was unsuccessful. In the other case,[179] by contrast, the challenge was successful, with the legislation in question attempting to exact a levy on employers in activities of industry or commerce.

It is interesting that MacCormick chose these two cases; certainly, he put the contrast between them to good use. In relation to the second case, MacCormick agreed with the House of Lords that 'statutes imposing or authorising taxation should be construed strictly', and that therefore the statute was rightly found to be ultra vires with respect to members' clubs, though he also added that no 'very serious injustice would have been done' had the *Industrial Training Act* 1964, which empowered Ministers to introduce the regulation they did, 'been held to apply to members' clubs'.[180] The regulation had effectively attempted to spread the cost of training certain employees – for instance, waiters – across various employers, including not just large hotels but also members' clubs. One of these clubs, the Royal Automobile Club (RAC), did not want to pay the levy and contribute to these training costs, and it is they that brought the case. Of course, this club, like others, stood to benefit from the employee training being provided. But, they argued, their activities were not 'activities of commerce or industry', for if they were, so were all private arrangements to employ, say, cooks or cleaners. MacCormick, however, saw things differently: 'From a waiter's point of view there is perhaps not

[178] *McEldowney* v *Forde* [1969] 1 All ER 1039.

[179] *Hotel and Catering Industry Training Board* v *Automobile Proprietary Ltd.* [1969] 2 All ER 582.

[180] MacCormick, 'Delegated Legislation' (1970), 180.

a great deal of difference between working in a hotel or in a club such as the RAC', and thus, given that all 'employers will benefit from an increase in the pool of properly trained people, all employers should be eligible to share in the burden of paying for training them'.[181] Here, substantively speaking, MacCormick's judgement was that social, distributive justice could justifiably outweigh the inroads into liberty.

The irony was that where the House of Lords was so keen to invalidate delegated legislation, heavily critiquing the use of a power to tax, in the other case, where what was at stake was the freedom of association, the Lords went out of their way to find a way to find the legislation valid. In the one case, where it arguably mattered less, civil liberty was protected from administrative convenience. In the other, where it mattered more, civil liberty was sacrificed. As MacCormick put it: 'It is said that a relatively trivial instance of the protection of citizens from unauthorised taxation should serve so sharply to contrast with judicial tolerance of an administrative invasion of freedom of association so sweeping that even the troubled condition of Northern Ireland can scarcely justify it'.[182]

In that first case, the Minister of Home Affairs had added, to an already existing regulation deeming certain named organisations unlawful, that equally unlawful would be organisations 'describing themselves as "Republican Clubs" or any like organisation howsoever described.[183] The regulation was indeed 'sweeping', with it being practically impossible, MacCormick argued, for 'any citizen' to 'know in advance of being prosecuted and convicted whether an organisation of which he is a member is or is not deemed to be unlawful by reason of being a "like organisation"'.[184] Finding such a 'vague and arbitrary' piece of regulation valid required 'a rather athletic feature of interpretation of the regulation', which is what the courts engaged in.[185] MacCormick did acknowledge that in cases as politically sensitive as this one, 'the courts ought to take great care not to substitute their opinion for the Minister's, provided he is not acting outside the limits of his lawful discretion'.[186] But he was equally clear that the majority in this case had erred in not invalidating the legislation. The sheer power given to Ministerial discretion was 'an alarming and

[181] Ibid.
[182] Ibid.
[183] Ibid., 172.
[184] Ibid., 173.
[185] Ibid.
[186] Ibid., 176.

remarkable one', all the more so given it was 'brought into existence by delegated legislation'.[187] And, he added:

> … in more general terms, it is not clear that a power which can legitimately be used to suppress violently revolutionary organisations explicitly named ought to be extended to cover large and indeterminate classes of organisations. Only the courts can stand between the citizen and such arbitrary extension of executive powers. If indeed a Minister believes that so wide and general a proscription of clubs is required in the interests of peace and good order, is it too much to ask that he have it enacted after full and proper deliberation in a Parliament…?[188]

In his reading of both cases, then, MacCormick spoke as an advocate for the ordinary citizen. In the first, in finding the delegated legislation valid, the courts were effectively neglecting, if not undermining, their own duties to citizens. These citizens were being deprived of the possibility of acting lawfully, being at the whim and mercy of an entirely unpredictable Ministerial discretion. In the second, citizens too were being deprived of what was a common, public good – the fair distribution of costs of training relevant employees – even if, on balance, it was indeed correct to narrowly construe such delegated legislation.

This early example is typical of MacCormick's approach to the protection of civil liberties (though also, more broadly, alongside social justice), exercising caution and sensitivity with respect to any attempt to extend executive power, and locating and evaluating either the benefits or the dangers of such extensions in the perspective of ordinary citizens (albeit potentially in extraordinary circumstances, such as in Northern Ireland).

Another typical example is MacCormick's response to the *Younger Committee on Privacy*, which reported in 1972.[189] MacCormick here made several analytical points in response to the Committee's Report one was to argue against the analogy that the Committee drew between a potential right to privacy and rights of free speech and of assembly, with MacCormick arguing that whereas the first could be understood to be a claim right, the latter two rights were better conceived as liberties, and that, as a claim right, a right to privacy was thus not about imposing vague or unlimited duties on the legislature (as the Report seemed to think) but instead specific duties in particular against 'corporate enterprise wielding great economic power' or 'agents of the greatest corporate enterprise of

[187] Ibid., 177.
[188] Ibid.
[189] See MacCormick, 'A Note' (1973); 'Privacy' (1974); and 'Privacy and Obscenity' (1978).

them all, the state';[190] a second, was again to argue for a 'fundamental difference' between 'the definition by legislation of a right' and the 'procedure and process' of 'the elucidation of a concept', it being possible to do the former even when the latter was difficult, thereby critiquing the Committee's reliance on the difficulty of the concept of privacy to argue against the desirability of introducing a right to privacy.[191]

Later, and this time also critically discussing some US cases, MacCormick argued against yet another obstacle to introducing a right to privacy: claiming that it would conflict with existing laws against obscenity.[192] Here, what MacCormick was doing was less making a certain existing area of the law morally intelligible, and more drawing on his analytical talents to clear any obstacles to the possibility of introducing a new legal right, and especially one that could restrict incursions into the goods of individuals by corporate and executive power.

Throughout the long 1970s, MacCormick did not shy away from controversy, deploying his skills to exercise difficult judgement, often amidst considerable disagreement and sometimes in the face of considerable pressure to fall in line. It was the task, as he saw it, of the jurist to denounce decisions by courts that 'enunciated an unjust rule', as he found that the decision in the Gay News trial[193] did when it 'laid down that blasphemy is still a crime by the law of England, and the editor of Gay News was convicted and fined heavily for publishing a poem found by the jury to cast scandalous aspersions on the person of Christ'.[194] It was, MacCormick argued, 'not to my judgement acceptable that the law's penal prohibitions should give special protection to the tenets of one religious faith' – that is simply 'incompatible with equality of liberty for all citizens'.[195]

Similarly so in relation to a then-heated debate on rights to the freedom of speech of bodies such as the National Front. Responding to one of the leaders of that group, who had indicated that the National Front was 'even more against liberals than blacks', MacCormick argued that it was wrong

[190] MacCormick, 'A Note' (1973), 26.

[191] MacCormick, 'Privacy' (1974), 77.

[192] See MacCormick, 'Privacy and Obscenity' (1978).

[193] *R* v *Lemon*, *The Times* 13 July 1977.

[194] MacCormick, 'Civil Liberties and the Law' (1977), 6. I quote here from the lecture MacCormick gave at Heriot-Watt University on 25 October 1977 and published by the Heriot-Watt University Special Lecture Series, but similar points are made in chapter 3 of LRSD (1982).

[195] MacCormick, 'Civil Liberties and the Law' (1977), 7.

to prohibit such speech, even if it was against everything he stood for, and he thus 'condemn[ed] most roundly the tactics deliberately avowed by the Socialist Workers' Party, of forcibly breaking up lawful meetings and processions held by the National Front'.[196] Any such attempt to obstruct the freedom of speech was 'highly dangerous to the cause of rightful liberty' – even if, MacCormick continued, he disagreed with the opinion entirely, 'I still respect the Nation Front's right to argue that my kind of liberalism be abrogated by law'.[197] Echoing the stance we saw MacCormick take above, namely that one can and ought to take a stand but not impose it on others, MacCormick said:

> He who believes only in the liberty of others to support and act in accordance with his own tenets does not believe in liberty at all but in his own tenets. The real challenge in my opinion is to take seriously and use unapologetically one's own moral tenets in approving or condemning acts of human beings without desiring that everyone share these tenets, save in relation to the delimitation of equal liberty for all. For me to have and to pursue my own tenets is a condition of my self respect; so I conceive it to be for others. Therein is the ground of the right to equal liberty for all, within those constraints in which liberty can be equal, subject to securing economic fairness.[198]

To exercise one's judgement and thus give one's considered moral view was a matter of self-respect: in doing so, one took oneself seriously as a moral agent. But this had to be coupled with respect for others and the possibility of them acting out of self-respect too. Law here played a vital role in securing liberty: far from being the opposite of liberty, law was 'a necessary condition of civil liberty and a better guarantor of rightful freedom than anything the opponents of legal order can offer'.[199] And it was the task of the jurist to make the case, and continue making the case, especially in the context of heated, controversial, matters, in favour of the possibility – but never guarantee – of law protecting civil liberty and thus playing a positive role in good government.

In MacCormick's view, part of this meant arguing in favour of 'adopting an entrenched and justiciable law guaranteeing fundamental rights and civil liberties'.[200] Speaking in 1977, MacCormick urged that Britain look 'for consideration and adaptation the European Convention on Human

196 Ibid., 9.
197 Ibid., 9–10.
198 Ibid., 10.
199 Ibid., 13.
200 Ibid., 19.

Rights'.[201] Prefiguring much of the debate to come, he added that if it was thought that entrenching such provisions would 'breach the traditional sovereignty of Parliament', then 'none the worse for that', for, in truth, the Parliament of Great Britain created in 1707 was, in fact, already limited, with assertions of 'absolute Parliamentary sovereignty' being an 'assertion of a usurped power'.[202] Even such a Bill of Rights, however, would not provide a guarantee of the safeguarding of liberty: it would only ever provide half of what is needed, and 'the other half would be a determined resolution among the people that such a Bill be enacted, sustained and, above all, most scrupulously observed'.[203] Incidentally, the view MacCormick expressed in this lecture echoed the Statement of Evidence made by the SNP on 2 August 1977 to the *Select Committee of the House of Lords on a Bill of Rights*, which was authored by MacCormick and which recommended the entrenchment of a Bill of Rights, arguing firmly against critiques of such a Bill on the basis of 'the dogma of the sovereignty of Parliament, a dogma which has led to the denial of the constituent states for the UK of the Articles of Union of 1706–7'.[204]

State Aid for Political Parties

MacCormick not only exercised difficult judgement in relation to recent court cases or matters of controversy in the public eye, but he also did so when participating more formally in committees or commissions of inquiry and reform.

An excellent example of this, and one which also illustrates MacCormick's commitment to preserving liberty and democracy in the face of attempts to consolidate and concentrate power, is his participation in the *Committee on Financial Aid to Political Parties*, chaired by Lord Houghton (and thus known as the Houghton Committee). On 8 May 1975, this Committee had been formed to consider the question of financial aid to political parties, and in particular 'whether, in the interests of Parliamentary democracy, provision should be made from public funds to assist political parties in carrying out their functions outside Parliament'.[205] The Commission operated very much in the glare of public

[201] Ibid.
[202] Ibid., 20.
[203] Ibid.
[204] See MacCormick, 'Is There a Constitutional Path' (2000), 723.
[205] *Report of the Committee on Financial Aid to Political Parties* (1976), iv.

opinion, with there being, at the time, a crisis in the public purse, necessitating – in the opinion of some – considerable cuts to public expenditure. Financial worries also hit a number of the bigger political parties – Labour and the Liberals especially, but also to a lesser extent, the Conservatives. The majority of the twelve-member Commission, however, sought to bracket out the current economic conditions – as 'it would be quite wrong for us to assume the role of arbiter on public expenditure'[206] – and argued instead for financial aid on the basis that 'political parties have long been essential to the working of our parliamentary system',[207] such that without such support, there was a danger that the democracy itself would not survive. The eight men in the majority, then, recommended a scheme where effectively 5p of the taxpayer for each vote cast would be available to the qualifying parties, estimating it would cost the public purse around 2.25 million pounds a year.

There was, of course, considerable pressure on the members of the Commission to produce a unanimous report. However, four men disagreed with the recommendations of the majority: Sir Tatton Brinton, a former Tory MP and Treasurer of the Conservatives from 1964 to 1974; Ian Aitkin, a *Guardian* journalist; Julian Haviland, a journalist at *Independent Television News*; and MacCormick. The ensuing Minority Report reads very much like something written by MacCormick. The dissent of the minority was based 'fundamentally' on differences in 'our conception of the nature and role of political parties'.[208] While accepting 'the importance of the survival of political parties – though not necessarily the present ones', the members of the minority asserted that 'we do not believe that political parties represent more than one among the several pillars which support our parliamentary democracy'.[209] The parties themselves were but an expression of something deeper: 'the commitment of the British electorate to parliamentary democracy, and its willingness to work it'; crucially, this was a 'voluntary' commitment, and this voluntariness was foundational to the flourishing of democracy.[210]

Not only would financial aid to political parties undermine the voluntariness of British parliamentary democracy ('even voting is not yet compulsory'),[211] but there would also 'be no guarantee that the provision

206 Ibid., xiii.
207 Ibid., xii.
208 Ibid., 75.
209 Ibid.
210 Ibid., 75–6.
211 Ibid., 78.

of state money would of itself "improve" the performance of parties'.[212] In fact, quite the contrary: 'the very activity of raising money has always been recognised as one of the cohesive forces holding parties together'.[213] Rather than protecting parties, they should instead be subject to the vagaries of the times, including economic conditions. If this meant some political parties collapsing and others forming, precisely in response to changing conditions, then so much the better: that was precisely democracy at work. To support struggling political parties 'would diminish the element of confrontation in British political life and lead to a greater degree of consensus between the parties',[214] but part of the point of having a democracy was that it enabled vigorous debate that subjected itself to the evaluation of the citizenry. At a time when 'cynicism about politics and politicians is already at an alarmingly high level', to see those politicians 'voting substantial sums of public money to their parties', especially at a time of economic crisis, with other cuts to the public curse, could 'only deepen this cynicism even further'.[215] Further, once begun, it would be difficult to stop financially propping up parties – especially the bigger ones who, for whatever reason, may struggle for members.

What Parliamentary democracy needed, then, according to the four men in the minority, was not more protection of existing political parties, consolidating their power, sheltering them from the conditions of the times and the emotions of public opinion, but instead competition between parties, including potentially the emergence of new ones, and thus a healthy fight for members and political allegiance. Far from protecting democracy, to support financial aid would be to undermine it: politics was a realm of contestation and change, and one in which nothing was sacrosanct, at least nothing that justified taxpayer money propping up struggling or failed political platforms.

Local Government Autonomy

MacCormick's stance in favour of pluralism and contestation, seeking to maximise the voluntariness of the citizen in the participation of politics, was echoed in his defence of local government autonomy. I shall be returning to this theme of decentralised political participation in the

212 Ibid.
213 Ibid.
214 Ibid.
215 Ibid.

chapters to come, for it was a central part of MacCormick's nationalism and his hope for Scotland in Europe, but it is worth noting that this was also very much on his mind in the 1970s when he was participating in a variety of SNP policy committees. One such committee, in which MacCormick took part, was focused on the Structure of Government in Scotland. This Committee saw itself as complementing the recommendations of Constitution Committee: the framework of a democratic constitution was vital, but not enough on its own. As was indicated in the Policy on the Structure of Government in Scotland, adopted by the SNP at its Annual Conference in 1978: '... there must be a commitment in practice to restoring real power to the elected representatives of the people in Parliament, to de-centralising the exercise of power within Scotland itself, and to giving every person and community in Scotland the opportunity to influence government at all levels'.[216]

To this end, the Policy took a stand against extensions to Ministerial power, as was becoming more and more prevalent in Westminster, recommending the setting up, 'in parallel to the main departments of state, Standing Committees of Parliament charged with keeping under review specific areas of governmental activity'. Via such Committees, every MP would be able 'to seek and obtain full and informative replies to questions about the conduct of government'.[217] Further, such Committees 'will also have the power to scrutinise and promote constructive discussion of Government proposals for legislation before they are formally drafted for enactment as law', thereby making 'constructive criticism' as effective as possible, and, via public hearings on such proposals, also enabling 'citizens in general and interested groups and organisations to make public comment on and criticism of proposals'.[218] The point, throughout the Policy, via such mechanisms, but also others (for instance, a special council for the Islands in Scotland), was to decentralise law-making and maximise political participation – to bring government down as much as possible to local theatres of active citizens.

Edinburgh University Settlement

Whether through academic publications and lectures, or as a participant in reform and inquiry commissions or policy committees, MacCormick

[216] *SNP Policy on the Structure of Government* (1978), Edinburgh University Archives, para 1.
[217] Ibid., paras 4–5.
[218] Ibid., para 7.

thus stood up for good government as a matter of protection of civil liberty and social justice by law, while also, at the same time, decentralising and devolving law-making as much as possible into local, active, participatory contexts. But MacCormick did not just do so as an academic voice, from high above in some realm of a heaven of concepts. He did so grounded in practical details amongst matters of controversy – and, importantly too, in local action in his own community.

A good example of this is his participation in the Edinburgh University Settlement. The Edinburgh University Settlement was part of the broader Settlement movement, which had begun in the late 1880s, with a view to bridging the gap between the rich and the poor, in particular by establishing 'settlement houses' in poor urban areas, where the poor would live with volunteers, who would help them to alleviate their poverty, and where they would also receive services such as English classes and healthcare.

For the Edinburgh University Settlement, which had been established in 1905, its aims were 'to bring education within the reach of ordinary people; to make provision for social research; and to give the community civic and social leadership'.[219] As further articulated later, in 1988, the Settlement sought to 'supplement public provision for the poor, deprived, disadvantaged and disabled in the Edinburgh area'.[220] It did this via projects such as the 'Ambassadors Project', which mobilised 'relevant professions skills from members of the University', 'developing special projects of a para-medical, social and educational kind', seeking to 'encourage among students a commitment to voluntary service', and, more broadly, 'helping the University … to retain an active awareness of the needs of the community around the University'.[221]

MacCormick was elected as Chairman of the Executive Committee of the Settlement in April 1988 and continued to serve as Chairman until 1994. This takes us, of course, well past even the long 1970s, but it is worth mentioning here, given its connection to the themes of this chapter. This was hardly a period in which MacCormick had little to do: he had just completed his second round as Dean of the Law School (1985–88) and, amongst other commitments, was also serving on the Broadcasting Council for Scotland. The Chairmanship of the Settlement was just

219 Edinburgh University Settlement, *Annual Report* (1994), i. These and other Edinburgh University Settlement Reports are available in the Edinburgh University Archives.

220 Ibid., 1.

221 Ibid.

another aspect of MacCormick's commitment, as a citizen, to his local community. And yet, it was an important one, for it echoed his philosophical defences of the pursuit of equality and fairness as part of good government, including his location of the point of view of the ordinary citizen – indeed, the poorest and most neglected of citizens – at the very centre of theories of justice.

MacCormick arrived at the Settlement at a time when it was in considerable financial difficulty, which necessitated a full review of its activities. It is telling that he remained at its helm for the next six years (the initial term was only for four, but the members of the Settlement persuaded him to stay on) and oversaw a period of stability and increased activity.[222] Indeed, it is perhaps no accident – though hardly of course attributable to MacCormick alone – that after years of reporting a budgetary deficit (£6,233 in 1987, and £3,034 in 1988), only one year into his Chairmanship, the Settlement reported a surplus of income over expenditure.[223] As MacCormick himself noted in his Chairman's Report in 1989, the Settlement had also stabilised its 'internal planning', liaising productively with the Social Work Department, and supporting not only the local community (for instance, after the tragedy of a gas explosion in Guthrie Street), but also beyond, raising money and resources for victims of the Armenian earthquake.[224]

In 1989, MacCormick indicated that he was especially proud of increased student participation, for instance in the Ambassadors Project, which now included students assisting with adult legal education. The Settlement did indeed provide numerous educational activities. Its 'Second Chance to Learn' educational programme – interestingly, in 1988, its theme was 'What is Scottishness?' – enabled persons from very deprived areas with a 'stepping stone on to further education or employment', including going on to study at Edinburgh University.[225] But the activities of the Settlement also went much further. They included, for example, a 'Companion Service', with visits to elderly and senile members of the public in their homes, as well as a 'New Wilkie Club', the aim of which was to create 'a social base and a programme of activities for people recovering from mental illness'.[226] Again, as vital as the provision of

[222] Following his term, MacCormick continued to support the Settlement, as its Representative in the University Senate as well as one of its Custodian Trustees.

[223] Edinburgh University Settlement, *Annual Report* (1988), 15.

[224] MacCormick, 'Chairman's Report', in Edinburgh University Settlement, *Annual Report* (1989), 1.

[225] Edinburgh University Settlement, *Annual Report* (1988), 4.

[226] Ibid., 9.

such services were for the local community, the Settlement also sought, wherever possible, to assist vulnerable groups beyond its territory – in addition to the above-mentioned assistance for victims of the Armenian earthquake, the Settlement encouraged local technology manufacturers to donate cameras and other equipment to communities in Romania, something MacCormick personally arranged and secured.[227]

It is no surprise that, writing in 1991, after only four years in the Chairmanship role, the Director of the Settlement wrote that 'members of the Executive, Staff and Volunteers realise how much is owed to Professor MacCormick'.[228] Thanks to his Chairmanship, the Director added, the Settlement 'continues to increase in profile through service and innovative projects', has a well-established planning and management structure, and in general, despite these reviews of its procedures and the loss of its premises in Guthrie Street, also 'increased its activities'.[229] It speaks volumes about MacCormick and his character that, amidst all the philosophical and political activity in which he was engaged in, he found time to dedicate himself, in grounded, practical detail, to an organisation like the Edinburgh University Settlement, helping it out of immediate financial difficulties and securing its longer-term future. Indeed, it may be possible to say that MacCormick's commitment to democracy, civil liberty, equality, fairness, and local government was as important in contexts like this as it was in his philosophical writings, which were now reaching an ever-wider global audience.

In fact, one could go further and argue that experiences such as this one, in a local, voluntary, community organisation, very much informed MacCormick's abstract defences of principles such as (later, in the European context) subsidiarity or, as in the 1982 collection discussed in this chapter, the compatibility of the rule of law, the protection of civil liberty by law, and the pursuit of equality, welfare, and social justice.[230]

Equally so, in the other direction: MacCormick's participation in the Settlement was consistent with his formation in the Scottish philosophical tradition. As Robin Downie, who participated in the Glasgow University Settlement, noted, 'the Settlement movement is interesting

[227] Ibid., 13.
[228] Ibid., 2.
[229] Ibid.
[230] There is a longer history in the background here as to the importance of local, voluntary associations to the 'decentralised, participatory system of welfare', and thus to the rise of the welfare state, including in the mid 1970s: see Thane, *The Rise and Fall of the British Welfare State* (2024).

philosophically', emerging from the 'Idealist movement which was the dominant philosophy in Scottish universities in late nineteenth and early twentieth centuries'.[231] An important figure in that movement was T. H. Green, and the person in Glasgow who wrote an *Introduction to Green's Moral Philosophy* was none other than W. D. Lamont,[232] who, as we saw, was one of MacCormick's most influential philosophy teachers. The Settlement, then, and its broader philosophical resonances, including about the very aim and value of philosophy in community, was very much part of MacCormick's formation and then ongoing negotiation of his role as a philosopher. All this reached deeply into MacCormick's character – both to its roots, with his inheritance of social welfare from his mother, through to his ongoing conceptual work on Scottish nationalism, Europe, the institutional theory of law, and reason's practicality.

[231] Private correspondence (on file with the author).
[232] See Lamont, *Introduction to Green's Moral Philosophy* (1934).

7

A Philosophically Credible Nationalism?

Constitutional Change in Scotland

Could nationalism be philosophically credible? This is a question that MacCormick asked himself from early on and then throughout his life as a philosopher. Born into, as we have seen in Chapter 1, an intensely political family – a family of Scottish nationalists – but being, also, a reflective young man, and becoming a philosopher, MacCormick could hardly help but set up a confrontation between the most parochial, immediate, and personal of loyalties and the self-searching and self-scrutinising mode of philosophical reflection. If we think of philosophy as a practice of self-reflection and self-critique in the name of (hopefully) better relations with others, then MacCormick's engagement with nationalism over many decades can be approached as MacCormick asking himself whether there existed a version of nationalism that was compatible with his other commitments and value orientations, e.g., to respect for persons, including reasoning together with civility, decency, and considerateness.

Put another way, we could examine MacCormick's lifelong wrestle with nationalism as part of the negotiation of his character, i.e., the manner or style with which he related with others. Nationalism, then, can be approached as a – if not 'the' – major, existential challenge for MacCormick's character: could one be a nationalist and still be a philosopher, and if so, what kind of philosopher? Could one be a nationalist and engage with others in the manner or style that MacCormick was disposed to, i.e., respectfully, but also joyfully? Could one be a nationalist and not embrace isolationism, domination over others, or demonising aliens and enemies? Could nationalism, in other words, be a way of enhancing, rather than lowering, the quality of relations with others?

To approach MacCormick's nationalism in this way is certainly to raise the stakes and, as potentially illuminating as I think such an approach might be, it must be tempered with something much more grounded: the everyday politics that MacCormick found himself very much embroiled in from the 1970s onwards. Indeed, the above stakes – especially for MacCormick's character – are in many ways best refracted in concrete circumstances, and thus in moments when MacCormick took the initiative in a certain particular scenario or over a certain issue or responded to a certain particular event in a certain way. It is of course impossible to cover all the significant events in which MacCormick participated in, or contributed to, that are related to how he lived Scottish nationalism and philosophically constructed it. My aim here is much more circumspect: to pick out a number of situations that are illustrative of MacCormick's engagement with nationalism, especially with a view to showing how they might illuminate his character.

Even with this more circumspect aim, this chapter traverses a long period: from the late 1960s and especially early 1970s, with MacCormick's editing of *The Scottish Debate* (1970), through to the mid-to-late 1970s, when MacCormick was involved in the drafting of a 'Constitution for a Future Independent Scotland' and numerous other issues surrounding constitutional change, then into the 1980s, when MacCormick participated in the decade-long debate on the Claim of Right, which in 1989 established the Scottish Constitutional Convention, right through to the early 1990s, when MacCormick further refined his view of nationalism and constitutionalism in Scotland.

An important aspect of these debates and reflections over constitutional change in Scotland, already from 1975 and the EEC referendum in that year, was the question of Europe. Although the place of Scotland in Europe was in many ways inseparable from the treatment – especially MacCormick's treatment – of Scottish constitutional change, nevertheless, to make the material manageable and digestible, I shall turn to Europe and the hope and promise it offered for Scottish nationalists in Chapter 8. Here, in this chapter, the focus is on how MacCormick lived Scottish nationalism politically, and how he conceived of it philosophically, especially in relation to constitutionalism. Indeed, as we shall see, very much integral to the issue of how to conceive of nationalism, for MacCormick, was the issue of what it meant to be a constitutionalist, i.e., what was significant and valuable about the constitutional register. Thus, as much as the main focus here is on nationalism, one eye is always fastened onto the meanings of constitutionalism for MacCormick. This, too, of course has a Scottish context: as we saw in Chapter 1, Scottish constitutional history was already a passion of his father's, as well as of a whole generation of politicians and historians of the time.

The Historiography of Scottish Nationalism

Before proceeding further, it is important first to consider the historiography of Scottish nationalism. Although once bereft of literature, the story of Scottish nationalism in the twentieth century has received a boost of attention in recent years. The work of Neal Ascherson, Cairns Craig, Stephen Finlay, Scott Hames, Christopher Harvie, Gerry Hassan, Ben Jackson, Michael Keating, Colin Kidd, Naomi Lloyd-Jones, James Mitchell, Murray Pittock, Malcolm Petrie, and Paula Somerville, to mention just a few, has changed the landscape considerably. This, in turn, should be set against broader changes in the historiography of Britain, including vitally important work on earlier centuries, and across a range of fields.[1] Of course, to this can be added many further contributions in relevant subsets of this historiography, most relevantly here, British constitutional history.[2] We encountered some of this scholarship in Chapter 1, and this book is not the place for a full-scale review of it. Nevertheless, it is important to return to it in the context of this chapter, for the historical framing of Scottish nationalism – especially as it includes the more recent history from the 1960s on – matters enormously to how one approaches MacCormick.

For a start, there is the very word – 'nationalism'. It is striking that the title that Kidd chose for his magisterial survey of 'political thought in Scotland, 1500–2000' was not nationalism, but instead 'Union and Unionisms'. Kidd was very much aware, especially at the time of writing his book (2008), that he was swimming against the tide: the historiographical tendency, he argued, was to see nationalism and unionism as two opposite sides of a rigid binary, much like England and Scotland itself.[3] Kidd acknowledged that, to some extent, this was understandable, especially in light of the 'narrow' version of unionism espoused by Margaret Thatcher: a lot of what was distinctive about Scotland was lost in the Thatcherite vision of Britain.[4] But, Kidd argued, there were other conceptions of unionism, including in Scotland. Unionism 'was not necessarily about capitulation, assimilation, integration or emulation'; it could,

[1] For instance, by David Armitage, Karen Bowie, Linda Colley, Tom Devine, Richard Helgerson, Lorna Hutson, John Kerrigan, Susan Manning, Roger Mason, J. A. C. Pocock, John Robertson, and Alice Taylor, to, again, mention but a few. Kerrigan's *Archipelagic English* (2008) and Manning's *Fragments of Union* (2002) were both especially formative for me in writing this book. More recently, Hutson's *England's Insular Imagining* (2023) shows what one can do with a constitutional history that takes geographical imaginaries seriously.

[2] See, e.g., the work of J. D. B. Mitchell, Duncan MacNeill, Geoffrey Barrow, T. B. Smith, Colin Munro, and, recently, Sionaidh Douglas-Scott, *Brexit, Union, and Disunion* (2023), and the two-volume *Cambridge Constitutional History of the United Kingdom* (2023) edited by Peter Cane and Harshan Kumarasingham.

[3] Kidd, *Union and Unionisms* (2008), 3.

[4] Ibid., 4–5.

instead, be 'about the maintenance of semi-autonomy or nationhood with Union, by means of compromise, adjustment and even nationalist assertion when required'.[5] To think in binary terms was, essentially, to risk missing so much of what was valuable and fascinating about Scottish political thought. In fact, Kidd argued, 'For much of modern Scottish political history there was an ill-defined – and neglected – middle ground where moderate unionism and moderate nationalism were in surprisingly close proximity'.[6] Indeed, it mattered greatly both what kind of nationalist, but also what kind of unionist, one was: just as there were many shades of nationalism, so with unionism. The two were often intertwined and could share deeper attitudes and have overlapping sensitivities.

Kidd's historiography is important for this book.[7] His careful and nuanced reading of the entangled history of Scottish nationalism and unionism, with attention to religion, jurisprudence, and literature, and always seeking to inhabit the difficult-to-articulate shifting sands of the middle ground, is very much in keeping with my reading of MacCormick in this book. As we have seen in the chapters thus far, and as we will see again in this chapter and the chapters to come, MacCormick's intellectual creativity was precisely often combinatory, synthetic, connective, inclusive, and attracted to hybrid, though also difficult, hard-to-capture, in-between zones, e.g., social democracy, post-sovereignty, legal institutionalism, and the limited practicality of reason. This very much extends to what we may call MacCormick's 'unionist nationalism' or 'nationalist unionism' – a kind of pragmatic and principled gradualism, a commitment to democracy and constitutionalism, a demand for self-respect but always alongside deep respect for others, and an almost unshakeable optimism that one could and should collaborate and compromise so as to live peacefully together.

It is, thus, no accident that Kidd positions John MacCormick, MacCormick's father, in the middle ground that his historiography seeks to illuminate. As he puts it, when tracing the history of Scottish political thought in the second half of the nineteenth and the first half of the twentieth centuries:

> …for much of the modern era the immediate object of nationalist agitation has not been the winning of independence for Scotland – a distant and, seemingly, unattainable goal – but to win self-respect for Scotland as

[5] Ibid., 5.

[6] Ibid., 6.

[7] See also Kidd and Petrie, 'The Independence Referendum in Historical and Political Context' (2016).

> a nation within the Union, and to put a stop to the wholescale anglicisation of Scottish life and to obtain a greater measure of autonomy for Scotland within Britain and its empire.[8]

John MacCormick's 'moderate nationalism' was thus precisely that: a kind of reformist unionism. As we have seen in Chapter 1, John MacCormick's Scottish Convention of the 1940s and 1950s was a call for greater Scottish democracy within the Union, albeit – here again we see the middle ground – accompanied by a passionate argument for the distinctiveness of Scottish constitutional history, as was indeed endorsed in the famous dicta by Lord Cooper (himself a unionist) in *MacCormick* v *Lord Advocate*. For Kidd, this 'moderate nationalism', this 'reformist unionism', was well and alive in MacCormick, the son, too: 'The central exponent of the nationalist interpretation of the Union state', Kidd argues, 'has been Neil MacCormick … who has some claim to being the most sophisticated and incisive of late 20th century Scotland's cadre of pioneering analytical unionists'.[9] Unionism, in this version, is very much Scottish, and certainly not exclusively, perhaps not even mainly, English, but it is a unionism very different from the kind of vision expressed by Thatcher. It is a nationalist unionism – a differential unionism of mutual respect and diffusion of power, rather than a project of centralisation, domination, assimilation, incorporation, and the concentration of power.

Despite Kidd's efforts at illuminating and attending to the middle ground – acknowledging but avoiding 'the extremes of anglicising unionism and Anglophobic nationalism'[10] – the historiographical pull towards a history of Scottish nationalism as a history of independence, of the pursuit of a Scottish sovereign state, remains magnetically strong. Although this book situates MacCormick much closer to the middle ground identified by Kidd, it is nevertheless also informed by these studies, especially in their more recent form, as argued, for instance, by Jackson (2020).

Jackson focuses on Scottish political thought since the 1960s, and in doing so reminds us – as indeed we saw in Chapter 6 – of the sustenance Scottish nationalism received by Thatcherite policies. As Jackson put it, in the 1960s and 1970s, 'Scottish nationalism began to present itself as a moderately social democratic ideology of community and decentralisation, commitments which nationalists argued had deep roots in Scottish history'.[11]

[8] Kidd, *Union and Unionisms* (2008), 261.
[9] Ibid., 298.
[10] Ibid., 300.
[11] Jackson, *The Case for Scottish Independence* (2020), 91.

This stabilised further in the 1980s and 1990s, such that, as Jackson observes, 'From the 1990s onwards, the SNP was skilful at positioning itself rhetorically and substantively slightly to the left of the Labour Party'.[12] Jackson's attention to the political positioning of the SNP, and in particular the centrality of arguments concerning economic policy – the argument, for instance, in the 1990s, articulated by Alex Salmond, 'that it would be possible to combine a vision for Scotland as an internationally competitive economy with support for a strong welfare state', somewhat like 'Nordic social democracy'[13] – is also important. These were, indeed, everyday political realities for the SNP, and for Scottish politics generally, and they duly form a crucial context for MacCormick too. We forget at our peril how much of Scottish nationalism in the 1970s, 1980s, and 1990s was a reaction to an over-centralised, right-wing, free market ideology and state practice.

However, as much as he recognises the importance of the above ideological context, ultimately, for Jackson, the story of Scottish nationalism is less an ideological story, and more a story of 'sovereignty'. As Jackson argues, this is a story that shows that 'a revived language of sovereignty and democratisation proved to have greater political vitality than a socialist language of economic transformation or a concern with the defence of Scottish culture'.[14] Certainly, as Jackson sees it, talk of 'sovereignty' and the pursuit of 'statehood' is softened, in particular in the 1980s and 1990s, by situating Scotland within transnational and global political orders – of Europe especially – but the language remains, and finds expression in the concept of 'popular sovereignty'. Thus, Jackson argues popular sovereignty 'took on a wider significance in the debate over Scotland's constitutional status during the 1980s and 1990s as it became increasingly central to the nationalist critique of the British state'.[15]

It is not that the political thought, as unearthed so clearly and helpfully, by Jackson, is not subtle and nuanced: quite the contrary, Jackson shows how 'Scottish nationalists have in fact developed a sophisticated account of how an independent Scotland would simultaneously enjoy self-determination in certain respects but in others share institutions, laws and society with foreign nations', acknowledging 'realistic limits to Scottish autonomy' and situating 'the quest for Scottish statehood in a more general interpretation of ideas about national sovereignty in the

[12] Ibid., 125.
[13] Ibid., 118.
[14] Ibid., 166–7.
[15] Ibid., 137.

wake of European integration and growing global economic interdependence'.[16] Jackson is very sensitive to the 'pluralistic', 'diffusionist', and 'anti-centralising' impulses and orientations of these visions of Scottish nationalism,[17] as indeed he is to 'gradualist' and 'utilitarian' approaches to nationalism,[18] especially in the 1980s and 1990s (some of which was still echoed, as Jackson notes, in the speeches of Nicola Sturgeon, First Minister of Scotland from 2014 to 2023). These are, of course, terms associated with MacCormick (amongst others), and Jackson's sensitivity to them means that he offers a subtle and nuanced reading of MacCormick's contribution to late twentieth-century Scottish political thought. For instance, Jackson recognises that MacCormick offered a critique of the language of 'sovereignty', calling instead for 'post sovereignty', and maintaining that 'there was no definitive logical relationship between the advent of "post-sovereignty" and an independent Scotland', with independence being just one choice among many.[19]

It is at this point, however, that Jackson's positioning of MacCormick, within a broader historiographical framing of the pursuit of independence and statehood, alongside an emphasis on 'popular sovereignty', begins to creak, even on its own terms. Jackson is in many ways very much aware of this: he notes, for instance, how the strategy – of a gradualist, pragmatic, flexible, post-sovereign, stance – changed following the 2011 Scottish Parliament election, with the ensuing 2014 Independence Referendum 'popularising independence as a rupture from the status quo'.[20] This was only exacerbated by the Brexit referendum, whereupon the exit from the EU posed, as Jackson puts it, 'a further dilemma for the advocates of "post-sovereignty"', forcing them effectively to make the choice they were trying to avoid in the 1980s, i.e., 'between an independent Scotland with unhindered economic relations with the rest of the UK out of the EU, or a Scotland separated from the UK's single market as a full member of the EU'.[21] Thus, Jackson signals he is aware that something fundamental changed in that shift post the 2011 Scottish Parliament election – perhaps part of the challenge is that it is very difficult, if not impossible, to avoid hindsight, and thus project back the language of sovereignty and

16 Ibid., 145.
17 Ibid., 146.
18 Ibid., 177.
19 Ibid., 159.
20 Ibid., 160.
21 Ibid. Douglas-Scott, *Brexit, Union, and Disunion* (2023), chapter 1, offers a similar reading: for her, the realities of Brexit undermine post-sovereignty as a concept.

statehood, as if it were bound to reach the popular heights it did in the twenty-first century.

The trouble, once again, is that neither MacCormick's philosophy – nor indeed his political interventions – fit well into the pursuit of independence and statehood for Scotland. Put another way, neither MacCormick's political life, nor his philosophical thought, are helpfully subsumed under a historiography that places independence, sovereignty, and statehood in the centre of the historical inquiry: his thought was both more creative and more deeply felt than this. It also did without sacred cows, such as sovereignty or the state; indeed, MacCormick worked hard to loosen the hold of these languages and their associated concepts, and to offer alternative terminologies and imaginaries. It is thus misleading to say, as Jackson does, that MacCormick's 'earliest writings on Scottish government confessed some ambivalence about whether he ultimately supported advanced devolution rather than independence',[22] for this projects back a choice that emerged later, but which MacCormick was working precisely to avoid earlier. Similarly misleading is the claim that MacCormick's 'analysis' (of post-sovereignty) 'left tantalisingly indeterminate how far it would indeed be desirable on these grounds for Scotland to secure independence rather than some form of advanced devolution'.[23]

Although perhaps less misleading, it is still ultimately not helpful to say that 'MacCormick's explicit commitment to Scottish independence became stronger over time', even when qualified, as Jackson qualifies it, by adding that MacCormick 'remained a gradualist with respect to devolution as a necessary first step towards full Scottish statehood'.[24] This masks more than it reveals, and neglects the particular political contexts in which MacCormick's statements (that supposedly reveal this change) were made. The historiographical framing here overburdens and occludes from view something more fragile that MacCormick was working towards. Although Jackson's reading of MacCormick's work is subtle and nuanced, what his broader historiographical framing risks losing sight of is just how conceptually innovative MacCormick's view was, precisely because it did not fit into that mould. In other words, rather than being undecided or ambivalent, MacCormick was articulating a well-worked out position. To some extent, this needed to be grounded in the political language of the time – hence references to 'sovereignty' – but this is not a position that

[22] Jackson, *The Case for Scottish Independence* (2020), 154.
[23] Ibid., 156.
[24] Ibid., 154.

can be easily slotted into a historiography that puts thinkers in opposing camps of pro- or anti-independence. That position is only 'indeterminate' or 'ambivalent' from a historiographical perspective in which the choice is binary: either for or against independence in the form of a sovereign state.

Part of the historiographical challenge is not to let party politics dominate the story. This is especially important with respect to MacCormick. As involved as MacCormick was in the SNP, he was never a 'party politician'.[25] MacCormick's was a more searching and more personal reflection of nationalist loyalties. In Walker's insightful phrase, this was a highly 'reflexive nationalism',[26] which cannot be squeezed into a battle of ideologies or political beliefs at party level.

This goes even for certain terms that were both rife within the SNP as well as to some extent beyond, in Scottish politics more generally, such as 'popular sovereignty'. The lack of sacred cows in MacCormick's thought, mentioned above, could be extended to 'popular sovereignty' too. The use of the term was, and is, often burdened by confusion. Thus, for instance, popular sovereignty should not be confused with internal sovereignty, i.e., in the UK, the idea of the law-making supremacy of Parliament (strictly speaking, the King-in-Parliament) vis-à-vis other internal law-making institutions. Nor should it be confused with external sovereignty, i.e., the sovereignty of the UK vis-à-vis other states.[27]

Popular sovereignty, in Scottish constitutional history, is a matter of the relations between the monarch and the people in Scotland, indicating that the king was subject to a contract with the people. But this by itself did not mean that the Scottish people were sovereign, vis-à-vis, for instance, the UK government. It meant solely that the Scottish people were sovereign vis-à-vis the monarchs that they elected to rule them. The Scottish tradition of 'popular sovereignty' could, then, be extended, not to claim independence, nor even to challenge the law-making supremacy of the Westminster Parliament, but instead to critique the idea of a legally untrammelled political power. Thus, insofar as Westminster parliamentary sovereignty is interpreted not as law-making supremacy, but as some kind of absolute power that is unlimited by law, then popular sovereignty

[25] This did not mean MacCormick was 'a political innocent': as Alex Salmond noted at his funeral, MacCormick was highly skilled in 'the political arts of compromise, artifice, and timing': Salmond, Eulogy at MacCormick's Funeral (17 April 2009).

[26] See Walker, 'Scottish Nationalism' (2012).

[27] See also Douglas-Scott, *Brexit, Union, and Disunion* (2023), chapter 6; Tomkins, 'The Constitutional Law in 'MacCormick v Lord Advocate' (2004); Tierney and Loughlin, 'Shibboleth of Sovereignty' (2018); McHarg, 'Declaration of Arbroath' (2020).

could be brought in to argue that, even if that were so in England, it was not so in Scotland. In Scotland, on this argument, the tradition of popular sovereignty showed that no law-making power in Scotland was above the law: instead, such powers were always granted on legal terms by the Scottish people.

The deeper point here is that, though loyal to a fault to Scotland, MacCormick was never loyal to ideas or labels for their own sake: what mattered to him was whether they enabled and enhanced, rather than detracted from, the quality of our relations with others. One could be Scottish, and proudly so, but this need not mean that one was wedded to any one particular political aim, nor indeed to any one political language, nor even to any one way of imagining a political order. One could stand up for Scotland and its interests, demand respect, and argue for its distinctiveness, including historically, but this need not mean that one had to pursue any particular political project, and certainly not a sovereign state for Scotland. This is not 'indeterminacy' or 'ambivalence'; nor is there here any change of political program over time; instead, there is a consistent and deep-running commitment to the flourishing of Scotland, which, in MacCormick's treatment, often requires the construction of difficult, in-between zones of political innovation, including building new political languages, and not being a prisoner of certain concepts.

The historiographical framing, thus, matters greatly. When its focus is on independence, on the pursuit of an independent sovereign state for Scotland, then there is a risk that some of what is valuable about Scottish political thought gets lost, neglected, or marginalised. This is not to say, of course, that there are no histories to be told of the above project for independent sovereign statehood, nor that these are not immensely valuable. As, for instance, Finlay has recently demonstrated, in his history of *Scottish Nationalism* (2022), there is a vital story to be told about the internal varieties and contestations within the pursuit of Scottish independence, especially at the level of party politics. Nevertheless, the adoption of the goal of independence, or the language of sovereignty and statehood, as the lingua franca of Scottish nationalism, and thus its distancing from unionism, with the subsequent loss or neglect of the difficult, almost inarticulable, middle ground, as identified by Kidd, does mean that, especially when we turn to individual thinkers and actors, as in this book with MacCormick, we must be on our guard that it does not obscure more than it reveals, and that it does not obstruct us from attempting to reach as deeply as we might into the soul-searching process that a confrontation with nationalism can occasion.

Finlay's book is, in this respect, is very valuable, for with regard to MacCormick it shows us clearly what MacCormick was not and how his thought was not hampered by any one particular political aim or political language.[28] If, in Finlay's definition, 'Scottish nationalists are nationalists because they believe in the primacy of the nation as a political unit and that statehood is the natural condition for nations',[29] then, on this definition, MacCormick was not a nationalist. If, as Finlay also defines 'Scottish nationalism', it means 'the endeavour to acquire (or as they would put it themselves, reacquire) independent, sovereign statehood',[30] then again, MacCormick was not an exponent or advocate of Scottish nationalism.[31] But, of course, this would be in many ways a paradoxical conclusion. MacCormick was, surely, a nationalist of a kind. We must, then, avoid a historiographical framing that would make it harder for us to see in what way nationalism, and of a particular kind, was central to MacCormick's character.

Time for Nationalism

Historicising Scottish Nationalism

It may be helpful to begin probing MacCormick's nationalism as a matter of character, i.e., as a matter of relating with others in a certain manner or style, by noting his early recognition that there were a variety of ways in which one could be a nationalist. In a piece written between the two general elections of 1974 – with the SNP having just won seven seats and, later in the year, unbeknownst to MacCormick at the time of writing the piece, going on to win eleven seats – MacCormick gave his own history of 'The Rise of Scottish Nationalism'.[32] MacCormick's starting point

[28] MacCormick himself receives two brief mentions in Finlay's book; see Finlay, *Scottish Nationalism* (2022), 128, and 261, fn. 38.

[29] Finlay, *Scottish Nationalism* (2022), 3.

[30] Ibid., 8.

[31] Finlay is very attuned to the complexities of the relationship between nationalism and unionism in Scottish thought, but he nevertheless treats the latter as a broader 'context', saying it is necessary to discuss, just as capitalism would be necessary to discuss in a book on socialism: *Scottish Nationalism* (2022), 121. Finlay thus thinks of nationalism and unionism as opposites, seeing unionism as 'an intellectual hurdle for the nationalist movement to overcome' (*Scottish Nationalism* (2022), 140), and arguing that 'unionist nationalism' is 'a contradiction in terms. A nationalism that does not seek statehood is not a nationalism as most people would understand it': *Scottish Nationalism* (2022), 140. As I am suggesting in this book, this historiographical framing risks missing the conceptual innovation present in MacCormick's work on nationalism.

[32] MacCormick, 'The Rise of Scottish Nationalism' (1974).

was to confront and dismiss claims that Scottish Nationalism was a 'mere protest vote', and thus a momentary frustration, or that it was based on nothing more than 'oil-fed greed', given the recent discovery of oil within the Scottish Area of the British sector.[33] MacCormick resisted such characterisations of Scottish Nationalism by telling a different history of it, and one that did not shy away from noting the various disagreements amongst nationalists, and thus also the different kinds and degrees of nationalism.

Drawing on the-then recent work by H. J. Hanham (*Scottish Nationalism*, 1969), James Kellas (*The Scottish Political System*, 1973), J. D. B. Mitchell (*Constitutional Law*, 1968), T. B. Smith ('The Union of 1707', 1957), as well as the memoirs of his father (*The Flag in the Wind*, 1955) and his own recent collection (*The Scottish Debate*, 1970), MacCormick offered an account of Scottish nationalism that begins with the frustration of the Scots in being ignored by writers of British constitutional theory and history, in particular in terms of the lack of recognition of the constitutional status of the 1707 Treaty of Union. As we have already seen in Chapter 1, and as we shall see further, attention to this Treaty was a recurring theme of MacCormick's treatment of Scottish nationalism. For now, what is significant is that MacCormick drew, with considerable self-conscious irony, on the work of A. V. Dicey and Robert Rait, in their *Thoughts on the Union between England and Scotland* (1920), to the effect, as he quoted them, that 'The permanent success of the Act of Union is shown in … the preservation thereby of English and Scottish nationalism'.[34]

Already here we see complexity in MacCormick's treatment of nationalism: there were two kinds, English and Scottish, and they were not only compatible with, but indeed secured by, a British Union State. Within that state, and thus under the Union, 'Scots and English people alike could find their separate identities secured while engaging themselves wholeheartedly in the common British enterprise of expanding, defending and governing a world-wide Empire'[35] – an early recognition, it should be added, of the important colonial context of the British constitution. Far from destroying Scottish nationalism, the Union of 1707 – as long as its effect is properly respected – preserved it, doing so by securing an 'institutional separation … in the spheres especially of law, religion,

[33] Ibid., 425.

[34] Ibid., 426; see Dicey and Rait, *Thoughts on the Union between England and Scotland* (1920), 319–45.

[35] MacCormick, 'The Rise of Scottish Nationalism' (1974), 426.

education and local government'.[36] But not only did the Union preserve Scottish nationalism in that sense – a kind of institutional nationalism, we might call it – it also helped to bridge the previously existing gap between Highland and Lowland Scots, thereby creating conditions 'for a new form of all-Scottish nationalism', which found its literary echoes in 'Sir Walter Scott, himself a sentimental nationalist but a strong political unionist'.[37]

MacCormick's linkage of the Treaty of 1707 to nationalism itself conveys a responsiveness to the complexities of nationalism, which, for MacCormick, took on different colours depending on the political context, including how this was experienced differently in different parts of the United Kingdom. Furthermore, this was clearly a nationalism that was capable of coexisting – without contradiction – with unionism. This does not mean that MacCormick downplayed the tensions among adherents of these varieties of nationalism: as he said, the kind of nationalism that one found, for instance, in 'Mr William Ross, currently Secretary of State for Scotland', which resembled that of Walter Scott, 'has long been an uneasy bedfellow to a stronger kind of nationalism … which has grown from a profound dissatisfaction with the complete centralisation of British and political activity … and with the corresponding, and steadily increasing provincialisation of the quality and style of life of Scotland'.[38] A key part, then, of the new nationalism that MacCormick was identifying – which was on the rise certainly in the early 1970s – was a 'stronger' nationalism that felt deeply about the provincialisation of Scotland, and thus saw the urgent need to 'stimulate enterprise and initiative', in particular by bringing 'significant spheres of politics and government' to Scotland.[39]

Having presented, already in a few pages, a complex picture of a variety of Scottish nationalisms, MacCormick went on in the piece to trace the 'modern history of political nationalism in Scotland', which he found began with 'the foundation in 1853 of the National Association for the Vindication of Scottish Rights', and subsequently the 'all-party Scottish Home Rule Association (1886–1928)'.[40] It is significant that MacCormick's historiography is not limited to party politics, though he did not ignore these: he noted, of course, the establishment of the National Party of

[36] Ibid., 427.
[37] Ibid.
[38] Ibid., 428.
[39] Ibid.
[40] Ibid., 430.

Scotland in 1928, and the subsequent merger in 1934 between it and the Scottish Party (which had been founded in 1932), which formed the SNP – a merger, as we know already, in which his father, John MacCormick, played a leading role.[41]

But although he noted the small gains, though, amidst mainly disappointment, of the electoral results of the SNP, MacCormick paid special attention, and placed considerable emphasis on the importance of, cross-party or all-party movements, such as his father's Scottish Covenant. Again, MacCormick notes the tensions within the party, e.g., between the members of the previous Scottish Party, which had favoured 'complete national independence', and who continued to voice that view in the SNP, and the remainder, led by John MacCormick, who fought for a more 'moderate' view, namely a policy of establishing a Scottish Parliament. Those tensions, which continued to bubble over, finally re-emerged, amidst others concerning conscription during the Second World War, resulting precisely in John MacCormick's departure from the SNP in 1942 and his establishment of the Scottish Convention.[42]

In MacCormick's judgement, 'the greater political initiative' at the time lay with the 'more "moderate" Convention than with the more "fundamentalist" SNP', with the Convention organising a number of Scottish National Assemblies, beginning in 1947, which culminated in an influential 'scheme of self-government': *A Blueprint for Scotland* (1948). Having collected over a million signatures in 1949 and early 1950, the commissioners appointed by the Assembly had requested an interview with the Prime Minister and the Leader of the Opposition, but both declined. This may seem minor, but it is important that MacCormick mentioned it, for it underlies a sense of disappointment and frustration at being ignored by the English establishment, despite 'the remarkable success' of the Convention.[43]

The same sense of frustration and disappointment is also present in MacCormick remarking that, following the endorsement of a devolutionary scheme by the Royal Commission in 1973, the response of the Commons was 'cynicism and hilarity', which, as MacCormick added, given the 1974 victories, 'proved misplaced'.[44] There is certainly no lack of feeling in MacCormick's history, albeit held carefully in check. This

[41] Ibid., 431.
[42] Ibid., 432–3.
[43] Ibid., 433–4.
[44] Ibid., 436.

affective history is a mixture of both hurt pride for the lack of recognition and respect, as well as sorrow for the current state of affairs and a passionate enthusiasm for reform.

It is also significant that, when MacCormick came to describe the advances of the SNP in the 1960s – beginning with William Wolfe's second place in the 1962 West Lothian by-election – and then of course Ewing's 1967 victory, he traced this back to his father's Covenant in 1949–51. As he put it: 'the developments of the 1960s are a very natural sequel to the rejection of the Covenant proposals in the 1950s'.[45] This is not a history that narrows Scottish nationalism to party politics. Quite the contrary: MacCormick even stated that 'We cannot yet tell what long-run momentum the SNP really has',[46] thereby suggesting that Scottish nationalism has its own history, independent of the SNP – that it is a broader political movement, a rising political consciousness, and at once a platform for a democratic and constitutionalist philosophy.

It is, then, important, that MacCormick's sense of nationalism was very much informed by its self-conscious historicization – a recognition that it was a temporally drawn-out process, which varied in kinds and degrees, depending on the events of the time, but also very much alive, even in times when it might have been expected to fizzle out (such as after the Treaty of Union). The very subtitle of the piece – 'A Case of Too Little and Too Late?' – signals awareness of the temporalities of the movement, with MacCormick cleverly – like a debater – turning this around to say it was not, as the opponents of Scottish nationalism might have it, that there was 'too little, too late' of Scottish nationalism, for this had a much longer history that was gaining further momentum, but rather that there might be 'too little, too late' of the 'desire' to preserve the Union.[47] A history of nationalism showed that it was unionism, not nationalism, that was more fragile.

The Scottish Debate

There is, as the above already attests, a fascinating – and, to my knowledge, little studied – link between Scottish nationalism and time.[48] This is, of course, visible in the very term 'gradualism', which offers a kind of

[45] Ibid., 437.
[46] Ibid., 436.
[47] Ibid., 437.
[48] Except for Walker, who recognised this as an important aspect of MacCormick's conceptualisation of nationalism: see Walker, 'Scottish Nationalism' (2012).

suspended, provisional, and defeasible temporality within which constitutional change can occur. This sense of time – of gradual time – is itself connected to the attempts made, both by his father as MacCormick saw it, but also in his own name, to rise above party politics, and to seek a unity, a consensus, however provisional and pragmatic, in order to keep the political momentum alive, to keep the political fires burning. This simultaneous orientation towards something that continues and that unites – that offers a consciousness of being part of something that outlives one, while also promising more, thereby again bringing people together, including a wide variety of views and sensibilities – is a large part of what MacCormick was searching for in his writings on nationalism.

This very much includes not only his own chapter on 'Independence and Constitutional Change', but also the very project of which this was part: *The Scottish Debate*, edited by MacCormick and published in 1970. This is a remarkable volume, certainly for its time – but even still today – for how inclusive it is of a wide variety of views on the prospect, possibility, and desirability of Scottish independence. Hosting ten chapters, with two extra replies to two of them (itself an interesting inclusion of genre: again, akin to a debate), the collection canvasses positions both strongly in favour of Scottish independence, such as the chapter by MacCormick's brother, Iain MacCormick, and those strongly against, such as the chapter by Donald Dewar (who nevertheless argues for devolution). The other chapters are by Douglas Young – the famous classicist who rebelled against conscription in the 1940s, citing the Treaty of Union as a defence; Robert McLaughlan, a journalist at the *Herald* T. B. Smith, the famous legal nationalist; David Steel, then a Liberal MP; Esmond Wright, a Conservative MP, who was also against independence; David Simpson; and K. J. W. Alexander, with these last two both being economists, though on opposite sides of the independence question.

MacCormick's conception of the volume was that it was, as signalled in the title, a 'debate, not the advocacy of any particular point of view' – an attempt to 'contribute to a clearer understanding of the nature of the Scottish national movement in historical and comparative terms, and to facilitate rational judgement of the issues at stake'.[49] As a 'Scotsman presently living and working in England' – he was, as we know, in Oxford at the time – there was an 'alarming unawareness of the matters with which the book deals', and he hoped that the book would find

[49] MacCormick, 'Introduction' to *The Scottish Debate* (1970), 1.

'some English readers'.[50] The point, once again, was to have views on the matter 'tested in the first of critical discussion', but at the same time, while creating room for disagreement, to avoid 'the polarisation which party politics produces', which 'tends to create artificial conflicts'.[51] In the result, he added, the collection showed that amongst all the disagreement, there was a 'middle ground', namely that 'some greater degree of local control of Scottish affairs is desirable',[52] and it is clear that in that sense, in his own mind at least, the collection was a success, for it showed that a middle ground was possible, and that 'a workable consensus may emerge out of the conflict'.[53] Movingly, the collection was dedicated 'to my parents, from whose labours on behalf of a humane and liberal Scottish Nationalism I have inherited my prejudice in favour of home rule'.[54]

Indeed, it is worth dwelling here on MacCormick's position, as articulated in this early piece in 1970. The delicacy of the challenge facing MacCormick in writing his chapter ought to be acknowledged: he was, after all, the editor, bringing everyone around the table. At the same time, he was a contributor, so he was wearing two hats: one which involved the arts of inclusion, of stepping back and finding a language to enable participation; and the other, an art of assertion, which called for an articulation of his own view in the debate, precisely as one of the participants in it. These arts, however, were never separate in MacCormick's writings: his mode of asserting was always at once a mode of including.

Thus, MacCormick begins his chapter by ruling out an option that would mean there would be no prospect of finding a middle ground: an approach to nationalism that sees it as 'an end in itself' – a kind of 'pure nationalist principle', which would entail 'metaphysical beliefs about the nature of nations, beliefs about which rational discussion can scarcely be conducted'.[55] This MacCormick firmly rejects – again, what he is after is precisely a rational discussion, and this requires creating a space in which others can find room for interaction with him. What is needed is thus something less metaphysical and more pragmatic, and this is exactly what MacCormick articulates, offering a 'utilitarian nationalism', which sees nationalism as a 'means to an end', where the end in question is 'the

50 Ibid.
51 Ibid., 2.
52 Ibid., 2–3.
53 Ibid., 3.
54 Ibid.
55 Ibid., 52.

well-being of the Scottish people'.[56] There is, throughout MacCormick's chapter – as in much of his work on nationalism – a very grounded, very practical orientation to 'realities', to detailed processes and mechanisms, to the nuts and bolts at issue.

This does not mean that there is an absence of feeling in the piece. Quite the contrary: MacCormick writes with visible, and yet restrained, passion, when he expresses alarm at 'centralisation', which 'in its present form will reduce Scotland to the worst sort of provincialism and parochialism'.[57] What he wants for Scotland is the opportunity to take 'responsibility for their own future'.[58] This is only appropriate, he adds, given that 'most Scots now regard themselves as belonging to a community of respectable antiquity, and wish to preserve its distinctiveness'.[59] This is, he says, 'the fact that matters'.[60] The depth of feeling here sits alongside a consistent emphasis on, precisely, 'facts', on 'realities', and on the value of a 'pragmatic approach'.[61] The two are not mutually exclusive: the emotion runs through the pragmatism, though with pragmatism as the lead partner in the dance.

It is also clear that as much as the depth of feeling is important, it does not yield to a natural or inevitable conclusion that the self-conscious nationalism of the Scottish people must lead to an independent state. Indeed, the very point of 'utilitarian nationalism' is to voice caution at jumping too hastily and embracing such a link without further reflection. What is important is to slow down – take time – and consider the benefits and costs of any one particular means to the above end, i.e., the well-being of the Scottish people. For instance, were independence to come at the cost of 'the very real values of the British way of life: traditions of tolerance and freedom', then this would be too high a cost to bear.[62]

Again, what MacCormick calls for – what his adoption of a utilitarian nationalism, precisely at this point in the fortunes of the issue of Scottish self-government – is to take time in placing the various means – 'devolution, federation, and independence within a customs union', these being the 'live possibilities'[63] – on the table and to assess their relative merits. Here, MacCormick drills down into the details, both of economic policy

[56] Ibid.
[57] Ibid., 53.
[58] Ibid.
[59] Ibid., 54.
[60] Ibid.
[61] Ibid., 63–4.
[62] Ibid., 54.
[63] Ibid., 55.

as well as constitutional mechanism. What sort of tax powers would be needed? What kind of electoral reforms? How likely was it that any proposed arrangements would be workable and sustainable? The whole essay is a subjunctive reflection on possibilities and probabilities, including long-term futures: 'suppose', such a scenario, then what, he asks?[64] No question is too speculative, but also all questions are grounded, particular, some more immediate, some far into the future.

However one turns it – and MacCormick turns the problems around in all directions, seeing indeed 'a multitude of … practical problems'[65] – it becomes increasingly clear to him, in the course of the essay, that any change would need to be done 'in stages', but then, he asks, 'what stages?'.[66] Again, he works patiently through the various possibilities – what would need to be changed first, and how. He goes out of his way to be 'constructive'[67] and to also propose a 'constructive' approach: one that would necessarily be 'gradual'.[68] Practically speaking, he says, if one looks at the details, if one really examines the realities, then it is clear that independence would need to be preceded by devolution, by 'the establishment of a limited Scottish Parliament whose powers should be successively extended up to the point of complete autonomy' – should, of course, independence be thought to be desirable.[69]

Throughout all this searching, all this questioning, MacCormick never loses sight of something that is always in his mind: the possibility of a middle ground, of avoiding 'collision courses',[70] of seeing that, in fact, there 'is a great deal more common ground between "separatists" and "devolutionists" than is commonly supposed by either group'.[71] This is pragmatism, certainly, but it is a deeply felt, constructive, upbeat, and inclusive pragmatism, and one which, again, is assisted by a creative approach to time – to political time, or the time of constitutional change, i.e., a kind of subjunctive gradualism, an 'open-ended'[72] process, a sense that certain things can be deferred and suspended, to be dealt with later, precisely an avoidance of finality or quick resolution.

64 Ibid., 58.
65 Ibid., 59.
66 Ibid., 60.
67 Ibid., 62.
68 Ibid., 60.
69 Ibid., 62.
70 Ibid.
71 Ibid.
72 Ibid., 63.

The temporal aspects of MacCormick's contribution combine with his inclusiveness, with his search for common ground – and thus avoidance of extremes, of false choices, of unnecessary binaries and collisions – as well as with the need for slow, careful judgement, for peaceful and orderly transition, for generating possibilities and evaluating them cautiously, for having a genuine debate, but in the spirit of collaboration towards a perhaps-never-to-be-completed end, that of the well-being of the Scottish people. One could characterise this as 'ambivalence' or 'indeterminacy', or even as contradictory or incoherent, but to do this would risk missing the point and the value of this approach. MacCormick's intervention here showcases practical reason at work – other-oriented, for always mindful of respecting the views of others and hearing them, and practically grounded, while still imaginative and forward-looking, hopeful, and optimistic. It was a difficult, delicate, art, but one which MacCormick was already, in these early years, proficient at. It is an art very much on display, too, in his final words in this chapter, which are worth quoting in full:

> In a book of this kind it seems particularly desirable to see how much common ground there is between varying approaches to the problem. In the midst of all the divergences of opinion and of emphasis which these essays exhibit, there are two threads which seem to run through all. One is the insistence upon the need for co-operation among the peoples of these islands; the other is the need for greater Scottish participation at a local level in Scottish affairs. The advantage of taking a pragmatic approach to our future is that it seems likely to secure both objectives, and in doing so to command a very wide degree of assent; and that is after all the vital element in the working of any constitution. Such a pragmatic approach follows from an appreciation of the realities of constitutional change.[73]

The essays collected by MacCormick in 1970 were to prove influential – they were one of the items considered by Lord Kilbrandon and the Royal Commission in their inquiry.[74] As has been mentioned in Chapter 4, MacCormick had discussions with Lord Kilbrandon about the subject matter of the inquiry, and he is indeed duly listed in the Report as a 'private individual' who contributed to the Commission by way of 'private discussion'.[75] Although, of course, there is no direct evidence of MacCormick's influence on Lord Kilbrandon and the Report, it is striking that the Report does in many respects echo both MacCormick's diagnosis of the

[73] Ibid., 63–4.

[74] Paper No: cc(we) 65; the book is cited, for example, on page 135 of the *Report of the Royal Commission of Inquiry* (1973), in relation to economics.

[75] *Report of the Royal Commission of Inquiry* (1973), 495.

problem – the increase in centralisation of government in Westminster and Whitehall,[76] and the resultant weakening of democracy, along with the strength of national feeling in Scotland 'who wish their distinctive national identit[y] to be recognised in the system of government'.[77] Interestingly, too, the Report notes also the 'complaint … that Scots law is not sufficiently understood in London or catered for in UK legislation'[78] and suggests that the solution to that would be to have a Scottish Representative Assembly as 'an appropriate means of recognising Scotland's national identity and of giving expression to its national consciousness'.[79] This would have been, one surmises, music to MacCormick's ears.

Against Anglo-Phobia

Lest it be thought that MacCormick only ever spoke in indignant tones about the mistreatment, the lack of respect or recognition, of the Scots and their distinctiveness in England, it is worthwhile, as a brief corrective, to consider his short reflection on a-then recently published article about Scottish universities. Entitled 'Provincialism and the Scottish Universities', and appearing in the important Scottish political journal, *Question*, in 1977, MacCormick took issue with an article that, drawing upon figures showing a rise in English-trained professors in Scotland, and a fall in Scottish-trained professors in England, inferred that care had to be taken to avoid 'de-Scottishness of Scottish universities' and thus that some policy of protecting Scots graduates and Scottish universities was justifiable.[80] MacCormick's reply to this inference and justification did not mince words:

> It really is the grossest of insults to ascribe such attitudes [of failing to attend to Scottish subjects] to the many gifted men and women from England and elsewhere who have over many years committed themselves to working in and for Scottish universities, dedicated themselves to their Scottish students, contributed enormously to learning in Scotland learning about Scotland … and indeed generally helped to dispel that sense of self-depreciation, oddly coupled with mere complacency, which I think characterised Scottish universities more formerly than now.[81]

[76] See ibid., 329–30.
[77] Ibid., 330.
[78] Ibid., 331.
[79] Ibid., 335.
[80] MacCormick, 'Provincialism' (1977), 3.
[81] Ibid.

It was, MacCormick continued, simply against 'fundamental decency' to make such claims about English-trained professors in Scotland. This was, however, not just a matter of being committed to 'academic freedom and to the autonomy of universities'.[82] As important as this was, there was something else at stake, i.e., Scottish nationalism:

> What Scottish nationalism in its true and honourable form is not concerned with is a carping and nasty attitude to English people or any 'outsiders' who have settled here and committed themselves to working and bringing up their families here and adding new threads to the rich and varied pattern of our history. It is concerned with restoring in Scotland that real security of self-respect which will consign such manifestations of a sense of inferiority to the unhappy past to which they belong.[83]

Far from it being the case that MacCormick's nationalism was ever Anglophobic, and far from it always or even mainly calling for respect from the English for Scotland and the Scots, MacCormick's nationalism in fact went both ways, i.e., respect in all directions: there was no room, for him, for a tone of complacency, protectionism, or hostility, and thus a politics of 'us and them'. No 'chip-on-shoulder provincialism'[84] for MacCormick, then. The very fact that, amongst a busy period, in 1977, MacCormick would take the time to respond to an article and do so with such passion – equal to any passion he expressed when he felt Scotland had been disrespected – speaks volumes, once more, about his character and the character of his nationalism.

The Invisible Union

From a certain perspective, the debate over the legal status of the Acts of Union of 1707 may seem irrelevant, or at best, minor and pedantic. Indeed, it could very easily be characterised as a parochial, navel-gazing, unrealistic and romantic indulgence by myth-spinning Scottish constitutional theorists and historians – perhaps especially MacCormick himself, given, as we saw in Chapter 1, the leading role that his father had in drawing on the legal status of the 1707 Union to counter the Dicyean orthodoxy of Westminster sovereignty in *MacCormick* v *Lord Advocate* (1953). MacCormick's interest in that case, and in its arguments, could thus all too readily be dismissed as but the unsurprising, but also disproportionate or

[82] Ibid.
[83] Ibid.
[84] Ibid.

even inappropriate, certainly biased, endorsement by a son of his father's doomed and naïve project.

To do this, however, would be a great disservice to the significance of the debate over the Union generally, but also in terms of its importance to MacCormick's politics and philosophy – indeed, to his character. At stake in the debate was not simply how to characterise the legal status of a particular Act – or more accurately, a series of domestic Acts that introduced, into domestic law, an international Treaty – and thus how best to describe the constitution of the United Kingdom. Further, by no means was this an antiquated debate of sole historical interest. Rather, and certainly for MacCormick, what was at stake was the very possibility of law as a limit on power.

As such, the status of the 1707 Union, and whether it could be said to have introduced limits on what the new Parliament of Great Britain could do with respect to Scotland (and the three protected Scottish institutions of religion, law, and education), was entangled with the very possibility of constitutionalism, i.e., of the project, which itself reached deeply into jurisprudence (and not just public or constitutional law), of the relationship between law and power. To put it crudely: was law the outcome of power – as many, such as Bentham and Austin, argued – or was power necessarily legally instituted and therefore legally limited? This was, it should be added, not only a question that emerged later – when MacCormick was writing – over the status of the Union, but was also very much present at the time, with the language of 'limitations', and thus the prospect of 'limited sovereignty', being closely debated amongst the adherents of natural jurisprudence in the seventeenth century[85] and in the debates surrounding the 1707 Union itself, especially via the figure of Andrew Fletcher of Saltoun.[86]

This question, of the relation between law and power, was, in turn, closely linked to the quality of relations that one could argue the Union of 1707 established: was it a Union that legitimated the domination of one nation (England) over another (Scotland), or was it a less hierarchical, more heterarchical, union? Was it a Union in which one party could ignore, disrespect, and ride roughshod over another, or was it a mutually respectful pact of two equally free nations, with their own distinctive traditions and institutions, that joined peacefully together in order to reap the rewards of collaboration (most especially, in the context of empire)?

[85] See Moore and Silverthorne, 'Protestant Theologies' (1995).

[86] See Robertson, 'An Elusive Sovereignty' (1995).

Just what kind of relation did the Union of 1707 establish: was its purpose to incorporate, swallow, and extinguish one state by folding into another, which simply continued as if nothing happened except its own swelling, or did it inaugurate a new political and legal entity – a new union – of, again, relatively autonomous and distinct, but nevertheless co-operating, parties? At stake, in other words, was precisely character, i.e., the manner or style of relating with others.

For all its seeming technicality and historical antiquarianism, then, this debate reached deeply into MacCormick's character and was of vital significance for him. It was no accident that it played such an enormous part in his engagement with nationalism, though, equally, constitutionalism, but extending, really, to the very depths of his jurisprudence. As such, the debate shows how so much can be at stake – politically and philosophically, but also existentially, in what appears, at first, to be nothing but an irrelevant or minor historical disagreement.

Historical Realities

To see this, we need to look closely at MacCormick's writings on the 1707 Union – of course, necessarily selectively so. Here, it is instructive to observe how early on in his writings the issues raised by the 1707 Union, if not explicitly the Union itself, were prominent in MacCormick's concerns.

Thus, for instance, in one of his first reviews, published in 1966, of *Sovereignty within the Law* by Arthur Larson and Wilfred Jenks (1965), MacCormick did not hesitate to assert that 'the question of the relationship between law and sovereignty is *from a legal point of view* [original emphasis] purely a logical one', i.e., 'it is analytically true that "sovereignty" is only legally significant in so far as it is a capacity defined by law, i.e., that the law is logically prior to the sovereign, whose power is in this sense necessarily limited by law'.[87] The analytical point, however, as important as it was, did not end the inquiry, and one had to go on, practically, to consider 'by what concrete provisions those who exercise that power [i.e., a power conferred by law] are limited in their exercise of it in the interests of municipal and international justice? How effective "is the rule of law" and by what means, if any, is it entrenched?'.[88] As always with MacCormick the analytical and the practical proceeded alongside each other and any answer to one did not determine the answer to the other.

87 MacCormick, 'Review of Larson and Jenks' (1966), 285.
88 Ibid., 285.

In the above review, the 1707 Union did not feature explicitly, but it was there, in the background, the prime example for MacCormick of a law that limited power. If it was not explicitly mentioned in that review, however, the 1707 Union certainly featured prominently in MacCormick's review of Stanley de Smith's account of the British constitution, *Constitutional and Administrative Law* (1971). Indeed, the review begins with the quote from Dicey and Rait already mentioned above and draws on it to observe that 'it is a remarkable truth that the literature of the British constitution exhibits a striking lack of unanimity or unity among its English, Scottish and (for that matter) Northern Irish exponents'.[89] This is because so much of 'British' constitutional history and theory is written as if 'British' was just another term for 'English'.

Key to seeing these disparities is precisely the question of the status of the Union or, in other words, where the starting point of the UK constitution lies. The 'Scots view', as MacCormick put it, 'strongly favours May 1, 1707, as the starting point, to which the Irish add the rider that 1800 marks a new and second point of departure'.[90] By contrast, the 'English view tends to fluctuate between acceptance of these propositions, and assertion of the contradictory view that the events of 1707 or 1800 are footnotes to a continual and legally unitary progression of one constitution (the English one) from dim antiquity to the present time, the latter opinion being predominant'.[91] De Smith's new book was very firmly present in the English tradition.

In his account – nevertheless characteristically generous and respectful, e.g., MacCormick indicated that he has already set it as 'the basic text for first-year students reading constitutional law'[92] – of just how 'exclusively English' is the story de Smith tells, MacCormick, as a counter, urged that 'any realistic account' of 'constitutional law' 'must take full notice of the acts of the political system which operates within its compass'.[93] This is one of many occasions on which MacCormick referred to facts, to reality, to seeing how things actually work on the ground. If one did pay such attention, MacCormick argued, then one would see that the Acts of Union were far from 'mere "scraps of paper"':[94]

89 MacCormick, 'Review of de Smith' (1971), 174.
90 Ibid.
91 Ibid.
92 Ibid.
93 Ibid., 175.
94 Ibid., 177 – arguably a reference to an article by his father: see chapter 1.

> What, then, are the facts? There is at least one clear case in which a government has altered its policy in response to critical pressure and demands for conformity with the terms of the Union. When in 1872 the Liberal Lord Chancellor Hatherley first introduced the proposal to abolish the appellate jurisdiction of the House of Lords and Privy Council, and to create instead an 'Imperial' Court of Appeal, Lord Cairns raised the objection (among others) that it was inconsistent with the terms of the several unions [1707, 1800] to create an English court which would hear appeals from the Scots and Irish courts.[95]

The citing here of a specific historical instance – a historical 'fact' – is significant. It was further supported by MacCormick quoting from later debates over the Supreme Court of Judicature Bill, in which again the terms of the Acts of Union were cited in objection to any such 'imperial court'.[96] The fact that the proposals were 'abandoned in view of such objections is', MacCormick continued, 'strong evidence of the recognition of the serious importance of conforming with the fundamental terms of the Union'.[97] There were other examples, too, such as the debate in the nineteenth century over Scottish universities legislation.[98] What these 'facts', these 'realities', showed was that 'the Articles of Union are "fundamental" in the strong sense that they give rise to a legal duty not to abrogate them save with specifically Scottish consent'.[99]

Attention to facts and realities, then, mattered, and could, in MacCormick's view, trump any overly legalistic argument as to the 'strict legal power to override' the Articles of Union – a view MacCormick acknowledged was the consensus amongst English constitutional theorists.[100] But attention to these facts and realities was not the only reason to adopt a more realistic, and at once geographically respectful, constitutional theory and history. The other reason was that the English position – this kind of 'English nationalism', evident in equating the 'British' constitution with an 'English' one – was based on defunct, 'bankrupt'[101] or 'bad jurisprudence'.[102]

It was, MacCormick argued, 'difficult to conceive of a coherent jurisprudential theory in the light of which the Union agreement is not seen

95 MacCormick, 'Review of de Smith' (1971), 177.
96 Ibid.
97 Ibid.
98 Ibid., 178.
99 Ibid.
100 Ibid., 179.
101 Ibid., 177.
102 Ibid., 179.

as being constituent, and therefore, however skeletally, constitutional'.[103] This was because the jurisprudence of 'English positivism' had been shown, by the English themselves, as especially Hart, to have been mistaken: law was not, as Bentham and Austin thought, the command of a sovereign. This was a theory, as is well known from Hart's criticisms, that failed to make sense of, for instance, the continuity of legal systems and reduced all forms of law to one unlikely and inadequate form, namely a command backed up by a sanction. In fact, MacCormick argued, even Bentham had an inkling that such a jurisprudence was inadequate, for he 'did conceive of the limitations laid down in the union as having real practical significance'.[104] Putting aside the exegetical question, the overall point was clear:

> In any event, given that sovereign power derives from rules (as modern jurisprudence has taught us), it is perfectly clear that the rules by which sovereign power is conferred may create exceptions to that power, thereby imposing certain legislative disabilities upon the sovereign body. A parallel duty may be imposed upon the courts to give effect to all valid enactments of the sovereign, but to declare ineffective and invalid any purported legislation trenching upon the area of disability.[105]

Interestingly, by 'modern jurisprudence', MacCormick did not just refer to Hart and his critiques of Bentham and Austin's theory of the relationship between law and sovereign power. He also referred to Kelsen. Adopting Kelsen's theory of the 'historically first constitution' – the *Grundnorm* (the Basic Norm) thanks to which a legal system can be presupposed to exist – the only option was precisely the 1707 Union:

> Had they [the Acts of Union of 1707] not been ratified the United Kingdom would not have come into existence as a state, not by peaceable means at any rate. The enabling legislation was validly passed by each of the two separate Parliaments, acting under each of two separate constitutions. Therefore it is either the case that the arrangement ratified was a new constitution of a new state, or it is the case that the United Kingdom has two constitutions; if either former constitution was validly abrogated in favour of a new one, both must have been, and if neither was, both exist. Since there are two separate 'chains of validity' before 1707 and but one after it, the United Kingdom either has two grundnorms, or a new one came into existence in 1707.[106]

103 Ibid.
104 Ibid., 177.
105 Ibid.
106 Ibid., 178.

But, of course, on Kelsen's own terms, a state or a legal system (the two are equivalent in Kelsen) cannot have two *Grundnorms*; therefore, it must be the case the Acts of Union of 1707 are the *Grundnorm* – the historically first constitution, the ground zero – of the UK constitution. This, it should be added, was not just a matter of good jurisprudence – whether Hartian or Kelsenian. It was also a matter, significantly, of 'respect': this 'Respect for the spirit of the terms of the Union' was a matter both of reality (as the examples above indicated), but also of good theory.[107] In other words, attention to reality, and good theorising, were part and parcel of good relations – in this case, respectful relations between England and Scotland (though also Ireland and Northern Ireland).

It is well to remember that the arguments adopted by MacCormick here were made in 1972 – much earlier, then, that is usually acknowledged. They continued, in various forms, in reviews that came soon after, e.g., the same theme of 'reality' being obscured by 'the traditional constitutional theory of the UK as a unitary state', that mythical consensus that 'derives from a mistaken over-concern with legal sovereignty at legislative level, itself based on the distinctive English tradition in positivist legal theory from Hobbes to Holland, of which the finest flowering was in Bentham's and Austin's writings', was repeated in MacCormick's glowing review of James Kellas's pathbreaking *The Scottish Political System* (1973).[108]

Kellas's book was important because it once again illuminated the reality of the diversity of British constitutionalism in a way that has been 'ignored' by 'the current traditional of constitutional jurisprudence'.[109] The tone here sometimes was simply one of exasperation, e.g., as in the 1974 piece on the history of Scottish nationalism discussed above, MacCormick said:

> It has been a source of persistent annoyance to Scotsmen and Scots lawyers [referring to Lord Cooper's opinion in *MacCormick* v *Lord Advocate*] that English writers on the British Constitution have so persistently asserted that Britain has no written constitution, in the teeth of the fact that the United Kingdom was first constituted by legislative acts of separate states adopting and putting into effect from an agreed date agreed Articles of Union.[110]

However one looked at it, whether realistically or theoretically, it was hard to see how the English consensus, the theory of the 'English' constitution,

107 Ibid., 179.

108 MacCormick, 'Review of Kellas' (1973), 27.

109 Ibid., 28; see also MacCormick, 'Review of Grant' (1976), where MacCormick refers to the '1707 constitution': 304.

110 MacCormick, 'The Rise of Scottish Nationalism' (1974), 427.

could be anything but an example of blindness, whether neglectfully or wilfully disrespectful of the Scots (and the Irish and Northern Irish).

Dicey and the UK Constitution

What is exasperation – or annoyance – in certain times appears, at other times, as almost resignation (though never quite that) and at times apologia. The latter is visible, for instance, in MacCormick's 1978 piece, delivered as a lecture at Queen's University in Belfast in 1976, on the occasion of the 25th anniversary of the *MacCormick* v *Lord Advocate* (1953) case.[111] Here, MacCormick acknowledged that 'I must frankly admit to having a personal as well as a scholarly motive' for asking the question he did, as per the title of his lecture – 'Does the United Kingdom have a Constitution?' – given that 'I am the son of the leading petitioner in that case'.[112] But any embarrassment is quickly sidelined, as MacCormick turned to analysing the case, and the status of the 1707 Union, in relation to 'some basic questions in legal theory'.[113] As he put it, 'All questions of the more fundamental sort in constitutional law necessarily involve questions of legal theory; and legal theory in turn must be testable by reflection on constitutional law and practice'.[114] That being so, he asserted, given he was 'by trade a legal theorist', his interest in the case 'is more than one of mere filial piety'.[115]

MacCormick's immediate critical target was Dicey. In particular, MacCormick confronted Dicey's claim that the doctrine of the sovereignty of Parliament is a 'logically necessary truth': for Dicey, 'limited sovereignty' was a 'contradiction in terms', for a 'sovereign power cannot, while retaining its sovereign character, restrict its own powers by particular enactment'.[116] There are two propositions that make up Dicey's theory: (1) 'a "sovereign" is by definition a holder of legally unlimited and illimitable authority'; and (2) 'no legal system can exist in which there is not some "sovereign" so defined'.[117] These propositions are similar to, but not identical with, 'Austin's science of jurisprudence'.[118]

111 MacCormick, 'Does the UK' (1978).
112 Ibid., 1.
113 Ibidl.
114 Ibid., 6.
115 Ibid., 7.
116 Ibid.
117 Ibid., 8.
118 Ibid.

For both theorists, legal limitations on the sovereign were logically impossible. For Austin, this was because prior to the existence of law, there had to be the social fact, the existence, of a sovereign, and a sovereign was someone who was habitually obeyed. For Dicey, by contrast, sovereignty was not a matter of 'social fact … certainly not fully'.[119] It was, instead, 'normative', meaning that the 'doctrine of the sovereignty of Parliament is itself a principle or norm of the constitution'.[120] But how could Dicey here have his cake and eat it – after all, if one wanted to insist that sovereignty was legally instituted, then could not those very 'legal norms which confer legislative power … subject it to limits'?[121] At best one could argue that it was 'contingently' true that the UK constitution, i.e., the legal norms that made the Parliament sovereign, did not contain limits. One could certainly not argue that it was a logical truth, for this was at odds with the normative reading of sovereignty, which Dicey explicitly endorsed.[122]

Now let us, MacCormick continued, run with the contingent claim, i.e., with a reading of the constitution as determined contingently by the norms that establish it. The best account we have of such rules as 'a complex matter of (contingent) social fact' was Hart's, which, as we know, is based on a rule of recognition, i.e., the acceptance, from the internal point of view, of the officials as to the ultimate criteria of validity.[123] Certainly, this meant that one needed to look historically at what the officials accepted and when, but history alone was not enough: 'geographical as well as historical factors' needed 'to be considered'.[124] After all, the UK was not England: there were also Wales, Scotland and Northern Ireland. And, if one wanted to know what the officials in Scotland thought, then there was hardly a better source than Lord Cooper's dicta in *MacCormick* v *Lord Advocate*, which, in MacCormick's reconstruction, noted that the rule of recognition, as Lord Cooper understood it, was 'Whatever the Queen in Parliament enacts, unless in derogation from the justiciable limits set by the articles of Union, is law'.[125]

To posit otherwise is to suggest that the internal point of view, and officialdom, in the UK was limited to the English officials. But, even if one did limit oneself to English officials, and insisted on those involved in the

119 Ibid., 9.
120 Ibid.
121 Ibid.
122 Ibid., 10.
123 Ibid., 10–11.
124 Ibid., 11.
125 Ibid.

legislative process, then even then one could argue, based on the examples already given above (e.g., in 1872 re the 'Imperial Court of Appeal' proposals), that as a matter of contingency, the British constitution did accept norms by which it limited its own sovereignty.[126] Thus, if one does accept Dicey's 'contingency' point, and a normative rather than a factual account of sovereignty, then, tracing that contingency historically and geographically, by reference to the Hartian internal point of view officials – English, Scottish, Welsh, and Northern Irish, but even potentially just English – yields the conclusion that the British Constitution does both institute and limit parliamentary sovereignty, from 1707 and thereafter.

Interestingly, and in ways that was to echo later for MacCormick when he tackled the question of sovereignty in Europe, MacCormick did not dismiss out of hand the possibility that there could be, within one state, more than one rule of recognition. In a state like the UK, it was perhaps possible that there were plural rules of recognition, with each of the various components – English, Scottish, Welsh, Northern Irish – having their own distinct, though overlapping, point of view, accepting slightly different ultimate criteria of validity. There was 'nothing', MacCormick added, in 'Hart's theory which requires us to conclude' that this was 'impossible, or logically absurd'.[127] Hart was 'alive to the possibility', via his core / penumbra principle, that any rule, including the rule of recognition, was subject to 'dubitable points, in relation to which there are competing versions of the "proper" criteria to apply'.[128] There was, then, some pluralistic potential in Hart's theory. But this would surely have hardly satisfied Dicey, who would not want to claim that there were different criteria of validity in the UK.

The upshot was clear: either one acknowledged that the Union of 1707 was a historically first constitution (in this case, of Great Britain, with the UK coming into being in 1800 after the second union), at which point one had to also concede that there were legal limits on the Westminster Parliament, or, one had to think, entirely implausibly, that 'England has a continuing identity into which have been absorbed Wales, Scotland, and Northern Ireland, with total loss of any distinct legal identity in all cases'.[129] That the latter was an untenable view was clear, if only for instance from the-then recent Kilbrandon Report, which acknowledged

126 Ibid., 11–12.
127 Ibid., 14.
128 Ibid.
129 Ibid., 18.

that the UK was 'a state comprising several national traditions, including legal traditions'.[130]

Ultimately, though, in this piece as well as others after it, MacCormick did not rest his argument on the geographical-historical filling in of contingent truths, as per a hypothetical Hartian-Dicyean argument. The acceptance of rules, including a rule of recognition, was not solely a matter of fact: such acceptance was made in the context of 'underpinning reasons' – which was MacCormick's reconstruction of the Hartian point of view. When one, as an official, accepted a rule of recognition then one did so with 'justifying or legitimating reasons for acceptance',[131] i.e., in light of the principles that made moral sense of those rules. This was a kind of moral (or at least politically moral) contingency account of the rule of recognition: the content of the rule was contingent, in any one time and place, but still had to make justifiable, legitimating sense.

There could of course be disagreement and contestation on what did make justifiable, legitimating sense, but any such reasons had to be intelligible: they still had to make an intelligible case for why acceptance of the rule was justifiable or legitimate. And, if one were to take, as surely one must, the importance of democracy for any legitimacy in contemporary states, then it would be difficult to make a case that the whole of Scotland could be ignored, as one would be doing if one insisted 'on the proposition that Parliament has in principle power to sweep away the Scots courts or Scots law or the Church of Scotland'.[132] But that was precisely what one was bound to insist if one claimed, as many English constitutional theorists and historians continued to claim, that the 1707 Union was not a constituent part of the British constitution.

Jurisprudence and the Constitution

There was, in this above more pronounced normative reading of the Hartian point of view, something difficult that MacCormick was trying to grasp: some kind of middle ground between geographical-historical contingency and political morality. In a later paper, in which MacCormick returned to the question of the relationship between jurisprudence and constitutional theory and history – originally an address at University College London on 9 December 1982, and published in 1983 as 'Jurisprudence and

130 Ibid.
131 Ibid., 19.
132 Ibid., 19–20.

the Constitution' – MacCormick sought to capture once more this middle ground. At stake was the question as to 'whether any positivist legal theory can give an adequate account of constitutional law'[133] – a question that was very much in the scholarly eye thanks to Dworkin's criticisms of Hart.

Without delving into the details of MacCormick's take, his position in this piece was that neither Dworkin on his own terms, nor Hart on his, captured what needed to be captured, i.e., precisely a jurisprudential theory that could provide an adequate account of the (British) constitution. On the one hand, Dworkin was right that no positivistic account of social facts could, without a supporting theory of institutional morality, make sense of a constitution. But, on the other hand, the Hartian intuition that contingent social facts mattered, as these were determined by the internal point of view of officials at particular times, in particular places, was also vital. The danger in Dworkin's view was that it was insufficiently grounded in contingent detail. The danger in Hart's was that it was insufficiently normative. Thus, one had to find a middle way. The language adopted by MacCormick in 1982 was that of a normatively infused concept of custom:

> Custom, as I wish to understand the term, is an emanation of the practical reason of human beings applied to the practical necessity of securing a stable framework of communal coexistence. It is constituted by a sharing of practical judgements as to how and within what limits ('rights') the coexistence and collective decision-making of a community ought to be carried on.[134]

This consensus, MacCormick hastened to add, 'is never perfectly achieved anywhere, is always in some degree precarious, and sometimes dissent resolved itself into the arbitrament of war'.[135] But the key point was that neither custom alone, nor an abstract, timeless morality, could do the trick: '…the custom which is fundamental grounding of any stable constitution is, in my submission, an exercise of practical reason issuing in assent by many and diverse individuals to an allocation of authority to regulate, adjudicate over and carry forward public administration in what those individuals envisage as an integral community'.[136]

Here, jurisprudence and constitutional theory and history were at one. At the core of both was an assertion, by MacCormick, of the importance of 'assent by many and diverse individuals', as grounded in the rules and

[133] MacCormick, 'Jurisprudence and the Constitution' (1983), 13.
[134] Ibid., 26.
[135] Ibid.
[136] Ibid., 27.

principles that gave the order they lived in stability. There was, in other words, a call here for 'respect' – as MacCormick puts it in this piece, 'steadfast respect toward which we ought to be governed by those who achieve positions of constitutional authority'[137] – and it was precisely this 'respect' that was missing from accounts that neglected to acknowledge as constitutional, thereby also making invisible, the terms of the 1707 Acts of Union. As a matter of both constitutional history and jurisprudence, to make the 1707 Acts of Union invisible, in this way, was to ignore and disrespect an entire population – Scotland – and ultimately to give up on the possibility of law limiting sovereign power.[138]

Living Constitutionalism

As abstract as some of the above points about jurisprudential methodology and constitutional theory must sound, they were deeply felt and connected to something central to MacCormick's character, precisely, as above, a sense of the importance of respecting persons, of being decent, of being basically considerate toward one another. Of course, put like this, it sounds bland and banal – a reduction of so many years of complex theorising, and circumstantial political action, down to a parent's desperate cry to a child, 'be kind!'. But even if bland or banal when put in these abstract terms, to live it concretely, whether in theory or in practice, was difficult and delicate, often requiring considerable bravery and determination, but also self-discipline.

In many ways, this was exactly what constitutionalism came to for MacCormick, as he lived it, both as a philosopher and as someone involved in politics: it was, at its root, a matter of respect, both for oneself and for others. But to secure respect, as we have already noticed, was not something

137 Ibid., 28.

138 MacCormick returned often to the issue of the status of the Union, e.g., as chapter 4 in *Questioning Sovereignty*, and in 2004, 'Doubts about the Supreme Court'. In 2008, when towards the end of his life, and writing entries for *The New Oxford Companion*, he made sure one of them was on the 'Treaty of Union', this time also adding that the union negotiations had been 'triggered' by a 'menacing army' that the English had marched in 1705, subsequently extorting a 'price', for the Union by 'complete suppression of the Scottish Parliament and separate Scottish Crown': MacCormick, 'Treaty of Union' (2008), 1192. It is interesting to compare MacCormick's account with others, e.g., MacNeill's *The Scottish Realm* (1947), chapter 16: MacNeill's account stresses how determined England were to get an 'incorporating union', accompanied by a 'desire to bring the recalcitrant nation [i.e., Scotland] under domination'. Of course, the historiography of 1707 is rich and contested: see Whatley, *The Scots and the Union* (2007), for an extended discussion.

momentary – it required stability over time, it was something that had to be consistent and coherent over time. Constitutionalism, for MacCormick, one could argue, was a mixture of respect and the slowness of time, the taking of time to show and demonstrate one's respect. It was, furthermore, a multi-directional and one might add hermeneutical respect: it was thus a respect for 'many and diverse persons', mindful of their perspective on one's own actions. This kind of long-term, never-ending, multi-directional, and hermeneutical respect was precisely what living constitutionalism entailed, and that, in turn, was inseparable from character – from how one lived, with what attitudes, in one's relations with others.

The Mandate Question

One important moment in which this attitude, this practice of constitutionalism, can be seen in MacCormick's case was in the mid 1970s debate over what constituted a 'mandate'. The debate needs to be put in context: following the Kilbrandon Report in 1973, and the election victories for the SNP in 1974, considerable enthusiasm, if not confidence, was rife within the party. MacCormick himself, to an extent, was swept up in the excitement, writing, in 1974, that 'Today, the question is not whether a Scottish Parliament will meet again, but where and how soon'.[139] In 1975, too, he wrote of the 'the devolution we are about to receive',[140] claiming confidently that 'Before 1980 a Scots Parliament will reassemble in Scotland'.[141] Nevertheless, though prophesising so confidently at times, MacCormick never let enthusiasm get the better of his commitment to democracy and constitutionalism.

There was a view, voiced especially loudly in 1975–76 by some SNP members, that a majority of SNP seats in Scotland in the Westminster elections was a 'democratic mandate' for independence.[142] Something like this policy had been included in the 1974 party manifesto, which had 'stated that such a majority would be committed to demand from the UK Government the necessary legislation to set up a Scottish Parliament with full control over all the affairs of Scotland'.[143] Now, after the elections wins, voices within the party wanted to adopt such a policy for the next election. The background to this, of course, was the continuing tension in the party

139 MacCormick, 'A Filial Look' (1974), 13.
140 MacCormick, 'We Need a New Politics' (1975), 18.
141 Ibid., 17.
142 See Harvie, *Scotland and Nationalism* (2004), 211–2.
143 'Nats Open Mandate Debate', *Observer* (5 September 1976), 3.

between those who backed devolution – as a necessary first step (the gradualists) – and those who argued for independence (the fundamentalists). Even though, in May 1976, in a well-attended conference (over 2,000 members) in Motherwell, the party had decided that it was 'prepared to accept an assembly with limited powers as a possible stepping stone',[144] tensions had been and remained high. This was all the more so given that in January 1976, a group broke away from the SNP to establish the Scottish Labour Party, adopting a fundamentalist platform, and attracting one of the SNP's future stars, Jim Sillars.[145]

The growing excitement, and the pressure from fundamentalists, must have been considerable. MacCormick, however, stood his gradualist ground. Writing in *Question*, in September 1976, MacCormick tackled 'the mandate question'. He dissented from the very language of a 'mandate': 'It is', he argued, 'a device for disguising respect for the internal democracy of the party itself as respect for the will of the popular majority. It is the rhetoric in which oligarchy masquerades as democracy'.[146]

Indeed, the language of 'respect' runs deep in MacCormick's piece, e.g., he argued that 'In one respect this [policy of an independence mandate based on the majority of seats] would be a more respectable use of the idea of the mandate than most', and there were, of course, many in the party, perhaps even a majority, that stood for independence, now or as quickly as possible.[147] But the SNP would really be getting ahead of itself by deploying the language of mandate, pretending, falsely, that a majority of seats allows it to 'conduct government'.[148] It was one thing to 'play the mandate game with the Government' and 'another thing altogether to play it as against our own people'.[149] A majority of Westminster seats was not equivalent to the will of 'a majority of the Scots' – pretending otherwise was to endanger 'the democratic rights of my fellow citizens':[150] 'It is surely an article of democratic faith that a people ought to be governed according to the will of the majority, saving the necessary respect owed to the rights of minorities. The more fundamental the issue, the more important is the principle. The constitution of a country is as fundamental a political issue as there is'.[151]

144 Mitchell, Bennie, Johns, *The Scottish National Party* (2011), 20.
145 See Pittock, *The Road to Independence* (2013), 77; Hames, *Literary Politics* (2019), 95–6.
146 MacCormick, 'The Mandate Question' (1976), 8.
147 Ibid.
148 Ibid.
149 Ibid.
150 Ibid., 8–9.
151 Ibid., 9.

MacCormick's view prevailed, and was soon followed by an announcement, by the party Chairman, Bill Wolfe, that 'no matter how strong the support for the SNP might be, a unilateral declaration of independence formed no part of its policy'.[152] Once more, a gradualist, constitutionalist, responsible, and democratic stance had won.

Such a stance, however, had to be continually fought for. For example, in 1977, following an address by the Queen to the Westminster Parliament, a number of SNP figures, with republican leanings, called for a republican referendum, questioning the legitimacy of the monarchy in Scotland, and arguing that 'a new titular head of state should be created instead of the Queen if Scotland gained independence'.[153] MacCormick's response, reported in the press, was that such arguments and claims only enabled the party's opponents to attach a 'separatist label' to it, and argued instead that 'a great majority of Scots were non-political and wanted to retain a symbolic link with the Crown'.[154]

Later, too, in 1978, when the SNP had been 'hostile to any form of agreement' with the Labour government, given all the difficulties with the passage of the Scotland and Wales Bill 1978, MacCormick once more stood up to argue, as reported in the press, 'that the SNP parliamentary group should consider a working agreement with the Government'.[155] The balancing act was delicate here: on the one hand, it was necessary to stand up to Westminster tactics, and not allow them to defeat the political momentum in Scotland – in this respect, the title of a piece by MacCormick in the press in 1977 is telling: 'Westminster Must Beware of Pushing the SNP into an All-Out Battle'[156] – but, on the other hand, any constitutional change must be precisely that, constitutional, and achieved 'by stages so as to secure a continued spirit of friendship and cooperation throughout Britain'.[157] Given the ingenious balancing act required, no wonder MacCormick was being named in this period in the press as a possible candidate for leading the SNP following the soon-to-come retirement of Wolfe.[158]

152 'Nats Open Mandate Debate', *Observer* (5 September 1976), 3.

153 Peter Hetherington, 'Queen's Unity Call Splits Nationalists', *The Guardian* (28 May 1977), 24.

154 Ibid.

155 John Kerr, 'SNP Seeks Deal With Cabinet on Devolution', *The Guardian* (18 July 1978), 4; see also Levy, *Scottish Nationalism at the Crossroads* (1990), who traces this disagreement within the party to debates at the SNP's 1977 conference: 78–83.

156 MacCormick, 'Westminster Must Beware' (17 May 1977), 14.

157 Ibid.

158 See *The Times* (18 November 1978), 3.

SNP Constitutional Policy

MacCormick's political interventions – precisely often outside the party's official stance, seeking to correct it, to bring it back into line, and thus fighting for its political reputation as a responsible, moderate, constitutionalist, and democratic party – were not, however, solely negative and critical of party policy. Rather, MacCormick also worked hard, in this period, behind the scenes, to positively and constructively articulate a constitutional policy for the SNP, and for Scotland more generally. In 1976, a Constitutional Committee, under the Convenorship of Robert McIntyre, and the Vice-Convenorship of MacCormick, took on the task of drafting 'A Constitution for a Future Independent Scotland'.[159] Some movements in this direction had been attempted before, e.g., in the 1960s, when Roland Muirhead had directed a constitution for a Scottish Provisional Constituent Assembly in 1964,[160] and then again in 1968 with proposals by P. J. Findlay and Arthur Donaldson.[161] Now, in 1976, the newly convened Constitutional Committee renewed the effort, completing a draft, and presenting it successfully, first to a series of meetings of the SNP National Assembly in 1976–67, and then at the 1977 SNP Conference in Dundee.[162]

Indeed, MacCormick himself presented the draft to the members of the conference in 1977. Notes available in his archive indicate that he began with references to 'George Buchanan and Lord Stair', stressing Stair's view 'on law as custom of the country from time immemorial, esp. as evidenced by court decisions and the customs recognised by courts'.[163] Buchanan, in turn, was brought in to remind the audience of elective, contractual kingship, where the 'King administers and adjudications under law, which is not his but the people's law' – a position that, he added, 'survives as a myth of popular sovereignty.'[164] Since the Union of Crowns in 1603, and then again since 1707, 'reality progressively diverges from these ideals' expressed by Buchanan and Stair, with 'centralisation and increase of government power' steadily from the nineteenth century.[165] What should be the SNP response to this divergence between reality and ideal? What constitutional arrangement should Scotland seek?

159 See MacCormick, 'An Idea for a Constitution' (1991), 159.
160 Bulmer, 'An Analysis' (2011), 676.
161 Ibid.
162 MacCormick, 'An Idea for a Constitution' (1991), 159.
163 MacCormick, Notes to 43rd Annual National Conference in Dundee, May 1977.
164 Ibid.
165 Ibid.

Others have written of the details of the new draft constitution and how it offered a contrast to the 'Westminster model' of constitutionalism, presenting a vision 'of a more consensual, balanced, power-sharing form of democracy', i.e., a 'constitutional democracy'.[166] Unlike the 'Westminster model', where 'the power to rule and decide is vested in Ministers who command a majority in the elected assembly', and thus expresses '"an elitist, hierarchical, top-down" conception of politics'[167] – a kind of 'winner takes all logic … with its parliamentary sovereignty and centralisation of power',[168] the 1977 draft (which was renewed, this time under the Convenorship of MacCormick, in 2002), was more along the lines of the approach 'developed in Scandinavia and the Low Countries'.[169] As Elliott Bulmer phrases it, the general principles of this constitution were: '…(i) power-sharing between the people and Parliament, and between Parliament and executive; (ii) the accountability of the executive to Parliament, and of the Parliament and of executive to the people; (iii) a more participative approach to the development, consideration and scrutiny of policy and legislation; and (iv) equality of opportunity'.[170]

This was to be achieved by 'proportional representation, fixed term parliaments, the formal election of the executive by Parliament, and the incorporation of human rights into constitutional law'.[171] The monarchy would continue, establishing a constitutional monarchy with a largely ceremonial role.[172] The commitment to proportional representation was especially significant, 'designed to encourage coalition government and bring to an end single-party majority rule'.[173] The standing and independence of the Scottish judiciary was to be strengthened, with 'the Court of Session to be given the status and authority of a proper Supreme Court, including the power to review the validity of legislation', and numerous Crown prerogatives, a staple of the Westminster tradition, even to the extent of war-making and treaty-making powers, were to be removed and 'vested in the Parliament of Scotland'.[174] Of course, it was also a written

166 Bulmer, 'An Analysis' (2011), 676.
167 Ibid.
168 Ibid., 678.
169 Ibid., 707.
170 Ibid., 680.
171 Ibid.
172 Ibid., 681.
173 Bulmer, *A Model Constitution* (2011), 14.
174 Ibid.

constitution – itself an important step given the lack of any one central, accepted text in the British constitution.[175]

This vision of a more consensual politics, one that was open and accountable, with diffused rather centralised power, stressing collaboration and co-operation, and protecting fundamental rights – again, very much a constitutional, liberal, democratic vision – remained as official SNP constitutional policy from 1977 onwards. Though there were changes in the early 1990s and then again in the early 2000s, these were relatively minor, relating to 'the addition of the sections on local government and the replacement of archaic language with more modern terminology' – the 'core' was 'largely unchanged'.[176]

This was a core – a symbolic core – that presented something pragmatically workable, a vision, certainly, but not a hopelessly romantic one with no connection to reality. As Bulmer notes, the draft did not contain 'a preamble, no stirring words about "national struggle", no ringing declaration of liberty, equality, and fraternity'; there was no 'flag or an anthem' specified; in many ways, it was 'a functional document, a basic framework of democracy, not an ideological statement'.[177] This, of course, has all the hallmarks of the MacCormick tone: restrained, moderate, and focused on producing something that many could endorse and that provided a practical, reliable road map for the future.

Hindsight can, however, be misleading, and the long-term survival of the draft, and the reputational gains this represented for the SNP for many years, masks what was both a very contested process within the party, but also a move that was in many ways radical, given the predominant constitutional orthodoxy of the time in the UK, and especially in England. The text was certainly subjected to considerable scrutiny inside the party during its drafting and was also subject to intense debate at the 1977 conference itself. An illuminating example of this, which also illustrates the kind of minor, but significant, quality of MacCormick's interventions in such debates, was that of an amendment, proposed at the 1977 conference, in favour of citizenship, under the future constitution, being tied to paternity. In answer to it, MacCormick said: 'Maternity is a matter of fact; paternity can never be more than a matter of inference'.

175 For further discussion, see also Bulmer, *Constituting Scotland*, 2018, which includes the texts of the various drafts, including the 2002 draft which became known as 'the MacCormick draft'.

176 Bulmer, 'An Analysis' (2011), 692.

177 Bulmer, *A Model Constitution* (2011), 9.

Amongst laughter, 'the amendment died, quietly'.[178] MacCormick himself was characteristically positive about the experience of the process within the party: 'As an experiment', he said, 'in rational collective decision-making, combining as much openness as possible with real deliberative effectiveness under constraints of time, the process seemed to me a great success', which, again characteristically, he attributed to the efforts of Isobel Lindsay.[179]

More generally, there is no doubt that, in 1977, the ideas expressed in the draft constitution were radical. As MacCormick himself put it, reflecting back in 2000 to those years:

> In 1977, this [SNP constitutional policy] was somewhat controversial. Unicamerality was regarded by some as doubtful; proportional representation was regarded with suspicion by the two larger parties of state; election of ministers rather than appointment by the Queen as Head of State was not favoured; the idea of a commission on judicial appointments was considered insulting in view of the historic powers of Lord Advocate and Prime Minister in advising the monarch. Entrenched Bills of Rights were considered anti-democratic by many, because of the discretion they removed from elected politicians and confer on judges. Now, however, there is evident consensus that a Scottish constitution should have these characteristics and other related ones.[180]

That was MacCormick's view in 2000. Somewhat earlier, in 1991, he was not yet so confident, proposing the draft, then made with some minor changes, as 'only a first stage of public debate', offering it 'to the ordinary rigours of scholarly criticism and public debate'.[181] Nevertheless, even then, somewhat hesitant as he was, MacCormick was clearly proud, and very much willing to defend, the vision contained in the constitution. He was proud that 'the constitutional is fundamental law, and justiciable as such'; he was proud that 'Rights of citizenship and of residence are conferred in plainly non-racial (and non-racist) terms'; he was proud of the retention of the 'forms of constitutional monarchy', given that 'these have proved well-adapted to securing stable democratic government in Northern Europe'; he was proud of all the devices for limiting the power of the executive, such as fixed-term parliaments; and he was especially proud of the entrenchment of fundamental rights, which was in many

178 Owen Dudley Edwards, 'Report of the 1977 Conference', *The Scots Independent* (July 1977), 8.

179 MacCormick, 'An Idea' (1991), 160.

180 MacCormick, 'Is There a Constitutional Path' (2000), 723.

181 MacCormick, 'An Idea' (1991), 161.

ways based on the European Convention of Human Rights, and which thus placed constitutional limits on government.[182]

Indeed, as MacCormick saw it in 1991, it was indeed the new Charter of Rights, embraced in Article V of the draft, that was 'the most vital and innovative of all'.[183] MacCormick was aware that 'this cuts against long-standing British practice', but he added, 'not without reason'.[184] The protection of fundamental rights was central to the very project of a possible future independent Scotland. In fact, although in many ways based on the ECHR, the draft sought to go further, e.g., by adding to those protections the Scottish 'hundred and ten day rule', which offers a 'spectacular strengthening' of the rights of a criminal accused, incorporating a 'guarantee against unduly long detention before or during a criminal trial'.[185] MacCormick clearly saw this aspect of the draft as the most significant, arguing, amidst all the talk of the value of democracy, equally powerfully for the centrality of protecting the rights of minorities.[186]

The Claim of Right

The service that MacCormick provided to the SNP in drafting and then defending, including amending over time, this constitutional policy cannot be underestimated. In surviving over time, it helped provide a sense of continuity of principle, which tapered over the rifts and divisions of the late 1970s, following the failed referendum, and the wilderness years of the 1980s. At the same time, it is clear that in writing the draft, MacCormick was not solely acting in the interests of the party – indeed, he saw himself as acting very much in the interests of Scotland and its future.

That this was so became very visible in the saga, especially for the SNP, that was the process culminating in the Claim of Right in 1989. MacCormick's participation in it, and his very public criticism of the SNP's decision not to, is yet another example of where MacCormick had to be brave, hold his gradualist ground, and stand up for principle in the face of considerable political pressure to do otherwise. In keeping with what has been said above, this was MacCormick acting and thinking in a different temporal register than everyday party politics and its short-term political tactics. This was classic MacCormick, the gradualist, the constitutionalist,

[182] Ibid., 161–2.
[183] Ibid., 167.
[184] Ibid.
[185] Ibid., 168.
[186] Ibid.

who had his eyes firmly on the long-term future, embracing a long and possibly hazardous evolution rather than a quick revolution, always tracking the majority democratic will, and thus always the voice of respect for many and diverse persons.

The roots of the Claim of Right were in the aftermath of the failed 1979 referendum.[187] On 1 March 1980, the first year anniversary of that loss, 400 people gathered in the Edinburgh District Trades Council, to recall that failure, but also to find a way of dealing with it constructively and prospectively. In the result, the 'Campaign for a Scottish Assembly' (CSA) was formed, led initially by Jack Brand (a member of the '79 Group). As Mitchell described it, Brand 'chaired the CSA as a "movement for Scotland" and not a political party'.[188] The aim was 'to set up a convention drawn from all parts of Scotland to consider detailed proposals for an assembly'.[189]

The CSA soon changed its name to 'the Campaign for a Scottish Parliament', with the change from 'assembly' to 'parliament' indicating, in Mitchell's estimation, 'a deeper level of commitment'.[190] Later, following the Claim of Right, in 1989, the Campaign was to become the 'Scottish Constitutional Convention', which was also a historically self-conscious choice, not only echoing past cross-party movements (most resonantly, in the present context, of John MacCormick's Convention and then National Covenant of the 1940s and 1950s), but also displaying a newfound confidence in the prospect of constitutional change in Scotland. At times, the nomenclature suggested that constitutional change had already arrived, or almost arrived, or was about to arrive, almost as if, by calling itself a 'Constitutional Convention', it had 'instated itself with a "provisional" representative authority drawn from outside the democratic process, in the name of the national community but without its electoral warrant'.[191]

The initiative had received a considerable boost in the 1987 elections, which although Thatcher won, also resulted in considerable Tory losses

[187] Incidentally, with respect the failed referendum, William Storrar recalled how he sat together with MacCormick in a room in Old College, keeping tabs on the results of the vote on the previous day, with MacCormick adding up totals: see Storrar's remarks at the *What Scotland Wants: Ten Years On* conference (25 February 1989), Unit for the Study of Government in Scotland; and see also Storrar, 'Scotland's Meridian' (2012), 224.

[188] Mitchell, *Scottish Question* (2014), 219.

[189] Ibid.

[190] Ibid.

[191] Hames, *Literary Politics* (2019), 168.

for the Scottish seats, falling from 21 to 10. In response, the CSA 'set up a Constitutional Steering Committee' – yet another body – 'of "prominent Scots" headed by Sir Robert Grieve', with Jim Ross, 'a retired Scottish Office civil servant who had been responsible for devolution in the 1970s' acting 'as secretary' and subsequently principal draftsman of the Claim of Right, but also including other figures, such as Isobel Lindsay, Paul Scott, and MacCormick.[192] It was this Committee that produced the Claim of Right text in July 1988, proposing, simultaneously, a Constitutional Convention.[193]

Given the echoes of his father's Covenant, it is perhaps unsurprising that MacCormick chose to participate in the process culminating in the Claim of Right. But he had to do so very much against SNP policy. In some ways, this decision by the SNP was also unsurprising. Labour, under Donald Dewar, embraced the Claim of Right and the Convention it established, and the SNP had to make a political decision as to whether it was more in its political interests to abstain. 'Fearing a Labour stitch up',[194] which would result in them being 'marginalised numerically but also politically, as the convention would discuss devolution but not independence',[195] the SNP declined to participate. Dewar, and Labour, by contrast, 'ultimately committed the party to the Claim's key recommendation of establishing a Scottish Constitutional Convention', albeit amidst awareness of the dangers, with Dewar 'saying that it would be like riding on the back of a tiger'.[196]

This statement by Dewar was made in October 1988, but just a month later, in November, Sillars won a famous SNP victory in the Govan by-election, very much Labour's electoral heartland in Scotland.[197] It is thus perhaps no great surprise that the SNP decided not to participate in 1989 – once again, it had gained (perhaps illusory) confidence in its own prospects. As Wilson recalled, opinion was divided, with the SNP receiving 'hundreds of letters … in criticism', though, equally, especially later, 'lots of letters saying it was the right thing'.[198] Either way, Wilson confessed, it was clear that the SNP had 'mismanaged the public relations dimension',

192 Mitchell, *Scottish Question* (2014), 235; see also Dudley Edwards, *A Claim of Right* (1989), 2, for the full list.
193 Hames, *Literary Politics* (2019), 168.
194 Ibid., 182.
195 Lynch, *SNP* (2013), 195–6.
196 Hames, *Literary Politics* (2019), 181.
197 Ibid.
198 Wilson (interview).

as 'the SNP did lose some public support as a result'.[199] Both MacCormick and Lindsay, who argued for participation at the SNP National Council (with Lindsay's motion being supported by MacCormick), were, in Wilson's words, 'flattened'; MacCormick, 'as a man of principle, wouldn't budge for political reasons', but Wilson added, 'his standing in the party did not wane as a result'.[200] This was a victory for the fundamentalists, with the gradualists being left to fight their corner outside the realms of the party.

In the glaring eye of the press, MacCormick did not mince his words. He is reported in numerous outlets of the period as stating that the SNP's decision not to participate was 'a mistake': 'The Convention', he is reported as saying on the front page of the *Scotsman*, 'can do the party no harm, even in its current proposed form. It could do the party and the country a great deal of good'.[201] A few days later, he repeated his view that even though the SNP is right to not 'disguise its commitment to independence in Europe', nevertheless, 'in the meantime it is also necessary to have a clear answer to the question what form of constitutional change is to be demanded while the Scottish electorate falls short of endorsing independence'.[202] For MacCormick, this time being reported on the front page of the *Observer*, under a title claiming that 'Convention impasse' was a 'victory for Thatcher', the Claim of Right offered an 'opportunity to get a common demand for substantial change – even though it is less than the SNP wants'; that was 'something that we shouldn't give up lightly'; to act otherwise, as the party was doing, was to risk 'injury' to the party.[203] These were, indeed, heady days, but MacCormick stood his ground, despite the potential for a serious rift with the party.

MacCormick's public pronouncements, criticising the SNP so openly, came only after he had already tried every avenue within the party, not only at the above-mentioned National Council meeting, but also earlier, at the SNP Annual National Conference in Inverness in September 1988. The speech he made on that occasion was one of his finest – a searing piece of oratory, at times reaching poetic proportions. Recalling his father's address, fifty-nine years ago, also in Inverness, then launching the National Party of Scotland in the Highlands, MacCormick remembered how his father then

199 Ibid.

200 Ibid.; see also Wilson, *The SNP* (2009), 243.

201 Alan Hutchinson, 'SNP Pulls out of Convention', *Scotsman* (31 January 1989).

202 Derek Bateman, *Scotland on Sunday* (5 February 1989).

203 Callum McRae, *Observer Scotland* (29 January 1989).

spoke to only 'a handful of people'.[204] He then reached yet further back, to his ancestors who lived in the Highlands – in particular his 'Macdonald grandmother' who 'had been born in Glenurquhart nearby' – adding that for her, seeing her own 'son speaking at that first National Party meeting', the occasion echoed her own eviction from 'a late clearance [which] made home no longer home', and 'evoked the sense of uprooted rootedness, of belonging in dispossession'.[205] Continuing this theme of dispossession, clearly also one that was personal to him – as indeed it would have been to many members of his audience – MacCormick then continued in this way:

> Out of dispossession we seek reclamation, a reclamation of the land for the people, and, no less, a reclamation of the people to this their land. Let it be repossessed; let empowerment supplant disempowerment. Vacant factory lots ought to be re-growing lusty and active communities, places of vigour and enterprise (but not in that de'il tak the hindmaist travesty 'enterprise culture' foisted on us by the zealots of the present regime). The vacant rigs of cleared crofts and the open emptiness of sporting estates ironically so-called ought to be filled again with people and ploughshares in reasonable balance to the land and its potential.[206]

These are ringing words, deeply felt words, and also deeply personal ones. Indeed, in that personal vein, the speech continued:

> My commitment to the cause this Party represents, and thus subordinately to the party itself, expresses itself to me in such images. In Mull in February 1974, after a Saturday of packed and rousing meetings everywhere from the Iona Ferry to Dervaig and Tobermory, meetings such as you can only get in a winning campaign on a flowing tide, there was a Sunday morning journey back to Grasspoint to catch the newspaper boat to Oban. After rain, the morning was of crystalline brightness and clarity, but the sun on that low trajectory that gives every shadow the sharpness special to the West on fine days just before the Spring. At one place, the road rose high along the hillside above a strath that was empty but for a few sheep grazing on pasture almost overgrown with fags and rushes. The shadows of the morning displayed with a deadly exactness line upon line the rigs on the land still there to be read as the enduring memorial of the people who made way for the sheep; on such a morning it is not to be imagined that they did so gladly.[207]

I quote these at length, not only because they are beautifully crafted passages – showing MacCormick at his poetic finest – but also because of

[204] MacCormick, 'Constitutionalism and Democracy', SNP Annual Conference (1988), 1.
[205] Ibid.
[206] Ibid., 2.
[207] Ibid., 3.

their political intelligence, here clearly designed to ease the ears of his audience, to prepare them for a particular message, which the speaker knows is likely to be controversial. MacCormick pulled out all the stops recalling not only his father, but also Neil Gunn 'and such other brave pioneers of Home Rule in the Highlands as Duncan McNeill, translator of George Buchanan and historian of our constitutional tradition',[208] going on to speak further of Buchanan, but also of David Hume, and the value of free government, i.e., government under a constitution that limits arbitrary power and protects fundamental rights. He reminds his audience how important this is, especially in the face of the 'elective dictatorship', the Thatcher regime, they are living under, with its 'perversion of democracy and a corruption of constitutionalism'.[209] As if they were not aware, he reminds them too of Thatcher's poll tax, 'thrust upon us',[210] and how this was 'contrary probably to the letter and certainly to the spirit of the Articles of Union'.[211]

And then, when the audience has been well and truly impassioned, and on a democratic high, proud of their tradition – their Scottish constitutional pedigree – MacCormick asks, almost innocently, 'What is to be done then?'.[212] His answer is that what 'stands out above all other immediate prospects' is precisely the Claim of Right and the Constitutional Convention it has established.[213] 'All parties', he tells them, 'indeed will have to swallow some pride of exclusiveness if such a scheme is to go forward', but it is vital that they come together in support of this initiative: it is 'our earliest best hope of a morally compelling protest for democracy and constitutionalism in Scotland … the best first step now available towards the making or remaking of a Scottish Parliament'.[214]

Unrepentant Gradualism

MacCormick's lyrical call fell, as we already know, on deaf ears. But he had tried, and in the aftermath he stuck to his guns, embracing an attitude he referred to, in his contribution to the Claim of Right collection,

[208] Ibid., 5.
[209] Ibid., 9.
[210] Ibid., 11.
[211] Ibid.
[212] Ibid., 13.
[213] Ibid., 14.
[214] Ibid.

as 'An Unrepentant Gradualism' (1989). This return to the language of gradualism, and its temporality, reminds us of the connection between time and constitutionalism. Indeed, as he had put in his 1988 speech, 'Gradualism is all but inevitable corollary of constitutionalism; but also a commitment to democracy, for we should seek to go at the speed of the greatest majority in promoting constitutional change'.[215] In his Claim of Right piece, he reiterated his view that there are no such 'shortcuts' to constitutional change.[216]

In a sense, gradualism was an echo of a long-standing Scottish respect for custom and tradition, one of the key 'discoveries of the Scottish Enlightenment', and one 'particularly well articulated by David Hume'.[217] It was not that the Claim, and its vision, was without its problems: in fact, MacCormick confessed that he should have 'contemplated yet more carefully', in considering the 'framing of convention proposals', 'the question what would be sticking points for other parties, particularly the SNP'.[218] The faults and imperfection of the initiative could not be disguised or excused in full.[219] Nevertheless, on the whole, and under the circumstances, we have to 'find a way of bringing together all those who desire home rule in Scotland' and thus get behind a 'concrete proposal for workable change' that can 'un-jam the present constitutional log jam'.[220] Hence, he was getting behind it.[221]

MacCormick's above reference to Hume was no outlier. The 'elective dictatorship' and 'enterprise culture' he and others saw Thatcher wielding went against the warnings made by F. A. Hayek of the dangers of 'constructivist rationalism', i.e., the idea that 'governments can design societies'.[222] Governments cannot go against the 'grain of the custom and tradition of the people governed', with the present government, Thatcher's, in

215 Ibid., 14–15.

216 MacCormick, 'An Unrepentant Gradualism' (1989), 100.

217 Ibid., 102.

218 Ibid., 107–8.

219 Ibid., 108. See also MacCormick, 'Constitutionalism and Constitutions' (1989), where MacCormick speaks of the 'mistakes' made in the process: 'I do think we bent over too far backwards towards placating opposition in the Labour Party to any idea of all-party activity': 7.

220 MacCormick, 'An Unrepentant Gradualism' (1989), 108.

221 The literature on the Claim of Right is large, and this is a complex and rich decade of debate, which is necessarily treated briefly here. See, e.g., Jackson, *A Case for Scottish Independence* (2020); Marr, *The Battle for Scotland* (2013); McLean, *Getting It Together* (2005): Hames, *Literary Politics* (2019); and the other chapters in Dudley Edwards, *A Claim of Right* (1989).

222 MacCormick, 'Constitutionalism and Constitutions' (1989), 7.

addition 'despis[ing] the custom and tradition of the people, so far as that has grown up in Scotland anyway'.[223] Hayek's view, in turn, did not come from nowhere: it 'grows partly out of reflections on Scottish legal thought of the 18th century'.[224]

Here, and in other publications of the time,[225] what we see is MacCormick embracing a theory of political time, of constitutional change, that is decidedly evolutionary, recognising 'the essentially traditional or customary quality of viable constitutional arrangements'.[226] This did not mean one could not approach matters with reason, but this was a customary reason – again, there were no shortcuts here, no magic wands, no quick and easy fixes, no way to achieve maximal efficiency.

One could speak of a 'Humean and Hayekian practical reason',[227] but for this one had to embrace the kind of slowing down of political decision-making that Hume embraced, for instance in his 'The Idea of a Perfect Commonwealth'. In that piece, Hume found a way of increasing democratic participation at every level of a political community, but the cost of this was dropping the need for immediate impact, quick change, rapid results, and short-term thinking.[228] Further, this came along with epistemic modesty, with awareness of the fragility of knowledge, and of the inevitable limitations of our capacities – thus, an acknowledgement that 'our knowledge claims have always to be tentative, grounded in probability rather than certainty, provable by experiential evidence rather than by recourse to innate ideas'.[229] None of this meant, again, that constitutional change was not the realm of reason: but it was practical, epistemically limited, imperfect, ideally stretched out over time, participatory, democratic, customary reason – very much the slow-going, hard-working, grounded, and practical reason of the democratic intellect. As we shall see, when we

223 Ibid.

224 MacCormick, 'Spontaneous Order' (1986), 1.

225 It is significant that MacCormick was, at this time, reading and re-reading the Scots, and also engaging with American constitutional history, connecting Scottish thought to the making of the American constitution, see e.g., 'Law and Enlightenment' (1982); 'The Idea of Liberty' (1984); 'The Idea of a Free Government' (1985); 'The Future of Legal Systems' (1990); 'Republicanism and Enlightenment Thought' (1992); and 'Constitutionalism and Democracy' (1993). These pieces form an important intellectual context and precursor to MacCormick's later theorisation of Europe and his development of his later institutionalism, in particular his theory of law as institutional normative order (see also chapter 9).

226 MacCormick, 'Constitutionalism and Democracy' (1989), 25.

227 See MacCormick, 'Spontaneous Order' (1986), 7.

228 See MacCormick, 'Constitutionalism and Democracy' (1989), 26–7.

229 MacCormick, 'Spontaneous Order' (1986), 4.

examine in particular MacCormick's later institutionalism, alongside his philosophical analysis of, and political action in, Europe, MacCormick would return to these ideas at a later stage.

Returning to Nationalism

Common Pasts, Common Futures

In closing this chapter, it will be worthwhile returning to the theme with which it opened: nationalism, and whether it could be philosophically credible. Crucial to this question was what we have also already witnessed above: a matter of the historiography of nationalism. Thus, for MacCormick, a large part of the philosophical interrogation of nationalism consisted in engaging with its history and that history has been framed and told. This is clear throughout his writings, but perhaps especially so in a piece published in 1979, 'Nation and Nationalism', which was later republished in his 1982 collection (LRSD), and which MacCormick drew on in years to come. The occasion for this piece had been a series of public lectures, culminating in an edited volume entitled *The Crown and the Thistle* (1979) – MacCormick did not himself give a lecture, but he wrote a piece and commented on that of another.[230]

Vital to MacCormick's argument was that 'nationalism' has had various historical meanings, and that many of its contemporary understandings adopted, too uncritically, understandings of nationalism that emerged following the 1789 French Revolution and took on momentum in the early nineteenth century. According to this 'orthodox theory', as MacCormick called it, nationalism is a morally intolerable doctrine, for it is 'coupled with ideas of patriotism, even chauvinism and xenophobia'.[231] According to this theory, a claim to nationalism 'necessarily and absolutely overrides every other possible claim on an individual'.[232] This is grounded 'on the thesis that the nation is the highest form of human association, through which and only through which human perfection can be achieved'.[233] Further, nationalism of this sort tends to be associated with the project of calling for – if one does not have it already, and thus is seeking potentially its colonial expansion – a sovereign state. This connection was made

230 Lord Hailsham, 'The Nation and the Constitution' (1979).
231 MacCormick, 'Nation and Nationalism' (1979), 105.
232 Ibid., 103.
233 Ibid.

especially strong in the revolutionary arguments of 1789 and thereafter, whereupon 'first of all subjects became citizens, the state became a nation and the sovereign nation arose to fill the void left by the demise of the absolute monarch'.[234]

For MacCormick, however, this was resolutely not the only understanding of nationalism available and certainly not the one he wished to endorse. MacCormick was clear that the above understanding would not be morally tolerable – it would not be a philosophically credible theory of nationalism. What, then, would? Here, interestingly, MacCormick delved further into history: there was, he argued, a 'pre-1789 sense of nationalism'.[235] This can be gleaned from numerous histories – including, importantly, English, e.g., by reading Spenser and Shakespeare and the way they are 'profoundly moved by a sense of the English nation and of pride in its qualities and achievements'[236] – but especially that of Scottish history.

MacCormick's sources of Scottish history were familiar: they included, e.g., the *Complaynt of Scotland* following sixteenth-century attempts by Henry VIII to 'procure forcibly a Union of England and Scotland'; Buchanan's *De Jure Regni apud Scotus*; Hector Boece's sixteenth-century history of Scotland; Barbour's *Bruce*; the *Declaration of Arbroath*; as well as contemporary historical takes on those sources, such as Barrow's *Robert Bruce* (1965) and Rosalind Mitchison's *A History of Scotland* (1970). What MacCormick saw in them was a political self-consciousness – a consciousness based on a sense of 'national distinctiveness', including awareness of the 'immemorial laws and customs of the Scots'.[237] This kind of nationalism involves 'relatively large grouping of people', on 'some tract of territory', that have a 'common name' (e.g., the Scots), 'a common language', and 'who conceive of themselves to have a communal past, including shared sufferings and shared achievements, from which past is derived a common culture which represents a form of cultural continuity uniting past and present and capable of being projected into the future'.[238]

The sense of the common past such a grouping might have may well be 'mythical', but did this change its importance for the people concerned? Not according to MacCormick: such a common past remained, however mythical, a 'shared consciousness' that 'inheres the sense of a common

[234] Ibid., 105.
[235] Ibid., 106.
[236] Ibid.
[237] Ibid., 108.
[238] Ibid., 100.

identity'.[239] What a reading of the Scottish sources of pre-1789 history shows, argued MacCormick, is a 'consciousness of belonging to a nation' – a 'sense of continuity beyond an individual's life-span'.[240] A sense of the past is clearly vital to this, but this sense of the past is entangled with a sense of the future –'a will or hope for continuity into the future' – a momentum towards future flourishing.[241] Once more, as we have seen throughout this chapter, MacCormick's conception of nationalism is linked with a dynamic sense of political time: something continuous, reaching back but also forward in time, and grounded in the self-understandings but also self-respect of persons, i.e., very much a normative time, loaded with identity.

Contextual Persons

Indeed, this grounding in 'popular consciousness'[242] was crucial for MacCormick. It was crucial not only historically, but also morally: for MacCormick, to fail to take seriously this aspect of a person's self-understanding – i.e., the contingent fact of it mattering to them that they belong to a nation – was to fail to respect them as persons. As he put it: 'The Kantian ideal of respect for persons implies … an obligation in each of us to respect that which in others constitutes any part of their sense of their own identity'.[243] The grounds of MacCormick's nationalism are therefore moral respect for the social conditions of human identity: 'our sense of individual personality and identity is derivative from a social context', MacCormick argued, and we thus 'place ourselves through family, local community, nation, citizenship, religious affiliation, education, hobby, work community and so forth'.[244]

It is not that nationalism is always what matters most to us, or even matters at all, but insofar as contingently it does – and the history of Scottish nationalism showed that was so – then it is a matter of respecting persons, these contextualised, social persons, that what these persons value is respected. 'Respecting other people', MacCormick argued, 'entails respecting the things they value'.[245] If that happens to include a sense of national belonging, as it might (though need not), then respect

[239] Ibid., 101.
[240] Ibid., 102.
[241] Ibid., 109.
[242] Ibid., 100.
[243] Ibid., 109.
[244] Ibid., 102.
[245] Ibid., 103.

ought to extend to that. MacCormick's nationalism here is decidedly a kind of respect for others, based on a hermeneutical understanding of what matters to them, as this is evidenced by contingent historical fact. This, incidentally, also shows how and why MacCormick may have gravitated towards emphasising Hart's internal point of view as his biggest contribution to jurisprudence, albeit combined with a moral reading of that point of view, as a deeper commitment to value than Hart allowed for – a reading MacCormick argued for precisely at this time, in his Appendix to *Legal Reasoning and Legal Theory* (1978) and then, as we have seen in Chapters 5 and 6, in his book on *Hart* (1981).

Moral respect was one aspect that was crucial, but this respect was not politically inert. Although it was not necessarily linked to the justification that such a grouping of people ought to have an independent sovereign state, it did have '*some* political implications'.[246] According to MacCormick: 'The mode of consciousness which constitutes a national identity includes a consciousness of the need for a form of common governance which recognises and allows for the continued flourishing of the cultural and historical community in question'.[247] This may express itself in various ways, i.e., in various forms of 'institutional expression', such as protection of 'church or of religious organisation', or indeed legal or educational institutions.[248] The protection of 'appropriate institutional forms', then, went part and parcel with a respectful, hermeneutic, even if contingent, recognition of national consciousness. Again, none of this meant that this protection must take the form of a sovereign state: in fact, MacCormick embraced – and we must remember this is 1979 – the potential protection offered by Europe:

> I would myself most warmly welcome the hesitant moves of the past two or three decades towards a new form of world order, of which, in our corner of the world, an example is provided in the supra-national confederation towards which the European Community is groping… A diffusion of governmental power among various levels of government, rather than a concentration of power in centres of local omnipotence, seems eminently desirable.[249]

Europe was thus, early on, seen by MacCormick as a potential political theatre for the contingent Scottish popular consciousness of national

246 Ibid., 108; original emphasis.
247 Ibid., 109.
248 Ibid., 108–9.
249 Ibid., 109.

belonging, with its political implications for some kind of protection of the institutional expression of that sense of nationalism, which necessarily included a mixture of self-government within nations and collaboration across and between them.

Characteristically, for MacCormick, this resolutely should not be anti-English: to adopt Scottish nationalism, in the way, he defined it, was not 'to dislike or disrespect England, English people, the English way of life, or any such thing'.[250] Quite the contrary: MacCormick went out of his way to look for commonalities between the nations of the UK, and embraced, for instance, the idea of a 'common loyalty to a common monarch': this was, he said, 'genuinely something in common among all parts' of the UK.[251] What did have to be avoided was 'the anglo-centric conception of Britain',[252] and this meant pursuing some form of political scheme that instituted conditions for national self-respect and mutual respect between nations, as well as national self-government, enabling national flourishing, combined with governmental as well as symbolic forms of co-operation and union. As difficult to articulate and hold as this may be, this was the ground one had to pursue: indeed, a properly understood nationalism – a nationalism supported by an appropriately sophisticated historiography – was coupled with considerable political creativity, itself informed by sociological perspectivalism and an underlying moral commitment to respect for contextualised, social persons.

Liberal and Civic Nationalism

MacCormick's 1979 vision of nationalism very much set the terms for his subsequent engagements with the question of just how nationalism could be philosophically credible. Although the language of these later treatments did change – MacCormick, in the early 1990s, began to speak in terms of 'liberal nationalism' and 'civic nationalism' – nevertheless, the substance of the argument, as above, remained essentially the same. There are a number of factors that can help explain the change in nomenclature.

One of them, as many observers have shown, was the intense cultural activity in Scotland following the failed 1979 referendum – a political vacuum filled precisely by civic voices. As Cairns Craig, for instance, argued

250 Ibid., 110.
251 Ibid.
252 Ibid.

already in 1989, 'Instead of political defeat [in 1979] leading to quiescence, it led directly into an expression of cultural creativity', with the 1980s emerging as 'one of the most significant decades of Scottish cultural self-definition in the past two centuries'.[253] Hames, who quotes this passage with approval, shows wonderfully how 'national civic bodies', from 'the Scottish Arts Council to the Confederation of Scottish Business',[254] along with many other forms of cultural expression – including many literary and cultural magazines, some student run – articulated the civic values of Scotland, creating an image of and a vision for a civic nation.[255] The writing of Scottish literature in this period was of course of immense importance – and MacCormick himself recognised this, recalling his own literary studies, and writing, for instance, about the significance of Neil Gunn, amongst other Scottish literary figures[256] – but this politico-literary partnership was not entirely limited to elites, and included, increasingly, the grassroots: it became, even if slowly, a broadly civic, cultural movement.

Another context, important certainly for MacCormick, was much soul-searching amongst liberals or exponents of liberal political philosophy. This is a context that is much too complex to be treated briefly, but it is important to at least link it here to MacCormick's conception of nationalism in the early 1990s. Despite many criticisms, both from without, as well as from within, liberalism was a robust political creed: it did not go gently into the good night, if indeed it went at all. As MacCormick himself put it, in his 1987 review of Raz's *The Morality of Freedom* (1986):

> Liberalism has a strange persistence. Denounced a thousand times for incoherence and internal contradictions, pilloried ten thousand times for parading the ethic or interest of the bourgeoisie as universal principle, yet eleven thousand and one times it comes back. Not always in the same form; not ever in the same form, indeed. Perhaps any creed whose special point is that each should work it out for himself or herself has to have as many versions as proponents.[257]

A little like nationalism itself, there were many versions of liberalism: it was an internally contested, rich tradition of debate, as it should be. Especially important for MacCormick – and in this respect applauding

253 Craig, 'Scotland 10 Years On' (1989), 9, quoted in Hames, *Literary Politics* (2019), 159.
254 Hames, *Literary Politics* (2019), 162.
255 Ibid., chapters 3 and 4.
256 MacCormick, 'Gunn' (1991).
257 MacCormick, 'Access to the Goods' (1987), 599.

Raz's account – was the disassociation of liberalism from 'untenable individualism'.[258] Here, it is worth quoting MacCormick in full:

> Liberalism is derided alternately as being the theory that society is a simple aggregation or 'consociation' of pre-formed persons, or as being the theory that nothing is purely and underivedly good save the subjective state of some individual (so that all social goods are resoluble without residue into some combination of individual goods). If it has to be such a theory, it fully earns the derision. For of course it is a matter of social achievement to develop social institutions in which individuals count for something; and what individuals count for is in turn explicable or statable only in social terms, not in some ineffably private language.[259]

This is in many ways a restatement of a view already held by MacCormick: as we saw above, respect for persons, as MacCormick saw it, entailed seeing those persons as social, as contextual, as embedded in places and times, holding contingent values, and with a cross-temporal consciousness that reached back as well as forwards in time. MacCormick was to restate this view, as he did in this 1987 review, many times in the future. Autonomy was a vital value – it is hard to imagine liberalism without commitment to individual autonomy – but autonomy was 'by no means a purely individualistic achievement'; to the contrary, autonomy was possible only under certain social conditions – autonomy was 'essentially a public or collective good'.[260]

Raz had captured this well, but he also did not go far enough in embracing the social: for instance, although Raz acknowledged the value of equality among persons, 'he has too little warmth for it as an ideal'; to be a liberal, then, meant looking for a way to square the circle of respect for autonomy and respect for equality.[261] As always for MacCormick, philosophy pursued an almost impossible middle ground; in the glare of that pursuit, labels, such as 'liberalism', often went up in smoke – what was important was the substance, grounded, practical, substance of respect for persons. If this was liberalism, it was a warm, social liberalism – one that edged very close to being socialism.

It became a kind of mantra for MacCormick that liberalism was compatible with nationalism, as long as one did not embrace the above 'methodological individualism'. He found confirmation of that view in multiple

[258] Ibid.
[259] Ibid.
[260] Ibid.
[261] Ibid.

sources – in particular, he spoke very highly of Yael Tamir's *Liberalism Nationalism* (1993), which had originated as a doctoral thesis at Balliol College, Oxford, that he had examined in 1990 – but this was, again, hardly new for him, and was instead precisely another way of stating a point he had already made in the late 1970s, i.e., that respect for persons entailed respect for them as members of communities, albeit with contingent, and thus far from social deterministic, orientations to value. The point that MacCormick emphasised and developed in these pieces in the early 1990s – such as his 1991 piece, 'Is Nationalism Philosophically Credible?' – was that this respect for contextualised individuals entailed the justification 'of some form of democratic self-determination.[262] As MacCormick put it in this piece:

> Some form of collective self-constitution, some kind of active participation in shaping and sustaining the institutions of social or communal government whose aim is to advance liberty and autonomy, seems to be a necessary part of the whole ensemble of conditions in which the autonomy of the contextual individual could be genuinely constituted and upheld. If autonomous individuals require the context of some sort of freedom-enabling society, then the collective autonomy of the society itself seems a part of the necessary context.[263]

Thus, for MacCormick, liberalism, although a vital intellectual context for his thought, was a really a stepping stone onto something else: a defence of the social conditions under which it could flourish. His conception of the individual, and his interest in the value of autonomy, was deeply social – indeed, again, almost as if it was a cover for what essentially a kind of socialism.[264] Our individuality was the outcome of social interaction: we are, MacCormick said, 'social products, not independent atoms capable of constituting society through a voluntary coming together'.[265]

Further, the prospect of our autonomy flourishing was not dependent on any of our individual wills; no amount of individual effort could, alone, give us access to our autonomy. Rather, individual autonomy – individual freedom – was dependent on social conditions, including equalising, as much as possible (without this itself becoming tyrannical), collective access to freedom and autonomy. It was articulating those social conditions that really mattered to MacCormick. This included 'schemes

262 MacCormick, 'Is Nationalism Philosophically Credible?' (1991), 14.

263 Ibid., 14–15.

264 In that sense, perhaps, similar to Mill: see McCabe, *Mill, Socialist* (2021); Ghosh, 'Mill before Liberalism' (2024).

265 MacCormick, 'Is Nationalism Philosophically Credible?' (1991), 13.

of redistribution, welfare provision and educational support',[266] but, crucially, it also included the presence of institutions – such as a Parliament – that enabled 'the activist and participative character of full autonomy',[267] and thus some scheme of self-government for communities that, contingently, considered themselves to be nations.

Thus, although sometimes couched in the form of 'liberalism', the value of liberty, freedom, or autonomy, MacCormick's focus, in substance, remained always firmly on associative conditions, on institutions, on the communal and social contexts in which individuals could participate and realise their self-respect. It is also in this sense that we need to acknowledge the primacy of the other key context for MacCormick's defences of nationalism in the 1990s (right through from the early to the late 1990s), i.e., Europe. Europe, and in particular the European Economic Community (and, later, the European Union), became this magic middle ground, this difficult-to-articulate space-time, in which one could try to think and realise nationalism, but also more broadly, this underlying respect for persons, precisely as social creatures. Europe, in all its grounded and detailed – often painfully detailed and technical – institutionality, became the political theatre in which one could philosophise about the credibility, the desirability, the possibility of nationalism. Europe was the social context in which nationalism could flourish, almost as if Scottish nationalism could not be credible without a European home. As articulated in later pieces, such as 'What Place for Nationalism in the Modern World' (1994) and 'Liberalism, Nationalism and the Post-Sovereign State' (1996), and of course in his 1999 collection, *Questioning Sovereignty* (1999), Europe, and its institutions, its future, was fundamental to the philosophical credibility of nationalism. This cannot be underscored enough: nationalism, for MacCormick, was simply inconceivable and indefensible without a larger social context, without a plurality of unions, into which it fitted. Nations did not need states,[268] but they did need relational, pluralistic, diffused political orders: without this, much like an individual without a society, a nation could not exist, let alone flourish.

Civil Nationalism

The European context will be the focus of Chapter 8, but it is fitting to end this chapter with a brief note of another aspect of MacCormick's

[266] Ibid., 15.
[267] Ibid.
[268] See also MacCormick, 'Does a Nation Need a State' (1999).

nationalism, i.e., the way he lived it as a SNP Parliamentary candidate. This was, not so much or not only, a civic or liberalism nationalism, as it was a civil one.

As has been mentioned before, MacCormick stood for election in Westminster elections five times: 1979, 1983, 1987, 1992, and 1997. He was unsuccessful in all. Perhaps the closest contest was in 1992. Here, MacCormick stood as a SNP candidate for Argyll & Bute – a place to which he was tied personally in many respects. But he faced a formidable – and, for MacCormick, an awkward – opponent: Ray Michie. Michie was a Liberal Democrat with a long-standing commitment to home rule for Scotland and to the promotion of Scottish Gaelic – causes that were of course both dear to MacCormick. There was thus little political room for MacCormick's view, precisely because he was not, despite being a SNP candidate and officially campaigning on a platform of independence, a hard-nosed fundamentalist. MacCormick, of course, was typically undeterred. As reported by Murray Ritchie in the *Herald* on 30 March 1992, reporting a speech given by MacCormick in Strone the previous week: 'You could almost hear the violins as he [MacCormick] lyricised about the springtime in Argyll, seeing it as a metaphor for a Scotland in blossom, a place where the buds are about to flower in a spirit of national renewal after the long, dark interlude. Even the daffodils were appearing, he noted, and doing so in SNP colours'.[269]

MacCormick's lyricism, coupled with his intellectual standing, as well as his family pedigree ('MacCormick boasted that the two of them [i.e., him and his father] could not travel to Campbeltown in Kintyre without meeting one of his cousins every 10 miles',[270] but also his energy and enthusiasm despite the odds – Ritchie also reports him 'working his way around Cowal in a car which seems certain not to survive the campaign'[271] – turned 'this campaign [in Argyll & Bute] into one of the most fascinating in Scotland'.[272]

'Fascinating', yes, but also, most significantly, one of the most 'civil'. As reported by David Ross, this time writing in 1997, but looking back to the 1992 contest, 'The lasting impression of the 1992 election … was of a civilised campaign'.[273] The 'tone' of the two candidates, MacCormick

[269] Ritchie, 'Breath of Fresh Air as Candidates Take Issue but Not Umbrage', *The Herald* (30 March 1992), 20.
[270] Ibid.
[271] Ibid.
[272] Ibid.
[273] Ross, *The Herald* (4 April 1997).

and Michie, was one of 'mutual respect' and their 'friendship was clear to all'.[274] This, by itself, speaks volumes about MacCormick's nationalism, which was not only liberal or civic, but also very much civil, i.e., always based on respect and considerateness for others. From the perspective of this book, what is important is that this is on display both in his philosophy and in his politics, both in the abstract and in how it was lived, i.e., deeply in his character.

[274] Ibid.

8

European Futures

Post-Sovereignty, Subsidiarity, and Constitutional Pluralism

Europe: the promised land. It is sometimes thought that MacCormick's interest in Europe begins in earnest in the early 1990s, receiving an early apogee in his 1992 Chorley Lecture at the London School of Economics and Political Science, and subsequent 1993 paper, 'Beyond the Sovereign State'.[1] That is an undoubtedly important moment, and it is true that within his jurisprudence, Europe comes to the fore in the 1990s, with numerous important milestones, including the publication of *Questioning Sovereignty* in 1999 (which brought together a number of influential papers published during the decade before), and then continuing with many articles and chapters.

However, in truth, MacCormick's interest in Europe began a long time before that lecture. As we have seen, MacCormick had indicated that, prior to his death in 1961, his father, 'saw the coming of a European Community, and at once grasped it as a crucial context along with the Commonwealth in which the Scots could finally come into their own'.[2] Europe's promise – the hope of Europe – for Scottish nationalism continued to be a topic of political discussion inside and outside the SNP, from the late 1940s onwards, and, as we have seen, it played a part also in the student debates of the 1960s, with MacCormick serving as the Prime Minister in a Glasgow Union debate on the motion 'To establish a separate Parliament for Scotland; and as the Government of Scotland, to join the Common Market regardless of British and Commonwealth ties'.

As we have also seen, and will see in more detail in this chapter, MacCormick was consistently optimistic about Europe, even when the

1 To give just one example, Richard Rawlings introduces a landmark collection of papers on *Sovereignty and the Law* (2013), with a paper that pays tribute to MacCormick, and especially to this lecture, saying that his lecture 'struck a chord. It chimed locally with the rich LSE tradition of treating law as a social phenomenon and of engaging with the economically and socially relevant and … with a range of contemporary legal and political occurrences in this part of the globe' (Rawlings, 'Introduction' (2013), 4); looking back, he adds, 'MacCormick's 1992 Chorley Lecture can now be seen as ahead of its time': 7.

2 MacCormick, 'Address on the 71st Anniversary of the SNP' (16 January 1999), 4.

SNP wasn't, e.g., he supported the 'Yes' vote in the 1975 referendum on whether the UK ought to remain in the EEC, while the SNP campaigned for 'No'. Many years later, and after decades of arguments for Scotland's future being in Scotland, MacCormick became a Member of the European Parliament (MEP) from 1999 to 2004. His period as MEP coincided with the Convention on the Future of Europe (2002–3), and thus also the drafting of the European Constitution. Throughout this time, and also briefly after his period as MEP, MacCormick continued to engage with the relations between Scotland, the UK, and Europe, becoming, in 2007, advisor on European Affairs to Alex Salmond, the-then First Minister of Scotland.

MacCormick's engagement with Europe, then, was intense, both philosophically and politically. Many volumes could be written about his attitudes to and theorisation of Europe – indeed, there is a large and still burgeoning literature on MacCormick's influence on theorising Europe as well as associated concepts, such as constitutional pluralism, subsidiarity, and sovereignty.[3] In this chapter, I tackle MacCormick's engagement with Europe, and these concepts, but I do so very selectively: my aim is to show how MacCormick's political and the philosophical engagement can be understood to be expressions, but also negotiations, of his character. In many ways, MacCormick really lived 'Scotland in Europe'.

But, for MacCormick, Europe was far from being merely a political opportunity for Scottish nationalism: it signified something deeper,

[3] See, e.g., the various chapters in Dickson and Eleftheriadis, *Philosophical Foundations of EU Law* (2012), where, in the introduction, MacCormick is described as 'the legal philosopher who examined' various questions regarding the legal theory of the EU 'with the greatest thoroughness and whose work has had most lasting effect': 4, fn. 4. See also: Menéndez and Fossum, *Law and Democracy* (2011); Avbelj and Komárek, *Constitutional Pluralism in the EU and Beyond* (2012); Davies and Avbelj, *Research Handbook on Legal Pluralism and EU Law* (2018); Walker, *Sovereignty in Transition* (2003); and Rawlings, Leyland, and Young, *Sovereignty and the Law* (2013). This influence ranges beyond the European context and extends more generally to transnational legal and political theory as well as to what has been called 'pluralist jurisprudence': see, e.g., Maduro, Tuori, and Sankari, *Transnational Law* (2014); Halpin and Roughan, *In Pursuit of Pluralist Jurisprudence* (2017); Krisch, *Beyond Constitutionalism* (2010); and Culver and Giudice, *Legality's Borders* (2010), which is dedicated to MacCormick. It is of course also important not to overemphasise MacCormick's influence; he was one voice among a number who were working on theorising law in a European context, and his work was also interpreted and taken in creative new directions by those inspired by him, e.g., by Neil Walker (MacCormick's eventual successor to his Chair in Edinburgh), who taught MacCormick's work at the European University Institute in Florence in the 1990s and who played a very important role in both disseminating MacCormick's thought while also making it creatively his own (see, for example, Walker's take on constitutional pluralism: 'The Idea of Constitutional Pluralism' [2002] and 'Revisiting Constitutional Pluralism' [2016]).

a hope for a new kind of political community – of political unity, but amongst the acknowledgement of differences (indeed, in many ways, a unity designed to protect differences, including local knowledge). For MacCormick, Europe was a deep political challenge, but in a positive sense: it carried the promise of a new beginning, for different kinds of political relations, and for creating a language and a new set of concepts (such as 'constitutional pluralism' or 'post-sovereignty') or giving new life to old ones (e.g., 'subsidiarity'). Conceptualising Europe – often, again, in the future sense, imagining new political possibilities via Europe – was vital to MacCormick's character: it is one of the key places – one of the central *topoi*, in rhetorical terminology – in which MacCormick wrestled with the question of how best to live with others. Europe, in short, showcases how MacCormick both lived and dreamed relations with others.

In what follows, I explore MacCormick's engagement with Europe in three steps: first, I turn to the roots, within his work on Scottish nationalism, but also in his contributions to SNP policy, and other interventions in Scottish politics, in the 1970s and 1980s, from which the more explicit theorisation of Europe emerged in the 1990s; second, I turn to MacCormick's theorisation of the constitutional aspects of Europe, how these were linked to his other philosophical interests (especially conventions, and the evolution of constitutional orders, generally), and to his contributions as an Alternate Member of the European Constitution; and third, having illustrated the sense of novelty, originality, promise, hope, and experimentalism that Europe offered for MacCormick, both political and philosophical, I turn more to the realities of being a MEP and the frustrations and disappointments these entailed for MacCormick, albeit arguably without him ever losing the underlying sense of Europe as a promised land. Throughout, we will see that MacCormick's characteristic attempt at articulating an optimistic middle space – that almost impossible to conceive middle space that allowed one to really think, to generate concepts – was at work here too, in the crafting of language such as 'the post-sovereign commonwealth' governed by 'subsidiarity', or in his defence of the possibility of 'constitutional pluralism'.

Of course, all this operated alongside other contexts: the increasing collaboration with European scholars following his taking up of the Chair in Edinburgh in 1972, which includes very much his work on institutional legal theory (see Chapter 9); and his also very European project of theorising practical reason, including, within the Bielefelder Kreis, comparative approaches to statutory interpretation and precedential reasoning (see Chapter 10). These contexts are entangled with his work on Europe: the approach to Europe as a *sui generis* order but also to European constitutionalism is informed by, and in turn informs, work on law as an institutional normative order – as an evolving political and legal order that does not necessarily need a sovereign and can, instead, be more genuinely democratic – as well as work on practical reason, which is also devoted to establishing the protection of difference within an overall principled coherence, but one that is always dynamic, always forward-looking, and only ever grounded in defeasible stability. There are some fascinating connections here, e.g., between the future-oriented treatment of Europe, the promise, the hope of Europe, but nestled within a conventional, stable, order, and the processes of practical reason, which, through defeasible universalisation, also look forward, disciplining present action by imagining oneself as part of potential new unities. These further contexts and connections, however, even if glanced at in this chapter, are taken up more thoroughly in Chapters 9 and 10 of this book.

Europe Emergent

Personal Contexts: Peace and Scotland

As has already been noted, there is an extraordinary excitement and sense of upbeat, optimistic energy, including conceptual inventiveness, that pervades MacCormick's engagement with Europe. There is also a deep recognition that Europe really matters. But this excitement, energy, and sense of importance did not come from nowhere. Even if MacCormick's Europe was sometimes utopian, it did not come from no place. It is telling, for instance, that when reflecting on 'Europe's Future, Scotland's Future' on St Andrews Day in Brussels in 2003, MacCormick began by recalling a memory that his mother told him 'on several occasions':

> ...after she took me home from the hospital where I had been born, she one evening took me out to the front garden in Stepps, just to the east of Glasgow where my family then resided. She held me up so that she and I could see the scarlet glow to the west of Clydebank in flames after the dreadful blitz there. That is clearly the world into which I was born, a world of catastrophic war.[4]

Thus, although he of course did not fight in the Second World War, or any other conflict, for MacCormick, peace was one of the roots of

[4] MacCormick, 'Europe's Future, Scotland's Future', St Andrews Day Speech, Brussels (30 November 2003), 2–3.

his engagement with Europe. He was part of a generation that still had a personal connection to war and its destruction. 'This is the world', he continued, 'which we Europeans have spent the last half-century and more, escaping, burying, and putting behind us'.[5] That is why, he argued, 'Scotland doesn't have a future that isn't also Europe's future'.[6] MacCormick was in many ways a conceptual poet of peace – of finding new, often ingenious ways of living together in less hierarchical, more heterarchical, more collaborative, more democratic political orders: concepts such as 'constitutional pluralism', 'post-sovereignty', and 'subsidiarity' belong very much in this conceptual poetics of peace. Europe was exciting because it offered – paradoxically, given its dense history – almost a blank slate onto which one could craft a new political imaginary, i.e., one that did without centralisation and concentration of power, and all varieties of top-down, coercive, and secretive forms of political domination. Europe offered the prospect of the diffusion of power, bringing law-making close to those who were most affected by it, set within defeasible, flexible conventions that people understood, and gathering together local knowledges while collaborating across difference. That was all exciting, but it was rooted in something of great, albeit fragile, value: peace.

The other root of MacCormick's engagement with Europe may seem paradoxical but is not: it is MacCormick's Scottishness. As MacCormick understood it and approached it, to be Scottish was also to be European. This, too, is articulated in the above quote, but the relations MacCormick saw between Scotland and Europe were by no means confined to the pursuit of peace and the avoidance of war. There was, in MacCormick's understanding – whether it be Scottish literature, or philosophy, or indeed law – a sense of interweaving Scottish and European histories, reaching far back in time.

In fact, Scots law was emblematic of this interweaving and a tradition that showed, too, that although of course there was much intermingling between Scots law and English common law, Scots law's deepest sources were European, and in particular Roman.[7] Similarly so with Scottish philosophy, especially in the Enlightenment (but not only: MacCormick was well aware that George Buchanan was a poet of European renown): Fletcher, Hume, Smith, and many others, were in many ways European thinkers, with long-standing links to the continent, and their work could

[5] Ibid., 3.
[6] Ibid.
[7] See, e.g., MacCormick, 'The Law Is a Mongrel' (1996).

not be understood, nor have been possible, without those European conversations.

MacCormick did not just think of this Scottish–European entanglement as a matter of history: he also lived it in his collaborations with scholars – as we shall see in Chapters 9 and 10, this meant translating from German and French to English, it meant cultivating friendships with scholars in Europe, it meant commitment to European academic institutions (such as the European University Institute in Florence), and it meant collaborating academically with European scholars in all kinds of ways (from the Bielefelder Kreis to jointly authored and edited papers and books). Thus, for MacCormick, there was never a contradiction between being a Scottish nationalist – in the sense in which he was that, as we saw in Chapter 7 – and being a European. Being Scottish and being European was not something MacCormick had to reconcile – as if it was a gap that needed to be bridged, or worse, a conflict that had to be managed. He lived it seemingly effortlessly and with great joy. This is evident, as we shall see in a moment, from the very first writings on Scottish nationalism in which MacCormick referred to Europe.

Europe and the SNP

It may be worthwhile to pause here to note just how remarkable it is that someone with MacCormick's sensibility – both so Scottish and so European – lived through the times he did, though of course, no doubt, the times also shaped the man. Still, it is extraordinary just to what extent the rise of Scottish nationalism proceeded side-by-side the rapid development of European politics, and how all this was interspersed with MacCormick's own political career.

To pick out but a few key moments: the Kilbrandon Commission on the Constitution, recommending devolution and a Scottish Parliament, reported in 1973; it was also in 1973 that the UK entered the European Economic Community (EEC); in 1974, the SNP made considerable electoral gains; in 1975, the referendum on the continuing membership of the EEC was held; also in the 1970s, the SNP drafted a Constitution for a Future Independent Scotland (which, importantly, included a Bill of Rights modelled on the European Convention on Human Rights); in the late 1980s and 1990s, the SNP came officially to adopt a pro-European stance; in 1993, the EEC grew to become the European Union (EU), also asserting itself as a sui generis legal order and, simultaneously, creating, in 1993, a Committee of the Regions (with, arguably, more scope for stateless nations to participate in European policymaking); in 1999, Scotland saw the return of its Parliament; in 1999, MacCormick was elected as MEP, serving not only in the European Parliament, but also in the Convention on the Future of Europe, which drafted a new European Constitution; in 2007, upon the SNP winning minority government in Scotland, MacCormick was appointed European Affairs advisor.

It is as if – through a remarkable string of coincidences – the age was made for MacCormick, just as much as MacCormick was made for the age. During all those years, Scottish and European affairs, including constitutional changes, went hand in hand. Once again, the rise of Scottish nationalism was very much entangled with the rise of European integration. MacCormick was in the thick of these changes: indeed, it seems, he could not help but be Scotland's Man in Europe and, at the same time, Europe's Man in Scotland.

The simultaneous adoption of Scottish nationalist and pro-European stances was not, it should be underlined, a widely shared attitude, at least not amongst SNP members, and certainly not in the 1970s. The historical picture is, of course, complex: in the late 1940s, Robert McIntyre did make a connection between 'Scottish self-government and European union',[8] going on to 'welcome', as a policy, 'steps towards the Federation of Europe', albeit only on the basis of 'equal co-operation of self-governing democratic countries'.[9] At this time, the party made numerous attempts to participate in European initiatives, sometimes successfully, e.g., in 1949, in Paris, it participated in the Congress of European Federalists, with McIntyre representing the party.[10] This organisation became, in due course, the International Congress of European Communities and Regions, though it is interesting that already then the SNP, once again through McIntyre, made it clear that they 'represented "nations" not "regions" or "provinces"'[11] – a linguistic reminder that was to echo later in the 1990s and 2000s. Further, in 1951, the SNP had urged membership of the European Coal and Steel Community,[12] and, in 1955, an article in the *Scots Independent* claimed that Europe could be a 'Safeguard for Small Nations' and be 'very different from that of subjection to a single and much greater nation'.[13]

[8] Lynch, *From Versailles to Maastricht* (1994), 47.
[9] Ibid., 48.
[10] Ibid.
[11] Ibid.
[12] Saunders, *Yes to Europe!* (2018), 351.
[13] See Laura Cram, 'Identity and European Integration' (2009), 118; see also Lynch, *From Versailles to Maastricht* (1994), 49.

Following the signing of the Treaty of Rome, in March 1957, this enthusiasm ebbed away, and continued to dissipate in the 1960s. In part in reaction to the position of Westminster parties, which were largely in favour of participation in the EEC in the 1960s, the SNP was markedly less enthusiastic.[14] This lack of enthusiasm in the 1960s turned, arguably, into suspicion in the 1970s, with widespread anxiety about Europe swallowing up both Scottish identity and Scottish independence: for the 'fundamentalists', who would settle for nothing less than a sovereign state, Europe was no horizon of promise, but instead yet another danger zone in which the dream of independence might slip away. Once again, we see a conception of nationalism being interlinked with a conception of Europe.

This was not the reason for suspicion of Europe in the post-war era among SNP members – as Eve Hepburn has noted, the 'EEC was viewed as centralist and elitist', and, equally, as a capitalist club (created by the rich for the rich) – but it was clearly a crucial one, e.g., 'it was unclear how Scottish interests would be represented if the EEC operated on an intergovernmental basis', it being thought, not unreasonably, that if the UK government was the sole representative in the EEC, then Scotland would only be marginalised further.[15] For many SNP members in the 1970s, the EEC was just the UK on 'a larger scale', with 'the same centralising tendencies, in political and economic terms, as the UK':[16] there would simply be no room for Scotland, including for its socialist outlook as well, more prosaically, its farming and fishing economic interests,[17] in such a centralised, elitist, capitalist order in which it had little, if any, political representation.

For these reasons, and although there were always some pro-European voices within the SNP,[18] the SNP opposed membership in the early 1970s, and it campaigned for a 'No' vote in the 1975 referendum. The 'No' campaign included figures like William Wolfe, Gordon Wilson, Stephen Maxwell and Isobel Lindsay, as well as future M. E. P. Winnie Ewing, who argued that a 'YES' vote would be a 'death warrant' for Scotland: 'The EEC', she said, 'was one of the most undemocratic bodies in the world. It was a political superpower and was unacceptable to the SNP'.[19] Wolfe, in turn, argued that 'It

[14] Saunders, *Yes to Europe!* (2018), 351; Lynch, *From Versailles to Maastricht* (1994), 50–2.

[15] Hepburn, 'Degrees of Independence' (2009), 193.

[16] Dardanelli, 'Ideology and Rationality' (2003), 275.

[17] See Saunders, *Yes to Europe!* (2018), 351.

[18] For example, in 1972, at the Annual Conference, a motion calling for 'Independence in Europe' was tabled, but not discussed for 'lack of time': Lynch, *From Versailles to Maastricht* (1994), 54.

[19] Quoted in Saunders, *Yes to Europe!* (2018), 354.

is the aim of the Common Market to establish political domination of the whole of Western Europe and to tolerate no deviations from this line'.[20]

Not all SNP members argued for leaving Europe as a matter of principle: for some, it was a tactical matter of gaining further ground (won in the 1974 elections) from the Westminster parties, especially Labour, given it was divided on the subject of the EEC. Thus, part of the SNP campaign involved arguing that the SNP could only agree to membership 'once it had negotiated its own terms as an independent country'; 'No Voice, No Entry' was the slogan in that respect.[21] Ironically enough, the slogan 'Scotland in Europe' was used in this period not by the SNP, but instead by a London-based 'Britain in Europe' campaign.[22]

It was only in the face of defeat in the 1975 referendum – with Scotland voting, much like the rest of the UK, in favour of retaining membership of the EEC (by 58.4 to 41.6 per cent)[23] – that the SNP slowly and, at first, quietly, shifted towards a pro-European stance. There was markedly less hostility to Europe amongst SNP members in the 1983 SNP Annual Conference, with both Gordon Wilson as well as Ewing having changed their positions after the 1979 debacle,[24] with the party 1984 Manifesto for the European Elections – in which the party had traditionally performed better than in the Westminster elections[25] – now cautiously saying that 'An SNP Government would [upon independence] approach negotiations with the Common Market in a positive manner'.[26] This cautious stance continued in 1987 with the SNP showing 'intention to work within the European Framework and to create "a Europe of Nations"'.[27]

The official turn occurred at the SNP Conference in 1988, when the SNP adopted the 'Scotland's Future – Independence in Europe' stance, and one which it was to hold steadfastly onto from then on.[28] By 1989, in

[20] Quoted in Jackson, *The Case for Scottish Independence* (2020), 148.

[21] Saunders, *Yes to Europe!* (2018), 352.

[22] Ibid., 354; 358–62. For a subtle reading of the SNP 'No' campaign, see Lynch, *From Versailles to Maastricht* (1994), 54–61, who notes the various disagreements behind the official party line.

[23] Ibid., 347.

[24] Dardanelli, 'Ideology and Rationality' (2003), 281.

[25] See Lynch, 'From Social Democracy' (2009), 623. In 1979: the European result was 19.4% in comparison to 17.3% for Westminster; then 17.8% to 11.4% in 1984; then 25.6% to 14% in 1989; and 32.6% to 21.5% in 1994.

[26] European Elections, SNP 1984 Manifesto.

[27] Valeria Tarditi, 'The SNP's Changing Attitude' (2010), 14.

[28] Macartney, 'Independence in Europe' (1990), 41; Lynch, *From Versailles to Maastricht* (1994), 66–7.

the elections to the European Parliament, the SNP argued for a vision of Scotland within the EEC as 'one of a confederal family of nations working together to improve the quality of life of its constituent peoples'.[29] Indeed, it is important to observe that it is in these years of the late 1980s that SNP talk of 'Independence in Europe' is being married explicitly and consistently to talk of 'pooling sovereignty'.[30]

That the history here is complex may be illustrated, briefly, by noting the changes in position, but also the influence of, Jim Sillars.[31] Sillars, who was born in Ayr in 1937, and thus grew up in working class Scotland, was, before he came to the SNP in 1981, a Labour man.[32] Indeed, in the 1960s, following Ewing's by-election win (from Labour) in 1967, Sillars argued robustly for 'the Union as a vehicle for working class advancement',[33] going on to win a by-election himself in 1970. During the course of the 1970s, Sillars came to be 'increasingly haunted by the structure of the Anglo-Scottish Union', which he felt 'marginalised Scottish interests and political preferences', and, in late 1975 he left Labour to launch, together with John Robertson and Alex Neil, the Scottish Labour Party (SLP, officially on 18 January 1976). The SLP argued in favour of an 'autonomous Scottish state within the [EEC]'.[34] But this had been an about-turn by Sillars who, in the 1975 referendum, campaigned for 'No', serving in the Executive of 'Get Scotland Out'.[35]

Having lost his South Ayrshire seat at the 1979 election, and with the SLP faltering, Sillars eventually made the jump to the SNP in 1981.[36] In joining the SNP, he drew on the material he had developed for the SLP – including one of its slogans, 'Independence in Europe', the title also of a later book in 1986 and then SNP party platform in 1989. His standing at the SNP received an enormous boost in 1988 when he won, from

29 Tarditi, 'The SNP's Changing Attitude' (2010), 14.

30 Ibid. Although there may be some resemblance to MacCormick's language here, it is also important to notice the differences, e.g., MacCormick championed 'Scotland in Europe', which is rather different to 'Independence in Europe', and he did not speak of 'pooling sovereignty' as much as thinking 'post sovereignty'.

31 See Jackson, 'From British Labourism' (2022), on which I here rely; see also Jackson, *The Case for Scottish Independence* (2020), 149–52.

32 Ayr, though not itself a mining town, had mining nearby in the east of Ayrshire. South Ayrshire, the constituency Sillars later represented as MP, had some mining villages. My thanks to Colin Kidd for discussion, who also noted that he and Sillars went to the same primary school in Ayr (Newton Park).

33 Jackson, 'From British Labourism' (2022), 235.

34 Ibid., 236.

35 Saunders, *Yes to Europe!* (2018), 350; Wright, 'The SNP and UK Relations' (2009), 179.

36 See Lynch, *From Versailles to Maastricht* (1994), 61–2.

Labour, the iconic Glasgow Govan seat in a by-election in 1988.[37] Sillars supported 'Independence in Europe', but without the gradualism: indeed, Sillars was instrumental in making sure the SNP did not participate in the Constitutional Convention set up by the Claim of Right in 1989.[38] Sillars eventually stepped back from frontline politics after losing Glasgow Govan in 1992.

The slight detour into the political life of a key SNP figure can offer an instructive contrast to MacCormick's attitudes. In light of the vacillations and conversions of figures like Sillars, it is striking that MacCormick's nationalism was never at odds with his pro-European attitude; there was no conversion, post 1975 referendum towards Europe.[39] Indeed, MacCormick was consistently pro-Europe long before any official adoption of SNP policy, including in periods when the SNP was positively against participation in the EEC. Unlike Sillars, MacCormick was also consistently a gradualist, including, as we have seen in Chapter 7, a participant in the Claim of Right and the ensuing Constitutional Convention. Rather than adopting the slogan 'Independence in Europe', MacCormick championed and lived a different one: 'Scotland in Europe'. The latter did not mean the pursuit of a sovereign or 'autonomous' state: instead, it meant something more conceptually and politically creative, i.e., a role for Scotland, alongside other nations, in a post-sovereign commonwealth governed by the principle of subsidiarity.

The 1975 Referendum

As mentioned above, MacCormick's engagement with Europe, and its prospects for Scottish nationalism, came early. Already in 1970, writing in *The Scottish Debate*, MacCormick canvassed the possibility of a 'customs union among the British nations', with Europe being drawn on as an 'analogy'; after all, he argued, as Europe shows us, 'a common market is necessarily a political and legal unit, however loose', and thus the EEC might be a model that a gradualist, like him, could endorse, for it could offer a workable

37 In 1973, this same seat had been won by Margo MacDonald, also in a by-election; later, in 1981, MacDonald and Sillars married, becoming a SNP power couple.

38 See Jackson, 'From British Labourism' (2022), 237.

39 One figure who was pro-Europe early on, including in the 1975 referendum, was George Reid, fellow gradualist, and a SNP MP, who received a rebuke for not towing the party line. Later, in the mid 1990s, Reid embraced 'post sovereignty', thus showing how close he was at various times, to the kinds of arguments put forward by MacCormick: see Jackson, *The Case for Scottish Independence* (2020), 158–9.

balance of self-government and collaboration.[40] In 1975, MacCormick campaigned for 'Yes' vote. Writing in February 1975, in a piece entitled 'We Need a New Politics', MacCormick noted that there was, in Scotland, 'a real and substantial consensus in favour of limited constitutional change'; the key term here was 'consensus': 'constitutions', MacCormick said, 'were not parking laws. You cannot make or change them on bare majority votes'; you had to always work within 'a broad consensus', and thus within the constitutional frameworks that existed.[41] Here, MacCormick added:

> Much depends on other parameters. If the European adventure is to continue (and how can Scotland not see her destiny entwined with Western Europe?), we will in the end, I believe, come to see our rightful place as one *patrie* among the *patries de l'Europe*, to invert a phrase of General de Gaulle's [de Gaulle had, of course, famously opposed UK entry into the EEC in the 1960s] in echoing a view of Mr Sillars.[42]

It was, however, in June 1975, just after the EEC referendum, that MacCormick gave his earliest and clearest argument for the importance of the EEC as 'the constitutional context in which now the argument over Scottish independence must be conducted'.[43] MacCormick was proud of the fact that 'In speeches at SNP meetings in various constituencies over the past two and more years, I have made no secret of the fact that my own commitment to the EEC, and to voting in any referendum for membership of it, was an unconditional one'[44] – not a political tactic, then, but very much a commitment of principle. But, equally, not one that MacCormick thought did any damage to the party: to the contrary, support for the SNP, and for some degree of Scottish autonomy, was not at odds with supporting the EEC.

Being in Europe, MacCormick argued, makes sense, especially historically, given the many 'strong links, for centuries stronger than England's, with Western Europe'.[45] Some of those links have been forgotten and neglected, and being part of 'the new institutions of Western Europe' can help Scotland 'to re-create something of our former cosmopolitanism'.[46] MacCormick placed emphasis on being part of something, on active

40 MacCormick, 'Independence and Constitutional Change' (1970), 58.
41 MacCormick, 'We Need a New Politics' (1975), 18.
42 Ibid.
43 MacCormick, 'Independence and Federalism' (1975), 1. This speech, available in the Edinburgh University Archives, was delivered to the Andrew Fletcher Society in Dundee in June 1975.
44 Ibid.
45 Ibid.
46 Ibid., 2.

participation in 'a larger political and economic community'.[47] The question now, he said, precisely for Scottish nationalism, were 'the terms of our togetherness'.[48] In this respect, MacCormick looked ahead to the constitutional changes being proposed and debated in Westminster (changes which were ultimately proposed in the *Scotland and Wales Act* 1978 and made subject to the referendum in 1979). He realised, he said, that any proposals were likely to be inadequate – at least from the perspective of someone committed to self-government in Scotland. The powers of any new Scottish Parliament, as granted by Westminster, at least initially, are unlikely to be sufficient.[49] However, and here keeping hold of his gradualism, 'the slow hard process of stage by stage incremental growth' can ultimately lead to the 'desired objective'.[50]

So what was the 'desired objective'? Well, that question had to be now, as MacCormick saw it in 1975 (though potentially already earlier, in the previous two years as he toured SNP constituencies), answered by reference to the EEC. MacCormick noted that 45% of Scots electorate 'now favour either some sort of federal relationship with the rest of the present UK (26%) or that form of independence which is the SNP's policy' (19%)'.[51] What the 'new location of the whole debate in the European context' shows is that there is, in practice, little practical difference between these two options.[52] Certainly, and assisted by the coming of a Scottish parliament, Scotland will need to find her place in the EEC and take part in deliberation and decision-making 'in the councils of the EEC': but there was no reason, MacCormick added optimistically, why matters should not evolve so that it could do so.[53] Further, given that the EEC works by requiring much intergovernmental co-operation and decision-making, there will need to be considerable 'community of policy' among the nations of the UK: the necessity for practical action will mean that 'there will not be the kind of radical clash or divergence of policy' as there might be under an internal-federalist approach.[54]

Speaking precisely in this future tense – as a kind of prophet, and an optimistic one – MacCormick's judgement was that there were reasons

[47] Ibid., 3.
[48] Ibid.
[49] Ibid., 6.
[50] Ibid., 5.
[51] Ibid., 3.
[52] Ibid., 6.
[53] Ibid., 7.
[54] Ibid.

to be hopeful about 'the possibility of Scotland's being with England and Wales (or England-and-Wales) a co-equal partner within a wider confederation', which would also offer a 'counterpoise to that natural tendency towards English pre-eminence'.[55] There was 'no reason in the world why the Scottish government should not establish its own links with Brussels along the lines of those enjoyed by the Federal German Länder'.[56] The point was, again practically rather than 'theologically',[57] that the kind of 'independence within the EEC' that is possible, if not likely, to evolve, would be precisely the kind that is needed: not federalism in the strict sense, and also not independence in the strict sense (of a sovereign state), but a workable, but still relatively autonomous, and equal partnership of nations in a new kind of confederation. Certainly, Scotland's membership of the EEC would be 'a matter for negotiation, not automatic right', and this would take time and patience, as all constitutional change does, but given Scotland's strategic importance for Europe (both militarily and economically, e.g., because of Scotland's oil), MacCormick had no doubt it could – indeed that it would – happen: 'I look forward', he said, 'to the day when an independent Scotland will take her rightful place as one among the European nations belonging to the EEC. I do not doubt that it will come'.[58]

This is – from the perspective of a reader many years later, with the advantage of having read the many speeches and publications of MacCormick on Europe – classic MacCormick, except that this is 1975. This is before the Scottish Labour Party and its slogan of 'Independence in Europe', which was then transplanted, via Sillars, into the SNP in the 1980s, culminating, as we saw above, in the 1988 formal adoption of this policy. It is also clear that 'independence', for MacCormick, meant something else here than the pursuit of a sovereign state– and certainly something else than, the 'the swift and (in at least a technical sense) revolutionary dash for independence'[59] that he saw being championed by some fundamentalist views in the SNP. This was a resolutely gradualist, but also thoroughly 'practical' approach: one which did not allow dogmatic commitment to concepts (such as sovereignty or the notion of a sovereign state) get in the way of desirable and workable practical solutions.

[55] Ibid., 8.
[56] Ibid., 9.
[57] Ibid., 6.
[58] Ibid., 9.
[59] Ibid., 4.

The important thing for MacCormick was not a slogan or a dogma – as if a trophy one could wave about – but instead a practically workable way of living together, of relating in ways that allowed for both collaboration and relative autonomy, a form of difference-in-unity. The inherited concepts, the philosophical language, which was deployed to political use (such as precisely 'sovereignty'), was, for MacCormick, like an iron ball, dragging us, not allowing us to grasp at the new political and philosophical opportunities Europe offered. Hence, perhaps, the emphasis on the future and the atmosphere of optimistic prophecy about this, and many other of MacCormick's pieces, on Europe: the key thing was a desire for, and an excitement about, the possibility of new political and philosophical horizons.

Hesitant Moves, Promising Signs

Although not a slogan or a dogma, there is a sense that the promise of Europe (for Scotland and, later, other stateless nations) does come to be reiterated by MacCormick, in his speeches and writings, as a kind of mantra. For instance, MacCormick's writings on nationalism in the late 1970s and early 1980s often end – typically after illustrating and arguing for the distinctive Scottish constitutional tradition (as we saw in Chapter 7) – with a statement about the promise of Europe. Conceiving of nationalism as a form of self-respect as well as respect for others as persons (as social, culturally and historically located, persons) was, MacCormick often argued, compatible with – indeed could only be enhanced by – 'the hesitant moves of the past two or three decades towards a new form of world order, of which, in our corner of the world, an example is provided in the supra-national confederation towards which the European Community is groping'.[60] Europe, MacCormick insisted, with its 'stability secured by the strength of common European institutions will [notice again the future tense] allow for the full and mutually respectful flourishing of the many diverse nationalities of democratic Europe'.[61] It is, in an 'emergent West European Confederation' that Scotland can find her 'rightful place … alongside of her sister British Nations'.[62] Likewise, in a passage that was repeated in numerous writings, especially in the 1990s, on nationalism, MacCormick once again pointed to 'the future': 'There are signs in

[60] MacCormick, 'Nation and Nationalism' (1979), 109.

[61] Ibid., 111.

[62] MacCormick, 'Constitution' (1979), 155.

the European Community that we are slowly learning how to transcend the sovereign state without dissolving the nation. In such a setting, the ancient nationalities of Europe can perhaps again come into their own, in conditions of mutual security, mutual respect and a whole variety of interlocking levels of non-sovereign government'.[63]

Having first been articulated in the 1970s, and then reiterated, through the 1980s and the 1990s, the view never changed – what happened is that over the course of the decades after the 1975 referendum, MacCormick raised the political, but especially the philosophical stakes, of these utopian-sounding European futures. This included the most basic questions one can ask about law and when it comes into existence, as well as the most basic questions about forms of political order, e.g., the concept of a state. Thus, for instance, in 1990, speaking at the David Hume Institute (of which he was then Vice President), and commenting on a speech by Judge Thijmen Koopmans, in which Koopmans spoke of what he saw as the 'internationalisation of legal systems' and the 'rapidly developing common law of Europe', MacCormick said:

> We in Western Europe for certain, and perhaps to a considerable extent we the inhabitants of the planet earth, are moving out of a particular phase of legal development towards a newer (and yet also older) understanding of the nature of law. After a period in which most thought about law has presupposed the sovereign state as the source, ground and home of law in its most authentic form, we are now rediscovering a ius gentium and finding in forms of non-state law the framework for a new economic order in world-wide markets.[64]

Conceptualising the promise of Europe, for nations like Scotland, was at one with reaching into the conceptual depths – into new conceptual futures – and thus thinking anew about law and politics. It meant loosening the shackles of conceptual habits: perhaps, in this new international world – a fourth stage, perhaps, from Smithian commercial society to 'radical internationalisation'[65] – we 'may be witnessing [here echoing Marxist visions] a post-socialist world in which it is the state that is withering away while the law comes into its own again here as a rational basis for the administration of things'.[66] But this was not just a matter of getting rid of an old, tired label – like the state or the sovereign state. It was

[63] MacCormick, 'Of Self-Determination' (1990), 19; 'Is Nationalism Philosophically' (1991), 18.
[64] MacCormick, 'Reply to Koopmans' (1990), 13.
[65] Ibid., 14.
[66] Ibid.

a deeper matter of re-conceptualising law, precisely not as a command issued by a dominant power for inferior subjects, but as something more like a customary reason that is constructed within an institutional tradition. As MacCormick put it, fittingly, given the forum, by reference to the work of Hume:

> David Hume's critique of ethical and jurisprudential rationalism dealt it a death blow; but the practical point of the rationalist debate survived in Hume. For in his view custom and tradition remain the essential vehicles of law and its development. The reasonable is not then something extraneous to law but something constructed by or within it… Like F. A. Hayek, I am of the view that a Humean critical rationalism is the best stance to adopt on the questions of practical philosophy.[67]

These are deep waters indeed: here, the promise of Europe points towards a rejection of the will-theory or pure-reason account of law – a 'voluntarist' or 'rationalist' account, as adopted by Bentham and Austin, and which found its way into 'Dicey's apotheosis of the dubious doctrine of Parliamentary sovereignty'[68] – and clears the way for an adoption of a theory that sees law emerging from, and being re-articulated within and by, a community of practice as inhering in its constructively reasonable institutions, especially that of courts.

MacCormick certainly dived, full-body, into these waters, and I will be examining them in Chapters 9 and 10, on institutionalism and practical reason, respectively. For now, what is important to see is the connection between the promise of Europe, as a new political theatre for nations (but not necessarily states, let alone sovereign states) and this search for a new conceptual language for law – 'new', of course, in the sense of unfamiliar and novel, given the dominance of the Benthamite–Austinian conception of law as the command of a sovereign, but not necessarily historically new (as the example of Hume illustrates). Of course, all this still left lots of details to be worked out, but the key thing is that law, as well as reason, could be re-conceptualised so as to be compatible with this new 'world of the post-sovereign-state'.[69] The key to this re-conceptualisation was precisely Europe and showing how its new political order was not at odds with nationalism, properly conceived:

> A part of the answer is clearly that the old (and morally objectionable) absolutism of nation-state nationalism based on doctrines of illimitable

[67] Ibid., 15.
[68] Ibid.
[69] Ibid., 16.

> sovereignty must be abandoned, and abandoned without regret. In turn as new confederations emerge, for example in the case of the European Community, these can and should create space for the flourishing of some of the nationalities which were wholly or partly submerged within the 'nation-states' of the 19th century. This would involve an upward and downward diffusion of power – a wholly good thing from the point of view of the rationalist legal order envisaged by Judge Koopmans. It may be that there is a kind of rationalism and a kind of nationalism that are not mutually incompatible. For my part, I favour them in their mutually compatible forms, but only in those forms.[70]

We see, in speeches like this one, how all these notions – of nationalism, of internationalism, of institutionalism, of rationalism, all this conceptual innovation in hunt of new (or old-new) ways of thinking of law and its role in political ordering – were entangled with the political promise MacCormick saw in Europe.

A New Lexicon for a New Commonwealth

Winds of Change

By the time, then, of the 1993 piece 'Beyond the Sovereign State', which many scholars have cited as inspirational, and which did indeed reach a wide audience, many of the ideas in it had already been articulated, in one form or another, in previous papers, in many articles in newspapers,[71] and no doubt also tested in the coal-fire of party politics, whether in his own name (when MacCormick stood for election to Westminster) or in support of others. Indeed, the period of the early 1990s were very fast moving, politically, and MacCormick was very much in the thick of it. There were two kinds of changes here that are important to underline: first, changes in Scotland, including the momentum in Scotland for constitutional change, which went beyond the SNP, as well as changes within the SNP itself; and second, changes in the way European integration itself was developing.

Within Scotland, matters had moved swiftly since the creation of a Scottish Constitutional Convention, on the back of the Claim of Right in 1988. This Convention had its first meeting in March 1989, and adopting a declaration, also called 'The Claim of Right'. In what proved to be a matter of considerable political significance, Thatcher's government introduced, on 1 April 1989, a new 'Community Charge', commonly referred to

70 Ibid., 18.

71 In terms of newspaper pieces, see, e.g., 'Time to Tear Ourselves Away' (1992).

as 'the Poll Tax', on Scotland, and one year ahead of it coming into force in England and Wales. Protests inevitably followed and injected further political momentum into the Constitutional Convention, which issued its first report, entitled *Towards Scotland's Parliament*, in March 1990. There were numerous rallies in this period, including, for instance, the 'Scotland United' rallies in 1992 in Glasgow and Edinburgh, which called for a multi-option referendum on the future government of Scotland. There were symbolic acts, too, which resonated personally for MacCormick, such as the 1996 return of the Stone of Destiny. But there were also important documents published by the Convention, such as 'Scotland's Parliament, Scotland's Right' in November 1995, which offered a blueprint for devolution.

All this culminated, after Blair's Labour swept into power in 1997, with a referendum on Home Rule on 11 September 1997, with 74% of Scots voting for a Scottish Parliament and 63% for that Parliament to have powers to vary the basic rate of income tax. In what cannot be sufficiently described as a profound personal experience for MacCormick, Scotland's Parliament was re-established by the ensuing *Scotland Act* of 1998 and first sat in Edinburgh on 12 May 1999, with its official launch on 1 July 1999. Scotland's inaugural First Minister was none other than Donald Dewar, MacCormick's long-time friend from Glasgow University days (Dewar died the year after in 2000).

Changes within the SNP were just as fast-paced. Having adopted, as we have seen, its official policy of 'Independence in Europe' in 1988, the SNP came to stabilise and solidify its commitment to the European Community. This was undoubtedly strengthened by Sillars' famous win of the Glasgow Govan by-election in November 1988, and his subsequent championing of the above policy while on the SNP executive till 1992. There was, in many ways, a sense of impatience within the SNP: the slogan in the 1992 manifesto was 'Independence in Europe make it happen now',[72] and some decisions were made for tactical reasons – such as, most prominently perhaps, the decision not to participate in the Scottish Constitutional Convention – but amongst the impatience and calls for rapid, even fundamentalist, change, the overall policy of the SNP stabilised.

Significantly, Europe was now talked about and portrayed as 'a confederal union of independent member states and contrasted with a unitary, centralised UK state with the obvious claim that the former was providing

[72] Tarditi, 'The SNP's Changing Attitude' (2010), 15.

a much more favourable framework for Scotland than the latter'.[73] And, perhaps most importantly, in 1990, the SNP renewed and reiterated its commitment to 'constitutional' change, recalling its Constitutional Policy Committee, slightly amending and re-publishing its Constitution for a Future Independent Scotland. It was also in 1990, at its Annual Conference in September, that Alex Salmond became the SNP's leader.

Europe was of course also changing rapidly. This had many aspects that resist quick description, but amongst such changes were the move, between 1979 and 1997, towards more 'substantial social and regional policies' – a move 'leftwards' and one 'which contributed significantly to dispel its [the EC's and then the EU's] image as a purely laissez faire, capitalist organisation'.[74] This was very important for the EC (and then the EU's) legitimacy in Scotland: as Pittock has recently argued, 'Social equality is a key – perhaps the key – area where Scottish social attitudes diverge strongly from those elsewhere in the UK'.[75] Significantly, too, Scotland itself benefited from those regional funds, 'especially those targeted to areas in industrial decline, which were just born in the late 1970s but commanded over 30% of the EU budget in the 1990s'.[76] These two factors help explain the increasingly popularity of the EC/EU in Scotland, e.g., in 1994, 'a poll showed that support for a joint Scottish and European identity "to some degree" was the identified preference of 64% of SNP, 55% of Labour, and between 25 and 30% of Conservative and Liberal Democratic voters'.[77]

Of course, there were also major changes in the overall structure of the EC, which, on 7 February 1992, via the Maastricht Treaty, made vital steps towards further political and economic integration, such as establishing a future single currency (finally launched into circulation on 1 January 2002). Various major structural changes quickly followed, such as the launch of the 'four freedoms' (i.e., the free movement of people, goods, services, and money), the creation of a European Economic Area in 1994, and further enlargement in 1995, as well as increasing foreign visibility (especially with the 1997 Treaty of Amsterdam). These changes were, unsurprisingly, given also their pace, often met with considerable

[73] Dardanelli, 'Ideology and Rationality' (2003), 277–8.

[74] Ibid., 280.

[75] Pittock, *Scotland: The Global History* (2022), 365; see also Jackson, *The Case for Scottish Independence* (2020), 149; and Ichijo, *Scottish Nationalism and the Idea of Europe* (2004), 117–129.

[76] Dardanelli, 'Ideology and Rationality' (2003), 280.

[77] Pittock, *Scotland: The Global History* (2022), 371.

opposition – or, at the very least, scepticism and caution – in Member States, including in some of their constitutional courts, most famously the German Constitutional Court.[78] They were also, of course, and stretching back to the 1960s, accompanied by numerous important cases, both in Member State courts and in the European Court of Justice (ECJ), articulating and again contesting the EC/EU's own legal sui-genericity,[79] with the ECJ becoming ever more assertive still in the early 1990s.[80]

Alongside these structural changes, one must also recall the various struggles over and movements within Europe towards secession by smaller groupings within larger political orders – most emblematically, in this period, the collapse of the Soviet Union from 1989 to 1992, and the new autonomy of Eastern European countries[81] as well as the break-up of Yugoslavia in 1991–92. To this, too, one should add the voices of protest and secession in Catalunya and the Basque Country in Spain, or Flanders and Wallonia in Belgium – in addition, of course, to what was happening in the UK, including in Northern Ireland.

These were all breathless changes, and their breathlessness was in many ways matched by the changes in MacCormick's political life. Somehow, MacCormick managed to combine participating in the Claim of Right and the Scottish Constitutional Convention alongside also serving the SNP in its various policy committees, especially its Constitutional Policy Committee. Convening this Committee from October 1990 to June 1991, MacCormick took the lead in amending and re-presenting the Constitution to SNP members and more broadly.[82] He continued to contest Westminster elections (in 1992 and 1997) and served on the SNP National Council becoming, in 1992, the SNP Scottish Cabinet Member for Home Affairs.[83]

[78] E.g., MacCormick, 'Maastricht Urteil' (1993); see Cruz, 'The Legacy of the Maastricht-Urteil' (2008), for an overview and history.

[79] In famous cases such as *Van Gend en Loos* (1963), *Costa* v *ENEL* (1964).

[80] With e.g., *Francovich* (1991) and *Factortame* (1991), amongst numerous important cases. Apologies are due to EU lawyers and legal historians for this caricature history; the point is to convey a sense of the rapidity and scale of the changes within which MacCormick was immersed.

[81] MacCormick was very conscious of this process, e.g., he visited Poland for the first time in October 1988: 'Everywhere', he wrote, 'one had a powerful sense of the Polishness of Poland, and yet of a frustration that this was locked into an inefficient and unpopular system of government', i.e., 'there was here a nation whose state was serving it ill': MacCormick, 'Is Nationalism Philosophically Credible?' (1991), 11.

[82] See MacCormick, 'An Idea' (1991).

[83] 1992 is the year, too, of many personal changes, with divorce from his first wife, Karen, and a new marriage with Flora, who was a crucial support for him in the years to come. Indeed, MacCormick and Flora were a formidable team, both in Scotland and in Europe, with

After his friend still from Glasgow University days, Allan Macartney, was elected MEP in 1994, he joined ranks with him, alongside Neal Ascherson, Michael Lynch, Malcolm Anderson, Mungo Deans, David Murray, and Roy MacIver (only two of whom, Macartney and MacCormick was SNP members), to serve on the Transition to Independence Working Group (which was established on 7 October 1995) and which published an important working paper in 1996.[84]

The collaboration with Macartney is very significant, with their views being complimentary in many respects, e.g., back in 1992, in his *Scotland – A European Nation*, Macartney had argued, much like MacCormick, that the emerging European confederation, which pooled sovereignty, could 'allow Scotland to exert equal influence over decision-making as other small member states'.[85] When Macartney died, suddenly, as a result of a heart attack, in August 1998, he was replaced by Ian Hudghton, with MacCormick himself subsequently becoming an SNP MEP candidate, duly elected on 10 June 1999.[86]

All through these years, in the 1990s, and thus amidst this flurry of political activity, MacCormick continued to write philosophically. In many ways, his philosophical writing allowed him to digest what was happening and happening so quickly. The philosophy, too, arguably

Flora playing an important role in MacCormick's MEP office. Although I do not dwell on this relationship in detail in this book, preferring to respect its privacy, there is no doubt that any account of MacCormick's character is greatly incomplete without proper engagement with it. This is, of course, only one of many ways in which this book's portrayal of MacCormick is partial and fragmentary.

84 The Working Group had a wide remit and considered: 'a) the constitutional and legal mechanisms of the dissolution of the Union between Scotland and England and the accommodation of the successor states in the EU; b) how the resulting reorganisation of the machinery of the central government and other joint UK institutions might be achieved; and c) the establishment of a framework for an Association of States of the British Isles, consisting of the present constituent parts of the UK and the Channel Islands, the Isle of Man and the Republic of Ireland': *Transition to Independence Report* (1996), 1–2. The Group traced arguments based on both 'legitimacy', which it tied to 'a clear, democratically expressed majority will in Scotland', and 'legality', examining the position under international law, Scots law, and English law: *Transition to Independence Report* (1996), 5–6. It also endorsed a referendum procedure, which would be based on a vote for an independent Scotland under a proposed, written constitution: *Transition to Independence Report* (1996), 9. The Report is sophisticated both technically – in terms of the legal machinery – as well as practically, in terms of the precise steps needed for 'independence in Europe'.

85 See Hepburn, 'Degrees of Independence' (2009), 194.

86 It is said that in his election speech, MacCormick was the eighth candidate to speak: 'he said that he felt like Elizabeth Taylor's eighth husband on his wedding night: he reckoned he would need to try something different': correspondence with Robin Downie (on file with the author).

became more abstract – raising the philosophical stakes, as mentioned earlier, of the political changes occurring around him to ever-greater heights. In a series of papers in the 1990s, MacCormick articulated his vision of Europe as a post-sovereign commonwealth governed by subsidiarity – a vision that he then carried with him into his role as MEP, and especially into the Convention on the Future of Europe (2002–3). Before, then, turning to his contributions in the Convention, it is important to consider the major arguments made by MacCormick in this period (collected, as mentioned above, in *Questioning Sovereignty*, 1999). Again, as we have seen, these are arguments that reflected MacCormick's re-conceptualisation of nationalism (alongside his re-conceptions of law and reason), but they also introduced a new political and philosophical vocabulary – a new lexicon – comprised of 'constitutional pluralism', 'post-sovereignty', and 'subsidiarity' for a new commonwealth.

Sovereignty Talk

It is important to emphasise here how much MacCormick cared about the quality of the political discourse over Europe. This is important, too, for some scholars have criticised MacCormick for being 'confused' about sovereignty. For instance, some scholars have argued that it did not make sense, especially when set against the longer European history of the concept of 'sovereignty', to speak of 'post sovereignty' and certainly not in the European context where Member States always retained the sovereign power to withdraw.[87] Some of these scholars have also argued that 'constitutional pluralism', another of MacCormick's terms, is a 'conceptual oxymoron'.[88] My point here is not to assess these criticisms, which are,

87 See McLoughlin, 'Ten Tenets of Sovereignty' (2003); and Walker, 'Late Sovereignty' (2003), who prefers, as signalled in his title, to speak of 'late sovereignty'; see also Troper, 'The Survival of Sovereignty' (2010). Later, in a piece called 'After Sovereignty' (1998), MacCormick responded more explicitly to some of these criticisms: characteristically generously (if not over-generously), he acknowledged their force, but insisted, especially in light of a 'political or mixed-jural-political reading' that 'while legalistically late sovereignty', via this right of withdrawal, 'is preserved, there remains a case for the "post sovereignty" thesis': MacCormick, 'After Sovereignty' (1998), 168. Clearly, MacCormick felt there was something of value worth fighting for in the post-sovereignty idea, even if this was difficult to articulate, especially when facing 'legalistic' arguments, and even if it had an air of wishful thinking about it.

88 See McLoughlin, 'Constitutional Pluralism' (2014).

in their own right, important contributions to the debate over these key terms; instead, my argument is that it is vital to see MacCormick's sensitivity about terms within the broader political context in which they were being used.

The language of 'sovereignty' was used by both the Scots and the English in this debate, and in particular ways. For the Scots, talk of sovereignty, including popular sovereignty – which was used by the fundamentalists in the SNP, but had also become more prevalent as a result of the Claim of Right in the 1980s – was associated with aligning Scottish nationalism with the pursuit of a sovereign state. It thus played a zero-sum game, and often resulted in impatient and democratically illegitimate – at least as MacCormick saw it – claims to quick, or even revolutionary, independence (including other ways of separating out Scotland, such as becoming republican). Talk of sovereignty in this way had the other consequence that it smacked of isolationism and separatism, positioning itself aggressively as against the English. For the English, on the other hand, to speak of sovereignty was to speak of the sovereignty of Parliament – of Westminster sovereignty. This was, in turn, tantamount – to MacCormick's ears, but also to many other Scots – to claiming political domination over Scotland and ignoring, for example, what the Scots saw as fundamental constraints imposed by the Acts of Union 1707.

Talk of 'sovereignty', then, was not conducive to what MacCormick saw as a positive, progressive, and gradualist process of constitutional change in the UK. It made the debate – politically and philosophically – too aggressively oppositional. It created unnecessary and unhelpful political tension. The resultant attitudes were extreme and, again, oppositional, with both sides kicking in their heels and shouting at each other: these were not the kinds of attitudes needed to work out, practically and reasonably, a more democratic future, which balanced self-government with the needs of international collaboration.

Thus, MacCormick's choice of lexicon needs to be read in this pragmatic light: as a matter of caring for the quality of the political discourse, and the prospects for productive conversations, surrounding constitutional change in the UK. Here, it must be again underlined just how often and how intricately – at what level of detail[89] – MacCormick was involved

[89] Insight into the level of detail that MacCormick engaged in can be gleaned from a visit to his archives: these archives reveal the many policy documents MacCormick drafted or commented on; they also show how involved he was in the details of local politics, e.g., leading a petition in 1996 for a new ferry service between Campbeltown and Ballycastle in Argyll (see MacCormick, Letter to the Secretary of State for Scotland, Michael Forsyth, on 20 February 1996) and an airport for Oban (*Oban Star*, 22 May 1996). It was, incidentally,

in policymaking within the SNP, but also more broadly in Scottish politics. Relations between Scotland, the UK, and Europe were MacCormick's bread and butter in SNP Council and Committee meetings and all around the country when campaigning for SNP seats in local, national, and European elections. MacCormick was working out, over the course of many years, the practical details of, say, SNP's constitutional policy, including the legal machinery of Scotland transitioning to becoming a member of the EC/EU. The point is that certain languages, which came along with certain attitudes, got in the way of crafting workable, diplomatic, and practical solutions, as well as a more promising future. This was, then, less a matter of abstract theory, or even accurate constitutional history, and more a matter of the quality of political discourse, including its prospects of enabling productive political action, both in the short term and especially in the long term.

For MacCormick, this was not simply a matter of good politics, echoing, say, the criticism of fanaticism and enthusiasm in favour of moderation by his compatriot from some two centuries previously, Hume.[90] All this was important, but the roots of this new lexicon lay deeper: the language mattered because it was a matter of character, i.e., a matter of how one related with others. To talk of sovereignty – whether popular or Westminster sovereignty – was to take up a stance of aggressive self-assertion as set against others. It was to jump up and down and insist on one's power and autonomy – an immature stance of someone who had not yet learnt the lessons of co-operation and compromise. To insist on 'sovereignty' was not constructively collaborative, but instead adopted an attitude of winner-takes-all. More resonantly, it was not a stance of respect for persons. Again, this was not a stance that was practically reasonable precisely because it was insufficiently relational. All this mattered enormously to MacCormick, as a matter of character.

Beyond the Sovereign State

As set against that background, then, let us return to these pieces in the 1990s. MacCormick's Chorley Lecture, 'Beyond the Sovereign State', was delivered at the LSE on 3 June 1992. The date is significant:

this same level of attention to detail, the sheer ability to absorb information, that many (e.g., Ian Hudghton, in an interview with the author) also commented on when observing MacCormick at work in the European Parliament.

90 Although this too played its part, given MacCormick's 'addiction' to Hume: see for example the early reference to Hume's 'Idea of a Perfect Commonwealth' in MacCormick, 'Constitutionalism and Democracy' (1989), 26–7.

the day before, on 2 June, Denmark, in a referendum, voted against the Maastricht Treaty – which had been signed in February 1992 (an agreement reached later, in December 1992 – called the Edinburgh Agreement – secured a favourable vote in a second referendum). Further, a year earlier, in 1991, in the *Factortame* decision,[91] the European Court of Justice had judged invalid a UK Act (and its regulations), the *Merchant Shipping Act* 1988, for the illegal (under EC law) restriction of fishing rights by non-UK vessels in UK waters. MacCormick taught this case in Edinburgh and it was of course also being discussed by his colleagues in Edinburgh, many of whom were becoming interested in the legal theoretical issues flowing from the EC/EU.[92]

The pedagogical context is significant and also explains why MacCormick drew on so heavily on Austin's understanding of sovereignty in the lecture. This made sense pedagogically: MacCormick discussed the *Factortame* decision alongside Austin's theory, using the former to test the latter. Much to his surprise, MacCormick's students in class did not think there was any particularly great conflict between Austin's theory of sovereignty and the case: the UK remained sovereign at all times, for it only delegated – via the 1972 *European Communities Act* – certain specific powers to the EC and it retained the power to 'unilaterally enact legislation directly revoking British membership of the EC'.[93] But – hold on, one can imagine MacCormick saying in class – just how likely is such a unilateral revocation? Would it not cause 'huge economic damage' to the UK?[94] But if that is so – if it is accepted as a matter at least of practicality and likelihood that the UK could not or would not unilaterally revoke their membership – then does this mean that 'Instead of the UK Parliament … being sovereign, the bureaucrats of Brussels are' and that 'instead of being delegates of the UK sovereign, the UK authorities are mere delegates of the Euro-sovereign'?[95]

There are several points to make here about how MacCormick sets up the problem. Of course, this is done in many ways for dramatic effect, first

[91] *Factortame* (1991) C-221/89 – 25 July 1991.

[92] There were various strands and manifestations of this; one important one was 'an interdisciplinary and inter-university seminar', funded by the Economic and Social Research Council (UK) on 'Legal Theory of European Integration', run by Zenon Bańkowski, Richard Bellamy, and Andrew Scott; see, e.g., MacCormick, Bańkowski and Scott, 'The European Union?' (1995).

[93] MacCormick, 'Beyond the Sovereign State' (1993), 3.

[94] Ibid.

[95] Ibid., 4.

in class, and now in a public lecture. MacCormick is well aware of the view that rather than being a giving up of sovereignty by the UK, the entering into the EC was an assertion of sovereignty, in particular, because the UK retained the power of exit – indeed, the view is elementary.[96] But it is interesting that, in raising potential doubts about it – again, just how likely would such a unilateral revocation be – MacCormick does not insist on a purely legal analysis, i.e., instead, he situates and relates the law to political and empirical reality, not of conceptual certainties but rather of political and economic probabilities.

Further, it is also instructive that MacCormick sets up talk of sovereignty as precisely a problem of relation – in practice – between two personified abstractions: the Member States and the EC. Talk of sovereignty, it seems – in the Austinian mould, at least – would mean that we would need to side with one entity as superior to, and thus politically dominant over, the other. Whatever the legality of this, in some strict, abstract, pure world of legal concepts, the question is: is this workable in practice? What kind of relation would this set up? How would it affect the political – even moral – quality of the relations between Member States and the EC? And is this not important, given the fragility of the situation – the tensions running high, in light of decisions such as *Factortame*? Could one, in such a politically fraught context, separate out the law into a heaven of concepts, and ignore the political theatre in which such arguments and languages were used, with what attitudinal consequences? Choice of language, and associated concepts, was also relational act, with communal repercussions, and this really mattered, especially if one was, as MacCormick clearly was, steeped in the everyday practical realities of ongoing political discussions, i.e., of policymaking and often delicate political negotiations.

It is telling that having set the problem up in the way he did – i.e., are we forced to choose between one side being sovereign and the other inferior? – MacCormick went on to analyse the situation as it might be viewed from both sides. The language that dominates this piece is that of 'point of view' – a kind of mutual perspectivalism, an exercise in practically grounded empathy, urging both sides to see how the other might see it.[97]

96 See also his later analysis: MacCormick, 'After Sovereignty' (1998); the reason why he argues that the 1972 Act was not a revolution because the UK retained this power: 36; this did not mean, however, that in practice, there was not complexity and indeterminacy here, which left much open, to be worked out as one went along: 36–8. Again, the practical complexities often mattered more than theoretical purities.

97 I return to and discuss in detail MacCormick's 'perspectivalism' about value in chapter 10.

Either side could see it in 'narrow' and 'monocular' ways: EC officials could claim EC sovereignty and see Member State governments as 'but the delegates of the Community'; equally, however, Member State governments can claim that 'they are not in the habit of deferring to Community decisions save on a restricted range of matters' and that their citizens, in any event, 'accept Community decisions as a matter of loyalty to their own governing authorities'.[98] This is possible, but is it 'satisfactory'? And is it necessary to 'imprison yourself within a particular point of view, one particular perspective'?[99] Here, MacCormick looks to jurisprudence to perform a particular function, i.e., to liberate us from such false choices, such zero-sum games, and thus allow us to escape the prison of a monadic, monocular view that fails to relate, respectfully, with another:

> One thing which it is necessary for jurisprudence or the philosophy of law to do in the present state of affairs is to guard against taking a narrow one-state or Community-only perspective, a monocular view of these things. The difficulty about sovereignty is that it seems to point inevitably in that direction. So the thing to do is to use the discussion so far as a springboard for looking at other models which may enable us to account for legal complexity in a different way.[100]

This is a deeply practical and deeply relational approach to the issue of conflicts between the EC and Member States. It also speaks volumes about what MacCormick thought was the role and value of philosophy, i.e., a matter of enabling better relations between us – something deeply set within one's character. In many ways, the very point of philosophical thought was its ability to allow us to step back from our own particular point of view – to universalise, as MacCormick was always emphasising practical reason did – and to see how another might see it. Philosophy, but also practical reason, was on this view a relational art, an empathic art: it was, in its most profound sense, an exercise in respecting others, a means for avoiding monological dogmas, and a pragmatic and flexible attitude that was always responsive to another's point of view. Philosophy was not, at its deepest, a monological defence of a set of theses one was committed to defending against all comers; it was not the grabbing and settling of conceptual territory that established impregnable castles in the sky. It was, instead, a self-reflexive discipline of reaching out to others.

[98] MacCormick, 'Beyond the Sovereign State' (1993), 5.

[99] Ibid.

[100] Ibid.

What were, then, these other models that jurisprudence might adopt in theorising the relation between the EC and Member States? Given his emphasis on 'points of view', it is perhaps unsurprising that MacCormick looked to Hart. No doubt his audience of legal scholars, and fellow legal theorists, would be quick to see the echoes of Hart's 'internal point of view'. Might there be an interpretation of Hart that would allow for a more relational reading – a more pluralistic reading – of what was happening in the EC? MacCormick thought there was, indeed, such 'potential' in Hart's theory.[101]

If one understood Hart's theory of the rule of recognition – the ultimate criteria of the validity of legal rules in a legal system – in evolutionary terms, i.e., as a 'rule which depends on deliberative practice and emergent custom', and thus something that 'can evolve and develop over time, and can be controversial or unclear on some points so long as it is not so on all',[102] then there is no reason in principle why such a rule could not evolve so as to enable 'interaction and overlapping between systems'.[103] Hence, one could see that what happened after the 1972 Act was that the UK incorporated, into its rule of recognition, a criterion of validity that made UK laws subject to tests of validity via EC law. There was complexity here, for what counted as EC law was subject to interpretation by EC institutions, such as the ECJ. Thus, there was a sense in which the new UK rule of recognition, after 1972, was now one that enabled overlapping and interlocking legal systems.

Of course, from the perspective of each system, their own rule of recognition would still constitute the 'ultimate criteria' for that system – there would still be, relative to each system, an 'internal point of view', no matter how overlapping or interlocking the systems were. But the theorist need not be a loyal official; indeed, perhaps a theorist ought not to be. 'Instead', MacCormick argued, 'of committing oneself to a monocular vision dictated by sovereignty theory, one can embrace the possibility of acknowledging differences of perspective, differences of point of view'.[104] Thus, one would also need to acknowledge the internal point of view of the EC officials and see how their rule of recognition has developed over time. This meant incorporating and tracing changes as between the various treaties, including the European Convention on Human Rights, as

[101] Ibid., 9.
[102] Ibid., 5.
[103] Ibid., 6.
[104] Ibid.

well as the ways in which the EC institutions were themselves developing, especially the ECJ.[105] It was possible – though not necessary – that the EC saw the grounds of its validity in Member States differently from the ways that the Member States saw it. Where this led to conflicts, then there were mechanisms in place to manage them, e.g., the process of reference to the ECJ. The important point was that 'Where systems overlap, neither is necessarily part of the ultimate reason for the validity of the other, nor do we have to presuppose some common reason for, or ground of, validity external to them both',[106] as might be the case if we say, along Kelsenian lines, that both the EC and the UK legal systems were part of an ultimately superior, unity-securing, international law.

What MacCormick was after here – whether successfully delivered or not – was liberation from the view, which he certainly saw at work in the political debates over Scottish nationalism, but which were also increasingly affecting the political debate over the EC, that 'all law must originate in a single power source, like a sovereign', and thus that the only kind of relations one could have between legal systems were ones in which one had to 'be subordinate or hierarchically inferior to the other or to some third system'.[107] Surely jurisprudence, the practice of philosophy, need not force us into such a position. Surely, we could recognise that at least there was a conceptual possibility of a way of thinking about law that did not require us to posit relations of hierarchy, subordination, and domination. Something like this might be complex and messy – it may not appeal to those who want to draw bright and clear theoretical lines in the sky – but if we can see it happening practically, then why could we also not conceptually? Should not philosophical concepts broaden rather than narrow our political horizons? Should not philosophy enable, rather than stand in the way, of enabling good relations between persons and communities?

There is an enormous sense of desire and hope in this 1992 lecture, an enormous sense of optimism and belief in law and its conceptualisation, as capable of creating new political opportunities, new ways of living together. There is, equally, a sense of the looming danger of believing in the necessity for sovereign states and thus stamping one's foot, thereby (as MacCormick saw it) insisting on relations of subordination and domination. Throughout this piece, MacCormick links certain concepts and their

[105] Ibid., 7.
[106] Ibid., 9.
[107] Ibid., 8.

associated languages with attitudes towards what are then deemed 'other' and 'inferior' normative orders, e.g.:

> A widespread belief in sovereignty as essential for statehood would fit well with a belief in state law as paradigmatic for law. The two would yield some predictable consequences in terms of attitudes, both practical and pedagogical as well as theoretical. For example, you would tend to marginalise international law. You would tend to marginalise primitive law, you would marginalise canon law and church law. You would marginalise what is sometimes called the 'living law' of social institutions like universities, firms or families… You also necessarily marginalise all those areas of illegal regulation which nevertheless make life possible in some situations [e.g., certain slum areas of Brazil].[108]

What is fascinating and important here is the link MacCormick draws between philosophical concepts and political attitudes, and especially consequences for 'othering' and then 'marginalising' those others. 'Tendencies' matter – not necessarily in the sense that we must begin with them and then work out philosophical theories from them, but in the sense that we should not foreclose certain possibilities, i.e., not force ourselves into adopting certain attitudes or tendencies for philosophical reasons. To do that is dogma, and that is the very opposite of philosophy.

In closing his 1992 lecture in the way he did – perhaps rather dramatically arguing that there were no longer any sovereign states in Western Europe, for there 'has now been a pooling or a fusion with the communitarian normative order of some of the state's powers',[109] MacCormick was very much echoing language that was being deployed by the more gradualist voices in the SNP and in Scottish politics generally. In what was a typical kind of debater's joke and one that could also be repeated on the campaign trail, MacCormick said: 'We must not envisage sovereignty as the object of some kind of zero sum game, such that the moment X loses it Y necessarily has it. Let us think of it rather more as of virginity, which can in at least some circumstances be lost to the general satisfaction without anybody else gaining it'.[110] Indeed, MacCormick did not hide away his 'personal political stance or attitude'[111] of a Scottish nationalist, but of a particular kind (as we saw in Chapter 7). Nationalism was not the problem here. Indeed, part of what

108 Ibid., 14.
109 Ibid., 16.
110 Ibid.
111 Ibid., 17, citing his 'Can Nationalism be Philosophically Credible?' (1990) paper.

made nationalism philosophically credible was the very possibility – philosophical and political – of a distinction between nationalism and the pursuit of the sovereign state. It was the latter project, not nationalism, that was to blame for the many violent conflicts Europe had seen in the last century.

There was, then, a lot at stake. Here, towards the end of his lecture, MacCormick was at his most lyrical, most hopeful, crafting a paragraph that was perhaps his most inspiring in all his academic writing:

> Can we think of a world in which our normative existence and our practical life are anchored in, or related to, a variety of institutional systems, each of which has validity or operation in relation to some range of concerns, none of which is absolute over all the others, and all of which, for most purposes, can operate without serious mutual conflict in areas of overlap? If this as possible practically as it clearly is conceptually, it would involve a diffusion of political power centres as well as of legal authorities. It would depend on a high degree of relatively willing co-operation and a relatively low degree of coercion in its direct and naked forms. It would create space for a real and serious debate about the demands of subsidiarity.[112]

Where MacCormick ended this piece – with a passionate cry for the possibility and desirability of a post-sovereign world governed by subsidiarity – was precisely where he took off in what can only be described as a flood of papers on the topic in the years that followed. Indeed, although many of the ideas in this 1992 lecture, and 1993 article, were not new, but rather outgrowths of his previous work on nationalism, the piece did spur both MacCormick on to develop further the concepts hinted at (especially subsidiarity) as well as inspired many others, including a new generation of constitutional theorists and scholars of EC/EU law.[113]

[112] MacCormick, 'Beyond the Sovereign State' (1993), 17.

[113] Michael Wilkinson described the 1993 piece as 'the article that launched a thousand more': Wilkinson, 'Beyond the Post-Sovereign State?' (2019), 6. The piece continues to generate scholarship, e.g., very recently, it was said to 'embody the spirit of the time': see Scarcello, *Radical Constitutional Pluralism* (2023), 18. 'Constitutional pluralism', which was said to be inaugurated by this article, has developed into a very large literature, e.g., see Avbelj and Komárek, *Constitutional Pluralism in the EU and Beyond* (2012); Jaklic, *Constitutional Pluralism in the EU* (2014); Krisch, *Beyond Constitutionalism* (2010) and 'Who's Afraid of Radical Pluralism?' (2011); and Flynn, *The Triangular Constitution* (2019). Part of the reason for the mushrooming of the literature was that the 1993 paper, and the very idea of constitutional pluralism, was controversial, generating both strong support and strong dissent, see, e.g., Loughlin, 'Constitutional Pluralism' (2014); Eleftheriadis, 'Pluralism and Integrity' (2010); and Walker, 'Constitutional Pluralism Revisited' (2016). The debate has continued into the 2020s, e.g., Canihac, 'Law and Virtue in a Post-Sovereign Commonwealth' (2021).

Subsidiarity: Making Democratic Europe Work

What was subsidiarity and how did it fit into MacCormick's vision for Europe as a post-sovereign commonwealth – a commonwealth in which nations, such as Scotland, could fully participate, but not necessarily in the form of sovereign states? From the outset, whether as mentioned in the 1992 lecture, or as repeated in, for instance, his 1994 acceptance speech on receiving an honorary doctorate at the University of Saarland in Germany, 'subsidiarity' was a kind of replacement language for 'sovereignty', a more practically oriented, problem-solving, language, which would help distribute 'decision-making ... at the most appropriate level'.[114] 'The demise of sovereignty' was an opportunity that the language of 'subsidiarity' could take up – a gap it could fill – thereby pointing the path towards a brighter future.

MacCormick was very conscious, it should be added, of the deployment of the language of sovereignty in the form of 'popular sovereignty' – including of course by the SNP, but also more broadly in Scotland via the Claim of Right and the Scottish Constitutional Convention – but he largely sought to steer this towards a defence of democracy via subsidiarity: popular democracy mattered, but it had to be properly managed and distributed across forms of collaboration and co-operation amongst nations. There were dangers in taking popular democracy too far, resulting in 'monolithic democracy', which was especially dangerous for minorities within states.[115] The prospect of subsidiarity within the EU offers precisely the opportunity of realising, but also carefully steering, the undoubted, but still qualified, value of democracy.[116]

Again, subsidiarity here operated as a kind of mirror image – a practical, political realisation, within Europe – of civic, liberal nationalism, i.e., a kind of nationalism that sought out unities that it could participate in rather than beating its breast and separating itself out from 'others'.[117] Once more, language really mattered, and MacCormick was encouraging us all to give up the language of sovereignty in preference to that of subsidiarity.[118]

114 MacCormick, 'Sovereignty, Democracy, Subsidiarity' (1994), 289.

115 See, e.g., MacCormick, 'Sovereignty: Myth and Reality' (1994), 237–8.

116 See ibid; but also many pieces in this vein in the mid to late 1990s, including: 'What Place for Nationalism' (1994); 'Sovereignty, Democracy, Subsidiarity' (1995); 'Sovereignty or Subsidiarity' (1998); 'Does a Nation Need a State' (1999). The sheer number of publications, alongside related speeches and presentations, shows how much this mattered to MacCormick: he spoke and wrote himself repeatedly and intensively into this new language, this new political imaginary.

117 MacCormick, 'Liberalism, Nationalism and the Post-Sovereign State' (1996), 566–7.

118 MacCormick did this not only in his academic writings, but also in pieces of journalism or more public-facing publications throughout the 1990s, e.g., see 'Independence has to be

In the piece that perhaps best articulated MacCormick's theory of democracy, via subsidiarity – 'Democracy, Subsidiarity, and Citizenship in the "European Commonwealth"' (1997), which began life as the Annual European Lecture at Queen Mary and Westfield College delivered on 11 November 1996 – MacCormick first situated discussions of democracy in Europe by tracing the 'evolution' of the latter. Every time there has been an enlargement, new treaties of accession were signed; in addition to these, there have been numerous 'amendments and consolidations', especially 'the *Single European Act* of 1983 and the *Maastricht Treaty* of 1992'.[119] Further, this evolution has proceeded in such a manner that, at least internally within the EC, neither the Member States, nor the EC itself, were fully sovereign: the powers previously 'vested in a sovereign state ... are no longer exercisable by a single power-structure with a single normative frame'; they have instead 'been diffused or parcelled out in a new distinctive way'; in other words, Europe developed into post-sovereignty.[120] Finally, post-sovereign Europe has, over time, developed into being a 'thing-of-its-own-kind', which MacCormick proposed to call a 'commonwealth', in homage to Hume's 'utopian jeu d'esprit, "The Idea of a Perfect Commonwealth"':

> The particular point of what we can call 'a commonwealth' is that it should comprise a group of people to whom can reasonably be imputed some consciousness that they have a 'common weal', something which really is a common good, and who are able to envisage themselves or their political representatives and governing authorities realising this or striving after it through some form of organised political structure, embodied in some common constitutional arrangements... Here, in Europe we have something which is a constituted order, which does have however imperfectly a legal constitution, whose members have certain vital interests in peace and prosperity that they can best pursue as common interests through policies oriented towards this common good.[121]

It may be that the overall self-consciousness in the EC was rather thin – perhaps mainly civic, and thus oriented towards institutions, but still, it seemed possible to say that this kind of communal self-consciousness had evolved.[122] In short, over time, Europe had developed into a sui generis

transformed from abstract ideal to concrete proposal' (1998); 'A Parliament once again?' (1998); as well as in public debates or policy documents.

119 MacCormick, 'Democracy, Subsidiarity, Citizenship' (1997), 335.

120 Ibid., 338.

121 Ibid., 339.

122 Ibid., 342.

legal order: a post-sovereign commonwealth. MacCormick's characterisation of Europe as an evolved constitutional order played a significant role, later during and after the Convention on the Future of Europe, with MacCormick arguing that Europe already had a constitution – the question was just whether and how to formalise it. But it was also important descriptively and normatively in other ways.

It was important descriptively because it allowed one to argue that Europe was a legal order not because – certainly not merely because – it was the outcome of a treaty between Member States, but rather, because it had acquired 'a close woven texture and a continuity' among its 'institutions and organs' alongside its 'self-referentiality', i.e., its reference to itself as a system.[123] It was, as we shall see in Chapter 9, an institutional normative order.

It was important normatively, in turn, because this kind of institutional development, which constituted it as a legal order (and was thus a kind of living, informal constitution of it), offered the conditions under which democracy, at least of a certain kind, could develop and flourish. As MacCormick put it in a piece published at the same time as this piece, democracy could be understood as something 'emerging from gradualist constitutionalism'; perhaps it could even be said it was 'more a consequence than a cause of constitutional government',[124] even if, in the case of Europe's evolution, one could still trace (however imperfectly) the democratic endorsement of the various treaties and amendments to them.[125]

So what kind of democracy, then, emerged from this evolved constitutional order, this post-sovereign commonwealth, as it had become? Well that form was what we might call 'subsidiarity' – a kind of exercise of deliberation, or practical reason, which asked:

> ...the question where it is best for the common good that a particular power be exercised, how far locally on a basis of local knowledge and understanding, how far centrally in a way that equalises the situation, at any rate the normative situation, in a very wide-reaching way but with a cost in the overriding of local knowledge. It is after all desirable as far as possible for people to be masters of their own destiny at the level of individual and local-communal life, without losing the power to operate in a large scale economy that can create the conditions for the kind of decent prosperity that may well be the necessary guarantee of durable peace.[126]

123 Ibid., 344–5.
124 MacCormick, 'Jurisprudence, Democracy' (1998), 1098.
125 MacCormick, 'Democracy, Subsidiarity, Citizenship' (1997), 335.
126 Ibid., 338–9.

Answering this question, as to the appropriate level of decision-making, was, MacCormick suggested, dependent on the kind of good that was sought to be protected. Here, MacCormick a four-fold distinction of different kinds of subsidiarity – and, at once, four different kinds of democratic processes – that could protect different kinds of goods, precisely within this post-sovereign commonwealth.

These four were: first, 'market subsidiarity', i.e., a kind of subsidiarity that protects 'market goods', and thus one that 'enables individuals and corporate groups of individuals to make their own free choices about matters they ought to be free to decide and contributes to enhanced if not always equal prosperity';[127] second, 'communal subsidiarity', which is responsive to 'the need to have a rich and varied range of institutions belonging quite as much to civil society as to the state within which individual self-realisation can be fostered and developed',[128] and which thus includes 'freedom of marriage and association, and a rich range of voluntary bodies open for participation' as well as 'forms of public self-government at a level local enough to support and reflect senses of civic and cultural identity';[129] third, 'rational legislative subsidiarity', which 'endorses the need for effective representative democracy expressed through legislation at provincial, federal, and all-Europe levels', discouraging 'all-Europe institutions that would unduly overshadow more local ones';[130] and, finally, as a fourth type, 'comprehensive subsidiarity', which MacCormick argued 'requires the adoption of practices and fora for deliberation that are as open and accessible as possible, even if rights of audience in particular fora are necessarily regulated and restricted'.[131]

This may be complex and dense, but that was because democracy itself, as a value, was not one-stranded or one-dimensional. As filtered through the deliberative procedure of subsidiarity in a post-sovereign commonwealth, it protected different kinds of goods, responding to different needs and requirements of individuals and communities. Further, this was precisely the kind of complexity that had evolved in the EC. The last thing the EC needed was a kind of constitution de-novo, some kind of grand design approach to constitution-making for Europe.[132] Instead, what the EC needed was a recognition of the complexity it had developed, i.e., a

[127] Ibid., 354.
[128] Ibid., 351.
[129] Ibid., 354.
[130] Ibid.
[131] Ibid.
[132] Ibid., 355.

complex, particular kind of democracy that was the singular outcome of its gradual constitutionalism. It is, indeed, this project that MacCormick took himself to be participating in when he became an Alternate Member of the Convention on the Future of Europe, and thus a drafter of the European Constitution.

It is interesting that, perhaps akin to his approach to Scottish nationalism, and his embrace of gradualism in that context, that MacCormick saw democracy in Europe, via the machinery of subsidiarity, as a kind of receding horizon, always in the future, always imperfect, and thus always something that was 'still-to-be-elaborated'.[133] It was as if, for MacCormick, the value in question was so complex that its perfect realisation had always to be deferred: all we could manage, in the here and now, was necessarily imperfect deliberation towards it.

This is certainly one aspect of what is significant about MacCormick's turn from 'sovereignty' to 'subsidiarity' in his lexicon for the emerging age. But another lies in the history of the word itself. In an unpublished lecture MacCormick delivered at the University of Iceland, on 1 March 1999, he looked again at subsidiarity, but this time in the context of academic governance. Significantly, in this context, he placed subsidiarity in dialogue with collegiality.

In examining the history of the term, MacCormick argued that its origins lay 'in the nineteenth century papal encyclical Quadregesimo Anno of Pius IX'.[134] Here, the Pope had described the way that the modern state had grown to such an extent that it was no longer serving humans; instead, it was oppressing them. This was the opposite of what the state was for: 'The state's proper function in relation to the individual, he [the Pope] said, is one of subsidium, of help'.[135] But this was not help that was at odds with human flourishing: it ought not to stand in the way, but instead enhance, flourishing. This sense of subsidiarity (as a form of respectful aid) was taken up 'during the twentieth century' by 'various Catholic moral theologians and political thinkers', including, within the UK, by John Finnis.[136] Within the EC, the term 'subsidiarity' was employed in ways that echoed these sentiments, namely to ward off the possibility of an 'over-mighty state', including both the prospects of a 'European

133 MacCormick, 'After Sovereignty' (1998), 38.

134 MacCormick, 'Subsidiarity and Academic Governance', University of Iceland (1 March 1999), 3.

135 Ibid.

136 Ibid., 4.

super-state', but also over-centralised Member States.[137] Now appearing in the *Maastricht Treaty*, including in its preamble, though without it yet being clear how exactly it would function, the prospect was there for it to protect the EC's evolved status as a post-sovereign commonwealth, and thus one that diffused power, relating it in more complex ways to the different levels of flourishing within the EC.

Conceived of as this form of respectful aid – helping others to develop their own self-respect, their own sense of identity, albeit still within a community, or indeed many levels of community (something that also echoes his mother's sensibility) – it is no surprise that MacCormick connected it, in this lecture, to collegiality. Collegiality, as defined by MacCormick, 'calls for a relatively egalitarian mutual regard among team-members, and a readiness to share, and over to interchange in the performance of, functions and responsibilities'.[138] In a way, collegiality, so conceived, was also an aspect of democracy – of the possibility of a democratic 'style of work and work management'.[139] Democracy within an academic institution is, as it is on a wider scale in a society, a complex business, and there are many different levels at which decisions need to be taken. Here, what is important to see is that subsidiarity and collegiality worked together – both were expressions of mutual respect and mutual regard and both enabled academic freedom (yet another, third value, interlocked with the other two). If such academic freedom is to flourish, then academic institutions, i.e., universities, must avoid adopting a kind of '"managerial" culture that threatens the primacy of subsidiarity and collegiality in academia'.[140] For MacCormick, when the relations between subsidiarity, collegiality, and academic freedom were lost, academia also lost its quality as an academic activity and became, instead, a business enterprise.

Reflexive Identities

This brief detour into academic governance allows us to see that, for MacCormick, subsidiarity was an ideal – a value – deeply set within his character: it amounted to a kind of respect for others; not a cold respect, but instead a warm and enthusiastic willingness to help (to be collegiate), but one that did not seek to overtake the identity of another, allowing the

[137] Ibid., 4–5.
[138] Ibid., 8.
[139] Ibid.
[140] Ibid., 20.

identity of another to flourish. This deeper association of subsidiarity with identity was, arguably, one of the reasons why MacCormick often stressed that 'subsidiarity' was 'a watchword for our times'.[141]

Further, this association was also clearly on the minds of his fellow colleagues in Edinburgh, for whom reflection on the legal theory of European integration was very centrally concerned with questions of identity, and with how complex such questions were.[142] What one could see, in one perspective, as a matter of conceptualising validity – seeing legal systems as interlocking and overlapping – one could also treat as a matter of identity, with identities too being seen precisely as interlocking and overlapping. In a way, the EU, and its pluralism – a pluralism governed precisely by subsidiarity, a kind of respect for persons and their flourishing within a community – offered precisely an opportunity for reflection on the complexities of one's identity.[143] MacCormick's colleague, Zenon Bańkowski, demonstrated it – if not performed it (in his trademark lyric-analytic style) – in the following way:

> In defining myself as Scots I do not thereby have to exclude because I can say that I am Scottish because I am not English but we are both European. This does not have to be a vertically layering of identities on the lines of the Russian doll model. I do not have to exclude the English for I can see it as part of the way that I define myself. For I bring in Englishness into my identity when I try and make sense of myself as European. But the point here is to see myself as *Scottish* European (and not the other way round) so that the identity is a local one at the start. In starting like this, I realise that my identity now consists, in part at least, of those whom I excluded in an earlier

[141] See MacCormick, 'Decentralisation, Devolution' (1999), 198, where the two are linked explicitly.

[142] These were of course also questions for many others: e.g., see Weiler's influential 'The Transformation of Europe' (1991).

[143] See Bańkowski, MacCormick, Scott, 'The European Union?' (1995); see also Bańkowski and Christodoulidis, 'The European Union as an Essentially Contested Project' (1998). There remains a story to be told about Edinburgh Law School in these years – especially in the 1990s – being a cauldron of philosophical activity on relations between law and Europe, in ways that were both informed by the detailed policy changes in European governance, but that also probed political and existential depths in new ways. For instance, work in Edinburgh on law and Europe in these years included extensive reflection on processes of legal reasoning in Europe, e.g., Bengoetxea, *The Legal Reasoning of the European Court of Justice* (1993). There were thus creative affinities being generated between what was happening in Europe, theories of private law, and work on legal reasoning, including the prospects of legal artificial intelligence (e.g., see Bańkowski, White, and Hahn, *Informatics and the Foundations of Legal Reasoning* [1995]). Edinburgh, in this respect, was a multi-dimensional centre of research on law in Europe in ways that were rare in England.

> operation, the English. For to think of myself as Scottish European means also that I have to accept that it means that part of my Scottishness is English for they are English Europeans. So my Scottish identity changes as also does my European one. The English, the French and the Germans and so on can do this, as do groups at levels below the nation state. This means that we come to nuanced views of our identities which in the many cross cutting intersections and inclusions and exclusions means that nobody is fully cut out. Moreover since this is always in flux I can never be in a permanent state of exclusion for no one can tell where the next encounter might lead.[144]

Here, then, is a performance of European identity – reflexive, existential, never-ending, set very much within interlocking relations and ever-new encounters – that was the corollary, at the level of individual character, of subsidiarity as an institutional value within the EU.

It was also the kind of identity that MacCormick often went out of his way to praise and admire in others, such as in his friend, Allan Macartney, of whom he wrote that 'He was a living embodiment of the nationalism that is tolerant, inclusive, and universalist in outlook and commitment. For him, the fundamental principle in politics was that of self-determination for individuals and for peoples.[145] Macartney, as MacCormick saw him, was as much a Scot as he was a European: in fact, the latter helped him be a Scot of a particular kind. MacCormick might just as well have been describing himself: to be European, for him, was to be able to express one's self-respect and identity, in his case as a Scot, while simultaneously working, helping, but always respectful, with due regard, to others and their own self-respect and sense of distinction. This was an identity of overlapping and interlocking differences – a kind of differential unity. In a way, the prospect of such an identity was the very point and promise of Europe, and philosophy, at its best, might help pursue that project, e.g., via the adoption and extrapolation of the language of subsidiarity.

An Imperfect Commonwealth? Europe's Practical Realities

Armed with this decade-long argument for a post-sovereign commonwealth governed by subsidiarity, MacCormick was suddenly catapulted from operating politically behind the scenes (at least with respect to party politics) and straight into a fiery political cauldron, right on the frontlines of European politics: the European Parliament. Not only, however, did he become an MEP, but, as luck would have it, his stint as a Parliamentarian

144 Bańkowski, 'The Journey of the European Ideal' (1999), 168.
145 MacCormick, 'Macartney' (1998).

coincided with the Convention on the Future of Europe and the drafting of a European Constitution. For someone with MacCormick's interests and skills, this was almost too good to be true: here, his philosophical vision, his new lexicon, and, most importantly, his character – his manner or style of relating with others – would be thrust into the limelight and put to the test. In this section, I want to, briefly and inadequately, say how he fared, including how he himself reflected on the experience.

In doing so, I pay particular attention to the mix of the continued enthusiasm for and belief in the European project that MacCormick so consistently espoused, but now placed alongside what were some hard-learnt lessons in its realities. Of course, MacCormick was no stargazing idealist, no matter how romantic and utopian he could at times be, and there were plenty of instances prior to his stint as MEP where he confronted the sense of the difficulty of reality within the EU. In fact, no one with an interest in, and hope for, the EU, could avoid such confrontations, for there were constant tensions between Member States and EU institutions, perhaps especially at the level of adjudication, and thus between the EJC and domestic Constitutional Courts. Sometimes, especially in relation to certain sensitive issues of special importance in certain states (such as debates over abortion in Ireland), the political discourse became particularly tense, and this was reflected in academic works that polarised the discussion. From MacCormick's perspective, given the hope placed in Europe as a theatre for a new kind of politics, such polarisation of the debate needed to be addressed and hope needed to be restored.

What Kind of Pluralism?

A good example of this, and of MacCormick's response to it, was his view of Diarmuid Rossa Phelan's *Revolt or Revolution* (1997). In this book, Phelan, with attention to both French and Irish – but especially Irish – constitutionalism, argued that matters had come to a head in the relations between the EU and Member States. According to Phelan, the ECJ was effectively forcing a 'judge-made constitution for Europe', which was corrosive of the sovereignty, including the constitutional identity, of the Member States.[146] This was being done, Phelan argued, without the consent of the Member States: the ECJ, with its claim for being a *sui generis* legal system, and its doctrines of 'supremacy, direct effect, transfer of sovereign rights, and the rest of it' had simply moved far beyond what had

[146] MacCormick, 'Risking Constitutional Collision' (1998), 523.

been agreed to with the accession treaties, and thus beyond the will of the contracting parties.[147] For Phelan, this meant that there was now a stark choice facing constitutional courts in Member States: revolt or revolution (hence the title of the book). As MacCormick summarised it:

> State constitutional courts or supreme courts with constitutional functions will be driven to the point where one or other of two paths must be taken. Either loyalty to Community law will force them to sanction a revolution in their own state, a constitutionally unauthorised change of the constitution that will effectively transfer the people's sovereignty to organs of the Union. Or loyalty to the constitution as expression of the people's sovereign mastery of their state will sanction a revolt against the constitution of the Community, and the decisions of the ECJ that have created it.[148]

For someone who espoused 'constitutional pluralism' – the view that it was not necessary, in theorising the relations between legal orders that each claimed constitutional status (such as the EU and the Member States), to posit one as superior to the other, with one validating the other, but instead to see them as overlapping and interlocking, with some inevitable indeterminacy, thereby paying regard and respect to how each saw themselves vis-à-vis the other – this was clearly a challenge. Could pluralism, as MacCormick had conceived it, hold back the kind of oppositional rhetoric that was emerging in views precisely like that of Phelan's? Was there too much of a danger that this kind of pluralism could reduce down to the kind of stark choice that Phelan argued for: revolt or revolution?

MacCormick, as we have seen, was averse to the language of 'revolution' – he had argued, for instance, that despite the profound changes instituted by the 1972 European Communities Act, there was no 'revolution' as such in the UK.[149] Throughout MacCormick's work on Europe, as indeed when theorising constitutional change in the UK, the emphasis was always on evolution, both descriptively and normatively. But what to do when the discourse – in popular politics as well as in academia – boiled over into this fiery language, this characterisation of a crisis? Faced with this, MacCormick clearly felt that he needed to inject extra resources into his pluralistic picture – to bring the parties to the table, showing them they did have some common ground, that the choice was not as stark as they thought, that there was no real crisis, but instead the usual kind of undoubtedly difficult, but not intractable, negotiation between equal partners.

147 Ibid.
148 Ibid., 522.
149 See MacCormick, 'After Sovereignty' (1998).

It was in this context, and responding thus to this kind of oppositional discourse, that MacCormick suggested that rather than 'radical pluralism' – according to which the law ran out in cases of conflict between Member State Constitutional Courts and the ECJ – there was another kind of pluralism: 'pluralism under international law'.[150] For MacCormick, the point of this was precisely to maintain 'pluralism', i.e., to avoid relating the Member States and the EU hierarchically. For instance, he did not want the kind of Kelsenian 'monism' that would see international law as superior, validating the EU, which in turn validated the Member States (nor the other way, with international law validating the Member States which then, via a treaty, validated the EU).[151] He was adamant that his analysis did not collapse into a theory that showed the 'constitutional dependency' of either the Member States on the EU or the EU on the Member States. The relations between the two had to remain 'interactive rather than hierarchical'.[152] This was not just a matter of abstract theory: it was a matter of character; it was deeply important for MacCormick to show that, for all the practical difficulties this may entail, one could have relations of mutual respect and regard between Member States and the EU such that neither was superior or dominant to the other. At stake was the possibility of peaceful and positive relations between communities.

To maintain such relations, then, MacCormick argued that it might be possible to see international law functioning 'in a kind of coordinate way … as a common ground of validity both of Member State systems and of Community, neither being therefore a sub-system of the other, but both cohering within a common legal universe governed by the norms of international law'.[153] The point here was not to offer a monistic theory of law, such that for there to be law, there had to be one, ultimate, superior criterion of validity, which validated all other legal systems. This was not MacCormick 'converting' from pluralism to monism.[154] This was MacCormick responding pragmatically to the kind of oppositional discourse being articulated by figures like Phelan – a discourse that risked making it seem as if there was no middle ground, but only stark conflict, only crisis. The point was to see if law could play the kind of role that MacCormick saw theory itself playing: recognising both sides as equal, relating them heterarchically.

150 MacCormick, 'Risking Constitutional Collision' (1998), 527.

151 Ibid., 528.

152 Ibid.

153 Ibid., 527.

154 As it has been read by numerous commentators: see, e.g., Eleftheriadis, 'Pluralism and Integrity' (2010).

Perhaps reacting over-generously to certain writings at the time, which sought to apply Kelsen to the EU and international legal order,[155] MacCormick called this 'pluralism under international law' an 'instance of "monism" in Kelsen's sense', though he then quickly added that Kelsen himself never did 'contemplate the kind of tertium quid between international and municipal law that the Community constitutes according to the "sui generis" interpretation here endorsed'.[156] This was, indeed, one of a number of examples where perhaps MacCormick's disposition to be inclusive, to be responsive to the voices of others, also obscured what he was really trying to say.

Indeed, we do a disservice to MacCormick's creativity – his pursuit of something resolutely relational and interactive, something possibly heterarchical rather than necessarily hierarchical – if we read the above statement, uncharitably, de-contextually, as an ultimate endorsement of monism. For MacCormick, the role and value of philosophy consisted, in large part, in how it enabled us to relate to one other: how it encouraged us to regard each other with respect, to avoid placing ourselves first or in a dominant position over another, and thus fail in our active considerateness towards them. If, at times, this required somewhat strange, odd, ambiguous, hard-to-articulate, conceptual footwork – such as arguably 'pluralism under international law' – then so be it: the point was that philosophy served the quality of relations in common life, not that it dictated them, standing above them, determining dogmatically what must be. It is in this spirit that we need to read MacCormick's suggestion of 'pluralism under international law'. The whole point was to avoid the kind of task that Phelan recommended to Member State Courts. As MacCormick put it:

> Simply to remit to state courts an unreviewable power to determine the range of domestic constitutional absolutes that set limits upon the domestic applicability of Community law may be to invite a slow fragmentation of community law; yet it is a clear international obligation of states not to fragment the Community by unilateral decisions either judicial or legislative (or, for that matter, executive). Ross Phelan's proposal gives an unsatisfactorily unbounded discretion to state courts in permitting, for the sake of the domestic constitution, limitation of the local effectiveness of Community law.[157]

155 Especially Richmond, 'Preserving the Identity Crisis' (1997); see MacCormick, 'Risking Constitutional Collision' (1998), 524, fn7.

156 MacCormick, 'Risking Constitutional Collision' (1998), 530.

157 Ibid., 531.

If, in order to avoid Member State Constitutional Courts behaving in this way, it meant placing under review any neat conceptual distinctions between monism and pluralism, then this was a price worth paying. Conceptual dogma could not stand in the way of good quality, workable, relations between either legal systems or persons. As always, there were no sacred cows. 'Pluralism under international law' was, as MacCormick put it, 'contextually more persuasive and appropriate';[158] what really mattered was precisely what was contextually appropriate (rather than conceptually pure). As he added, later, when revising this piece for inclusion in *Questioning Sovereignty*, this called on parties to exercise 'wisdom' when approaching 'problem situations', encouraging them to look for resources (e.g., in international law), rather than resolve to either revolt or revolution.[159] However difficult conceptually, one could always strive to facilitate the exercise of practical reason: a relational reason, which kept the conversation going, kept the relationship working, and thus showed mutual respect, regard, and considerateness towards each other.

European Law-Making

Of course, this was 1998, and, in 1999, MacCormick would not only witness the inauguration – the return – of the Scottish Parliament, but also his own personal elevation into active politics, being elected as a SNP MEP on 10 June 1999. That this was an emotional moment for MacCormick goes without saying: writing in 2002, reflecting on what it meant to be Scottish, MacCormick first recalled: 'Seldom if ever have I felt such exhilaration as on 1 July 1999, on the occasion of the formal opening of the Scottish Parliament, and the celebrations throughout Edinburgh on that mild July evening. Everybody around was happy, and everybody positive. We hadn't got a parliament to score a point against somebody else, but just to affirm ourselves'.[160]

After tracing his own family roots in Scotland, he finished this brief piece by saying:

> In my professional life, as in the European Parliament, I move in a completely international milieu, while remaining consciously an heir of the massively significant philosophical tradition of the democratic intellect

[158] Ibid., 532.
[159] MacCormick, Q. S. (1999), 121.
[160] MacCormick, 'Being Scottish' (2002), 152.

> and of Scots law. I hope that means that I am very Scottish, but not narrowly so, and that my highly liberal nationalism is the other face of my internationalism.[161]

There is no doubt that MacCormick carried this universalistic Scottishness with him into the European Parliament – combining a genuine pride in being Scottish, wearing the kilt and playing the bagpipes,[162] with working for, as he saw it, the good of the EU.

'Work' is, indeed, the operative term, for to say that MacCormick's time in the European Parliament was busy would be a very considerable understatement: as an SNP MEP, he became a member of the Green/European Free Alliance Group, and came to serve as their Ombudsman;[163] he served, too, as Vice President of the 'Intergroup on Stateless Nations'; from 2002 to 2003, as has already been noted, he was an Alternate Member of the Convention on the Future of Europe, tasked with drafting the European Constitution;[164] he was also a member of numerous Parliamentary Committees and official delegations;[165] and, in addition to all this, he was of course a Parliamentarian for his constituency[166] as well as a vital

161 Ibid., 154.

162 Many have commented to me on how MacCormick took every opportunity to joyfully express his Scottishness at the European Parliament, including to passersby in the street (Hudghton, interview).

163 For more in his role in the EFA, see Dauwen and Vanhaelewyn, *European Free Alliance* (2006). Catherine Stihler, who was Labour MEP in the same period as MacCormick, recalled MacCormick championed the phrase 'internal enlargement', and that his combination of attention to 'detail', 'gregariousness', and 'reasonableness' meant he was able to play the role of reconciling tensions, e.g., between Greens and the EFA, making him the ideal Ombudsman for the group (interview). Numerous others who worked alongside him in this period commented on how he was a 'wordsworth' (though also often spoke 'too fast'), that he was always 'comfortable looking at texts', that he was 'level-headed', and that his 'enthusiasm' was infectious (interviews with author from a visit to the European Parliament).

164 Officially, he represented EFA with Johannes Voggenhuber of the Austrian Greens representing the Greens. It was acknowledged by the EFA that MacCormick voiced the 'standpoints of the EFA subgroup' numerous times, perhaps especially in his 'Democracy at Many Levels': see Dauwen and Vanhaelewyn, *European Free Alliance* (2006), 82.

165 Including the Committee on Legal Affairs and the Internal Market; the Committee on Constitutional Affairs; the Temporary Committee of the Echelon Interception System; and Parliamentary delegations to Japan and Romania.

166 There are many examples of the detailed work he did here, e.g., speaking to the Argyll & Bute Council on 2 May 2002, MacCormick covered policy changes, including his efforts at influencing them, with respect to ferries, live animal transport (and generally higher transport costs for the islands), depopulation, Gaelic, structural funding, Common Agricultural Policy, renewable energy, tourism, and environmental law.

liaison between policymaking in the EU and in the SNP,[167] serving as the SNP Vice President (from 1999 to 2004), amidst what were important changes in this period, directly affecting Scotland's voice in Europe.[168] By all accounts, he performed all these tasks with incredible skill and flair, and with almost infinite energy, resulting, for instance, in his being voted Scottish Euro MP of the Year three years in a row.

Telling the full story of MacCormick's period as MEP, and his contributions to the many committees and issues he engaged with in these years, is a task for another time. My aim, instead, is to give just a taste of this, with a view in particular for considering how his involvement can be said to be related to his character, and thus to his manner or style of relating with others. I begin first with his experience as a Parliamentarian, and then go on to discuss his role in the Convention on the Future of Europe as well as his evaluation of this constitutional project.

In a 2005 paper, MacCormick reflected on his time in Parliament.[169] Looking back, he characterised his own view expressed in the 1990s, in particular about the democratic credentials of the EU, as 'an optimistic one, even perhaps a naively complacent one'.[170] Back then, as he now saw it, he had 'suggested that the European Union did provide a setting in which these values [the various goods, as we saw, that the EU order sought to protect] could flourish through a distribution of powers guided by the principle of subsidiarity'.[171]

For this to work in practice – to be instantiated in reality – those who exercise such powers had to be answerable to those whose lives they affect, precisely by exercising such powers. But were they? Here, MacCormick

[167] Including a re-issue, with changes, of the 'SNP Constitution for a Future Independent Scotland' in 2002, and generally advising the SNP on the machinery for independence in Europe: see MacCormick, 'Is There a Constitutional Path' (2000). This also included voicing concerns of the SNP with respect to certain matters in the draft European Constitution, especially in relation to fisheries, e.g., writing to Jack Straw, then Secretary of State, on 28 May 2004, Alex Salmond quotes an opinion of MacCormick's, relying explicitly on his expertise as a 'Professor of Constitutional Law', as to how detrimental it would be for the EU to have exclusive competence over marine biological resources.

[168] For example, e.g., relating to calls for greater participation by 'constitutional regions' in EU policymaking, as was articulated by the 2001 Flanders Declaration: see here, for example, MacCormick's 'Comment on the Governance Paper' (2001), a comment on the European Commission's White's Paper on Governance.

[169] MacCormick, 'Legislative Deliberation' (2005). This was initially delivered, in a slightly different version in 2001: 'Can Europe be Democratic?', Ledingham Chalmers Lecture, University of Aberdeen (10 May 2001).

[170] MacCormick, 'Legislative Deliberation' (2005), 286.

[171] Ibid.

argued that one of the biggest deficiencies of law-making in the EU was its proneness to being done 'in camera', i.e., secretively and behind the scenes, with no real prospect of accountability, transparency, or answerability:

> ...too much of the work is in effect done by the Committee of Permanent Representatives, and delegated bodies subordinate to it. National civil servants meeting in private hammer out mutually acceptable proposals in the light of governmental instructions. Ministers in Council then effectively confirm what is already mainly a done deal. This protected Ministers-as-European-legislators from being made effectively answerable to their home parliament and electorate. The proper role of the Member State parliaments as part of the process of democratic checks on the governance of Europe was thereby substantially undermined.[172]

There were issues here both with the Council and the Commission. The Council, at least before 2002, 'deliberates in secret even when it is engaged in the enactment of laws'.[173] The Commission, in turn, which is 'an extra-parliamentary executive on which the Treaties confer ... the principal power of legislative initiative' is only 'indirectly elected, through a process of Council nomination and parliamentary confirmation'.[174] There were checks in place, especially via the Court of First Instance and the European Court of Justice, and MacCormick was positive about these institutions, saying of them that they 'do effectively secure the rule of law at European level'.[175] Overall, there were serious issues with, though some positive aspects and further prospects for improvement in, the democratic legitimacy of the European law-making process.

MacCormick's tone in these reflections was a mixture of practical frustration and cautious optimism. Yes, it was 'extraordinarily busy and demanding ... full of interruptions ... with far too little time to think' through the issues and questions that came before one; 'You are called upon to cast vote after vote without always being comfortable that you have grasped what is at issue and are voting with proper reflection'; in addition, 'requests pour in from constituents and lobbyists'; it is 'all very hectic, but you survive it somehow'.[176] Despite this lack of time, the process was such that one could exercise one's judgement and engage in genuine scrutiny and

[172] Ibid., 287.
[173] Ibid.
[174] Ibid.
[175] Ibid.
[176] Ibid., 289–90. For a further insight into this, see MacCormick, 'MEP for a Day', and other speeches around this time (in late 2003/early 2004), where MacCormick speaks of the 'four main things' 'we do' as MEPs: 'We make laws, we influence policies, we hold the

debate, though necessarily on a narrow, selected range of issues, i.e., those that came before the Committees that one was part of.

Perhaps in part because of the lack of a link between the Parliament and the Commission – there being no government supporting this effective executive in the Commission – no party in the Parliament measures its success 'by reference to the degree to which the Commission's programme goes forward unscathed and unchanged'.[177] This meant that there was considerable scope for exercising 'one's own judgement on a balance of considerations', including 'one's own sense of the rightness, justice or wisdom of a given measure', and then to test this judgement in debate in Committee.[178]

The Committees worked by appointing rapporteurs on particular issues, which was subject to debate and further amendments, and finally a vote. This report, as voted for by a Committee, was then put forward to the Parliament in plenary, where it was further debated, amended, and voted on. Whereas genuine debate in Parliament was difficult (when MacCormick was an MEP, there were 662 members), the process within the Committee was robust and, thus, the overall 'structure and procedures of the parliament give space to individual members as such to play a considerable and active role, exercising responsible but independent judgement'.[179] There was, MacCormick thought, 'a rational and discursive quality' to legislative processes in the European Parliament, even if this fell 'well short of perfect rationality'.[180]

It is significant, though also unsurprising given his interests in practical reason, that the quality of deliberation in the European Parliament mattered so much to MacCormick. But, also characteristically, MacCormick examined this quality very much in the detailed and practical context of the relevant institutions. Thus, for instance, in the version of the above paper delivered as a speech in 2001, MacCormick focused specifically on the lack of transparency in deliberation in European governance. He noted that the 'present unreformed Treaties yield much obscurity and lack transparency'.[181] Part of the problem with how the EU worked was that 'in its intergovernmental aspects it has tended to shift the power

European Commission to account, and we use the platform of the EP as a lever to help solve problems': 1.

177 MacCormick, 'Legislative Deliberation' (2005), 289–90.

178 Ibid., 290–1.

179 Ibid., 294.

180 Ibid., 295.

181 MacCormick, 'Can Europe Be Democratic?' (2001), 16.

balance insider Member States in favour of the executive and against the legislature'[182] – this made law-making in Europe more a process of untransparent dialogues between executives (in the Member States and in the EU). 'Secretive legislation in a Council of Ministers', MacCormick added, 'whose work is prepared through a Committee of Permanent Representatives (COREPER), that is by the permanent servants of the executive branch, takes lawmaking away from elected lawmakers and puts it into what is in effect the foreign affairs portfolio of the executive'.[183] As he put it in another context, this was part of the problem with how the EU Arrest Warrant came into being: even if the idea was a 'perfectly reasonable one', 'it should never become law just on the say-so of Ministers set up for doing it by COREPER, insulated from parliamentary answerability either in their home parliaments or in the European Parliament'.[184]

Thus, the difficulty was that often the European Parliament was effectively bypassed, or not properly consulted, and neither were the national legislatures properly involved. All too frequently, law-making in Europe was a matter of 'executive intergovernmental collaboration', operating outside the 'loop of accountability'.[185] 'We need', MacCormick argued, 'more co-decision, and better co-decision that empowers national parliaments', including regional parliaments, like Scotland's.[186]

A little later, when delivering the 2006 Annual Lecture of the David Hume Society, on the prospects for democratic law-making in Europe, MacCormick found himself reaching for the slow, in many ways deliberately inefficient, process that Hume had articulated in his 'Idea for a Perfect Commonwealth'. Recalling again the process by which the European Arrest Warrant was created, including how it was incorporated into UK law (e.g., via the *Extradition Act* 2003), MacCormick argued that the issues raised by such legislation 'needed much greater testing before our democratically elected representatives'.[187] As it was, the law here came into being via 'a cabal of executive, through a unanimous agreement at the Council of Ministers', without any opportunity for 'amendment by Parliament'.[188] This was not good enough. It was because of processes

182 Ibid., 18.
183 Ibid.
184 MacCormick, 'A Common Approach to Crime' (2007), 538.
185 MacCormick, 'Can Europe Be Democratic?' (2001), 20.
186 Ibid., 21.
187 MacCormick, 'The EU and the Idea' (2006), 8.
188 Ibid. At the time, MacCormick had proposed an amendment, based on the Scottish one-hundred-and-ten-day rule, but this was ignored.

like this that democracy was lacking in Europe, resulting in Europe being 'not well understood and currently not well loved among its citizens'.[189] It was, MacCormick argued, 'vital that in some sense the European Union becomes better connected to European people'.[190]

Could Hume offer a solution? Possibly: the point of Hume's scheme, even if it was a jeu d'esprit, was to offer a scheme for decision-making that slowed it down and fragmented it into smaller parcels of genuine debate. In the context of Great Britain at the time, Hume argued for a 'Senate' alongside a 'popular assembly', but where the latter was subdivided: you first divided the country into one hundred counties, and then you divided those counties into one hundred parishes. These parishes would select representatives to the county assembly. This county assembly, in turn, would choose a representative to represent it in the Senate. What you had, in the result, was a Senate composed of representatives from the county assemblies, as well as of course the county assemblies themselves. Law would be made when the Senate and the majority of the counties supported it. Although complex, the point was to create a system of slow deliberation and considered judgement that was also localised, retaining a close link to the people, and creating institutions where genuine debate was possible (rather than a chamber composed of hundreds in one room). As MacCormick put it, this was a 'kind of government which can't be hurried into rapid and rash decisions'; indeed, it was 'effective' not by being 'efficient', but by being 'deliberately inefficient'.[191] Democracy, in Hume's conception, and endorsed by MacCormick, was 'a complexification device': 'if', MacCormick added, 'you believe in democracy, you necessarily believe in complex and slow decision-making in government'.[192]

How did the European Parliament fare in light of Hume's proposals? Well, in some ways it failed, for it deliberated in a chamber that was too large (732 members by the time of MacCormick's 2006 speech). On the other hand, the Parliament really worked by being subdivided into many committees. Within such committees, there are only 'about forty to fifty' people in the room at any one time that have 'speaking or voting rights'.[193] The debate, on any one issue, 'goes on typically over many weeks with numerous interchanges of views', including, as was already noted above,

189 MacCormick, 'The EU and the Idea' (2006), 10.
190 Ibid.
191 Ibid., 16.
192 Ibid., 16–17.
193 Ibid., 22.

'many writings and redraftings of reports with amendments and compromises among political groups'.[194]

Set up in this way, there was something of an echo of Hume's complexification of democratic reason in the European Parliament. But what was missing was the connection with the people. A large part of the problem was the media: as MacCormick recalled with respect to the vote on the Takeover Directive, which he was involved in, in 2001, the final vote on it in the plenary session of Parliament was thinly attended. But this was after a long and drawn-out process of debate within the relevant committees, including a long conciliation procedure between Council and Parliament. As reported, however, in the *Scotsman* at the time, all that was communicated to the public was the very thinly attended vote at the end. Nothing was said about all the prior scrutiny and debate.[195] What this meant was that citizens had no idea about how decision-making in the EU really worked. The 'information deficit' – as significant as, and related to, the 'democratic deficit' – meant a loss of legitimacy: 'Citizens who have only a vague idea what is going on are in a weak position to secure accountability of their representatives'.[196] Feeling that they are politically immobile – inert in part for lack of information – and thus without connection, citizens become disconnected.

When combined with the already problematic law-making processes mentioned earlier (the secrecy of the Council, the lack of any real consultation with the Parliament), all this combines to seriously harm the political meaningfulness of the EU. There is simply no 'common enterprise', no 'community', no 'peoplehood'.[197] It is not, it should be noted, that Europe needs 'a collective popular selfhood', a 'single personified demos', to be politically meaningful; but it does need some process of meaningful 'political participation',[198] and that was what was missing, at least as matters stood at present.[199]

[194] Ibid., 23.
[195] Ibid., 24.
[196] Ibid., 26.
[197] Ibid., 28.
[198] Ibid., 29.
[199] See also Armstrong, *Governing Social Inclusion* (2010), who argued that MacCormick's work on the EU as a '"civic political community" in which membership is voluntary and reflects a willingness to participate in and uphold common civic institutions' (which he traced to MacCormick, 'Liberalism, Nationalism' (1996)), offered a promising account of 'solidarity and social justice' in the EU, precisely because it did not require 'a singular EU vision of how these values might be realised', filtering down, instead, debate over, and 'practical expression' of, this into lower levels: 236–7.

Constitutionalising Europe

That was March 2006, and it came after the failure of the European Constitution. Even then, MacCormick was not forlorn: there was still a 'serious possibility' for political participation in Europe, for democracy within the EU. 'Current and still improvable constitutional arrangements' pointed to that.[200] MacCormick was not someone who gave up hope easily. Indeed, in the Convention leading up to the draft Constitution, MacCormick threw himself into the process with characteristic energy and optimism, as he did, after the process, when attempting to justify the Constitution, even if he was not wholly happy with it (most tellingly in *Who's Afraid of a European Constitution*?, 2005). A gradualist to the end, MacCormick thought the Constitution was a step in the right direction, even if the road ahead was long.

MacCormick made three key sole-authored interventions in the Convention (alongside making other contributions). These were: 'Subsidiarity, Common Sense and Local Knowledge' (18 September 2002); 'Democracy at Many Levels: European Constitutional Reform' (24 September 2002); and 'Stateless Nations and the Convention's Debate on Regions' (31 January 2003). Though short, these are fascinating philosophical works in their own right: individually and collectively, they illustrate MacCormick, the grounded, practical, detail-absorbing, and yet at the same time forward-looking, universalistic, and morally sensitive philosopher at work. In many ways, their titles speak for themselves: in the first, MacCormick asked whether the 'principle of subsidiarity' can 'be refined in a way that would help to solve citizens' resentment of the improper exclusion of local knowledge and common sense from playing its part in the application of European law?'.[201] He answered that it could and offered a related proposal, calling for Community measures to 'take due account of specific local circumstances'.[202] If local knowledge was not enlisted, and was instead ignored, then this would, MacCormick argued, 'contribute to undermining confidence in the usefulness and value of European laws'.[203]

In the second of his contributions, MacCormick argued forcefully for 'democracy at many levels', including the Union level, the Member

200 MacCormick, 'The EU and the Idea' (2006), 29.
201 MacCormick, 'Subsidiarity, Common Sense and Local Knowledge' (18 September 2002), 3.
202 Ibid.
203 Ibid., 4.

State level, the internal territorial level, and the level of local authorities.[204] If the EU was to avoid claims it was becoming a 'super state', then it had to take all these levels seriously. There was a need, within this 'supranational union of a unique kind'[205] to recognise 'the right to self-government of all those territorial entities in the Union whose citizens have a strong and shared sense of national, linguistic or regional identity'.[206] Crucial to this was stronger protection for subsidiarity. This was in part a matter of procedure – including imposing obligations on the Commission to consult with legislative authorities at various levels, as well as standing for territorial entities before the ECJ – but it was also a matter of language, e.g., precisely avoiding terms such as 'regions' and referring instead to 'territorial entities within the Union, which their citizens regard as "nations"'.[207]

The call for this sensitivity – this respect and regard – was very much echoed also in the third contribution, on 'Stateless Nations', where MacCormick argued for 'parity of esteem' for nations, such as Scotland, Flanders, Catalonia, Wales, and Galicia.[208] The protection of 'minority languages' was a key part of this call for esteem.[209] Throughout, by a combination of more abstract as well as more concrete proposals, MacCormick championed participation, consultation, and in general respect and regard for the diversity within the EU.

In addition to these contributions, MacCormick also made eighty proposed amendments to the text of the draft Constitution, authoring thirteen of these by himself.[210] Although tracing direct causal influence is always tricky, some have argued that both the resulting text of the Constitution and, after its demise (following the referenda on the Constitution in France and Holland in May 2005), the text of the Lisbon Treaty (which incorporated many provisions from the Constitution), include aspects, even sometimes the precise wording, that had been proposed by MacCormick in these amendments. Thus, for example, Article 3(3) of the Lisbon Treaty 'now requires that the EU respect its rich cultural and linguistic diversity',

[204] MacCormick, 'Democracy at Many Levels: European Constitutional Reform' (24 September 2002), 3.

[205] Ibid.

[206] Ibid., 2.

[207] Ibid., 5.

[208] MacCormick, 'Stateless Nations and the Convention's Debate on Regions' (31 January 2003), 3.

[209] Ibid., 5.

[210] See Scott, 'Stateless Nations' (2012), 193, fn.12.

and this emphasis has been argued to have been 'a direct result of several amendments proposed by MacCormick'.[211]

Similarly so with changes introduced in the Lisbon Treaty with respect to subsidiarity: here, 'The very definition of this principle has been imbued with a strong sub-state theme', laying down that 'EU level action can only be justified where the objectives of the proposed action cannot be sufficiently achieved by member states, acting "either at a central level or at regional or local scale"' (Article 5(3) of the Lisbon Treaty); this 'wording', it has been said, 'is the same as that proposed by Art III-9 of the Constitution', which had incorporated 'the substance of the proposed amendment put forward by MacCormick'.[212] Further roles for regional parliaments, and the requirement to consult them on legislative proposals, were also added to the Protocol on Subsidiarity and Proportionality, which again was traced to certain amendments proposed by MacCormick.[213]

As Joanne Scott, who traced these connections, has argued, these and other amendments made by MacCormick, even if they did not go as far as he would have liked, constituted an 'important first step in recognising the downwards diffusion of political power within Member States and the implications of this for the exercise of competence by the EU'.[214] Through these amendments, MacCormick contributed to our understanding of the EU – in promise, if not entirely in reality – as a 'pluralist, multi-level' commonwealth,[215] 'based not on ethnic association but a production of deliberation in Europe's organised political space',[216] and one that need not 'suppress a vibrant local politics below',[217] but even potentially enhance it.

Scott's judgement echoes that of others, including those that worked side by side with MacCormick in the Convention and the Parliament, e.g., Andrew Duff, who was a Liberal Democratic MEP at the time, observed that MacCormick was 'particularly keen to impress on the Convention the importance of recognising Europe's huge diversity, and of catering for that diversity in constitutional terms'.[218] MacCormick's many contributions, both in the Convention and in Parliament, all speak to this

211 Scott, 'Stateless Nations' (2012), 194.
212 Ibid.
213 Ibid., 195.
214 Ibid., 194.
215 Ibid., 195.
216 Ibid., 202.
217 Ibid., 198.
218 Duff, Edinburgh University memorial website (2009), link no longer working.

defence of pluralism, diversity, and diffusion of power, working tirelessly, including at the smallest level of detail, in the service of local voices, which often risked being made invisible in and disconnected from the huge bureaucratic juggernaut of the EU.[219] In addition to the substantive importance of this view, what was also striking was MacCormick's combination of attention to intricate detail with philosophical reflection: as Scott recalled, MacCormick was 'the only legal theorist I have known who was as happy discussing the intricacies of the Water Framework Directive as he was theorising about European constitutional law.[220]

All a Great Mistake?

Did MacCormick's own experience of the Convention match these accounts of his contribution? In various lectures and publications, MacCormick certainly argued that a Convention – and thus also a formal, written constitution – was much needed, though not because it offered the opportunity to create, de novo, as if it were a blank slate, a new political order, but because it was a step in the right direction, capturing, for the moment, in a broader evolution, what was already a functioning, informal constitution.[221] This was needed because 'the processes of government at the all-Europe level are opaque to most citizens', even to the 'active political classes' amongst those citizens.[222] In that sense, 'all is not well with the condition of Europe',[223] and a written constitution could help mend that. Speaking in the House of Commons, in the Select Committee on European Scrutiny, he similarly argued that the Constitution is 'essentially a process of adjustment and improvement', not wholescale redesign

[219] See, further: Hunt, 'Devolution and Differentiation' (2010); Bourne, 'Bringing Europe Closer to the Citizen' (2006); Edward and Bengoetxea, 'The Status and Rights' (2011); Drew, 'Public Intellectual' (2012), specifically on MacCormick at the Convention, 215–19.

[220] Scott, 'Stateless Nations' (2012), 202.

[221] See MacCormick, 'European Constitutional Process' (2005); 'On the Very Idea' (2001–2); 'Europe's Future' (2003); 'The Sovereignty Issue' (2003); 'The New European Constitution' (2003); 'The European Constitutional Convention' (2004); 'Review Essay: How to Have a Healthy Constitution?' (2003); 'The Health of Nations' (2004); *Who's Afraid* (2005). The way MacCormick spoke of and conceptualised the European Constitution deserves much more attention than I can bestow upon it here. For instance, the biological metaphors (references to 'health') are interesting. It shows, once again, how much time was an aspect of MacCormick's constitutional theory: a constitution was something alive, which needed the support of theorists and citizens alike to stay 'healthy'.

[222] MacCormick, 'On the Very Idea' (2001–2), 536.

[223] Ibid.

'from the beginning'.[224] Improvement here very much included bringing the EU closer to its citizens, precisely via enhancing subsidiarity. Citing Adam Ferguson, MacCormick argued that changes in procedures of law-making in the EU needed to be more consultative because 'legislation ... is a treaty between citizens determined to live together as free persons'; it is 'not a top-down process at all, it is a dialogical process which emerges in an agreed product'; at the moment, though, it is 'too top down', but that could be changed.[225]

There was, in these years of 2002 and 2003, when MacCormick travelled, all over Europe, and up and down the UK, in universities as well as in local SNP meetings, in Parliaments and in various committees, a resounding optimism, even if qualified by his trademark gradualism: all this, as important as it was, was only ever an adjustment and improvement; more work was needed, but this was a step in the right direction. As he put it, too, in his 2005 book, *Who's Afraid of a European Constitution?*: for all its faults and deficiencies (one of which included the 'special problem' of fisheries),[226] 'the Constitution represents a large step forward in the enhanced democratisation of the Union'.[227]

This mainly optimistic gradualism does capture a good deal of what excited MacCormick about constitutionalism. There was a sense in which it could galvanise us all together, help us join forces, as a community: addressing a Scottish audience, for instance, MacCormick said that 'we together with all other Europeans, have been engaged, and are engaged, in this project of building a continental confederation', linking the building of that to the continually necessary defence and pursuit of peace.[228] But there was also something else, which was also fundamental: the sense in which constitutionalism offered an opportunity for 'interaction', for

224 Select Committee on European Scrutiny, House of Commons, Minutes of Evidence (26 February 2002), 193.

225 Ibid., 197. See also, MacCormick, 'Adam Ferguson: How Civil Will Future Society Be?' (2005), which was delivered as a lecture in Glasgow on 25 February 2002.

226 MacCormick, Who's Afraid? (2005), chapter 12.

227 Ibid., 90. Somewhat less optimistic was a pamphlet MacCormick produced in 2004, 'A Union of Its Own Kind', where, in particular by reference to fisheries and the Constitution's lack of formal recognition of how this sector mattered in particular ways to certain territorial entities, MacCormick said: 'I am very sad that in consequence I cannot actively support, or persuade my friends to support, a constitution whose main message I consider to be wholly positive. The two cheers of the preceding chapter diminish to a single insufficient one': 38. In the later *Who's Afraid* (2005) this was deleted, and MacCormick did find a way to be more positive about the impact on fisheries: see 88–9.

228 MacCormick, 'Europe's Future' (2003), 2–3.

'exchange', for the construction of 'a collective social and political space to address each other'.[229] Indeed, the two aspects went hand in hand: the common good of a community was never truly realised – it was always 'emergent'; the important task was to create structures, living structures, in which genuine debate could lead to the always imperfect and momentary instantiation of that common good. Writing a constitution need not get in the way of that, at least as long we are modest about our role, as but small-scale guardians of something fragile and evolving.

In the end, as noted above, the Constitution did not make it. Does this mean – as he called a piece of his published in 2008 – that it was 'All a Great Mistake?'. MacCormick was frank that mistakes were made. For instance, the ratification procedure effectively made it the case that there was never a Europe-wide referendum in which voters could vote as European citizens – instead, there were only nation-state referenda in which voters voted as French or Dutch voters.[230] This was a missed opportunity and MacCormick went on to consider what an all-Europe referendum might look like.[231] Another mistake was the inclusion of the bulky Part III in the Constitution text – this was unnecessary (that matter could have been 'annexed') and detracted away from the text as a constitution; a constitution was something that 'quite ordinary citizens could comfortably read on a Sunday afternoon'; in that sense, the Constitution, as it was presented, was a mistake.[232]

There were, then, mistakes, but was it 'all a great mistake?'. Here MacCormick answered 'no': the work that went in was necessary anyway, and perhaps it might be possible to see some aspects of it come to fruition. Indeed, MacCormick lived long enough, just enough, to see the Lisbon Treaty at least signed (it was signed on 13 December 2007), though not enough to witness it come into force (on 1 December 2009).

As we have seen, both with respect to the constitutional project, but also more broadly in his experience as an MEP, MacCormick's practical exposure to the realities of European governance did pose a serious challenge to his natural optimism. In response to those realities, and sometimes voicing his frustration – especially at the media portrayal of the work of MEPs – MacCormick found himself adopting a tone he rarely

[229] Ibid., 5–6.
[230] MacCormick, 'The Convention' (2008), 20.
[231] Upon reflection, he said, this idea was 'totally unrealistic in present circumstances': ibid., 26.
[232] Ibid., 24.

expressed: a tone of disappointment, perhaps even anxiety. Arguably, however, as cautious and qualified as it became, this optimism never quite left him. Europe, for all its faults, remained the promised land: a place where politics could be different, and where, both politically and philosophically, we could speak a different language, relating to each other in mutually respectful ways, working together to create a democratic paradise. Our understanding of law, too, could be transformed by this context: law, in its European guise, could become not the imposition of top-down governance by a distant power, but something more complex and valuable: a kind of customary order of differential unity.

9

The Relational Life of Institutional Legal Theory

There are many institutionalisms – many strands of self-styled 'institutional' legal theory. The very term 'institutional' is rich with resonances, e.g., with the 'institutions' of Justinian and thus with Roman law theory and practice, including the art and science of 'jurisprudence' in that tradition;[1] with the 'institutional writers', which includes the institutional tradition in Europe, as linked to programs of national legal development, especially in Scotland, where jurists – just like on the European continent – had an arguably more prominent and influential role in legal development than in the English common law;[2] with the Scottish 'institutions' of religion, education, and law, which were preserved in the Union of 1707, and thus which retained a vital dimension of Scottish identity; with 'institutional facts', as this term was theorised by late twentieth-century English-speaking analytical philosophy, in particular Elizabeth Anscombe and John Searle, and as it went on to influence legal and social philosophy;[3] with sociological theories of 'institutions', which includes more sociologically oriented treatments of law, especially those that do not tie law necessarily to the state, but see law as something that emerges from and develops in clusters of normative practice, including religion;[4]

[1] See MacCormick, 'De Iurisprudentia' (2001).

[2] See, e.g., Cairns, 'Institutional Writings' (1983); Cairns, 'The Moveable Text' (2001); Cairns, 'Legal Theory' (2019).

[3] Anscombe, 'Brute Facts' (1958); Searle, 'How to Derive' (1964); Searle, *Speech Acts* (1969). See, e.g., Ruiter, *Institutional Legal Facts* (1993); Lagerspetz, *Opposite Mirrors* (1995); Morton, *An Institutional Theory* (1998); Hartogh, *Mutual Expectations* (2002); Atria, *On Law* (2002); La Torre, *Law as Institution* (2010); and the essays in Del Mar and Bańkowski, *Law as Institutional Normative Order* (2009).

[4] Ross, *Law as a Social Institution* (2001); Tamanaha, *A General Jurisprudence* (2001). To this one could add the earlier work of Maurice Hauriou and Santi Romano; MacCormick was aware of this earlier line of work, but also distanced himself from it, never being completely persuaded by it.

and with more contemporary references to 'institutions' in jurisprudence, sometimes alongside the language of 'artifact'.[5]

These are just some of the resonances of the term 'institutions' – no doubt others could be found. Part of the difficulty, then, of writing about 'institutional legal theory' is that it is all too easy to mix up a whole range of otherwise separate debates and self-contained scholarly literatures. What is at stake in calling a legal theory 'institutional' thus depends very much on the specific context of debate and usage within which that term is used. Does this mean that nothing at all can be said in general of what an 'institutional theory of law' might entail? I do not think that necessarily follows, but it does entail that one needs to be especially careful to make any such general accounts responsive to contextual differences.

In this chapter, I seek to do both, i.e., to give a general account, which nevertheless tries to be contextually responsive, of MacCormick's appeal to 'institutions', thereby exploring what were the more general and substantive elements of his institutional legal theory, including as these changed over time; and second, to examine what MacCormick did with the theory in the context of the various communities he participated in. We shall see that in both parts what is being illuminated is the 'relational life' of institutional legal theory and thus the sense in which the theory is both an expression and a negotiation of MacCormick's character, i.e., his manner or style of relating with others.

In the first part, this 'relational life' connects to the general and substantive features of MacCormick's institutional theorisation of law, of which there are four: first, the sense in which norms and oughts (as well as, ultimately, law) emerge from, but also regulate, relations (where these 'relations' are conceived of in a particular way, often so as to avoid superior-to-inferior command-based relations); second, the sense in which these relations, from which law emerges and which it regulates, are also relations in time, and thus the importance of theorising law as a temporal phenomenon; third, the sense in which law exists and can be said to be knowable, and by whom (officials, scholars, citizens); and fourth, the moral and political significance of legal institutionalism.

In the second, shorter, part, I turn to the other sense of the 'relational life' of MacCormick's institutional legal theory, here also with four aspects, though with all four situated in the responsibility he was very conscious

[5] See, e.g., Burazin, Himma and Roversi, *Law as an Artifact* (2018); Ehrenberg, *The Functions of Law* (2016); Marmor, *Foundations of Institutional Reality* (2023).

of undertaking when he was appointed to the Regius Chair of Public Law and the Law of Nature and Nations in Edinburgh. Here, the focus is on how MacCormick's theorising of law institutionally enabled him to relate, in particular ways, with other persons.

The four aspects in this second part are: first, the sense in which theorising law institutionally was part of his role as a teacher and thus found expression and value pedagogically; second, the sense in which theorising law institutionally enabled MacCormick to connect philosophical and sociological approaches to law; third, the sense in which the institutional theory of law connected contemporary jurisprudence to work in the history of jurisprudence, especially the history of the law of nature and nations in the Scottish Enlightenment; and, fourth, the sense in which the institutional theory of law enabled MacCormick to bring together general and particular jurisprudence, stretching, in the latter case, from public to private law, and including the emerging interest in EU law, thereby also bridging gaps between philosophers and legal professionals. What we see in this part is how the very choice of both theoretical language ('institutionalism') and methodology is also a relational act: a way of relating members of communities together and thus also negotiating a role for oneself as a philosopher within and between numerous communities.

Inevitably, read this way, MacCormick's institutional legal theory bristles with complexity – almost to the extent that it is very difficult to treat it holistically as one theory. In its relational life, across a number of decades, the theory refracts many concerns – many particular problems and a diverse range of agreements and disagreements. But amidst all the complexity and change over time, what is constant throughout this reading, and thus what holds it together, is the sense in which, to repeat, the theory is an expression and a negotiation of MacCormick's character, i.e., his manner or style of relating with others. This attention to character – to reading with character – allows us to see how relations were crucial to both the substance of the theory as well as the relational functions of the theory, i.e., how the theory allowed MacCormick to craft for himself a certain role in a variety of communities. Put another way, MacCormick's institutional legal theory did not just normatively emphasise relations of a certain kind in the substance of the theory; it also allowed him to act relationally in particular ways, mediating across oppositions, and creating middle spaces between extremes where one could think creatively and inclusively. MacCormick's institutional legal theory was relationally generative in more ways than one.

The Relational Existence and Value of Law

MacCormick's institutional theory of law develops over many decades. It begins, arguably, with his Inaugural Lecture as Regius Professor of Public Law and the Law of Nature and Nations in 1973.[6] It picks up again, in the early 1980s, perhaps after the impetus of meeting Ota Weinberger at the Congress of the International Association for Legal and Social Philosophy in 1979, after which they continued to correspond and during which time Weinberger visited Edinburgh in 1981.[7] Some of this correspondence involved extensive discussion of language, in particular about the translatability of certain terms (such as how to translate the 'rule of law' into German).[8] These discussions were by no means abstract: already in 1983 MacCormick was assisting Ruth Adler in her translations of Weinberger's papers into English.[9] This correspondence and translation were to culminate in two collections: one joint one, entitled *An Institutional Theory of Law* (1986), with selected previously published papers by MacCormick and Weinberger combined into one volume, and then, a year later, a collection of Weinberger's papers alone.[10]

Undoubtedly, MacCormick was flattered, as the much more junior scholar, with all this attention from Weinberger, and the opportunity of working and publishing with him. It was important for MacCormick to make Weinberger's work available in English – it was, he observed, little known in the English-speaking world and would be of 'particular interest' to it.[11] This was not only because of the substance of the theory, but also because of its history: Weinberger's jurisprudence developed in the

[6] The lecture was published in the *Law Quarterly Review* in 1974. It is worth noting that MacCormick was considering numerous topics at the time for his Inaugural Lecture, including 'principles and precedent' or 'something on Justice': see MacCormick, Letter to T. B. Smith (17 October 1972).

[7] MacCormick wrote to Weinberger on 24 April 1981 to say how he 'greatly enjoyed your visit to us, and only regret that it was so short'.

[8] In 1981, after Weinberger's presentation in Edinburgh, MacCormick wrote to query Weinberger's use of the term 'Zurechnung': he wrote that for him it signified 'a speech act or a mental act – and what is more, an act which can be applied to causal situations as well as to normative ones'; this, he continued 'made me wonder whether, at the verbal level, contrast between causality and normativity is well made by appropriating Zurechnung to the latter only', as Weinberger appeared to have done in the course of his presentation in Edinburgh: MacCormick, Letter to Weinberger (24 April 1981).

[9] See MacCormick, Letter to Weinberger (10 October 1983), in which they discuss the headings and parts of their joint collection.

[10] Weinberger, *Law, Institution and Legal Politics* (1991) [1987].

[11] MacCormick, 'Foreword', Weinberger, *Law, Institution and Legal Politics* (1991), ix.

Brno school of Kelsen's Pure Theory of Law under the watchful eye of Frantisek Weyr. Unlike the Vienna school, according to MacCormick, the Brno school had affinities with 'British work in the Hartian style', namely, by its 'insistence on the dual character of legal norms – both as genuinely normative and yet at the same time having real social existence'.[12]

MacCormick also admired Weinberger for his contribution to the 'development of norm-logic and deontic logic', a long-standing interest of MacCormick's, and this was in turn connected to Weinberger's theory of action, in particular via a 'formal teleology', i.e., 'a distinct form of deontic logic, which formalises the treatment of norms as possible action-guiding thought contents'.[13] In addition, Weinberger had a remarkable life story, as MacCormick noted, having survived a number of Nazi concentration camps during the Second World War, as well as the years of 'Stalinism and repression in Czechoslovakia', escaping at the time of the Prague Spring.[14] Weinberger, then, was a formidable philosophical and historical presence, and one that MacCormick was clearly proud to be associated with, especially at this stage of his career.

MacCormick did not cease to theorise law institutionally after his collaboration with Weinberger, but he did so largely in different terms, coming to emphasise, this time by the mid 1990s, a different kind of institutionalism – one less concerned with establishing how law exists and how it is knowable, which were more the concerns of the earlier institutional theory of law, and one more interested in showing how law (and its practices of norm-giving) emerged out of, and always retained a link to, customary of normative ordering (or practices of norm-using). A number of papers in the late 1990s, such as 'Norms, Institutions, and Institutional Facts' (1998), created sufficient intellectual momentum such that, after his period as Member of the European Parliament (from 1999 to 2004), MacCormick returned to his institutional theory, publishing what he, at the time, described as his 'magnum opus', *Institutions of Law* (2007).[15]

The sheer span of time here – from 1972 to 2007 – should give anyone pause about the wisdom of attempting to examine the whole; there are many changes across the body of work in this vein, unsurprisingly so, given the many different interlocutors with which MacCormick engaged and thus the many different kinds of disputes and issues at stake. And

12 Ibid.
13 Ibid., ix–x.
14 Ibid., ix.
15 See MacCormick, 'Concluding for Institutionalism' (2009).

yet, in what follows, in this first part, I do attempt to look across this body of work, being mindful of change over time, but still considering what held it together as an institutional theory of law. As intimated above, I do so by reference to four themes, each of which seek to pick up on some 'relational' aspect of the theory: first, the very situating of law (and more broadly norms and the normative) in certain kinds of relations; second, the interest in how such relations were relations-in-time, and thus also law's temporality; third, the importance of the question of law's existence and knowability, especially in connection precisely to law's temporality; and fourth, the various values – moral and political – that were at stake in MacCormick's theorisation of law institutionally over almost four decades.

Relations of Non-domination

In previous chapters, we have seen how MacCormick, prior to his exposure to Hart and jurisprudence in Oxford, was steeped in Glaswegian moral philosophy, which did not ignore law – for it was an intensely practical, grounded, practice-oriented approach to morality, as for instance in the work of MacCormick's teacher in Glasgow, W. D. Lamont – but instead embraced law as a particular kind of normative practice. This was an approach that saw law as contingently a matter of respect for persons: law could be conceived of as an exercise in universalisation, i.e., a particular kind of justificatory practice. Throughout, law always had two faces: it was a social practice and it was normative. The challenge was how to articulate both sides so as to make them compatible with each other. To attempt to reduce law to something that was non-normative, explicable solely on the basis of impulses or coercive forces, with normativity as at best a mystification – a kind of false consciousness – was to fail to respect persons: it suggested human beings were but cogs in a machine, tossed about by the waves, without agency or responsibility for their actions. But to attempt to reduce law to a set of objective moral grounds – as if, in its pure form, it existed in some moral heaven of concepts – would also not do, for this failed to respect the complexity and reality of normative disagreements amongst persons and communities, as well as smacking of arrogance, for it failed to confront the limits of our moral knowledge.

For MacCormick, however, the principle of respect for persons lay deeper still. We have seen, again in prior chapters, how, when analysing technical questions of private law – whether that be contract law (and thus the practice of promising) or tort law (e.g., in his analysis of the obligation of reparation)[16] – MacCormick's fall back position was always to appeal to a sense of inter-personal duty, of not letting others down, of treating others decently, with considerateness and, precisely, respect. In addition to its manifestation in private law, this basic relational normativity was also ever-present, as again we have seen in prior chapters, in MacCormick's approach to nationalism and constitutionalism: sovereignty, as the source of law, was an idea we could, and should, move away from, because it reduced law to a relation of domination, of a command issued from a superior to an inferior, e.g., in the context of the United Kingdom, it generated a view of Westminster sovereignty as untrammelled and unlimited in its legal power, capable of entirely ignoring the limits placed upon it by the 1707 Acts of Union. This sensitivity to the dangers of political domination, and to law as a means to such domination, was strong in MacCormick a long time before he came to Oxford and became more steeped in Hartian jurisprudence, but, as we have seen, it also made Hart's non-authoritarian, hermeneutic, approach attractive to him, albeit not wholly, for MacCormick thought it stepped back too far from normativity.

The basic point is that for MacCormick, what lay at the heart of the normative – at the heart of theorising norms, but also other features of the normative universe (reasons, values, aims) – was an ideally non-hierarchical relation, a relation of mutual regard and respect, and not a relation of domination. This forms one of the foundations of his institutionalism and is present throughout all the various changes of examples and terminology: from the earliest accounts in the 1970s to the latest in the 2000s. Norms, for MacCormick, could not be reduced to coercive impositions of the will of a superior onto an inferior. Norms were not a sheer matter of power or force. Instead, norms emerged from interaction between persons who were looking to collaborate with each other or who ended up collaborating, for instance, because they were both pursuing a similar end. As he was to say later (e.g., in his *Institutions of Law*, 2007), in a kind of chant, 'norm-users' had priority over 'norm-givers' – we were norm-users before we became norm-givers, and norm-giving was always secondary to and derivative from the practices of norm-using.

A good, early example of this view is a piece on 'Legal Obligation and the Imperative Fallacy' (1973). What was crucial, MacCormick here argued, was not to confuse the 'imperative' with the 'normative': norms, particularly those 'norms which impose obligations', could

16 MacCormick, 'The Obligation of Reparation' (1978).

not be presented 'as deriving from commands or other imperatives'.[17] MacCormick argued that one could see the distinction if one noted the kinds of relational contexts in which 'commands' were issued: commands were addressed to others where those others were called upon to obey; the 'call to obedience', in turn, 'involves asserting one's superiority over another':

> There are certain relationships of superiority and inferiority, which may exist between persons, such that the inferior is in one sense or another required to comply with the expressed wishes of the other in relation to his conduct... This leads to the crucial observation that there are only certain relationships in which requesting is appropriate. Commanding is only appropriate in a context of superiority, whereas requesting is appropriate (though not only appropriate) between people who acknowledge each other as equals, provided that they are on friendly or at least courteous terms with each other.[18]

Here, one could contrast two kinds of examples: the bank robber who 'commands' the bank clerk to hand over money, and the solicitor who advises his client 'that he ought not to defraud the Inland Revenue by making a false tax return, or that he ought to have his will signed by two witnesses'.[19] The difference between the two is that in the first, the 'command' involves an assertion of superiority, backed up by the immediate coercive force of the gun, whereas, in the second, the 'ought' is not made in the context of a relation of domination – it is better understood as an expression of respect for that person's aims, i.e., if they want to have a valid will, then they ought to have it signed by two witnesses.

All well and good for these two contrasting cases, you might say, but what about the situation of a bank clerk being told what to do by the bank manager, e.g., that he ought not to bank the cheque of a certain client?[20] Is this not effectively a 'command', dressed up in the language of 'ought'? If so, does it not show that the 'ought' here presupposes a relation of domination, albeit in this context one allegedly of legitimate authority rather than sheer coercive power? And might not that 'legitimate authority' be in any event analysed down into some kind of coercive reality, e.g., that if the bank clerk disobeys, then he will lose his job? MacCormick's answer to this possible objection is telling. The first step

17 MacCormick, 'Legal Obligation and the Imperative Fallacy' (1973), 102.
18 Ibid., 106.
19 Ibid., 109.
20 Ibid., 107.

is to see that legitimate authority may coexist with coercive power, but also may not:

> For example, two friends on a sailing holiday in a jointly hired yacht might take it in turns to act as skipper. Whoever is for the moment skipper has a right to be obeyed by virtue of the principle underlying their arrangement, so if he says 'slacken the jib', the other ought to slacken it. His only motive for obedience is respect for the principle tacitly or expressed adopted. His companion has no power over him, though doubtless respecting the principle is important in ensuring the safety of both of them.[21]

The reference to a pragmatic arrangement between two friends is typical of MacCormick: he looks for a phenomenological grounding of the concept of authority that shows us how relations of authority are possible, but without being reduced to relations of domination or power over another. But how does this help analyse the above example of the bank clerk and the bank manager? The key is to see that when the bank manager makes a request to the bank clerk that he 'ought' to do X, he is not necessarily asserting that the bank clerk ought to do so 'in recognition of A's superiority over him'.[22] The basis, the ground, of the bank manager's ought is not that of his superiority over the bank clerk, backed up by coercion, such that if the bank clerk does not obey, he will lose his job. Rather, in virtue of the bank's rules and principles – its normative structure – if the bank clerk wants to do his job in accordance with those rules and principles, then he 'ought' not to cash the cheque of that client. If, for example, the bank clerk was to (no doubt unadvisedly) question the bank manager's request – 'why should I do this?' – then the bank manager can answer: 'because cashing the cheque would be to potentially breach such-and-such a duty of the bank'. That, at least, would be the reasonable reply (not, say, 'because I am the bank manager and you have to obey me'!); if the bank manager were to utter that latter statement, then the relation might well reduce to one of domination, where the 'ought' becomes 'a command'. But that is also not necessary: indeed, the more likely scenario is the former. The point is that some sense of reasonableness in relations – of mutual regard and respect – is built into an analysis of the 'ought'.

Of course, MacCormick's account of the 'ought' is not so unrealistic as to posit only relations of friends, even in situations such as the above, where some temporary arrangement of authority exists between them. There can be, and are, standing authority relations, such as the enactments

[21] Ibid.

[22] Ibid., 108.

made by a legislature to its citizenry. But these standing relations of authority do share something of the relations between friends: neither is reducible to relations of domination backed up by sheer coercive power.

Legislation, then, is not best understood as an act of will: rather, it is better understood as an act of presumptive authority that generates 'oughts' for the community, where the 'oughts' it generates themselves rest on the pre-existence of another 'ought', namely that set of rules and principles that confer authority on the legislature to issue legislative acts. In that sense, legislation is better analysed as 'a formal act: the acts of certain conventionally identified persons which conform with conventionally prescribed criteria thereby count as legislation'.[23] Legislation ceases to become so when it is issued, as it might be by a tyrant, to be obeyed simply because and in virtue of the tyrant's coercive power over its subjects (i.e., the subject ought to obey in virtue of the recognition of the superiority of the command-giver). Such a transition effectively marks the denigration of one's status from citizen to subject: the 'oughts' that one faced earlier, when issued in virtue of certain conventional criteria, making certain acts of the citizen possible that were not there before, have become nothing but commands issued by a superior to an inferior, dominated now by the sheer will of another.

How, then, might we analyse the kind of obligation that a law – for instance, one issued by a legislature – imposes on a citizen (as distinct, precisely, from a subject)?

> I as a citizen may or may not be disposed to accept each and every law in itself and for itself. I may disapprove of the content of particular laws, but insofar as the majority of citizens continue to accept that the law can only be made or changed by settled procedures, and in so far as the officials who administer it continue in fact to acknowledge and honour a duty to apply it scrupulously, the law binds me whether I like it or not. I cannot change bad or inconvenient laws, and the officials are not free to apply them or ignore them according to my likes and dislikes, or according to their own. The law, because it is the accepted law of the community, must be applied by officials. That is the duty of their station. So long as that duty is generally honoured by them, the legal system will remain a working order. If they cease to honour that duty the system will break down into a wilderness of arbitrary power.[24]

The rules – the 'settled procedures' – themselves make sense in light of relations: the relations between citizens, and the relations between, on the

[23] Ibid., 115.
[24] Ibid., 128.

one hand, officials, and their 'station', and the manner in which they exercise their office, and, on the other hand, that of citizens. Citizens have an obligation to obey in virtue of respecting the position of other citizens, as set within the authority of officials, but where this authority is qualified by the officials performing the duties of their station. The obligation to obey law is built on a set of relations regulated by rules, and, in particular, the duties of 'officials towards the law'.[25] In any event, it is certainly the case that for MacCormick, law and the obligations it generates are not reducible to commands backed up by sanctions, and thus to relations of domination or the imposition of one will onto another. One could put it another way: law exists only insofar as there are rule- and principle-created relations of authority, which are, in turn, dependent on officials exercising the duties of their station and thereby respecting their addressees as citizens, rather than treating them merely as subjects. Whether it is citizens acting out of respect for other citizens, or officials acting out of respect for citizens, the basic other-regarding relations of respect lie, for MacCormick, at the basis and heart of norms and oughts.

In his early work, in the 1970s and 1980s, but then consistently through to the 1990s and beyond, MacCormick always held on to the idea – which in many was the basis of his optimistic belief in law[26] – that law was not reducible to relations of domination backed up by coercion. Even the most seemingly coercive of laws, e.g., civil or criminal penalties, were not reducible in this way. Coercive enforcement may well be, MacCormick acknowledged, 'a practical necessity in a world in which some people (whether justly or unjustly) will not voluntarily respect the rights instituted by positive law (whether justly or unjustly) in favour of others',[27] but this did not mean that coercive enforcement was a necessary conceptual ingredient of the very notion of 'penalty', e.g., one could speak of 'unenforced penalties or even of voluntarily undertaken penalties'.[28]

Typically, those who claim that criminal law, for example, is necessarily coercive, build into the 'definition of penalties one particular theory of the justification of punishments, the theory of general deterrence', i.e., they claim that criminal law is somehow defined by its aim of deterring people from breaking the law.[29] But, MacCormick says, this is to include

[25] Ibid., 130.
[26] MacCormick once began a self-reflective piece with the assertion: 'I believe in law': see MacCormick, 'My Philosophy of Law' (1998), 1.
[27] MacCormick, 'Coercion' (1982), 265.
[28] Ibid., 266.
[29] Ibid., 267.

in the definition something that is inherently controversial and contested, namely the justification of criminal punishment. This is something to be debated, and not something to be simply stipulated in the definition of what constitutes a crime. Although MacCormick of course recognised the arguments for 'practical necessity', he insisted on some level of 'logical' or 'conceptual' necessity that protected the concept of law from being reduced to just violence or power.[30] It is not that, in MacCormick's perspective, coercive enforcement mechanisms do not add something to the creation of obligations by legal rules and principles; indeed, it is very important to see that they do, and that their so doing requires that we engage in the difficult task of seeing when, if ever, such coercion is justified. But, he wanted to insist, none of that means that law itself is necessarily coercive, i.e., that it is necessarily a means via which one person dominates another, erasing the latter's autonomy, and subjecting them to their whims and fancies.

The same insistence on situating law in relations of mutual respect is visible in the various criticisms MacCormick made of the Benthamite–Austinian conception of law as the command of a superior to an inferior, backed up by a sanction. MacCormick's label for what he rejected from Bentham and Austin, albeit with acknowledgement that the two theories differed substantially as between each other, was 'voluntaristic positivism', i.e., the view that law was a creation of a sovereign, who was habitually obeyed and did not habitually obey any other, and where, thus, it was 'logically impossible … for the sovereign itself in its corporate and law-making capacity to be bound by anything that could strictly be called a "law"'.[31] For MacCormick, despite differences, sometimes great ones, this was a strand of thought that continued in Dicey, with his theory of Westminster sovereignty,[32] and that reached a certain 'apogee' of 'decisionist positivism' in the work of Carl Schmitt.[33] Interestingly, 'voluntarism', i.e., the view that law was 'the will of the powerful',[34] also affected Kelsen,[35] and especially in later articulations of his theory (in the second edition of his *Pure Theory of Law*, 1967), where, according to MacCormick, he went 'deeper into a voluntarist view of the norm, whether of law or

[30] See ibid., 267–8.

[31] MacCormick, 'Dialectic of Might and Right' (1998), 45.

[32] But see, recently, Walters, *A. V. Dicey* (2022), with respect to the difficulties of drawing genealogies between Austin and Dicey.

[33] MacCormick, 'Dialectic of Might and Right' (1998), 47.

[34] Ibid., 39.

[35] Ibid., 46–7.

morality', seeing all 'norm-creating acts', including legislation and even the *Grundnorm* (in its fictional guise), as 'acts of will'.[36] It is not an exaggeration to say that 'institutionalism' was in many ways offered as an alternative to 'voluntarism': indeed, MacCormick himself sometimes put it that way, creating an opposition between 'institutional versus voluntarist conceptions of law's existence'.[37]

Part of the point for MacCormick, in this piece on 'The Dialectic of Might and Right', as well as in many others, was to convey the possibility that law could be conceived not necessarily in situations where there was one, ultimate, source of power, from which law emanated – a kind of 'sovereigntist tendency', as he called it, which situated law in this monadic, self-sufficient, non-relational exercise of a will – but instead, in the spirit of a 'diffusionist tendency', something that could be better analysed as creating 'spheres of responsibility' in relations of 'ongoing dialogue' and collaboration.[38] But this was not merely an argument for pluralism; the deeper reason for this diffusionist tendency – this potential compatibility between jurisprudence and constitutional pluralism – was the desire to avoid situating law, and the normative more generally, within relations of domination (hence also the shunning of the language of sovereignty and replacing it with subsidiarity). It had to be possible, MacCormick thought, to situate law instead in relations of collaboration – of decency, considerateness, and respect. This was, ultimately, a matter of character.

It was in such moments, when MacCormick found himself articulating this alternative possibility, that he reached – in the late 1980s and early 1990s,[39] then increasingly so from the mid 1990s on – to the notion of 'normative order'. This concept of 'order' appears already early on in MacCormick's work – for instance, in the above-mentioned 1973 piece on the 'Imperative Fallacy', where appeals are made to the value of order. But it is important to see that, even in such early instances, MacCormick's concept of order is always imbued with more than just regularity: indeed, the regularity itself is precisely the outcome of attitudes of respect and mutual regard, a kind of quotidian decency towards each other, e.g., of not

36 See MacCormick, 'Review of Kelsen' (1991). It also worried MacCormick that Kelsen's theory led to an identification of law and state. This blunted, MacCormick argued, 'the critical cutting edge of the demand that States be subjected to law': MacCormick, 'Dialectic of Might and Right' (1998), 47.

37 MacCormick, 'Foreword' to Amselek and MacCormick, *Controversies about Law's Ontology* (1991), vii.

38 See MacCormick, 'Dialectic of Might and Right' (1998), 48–55.

39 See, e.g., MacCormick, 'Spontaneous Order' (1986); and 'Further Thoughts' (1991).

letting each other down, of each of us taking our turn, of protecting each other's mutual expectations, of co-ordinating our activities together in the pursuit of common aims.

In, for instance, the above-mentioned piece on 'The Dialectic of Might and Right', when MacCormick critiqued what he saw as the tradition of 'voluntarist' or 'decisionist' positivism, he appealed precisely to 'our ability to co-ordinate our activities', as, for example, when we build languages that allow us to communicate with each other.[40] Language was indeed one of MacCormick's favourite examples, for it allowed him to capture the complexity of a normative order – that 'notorious elusiveness and complexity of grammars'[41] – while at the same time avoiding seeing normativity as the outcome of domination. Language was a complex normative practice, but it was not, of course, something that came into being as a result of someone, somewhere, dictating the norms of good usage – the rules of grammar – to which we then all complied. Language was a paradigmatic example of how we were norm-users first, working out – all very indeterminately, with the whole thing being always a work in progress (a point to which I return in a moment) – what was appropriate or not in the course of interacting with each other. The point, again, was the value of interaction, but interaction imbued with certain attitudes towards each other.

Whether 'as speakers of the language, as users of clocks and watches, as people who try to keep their appointments, as reasonably conscientious university lecturers, as folk who take our turn in the supermarket queue or at the airport check-in', we were creatures, MacCormick argued, capable of creating 'regularities'.[42] But these were 'regularities' because they were 'referable to some implicit but possibly quite vague norms or standards which are in a large manner shared'.[43] There was an order, certainly, but this order 'depends on the dispositions and, to a degree, the efforts of all involved'.[44] The concept of the 'normative' came along with the concept

[40] MacCormick, 'Dialectic of Might and Right' (1998), 55–6.

[41] Ibid., 55.

[42] Ibid., 56. An entertaining anecdote was told by Hector MacQueen, who recalls MacCormick, in a lecture in 1975–76, removing what was 'evidently a lady's watch', in order to make sure he kept to his allotted fifty minutes. When this was met with 'catcalls' in the teasing audience, MacCormick responded, with characteristic 'instant humour', with an account of social rules based precisely on the conventionality of men's as distinct from women's watches, or indeed the limit of fifty minutes placed on his lecture: MacQueen, Edinburgh University memorial page for MacCormick (2009), link no longer working.

[43] MacCormick, 'Dialectic of Might and Right' (1998), 56.

[44] Ibid.

of 'order': both were support acts for the other, and neither was, alone, the star of the show.

For MacCormick, what lay at the basis, the very possibility, of normativity, was interaction between persons who, in their mutual relations, respected each other's emerging and emergent, possibly also changing, expectations. This was not a matter of belief or knowledge, e.g., a knowledge of the rules one might claim, if one had to (as a result of a dispute for example), governed the interaction. At bottom was something less demanding epistemically, but more demanding morally: an interpersonal attitude, a readiness to co-operate and collaborate, a kind of mutual respect and considerateness towards one another; ultimately, a disposition not to disappoint each other. It was from such relations, and in support of them, that norms – and indeed the very possibility of normativity – emerged.

In the mid-to-late 1990s, and from then on into the 2000s, MacCormick would return again and again to one paradigmatic example of normative order: the queue. Thus, for instance, in a restatement of his institutional legal theory in 'Norms, Institutions, and Institutional Facts' (1998) – a piece that also marks a change of pace in MacCormick's writing, displaying great patience in description of ordinary events – MacCormick deployed the running example of the queue to illustrate what he called, tellingly, a 'socio-moral institution'.[45] Queues could be found in numerous places – 'at a supermarket checkout or at a bus-stop, or when approaching a hold-up or bottleneck in a busy road',[46] but in all of them, what we see is a kind of ethic of taking one's turn – one which operates imperfectly, which is important, but one which is nevertheless relatively stable and predictable, for it is held together by this kind of mutually respecting and other-regarding relation:

> To the extent that people 'take their turn', there is an orderly movement through the check-out, or on to the bus, to the limit of places available on board, and then on to the next bus that calls at the stop; an orderly procession of vehicles through the traffic bottleneck. Weaker or less forceful individuals are not forced out or 'jumped over' till nobody else is left trying to get through. From nearly everybody's point of view a kind of fairness and efficiency prevails. Nor does this have to work perfectly. There may always be somebody around who jumps the queue, or who speeds up the fast lane to the very last point then edges into the slow lane through

[45] MacCormick, 'Norms, Institutions, and Institutional Facts' (1998), 304.
[46] Ibid.

> the bottleneck, effectively challenging other drivers to put up with a pretty severe bump to their car (at least) or let him (usually 'him', I am sorry to say) cut in.[47]

It is interesting that MacCormick came to emphasise the queue as the paradigmatic example of normative order. The basic, underlying normative reality – and, again, it is at once a reality and something normative – is enabled by other-regarding, interpersonal attitudes of collaboration and co-ordination.

The details that MacCormick employed in describing the regular dynamics of the queue may seem trivial, but they are important: it is significant that MacCormick thought the 'normative order' in question was imperfect, and that there were often particular cultural 'nuances' at play in different kinds of queues.[48] This includes both some room for toleration (of the illegitimate queue-jumper), but not too much, and also a sense of when it is appropriate to give up one's turn, e.g., for someone who needed to get ahead of you in the queue for some good reason,[49] for instance: 'special considerations for very old people' or for 'disabled war veterans'.[50] Again, throughout MacCormick, stresses all kinds of imperfections as well as variations in the practice; there is no determinacy, no moral perfection, no ideal picture, no blueprint, no perfect shared knowledge – this is, at bottom, a practice, though, as above, a 'sociomoral' one.

Warts and all, with imperfection and indeterminacy built in, and thus dynamic and alive, this is not a 'normative order' made up of exceptional relations of exemplary virtue, but instead mundane, ordinary, and commonplace (but no less valuable for that) relations of decency between persons. Participating in such a normative order was a capacity available to all, or almost all, human beings. Again, what was crucial was less knowledge of the norms that may be made explicit, but more the interpersonal attitude, i.e., the orientation towards protecting one's own but also each other's participation in the relevant normative order. Underlying normativity was a kind of disposition or readiness towards collaboration and co-operation – towards mutual respect and considerateness. This may manifest itself in a kind of disposition to follow what one took (if one reflected on it) certain implicit norms of the normative order, but this was

47 Ibid.
48 Ibid., 308.
49 Ibid., 304.
50 Ibid., 308.

itself secondary to what lay underneath it all: again, relations of mutual respect, of non-domination, of 'broad commonality of attitude'.[51]

Queues are a wonderful example of quotidian turn-taking (also so important to communication via language) and thus of the basic – because, once again, so mundane – relations of mutual respect. Their existence, certainly for MacCormick, shows that normative communities are possible in the absence of any prior directing power. Monadic imposition of the will of one onto others need not be at the basis of the normative. Equally, though, the queue, as imagined and described by MacCormick, is no ideal blueprint that establishes – that constitutes in some static way – the appropriate moves possible within the order. This is an order that is very much bristling with possibility, anchored in something more dynamic than a set of constitutive rules, i.e., precisely the practice of interpersonal attitudes.

Within such an order, for MacCormick, there is no 'single right' way of articulating or interpreting the norms that one might come to articulate for it.[52] This is important, for it shows that MacCormick was willing to conceive of a realm of the normative that built-in, from the start, a sense of the realities of interaction: communities could be loose, rough, permeable, to a degree, but still be communities – they could still be normative communities in which there were generally 'wrong' ways of doing things. But what counted as 'wrong' had to be worked out, in practice, by the participants in the normative order.

Once again, this was a normative order that was alive and dynamic; perhaps one could say that it was normative because it was alive and dynamic – because it was an imperfect work in progress, held up by a basic interpersonal orientation towards mutual considerateness. This emphasis on imperfection as part of the normative was a point MacCormick often stressed, e.g., when distinguishing his view from Dworkin's notion of 'integrity', which MacCormick thought 'postulates a much more far-reaching degree of consensus' than was necessary and failed to be sufficiently realistic about the dynamics of social life.[53]

One could, then, posit a normative order that was normative and orderly without being pre-established by a power or authority and that did not require universal agreement or consensus. Perhaps we could say – although this is not explicitly the way MacCormick articulated it – that there were three aspects of what held up this normative order. First,

[51] Ibid.
[52] Ibid.
[53] MacCormick, 'Open Texture' (1991), 82.

there was a sense in which the participants were – again, generally, overlappingly, imperfectly – oriented to a 'common point' or an 'underlying idea', e.g., in the case of the queue, 'aimed both at attaining a service or opportunity that others seek at the same time, and at facilitating its attainment in mutual civility rather than through open conflict'.[54] Second, there was a sense in which (again imperfectly, with room for toleration) certain things were wrong to do, e.g., it was generally wrong to jump the queue.[55] And, third, but really most basic of all, was the very capacity, but also willingness, to not disappoint each other, to protect each other's expectations, and thus to relate considerately with each other.

It is significant that, in his conception of the 'socio-moral', of 'normative order' as a phenomenon that was both normative and orderly, MacCormick was adopting a view of the social that was thicker with normativity than that of Hart's. We know already from previous chapters that MacCormick did not think Hart's view sufficiently normative: that MacCormick thought, for example, underpinning reasons were part of the internal point of view, that there was a sense of orientation to the value, point, aim, or normative idea without which order itself would be unintelligible. It was not enough, for MacCormick, to posit a critical reflective attitude, as Hart did, at the foundation of social rules. Social order was, from the outset, more thickly normative, more imbued with an imperfectly shared sense of what was appropriate and not, but also, as above, a capacity and willingness to relate decently with each other. MacCormick was certainly attracted to Hart's avoidance of a dominant power as a condition for the existence of social (or indeed legal) rules, but ultimately, for MacCormick, as a Glaswegian moral philosopher, Hart stood too far back from morality. Of course, as above, one could also go too far (as MacCormick often thought Dworkin did): one had to always temper the normative with a good dose of the realistic, the practical, the messy and imperfect life of interaction.

Normative order was, of course, only a part of MacCormick's 'institutional legal theory', for MacCormick went on to claim that, for law to come into being, a process of institutionalisation needed to occur. This was a contingent process – and it is once again significant that it is a process – which

[54] MacCormick, 'Norms, Institutions, and Institutional Facts' (1998), 305.

[55] In work in the 1990s and later, MacCormick came to think that wrongness in a normative order was perhaps even more basic than the notion of its 'common point' or 'underlying idea', although it is also the case that that wrongness only made sense in light of that common point or underlying idea. See MacCormick, 'General Legal Concepts' (1991), 361; 'Wrongs and Duties' (2000), which is reworked as chapter 6 of *Institutions of Law* (2007).

involved, for example, a standing third-party (not involved directly in the interaction) regulating a normative order, and also, potentially, a second set of norms, which regulated the making and administering of those first-level norms. What emerges, then, is a 'two-tier normative practice':[56] in the case of the queue, there are now 'the queuing norms themselves' as well as 'deciding-about-queuing-norms'.[57] This entailed a view about the decision- and judgement-making of that third party, which was of course a theory of legal reasoning. I will turn to that topic in Chapter 10, but for now, the key point is MacCormick's insistence on seeing law emerge from, and always exist in relation to, a normative order. Law may be identified in large part with the process of institutionalisation, but this came later – any norm-giving that it entailed was secondary – and was always rooted in an underlying normative practice, i.e., tradition or custom.

Thus, MacCormick's theory of law as institutional normative order did not shy away from acknowledging the presence of authority or indeed the complexity of rule-making (e.g., in the form of legislative acts) that we see in contemporary legal systems; this had to be acknowledged, but what remained crucial for MacCormick was to present authority and second-tier norm-making as emerging from, and being part of, rather than inaugurating or constituting, normative order itself. The details of how institutionalisation emerged from, and then how it related – especially how it ought to relate – to normative order were complex and contested, but the important point is that for MacCormick, the connection was vital (similarly so, as we have seen, with his approach to constitutionalism: the European Constitution, for example, did not create a blueprint on a carte blanche, which was not an idea MacCormick endorsed, but instead imperfectly systematised an already-existing practice).

Caterpillar Tracks: Law's Temporality

I have now had frequent occasion to refer to 'emergence', 'development', 'process', and other such terms. Time was indeed an essential part of MacCormick's institutional legal theory. This had many manifestations, and it is important to say something about them.[58] In part two of this chapter, below, I will have occasion to relate MacCormick's emphasis on

56 MacCormick, 'Norms, Institutions, and Institutional Facts' (1998), 312.

57 Ibid., 313.

58 See also MacCormick's revised version of 'Stair's General Concepts' (2008), where he lists numerous ways in which temporality matters to law: paragraphs 115–120.

temporality – his awareness of this as such a significant aspect of theorising law – to his reading, which he had already been immersed in while in Glasgow, but which became increasingly intense from the late 1970s on – in Scottish Enlightenment thinkers. The inspiration he found there – in the work of Smith, for instance, on the historical development of legal institutions, or in the work of Stair and his insights into the incremental development of law by courts, as well as the critiques made by Hayek of blueprint-like, constructive rationalism, which was itself informed by readings in Scottish thinkers, especially Hume – was a vital spring for MacCormick's temporal sensitivity.

My immediate focus, however, is on how temporality features in MacCormick's institutional legal theory. What is important to keep in mind is that his reference to time is not some kind of optional add-on to an otherwise basically static picture of law. Rather, temporality is a crucial, foundational element of MacCormick's conception of the normative (just as, arguably, the temporal was a crucial element of his Scottish nationalism where, as we have seen, he was an 'unrepentant gradualist'). Seeing that law necessarily exists over time was crucial pragmatically, enabling legal theory to be more hermeneutically realistic, for it connected to how persons used law and experienced it. But its significance was arguably even deeper than that.

As we shall see, in particular, by reference to MacCormick's notion of defeasibility, incorporating temporality into one's account of law conveyed the sense in which law – but really any realm of the normative – was always imperfect. This was in part because it is under development, in part because of the limit of our capacities, and in part because of the sociality of the normative. Only monadic views of perfect (blueprint-like) normativity are possible: in social life, such universal assent is not possible.

Social life is simply too unpredictable, too complex, but also too much a matter of collaboration between persons who often do not agree universally, to be captured by some normative scheme – to be, to use another technical term, 'constituted' by rules. MacCormick was never convinced of such claims to the 'constitutive' structuring of social reality (as we shall see, it is an entirely different point to say society is 'instituted'), just as he was not convinced about claims for access to some Platonic realm of value by pure reason. Attention to the element of time in MacCormick's institutional legal theory thus helps to capture this sense of modesty and reflexivity about the normative that MacCormick consistently acknowledged, but also the sense in which it was never the work of one person, but always many, collaborating with each other.

The emphasis on the temporal dimension of institutional legal theory was present already in MacCormick's Inaugural Lecture in 1973 (published in 1974), which was the first time MacCormick articulated the idea of 'law as institutional fact'. Here, MacCormick set out to offer an explanation of what he called 'legal institutions', such as 'ownership, trust, testation, rights of intestate succession, incorporation, personality, obligations of reparation, real security … marriage, adjudication and a host of others'.[59] One immediate motivation for offering such an account was to articulate a solution to what became known as the 'individuation problem' in legal theory at the time, i.e., the challenge of offering an account of what counted as a single law. Bentham had raised the problem at the end of chapter 27 of *The Principles of Morals and Legislation*, when he asked:

> What is a penal code of laws? What is a civil code? Of what nature are their contents? Is it that there are two sorts of laws, the one penal the other civil, so that the laws in a penal code are all penal laws, while the laws in a civil code are all civil laws? Or is it, that in every law there is some matter which is of a penal nature, and which therefore belongs to the penal code; and at the time other matter which is of a civil nature, and which therefore belongs to the civil code? Or is it, that some laws belong to one code or the other exclusively, while others are divided between the two?[60]

These slightly breathless questions were only answerable, according to Bentham, with a theory of 'what a law is; meaning one entire but single law'.[61] When Hart, upon his retirement in 1968, took on the task of editing Bentham's works, so much of which remained unpublished, he fastened onto the manuscript *Of Laws in General*. This manuscript, in turn, was devoted precisely to answering the 'complex problem of the individuation of laws, that is, the criteria for deciding what should be treated as merely part of a law and what as a single complete law' that Bentham had left hanging at the end of *The Principles of Morals and Legislation*.[62] Although, of course, Hart had criticised Bentham's command theory of law, he very much admired Bentham's insights, supported by his 'logic of the will' – which Hart thought 'anticipated a form of modern logic known as deontic logic'[63] – and he worked, in a series of papers throughout the 1970s, on reconstructing Bentham's analysis, e.g., of powers and rights.[64] The

59 MacCormick, 'Law as Institutional Fact' (1974), 105.
60 Bentham, *An Introduction* (1996), last paragraph, chapter 27.
61 Ibid., chapter 27.
62 Hart, 'Bentham on Legal Powers' (1972), 814.
63 Hart, 'Jhering's Heaven of Concepts' (1983) [1970], 272–3.
64 See Hart, *Essays on Bentham* (1982).

problem itself was hardly new to Hart, for he had confronted it in his *The Concept of Law*, where he proposed his famous 'key to the science of jurisprudence', namely the union of two distinct kinds of rules, i.e., power-conferring and duty-imposing rules.

Roughly at the same time as Hart was reigniting his own interest in the 'individuation problem', with a particular focus on Bentham, Raz was pursuing his doctoral research (completed in 1967), which had culminated in the publication, in 1970, of his *The Concept of a Legal System*. Confronting and critiquing both Bentham's and Kelsen's answers to the individuation problem, Raz not only offered his own answer, but he also developed a meta-theoretical account of what kind of features, ideally, such an answer would possess. These included, first, some negative exclusions, i.e., that 'The laws individuated by the principles of individuation should not deviate too much or without sound reasons from the ordinary concept of law'; that they 'should not be over-repetitive'; and that they 'should not be redundant'; as well as some positive markers, i.e., that they should, instead, be 'relatively simple', for creating 'simple small units' would 'facilitate discourse about' the legal system and 'promote the analysis of law'; that they 'should be relatively self-contained (or self-explanatory'; that 'every act-situation … that is guided by a legal system should be the core of a law'; and that 'the principles of individuation should, as far as possible, make clear important connections between various parts of a legal system'.[65] We shall see in a moment that these meta-theoretical considerations were also important for MacCormick.

Being in Oxford at the same time and engaging with Raz in debate – at the Aristotelian Society,[66] with Raz recalling that it was MacCormick who made sure he was invited, and that they drove to the meeting together[67] – MacCormick was of course fully aware of Raz's work on the individuation problem. Indeed, reviewing in 1971 Raz's *The Concept of a Legal System*, MacCormick said of it that it was 'a work of major interest and importance which opens up a whole range of new and fascinating topics in analytical legal philosophy'.[68] These included the three questions that Raz had tackled in the book and that were key to understanding the concept of a legal system:

> a) the problem of existence, that is of establishing what are the criteria for settling whether or not a legal system exists, and for distinguishing

[65] Raz, *Concept of a Legal System* (1980) (first edition in 1970), 144.
[66] MacCormick, 'Voluntary Obligations' (1972).
[67] Private correspondence (on file with the author).
[68] MacCormick, 'Review of Raz' (1971), 380.

> between systems which once existed but no longer exist… b) the problem of identity – what are the criteria for determining which laws form a given system?; [and] c) the problem of structure, that is, the question whether or not there is any pattern of relations between types of laws which is common to all legal systems.[69]

These three problems of existence, identity, and structure were used by Raz to both group together and critique his predecessors as well as to provide his own theory of a legal system. The details of Raz's own answer cannot be analysed fully here, but it is significant that Raz retained much of Hart's analytical schema, and in particular the distinction between duty-imposing (*D*-laws) and power-conferring (*P*-laws) rules. Also interesting is that Raz found that, in some cases, *D*-laws and *P*-laws could be understood as two species of one class ('*O*-Norms'), and that, when he came to speak of 'laws instituting rights, which are internally related to groups of *D*-laws and *P*-laws',[70] these could be analysed into a tripartite structure, including: 'investitive laws' (which 'specify the ways in which rights can be acquired'), 'divestitive laws' (which 'determine the ways in which rights can be disposed of'), and 'constitutive laws' (which 'specify the consequences of being a right holder'.[71] As he continued to develop his theory, Raz deployed it to critique Dworkin's attack on Hart, e.g., by arguing that 'Dworkin is only dimly aware of the problem of individuation' and that, as a result, 'he disregards the fact that some statements by courts which look like statements of legal principles are in fact no more than abbreviated references to a number of legal rules', thereby taking the sting out of Dworkin's critique of Hart.[72]

That this problem, and these debates, were in MacCormick's mind at the time of his Inaugural Lecture in 1973 is evidenced not only implicitly by the lecture's arguments themselves, but also explicitly by MacCormick, who indicated, in 1992, that in the early 1970s 'the focus of my attention was on a puzzle in relation to analytical legal positivism, concerning Hart's picture of law as comprising primary rules (of obligation) and secondary rules (mainly power-conferring), as further elucidated in Joseph Raz's rediscovery of the need to articulate "principles of individuation"'.[73]

[69] Ibid.

[70] Ibid., 381.

[71] Raz, *Concept of a Legal System* (1980), 181.

[72] Ibid., 176.

[73] MacCormick, 'Further Thoughts' (1992), 7; see also MacCormick, 'Voluntary Obligations' (1972); and 'Legal Obligation' (1973) – the individuation problem appears in both of these; see also 'Preface to Raz' (1989).

Offering an answer to the individuation problem, then, was certainly one immediate motivation in MacCormick's Inaugural Lecture.

What, then, was his answer? Crucial to it was acknowledging the presence of something that he found missing in Hart or Raz, i.e., precisely temporality. For MacCormick, what was crucially common to the above 'legal institutions' was that 'they all denote things which for legal purposes we conceive of as existing through time'.[74] Institutions of law, he added, have 'temporal, though not spatial, existence'.[75] What was crucial to the manner in which these institutions existed – and what gave them identity as single laws – was precisely how they persisted through time, how they stitched time together into one coherent package.

This, however, was no abstract, idealised stitching of time: it was a stitching of time into 'small units' that corresponded to 'ordinary usage', as indeed Raz had recommended. 'Ordinary usage' here, at least as MacCormick saw it in 1972, was to refer mainly to the usage of legal institutions by lawyers – not citizens, for MacCormick thought that 'we do not know nearly enough about the way in which people in general perceive, or the extent to which they understand, the law, to rest any theoretical account of the structure of the law upon such grounds'[76] – though MacCormick did want his theory to 'make as much sense as possible to the non-professionals whose lives are regulated' by law.[77] Indeed, when, in the late 1980s, he returned to look again at the institutional theory of law, he paid special attention to how legal institutions, as he conceived them, could feature in 'citizens' legal reasoning'.[78] For example, in 'Institutions, Arrangements, and Practical Information', he set out to show how legal institutions created 'a kind of normative stability', enabling 'deliberations ... not only about what to do at any given moment', but also 'planning in a diachronic way'.[79]

But whether anchored in the practice of lawyers or the practical experience of citizens, the general desideratum of locating an answer to the individuation problem in pragmatically oriented 'ordinary usage' was vital for MacCormick. Temporality and practical, ordinary usage and experience were intertwined. Put another way, temporality was

[74] MacCormick, 'Law as Institutional Fact' (1974), 106.

[75] Ibid.

[76] Ibid., 116.

[77] Ibid., 118.

[78] MacCormick, 'Citizens' Legal Reasoning' (1989).

[79] MacCormick, 'Institutions, Arrangements, and Practical Information' (1988), 75; see also 'Time, Narratives, and the Law' (1995).

anchored in something of value – including something that a theorist needed to ensure – namely that any theory of law, including any answer to the individuation problem, had to resonate with and make sense of how laws were perceived, used, and experienced by those who utilised them and were affected by them. This was a theory of law (or, more accurately in this context, a theory of 'a law') for norm-users (to use MacCormick's later terminology) and an acknowledgement of temporality was key to that.

MacCormick's temporally oriented individuation of law posited three rules – institutive, consequential, and terminative rules – which, he argued, together comprised any one 'institution of law'. Thus, the institutive rule 'lays down when a contract, a right of ownership, a trust', etc, 'comes into existence', i.e., 'the law lays down that on the occurrence of a certain (perhaps complex) act or event a specific instance of the institution in question comes into existence'; once instituted, the institution generates consequences, 'in the way of rights and powers, duties and liabilities', which is precisely what the 'consequential rules' of the institution provide for; finally, the institution in question continues, persisting through time, until the law provides 'for its termination at some point in time', it being the point of the terminative rules to do precisely that.[80] It is these three rules together that gave an identity to an individual law; indeed, attention to these rules made the complexity of the law simpler, i.e., it made 'possible the individuation of the normative material into simpler units'.[81] This 'simplicity' was, as noted above, pragmatically anchored in 'ordinary usage'. MacCormick never tired of emphasising this:

> Lawyers and legal writers do in fact and do manifestly use institutional concepts in precisely the way I have suggested. They do take separate account of how contracts or trusts or wills or corporations are made, or how rights of property are initially or derivatively acquired… Having established these institutive conditions [e.g., in the case of wills, who has capacity, the procedural formalities, etc.], lawyers then turn to consideration of the complex legal consequences which follow immediately or subject to a further condition whenever an instance of such an institution exists… Once all that is attended to, there remains the matter of expounding the various modes of discharge of contract, or winding up of trusts, estates or companies, none of which is a subject wholly free of complexity or technicality.[82]

[80] MacCormick, 'Law as Institutional Fact' (1974), 106–7.

[81] Ibid., 114.

[82] Ibid., 113.

Without these tripartite rules, MacCormick claimed, it was really 'impossible to account for the legal use of such concepts as "contract", "trust", "will"' and all the others'.[83]

MacCormick also thought that these tripartite rules offered a better answer – better precisely because more anchored in ordinary usage – to the individuation problem than those offered by Hart or Raz (or, for that matter, Bentham or Kelsen). Indeed, organising laws into these units composed of institutive, consequential, and terminative rules, allowed one to see that the same law could include both power-conferring and duty-imposing rules, e.g., the legal institution of contract included rules that conferred powers on those who had capacity to enter into contracts, but also showed how, once brought into existence, such an institution created consequences, resulting in certain duties and rights.[84] Not only was this helpful, but it also avoided the obfuscatory effect of insisting that 'every legal power' was 'conferred by a separate legal rule', or indeed that 'every institutive or terminative rule' was 'power-conferring'[85] – as one might if one posited power-conferring and duty-imposing rules as the basic, foundational distinction for legal theory.

That the former view could not be true could be illustrated by various examples, e.g., in certain circumstances, persons are able to consent to physical interference (for example, in sport), which rendered such interference immune from being civilly and criminally wrongful. But it 'would be absurd here to suppose that there are two distinct legal rules in operation, one of which imposes a duty not to interfere physically with other people, the other of which confers upon persons generally a power to license certain forms of interference with themselves'; instead, 'what the law does is impose a duty not to interfere with the persons of other except with their consent'.[86] There are not two different kinds of rules here – as one would force oneself to think if treating duty-imposing and power-conferring rules as essentially different and basic – but instead one rule, which is both duty-imposing and power-conferring at the same time. Similarly, in terms of the latter point: it was not the case that every institutive or terminative rule was power-conferring, e.g., with respect to institutive rules: 'the existence of rights of intestate succession depends solely upon the occurrence of an event, somebody's dying without leaving a

83 Ibid., 107.
84 Ibid., 114.
85 Ibid., 118.
86 Ibid.

valid will, which is not always or even commonly a deliberate or voluntary act', and thus not the exercise of anyone's power;[87] and, in the case of terminative rules: 'contracts may be discharged by frustration' but that 'does not mean that anyone has power thereby to discharge them, for self-induced frustration is not frustration in the strict sense'.[88]

These arguments may no doubt be subject to further debate, but the overall point is another one: what MacCormick was after was an explanation of 'the structure of legal systems' that 'make[s] clear the distinctions and interrelations between various types of rule'.[89] As helpful as Hart (and Raz's) distinction between power-conferring and duty-imposing rules was, if one really sought to anchor legal theory in the practical, ordinary usage of lawyers and (to the extent possible, citizens), then it was misleading to treat it as a basic one. Hart, in particular, got himself into difficulties on that score, perhaps especially with respect to associating secondary rules with power-conferring ones (as many have pointed out, for instance by reference to the rule of recognition). It was simply clearer – pragmatically clearer – to organise laws into units composed of institutive, consequential, and terminative rules, such that, particular laws could include both power-conferring and duty-imposing rules, or even combine them into one rule. Key to that, in turn, was recognising the temporally extended experience of law by norm-users.

Law's Existence and Knowability

There was another sense in which temporality connected to pragmatic usage and pointed to something of value, with consequences, too, for what legal theory ought to aim for and how it should be conducted. This feature, also, sits at the intersection of two of the aspects I am suggesting are crucial to MacCormick's institutional theory: the temporal and the sense in which he wanted to show that law existed as a pragmatically knowable fact. This feature is MacCormick's theory of defeasibility of the rules that comprised institutions of law. Put another way, MacCormick's insistence on institutive, consequential, and terminative rules being defeasible is not only a significant part of his temporally oriented institutional theory, but also crucial to his theory of how law exists and how knowable it is.

87 Ibid., 119–20.
88 Ibid., 120.
89 Ibid., 121.

That, in turn, is closely related to what MacCormick took, but also how he distinguished himself, from the work of John Searle. Put pithily, MacCormick's theory of law's defeasibility was one of the grounds upon which he rejected Searle's notion of 'constitutive rules': law did not exist, as a special kind of fact, in the sense of being constituted by rules. Its existence, instead, was much more pragmatic – much more grounded and practical, administered necessarily imperfectly and incompletely by legal officials in social institutions – but, importantly, without thereby rendering it unknowable or hopelessly indeterminate. As with so much of his conceptual work, MacCormick here found a way, via the notion of defeasibility, to hold on to and balance multiple values at the same time – in this case, positing law as a kind of knowable fact, but without turning into a Platonic reality that was disconnected from practice.

That MacCormick was keen to offer a 'realistic' theory of law was visible from the outset of his Inaugural Lecture: indeed, he claimed, it is difficult to imagine anyone indulging in 'unrealistic jurisprudence'.[90] 'The problem', he said, 'is not whether to be realistic, but how, not whether we portray law as fact rather than fiction, but what counts as a fact and what, therefore, as a factual portrayal of it'.[91] This was to be jurisprudence in the realistic register, determined to give an account of how law exists in fact. However, if law, for MacCormick, was a fact, it was a most peculiar one: a made one, an incomplete one, and one loaded with normative aims or underpinned by values. MacCormick's 'realism' or 'naturalism', if one may call it that, was not a reductionist one: it did not seek to explain law by reference to 'physics, physiology, and behavioural psychology'.[92] Neither did it locate its facticity in the subjectivity of individuals – law could exist, e.g., a contract on a bus, between a passenger and the bus company without any awareness by the individual passenger in question. Here, continuing with the example of the contract, MacCormick said:

> It is obvious what makes it possible to know (or, therefore, to say) that such an act [as 'getting on and paying the fare'] brings a contract into existence. What makes it possible is that the act in question belongs to a class of acts whose performance the law treats as operative to make a contract. And what makes that matter is that the law ascribes certain rights and duties to individuals conditionally upon the existence of contracts.

[90] Ibid., 103.
[91] Ibid.
[92] Ibid.

> And what makes that matter is that sometimes people wish to assert legal rights and enforce legal duties, the procedures for doing which are established by further legal rules. And all that depends on the existence of organised groups of people, the legal profession, the courts, and enforcement officials, whose function is to give effect to such rules and whose actual practice is tolerably consonant with the announced rules. To say that a contract exists between parties as a result of certain acts is to adopt one particular frame of reference in terms of which these acts can be considered, namely that of the law, or more specifically of an interrelated set of legal rules. And as Professor Searle tells us, a proposition whose truth depends not merely upon the occurrence of acts or events in the world, but also upon the application of rules to such acts of events, is a proposition of institutional fact. So the existence of a contract is, in a philosophical sense, a matter of institutional fact.[93]

This helps explain how it is that a contract exists – a particular contract, and thus a particular kind of institutional fact – but only as a particular instance of the 'the institution itself',[94] the object of thought, or concept, that is the institution of contract, along with other such concepts, e.g., as above, ownership, trust, and testation. The above passage refers to Searle, but having invoked him, MacCormick quickly distinguishes his own position from his: institutions, in his sense, MacCormick argues, are not 'constituted by rules': they certainly have 'something to do with rules, but are not identical with them'.[95] This needs to be carefully unpacked.

MacCormick's view, as articulated in the Inaugural Lecture, was not helped by a couple of casual Platonic jokes (of concepts lurking behind facts, for example),[96] for it is clear that on his conception, the institutions themselves – the concepts, the thought objects – are also institutional facts, just universals (logically) rather than particulars. Particular contracts are institutional facts, but so is the institution of contract: that is precisely how law exists, as a peculiar kind of fact. Indeed, as MacCormick later said, in the 1986 version of his Inaugural Lecture, the reference to Platonism 'is intended in somewhat jocular vein, at least in that neither of the present authors [Weinberger or MacCormick] is platonistic in belief or inclination'.[97]

For MacCormick, legal institutions have a dual face – they are institutional in two senses simultaneously. They are, at once, 'institutions in the

[93] Ibid., 104–5.
[94] Ibid., 105.
[95] Ibid.
[96] Ibid., 105 and 109.
[97] MacCormick and Weinberger, ITL (1986), 75, fn. 7.

philosophical sense'[98] and 'institutions in the sociological sense'.[99] One can state institutions in the philosophical sense by articulating the rules that make them up – the tripartite rules above. But these rules are themselves made and administered in the imperfect and ongoing work of social institutions. It is important to emphasise here that MacCormick is not positing a world of ideal blueprints – a heaven of legal concepts – which are merely applied by social institutions: he is after something much more grounded in practice than that. He is very much aware that that is a risk that he will be read this way – again, the Platonic jokes do not help – and so he emphasises that positing such a heaven is not his view: 'There is a risk that the view which I have here presented … may seem to involve a belief on my part in a formalistic heaven of institutions, each with its polythene-wrapped set of essential rules which nicely settle all questions. That would, however, be a grossly unrealistic belief, and I do not hold it'.[100]

MacCormick's view is thus 'realistic' in two ways. First, he wants it to be possible to articulate institutions of law in a 'sufficiently clear' manner[101] and 'with *some* consensus'.[102] This goes not only for first-tier rules, such as the rules of contract, trusts, or succession, but also for second-tier rules, such as criteria of validity, or rules concerning how laws are made by parliament, or rules concerning the jurisdiction of courts. We can say that law exists and articulate, sufficiently clearly with some pragmatic consensus – or, as he put it in another way, 'in moderately vague and open-textured ways'[103] – how it does (again, by reference to the simple units made up of tripartite rules). I will return below to why being able to articulate law's existence is so important for MacCormick.

But law is also 'realistic' in another sense, and recognition of this other sense by MacCormick is what distinguishes him from Searle (at least as MacCormick understands him). For law is also the work of social institutions. When we pay close attention to how these institutions operate we will see that there is much more at work than 'rules', at least rules in that 'constitutive' sense, where X counts as Y and would not be Y were not for those rules. Institutions, in the philosophical sense, exist, but they do not exist in this watertight way, as if sealed off from changes in practice. What we can say, at best, is that such rules are 'regulative' rather than

98 MacCormick, 'Law as Institutional Fact' (1974), 105.
99 Ibid., 110.
100 Ibid., 121.
101 Ibid., 112.
102 Ibid., 121; original emphasis.
103 Ibid., 122.

'constitutive', where we understand 'regulative' as a matter of pragmatic reconstruction as we go along.[104]

It is here that the concept of defeasibility comes to play a vital role. The idea that legal institutions are 'constituted' by rules is much too static: it does not properly acknowledge the temporality of law, i.e., the sense in which it is a work in progress. When we really acknowledge this temporality, we will come to see that any articulation of the rules that make up the institution in question can only be 'ordinarily necessary' or 'presumptively sufficient',[105] and even then, only in relation to 'some' 'criteria'.[106] Take any 'institutive rules' of some institution, e.g., a contract for the purchase of a house: it is always possible that any such conditions will be shown to be either unnecessary or insufficient, e.g., all such contracts ordinarily need to be in writing, but what about the case of a person who sells his house in a pub, trying to save on conveyancing fees, and whose position, in certain circumstances – themselves only defeasible – may be protected by equity?[107] 'It would be foolish', MacCormick says, 'to suppose

[104] See also MacCormick and Weinberg's joint 'Introduction' to ITL (1986), where there is a more extended and explicit critique of Searle, though said to be 'largely' in 'Weinberger's terms': 21. Here, Weinberger and MacCormick express dissatisfaction with the 'definitional/identificatory character' of Searle's constitutive rules, adding: If one adopts the view that constitutive rules have only a definitional character [as distinct from a regulative reading of the constitutive rules, so adopting a regulative reading of the constitutive], one finds oneself saddled with the thesis that the rules of games (e.g., chess) can never be wholly broken. For someone who does not conduct himself as the rules require (e.g., by making diagonal moves with his knight) is by definition failing to play this game, viz., chess. So cheating at chess would be possible. This paradoxical conclusion, however, both can and should be rejected. Both chess itself and its internal institutions – knights, pawns, bishops, and so on. – are defined and constitutive not only by stipulative/definitive but also at least in part by regulative/normative rules. It is part of something's being a 'bishop at chess' that it may only be moved diagonally – and hence that any non-diagonal moves amount to (perhaps innocent) breaches of the rules, and such moves made deliberately in the hope of going unnoticed amount to cheating': 24. The normative and the pragmatic go hand-in-hand here: there is a more situated, grounded, dynamic, practice-based conception of games, and social life more generally, than a stipulative/definitive/imperative/constitutive account allows. MacCormick was corresponding with Weinberger about Searle on promising already in the early 1980s, e.g., in a letter in 1981, he wrote: 'I quite agree with your remarks about Searle. His whole argument in the theory about using a promise to derive an "ought" from an "is", is vitiated by the way in which he overlooks the presupposed general norm without which promising would not be a normative institution at all': MacCormick, Letter to Weinberger (24 April 1981). This is of course a live debate, see, e.g., recently, Marmor, *Foundations of Institutional Reality* (2023), but without any reference to MacCormick or Weinberger.

[105] MacCormick, 'Law as Institutional Fact' (1974), 123.

[106] Ibid., 122.

[107] Ibid., 122–3.

that the range' of possible grounds for exceptions to such institutive conditions 'might not be extended tomorrow (or indeed reduced)'; the law is inherently 'capable of expansion or indeed contraction'.[108]

Many other examples can be stated – MacCormick briefly mentions Dworkin's *Riggs* v *Palmer*; several examples from administrative law; and the notions of mistake and frustration in English and Scottish contract law.[109] Indeed, this is the bread and butter of the work of courts. The courts, faced with a new case, find themselves spotlighting a particular area of law where any received understanding is placed under scrutiny, and, in light of further reflection of the aims and values relative to that area, changed. It is important for MacCormick that such examples involve the courts examining the law in light of social conditions and values:

> It thus appears that no formulation, however detailed, of the institutive rule of an institution can be taken as giving a complete list of sufficient conditions for the validity of a purported instance of the institution, any more than as stating conditions each of which is in all cases necessity. Any such formulation of a rule has to be read as subject to possible further exceptions, has to be read, if we would be realistic, in the light of relevant legal principles already established and of possible new ones based on conceptions of the purpose of the institution in the context of changing social conditions and values.[110]

The list of 'vitiating factors' is never 'closed'.[111] Perhaps, at best, we can be more confident in some areas of law rather than in others that we have a clearer sense of the applicable rules than in others; but, in many, 'there is at any one point of time a considerable degree of flexibility and unpredictability', and even in those where we are confident, 'there is no area of law in which we can ever state with certainty that there is' no such flexibility and unpredictability.[112]

Any articulation of the rules, as they are said to exist at any one point in time, must be seen in light of their temporal development – their potential expansion or shrinkage – and thus their 'defeasibility'. To see this is precisely to see that 'the concept of law cannot be tied down to being

108 Ibid., 123.

109 Ibid., 123–6. See also the account of the development of the wife's equity in MacCormick and Weinberger, 'Introduction' to ITL (1986).

110 MacCormick, 'Law as Institutional Fact' (1974), 126.

111 Ibid.

112 Ibid., 127.

simply an institutional concept in the philosophical sense';[113] courts, in particular, are institutions in which persons employ, and must employ, the realms of principle and policy, subjecting 'moderately vague and open-textured' rules to reflection on their purposes and values. Law, as MacCormick insisted towards the end of his Inaugural Lecture, 'spills over the edges of the rules'; 'Rules as institutional facts are not the whole of the law'.[114] Law may be institutionalised – defeasibly, pragmatically – in the form of tripartite rules, in institutions understood in the philosophical sense – but these are made and remade, purposed and repurposed, expanded or contracted, by social institutions.

The 'spilling-over' of law is a telling image – a sense of something important MacCormick was trying to grasp, but which perhaps also eluded that grasp. Perhaps it also marks the vague, dynamic boundary between theorising law institutionally and theorising it as an activity of practical reason. Law could not be articulated in a metaphysical heaven of concepts, for this would ignore the sense in which it was made and remade, dynamically, by social institutions, including by reference to values (e.g., in the form of principles rationalising rules). Law could not be seen to be a pure matter of normative rationality, unanchored in any grounded practice, but that did not mean there was no scope for reason, as long as that was properly situated and limited. There had to be some middle space – some difficult to articulate compromise – between the sense in which law could be said to exist, and thus be knowable, and the sense in which it was a dynamic activity of necessarily limited agents working things out as they went along, dependent in many ways on the kinds of problems (the kinds of cases) coming before them.

Whether 'defeasibility' is sufficiently pragmatic for what MacCormick was reaching for here could be debated. He returned to this concept later, e.g., in the mid 1990s, when he spoke of how 'implicit defeasibility afflicts all instances of legal institutions',[115] but this time arguing that it was not the institution itself that was defeasible but the 'claim made to the right'.[116] This suggests he wanted to protect the philosophical sense of institutions more than he arguably did in his Inaugural Lecture. On the other hand, in his work on legal reasoning – certainly in *Legal Reasoning and Legal Theory* (1978), but in later work, too, in the papers collected in *Rhetoric*

[113] Ibid.
[114] Ibid., 128–9.
[115] MacCormick, 'Defeasibility' (1995), 100–1.
[116] Ibid., 102.

and the Rule of Law (2005) – as indeed, in the 1995 paper on defeasibility, he kept insisting on law not being 'exhausted by reference to the whole set of legal rules', and of any rules (whether first- or second-tier) only ever being capable of being 'verbally stated' with 'relative clarity'.[117] This was not just a matter of recognising that law was infused with 'underpinning reasons', 'underlying values', or that reasoning was a matter of principles as much as it was of rules – that it was a more normative practice than many positivists allowed. This was important, and I shall be returning to it in Chapter 10, but for now it is important to emphasise that it was also a matter of recognising the temporality of law: that law existed more dynamically, more pragmatically, than any purely analytical articulation of its existence in the form of rules might yield.

Another way to see this might be to show that there are at least three different ways one could understand the notion of defeasibility:[118] one would mean simply that any statement of the criteria of a rule is always subject to certain defeaters or exceptions, under which the ordinary application of the concept is defeated, but where the list of such possible exceptions is understood to be closed (the law being statable fully and completely as it is); a second would refer to there being exceptions to rules, but say that the list of potential exceptions is open, it not being predictable what those exceptions might turn out to be, but still insisting that law can be stated as it is at present; and a third option would be to say that law is inherently incomplete: that the fact that we cannot predict the exceptions to come show that law, at any one time, is necessarily incomplete, and so must be conceived of dynamically as a work in progress, with all its potentialities.

These are arguably three different temporalities: for the first two, law is statable as it is at any moment in time, though in the second it is recognised that things may change in the future; for the third, however, law is not statable – certainly not completely – at any one point in time, for it necessarily exists stretched over time, e.g., something more akin to custom or tradition, and perhaps more analogizable to a melody than a photograph, i.e., something that one can only appreciate by hearing it as it unfolds, though with the proviso that one never does get to hear it in its entirety.[119]

117 MacCormick, LRLT (1978), 245.

118 Upon which, of course, there is a large literature, beginning with Hart, 'Ascription' (1949).

119 See also Postema, 'Melody' (2004). Perhaps there is a way of reading Anscombe's famous 'Brute Facts' (1958) paper, which was also an inspiration for MacCormick, in this more radical manner: with her point being that it was never possible to be wholly confident that what one was seeing was what it was, not because it could be defeated by some other description in the future, but because it was inherently impossible 'to mention all

Situating MacCormick within these three possibilities is not straightforward. Sometimes, the way he speaks emphasises the existence of law at any one time, and thus the capacity for us to state it relatively clearly as at that moment in time. On other occasions, MacCormick's language and imagery points to something more radical. The notion of law 'spilling over' the rules might suggest this sense in which he was dissatisfied with the explanatory power of rules, not only because they were normatively inert by themselves, and thus required animation by aims, values, and principles, but also because reference to them alone was not sociologically sufficiently realistic or adequately pragmatic. It is useful, in this context, to point to another image MacCormick employed:

> It is as though the law were to be compared to the tracks of a 'caterpillar' tractor; an endless belt which is continuously moving through time. Endless, but not gapless, the gaps being filled in by extrapolation from what is already there. If the phenomenon we describe is circular, a circular explanation of it is not vicious, but required by veracity.[120]

Here, the imagery does point to something necessarily stretched out over time: being both 'endless' and full of 'gaps', even if those gaps are 'filled in' by social institutions as time moves on. As with so much of MacCormick's work, MacCormick was here grappling with something difficult to articulate – a space in which philosophical language and concepts almost broke down, and he found himself resorting to images that might help capture the intuition. In grappling with this almost impossible space, MacCormick drew on the philosophical terminology around him – 'defeasibility', 'institutional facts', 'rules', and 'principles' – but these were never wholly satisfactory. Still, that is where MacCormick dug: at this tremendously difficult intersection of law's institutionality and its practicality.

Valuing Institutionalism

There is also another way to read the sense in which it is not easy to position MacCormick consistently as to how he conceived of the temporality

the things that were not the case, which would have made a difference if they had been': Anscombe, 'Brute Facts' (1958), 72; our understanding of reality was always incomplete and never wholly stable, in part because of our limitations but also in part because our understanding was always in development and thus more dynamic than any static account of knowledge can provide. Again, this is not just a matter of unpredictability or the future being uncontrollable; it is a matter of the relativity of description or understanding, which shows we are creatures who live in time.

120 MacCormick, LRLT (1978), 246.

of law. This, in turn, is related to the fourth dimension of his institutional theory I wish to examine here, i.e., its connection to value. What, in one perspective, appears as philosophical indecision or inconsistency, appears, in another perspective, as a delicate matter of balancing multiple values. Thus, it can be argued that MacCormick found himself responding, pragmatically, to the interventions of others, at times emphasising one aspect or one interpretation of his institutional theory, and at times others. In all cases, what he was doing was trying to protect something of value.

Thus, for example, when MacCormick pointed to 'legalism' as a 'virtue' rather than 'the vice it is commonly treated as being'[121] what he was responding to were arguments, made in particular by Critical Legal Studies (CLS) scholars, but also more broadly those of an anarchist or more communist persuasion, that either the rule of law was a mirage – an obfuscation, a mode of false consciousness, a way of selling the illegitimate power of class rule to the hapless and naïve masses – or that it was a wholly unrealistic, purely analytical story of the determinacy of law (as if not mediated by real people exercising real power).[122] When set in light of such arguments, MacCormick did emphasise the sense in which law existed by way of largely predictable sets of rules via which citizens could hold those wielding power to account:

> ...legalism is to be understood as the stance in legal politics according to which matters of legal regulation and controversy ought so far as possible to be conducted in accordance with predetermined rules of considerable generality and clarity, in which legal relations comprise primarily rights, duties, powers and immunities reasonably clearly definable by reference to such rules, and in which acts of government however desirable teleologically must be subordinated to respect for rules and rights.[123]

One could and should tell a story about law's existence and knowability, for this was valuable politically: without it, it was difficult to make a normative case for the importance of conducting government in a certain way, i.e., by reference to acts of power being justifiable by rules. If the rule of law was a mirage, a myth, and law was nothing but power in another name, then on what basis could one argue that acts of the government could be illegal, i.e., operating either under wholly unreasonable – untenable – legal justifications or indeed occurring entirely without legal justification?

121 MacCormick, 'Reconstruction' (1990), 541.
122 See ibid.
123 MacCormick, 'Ethics of Legalism' (1989), 184.

Faced with a British government, for example, who shot 'three persons presumed to be engaged in bomb-planting on behalf of the IRA' in Gibraltar,[124] it was vital that such acts not be allowed to operate in some unregulated zone of pure power, but instead subjected to the requirement, as with all government acts, of justification by law. Was there 'adequate legal justification under predetermined rules' for what the officials did in this case?[125] It was vital that we ask this question, but how could we do so if law meant nothing, for it was so indeterminate, or because it was but power in another name? Here, in order to support this possibility of the critique of power – and thus the value of keeping the government in check – MacCormick argued against the 'scepticism' of certain voices, even against 'anti-foundationalism'.[126] After all, with the kind of 'adequate determinacy in practical discourse in community or polity' that law can 'generate', we would risk having no ground to stand on when faced with arbitrary power.[127] For MacCormick, in this context, 'law' has also the value of promising to make politics safer, helping to prevent Leviathan from becoming Frankenstein's monster, since those who exercise political power themselves have to exercise it under laws which are sufficiently clear and determinate to impose real restraints on arbitrariness of despotic conduct.[128]

Of course, one could take this argument too far: one could treat law, for example, as 'though it were a simple description of a natural datum' or as 'the plain fact of a scientific or speculative matter, an ontological or epistemological given'.[129] But this was manifestly not MacCormick's position. To go that far would be to remove law too far from its grounding in a particular kind of normative practice – the practice of institutions reconstructing the rules of law by reference to the law's aims and values. But the fact that law was based in such a normative practice, and thus not an ontological or epistemological given, did not mean it was an indeterminate exercise of power; law did not have to be 'determinate' in the sense in which CLS scholars argued it needed to be, for it to be a meaningful constraint on power. We needed just enough 'relative fixity',[130] just enough pragmatic determinacy, just enough belief in law for it to make a practical difference.

124 Ibid., 185.
125 Ibid., 186.
126 See also MacCormick, 'Smashing the Two Way Mirror' (1987).
127 MacCormick, 'Ethics of Legalism' (1989), 188.
128 Ibid.
129 Ibid., 189.
130 Ibid., 188.

After all, on the CLS's own views, believing in something did make a difference – hence precisely the power of false-consciousness; thus, if law was a matter of collective belief (e.g., in the form of institutional facts), then there was some reality to it, and thus some sense in which 'it can yet make a real difference for the better where it hedges official action against alleged wrongdoers and judicial moralising over unprohibited ill-doing'.[131] Legalism, as a creed, could be taken too far – at which point it undercut the possibility of the kind of critique it really was invested in, becoming naïve and too-readily complacent about law's capacity to restrain power – but, if it was kept in check, if it did not pass 'beyond certain thresholds',[132] if it did not collapse into a wholly unrealistic formalism or some unanchored pure normativism, then it was both real and very valuably so, precisely in order to thwart Leviathan becoming Frankenstein.

Thus, when faced with scepticism, cynicism, or outright anarchism that saw no value in law, but only obfuscatory masks for naked power, MacCormick did find himself emphasising the sense in which law really did exist – the sense in which it 'really does and really can settle issues of priority between principles by fixing rules'.[133] There is, in passages like that one, but also in others, a certain stamping of the foot, or thumping on the table: law 'really', 'really', even if with qualifications and softening, did exist, was knowable, and made a practical difference. It really was determinate (relatively), fixed (relatively), predictable (relatively). In such contexts, and precisely in response to such scepticism or cynicism, MacCormick found himself insisting, if not on 'the ethics of legalism', then for 'ethical positivism' and the 'practical force of rules'.[134] But it is vital to see that he did so precisely in the name of protecting critique – in the name of the possibility and plausibility of jurists and citizens alike questioning the grounds upon which power was exercised.

The above reference to 'citizens' points to two other realms of value that MacCormick was keen to protect with his institutional theory of law: the first was the possibility not only of critiquing power and holding it to account, but also of changing the rules via which it governed; and the second was the possibility of law enabling persons to plan those lives with

131 Ibid., 191.

132 Ibid., 192.

133 MacCormick, 'Reconstruction' (1990), 554.

134 See MacCormick, 'Ethical Positivism' (2000); see also the section on 'Why Rules at All?' in MacCormick, 'Reconstruction' (1990), 547–51.

more predictability than might otherwise be available. These have already featured above, but it is worth restating them in this context.

The very point of the emphasis on defeasibility, and likewise of stating that law was institutional not only in the philosophical sense but also in the sociological, was that one could show how law could be, and should be, responsive to contestability and pluralism of value as well as to social change more broadly. The language in which MacCormick articulated these points of the value of law being said to exist and being knowable could vary, e.g., MacCormick did sometimes speak of the 'rule of law' in addition to 'legalism', but the core idea arguably did not change: thus, part of the value of the 'rule of law' was precisely the sense in which citizens could challenge the rules as they were understood by officials, arguing for a new exception or a new defence, whether in court or as part of parliamentary politics.[135] The rule of law, on this conception, was less an 'ontological or epistemological given', and more a space for practical reasoning – an institutionalised space, yes, not a raw moral debate, but all the more valuable for that, enabling more focused and disciplined discussion, even if only ever yielding imperfect improvements.[136]

Arguably, this is another moment in which the institutional theory overlaps with, if not spills over into, a theory of practical reason, and indeed, much of the later work (as we will see in Chapter 10) in the 1990s was framed precisely as a theory of legal reasoning, with many of those papers collected in *Rhetoric and the Rule of Law* (2005). Nevertheless, this never lost connection entirely with the institutional theory of law: that

135 See MacCormick, 'Rhetoric and the Rule of Law' (1999), and generally in RRL (2005).

136 It is an interesting question whether the rhetorical tradition offered MacCormick a way of conceptualising the rule of law that would have been difficult otherwise; for example, a common exercise in rhetorical pedagogy was to take two commonplaces, in apparent contradiction, and reconcile them; in general, play with commonplaces – turning, twisting, reframing, extending, and contracting them – and of course, the very notion of reasoning from and thanks to places (rhetorical *topoi*), was part and parcel of rhetorical invention and ingenuity. If that is so – and there is evidence, from the first chapter of RRL (2005) that MacCormick thought of it as so – then one might argue that this is a distinctively rhetorical conception of the rule of law, i.e., precisely a space for reconciling apparent opposites. Such a conception might also be entangled, historically, with a kind of musical aesthetics, which also informed legal thought, e.g., through the notion of harmony, and the challenge of creating harmonies amongst seemingly disparate sounds. There is scope here, certainly, for a rhetorical and aesthetic theory and history of the rule of law, perhaps one that has a particular Scottish flavour (on rhetoric and legal education in Scotland, see Cairns [1991]). I return to rhetoric and the creation of inter-subjective spaces in Chapter 10.

theory always enabled a certain fallback, for all the stress on the argumentative character of law, on its twin, the institutional character, and thus the sense in which it did exist and was knowable, and was a fact, though of a peculiar kind.

The sense in which law could also enable citizens to plan their lives with more predictability also mattered to MacCormick and came to be emphasised in subsequent developments of the institutional theory – as we saw above, by reference to institutions functioning as a kind of 'diachronic legal information', which allowed persons to make 'practical arrangements' that could 'persist through periods of time'.[137] Where, in the earlier version, for instance in the Inaugural Lecture, MacCormick emphasised the value of his tripartite rules for being anchored in the usage of lawyers and legal officials, he later raised its stakes, and presented it precisely as something usable by citizens, and thus 'part of the structure of their reasoning about how to live their lives'.[138] When MacCormick did so, he was always careful not to take things too far: law, he said, 'can rarely provide all the answers'; it operates, at best, as 'a side-constraining element upon, rather than the totality of, actual practical reason'.[139] But, nevertheless, even if of 'limited relevance … in ordinary practical reasoning',[140] that was a relevance that still really mattered: law really could allow us to do better in avoiding doing wrong to others, or in collaborating more effectively. Certainly, this was another reason why it was important to have a theory that showed law was real – in a particular sense – and knowable – to an extent – not only by jurists and lawyers, but also by citizens.

There were, thus, numerous occasions in which what MacCormick emphasised was law's existence and reality, its practical force as a system of rules, its capacity to produce predictable order, and even its authoritativeness. This included the value of line drawing, sometimes arbitrarily, and making decisions in circumstances of disagreement and contestation, thereby defending the capacity of legal institutions to 'settle disputable practical issues in an authoritative way for all persons who fall under their jurisdiction or legislative competence'.[141] Law was often nestled in amongst matters of moral controversy, and was never wholly distinguishable from them, but at the same time, as an institutional practice, it was

137 MacCormick, 'Institutions, Arrangements' (1988), 74–5.
138 MacCormick, 'Citizens' Legal Reasoning' (1991), 15.
139 Ibid., 17.
140 Ibid., 19.
141 MacCormick, 'Relative Heteronomy' (1995), 78.

not raw moral debate, but instead, a form of collaboration that allowed persons 'to live by some common public standards that are settled and determinate'.[142]

In that sense, if we conceived of ourselves as autonomous moral agents – as agents who participate in morality conceived of 'autonomous, discursive, and controversial' – then, living under law, we were confronted 'with categorical requirements in the form of duties, obligations, and prohibitions that purport to bind the agent regardless of the agent's own rational will as an autonomous moral being', i.e., we were confronted with law in the form of 'heteronomous demands'.[143] Such statements, contrasting morality with law now conceived of as 'authoritative, institutional, and heteronomous',[144] could, if taken out of context, be seen to be at odds with MacCormick's insistence on seeing law as institutionalised practical reasoning and his stress on the dynamic making of law by social institutions, including its contestability by citizens (e.g., in court, as part of a claim for a new ground of defence). But, placed in context, they are better approached as MacCormick wanting to protect something that he saw of value: precisely law's capacity to reach some kind of pragmatic agreement, even if provisional, and thus securing some kind of order, which was not reducible to either power politics or to all out moral controversy.

That this was so with respect to this paper on 'The Relative Heteronomy of Law' (1995),[145] can be gleaned from the kinds of examples discussed in that paper, especially matters of life and death, including abortions.[146] Arguably, within that context and on such matters, what was worth preserving was both the capacity of individuals to decide with their conscience, while also protecting the capacity of communities to draw lines in moral sands. Further, having initially prised law and morality apart in the above-mentioned ways, MacCormick then effectively retraced his steps, not destroying the distinction he set up, but qualifying it extensively (hence only 'relative heteronomy'). Once again, his thought proceeded often by way of setting up contrasts, and then working to show they were more entangled and more connected than hitherto appreciated. The effort was always to try to balance values, even if they could not be perfectly

[142] Ibid., 76.
[143] Ibid., 78.
[144] Ibid.
[145] Republished, with some amendments, as chapter 14, 'Positive Law and Moral Autonomy' in MacCormick, IL (2007).
[146] MacCormick, 'Relative Heteronomy' (1995), 73–4.

reconciled: in this case, the value of individual moral conscience and the value of social co-ordination.

A good deal of the time, though, MacCormick did not emphasise law's existence and reality in the sense that it imposed itself on individuals. Indeed, very much to the contrary: as we have seen, much of the point in insisting, as in the later development of institutional legal theory, on law being a process of institutionalising normative order, was to protect the potential of law being democratically valuable. Institutionalism, as we have seen, especially in the writings in the 1980s,[147] and increasingly so in the 1990s,[148] and then programmatically in the 2000s, was contrasted with 'voluntarism' or 'decisionism', i.e., with a view of law as necessarily imperative, a command by a superior to an inferior, with no concern as to the connection between ordinary persons and the laws that governed them. This was arguably the strongest concern for MacCormick in his institutional theory, even more so than establishing that law exists and was knowable, or indeed that it was dynamic rather than static, or even that, in being so knowable, it was usable by ordinary persons in their practical affairs. What mattered most was that a conception of law did not stack the cards in favour of, from the outset, a view of political order as involving a remote, centralised, and coercive power ruling over a passive, alienated, and disenchanted mass.

For MacCormick, retaining and protecting law's democratic potential never meant doing without authority or even authoritatively imposed order altogether. There had to be scope for the exercise of authority in a community: without that, it could not function as a community. But this was neither how communities came into being, and nor did it lie at the foundation of what made communities work. The exercise of any authority had to be seen as part of something much larger and then ideally also distributed – diffused – in appropriate ways, so as to enable collaboration while bringing law as close as possible to those it affected most, thereby enhancing rather than drowning out the voices of persons with local knowledge.

In the 1980s, this sometimes meant drawing on the idea of 'custom as shared practical reason', which included persons acknowledging 'the practical necessity of securing a stable framework of communal

[147] See, e.g., MacCormick, 'Jurisprudence and the Constitution' (1983); then in 'Institutional Morality and the Constitution', a chapter in MacCormick and Weinberger, ITL (1986).

[148] See, e.g., MacCormick, 'Dialectic of Might and Right' (1998), reworked as 'The Benthamite Constitution – Decline and Fall?', chapter 5 of MacCormick, QS (1999).

co-existence',[149] with members of communities thus 'assenting to the need for an allocation of authority'[150] but still being involved, actively, in 'seeking to establish the principles by which we ought to live'.[151] Custom could still contain coercion – 'one person's custom can be another person's coercion'[152] – but this was still a world away from a view of law as the efficient exercise of a prior existing power, with a population blindly obeying that power.

The language of 'institutional normative order', which MacCormick emphasised from the mid 1990s onwards, needs to be seen, thus, in this light: less a matter now of establishing that law exists, or how we know it, and more a matter of emphasising how law can be, if not must be, at bottom, a matter of co-ordination amongst norm-users, and not a matter of norm-givers imposing their might upon a hapless, potentially distant population. Law was not necessarily a means of political domination – of establishing societies and order via rationalised, ideal blueprints, which persons had to conform to. It was not necessarily an instrument of imperial power. The negative theses were, however, easier to prove than the positive: if law was not that, then what was it? Well, it was a form of norm-giving, but nestled within norm-using; it was a process of institutionalisation, and thus stabilisation, as well as of exercising authority, but within dynamic, reflexive, and responsive communities of practice. If luck was on one's side, law could be a form of constitutionalising power, while expressing, negotiating, and balancing the voices of persons.

The very concrete expression of this, of course, was, in MacCormick's case, Scotland in Europe, i.e., a nation, with its own Parliament, in a post-sovereign commonwealth. It is not the lot of many general jurisprudential theories to be included, as an epilogue, in political pamphlets, but MacCormick's was: he included a two-page summary of 'The Institutional Theory of Law' and 'its Relevance to the European Union' in an overall argument, made while he was an MEP, in support of the Proposed Constitution of the European Union.[153] The EU was an institutional normative order: an order in which constitutional and democratic law-making was not only possible, but could flourish. Yes, this was

[149] MacCormick, 'Institutional Morality and the Constitution', a chapter in MacCormick and Weinberger, ITL (1986), 184–5.
[150] Ibid., 185.
[151] 'Ibid.
[152] Ibid., 184.
[153] See MacCormick, 'A Union of Its Own Kind?' (2004).

'optimistic',[154] as MacCormick was the first to acknowledge, but why should jurisprudence not be? Why could jurisprudence not offer grounds, however qualified, for believing in law, and its potential for enabling peaceful co-existence that protected self-organisation, and thus also self-respect, rather than political domination, and thus self-abnegation?

Thinking Institutionally, Acting Relationally

In the above, I have sought to read MacCormick's institutional theory of law substantively, with a view to exploring the ways in which MacCormick theorised law institutionally and what was at stake for him, morally and politically, in doing so. I have sought to capture something of the cross-temporal themes over many decades of MacCormick's institutional reflections on law, while still seeking to be sensitive to changes, whether in the leading examples used or in emphasis on particular values rather than others. This has already involved reading with character, and thus noticing how MacCormick's manner or style of relating with others was imbricated in the substantive ways in which he theorised law institutionally. I now want to switch focus, while still reading with character.

MacCormick's choice of theorising law 'institutionally' – the very choice of term, but also the way in which he articulated both the substance and the method of his theorising – was not a choice made in an abstract, monadic vacuum, but rather one that was embedded in and itself helped shape various academic communities that MacCormick was part of. Thus, one can read the institutional theory of law not only as a set of arguments and beliefs about law, but also as a relational act, as a way of contributing to a scholarly community, and thus negotiating and expressing one's role in it.

I am very conscious that this is a task that is filled with danger, and it is important that I indicate what I am not doing. I am not arguing that MacCormick always or even sometimes used the theory in order to bring together theorists from opposite camps. I am not suggesting his theory was strategic in this sense, used intentionally for this purpose. I am also not trying to explain away the details – the subtleties, the nuances – of the theory by reference to them being nothing but relational, communal acts, or acts of character, such that all such details are explicable on the basis of the relational or communal difference they made. Of course, this is not so: MacCormick was too dedicated a thinker, too much of an honest seeker of the truth, too intellectually curious, to be so strategic. Instead, I

154 Ibid., 40.

want to see how I can illuminate the theory, and thus read it more carefully and slowly, from alternative angles, by situating the theory in a variety of relational and communal contexts. At work here is a different kind of intentionality: not the entirely self-conscious, deliberate, and strategic sense of intentionality, but something that is harder to grasp, that operates somewhat beneath the surface of the exercise of will and choice – something more nebulous, which I am referring to precisely as 'character'.

I read MacCormick's institutional theory as a relational act in four sections, i.e., as: first, negotiating his role as a teacher and thus relating to his students; second, relating, as a philosopher, to his colleagues with interests in sociology; third, relating, as a contemporary jurisprude, to the history of jurisprudence; and fourth, relating general and particular jurisprudence, but thereby also connecting lawyers and legal professionals with philosophers. Naturally, more mediations and connections could be found, e.g., an important one was that through the language of institutional legal theory MacCormick connected Anglo–American and European–Continental jurisprudence, e.g., by translating and publishing together with Ota Weinberger. Further, it is important also to emphasise that within each of these four sections, my aim is not to be comprehensive, but merely to briefly illustrate how the theory was not only a matter of substantively theorising law, but also, at the same time, often via its methodology, a relational act.

Before turning to these four sections, however, it is important to emphasise the institutional source from which in many ways they all stem, i.e., MacCormick's position, to which he was appointed in 1972 at the age of thirty one, as Regius Chair of Public Law and the Law of Nature and Nations at the University Edinburgh, and which he continued to hold for another thirty-six years until his retirement in February 2008. As we shall see, the relational life of MacCormick's institutional theory of law is set within MacCormick's often very self-reflexive sense of the 'duties of his station'[155] – that sense, as MacCormick lived it, of not letting others down, of respecting others in the course of the exercise of one's duty.

[155] In F. H. Bradley's famous phrase, and one which MacCormick was very much aware of. See MacCormick, Letter to Dr. R. S. Bhalla (5 January 1979), where MacCormick recommends, as a reading on the concepts of 'duty and obligations', Bradley's 'My Station and its Duties', adding: 'I have the feeling that the concept of duty, is most familiarly associated with offices, positions or roles – the duties of a lecturer, the duties of a porter, the duties of a father'. Interestingly, MacCormick adds that '"obligation" … certainly in its historical use, in law, depends on the conception of a relationship, such as the relationship between

This sense of responsibility can be illustrated in numerous ways. For instance, during the period of his tenure in the Chair, MacCormick often took on very considerable administrative burdens for the Law School, serving as Dean twice (from 1973 to 1976 and 1985 to 1988), as well as acting for many years as Head of the Department of Public Law and Jurisprudence and co-founding (in 1983) the Centre for Criminology and the Social and Philosophical Study of Law.[156] Within the University he was equally active, as Provost of the Faculty Group of Law and Social Science and Dean of Social Sciences from 1994 to 1997, Vice Principal for International Affairs from 1997 to 1999, and Chairman of innumerable committees, from the University Staff Club to the Edinburgh Festival Club, and including too, as we saw in Chapter 8, the Edinburgh University Settlement. By all accounts, he took these administrative responsibilities and burdens (and burdens they were) as seriously as any other task he undertook in his political life, where, as we have seen, he was equally – and often at the same time as the above posts – a participant in innumerable policy committees for the SNP, in Parliamentary committees and inquiries, and in non-party political movements.

The above may sound like a trite tribute, combined with a list of achievements from a Curriculum Vitae, but it is not intended as so: again, MacCormick's sense of his responsibility cannot be underestimated. It extended, for instance, to a lifelong reflection on the history and very title of his Chair: 'Public Law and the Law of Nature and Nations'. Thus, for example, although there were naturally many reasons for MacCormick's increasing engagement, from 1972 onwards, with seventeenth and eighteenth-century thinkers – philosophers, precisely, of the law of nature and nations – one of them certainly was that, as MacCormick saw it, it was part of the duty of his station that he become knowledgeable about that intellectual tradition.

The law of nature and nations, it should be emphasised, is very much a European tradition. As MacCormick recalled, speaking about the history of the Chair on its tercentenary in 2007, the first holder of the Chair, Charles Areskine (or Erskine), began his tenure by studying in the Netherlands for four years,[157] as indeed did many Scottish lawyers and jurists of the time.[158] In a letter, in 1982, to an inquirer from the US

those who have exchanged promises … or the relationship between somebody who has done wrong and his victim'.

156 The name of the centre was coined by Bańkowski.

157 MacCormick, 'On Public Law' (2007), 151.

158 See Cairns (1996). Scottish lawyers went not only Netherlands, but also to Germany, and France.

about the history of the title of his Chair, MacCormick wrote, with quite some enthusiasm:

> In that title [of his Chair] there is of course an echo of the contemporary work of Christian Thomasius. No doubt more important in the general tradition is Pufendorf's *De Iure Naturae et Gentium*. The latter was no doubt the most influential work of its period both for Moral Philosophy and for Jurisprudence, insofar as the two subjects were then differentiated at all. When Gershom Carmichael gave his lectures as Professor of Moral Philosophy in Glasgow in the early 18th century, his lecture comprised commentaries on Pufendorf.[159]

In light of the history of his Chair, it was indeed important to MacCormick that his 'institutional theory of law' echoed the efforts of the institutional writers: Stair, certainly, with his *Institutions of the Law of Scotland* published in the late seventeenth century, which was inspired, as MacCormick saw it, by Grotius and Pufendorf, and which set the stage for a tradition of rationally reconstructing law by reference to a coherent set of moral and political principles 'derived from the law of nature'.[160] Right at the outset of this institutional tradition, then, was the question of how, and the extent to which, law – and in particular Scots law – could be 'the dictate of reason', in Stair's phrase, which MacCormick was fond of repeating.[161] This was, however, not unanchored, abstract, ideal reason, but instead very much a carefully incremental and institutionalised reason, exemplified, for Stair, by the gradual work of the courts. It would not be an exaggeration to say that MacCormick spent a scholarly lifetime understanding and extrapolating from this understanding of law as institutionalised practical reason – a view which very much echoed the tradition that he was an inheritor of, i.e., the law of nature and nations.

Of course, it does not do MacCormick justice to say that he read his way into this tradition – from Stair through to Kames, Hume, Smith, Millar, and Ferguson, amongst numerous others – out of a sense of duty; his engagement with these thinkers was too nourishing, too careful, too long-lasting, and also too pleasurable for him, for that to be either the sole

[159] MacCormick, Letter to William F. Swindler (27 May 1982). MacCormick went on to point out that one of his predecessors, Andrew MacConochie, one of the few successful lecturers in the history of the Chair, probably pirated Smith's *Lectures on Jurisprudence*, and also repeated something he was to return to in subsequent work, namely that there was a connection between the work of the Scots in the eighteenth century and the drafters of the US Constitution; see, e.g., MacCormick, 'Republicanism' (1992).

[160] MacCormick, 'On Public Law' (2007), 151.

[161] Ibid; and, e.g., 'The Rational Discipline' (1981).

or the dominant motivation. However, it is fair to say that in this case, as with so much of his work, MacCormick was very conscious of being, and also very much desiring to be, a member of an intellectual tradition, i.e., an exponent, especially a Scottish–European one, of the law of nature and nations.

There was, too, another echo of the title of MacCormick's Chair in his own work. Not only did he read his way into the 'law of nature', but he also sought to relate jurisprudence to 'the law of nations', which, as we saw above, he recognised was hardly distinguished in the eighteenth century from the 'law of nature'. This 'law of nations', in MacCormick's case, included public international law, the constitutional law of the UK (for this, too, was a law of nations), and European Union law.

In this respect, MacCormick was conscious of his nineteenth-century predecessor, James Lorimer, who was known as a scholar of private and public international law, having published, for instance, *The Institutes of the Law of Nations: A Treatise of the Jural Relations of Separate Political Communities* (1884). As MacCormick saw this, Lorimer kept alive, in Scotland, a newly German-inspired natural law theorising (via Kant and Hegel), himself having studied in Germany, at a time when, in England, a different kind of tradition – utilitarianism – was taking root, via Mill, Bentham, and eventually Austin.[162] Lorimer was also important in nineteenth-century legal education debates, once again seeking to revive the German tradition of the research and teaching of *Rechtwissenschaft*, or 'science of law'[163] – a topic MacCormick thought significant enough to choose as his contribution to the festschrift for George Davie.[164] Here, too, there was a Scottish–European intellectual tradition – the link to German-speaking scholarship being of special importance – which very much combined investigation into the law of nature with an inquiry into the law of nations.

The historical echoes of his Edinburgh Chair surely, then, mattered for MacCormick, even if we have to be careful not to overstate the case. It should not be thought, however, that MacCormick somehow painted himself into a gallery of scholarly stars, setting a distance between himself and his colleagues. Nothing could be further from the truth. For all his willingness to reflect on himself as part of broader historical currents, MacCormick was a hands-on grafter: someone who saw his task

162 MacCormick, 'On Public Law' (2007), 149–50.
163 Ibid., 156.
164 See MacCormick, 'Idea of Liberty' (1984).

as set within the practical, grounded details of the day-to-day work of a law school. He was not someone who sat in a room contemplating, and re-painting, his own portrait. Thrust into the Deanship one year into his appointment, MacCormick was conscious of the changes made by his immediate predecessors and, in some cases, colleagues, including Archie Campbell (the Regius Professor of Public Law and the Law of Nature and Nations just prior to MacCormick), John Mitchell (Professor of Constitutional Law), and TB Smith (Professor of Civil Law): these figures, as MacCormick saw it, established a 'new style Law Faculty', focused on research, but also making considerable changes in the law curriculum (which echoed recommendations made by Lord President Cooper).[165] He paid tribute to them, as he did, when looking back after eighteen years in the Law School in 2002, to others who took on the Deanship since 1972, including Bill Wilson (Lord President Reid Professor from 1972), Derick McClintock (Professor of Criminology from 1973), and Tony Bradley (Professor of Constitutional and Administrative Law from 1968), recalling that for them, as for him, what brought them together was 'an unshakeable common view' that what Edinburgh needed was 'a balance between liberal education in legal concepts and values and a rigorous grasp of the current law of the land'.[166]

Seekers of Legal Knowledge

Indeed, a crucial part – with implications for how he theorised law – of MacCormick's sense of his responsibilities, including as a holder of this Chair, was his role as a teacher of jurisprudence. This points us to the first aspect I would like to highlight through which one can see the institutional theory of law as a relational act, i.e., as an act of relation to his students – an act of respect paid to his students.

There is no doubt that MacCormick thought philosophical reflection on law key to legal education. Nevertheless, he did not take this for granted, but instead made an explicit case for it, both when addressing his students, as well as in academic papers, or even in the press. In fact, he thought it was 'incumbent on us', as teachers, 'to justify what we do, and even more than usually incumbent on us to be attentive and responsive

[165] MacCormick, 'On Public Law' (2007), 156–7.

[166] MacCormick, 'On the Very Idea' (2002), 228.

to our students' criticism of what we do and how we do it'.[167] Here, too, MacCormick was aware of a Scottish pedagogical tradition, which, as we saw in an earlier chapter, he had been exposed to as a philosophy student, with the publication of Davie's *The Democratic Intellect*. Writing in 1974, so soon after his appointment, MacCormick referred to the Scottish tradition of teaching jurisprudence, and characterised the challenge facing teachers of jurisprudence in the following way:

> We have a balancing act to perform: we have to encourage rigour and accuracy in knowing what has been laid down as law, and in stating what one knows or thinks; yet at the same time we have to instil an awareness of how much that may be said about the law or in the law is intrinsically contestable and dubitable and always subject to change. We have to show how the law is, from one point of view, an objective normative order, and yet how it is, at the same time, and from another point of view, inevitably permeated by some prevailing set of political and moral values which is itself far from incontestable. We are concerned both with rigorous accuracy and with rigorousness as to the limits of accuracy in any pronouncement about the ordering of human affairs.[168]

An important feature of the above 'balancing act' – itself typical MacCormick – is the duty to teach law as something knowable. Speaking to his students, in 1973, in his first lecture of the Jurisprudence course in that year, MacCormick recalled that 'the word "jurisprudence"' originally meant 'knowledge of law', with a 'jurisprudent' being someone 'who held himself out as having knowledge of the law such as to enable him to advise other people, officials or private persons, about the law'.[169] Jurisprudence was a kind of 'science' of knowledge: indeed, MacCormick referred explicitly to jurisprudes 'as perhaps most like scientists as well as being philosophers, for we must start out with the assumption that there are connecting generalities, such that law as a concept, law as a whole, does make sense'.[170]

As MacCormick saw it already then, this science of knowledge, jurisprudence, involved 'rational reconstruction', working with the materials we have to construct 'a model of what a legal system is' in a way that makes 'clearer the point of those very elements and above all their mutual

167 MacCormick, 'Jurisprudence' (1974), 360.
168 Ibid.
169 MacCormick, 'Introductory Lecture to Students', Jurisprudence course at Edinburgh Law School (1973), 17.
170 Ibid., 19.

inter-relationships'.[171] Drawing variously on analogies with 'grammar' or 'geography',[172] MacCormick characterised this science of knowledge, jurisprudence, as a matter of presenting the normative grammar or making a normative map of the law, in all its various parts and elements, with particular attention to their point or value.

These were no mere throw away lines given to students in their first lecture on jurisprudence – these characterisations of the teaching of jurisprudence, but also its broader tasks, were to be consistently repeated, including in papers explicitly on teaching, such as in his Presidential Address to the Society of Public Teachers of Law on 19 September 1984, tellingly entitled 'The Democratic Intellect and the Law' (1984).[173] For MacCormick, part of being a jurisprude – though also, in general, a law teacher – was taking seriously the issue of positively constructing an account of law's existence, such that one could present it as knowable, but also valuably knowable. For MacCormick, this meant showing how law as a whole – here echoing, surely, the Scottish institutional tradition – could be rationally reconstructed to form a coherent body of principle, with different parts or elements of the law aiming at realising different values, but all combining together to constitute a kind of practical philosophy for a community. At stake, in questions about the place of philosophy in a legal curriculum, was not just legal education, but very much the meaning and value of 'philosophy' itself. As MacCormick saw it at the time of this lecture, there were six questions that a philosophical education in law schools would ask:

> (1) What is there? (2) What is the structure of the things there are, and how do different kinds of existence interrelate? (3) How do we know what there is, and how do we have acquaintance with the things that exists? (4) By what method should we explain and expound the various matters open to our knowledge? (5) What is the place of human beings as rational agents in relation to whatever else there is? and (6) In the light of all this, how are we to live and conduct ourselves?[174]

[171] Ibid., 24.

[172] Ibid., 24–5.

[173] See also MacCormick and Twining, *Theory in the Law Curriculum* (1986): this was also an exercise in relation, involved a kind of dialogue and negotiation between MacCormick and Twining. There is no doubt that an ongoing conversation and friendship with Twining – who was and is passionate about legal education – was important for MacCormick: see, generally, Twining, *Jurist in Context* (2019); and Twining's account of MacCormick's life and work for the British Academy, 'MacCormick' (2012).

[174] MacCormick, 'The Democratic Intellect and the Law' (1984), 177.

The point lies more deeply than philosophy simply asking big and abstract questions.[175] The point is MacCormick's vision of the responsible philosopher – in this context, responsible to the students he was teaching. The above six questions were clearly interrelated, but it is also true that in this lecture, and in the early 1970s generally when he was beginning to teach in Edinburgh, MacCormick emphasised especially the 'crucial task' of providing 'a theory of legal knowledge, an epistemology of law'.[176] This, however, was no pure scientific job: it involved a responsible act of duty, which included respecting his addressees – the prospective knowers of law he was addressing – namely, his students.

In this respect, it is telling that, having asked these questions, MacCormick quickly followed them up by expressing dissatisfaction with an approach to them, for instance from within Realist (citing Axel Hägerström and Karl Olivecrona) or Marxist theory. Within these broadly 'materialist' philosophies, for whom 'only material things are real', 'consciousness of law has to be false consciousness mirroring', for instance, 'an ideological superstructure rather than a real base; or being a kind of 'fiction'.[177] For MacCormick, this was unsatisfactory, because it was at odds with what he saw as his duty, as a jurisprude, but also as a teacher of law, i.e., to show how law really does exist and really is knowable, and in ways that do not reduce those who know it, such as precisely his students, to mere carriers of false consciousness or victims of self-deception, or him to being a mere peddler of such false consciousness or false deception.

There was, here, a real duty – but also a real problem: to articulate how law exists and how it is knowable, and to do so in a way that respects his addresses as knowers of law. It is, then, in part in answering this call of duty, and seeking to offer a solution to this problem, that MacCormick can be understood as engaging in the institutional theory of law, especially in its earlier manifestations. In other words, in the early 1970s, the articulation of this theory – especially via the language of 'fact', albeit, as we have seen, a peculiar one – was informed by what and how MacCormick saw as the duties of his station: showing how law existed and could be knowable, and valuably so, i.e., precisely as a body of coherent principle, aiming at the realisation of certain values, and thus also being of service to

175 Some scholars read this as a kind of 'foundationalism' and criticised it accordingly, in particular for being too 'liberal' and not 'radical' enough – see, e.g., Hunt, 'Jurisprudence, Philosophy and Legal Education' (1986).

176 MacCormick, 'The Democratic Intellect and the Law' (1984), 179.

177 Ibid., 178.

the community, enabling persons to live well together. Equally important was presenting law as existing and knowable in ways that formed genuine objects of knowledge for those invested in the legal life – most immediately, his students, but ultimately also officials, scholars, and citizens. To do anything else was to disrespect persons and their point of view: again, this was arguably part of how MacCormick saw his duty, both as a jurisprude, and as a teacher of jurisprudence.

The mid 1980s were clearly a moment in which MacCormick was reflecting deeply on his duties as a teacher of jurisprudence, and in particular, the role and value of 'analytical jurisprudence' in legal pedagogy. Addressing the College of Law at the University of Saskatchewan in 1984, MacCormick made a case for the importance of analytical jurisprudence basing it precisely on how it can help answer the question as to what made the knowledge of law possible. Interestingly, here, MacCormick recalled – as he often did, with his papers regularly containing anecdotes – a scene from his own experience when addressing an 'audience in a Scottish rural community interested in the law of employment'.[178] As MacCormick described it:

> One unbelieving and indignant farmer asked me at the end of it: 'Is it a fact that I have to give each of my farm-hands a written contract of employment?'. Since the meeting took place some time after the coming into force of the *Contracts of Employment Act* 1961, I took on myself to answer his question with a simple 'Yes'. I am not sorry I did so. To have said anything else would have been to have misled him, pace Olivecrona et al and their worry about 'facts'.[179]

Philosophical worries and scepticisms had to be put in their place: they were in the service, after all, of the needs of persons, including ordinary persons and their everyday problems. This did not mean uncritical acceptance of everyday life by a philosopher, but it did mean keeping in mind that a philosopher was a member of a community and had a role to play in it. For MacCormick, this included presenting law as something knowable – as indeed a realm of facts, though of a particular kind – and thereby not misleading persons for whom a certain kind of practical knowledge really mattered. It was a matter of relation: of respecting those who were keen to know. The institutional theory of law was, in that sense, a matter of social responsibility – a matter of character.

178 MacCormick, 'Analytical Jurisprudence' (1994), 5.

179 Ibid.

It is worth pausing here for just a moment to note that the pedagogical context is an underestimated one in the historiography of philosophy. This is in many ways surprising given how important an 'office' or 'station' this was for many philosophers. For some this was directly so, in terms of teaching their students, but even for those who did not do any university teaching, pedagogy was arguably often an integral part of their philosophical practice. Many philosophers saw themselves as teachers of a kind to the general public. A good example of the latter is David Hume, who though never holding a university post, served for a time as a tutor, but even more importantly, saw himself as 'an ambassador' from the learned world to the world of conversation, and thus a kind of teacher.

The history of philosophy is impoverished when we fail to pay attention to the 'offices' that philosophers take on, and in which they negotiate particular roles for themselves (and, of course, also for philosophy). As Knud Haakonssen has argued, this is particularly important in the case of eighteenth-century philosophy, where it 'has until recently been forgotten that moral philosophy very often had a pedagogic propriety as a "foundation course" in university studies'.[180] This forgetting has meant marginalising moral philosophy, and treating as a secondary topic to epistemology and metaphysics, whereas, in fact, treating the pedagogical context seriously would show that for these thinkers moral philosophy was primary, with epistemology and metaphysics coming in to solve particular problems within moral philosophy.[181] The pedagogical context, then, can be vital for understanding the formation and significance of philosophy, including theories of law.

Philosophers and Sociologists

Doing one's duty as a teacher, and thus relating with students, but also others who may wish to know the law, was, thus, an important aspect of the relational life of MacCormick's institutional legal theory. A second aspect of this relational life is connected to this, but also has its own particular relational dimension, i.e., MacCormick's relations with those of his colleagues who were not philosophers, but were instead oriented towards the sociological study of law. The pedagogical side of this was that MacCormick argued forcefully for the importance, within the curriculum, of sociologically

[180] Haakonssen, 'The History of Eighteenth-Century Philosophy' (2008), 14.

[181] See also Hochstrasser, *Natural Law* (2000); and more generally, on 'offices' or 'personas' of philosophers, see Condren, Gaukgroger, and Hunter, *The Philosopher* (2009).

oriented legal courses, including professional posts. This view was sometimes articulated directly to the students. Thus, in the above-mentioned lecture in the Jurisprudence class in 1973, MacCormick noted that jurisprudence was indeed 'a philosophical subject', with its object being 'to promote a coherent and articulate understanding of a vitally important area of human experience', i.e., law, but that, in the study of this object, it 'would be wrong … to suppose that law is the only factor in our society which secures an ordered mode of existence for all of us'.[182] This, in turn, meant it was necessary to place jurisprudence, as a philosophical enterprise, within the broader context of a sociological study of law:

> Law may indeed be necessary to the maintenance of society as we know it, but it would surely be rash to suggest that it is also sufficient for the maintenance of such society. It would therefore be impossible and highly undesirable to try and construct a picture of law which wholly ignored the relationship of the law with other aspects of life in society, especially with other social controls as I have called them. And so, in the second place, jurisprudence as the general and theoretical study of law, is in a wide sense a sociological inquiry concerned to put law in its proper setting as one of the factors shaping and influencing life in society.[183]

The reference here to 'social controls' was not a loose way of talking, but in fact echoing the title of his contribution – 'Social Services and Controls' – to the *Annual Survey of Commonwealth Law*. In a letter written soon after his appointment in Edinburgh, in October 1972, and addressing Mr Yasin, the Secretary of the Social Sciences Research Council, MacCormick noted, striking a personal tone, that although 'I am myself primarily a lawyer and legal philosopher … I firmly believe in the value and importance of the works here in progress in sociology of law'.[184] He finished the letter continuing in this first-person manner:

> From my own particular point of view, I believe that the development of jurisprudential and legal philosophical studies must be in the direction of, and certainly must come to terms with an learn from, sociological work on law and indeed work from the viewpoint of the social sciences generally. I should perhaps mention, although I pretend to no sociological expertise, some of my own work has been at least on the fringes of the area which may be described as socio-legal, namely the chapters on 'Social Services and Controls' in the *Annual Survey of Commonwealth Law* for 1971 and 1972.

182 MacCormick, 'Introductory Lecture to Students', Jurisprudence course at Edinburgh Law School (1973), 1.

183 Ibid., 1–2.

184 MacCormick, 'Letter to Mr Yasin' (23 October 1972), 2.

> At the moment, too, I am working on a book about legal reasoning which although philosophical in intent must necessarily bear upon and perhaps contribute to understanding of problems about the judicial process.[185]

I will return, in a moment, to how MacCormick saw his own work, either, as he says, on the 'fringes' of sociology or in partnership with it. For what is just as significant as the way in which he characterised his own work is what he did, administratively, both in terms of curriculum and research administration, in order to support legal sociology in Edinburgh. In the above letter, MacCormick carefully observed what kind of legal sociology teaching and research was going on: there were, for instance, four PhD students in the field and one master's student; and within the undergraduate program, there were honours courses in sociology of law (taught by C. M. Campbell and R. J. Wilson). Further, research-wise, there were numerous projects on the go: Campbell and Wilson had recently received funding to study 'Social Research Methods for Lawyers', and there were projects in progress or development on 'Public Attitudes Towards the Legal Profession' and 'a comparative study of the adversarial and inquisitorial systems of criminal procedure'.[186] MacCormick took careful note of all this activity and intimated, as we have seen above, full support of it, including adding that 'I very much hope that a further appointment may be made by the Department' within this field.[187]

MacCormick did not mean these as empty promises or hopes. In February 1973, MacCormick wrote a powerful argument in favour of retaining the Chair of Conveyancing in Edinburgh. Confronted by suggestions, by other colleagues, that the Chair should be abolished, MacCormick said, not mincing his words, 'I disagree profoundly'.[188] Referring to his experience of teaching property law in Oxford, he said:

> Having spent five years teaching the English law of Real Property in total isolation from and abstraction from any element of Conveyancing practice, I am convinced that such an approach to the teaching of any property law anywhere is bad in principle and worth very little in execution. Far

[185] Ibid., 3. In this letter, MacCormick suggests he contributed twice, in 1971 and 1972, but he appears to have only done so once in 1971, with the 1972 entry written by D. J. Bentley. The *Survey* was an initiative of the Oxford Law Faculty, and it is likely MacCormick was commissioned by H. W. R. Wade to write this piece. MacCormick covered topics such as social welfare and security, housing and health, education, pollution and conservation, and economic and industrial development.

[186] MacCormick, 'Letter to Mr Yasin' (23 October 1972), 2.

[187] Ibid., 2.

[188] MacCormick, 'The Future of the Chair of Conveyancing' (1 February 1973), 1.

> from giving students a sound academic grounding in the subject it gives them a grossly distorted picture of that branch of law. I confess to being an 'American Realist' in relation to the teaching such subjects: only by learning what lawyers actually do in practice can one grasp the point of property law.[189]

This did not mean that the post-holder, in teaching such a course, should focus solely on 'technical aspects of drafting documents' – the point was to combine:

> ...the law of property together with that considerable element of conveyancing practice which is as essential to a proper understanding of the concepts of property as is discussion of the social basis and social effects of present property law; neither the practical matter of conveyancing nor the practical questions of social effects should be ignored. To say that such elements would make it impossible to cover the 'whole course' is simply to beg the question, What ought properly to be considered a 'whole course' in property?[190]

Accordingly, MacCormick advised, the name of the Chair should be changed to the 'Chair of Property and Conveyancing'. Soon after, in April 1973, MacCormick argued that the Law School should establish a 'Committee on Social Sciences and the Law', precisely in order to enable research and teaching in 'socio-legal studies' to flourish.[191] Such pronouncements were not outliers – there are numerous other examples, both in MacCormick's tenures as Dean, but also when engaged in other practical issues, such as the organisation of the jurisprudence curriculum, when MacCormick went out of his way to support sociological scholarship in its own right, but also the prospect of a partnership between legal philosophy and legal sociology.

To give just one further example, writing in 1982, in answer to a 'problem' that 'has come up in a couple of my tutorials' in the Ordinary course on Jurisprudence, with students not understanding the relationship between 'questions about Sociology of Law' and the 'preceding lectures on Natural Law and on Positivism', MacCormick, clearly concerned about this, argued that perhaps there was a way to present Positivism as more

[189] Ibid. Reading passages like this, one inclines to the thought that MacCormick's institutional theory could just be described as a kind of non-reductionist, normative realism. MacCormick's institutional theory consistently sought to balance realism and normativism about law.

[190] MacCormick, 'The Future of the Chair of Conveyancing' (1 February 1973), 2.

[191] MacCormick, 'Socio-Legal Studies', addressed 'To All Members of the Faculty of Law' (30 April 1973).

closely related to legal sociology: after all, were not both concerned with 'social sources'? 'Should we not', MacCormick continued, 'therefore be running in to Sociology of Law via the argument that Positivism necessarily presupposes, but nowhere properly elaborates, a theory of society into which to bed the notion of "social sources"?'.[192] Further, perhaps, MacCormick suggested, we could offer 'sociological explanations of why the various Natural Lawyers and Positivists might have chosen to write about law as they did'.[193] Indeed, MacCormick even argued for contextual legal pedagogy in the press, writing in a Letter to the Editor in *The Times*, in answer to an article by Roger Scruton, that 'Properly studied, it [the law] cannot but be viewed in its historical, sociological, political and economic relations, and with due regard to the practical philosophy which it embraces'.[194]

It is in such actions that we see MacCormick relating philosophy and sociology in practice, keen not to allow philosophy to lord over sociology, but instead raising the estimation and intelligibility of the latter and looking for ways in which they could profitably form a partnership.[195] Such actions are, in turn, very much on a par with what MacCormick argued for in his published philosophical work. If, as we saw above, it was possible to take 'materialism' too far – thereby rendering the knowledge of law either a matter of false consciousness or a form of fictional self-deception – then it was also possible to go too far in the other direction, i.e., in the direction of 'idealism' or a purely analytical theory of law. To do this would be to disconnect law from its grounded, practical existence in social institutions and in the lives of persons. In his lecture to Law Teachers in 1984, MacCormick argued just as passionately in favour of philosophy being part of jurisprudence, as he did in favour of sociology. As he put it, 'The question whether sociology of law is necessarily part of jurisprudence is accordingly answered with a speedy affirmative, the more urgent question being what is the right way in which to study law sociologically'.[196]

It is clear that this relational context – both in terms of the relations between disciplines, but also in terms of MacCormick's relations, as

192 MacCormick, 'Memorandum' (30 November 1982), addressed to Bańkowski, Kinsey, and Nelken.

193 Ibid.

194 MacCormick, 'Education for Judges', *The Times* (18 January 1984), 11.

195 Another early example is the appointment, by MacCormick, when he was in his first stint as Dean, of legal philosophers who were open to dialogue with sociology, e.g., Zenon Bańkowski in 1974 whose work was, especially then, in dialogue with Marxist sociology.

196 MacCormick, 'The Democratic Intellect and the Law' (1984), 179.

a philosopher, with his more sociologically oriented colleagues – was important for his institutional theory of law. This was visible not only in the sources he referenced as inspirations for his lecture – which included Karl Llewellyn's, 'The Constitution as an Institution' (1934),[197] Julius Stone's *Social Dimensions of Law and Justice* (1966),[198] and the work of Robert Summers[199] – but also in the concrete arguments MacCormick makes. It is not an accident that the very last paragraph of MacCormick's Inaugural Lecture, in 1973, is as follows:

> It seems clear that the way in which general principles are superimposed upon rules, making them into a coherent unity, justifying the limitation of their effect in some areas, and justifying extensions or innovations in other areas, is fully explicable only in terms of a full understanding of the mode of operation of the social institutions which are charged with the tasks of making, sustaining, interpreting, applying, and enforcing the law. Here, the philosopher may still pose questions, but he will have either to become a sociologist to answer some of them, or alternatively, have to wait for his sociological colleagues to give him the answers. The latter course seems the more properly modest one, so with becoming modesty I shall, for the moment at least, content myself with a modest conclusion: many important elements of law can be profitably contemplated as institutional facts in the philosophical sense, but we cannot squeeze the whole of the law into that category; in other aspects, it can only be comprehended as an institutional phenomenon in the sociological sense. Jurisprudence is, and must remain, a joint adventure of lawyers, philosophers, and sociologists.[200]

Although powerfully and passionately stated here in 1973, it should not be thought that this was either a particularly new position for MacCormick, or that it was one he quickly forgot, using it merely as a friendly introduction to as many of his colleagues as possible. It is arguably a position that harks back not only to, for example, his days in the Dundee Law School, where Ian Willock had espoused a broad approach to jurisprudence, which very much included sociology; or to the close relationship he developed with Donald Harris while a law student in Oxford; but even further back, to his studies in philosophy in Glasgow, where, as we have seen, the

[197] See also MacCormick, 'Lewellyn Revisited' (1992).

[198] Especially chapter 11. That MacCormick read and appreciated Stone's work can be gleaned from his early reviews, e.g., see 'Review of Stone, *Human Law and Human Justice*' (1966).

[199] Summers, 'Professor Hart's Concept of Law' (1963). Summers soon became a close friend of MacCormick's. MacCormick corresponds with him already from 1973: see MacCormick, Letter to Summers (9 May 1973); it is possible, if not likely, that they already met as students listening to Hart's lectures in 1964–5.

[200] MacCormick, 'Law as Institutional Fact' (1974), 129.

approach to moral philosophy was very much to examine it in operation, at work in the grounded practices of social life, such as law and economics. Within that Glaswegian, and more broadly Scottish tradition, one could be a moral philosopher and a social scientist at the same time – in fact, moral philosophy was a kind of social science, though one practised with respect for persons, and thus treating them not as vectors in behavioural regularities, but as persons with needs, dreams, hopes, and perspectives (treating them, in other words, hermeneutically).

MacCormick had numerous later occasions in which he either collaborated with or referenced legal sociologists, criminologists, or those who were sympathetic to socio-legal studies – such as many of his one-time colleagues, including Mike Adler, Beverley Brown, Eric Colvin,[201] Colin Campbell,[202] Derek McClintock, David Nelken, Lesley McAra, Richard Kinsey, David Garland, Joxerramon Bengotxea, David Smith, Emilios Christodoulidis – and many of these colleagues, as well as others, clearly appreciated MacCormick's call for a partnership between philosophy and sociology,[203] including differentiating him on that score from many other prominent legal philosophers of his day, such as Dworkin.[204] Clearly, the institutional theory of law was seen as a body of theory 'profoundly influenced by a general sociological theory of institutions and legal realist ideas of law as a means of social integration and change and as a normative reflection and institutionalisation of human political and social imagination'.[205] That this corresponded with MacCormick's explicit wishes can be clearly seen not only from the above Inaugural Lecture, where MacCormick spoke of institutions in the philosophical and the sociological sense being two sides of the one coin, but also, for example, in the joint introduction by MacCormick and Weinberger to their influential collection of otherwise single-authored articles, *An Institutional Theory of Law* (1986).

Here, MacCormick and Weinberger were at pains to point out that it is wrong to approach sociology as necessarily a 'reductionist programme', reducing legal phenomena to behavioural regularities; whether it could be so reduced, and what the alternatives were to that reduction (and there were many), were active debates within sociology, and sociology had its

[201] Colvin, 'The Sociology of Secondary Rules' (1978).

[202] Campbell, 'Legal Thought and Juristic Values' (1974).

[203] See, e.g., Bengoetxea, 'Legal Theory and Sociology of Law' (2020).

[204] See Schauer, 'Institutions and the Concept of Law' (2009).

[205] Priban, *Sovereignty in a Post-Sovereign Society* (2015), 98, quoted in Bengotxea, 'Legal Theory and Sociology of Law' (2020), 16; see also De Groot and Vrielink, 'Legal Theory and Sociological Facts' (1998).

own rich non-reductionist versions of explanation, such as for instance Max Weber's concept of Verstehen.[206] The institutional theory of law was, then, clearly to be distinguished from projects such as Kelsen's, the 'purity' of which was intended to bracket the analysis of law from empirical research,[207] but it was also not quite on a par with Hart's, which did take, in Hart's own words, a more 'descriptive sociology' approach to theorising law, but often at the cost of not being normative enough (something that could be corrected, as indeed it was, through MacCormick's insistence on law as a kind of practical reason).

Law could be theorised as both something that existed in fact and something that was normative. Further, to study it this way was not the purview of either philosophy or sociology, but rather very much a collaboration between them both. In treating law 'as an institutional fact, a matter of what is actually existent in social reality', the institutional theory of law, MacCormick and Weinberger wrote, 'emphasises the interplay of socially existent norms and observable features of social life, and takes the basis of legal dynamics to lie in this very interplay'.[208] In Weinberger's words, to theorise law 'without consideration of social reality is unthinkable'.[209]

None of this is to say that MacCormick deferred blindly or passively to sociology. His relations with sociology as a discipline, but also with his sociologically inclined colleagues, were richer than that – more respectful than mere passive acceptance of sociological doctrines would be. This extended to defending the role and value of philosophy when this discipline was 'castigated' or 'dismissed' as irrelevant or unhelpful to understanding law's role in society.[210] Just as it was incumbent upon philosophers to reach out, with 'modesty' as we saw above, with a sense of the limits of one's discipline, to other disciplines, including sociology, so it was imperative that sociologists truly engage and appreciate what philosophy can offer. While philosophers, like himself, would make mistakes if they thought for instance, that the term 'contract' 'must be the same for all systems and all times' – a mistake that could be corrected by paying attention to the sociological insights of thinkers such as Adam Smith, Karl

206 MacCormick and Weinberger, 'Introduction' to ITL (1986), 5–6.

207 This was an idea repeated many times, see, e.g., MacCormick, 'The Maastricht-Urteil' (1995), where MacCormick argued that the institutional theory insists on a degree of sociological realism, hence is not in the Kelsenian sense a pure theory.

208 MacCormick and Weinberger, 'Introduction' to ITL (1986), 20.

209 Ibid., 7.

210 MacCormick, 'Sociological Definitions' (1977), 87–8.

Marx or Max Weber[211] – the same would go for sociologists, who did not try to learn from philosophers.

Indeed, MacCormick said, it was precisely as a philosopher, but as one eager to collaborate with sociologists, that he offered his view of the institution of contract, with its tripartite structure. 'That model', he said, 'makes it easy to specify different conceptions of contract: at different times there may be significant differences in the specific institutive, consequential or terminative rules presented by a given legal system'.[212] The point is less whether this really works for sociology; rather, the point is that it really mattered to MacCormick that it might work. MacCormick would go on to call for methodological collaboration between the philosophy and sociology of law often, sometimes by reference to the institutional theory of law, and sometimes by reference to other frameworks – such as the notion of 'rational reconstruction'[213] – but in whichever form, it is clear that MacCormick's theorising here, both substantive and methodological, was, in part, a relational act, an expression and negotiation of his own role as a philosopher in a broader community of legal scholars, and thus very much a matter of character.

Voices from the Past

Unlike with his various arguments for the importance, as he saw it, of collaboration between philosophers and sociologists, MacCormick never explicitly argued, certainly not in any consistent methodological way, for collaboration between historians of jurisprudential thought and contemporary jurisprudes. There is an air of paradox about this, for he wrote an awful lot both about past thinkers – especially the Scots, including Stair, Hume, Smith, Ferguson, Fletcher, Millar, Lorimer, and others – and a case can be made that much of his own philosophical work was in constant dialogue with these thinkers. In terms of the latter, sometimes this was acknowledged, as when MacCormick argued with and drew from, in the context of his theories of legal reasoning and practical reason, Stair, Hume, Smith, and Kant especially (a point to which I return in Chapter 10). But, often, and strangely perhaps particularly with respect to his institutional theory of law, though there might be the odd reference, the theory

211 Ibid., 93.

212 Ibid., 94.

213 See, e.g., MacCormick, 'Four Quadrants of Jurisprudence' (1994); and 'The Ideal and the Actual' (1997).

seemingly developed without being nourished by – whether in agreement or disagreement with – the seventeenth and eighteenth-century philosophers that, again, MacCormick was clearly reading.

This is all the more perplexing when one realises that from very early on in his return to Edinburgh, MacCormick was engaged in the teaching of the history of legal thought, particularly Scottish Enlightenment thought, as well as in frequent correspondence with colleagues working on the history of natural law thinking. Further, on top of this, MacCormick participated in numerous academic societies dedicated to certain figures, such as the Andrew Fletcher Society (where MacCormick was a member since 1975), the Stair Society, and the David Hume Society (of which MacCormick was a sometime President). And yet, within his philosophical circles, whether in the Anglo-American world or in the European-Continental, these Enlightenment figures, which MacCormick was clearly in dialogue with, were often either absent or lurking quietly in the background.

In 1973, when MacCormick began teaching in Edinburgh, there were four honours courses in jurisprudence on the books: *Legal Rules and Legal Reasoning*; *Natural Law and Theories of Justice*; *Legal Institutions and Legal Values*; and *Scottish Legal Thought in the Eighteenth Century*, with *Sociology of Law* as a course also recommended for anyone interested in jurisprudence. MacCormick taught the first three in 1973, with the fourth being left over to begin in 1974. The second of the above, on natural law, did contain some historical material, with readings from Aquinas, Hobbes, Locke, Rousseau, and Kant, and it is also clear that, in his treatment of the material for the third course, MacCormick took into account the development of legal institutions – such as 'contract, person, corporation, property, delictual responsibility' – in 'their development under the influence of social and technological change', presumably by reference to some of the figures who shed light on this development (e.g., Smith, Marx, Weber). But it is the fourth course that is of particular relevance for present purposes.

Writing to William Twining in 1976 and encouraging him to become an external examiner for honours courses in Jurisprudence in Edinburgh, MacCormick provided further information on the syllabus for this course on *Scottish Legal Thought in the Eighteenth Century*. The 'primary intention' of the course was 'to consider the contribution of legal and philosophical writers in eighteenth century Scotland to the discussion of some perennial and important questions about law in relation to human nature and society'.[214] As this already suggests, though some effort would

[214] MacCormick, Letter to Twining (7 September 1976), 2.

be made to place these thinkers 'in a historical context', they would be considered 'not simply as historical figures', but also as philosophers, with their work evaluated 'in terms of the value and tenability of the theories they propound'.[215]

These figures were Viscount Stair, George Mackenzie, Francis Hutcheson, Lord Kames, Lord Bankton, Lord Erskine, Thomas Reid, David Hume, Lord Monboddo, Adam Smith, Adam Ferguson, John Millar, and Dugald Stewart, with some 'background references' to other thinkers, such as 'Hobbes, Locke, Grotius, Pufendorf, Cudworth, Clarke, Montesquieu, Goguet, and Blackstone'.[216] Amongst the secondary literature, was work by Nicholas Phillipson,[217] a figure with whom MacCormick corresponded,[218] Peter Stein, Ian Ross, Gladys Bryson, and Louis Schneider.[219] The course clearly did run in the mid 1970s, e.g., there is a record of the exam in the course in 1977, including questions about third-party rights in Stair (which MacCormick, as we have seen in previous chapters, was interested in and published on), about Stair and Hume on law's relationship to reason, about the concept of natural rights in Smith, and about the state of nature and its critique. The course received a boost in 1985, with the appointment of a former student, John Cairns, with MacCormick and Cairns co-teaching the course in certain years, e.g., in 1995, by which time the course was called the 'History of Legal Ideas'.

Throughout this time, as mentioned above, MacCormick was not only publishing on certain aspects of these various figures, but also engaging in correspondence about them, sometimes with colleagues that he knew from his days as a student in Glasgow, including David Raphael and Tom Campbell, or with former colleagues, such as T. B. Smith, or past teachers, such as Alan Watson, Ian Willock, and W. D. Lamont. Relations with these colleagues clearly mattered enormously to MacCormick.

There is a particular flurry of correspondence, matching a burst of publications, about Fletcher, Smith, Stair, and Hume, in the late 1970s and early to mid 1980s, at precisely the same time as MacCormick is finishing his book on *Legal Reasoning and Legal Theory* (1978), his book on *Hart* (1981) – a serious alternative to which, at the time, was a book

[215] Ibid.
[216] Ibid.
[217] Phillipson and Mitchison, *Scotland in the Age of Improvement* (1970).
[218] E.g., in the 1980s, as to links between Fletcher, Ferguson, and Buchanan: see MacCormick, Letter to Phillipson (24 June 1982).
[219] Schneider, *The Scottish Moralists* (1967); Bryson, *Man and Society* (1945); Ross, *Lord Kames* (1972); Stein, 'Legal Thought in the Eighteenth Century' (1957).

on Smith – and various papers that culminate in the collection with Weinberger, on *An Institutional Theory of Law* (1986). In the 1970s and 1980s, this correspondence relates, for instance, to discussions of Smith's and Kames's reliance theory of promising;[220] whether and to what extent Smith read Stair;[221] and the roots of Smith's work on natural rights, in particular in Stair, Locke, and Pufendorf.[222] Indeed, so deeply steeped does MacCormick get in the thought of these figures that, in writing to Alan Watson in 1981, he laments that 'the more I grow familiar with the work of the Enlightenment (not only in Scotland) and what it built on, the more I am aware of the narrowing of focus which the Austinian and post-Austinian tradition implied'.[223]

Further, MacCormick's publications on these figures in this period, in the late 1970s to the mid 1980s, are not incidental or cursory; they include substantial work on Smith's views of law ('Adam Smith on Law', 1980–81), two wonderful pieces on Stair as 'an analytical jurist' (1981) and his 'rational discipline of law' (1981), and various overview pieces of Scottish Enlightenment thought (e.g., 'Law and Enlightenment, 1982) and the influence of this on American constitutionalism (e.g., 'The Idea of a Free Government', 1985), amidst numerous reviews of books in the field.[224] Though not as intense in all periods, MacCormick's writings on these theorists continued throughout the late 1980s, all through the 1990s, and right up until his very last works, which returned, especially, to Smith,[225] Fletcher,[226] Ferguson,[227] Hume,[228] and Stair,[229] and to Stair, Hume, and Smith in his last book, *Practical Reason in Law and Morality* (2008).

It is, then, somewhat of a paradox that it is only on certain occasions, and even then without much detailed engagement, that MacCormick draws explicitly on these figures when theorising law institutionally. The reasons for this may be ones that MacCormick himself intimated, in the letter mentioned above, when he referred to the narrowing of the discipline following Austin, which also manifested itself in a general reluctance to engage

220 E.g., MacCormick, Letter to David Raphael (9 March 1977).
221 E.g., MacCormick, Letter to Donald Winch (30 April 1980).
222 E.g., MacCormick, Letter to Tom Campbell (12 March 1981).
223 MacCormick, Letter to Alan Watson (9 October 1981).
224 E.g., MacCormick, 'Review of Meek, Raphael and Stein' (1978); 'Review of Haakonssen' (1982).
225 MacCormick, 'Reasonableness and Objectivity' (1999).
226 MacCormick, 'Republicanism' (2003).
227 MacCormick, 'Ferguson' (2005).
228 MacCormick, 'Constitutionalism and Democracy' (1993), 'Idea of a Perfect' (2005).
229 MacCormick, 'General Legal Concepts' (1990); 'Law' (1993).

with the history of jurisprudence, especially with the history of Scottish jurisprudence. Exceptions to this were relatively rare, e.g., Postema's inclusion of Hume in his account of *Bentham and the Common Law Tradition* (1986)[230] or David Lieberman's *The Province of Legislation Determined* (1989).[231] Partly, then, MacCormick was mirroring a disciplinary norm – to keep the history of thought separate from philosophical analysis, or, when engaging with the history of thought, to treat the figures one was reading as if they were contemporary interlocutors on perennial questions.

Nevertheless, despite this, MacCormick's institutional legal theory can be read as a kind of relational act: a linking or connecting, even if subliminal, between contemporary jurisprudence and the history of legal thought, especially Scottish. This more subliminal relation, in turn, was mediated by another more immediate one: MacCormick's relations with scholars, some of whom were close friends, working on Scottish Enlightenment thought, and his participation in the above-mentioned scholarly associations and communities. Although I cannot make a full case for this here – and will be treating Stair, Hume, and Smith more in Chapter 10 – it is worth mentioning briefly how some of those links and connections may be unearthed.

As I have been intimating above, between the 1970s and 1990s, MacCormick's institutional theory of law underwent a transition: rather than being concerned so much with the existence and knowability of law, MacCormick came to emphasise more its customary emergence, and thus its dynamic development over time. To put it crudely, there was less talk of 'institutional facts' and more talk of 'institutional normative order'. The transition here can, however, be overdrawn, for, despite the Platonic jokes in the Inaugural Lecture in 1973, MacCormick was from the outset keen to see legal institutions – even in the philosophical sense – as temporally extended phenomena, occasionally and defeasibly constructed and reconstructed by social institutions, especially courts. However, there is a sense that in the 1980s, thinking again about his institutional theory of law, MacCormick came to emphasise much more the customary emergence of legal institutions.

There are many reasons for this shift. This includes responses from scholars at the time.[232] However, one of the factors that plays a crucial

[230] Postema corresponded with MacCormick, and they also sparred in debate on normativity in 1987.

[231] Which MacCormick reviewed enthusiastically, see MacCormick, 'Review of Lieberman' (1991).

[232] For example, Arnold, 'Institutional Aspects of Law' (1979); much later, in 1998, a similar critique, of a greater need for an evolutionary story of legal institutions, was made by Hulsen, 'Back to Basics: A Theory of the Emergence of Institutional Facts' (1998).

role is MacCormick's deep dive, precisely in the late 1970s and early 1980s, into the thought of the Scottish Enlightenment. One manifestation of this is MacCormick's overview of that body of thought in 1982.[233] Decrying again the 'undue attention' given to Bentham and Austin, MacCormick writes with great enthusiasm, if not passion, about the 'great themes of the general philosophy of human nature and society explored by such as Hutcheson, Hume, Ferguson, Smith, Reid, and Stewart' with Kames as a 'direct personal link' between them.[234]

A large part of the debate that fascinates MacCormick is the period's debate over the role and limits of reason – a point to which I shall return in Chapter 10. But an equally important part is the significance attributed by these thinkers to custom. This is especially prominent, as MacCormick describes it, in Hume, for whom the 'real basis of positive law is custom',[235] and then becomes evermore pronounced, in part via Montesquieu's reception in Scotland, with a generational rise of 'philosopher-historians' who pay attention to 'the process of legal development and interaction of legal forms with the economic organisation of societies', such as Ferguson, Smith, and Millar.[236] Perhaps, MacCormick muses, this 'historical sense' had really been present all along in Stair, with his view that law is better developed incrementally by the courts,[237] although it is also true that, for Hume, any such custom is not 'evidence of independently existing principles of justice', steeped of course as Stair was in a theological tradition (unlike Hume).[238]

There is no doubt that a key – albeit also ambivalent – figure in all of this for MacCormick was Hume. Hume was a constant companion for MacCormick – what MacCormick saw as a kind of scepticism about reason's practical role in Hume was very much a spur to his own theories of practical reason. Throughout his intellectual life, MacCormick, who confessed to being 'addicted' to Hume's works,[239] was both drawn to and, to an extent, reacted against Hume. Like for so many – Kant included – Hume was the best of all possible provocations to thought. MacCormick found he could not swallow Hume whole, e.g., he was attracted to Smith's corrective of Hume's artificial theory of justice, with the former's emphasis

233 MacCormick, 'Law and Enlightenment' (1982).
234 Ibid., 151.
235 Ibid., 159.
236 Ibid., 160.
237 Ibid., 162.
238 Ibid., 159.
239 MacCormick, 'Is Law Really' (2006), 19.

on 'natural rights', as encapsulated in the figure of the impartial spectator. He looked, one might say, for something normatively stronger than he thought Hume provided.

However, equally, MacCormick was enormously attracted to Hume's explanations of the customary emergence of norms – indeed, given MacCormick's disposition to see normativity in relations of non-domination (as we have seen above), Hume's examples, such as the famous example in Hume's *Treatise* of a normative, expectation- and reliance-generating convention arising from two strangers rowing a boat together to get to the other side of the river, were music to MacCormick's ears. MacCormick kept returning to scratch that itch: the sense in which normativity, perhaps knowledge too, derives from such non-authoritarian interactions between persons, from relations of a kind of basic civility or dialogical decency. Indeed, for MacCormick, as for Hume, language was precisely a key example of something that was both normative as well as real, but conventionally so: a complex practice, packed full of non-imposed norms, that resulted from innumerable interactions between persons over time.

There was something deeper, too, that attracted MacCormick to this customary or evolutionary explanation. In a paper on 'Spontaneous Order and Rule of Law',[240] MacCormick drew on what he argued was at the root of Hayek's critique of constructive rationalism, i.e., precisely Hume's notion of convention.[241] Hayek was concerned, of course, with 'the alarming spectacle of an ideal state issuing the most specific and particular instructions to each of its citizens, aimed at securing the maximum good for each through perfect co-ordination for all'.[242] The idea that one could rationally construct an ideal society was nothing but a recipe for tyranny and domination. Further, this kind of 'rigorous centralism' of policymaking simply did not work, as experience has shown time and again, and that was irrespective of whether the government in power was on the left or on the right.[243]

The point for MacCormick was that all this could be traced back to the kind of epistemic modesty and humility present in 'Hume's metaphysical antirationalism' and its 'critique of all claims to innate knowledge and

240 Originally given in 1984, at a conference in Turin, and then reworked and republished on numerous occasions, including at a Liberty Fund colloquium in Gleneagles, in Scotland, in 1986, as well as, tellingly, by the David Hume Institute.

241 MacCormick, 'Spontaneous Order and Rule of Law' (1986), 1.

242 Ibid.

243 Ibid., 9.

to self-evidence in empirically testable propositions'.[244] 'Our knowledge claims', MacCormick continued, echoing Hume, 'have always to be tentative, grounded in probability, rather than certainty, provable by experiential evidence rather than by recourse to innate ideas'.[245] Anything else involves 'playing God', but 'humans are not Gods and cannot act as though they had divine knowledge'.[246]

The point is important and goes to the heart of MacCormick's 'addiction' to Hume. What MacCormick found in Hume was precisely a kind of epistemology of respect: knowledge was social and emerged from interaction over time between persons; it was not, for it could not be, the imposition of the alleged wisdom of one supposedly epistemically superior person (a commander, a central institution, an enlightened sovereign) onto the ignorant masses. To assert such an epistemology was to practice monadic self-deception, which was dangerous both to oneself and to others. This was not how one could or should relate with others. Matters like knowledge, or normativity (including justice, the kind of justice that law seeks to protect), were not monological inventions made by someone in a flash of genius: they were, instead, necessarily imperfect, and at times arbitrary, incremental developments that were generated by many persons interacting with each other, each with an important but also necessarily limited contribution to make.

At the heart of what attracted MacCormick to Hume was, thus, a matter of character: the manner or style with which one related to persons. Underneath all this fancy critique of metaphysics and all this epistemological footwork was, ultimately, a basic respect for others – a moral orientation, but one that was deeply social and practically grounded, and accompanied always by a sense of one's own limitations and dependence on others. Put another way, theories of knowledge were ultimately about trust and civility, about the ethics of not letting each other down and not seeking to dominate one another.[247]

It may be possible to push this even further and argue that, already when he was a student, engaging with the theory of speech acts (in Austin, in Searle), MacCormick read these in light of Hume's own reflections, in Book 3 of the *Treatise*, on the power and magic of language, which can

[244] Ibid., 3.
[245] Ibid., 3–4.
[246] Ibid., 4.
[247] See also MacCormick, 'On Public Law' (2007), 159, where MacCormick relates theories of the development of language with civility and trust.

generate normative expectations, as with Hume's theory of promising. There was, in Hume's account, acknowledgement of the normative power of 'a certain form of words invented … by which we bind ourselves to the performance of any action'.[248] There is even, in Hume's terminology, reference to how 'these signs [of promising] are instituted', such that 'whoever uses them is immediately bound by his interest to execute his engagements, and must never expect to be trusted any more, if he refuses to perform what he promised'.[249]

Thus, it might be the case that Hume's civility- and trust-oriented account of norms generated by certain conventional uses of language may well have informed – even if only subliminally, for MacCormick does not put it in those terms – even the earliest of MacCormick's institutional intuitions, as in his Inaugural Lecture.[250] Hume's notion that justice, including the very specific, and often arbitrary, rules of law that support it,[251] is a kind of projection of the customary imagination, supported by language, may, then, be said to be at the deepest root of MacCormick's institutionalism. Hume's further idea that, although this is artifice, it is no less natural than that, may well echo MacCormick's early attempts to argue for law's existence and knowability, albeit not as a brute fact but precisely as an institutional fact.

Be this as it may, these are not the terms in which MacCormick explicitly explains his institutional theory. And, again, any such links would in any event not be straightforward, for MacCormick was clearly also drawn to Smith's corrective to Hume, with its emphasis on natural rights. It is perhaps in this sense that we need to read MacCormick's invocation, this time in a collaboration with Zenon Bańkowski, that there was such a category of speech acts as 'informal speech acts'.[252] An informal speech act was one that was made 'by reference only to the utterance of words … and to the complex intention disclosed by the utterance'.[253] As Bańkowski later put it:

> While some have argued that it is impossible to account for our ability to 'do things with words' except in terms of pre-existing pragmatic conventions, we think that some doings-with-words are possible apart from prior

248 Hume, *Treatise* (2000), 3.2.5.10.

249 Ibid.

250 See also the reliance theory of promising in MacCormick, 'Voluntary Obligations' (1972).

251 Rules concerning possession, accession, succession, and others, as in his analysis in the Hume, *Treatise* (2000), 3.2.

252 MacCormick and Bańkowski, 'Speech Acts' (1986).

253 Ibid., 126.

> or presupposed conventions; out of and around such 'natural' speech acts, conventions might grow and the action might become conventionalised and partly transformed in the process. Such acts in respect of which illocutionary intentions can be defined in terms of complex perlocutionary intentions and the conditions of their intelligibility will not be conventional or institutional but what we have called 'natural'. For example, it would be intelligible that someone should intend to get someone else to rely on him/her for some future performance even if there were no social or linguistic conventions about using such phrases as 'I promise' for this purpose; and where someone has been led to rely on someone else, there are good, non-conventional moral reasons for not disappointing such reliance. Such informal acts can and do become socially and morally institutionalised as the theory of speech acts says, but some of them, as in the case of contract can become yet further institutionalised by being brought within the sphere of adjudication – the sphere of judicial institutions.[254]

This harks back to MacCormick's reliance-based theory of promising,[255] and the idea that such a normative convention could arise from more basic, somehow more natural, relational needs, i.e., mutual trust and considerateness between persons. This may seem to be in opposition to Hume's emphasis on the artificial character of justice, but it is arguably not: after all, for Hume, such conventions, even if they are artificial, arise out of human nature, and in particular a basic kind of sympathy-based responsiveness to each other, as indeed in the example of the two men rowing a boat.

We do have natural ties with others, and, in the course of these interactions, certain normatively loaded conventions arise – precisely as with the queue, as MacCormick was to later show. These, in turn, over time, thicken institutionally – though always contingently, incrementally, and pragmatically, rather than in a planned and deliberate way – and come to form quite complex sets of rules, which make moral sense (for they are linked to those basic relational realities). In other words, law forms in this way, a strange kind of natural, including normative, artifice – a kind of 'institutional fact', but one now seen as part of a longer story of evolution, of customary emergence, of institutional normative order.

Such, then, might be the kind of story – only sketched here – that underlies MacCormick's transition, if it really is a transition, from talk of 'institutional facts' to 'institutional normative order'. We know that in the early 1980s, MacCormick was thinking of writing a book on Smith and did publish, albeit only articles, on Smith at this time, emphasising Smith's

254 Bańkowski, 'Institution of Law' (1991), 83.
255 See MacCormick, 'Voluntary Obligations' (1972).

interactional account of natural rights;[256] we know he read with enormous enthusiasm the publication of Smith's *Lectures on Jurisprudence* in 1978;[257] we also know he read Knud Haakonssen's *The Science of a Legislator* (1981), reviewing it, again with great enthusiasm, in 1982;[258] we know that he was re-reading Hume, in part by reference also to how he was redrawing, in his mind, the relations between natural law and positivism, in part due to the publication of Finnis's *Natural Law and Natural Rights* in 1981;[259] and we know how deeply he was venturing into Stair, writing on his conception of incremental, grounded, imperfect reason,[260] as well as considering, and admiring, the sense in which Stair was both a natural lawyer, of a kind, and at the same time an analytical jurist.[261]

In all of this, MacCormick did arguably see in the eighteenth-century tradition of the law of nature and nations an amalgamation of positivism and natural law, and thus yet another sense in which one could perform a kind of relational act, bringing about a communal peace, this time between contemporary legal positivists and natural lawyers. The roots of such potential reconciliation, it seems, lay in returning to our intellectual history: it was just a pity that the anti-historical attitudes of so many contemporary jurisprudes were not willing to accompany him there.[262]

Scholars and Practitioners

In the earlier-quoted last paragraph of MacCormick's Inaugural Lecture, 'Law as Institutional Fact', MacCormick argued for a partnership not only between sociologists and philosophers, but also with lawyers. His emphasis, in that lecture, on social institutions, and the officials in them, was no accident or something on the margins of his theory. It was, instead, central to his conception of law's institutionality: law was something that, for all its scholarly reconstruction as a system that made normative sense, was a matter of practice – messy, contested, occasional, pragmatic, and thus grounded in particular controversies as these came before the courts. This

256 See, e.g., MacCormick, 'Smith' (1981).
257 MacCormick, 'Review of Smith' (1978).
258 MacCormick, 'Review of Haakonssen' (1982).
259 See MacCormick, 'Natural Law Reconsidered' (1981); 'Law, Morality, Positivism' (1981).
260 See MacCormick, 'Rational Discipline' (1981).
261 See MacCormick, 'Stair, Analytical' (1981), 198.
262 For further appreciations, not necessarily in this same vein, of MacCormick's reading of the Scottish Enlightenment, see MacQueen, 'A Post-Positivist' (2012), and more recently, Bogle's account of Stair in his 'Morality before the Enlightenment' (2023).

attitude to the importance of institutions was to be found, too, in a number of the sources he cited as inspirations for his theory.

Thus, for example, in his essay on Hart (1963) Summers argued that one could not see law solely as an abstract system of rules: 'rules alone cannot do the job'.[263] Too much 'emphasis on the concept of rule rather than on the concept of functioning social institutions may, in some cases, obscure the true character of "legal" action, including 'the personalities of the officials who administer the system'.[264] One had to take note – realistically – of how legal officials in social institutions needed to 'resolve uncertainties' and thus make judgements.[265] Further, there was typically never one such institution, but many, and these were often in competition with each other: social institutions were 'bidding for power' and this was important to consider when theorising law.[266]

This was, in many ways, a realist-inspired point: do not get trapped in formalistic dreams, remember the real, that power-based, personality-driven, realm of persons working in institutions. A similar kind of realism was present in Llewellyn's 'The Constitution as Institution' (1934), which MacCormick also cited as inspiration. A constitution, Llewellyn said, was 'not a document, but a living institution built (historically, genetically)'.[267] If one focuses solely on the text, then one cannot understand what constitutionalism in a society entails: such a focus 'leaves wholly uncovered a mass of fundamental governmental structures and norms which do not happen to be mentioned in the document'.[268] Institutions really matter: 'it is institutions which test whether there is still force in the words, and how much force, and what that force is. It is institutions which validate the words, not the words which validate the institutions'.[269] It is instructive here to see how Llewellyn describes what an institution is and how he then relates it to the constitution:

> An institution is in first instance a set of ways of living and doing. It is not, in first instance, a matter of words or rules. The existence of an institution lies first of all and last of all in the fact that people do behave in certain patterns a, b and c, and do not have in other conceivable patterns d to w. And the probability that an institution will continue coincides with whatever probability there is that people will continue so to behave. Every living

[263] Summers, 'Professor Hart's Concept of Law' (1963), 644.
[264] Ibid.
[265] Ibid., 644–5.
[266] Ibid., 645.
[267] Llewellyn, 'The Constitution as Institution' (1934), 3.
[268] Ibid., 17.
[269] Ibid.

> constitution is an institution; it lives only so far as that is true. And the difference between a written and unwritten constitution lies only in the fact that the shape of an action in the former case is somewhat influenced by the presence of a particular document, and of particular attitudes toward it, and particular ways of dealing with its language.[270]

For Llewellyn, the key point was not whether a constitution was written or not; what really mattered was whether the constitution was alive, i.e., that it was a 'living and doing' in a whole 'complex' array of interactions between 'diverse categories of people',[271] including not only courts, but also various forms of 'machinery', such as the 'party system and campaign fund, protective tariff and secret ballot, patronage and Senatorial filibuster, judicial review and national banking'.[272] This was an expansive concept of a constitution, for sure, and it was also highly pragmatic, recognising that such an 'institutional structure' had to 'contain[] within itself the wherewithal for give, for readjustment, for self-sanitation'.[273] In a sense, one could say, the 'constitution as institution' was a form of customary practical reason situated within complex ways of living and doing.

Both Summers's and Llewellyn's realist orientations were present in MacCormick's account of social institutions in his Inaugural Lecture – as they would be later, for example, when MacCormick emphasised the sense in which the European Constitution was but a necessarily imperfect formalisation of an already-existing, complex, functional constitution in Europe. This was not, of course, to say that written constitutions did not matter – they mattered for Llewellyn too – but it was to say that there was always a link, for there had to be, between any such formalisation (or institutionalisation) and the imperfect normative practices from which it emerged and within which it stayed alive. It is, then, against such a background that we can understand MacCormick's call for a 'joint adventure' between philosophers, sociologists, and lawyers. Legal practice really mattered: it was not an outcome of some scholarly dream, but instead formed the material that scholars needed to rationally reconstruct and make some more systematic sense of.

This was a theoretical point, but there was also a more immediate, more local, impetus for such a view, i.e., for a recognition of the vital element of legal practice. Scotland was a small jurisdiction. Within such small jurisdictions, the relations between lawyers and scholars were close – indeed,

270 Ibid., 17–18.
271 Ibid., 21.
272 Ibid.
273 Ibid., 31.

the scholars had to be pseudo-practitioners and the lawyers had to be pseudo-scholars, as indeed the ambiguous term 'jurist' arguably seeks to capture. This was the case historically as much as it was still very much so. Certainly, the Scottish thinkers we saw MacCormick reading so enthusiastically above were very practically oriented – they may have offered theories of morality and society, but this was often in connection with theories of law in practice: Kames was a good example, being a scholar and a judge, but he was really one of many – the 'connections among the lawyers and the philosophers' of the Enlightenment were vast and rich.[274]

But there was more: as Phillipson had shown in his historical work,[275] lawyers were vital to the civic development of Scotland post-1707, being centrally involved not only in the day-to-day administration of the polity, but also in the kind of polite and learned conversation from which the Scottish Enlightenment emerged.[276] Lawyers in Scotland, then, were always more than practitioners: they were enmeshed in the civic dynamics of the polity. Lawyers had civic responsibilities: they were not so much 'captains of industry' as 'under-labourers of welfare'. Lawyers, as Phillipson put it, were 'custodians of Scotland's *virtu*'.[277]

That quote from Phillipson comes from a collection of essays MacCormick edited (though did not contribute to), entitled *Lawyers in their Social Setting* (1976). This was a volume dedicated, as MacCormick put it, 'to two distinguished citizens of Edinburgh and of its University, to Sheriff John G. Wilson Q. C., sometime Sheriff of the Lothians and Peebles at Edinburgh, and Dr Nan Wilson, sometime Lecturer in Social Anthropology in Edinburgh'.[278] It contained a series of papers that had been given as lectures between 1972 and 1975, each exploring the social role and value of lawyers. Very much a European collection, comprising accounts, either historical or sociological, of lawyers in Norway, France, South Africa, United States, Germany, Italy, and Scotland, and including, in addition to Phillipson, contributors such as Max Gluckman, Philip Selznick, Niklas Luhmann, Colin Campbell, and T. B. Smith, the papers focused on the relations between politics and the legal profession, including how lawyers contributed to the well-being of their societies, e.g., by becoming more involved 'in the problems of the underprivileged and the

274 MacCormick, 'Law and Enlightenment' (1982), 151.

275 E.g., Phillipson, *The Scottish Whigs* (1990); 'Lawyers, Landowners' (1976).

276 See also Kidd, 'The Phillipsonian Enlightenment' (2014); and Squibbs, *The Urban Enlightenment* (2014).

277 Phillipson, 'Lawyers, Landowners' (1976), 171.

278 MacCormick, 'Foreword' to *Lawyers in Their Social Setting* (1976), vii.

poor'.[279] As Selznick put it in his contribution: lawyers, as social advocates, were an integral part of a 'responsive legal order'.[280]

Lawyers could, then, be citizens of great value to a polity and in this sense mirrored the kinds of public duties that scholars might have (and we saw, in previous chapters, how seriously MacCormick took these, e.g., with his role in the University Settlement). For this reason, too, the prospects for collaboration between scholars and practitioners mattered. An interesting manifestation of the potential for such collaboration was the Scottish Law Commission to which scholars, certainly from Edinburgh, were often seconded. Indeed, in the early 1970s, the offices of the Commission were still in Old College, the Law School's home – though, writing as a Dean, it is with some relief that MacCormick notes, in 1976, that the Commission was moving out in June 1976, for this will clear 'some more nice rooms for our use, which will be a blessing while we are short of space owing to the building operations'.[281] In any event, one need not rely on such physical proximity: again, the reality of a small jurisdiction, like Scotland's, is that there were many and deep connections between theory and practice. As far as MacCormick was concerned, this was all to the good and needed preservation: as we have seen, MacCormick did precisely that, campaigning for the retention of the Chair of Conveyancing in Edinburgh, and arguing that attention to the practical, technical detail of law's everyday operation was vital to any philosophical understanding of law.

It is well to remember, in light of all this, that MacCormick himself for a long time contemplated a career in practice. As we have seen in previous chapters, MacCormick was initially set on qualifying as an advocate in Scotland, and took the job as Lecturer in Dundee in 1965 as a step onto that career (he later qualified as a Barrister of the Inner Temple in 1971, though he never practised). MacCormick's publications in the 1960s and early 1970s were often on matters concerning direct implications for legal practice. Even, however, when he decided that the academic path was, in the end, his calling, he still retained a lawyer's predilection for cases: his *Legal Reasoning and Legal Theory* (1978) was, in ways that were unusual for legal theory of the time (or arguably since), packed with cases. Even right at the end of his life, when writing *Practical Reason in Law and Morality* (2008), MacCormick situated his reflections on practical reason within controversial cases. MacCormick's theorising, then, was never far from practice.

279 Ibid., ix.

280 Selznick, 'Social Advocacy' (1976).

281 MacCormick, Letter to I. C. MacGibbon (24 May 1976).

We can see this, too, in the collection that completed his institutional theorisation of law: *Institutions of Law*, published in 2007. Here, much like an institutional writer, MacCormick adopted a panoptic perspective on all areas of law, thereby arguably seeking to relate not only theory and practice, but also general and particular jurisprudence. Throughout MacCormick's oeuvre, there was hardly an area of law that did not interest him: from all aspects of public and constitutional law right through to virtually all areas of private law, including contract[282] and tort, but also, for example, intellectual property law.[283]

In *Institutions of Law*, we see him returning to some of these interests, writing precisely on the 'law of obligations' alongside a chapter on 'property', but encompassing also the 'law of persons', including the powers of corporations, as well as a chapter on criminal law.[284] Analysis of public powers is placed alongside, and related to, relations between private law, commerce, and the economy. It is a work of breathtaking scope, worthy surely of any institutional writing, though also difficult, precisely because of how much it takes on, to process as a whole.

An analysis of MacCormick's efforts in particular jurisprudence must await the treatment of specialists in those areas. What I would like to emphasise here is that this holistic vision was yet another sense in which the institutional theory of law was a relational act: relating both scholars and practitioners, as well as those interested in general jurisprudential issues and those analysing particular areas of the law. As with so much of MacCormick's theorising, including institutionally, this was valuable not solely because of the particular insights he offered on the issues he addressed, but also because of the way the theory was a way of mediating relationships, constructing links, enabling conversations, across otherwise often separated communities. This was, precisely, a matter of character and shows, once more, the value of philosophy: Hermes-like, a kind of Humean ambassador, travelling between communities, bonding persons together, and creating the potential for relations of mutual respect, regard, civility, and decency.

282 See also the section on good faith in MacCormick, 'Stair General Concepts' (2008), section 12.

283 MacCormick, 'On the Very Idea of IP' (2002).

284 MacCormick's work on persons is significant and deserves further attention in its own right; he pays attention to how persons exist over time, and offers a realistic, rather than fictional, account of corporations as persons, arguing it is natural for human beings to collaborate in and act as collectives: in addition to the chapter in IL, see MacCormick, 'Persons as Institutional Facts' (1988); see the section on persons and personhood in MacCormick, 'Stair General Concepts' (2008).

10

Reason, Philosophy, and Character

A Matter of Civility

Any reader of MacCormick's philosophy is soon confronted with a basic puzzle, i.e., the relation between two bodies of thought in his oeuvre: institutional legal theory on the one hand and the theory of practical reason on the other. What exactly is the relation between these two theoretical orientations in MacCormick's work? Did he think that law was a kind of institutional phenomenon *or* a branch of practical reason, or did he think law was both at the same time? If both at the same time, then are these two bodies of theorising law at odds with each other or is there complex unity between them?

One could attempt to deflect the question by arguing that the two bodies are answering different problems: for example, whereas the first is concerned with questions about the ontology and epistemology of law, the second is concerned with questions about reasoning. This does not quite work, however, for, as we saw in Chapter 9, when MacCormick reflected further on the institutionality of law, coming to stress its dynamic and evolving character, he often ended up in a place that emphasised precisely the reasoning practices of social institutions. Similarly so the other way round: when, in theorising reasoning, MacCormick found himself too far in the sphere of indeterminacy, he looked for ways to anchor reasoning in something more stable, e.g., the existence and knowability of certain rules. It also does not work to say that whereas one body of theory (institutionalism) is more concerned with law, the other (practical reason) is more concerned with morality, or at least with the relationship between moral and legal reasoning. For, again as we have seen in Chapter 9, institutionalism was itself a language chosen to avoid splitting apart natural law and positivist traditions, finding instead a middle space between them where there were connections between law and morality.

One could, then, argue that there is a real puzzle here, and indeed, at times in this chapter I return to it, and consider the relations between these two bodies of theory. But the puzzle can also be taken too far. At stake is how to understand the very practice of philosophy, but also how to approach it as a reader. The bite of the puzzle depends on taking the view that the practice of philosophy, including its value to others, is reducible to the theses it defends and the quality of arguments made in support of them. This view takes it to be desirable that a philosophy be systematic and internally consistent – that a philosopher's oeuvre be so, in part so we can also slot it more easily into an overall map of philosophical views (e.g., characterise it as a positivist or an anti-positivist view). On this approach to philosophy, and its value, philosophy is a matter of arguing for, articulating, and defending, a thesis or set of theses, thereby forming an overall systematic and internally consistent answer to certain philosophical problems.

While acknowledging the importance of the quality of argument, and systematicity, consistency, and clarity in philosophical practice, this book does not accept that the practice of philosophy, or its value, can be reduced in this way. There is something else that lies deeper – that captures more of the complexity and the value of philosophical work. That something else is precisely character.

When approaching philosophy as a matter of character, and reading it in this way, one need not treat bodies of thought in a philosopher's corpus as merely instruments for articulating a thesis or a set of theses. Rather, such bodies of thought also become genuine explorations that a philosopher struggles over, both in dialogues with herself, but also and indeed especially in dialogues with others. On this view, inconsistencies, or even contradictions, are not errors or bugs, but features in philosophical practice: they show a philosopher at work, exploring a certain subject matter, returning to its difficulties, sometimes moving in one direction and sometimes in another.

On this view, a philosophical text is not worse because its author is undecided, or because it has failed to produce a clear and systematic thesis that defeats all other opposing views to it. Philosophy is not necessarily this kind of macho battle for domination, with winner takes all stakes. Philosophy can also be approached, and read, as a struggle with oneself, which centrally involves reflecting on how to live with others. It may be thought of as more like a confrontation of the self with a view to hopefully improving the quality of one's relations with others. Philosophy, in other words, can also be read with character – with attention to the manner or style with which one relates with other persons, including negotiating one's role in a community, which is a process that is complex and may involve indecision, ambivalence and difficulty. Reading philosophy with character, then, is an attempt precisely to illuminate this complexity, and to recognise value in that complexity.

In Chapter 9, I sought to read MacCormick's institutionalism with character. For instance, I tried to show how the very language of 'institutions' allowed MacCormick to relate with others in complex ways, including both his peers and his predecessors. From this perspective, institutionalism is better thought of not as a set of theses, but as a space in which MacCormick conducted conversations with himself and with others, thereby also finding his footing in various communities, often, in his case, relating groups that were at odds with each other or traditionally separated in some way, e.g., philosophers and sociologists, officials and citizens, and scholars and practitioners.

This does not mean that there are not substantive things one can say about MacCormick's institutionalism: indeed, reading with character is not about reducing or explaining away the details (including arguments and stances) of a theory, but instead illuminating them. In Chapter 9, I tried to do that by pointing to numerous themes that, for all the changes in the theory over time, also functioned as smaller spaces within the overall complex space of institutionalism that MacCormick kept returning to and exploring, such as the issue of relations being at the heart of the normative, or the temporal dimension of law-as-institution, or articulating how law exists and how it is knowable.

In this chapter, I try to do something similar, but this time with the theory of practical reason. Like institutionalism, this is a body of thought – including a vocabulary – that develops over five decades of a busy scholarly life. Also as with institutionalism, this involves dialogues that MacCormick engaged in, both with peers and with predecessors. With respect to peers, this is by no means only a dialogue – as it is unfortunately often presented or understood in the Anglo-American jurisprudential world – with Hart and Dworkin, where MacCormick is often positioned, especially in his first book, *Legal Reasoning and Legal Theory* (1978), as a loyal Hartian disciple, defending Hart against the youthful onslaught of Dworkin.

Although the polemics of the Hart–Dworkin debate do play an important role, they are only one part of a much larger story. This includes dialogues with many other figures in the Anglo-American world itself – for instance, conversations with fellow friends, colleagues, and doctoral students in Edinburgh[1] – but also with a whole generation of European

[1] The doctoral students included (this is not an exhaustive list): Ruth Adler, Fernando Atria, Claudio Michelon, Scott Veitch, Emilios Christodoulidis, George Pavlakos, Stefano Bertea, Joxerramon Bengoetxea, and Sundram Soosay.

philosophers and jurists. This included, for MacCormick, relations with Chaïm Perelman, Robert Alexy, and members of the Bielefelder Kreis, a group of legal philosophers who, over the course of two decades in the 1980s and 1990s, engaged in a comparative and philosophical inquiry into statutory interpretation and precedential reasoning. The story of this European conversation deserves to be told in full, but even when alluded to inadequately, as I do in this chapter, one sees just how important it was for MacCormick, and thus how much is lost from view when one's jurisprudential historiography is confined to certain debates that are said to dominate the Anglo–American world of jurisprudence.

Equally important, and even more so than in the case of institutionalism, is the fact that MacCormick's exploration of practical reason was conducted, as noticed for instance by Jeremy Waldron, 'in the company of philosophers such as Adam Smith and Immanuel Kant' and their 'inquiry into the nature of moral reasoning'.[2] In other words, a large and crucial part of MacCormick's theory of practical reason is the sense in which it provided him with an opportunity to read and re-read the philosophers of the long eighteenth century, especially Stair, Hume, Smith, and Kant. MacCormick's engagements with these thinkers is not best approached as an exercise in intellectual history: as much as he clearly appreciated the historical significance of the work of these thinkers, his aim was not to offer authoritative and historically contextualised interpretations of their work, but instead to engage with them in philosophical reflection on reasoning about what one ought to do, including the role and limits of rationality, the importance of emotion in value judgement, and the social dynamics of reasoning.

This aspect of MacCormick's theory of practical reason cannot be underestimated and so bears emphasising. As we have seen in previous chapters, MacCormick was educated, initially, as a Glaswegian moral philosopher. The questions that were alive for him, as a student in the late 1950s and early 1960s, were indeed questions concerning what it is to reason morally – which were, in turn, wrapped up in questions about what it is to do moral philosophy and be a moral philosopher. These were questions he confronted together with his teachers: Lamont, Maclagan, Horsburgh, Raphael, and Downie, amongst others.

Although, as one would expect, much of the teaching in Glasgow was oriented to reading Scottish moral philosophy – Hutcheson, Hume, and Smith especially – though of course always in dialogue with English and

[2] Waldron, 'Legal Judgement' (2011), 107.

European figures, a very large part of both the pedagogical and philosophical research culture concerned the place of Kant vis-à-vis the Scottish moralists. Accordingly, Kant loomed large in MacCormick's early reflections on moral reasoning, and it is from here that his interests in justification, especially in the Categorical Imperative and in universalisability – as further elaborated and interpreted by Hare, Paton, Lamont, and others – flowered and then continued as a life-long interest. However, what is crucial to remember is that the interest in Kant was set within a broader Scottish tradition of moral philosophy and the question, in many ways, both for him and for many others in Scotland, was how to read and interpret Kant in light of that tradition. Thus, reflection on Kant was always conducted alongside debates and discussions about Kant's relations with Hume and Smith.

It also important to remember, with respect to MacCormick's engagement with the Scottish tradition of moral philosophy, that MacCormick lived through a period of exciting discoveries, especially the publication, in 1978, after new student notes were found, of Smith's *Lectures on Jurisprudence*. Surrounding this discovery, there was a flurry of scholarly activity, including work by Tom Campbell, Knud Haakonssen, and David Raphael, with whom MacCormick corresponded and related over many years.

A further vital addition to this scholarly community was the growing interest, in Scotland, in the work of Stair, and the continuing research on Scots law and the history of its practice, for instance, via the Stair Society. MacCormick had a life-long interest in Stair, both in terms of how Stair illuminated the allegedly more principled approach to law-making in Scotland (than in England), and in terms of his overall theory of law, including law's reasonableness. Stair appears in MacCormick's earliest publications, in 1966, and in his latest, in 2009.[3] Indeed, Stair's *Institutions* was on the shelf at home in Glasgow when MacCormick was a boy, with his father recommending it to MacCormick already then.[4] One cannot, then, ignore the importance of Stair as a companion to MacCormick as he reflected on practical reason and its relationship to law.

As if all this were not enough, to it we must add MacCormick's own plans, at one point, in becoming a barrister, first in England, where he became a member of the Inner Temple, but always ultimately with a view

[3] MacCormick, 'Stare Decisis' (1966); 'Stair – Still Relevant' (2009); and see also the discussion of Stair in PRLM (2008).

[4] MacCormick, 'Rational Discipline' (1981), 146.

to practising in Scotland. Although MacCormick soon committed to life in academia – alongside, as we have seen, his involvement in politics (where, it is also important to remember, MacCormick was often called upon for his legal opinion) – sensitivity to the realities of legal practice never quite left him and accompanied his theorisation of legal reasoning. This is visible in many aspects of the style of his writing on legal reasoning: the sheer numbers, for instance, of cases in his philosophical work, including his orientation to the most controversial and difficult of them. Also significant is that the examples stretched to all areas of law – an effect, in part, of his teaching in Oxford, as tutors then taught so many law subjects – extending to English and Scottish private and public law, but also encompassing transnational and international legal orders. MacCormick thus pays attention to numerous courts in theorising legal reasoning, including the Scottish Court of Session, English courts, and the European Court of Justice. This range and scope, within systems and across systems, and this detailed engagement with cases, is significant, and also arguably unique among his peers.

And there is one more piece of the context that we must take into account when reading MacCormick's work on practical reason: his experience as a debater. It may be thought, because MacCormick's participation in debating was a feature of his student days, that it is something he left behind, and thus that it is of limited importance in reading his later work. If tempted by this thought, one does well to remember just how intensively involved MacCormick was in that student debating culture. If we recall, for instance, that Glasgow's debating was structured in the form of six parliamentary clubs, with each fighting their corner on the most controversial of subjects, and that MacCormick participated in this over the course of many years, accompanied by intense scrutiny of debating skills and styles, then we have before us what is nothing other than a cauldron of practical reason in which MacCormick is steeped at a very formative stage of his life.

Importantly, this cauldron is a deeply social one. If this is practical reason, it is so not in the sense of a lonely figure musing about what they ought to do, but instead very much a participatory, affective, oratorical, physical, and dynamically social activity of the exchange of arguments, tones, attitudes, and sensibilities. Again, MacCormick was a reflective participant in this practice: as we have seen, he often wrote reports of debates, and he also read reports of his own performances. Not only did he himself participate, but so did his family members – his father, his brother, his cousins – as well as his many friends, many across the political spectrum.

We thus ignore this context at our peril; indeed, I would argue, it is a vital context for understanding MacCormick's interest in the ethics of debate, but more broadly too, in the political dynamics of deliberation and persuasion – in the life, most generally put, of the democratic intellect.

Of course, all these dialogues and contexts make for a complex picture – an almost impossibly complex one. Accordingly, I do not aim to be comprehensive – this chapter is but one, partial and inadequate, reading of MacCormick's theory of practical reason. While I attempt to pay attention, as much as possible, to these various dialogues and contexts, I organise this chapter thematically into two parts that together illustrate MacCormick's theory of practical reason. Perhaps inevitably, there is in this discussion a certain emphasis placed on MacCormick's early formulation of his theory, with particular attention to *Legal Reasoning and Legal Theory* (1978) and various papers published in the 1980s, though supplemented with some attention to his final book, *Practical Reason in Law and Morality* (2008). In between, MacCormick responded to numerous criticisms of his account, and these responses found their way into his 2005 collection, *Rhetoric and the Rule of Law*. This is, of course, important too – especially in its conception of the rule of law – but arguably, the basic structure, which was modified but not radically altered, was set early, in the above-mentioned 1978 book.

In the first part of the chapter, I tackle MacCormick's approach to value in general. My argument, in keeping with this book's attention to character, is that what matters most to MacCormick when theorising value is respect for persons and their particular, potentially very different, orientations to what is valuable. Thus, there is, at the starting point and base of MacCormick's reflections on practical reason, a kind of civility: an awareness of, and sensitivity to, perspectivalism about value. This includes recognising that persons can have a strong normative commitment to value, which includes a complex mix of will (or desire), affect, and reason.

The perspectivalism in question, then, is a normatively thick one (and thicker, as we shall see, than Hart's). The perspectivalism is normatively thick because that is what is required by a genuine respect for a person's point of view: the commitments of others cannot simply be dismissed as entirely conventional (a matter, say, of following what others do); instead, they are, as above, complex mixes of desire, emotion, and reason. This normatively thick perspectivalism, read as respect for a person's point of view, is, however, restrained. In other words, it never embraces a metaphysics or epistemology of value (e.g., realism or ultra-rationalism) that would flatten or collapse that perspectivalism into a transcendental scheme of self-evident values or one right answer to hard cases. It remains, always, moderate and pragmatic, as well as generatively and constructively sceptical – arguably much like the figure to whom MacCormick often found himself resorting when theorising value: David Hume.

Informed by this perspectivalism about value, I turn, in the second part of the chapter, to MacCormick's account of the workings of practical reason. This has two stages: first, the requirement of justification, and in particular universalist justification. Persons, whether citizens or officials (but certainly especially judges), may be called upon to justify their actions to their fellows. When they do so, it is part of the ethics of reasoning together that this is done with a view to translating one's particular claim in a particular dispute into a language that others can find intelligible. This process includes imagining the potential effects on others, now and in the future, of one's adoption of a certain criterion of action. Without this universalist justification, debate cannot begin. Thus, in many ways, the very point and value of universalist justification is to create an inter-subjective space (a space that, later, in the 1990s, MacCormick calls the rule of law) where persons can bring their particular claims into the communal realm. MacCormick develops this view in the company of Kant's Categorical Imperative, later amended via Smith, and in dialogue with numerous teachers and peers. A role, too, is played by deductive logic; together with universalisability, the whole package, of this first stage, constitutes the first-order level of justification.

Once we have generated a number of candidate universal justifications, and thus created an inter-subjective space, we then proceed to the second stage of practical reason, i.e., the testing of these candidates and the making a choice between them. MacCormick refers variably to this process as second-order or second-tier justification, or also as the practice of non-deductive justification. MacCormick is fascinated by the complexity of this process, especially as it features in the details of the cases he explores. It is this complex process of testing that occupies the majority of his attention.

There are three such tests in the second stage: consistency, coherence, and consequentialism. The relations between them are not always clear in MacCormick's work, e.g., sometimes coherence and consequentialism appear to collapse into each other; sometimes consequences are considered first, and sometimes they are considered last. But more important than this internal systematicity in his thinking is his deep exploration of these second-tier, non-deductive forms of justification, perhaps especially the role and importance of consequential arguments in legal reasoning.

Having survived the various tests, one candidate justification ends up being chosen. That one is chosen is of special importance in the legal context, where a court must, after all, come to a decision. However, as important as that might be, MacCormick is also careful about the status that is attributed to any such decision. Here, MacCormick emphasises the defeasibility and revisability of decisions, especially with respect to precedent. Authority – or, put in other ways, the heteronomy – of law is needed, but this is set within a much broader social and dynamic context of contestation, debate, and change. We only ever have relative and defeasible stability in law. For all the necessarily practical importance for authority, law remains embedded in a long-term, incremental, on-going, never-ending, imperfect, and collective process of rational reconstruction.

That, then, is the plan for the chapter. Together, via the two parts – the first on MacCormick's perspectivalism about value, and the second on the two stages of the construction, deliberation and decision-making in an inter-subjective space (a communal space that MacCormick also conceives of as the rule of law) – I seek to shed some light on MacCormick's theory of practical reason. It is a complex picture, and perhaps not always an internally consistent one. However, as noted above, it is not for consistency and systematicity, or even the evaluation of the various beliefs and arguments in it, that I read it: I read it, instead, with character, and thus with how it was a negotiation of MacCormick's role, as a philosopher, in the various communities he participated in.

Speaking about MacCormick at his funeral, Neil Walker spoke movingly of how he had 'never met a more considerate human being' than MacCormick.[5] Similarly, others, reflecting on MacCormick's legacy after his death, have frequently written of MacCormick's basic 'decency'.[6] These are no accidents; nor are they merely the words of grieving friends. They pick up something of deep importance to MacCormick's character, i.e., the manner or style with which he related with others. There is, throughout MacCormick's work on practical reason, a basic and recurring orientation to respecting the other person, to being considerate to others, to being decent.

This, however, is no passive, joyless, task – you will find no sour or cynical tolerance here; instead, there is a most cheerful, joyful, and active curiosity in and warm regard for the views and opinions of another person. Indeed, it speaks volumes about MacCormick that, when writing his last

5 Neil Walker, 'Eulogy', Funeral Service for Neil MacCormick, Greyfriars Kirk (17 April 2009).

6 See, e.g., La Torre, 'A Flag in the Wind' (2010).

book – *Practical Reason in Law and Morality* (2008) – all the while staring death in the face, knowing that he will soon die from an incurable cancer, what he wrote about was the importance of not letting others down (keeping his promise to write a fourth book in his series), and of taking seriously, via the Smithian Categorical Imperative, the emotional experiences of others. It is this basic other-regarding sensibility, this considerateness and decency, this matter of civility – a joyful, warm, curious civility – that lies at the heart of MacCormick's theorisation of practical reason, and it is this that I ultimately seek to illuminate by reading this body of thought with attention to character.

Perspectivalism about Value

The question with which I began this chapter can be given another spin: if one is interested in ethical and moral questions – in questions about matters of value – must one, first, have a clear ontological position, i.e., a clear view of the metaphysics of value, and a clear epistemological position, as to what it is to know value, before one proceeds to tackling any particular ethical or moral problem or scenario? Put another way, is ethics dependent on meta-ethics?

If one is tempted by this thought, then one might well think that there is, for there needs to be, a tight relation between MacCormick's ontological and epistemological statements (for instance, defending law as institutional fact, but also, later, his accounts of institutional normative order) and his theory of practical reason, or how we reason about matters of value. This is a recipe for dissatisfaction, for one is likely to quickly come to the conclusion that although MacCormick did have a well developed theory of law's ontology and epistemology, he did not really have a well developed account of the ontology and epistemology of value in general (his account of normative order, one might say, is just an inadequate prolegomenon to a theory of law as institutional normative order).

To approach matters this way, however, would, I think, do a disservice to MacCormick. There are two points to make here: one is that we need to consider the possibility that a focus on reasoning about matters of value, rather than a focus on the ontology or epistemology of value, is a choice, and not a defect or an oversight; and the other is that perhaps MacCormick did have a theory of value's ontology and epistemology, but one that takes a more nuanced approach to what it means to theorise the ontology and epistemology of value. In a sense, the two go hand-in-hand. What I want to argue is that MacCormick did have an account of the ontology and epistemology of value – one largely based on perspectivalism about value – but that it is difficult to read this straightforwardly as ontology and epistemology, and that there are good reasons for that. In other words, there are good reasons why MacCormick emphasised the question of practical reason, i.e., the question about the role and limits of reason in relation to matters of value. MacCormick was always fascinated by both meta-ethical and metaphysical questions, but he did not think philosophy was doomed to stay within them: philosophy was simply too practical, too grounded, too social for that.

Humean Conversations

A good place to start is with how MacCormick frames his inquiry in *Legal Reasoning and Legal Theory* (1978). In the very first line of the book, in the preface that is explicitly dated 2 May 1977, MacCormick says the following:

> In this book, I try to describe and explain the elements of legal arguments advanced in justification of decisions, or claims and defences put to the courts for decision; to relate that to the general theory of law; and to do all that in the framework of a general theory of practical reason which owes a great deal to David Hume.[7]

Very much at the outset, then, MacCormick signals a certain allegiance to Hume's approach to practical reason. What does he mean? In what sense does he 'owe a great deal to David Hume?'

To answer this, we must look to see how MacCormick brings Hume in. Hume enters the fray as someone who expresses 'the most fundamental scepticism about the limits of reason in practical affairs'.[8] Prior to Hume, MacCormick says, there was a prominent defence of practical reason articulated by Stair: 'Law is the dictate of reason determining every rational being to that which is congruous and convenient for the nature thereof'[9] – a phrase that MacCormick did not tire of quoting.[10] I will be returning to Stair, but for the moment, what is important is that MacCormick sees Hume as challenging this view. Hume's argument, summarised by MacCormick, was as follows:

> Reduced to its essentials, his [Hume's] argument is that our faculty of reasoning can operate only upon given premisses; assuming certain premisses,

[7] MacCormick, LRLT (1978), i.

[8] Ibid., 2.

[9] Stair, *Institutions* (1981) [1693], 1.i.1.

[10] MacCormick, LRLT (1978), 1–2; see also 'Stair, Still Relevant' (2009).

> we can by reason ascertain the conclusions which follow from them. And indeed reason can guide us in seeking to verify or falsify assertions concerning matters of fact or existential propositions generally. In the latter case, however, reasoning has a secondary role, since it can work only with evidence already given in our various sense impressions.[11]

Reason, in short, could not lead us to prefer one premise or another – it could connect premises to certain consequences – it is an inferential faculty and of course very important in being so – but it cannot, by itself, make us prefer any one premise, e.g., that one ought to keep one's promises, or, more spectacularly, in Hume's example, from the *Treatise*, that one ought to prefer the destruction of the world in preference to the scratching of our finger. For Hume, according to MacCormick, such attachment or commitment to these basic premises was not a matter of reason, but instead 'a matter of a disposition of the will founded upon simple sentiment of preference or appropriation which we feel toward' some 'state of affairs'.[12]

Assume, for a moment, that one agrees with this view. Does it, however, follow that there is no role for reason other than making inferences from such basic premises? Here is where MacCormick sees himself as departing from Hume. MacCormick puts it this way, also bringing in Thomas Reid:

> Hume was correct in asserting that reasons cannot be given for ultimate moral premisses; there are no statements of 'pure fact' which we can give to back up whatever we set forth as our ultimate premisses in moral arguments. Moreover, it is the case that these ultimate moral premisses are necessarily associated with dispositions of the affections and of the will. But it is not true that they are not also apprehended by reason and in that sense rational. Our adherence to general principles – e.g., that no acts of violence ought to be perpetrated on human beings save in certain justifying or excusing circumstances – is a manifestation of our rationality, by contrast with our merely impulsive and animal reactions to circumstances.[13]

This is an important moment in MacCormick's theory. In one sense, MacCormick agrees with Hume, namely that, as he puts it, 'any mode of evaluative argument must involve, depend on, or presuppose, some ultimate premisses which are not themselves provable, demonstrable, or confirmable in terms of further or ulterior reasons'.[14] On the other hand, he also seems to disagree with Hume: there is, for MacCormick, some sense

11 Ibid., 2.
12 Ibid., 3.
13 Ibid., 3–4.
14 Ibid., 5.

in which our acceptance of and commitment to those 'ultimate premises' is 'also apprehended by reason and in that sense rational', or, as he puts it, matters of value not being 'provable' does not mean that 'no reasons at all can be given for adhering to such normative premisses – "principles" – as grounds for action and judgement'.[15]

This is a conceptual space of some difficulty and delicacy. On a less generous reading, MacCormick might be said to be wanting to have his Hume and eat him too (with apologies to the idiom). To some extent, he appears to embrace a certain kind of scepticism about the kind of rational access we can have to value: there are no matters of fact, he wants to say, via which we can rationally force another to accept that such-and-such is valuable. There is, it appears, some kind of constitutive link between a person's will and emotion to value. On the other hand, any acceptance or commitment to value, MacCormick wants to say, is also a 'manifestation of our rationality'. There is more to reason than Hume thinks, although he is also right that there are limits to reason.

Here, we must exercise care in how to read MacCormick. Again, one could argue there is something contradictory about MacCormick's position, i.e., that it is not a systematic or internally consistent ontological and epistemological thesis about value. However, once more, I think this would be a mistake: it would be rushing to read MacCormick's philosophy as valuable for the sole reason that it generates a clear and consistent thesis. There is another way to approach it: to try to grapple with the difficulties that MacCormick sees. To do that, we need to consider what is relationally at stake in MacCormick grappling with this difficulty, with him wanting, as it were, to have it both ways.

In trying to read this in another way, it is good to ask why it is that MacCormick does not want to go all out and argue that value is accessible by reason alone, such that, via reason alone, we could say something was self-evidently valuable. Put another way, we could ask: why is MacCormick reluctant to accept that matters of value are 'provable, demonstrable, or confirmable' by further reasons, or, alternatively, that there are matters of fact we could point to, as if there were moral realities there, awaiting our discovery? Why is MacCormick drawn to the sceptical aspects of Hume's philosophy?

Crucial for MacCormick is the following point: that 'honest and reasonable people can and do differ even upon ultimate matters of principle, each having reasons which seem to him or her good for the view to which

[15] Ibid.

he or she adheres'.[16] This is what lies at the heart of MacCormick's view about matters of value: respect for persons. This is not a trivial tolerance, but instead a deep, genuinely felt, regard for another person's perspective on value. There are two aspects to this respect: first, we cannot have a transcendent, objective view of value's existence or knowability, for if we did, this would endanger the respect we need to show to persons; and second, another person's acceptance of, or commitment to, value is not merely a matter of will and emotion, but rather, also, in addition, a manifestation of their rationality.

Neither moral realism nor moral expressivism is an acceptable meta-ethical position about value. The first would mean that we treat the moral views of others, when they differ from ours, as mistakes – they are simply mistaken, operating outside our community, alien to it, for their view does not agree with our account of the objectivity of value. The second would, in turn, cheapen the genuineness of the acceptance and commitment each person has to what is valuable for them, but it would also mean that persons are sort of monads to each other, their wills and emotions passing each other by like ships in the night, with no prospects for any sort of inter-subjective communication (i.e., reasoning) about value.

This middle position is indeed a difficult and delicate one. It is another manifestation of MacCormick's 'both and' rather than 'either or' style of thought. This, in turn, could itself be a matter of MacCormick negotiating his character, i.e., the manner or style with which he relates to others. Notice, in that respect, that the above can be understood precisely as a matter of relational attitude: if I insist on a transcendent view of value, then I will exclude others, seeing them as outsiders to my theory; if, on the other hand, I insist on a purely subjectivist, expressivist, view of value, then I also exclude them in a way, for then I do not relate to them, do not try to communicate with them, but instead simply tolerate them and move on. On either approach, there is a failure of relation – there is no connection, and certainly no respectful, mutually regarding, or considerate connection. That is, then, one sense in which what is at stake in MacCormick's theory of practical reason is his character.

One might be tempted, at this point, to say, that this shows that MacCormick had no real, consistent meta-ethical theory, or no well-worked out theory of the ontology or epistemology of value. But I think this would be too quick. That is because underlying the relational

[16] Ibid.

sensitivity above is something that one might treat precisely as a meta-ethical theory, or a theory of the ontology and epistemology of value. We could call this perspectivalism about value.[17] That there is evidence for the idea that MacCormick thought about value in this way is clear from his work, not only *Legal Reasoning and Legal Theory*, but many subsequent publications too.

In the 1978 book, this perspectivalism can be seen in two ways: first, in the way MacCormick reads Hume and thus in the way he pays his respects to Hume's point of view, making it, at the same time, reconcilable with what might otherwise be seen to be the opposing, contradictory views of Reid and Kant; and, second, more explicitly, in what he says, in his famous Appendix on 'The Internal Aspect of Norms', and thus how he modifies Hart's account of the internal point of view.

As we shall see, in relation to the latter, MacCormick normativises the internal point of view – he makes it morally stronger than Hart had characterised it – and that is precisely because he is attempting to pay his deep respects to persons and their acceptance of and commitment to value. Notice, however, that in pushing Hart's internal point of view in this direction – pointing, for instance, to there being underpinning reasons why officials accept the rule of recognition (again, normatively strengthening the official point of view in this way) – MacCormick nevertheless stops short of Dworkin's 'right answer thesis' or indeed Finnis's arguments concerning 'self-evidence' about value. In other words, MacCormick tries to find a middle path: acknowledging the normativity of a person's perspective, but not so far as to collapse it and flatten it into something everyone must conform to. MacCormick's pulse is always on the intersubjective space in between, i.e., on maintaining a genuine, respectful relation with others.

To return to the reading of Hume: MacCormick, as above, wants to read Hume in a way that includes him, while also including what he sees as valuable in Reid and Kant's responses to Hume. On this account, neither ultra-rationalism (of the kind Hume was combating) nor irrationalism (of the kind Reid and Kant were fighting against) are appropriate. Here is how MacCormick puts it, again trying to reconcile Hume, Reid, and Kant:

> Hume has indeed too passive a view of reason. On at least this point Reid and Kant are right. Reason imposes an order and structure on the phenomenal world of our experience – whether there is in it a real order answering

[17] See also, Bohlin, 'Effects on the Mind' (2014); and Waldow, *Experience Embodied* (2020), chapter 3 on Hume.

> to that which our reasoning makes for us in the phenomenal world is in the nature of the case a question of faith, not knowledge.[18]

This is a compact statement, but it captures the two sides: on the one hand, reason is active – it is practical – and more so than Hume acknowledges. This means that Reid and Kant are, on that point, right. But Hume is also right, and in this sense, Reid and Kant need to make way for Hume. That's because we can, and indeed must, live without knowing – in any certain, demonstrable, provable way – whether there is a 'real order answering to that which our reasoning makes for us'. Again, on the one hand 'it is possible for us to order the world of our activity: to shape it in accordance with rules and principles of action and to secure that the rules and principles of our action are mutually consistent and form a coherent set'.[19] This is what the 'irrationalist is blind' to.[20] Reason can 'limit the set of norms we can have all together',[21] at least, as we shall see later, for the moment and thus defeasibly so. But reason also has its limits, e.g., with respect to the commitment to reason itself:

> ...here we touch on the truth which Hume was probably the first philosopher fully to grasp, the truth which ethical and legal irrationalism as theories distort. My belief that I ought to strive to be rational is not a belief which I can justify by reasoning. Of course, it can be explained why somebody with the kind of social and familial background which I have, brought up in a 'professional' family in twentieth-century Scotland, is likely to hold such a belief. Of course it can be conjectured that all human beings have a biological nature of which the propensity to favour rationality is an essential part however occluded by misfortune or adverse circumstances. But these are explanations, not justifications.[22]

We must reject the idea of the irrationalist that reason has no role to play in shaping values, including constructing it as a 'rational order'.[23] However, we must also reject ultra-rationalism, or the view that 'there is some way of establishing by reasoning and reflection an objectively valid moral or legal order'.[24] In this respect, again by reference to Hume:

> For although Hume is wrong about the passivity of reason, he is not wrong in contending that our affectively valuing anything belongs to the realm of

18 MacCormick, LRLT (1978), 267.
19 Ibid.
20 Ibid.
21 Ibid.
22 Ibid., 268.
23 Ibid., 269.
24 Ibid.

> our attitudes and pre-dispositions; even in the case of reason, it is not reason which is expressed if we set value on rationality. If we set value on it, we shall follow it in trying to secure consistency and coherence at a given time and over time in our general attitudes to our own and others' conduct. But it is because we have affective attitudes (including, maybe, a favouring of reason and rationality) that we care about what happens to ourselves and other people, or that we *care* about anyone's acting reasonably or rationally. It is grossly overstating that to say that 'reason is and ought to be the slave of the passions' [as Hume did at one point in the *Treatise*]. But the arresting overstatement has its place even in philosophy.[25]

Lest it be thought this is an acceptance of expressivism, i.e., that value is but a matter of subjective emotional preference, immediately after the above paragraph MacCormick insists that 'Shaping these attitudes of "caring" into norms – rules and principles of action – involves the exercise of reason in framing the "universal" formulation of a guide to action'.[26] But, once again, reason can only take us so far, and in the 'testing' process, when we engage in 'consequentialist argument' what 'is at stake is how we are to live, how we are to satisfy our long-run propensities (what Hume called "calm passions")'.[27]

The dialectical, almost dizzying, movement of MacCormick's thought is on show here. In a way, language itself forces us into this dialectic: we cannot say two things at once, although MacCormick tries hard to pull off that trick. Hume is right, but so are Reid and Kant. Hume is wrong, but so are Reid and Kant. There is partiality and incompleteness in everything. And that is because, at the centre, is the relation: it is about finding a conceptual space in which Hume, Reid, and Kant can all sit at the table, and converse with one another.

It is the same with respect to matters of value: the world of value is a matter of perspective. It is not an undifferentiated, homogeneous unity. But neither is it a set of unrelated, monadic perspectives passing each other by. It matters that we respect each perspective by seeing how it is both reasoned and affective, but we cannot push this so far as to mean that perspectives can never connect, as if they were each perfect and could not be transformed in social exchange. What matters is that the realm of value is one of interlocking, overlapping, interacting, communicating, and thus inter-subjective perspectives. What matters is precisely civility: maintaining active, considerate, decent, and respectful relations between persons.

[25] Ibid., 269–70; original emphasis.
[26] Ibid., 270.
[27] Ibid.

Points of View

Just as with his reading of Hume (alongside Reid and Kant), so with his reading of Hart's internal point of view, as articulated in the Appendix to the 1978 book. According to MacCormick, Hart is in part right and in part not right. This also means that what may be traditionally associated with a natural law position is, likewise, in part right and in part not right. Hart's account of the internal point of view does not go far enough – it is not normative enough, as we shall see in a moment – but recognising its normativity need not collapse perspectivalism about value, as in certain versions of natural law. The point, as always with MacCormick, is delicate and difficult – it is about articulating a space where one can think further, but always inclusively with others, in this case, both those with positivist intuitions and those with anti-positivist ones.

The perspectivalism about value that MacCormick articulates in the 1978 Appendix is not unrelated to his institutionalist intuitions. There, too, in the concept of institutional fact, attention is given to the importance of attitudes as an explanation of how certain aspects of social reality can exist. Indeed, MacCormick's example in this Appendix is one that he sometimes employed to explain how facts exist institutionally, i.e., clocks and watches. Drawing on Swift's *Gulliver's Travels*, MacCormick quoted the description, made by the commissions of the King of Lilliput inspecting Gulliver, of the physical features of that 'great silver chain with a wonderful kind of engine at the Bottom'.[28] It is significant that this is an encounter between cultures – between persons who may need to learn about each other in order to form a relation with one another. The commissioners provide a very detailed description of the 'brute facts', as we might call them, of Gulliver's watch. But they do not yet understand it, no matter how accurate their description. What is missing from their understanding is the point of view within the culture (Gulliver's community) in which the watch makes sense.

But what is it for the watch to make sense in that culture? Just what is the content of this 'internal point of view' – one which MacCormick, of course, acknowledges Hart recognised, but which, as he also notes, was not an uncommon methodological point in the philosophy of the social sciences, made, for instance, by Peter Winch, Ludwig Wittgenstein, and Max Weber, each of whom were influential sources for Hart?[29] Here,

[28] Ibid., 275.
[29] Ibid., 278–9.

MacCormick recognises that one aspect of this internal point of view is a matter of understanding – of knowing the conventional norms that regulate the uses to which this device is put in a culture. We learn these norms in a community – we learn to use watches – and thus one aspect of this internal point of view is a kind of know-how, a skill of 'telling the time'.[30]

For Hart, this know-how or skill, is not without some normative orientation, but it is a very weak one. Thus, those who have the internal point of view also have a 'critical reflective attitude to certain patterns of behaviour as a common standard'.[31] This means that we are disposed to criticise anyone who deviates from the norms that regulate the use of telling the time, including ourselves if we find ourselves tempted to so deviate. This is, for Hart, what differentiates such a rule-governed practice from one that is merely habitual, i.e., precisely, the presence of a critical reflective attitude to the practice in question. For MacCormick, however, this weak sense of the normative content of the internal point of view is not enough. He drills down further into what is meant by the idea of a 'critical reflective attitude':

> Let us consider what must essentially be involved in our having a critical attitude to, or making a critical appraisal of, the actual conduct of oneself or other people. In this there must be some element of appraising the actual against some other possible configuration of action in the given circumstances which confront us. We must indeed have in view some 'pattern of behaviour'; that we use such a conceived 'pattern of behaviour' as that against which to appraise actual behaviour is indeed what *constitutes* the pattern as a standard for us. But only given a certain sense of the term 'appraise'. When we speak here of appraising we mean more than merely indulging in some quite neutral comparison as between the actual and the conceived state of affairs, followed by a recording of any divergence between the two. The conceived pattern must be a pattern of preferred or approved as against disapproved conduct. What makes 'not wilfully attacking other people' or saying 'It is 12 o'clock' only when both hands of the clock are aligned with the 12' standards of conduct? Not just that these are possible patterns against which we could conceivably appraise actual conduct, but that these are patterns of conduct actually willed, desired, preferred, approved as patterns *for* conduct and its appraisal in our own society just now. The relevant appraisal for conformity or not with some pattern which is envisaged as a pattern of preferred conduct.[32]

For MacCormick, then, the internal point of view – including Gulliver's and others in that community that use watches – must be normatively

[30] Ibid., 285.
[31] Ibid., quoting Hart.
[32] Ibid., 285–6; original emphasis.

stronger than Hart suggests. It cannot be a mere understanding that is somehow propped up by a critical reflective attitude. Or, put another way, that critical reflective attitude is not a mere going-along with whatever others happen to be doing. There must be, as he says, a 'preference', indeed to an extent a 'shared preference', for 'certain modes of possible action over others; the pattern in question must be one that is 'being willed by somebody'.[33] In relation to Hart, one might claim that this is but an interpretation of his view, or one might claim that MacCormick thinks that Hart does not go far enough. Either way, the point is that, for MacCormick, more needs to be said about the internal point of view: in addition to the 'cognitive' element of understanding the norms or rules that govern the practice, there is also a 'volitional', or affective element – a genuine commitment to it as something of value in a community.[34]

MacCormick is not so naïve or unrealistic as to think that everyone in a community must – for the practice to have meaning in it – adopt this central case of an internal point of view, with both cognitive and volitional elements. He recognises that there will be a variety of ways of participating in this practice, e.g., 'playing along', 'delinquent', and 'rebel' positions amongst others.[35] However, all these 'are all comprehensible only in apposition or opposition to the volitionally committed position'.[36] Very significantly, this also goes for the position of the theorist – the philosopher – who may take up the cognitive, but not the volitional, element of the internal point of view. However, this philosophical point of view is itself not possible without the full internal point of view. As MacCormick says, the hermeneutic point of view (the cognitive-but-not-volitional-point-of-view) is dependent on the full participatory point of view (the cognitive plus volitional view):

> There is [a] 'cognitively internal' point of view, from which conduct is appreciated and understood in terms of the standards which are being used by the agent as guiding standards: that is sufficient for an understanding of norms and the normative. But it is parasitic on – because it presupposes – the 'volitionally internal' point of view: the point of view of an agent, who in some degree and for reasons which seem good to him has a volitional commitment to the observance of a given pattern of conduct as a standard for himself and for other people or for both.[37]

33 Ibid., 286–7.
34 Ibid., 289.
35 Ibid.
36 Ibid.
37 Ibid., 292.

Notice, in the above, that MacCormick includes, as part of the volitional, a person – an agent – acting 'for reasons which seem good to him'. This is perspectivalism about value, but a complex one: it is stronger than any weak sense of conformity to something everyone else does, for it includes a genuine preference for something, and thus something that is willed and affectively supported. However, it is not entirely without reason either: an act made in accordance with it can be seen as a kind of manifestation of reason. For MacCormick, then, perspectivalism about value must include, as a central case, as the foundational case, a point of view with both cognitive and volitional aspects, but where these aspects, combined, give us a picture of an agent acting both affectively (to a degree) and rationally (to a degree).

The centrality of this point of view – more strongly normative than Hart allowed, at least explicitly so – is key to MacCormick's argument in the 1978 book. Indeed, MacCormick recognises that his insistence on it poses a 'problem for positivism'.[38] Within the practice of adjudication, someone can always ask: 'Why ought we to treat every decision in accordance with a rule valid by our criteria of validity as being sufficiently justified?';[39] analogously so with watches: why ought we to conform with the rules by which watches, as a technology for telling time, work? When asked, judges may well say that, indeed, they do have reasons for accepting such-and-such criteria of validity (i.e., such-and-such a rule of recognition):

> E.g., 'it is good that judicial decisions be predictable and contribute to certainty of law, which are and do when they apply known rules identified in accordance with commonly shared and understood criteria of recognition'; 'it is good that judges stay within their assigned place in the constitutional order, applying established law rather than inventing new law'; 'it is good that law-making be entrusted to the elected representatives of the people, not usurped by non-elected and non-removable judges'; 'the existing and accepted constitutional order is a fair and just system, and accordingly the criteria of recognition of laws which it institutes are good and just criteria which ought to be observed'; and so on.[40]

These are amongst the answers that could be given – and it is significant that MacCormick recognises a plurality of them – but what is most significant is that MacCormick thinks that the practice itself would be

38 Ibid., 62.
39 Ibid., 63.
40 Ibid., 63–4.

unintelligible without them. In other words, we cannot give a purely conventionalist answer to the question of how law exists: any such convention, as important as it is, must always be animated – at least in its central case – by such 'underpinning reasons'; the reasons that 'for many honest men and women must underpin their acceptance of a legal system all and whole'.[41]

These 'underpinning reasons', however, are not just relevant as and when they come to the surface, on the occasions in which a person is asked to supply them. They are, MacCormick says, 'always relevant'.[42] These 'reasons for accepting the system's criteria of validity, have an importance which cannot be overlooked'[43] – even if they rise to the surface only in certain cases, perhaps of particular difficulty and at a particularly high level of constitutional controversy. But even when they are not being explicitly articulated and scrutinised – and contested, for it is important for MacCormick that they can be not only formulated in different ways but also challenged and potentially changed – they remain 'always tacitly relevant to justifying the decision or accepting it as validly justified'.[44] Again, these 'underpinning reasons' can take many different forms, including values based on 'justice' or 'common sense',[45] but whatever form these take, they are fundamental to the conventional existence of law: 'What must be essential to the "internal aspect" of the rule of recognition is some conscious commitment to pursuing the political values which are perceived as underpinning it, and to sustaining in concrete form the political principles deemed inherent in the constituted order of the society in question'.[46]

This very significant amendment to Hart's picture – or reinterpretation of Hart – shows sufficiently that MacCormick was no mere passive disciple, no little insignificant footnote, to Hart's jurisprudence. MacCormick simply has a distinct approach to value: his is, in the end, a much more normatively thicker perspectivalism about value than Hart allows. This normatively thicker perspectivalism is in keeping with the deep-set orientation to others that I have been arguing is key to his character, i.e., his respect for persons. Conventionalism, on its own, is not enough to capture the sense in which value matters to persons. Conventionalism must

41 Ibid., 64.
42 Ibid.
43 Ibid.
44 Ibid., 65.
45 Ibid., 138.
46 Ibid., 140.

be animated by perspectivalism, and this, in turn, must be articulated thickly, as being a complex composition of desire, affect, and reason.

The view that MacCormick expressed in his 1978 book did not disappear. It returns, in various guises, in his later work. Arguably, it is part of what attracts him to Robert Alexy's work, which MacCormick discovered after he had written his, and which emerged from Alexy's doctoral dissertation. Published also in 1978, Alexy's *A Theory of Legal Argumentation*, which Ruth Adler and MacCormick translated from the German into the English (published in 1989), also recognised – as MacCormick saw it – that underlying any conventionalism must be some kind of commitment to value, even if that remains unrealised.

Writing in 1982, about the importance of 'practical reason' to theorising law and legal reasoning, MacCormick lambasted 'the almost total disregard in contemporary British and American legal writing … of contemporary European legal philosophers', including Alexy.[47] What attracted MacCormick to Alexy, amongst other things, were two features of his theory of argumentation: first, that Alexy argued for a 'pretension to correctness' being fundamental to 'practical discourse', and thus something akin to his own view about 'underpinning reasons'; and second, that although Alexy recognised this aspect, he did not take it so far – as did others, especially Dworkin – as to claim that there was one 'right answer' to hard cases, but instead stayed on the pragmatic level of practical argumentation, recognising that 'rival contentions' in hard cases 'depend upon rival theories about the meaning and point of law' with 'neither of these theories being capable of refutation except on the contested assumption that the other is better'.[48] As MacCormick further put it, articulating how he understood Alexy: 'For any practical dilemma, more than one proposed resolution may satisfy the requirements of practical reasonableness. The "pretension to correctness" in practical discourse is not the pretension that one's arguments can always yield uniquely acceptable conclusions'.[49]

It is crucial to see what MacCormick is balancing here – how he is creating this difficult and delicate space in which a number of considerations are being acknowledged. It is a complex space, for sure, and one can try to puncture it and flatten it by reference to rival meta-ethical theories. But to do that would be to miss the point. MacCormick's perspectivalism about value does want to capture – as it is important to capture if one is to respect persons – the

[47] MacCormick, 'Legal Reasoning and Practical Reason' (1982), 272.

[48] Ibid., 276.

[49] Ibid., 280.

genuine, honest, sincere, affectively felt, and desired commitment to value as part of the way persons participate in conventional, rule-governed practices. This goes, too, for officials in a legal system: their work is only intelligible to them, and also really only intelligible to all citizens, when their conformity with certain conventional practices (such as the rule of recognition) is underpinned by certain reasons, and thus aims for certain values.

However, recognising this aspect of value, does not mean that such reasons or values must be perfectly shared, such that the whole edifice collapses into an undifferentiated, homogenous unity of some transcendental level of value or some ultra-rationalist 'one right answer'. It must remain a most practical, and thus diverse, differentiated normative unity or order – it is a value-oriented order, certainly, but it remains a practice: rough, imperfect, in-progress, something that is worked out pragmatically over time. In that sense, it retains a connection to conventionalism, or Hartian positivism, while also stretching it, extending it such that it overlaps with many of the intuitions articulated by natural law theorists.

Perhaps this was part of the motivation for calling it 'post-positivism' in later work.[50] Typical of MacCormick's intellectual inclusiveness, he does not want to leave positivism entirely behind. In other ways though, the 'post-positivist' label is a misnomer: MacCormick was never a straightforward positivist from the outset – there is no later conversion here; he was, from the outset, a Glaswegian moral philosopher, who looked for, and found, in law a certain kind of moral intelligibility and significance – but only a certain kind, and thus one very much rooted in social practices.[51]

Right Answers and Self-Evident Truths

That MacCormick did not go the whole way with, while still deeply respecting and trying to learn from, those peers of his who identified as either anti-positivists (e.g., Dworkin) or natural lawyers (e.g., Finnis), can be gleaned from his various writings on those figures.

[50] See MacCormick, *Institutions of Law* (2007).

[51] It is also significant that MacCormick was very keen on this Appendix being published as a paper, and early on already in the mid 1970s, if not earlier. For instance, in a letter to Raz, on 17 October 1975, he says: 'I really would like your advice as to whether… I should try to publish the "Internal Point of View" essay at all. Or should it be put to the bottom of a drawer and left for a while? No hurry about an answer. But there is certainly no advice which I would welcome more than yours'. The piece mattered to him, though it was one he was also clearly anxious about, given that it was precisely a realisation that he was not a Hartian after all.

Thus, for instance, in the 1978 book, MacCormick agrees with Dworkin that 'matters of moral and political right come[] to be filtered into the law'; that 'the law is not hermeneutically sealed from morals and politics'; that principles do play a vital part in legal reasoning;[52] but he brings (as he sees it) Dworkin back down to earth, insisting that any articulation of such principles is embedded in an ongoing and necessarily imperfect task of rationally reconstructing the materials one has at one's disposal, i.e., in particular, the rules and earlier attempts at making them principled, which means that law is thus 'a constant dialectic between what has been and is taken as settled, and the continuing dynamic process of trying to settle new problems satisfactorily and old problems in what now seems a more a satisfactory way',[53] but also, most significantly, that there is 'no right answer' to 'hard cases' – even in the idealised world of Hercules – because there are simply base-level 'practical disagreements'. As MacCormick put it, in hard cases:

> ...we find ourselves faced with a disagreement which it is in principle impossible to send to any theoretical 'Hercules' for objective resolution by delivery of the right answer. We have reached that point of pure practical disagreement at which we have to reach out beyond that which is already settled among us and decide how we are to live, how our society is to be organised. Between two possible rational extrapolations from our legal and political tradition a choice has to be made, and not merely are the parties stuck with the specific decision, but the judges and all of us in the society have to live (pro tem. at any rate) with the ruling and its manifold practical effects on social and commercial life. Here we find ourselves beyond that which can be reasoned out, although we got there for reasons.[54]

For MacCormick, there is no idealised realm in which there is no disagreement. What we have is the hard work of reasoning together – the hard work of creating and recreating, in moments of controversy, an inter-subjective space where we can hear each other and have a debate. Such debates must reach a certain resolution, but these are resolutions reached out of practical necessity, by certain institutional means – such as voting by a majority (of judges or parliamentarians) – and though these must be respected, they are not evidence of any uniformity or transcendental unity. It is, as it were, the hard work of respect all the way up and all the way down.

A similar kind of respectful disagreement marks MacCormick's relation with Finnis's work. Though he admires Finnis's *Natural Law and*

52 MacCormick, LRLT (1978), 236–7.
53 Ibid., 45.
54 Ibid., 254.

Natural Rights (1981) – he says of it, for instance, that 'I have seldom read a work of philosophy with a greater sense of excitement and discovery ... it remains for me an intellectual landmark; one of those few books which bring about a permanent change in one's understanding'[55] – nevertheless, in the end, he expresses being 'uneasy with claims of self-evidence'.[56] There are no 'seven basic goods' – 'more probably than any list of basic goods' what we 'produce will be a construct achieved by the application of practical reason to actual and possible aims and interests we impute to individuals'.[57] There is no great, ideal, blueprint in the sky: discourse about value 'does not invent goods or ends in abstraction from people as they appear in historical and social settings'.[58] For all his admiration of Finnis's attempt, and there is no doubt this admiration is honest and sincere, MacCormick confesses that 'I remain in search of a different and more constructivist account of the good', being inspired in that respect, by 'ideas derivable from Hume and Smith'.[59]

Of course, MacCormick's relations with Dworkin and Finnis – and with other anti-positivists or natural lawyers – are complex ones, and MacCormick articulates different kinds of attitudes to their work at different times. His position on Dworkin, in particular, softens with age, to such an extent that later he expresses his regrets at his earlier criticisms and says his view is really at one with Dworkin[60] and, as we have seen above, he is very complimentary about Finnis and the impact his work had on him.

However, for all the softening and compliments, it remains the case that MacCormick did not go the whole way with them. Even when he found himself using language that might be mistaken for a kind of natural law position – e.g., when, in 1982, he speaks of endorsing 'foundationalism', this is quickly modified as being a 'moderate or sceptical foundationalism'.[61] What mattered, at such moments, to MacCormick was that the theory was normatively constructive: he did not take to views that were overly critical and saw nothing but domination of the powerful over the powerless, because for him this gave up too quickly and did not try hard enough to build an inter-subjective space. However, even when he emphasised some kind of 'foundationalism', he never pushed this so far as to exclude a basic

55 MacCormick, 'Natural Law and the Separation' (1992), 106.
56 Ibid., 128.
57 Ibid.
58 Ibid.
59 Ibid.
60 See MacCormick, 'MacCormick on MacCormick' (2008).
61 MacCormick, 'Smashing the Two Way Mirror' (1982), 205.

perspectivalism about value – a basic respect for persons, a basic sense of the limits of his or anyone else's reason or vision for the good life, a basic matter of civility towards others.

Finally, it might be argued that in his last book, *Practical Reason in Law and Morality* (2008), MacCormick was more confidently objective about value. Certain passages in the book can be lifted to argue for this, e.g., returning once more to Finnis, MacCormick says that 'there are some ideal goods that are ... good in and for themselves' for humans 'as thinking, speaking and social animals'.[62] It is possible to say that 'there really are objective human goods, of a kind which it is rational for anyone to take as good reasons for decisions, acts, activities and grand projects within some plan of life'.[63] We are creatures, MacCormick here argues, who have a certain 'human nature', and for us, being as we are, 'there clearly can be genuine reasons for doing things, for there are genuine objective values'.[64]

Such arguments could, it might be further added, be shown to be far from incidental or outliers in his work: one might be able to tell a narrative, for example, about how the view expressed in this last book was the culmination of work in the late 1970s and early 1980s, after *Legal Reasoning and Legal Theory* (1978) had been completed, when MacCormick was: delving deeply into Adam Smith (1981) and his defence, in response to Hume, of a natural foundation for rights; reading Finnis's *Natural Law and Natural Rights* (1981); commenting on Lamont's last book (1981), which closely related law and morality; departing further from Hart (in his 1981 book on him); and in general arguably recovering the possibility of a kind of natural law theory in the tradition of the law of nature and nations.[65]

Thus, one could try to tell a story about MacCormick as, all along, a moralist who was, in fact, committed to realism and objectivity about value, but who was too shy to articulate it – to come out, so to speak, as a natural lawyer – which is why it took him so long to do so, finally so clearly, in his last book. Although not wholly implausible – after all, these issues were alive for MacCormick and, like most if not all of us, he sometimes veered one way and sometimes another way – in the end, this would, in my mind, be a misleading reading. It would pick up on passages and focus too much on surface-level arguments and beliefs. It would not be

62 MacCormick, PRLM (2008), 35.

63 Ibid., 36.

64 Ibid.

65 This could be further supported by, for instance, quoting MacCormick's statement in the 1994 'Foreword' to LRLT that 'the Humean stance taken in my last chapter [that is chapter 10 of LRLT (1978)] needs to be radically reconsidered': LRLT (1994), xvi.

reading MacCormick with character. It would also return us, even more forcefully, to the puzzle with which I opened this chapter: namely, the relation of MacCormick's theory of practical reason to his institutionalism. It would, in other words, insert a very large contradiction in between two bodies of thought in MacCormick's oeuvre.

But there is another way to see this, including the relation between MacCormick's institutionalism and his theory of practical reason. The former, after all, also features in various chapters in MacCormick's last book. Indeed, for all its talk of the objectivity of ideal goods, when MacCormick comes to discuss Smith, he emphasises that, for Smith, as natural as natural rights might be, there is 'no assumption' in his work 'about a pre-existing or complete moral rule-book' – no ideal blueprint of a moral code.[66] What we find in Smith, instead, are two stories: first, at the individual level, a story about how we come to acquire moral knowledge as a result of social interaction over the course of a lifetime, thereby growing into a kind of moral autonomy; and second, at the level of cultures, about how what is known to be right and wrong, and good and bad, changes over time, being dependent on economic and other social conditions. Thus, arguably, even when he is talking about the objectivity of ideal goods, MacCormick's account is still situated within an acknowledgement of the connection between the ontology and epistemology of value on the one hand, and the development, at the individual level and the cultural, of value over time and in social contexts.

Put this way, one could argue that MacCormick's perspectivalism about value is precisely compatible with his institutionalism because, for both, what matters is the generation of value in interaction – in civil interaction – with others. Thus, a kind of civil perspectivalism about value is at the root of both bodies of theory: both are ultimately concerned with not letting others down, with showing others due respect and regard, with being considerate and decent towards others. Indeed, it is not an accident that immediately following his claims about the objectivity of value in *Practical Reason in Law and Morality* (2008) he quickly finds himself saying:

> Of course, we can be mistaken. The facts may turn out to be otherwise than we thought. Matters that were uncertain at the commencement of action may clarify themselves in a sense adverse to our project... Our own capability for or interest in a particular line of activity or endeavour may prove insufficient... Reasonableness and rationality require a continual 'executive monitoring' of one's activities to ensure they continue to be

[66] MacCormick, PRLM (2008), 60.

> supported by either the very reasons that initially supported our deliberative decision(s) or other supervening reasons that turn out to be more satisfactorily supportive of one's activity.[67]

Arguably, then, even at its most robust, MacCormick's defence of reason – and what is naturally good for human beings – is set within a self-reflexive ethic that very quickly moderates itself, pulls itself back, comes to think about the impact of a certain attitude (toward value, for instance) on others and their views, and thus returns, invariably, to the complexity of reasoning about value together. Put another way, philosophical reflection always had to be brought back down to earth, shown to be but another – albeit no less important for that – contribution to the difficulty of living together.

An Inter-Subjective Space

If recognition of perspectivalism about value lies at the base of MacCormick's theory of practical reason, then what is built on top? Here is where the work of practical reason really begins – but it is important to remember that it is enabled by the above attitude to value, i.e., perspectivalism. Thus, always operating in the background, and indeed in many ways the motivation for providing an account of the workings of practical reason (of which the detailed theory of legal reasoning is a part) is recognition of the above perspectivalism about value: persons have genuine, honest, desire-affect-reason-infused orientations to value and, as such, they can and frequently do disagree, sometimes intractably so.

Of course, persons in communities must find ways of co-operating and collaborating sufficiently and thus communal life cannot be based on wholescale and intractable disagreement alone. But the solution to that is not to collapse difference into uniformity, forcing everyone to accept the same theory of the good life or otherwise pretending the disagreement is not there. It is, instead, to construct and remain in an inter-subjective space where we can hear each other, contest our views, and reach a decision, no matter how provisional, so as to be able to live together peacefully. Any such decision does not destroy the underlying perspectivalism – that is always there. The point is to offer a way in which we can make practical decisions about how to live together, including resolve disputes, while not collapsing perspectivalism about value into an undifferentiated unity. To do that would be to dominate or oppress persons, failing to respect them.

[67] Ibid., 36.

How, then, might such an inter-subjective space be built and then dwelt in? Here, there are two stages that deserve our attention: first, there is the very construction of the inter-subjective space in which we can debate – a process that MacCormick theorises, via Kant and his various interpreters, as the practice of universalist (or first-order) justification; second, once we are in this inter-subjective space, which we have constructed thanks to making each other's particular claims intelligible to each other (precisely in universalist language), then we start to debate, testing, contesting, deliberating, which we do, according to MacCormick, thanks to a trifecta of arguments – consequences, consistency, and coherence (so-called 'second-order justification') – finally reaching a decision, i.e., choosing one amongst the possible rival universalist justifications. This second stage contains within it a question about what attitude to take to the status of any decision made, any ruling finally decided, which is a question that entails a theory of the authority of law (for instance, in the form of the authority of precedent).

In this part of the chapter, I thus turn to these two stages, and thereby to the bulk, the practical workings, of MacCormick's theory of practical reason. However, as I do so, it is once again important to remember that this process is built on, and always infused with, what also constitutes MacCormick's theory of value, namely his basic orientation towards others as persons deserving of respect, consideration, and decency.

Universalisation: The Value of Formal Justice

Practical reason begins with a duty to justify. The process starts, pragmatically, with a relational scene in which one person asks another to justify their actions or the basis of their decision to act in some way:

> In relation to all manner of acts and activities, claims and rebuttals, citizens of a society may be called on to show legal justification for what they do. In particular, since judges are required to give only such decisions as are justified according to law, they must apply thought to the question which of the decisions sought from them by the parties to a case is so justified.[68]

Justification, then, emerges as a pragmatic necessity in the process of persons relating with each other. This is all the more so in the institutionalised context of legal argument. The key point, in that context, is that particular

[68] MacCormick, LRLT (1978), 19.

persons in a particular dispute must, if they wish their claim to be heard and their dispute debated and resolved, justify their claim: they need to, in other words, translate their particularity into terms that others will find intelligible and that can be accepted in a community. As MacCormick was to point out many times: 'Particulars are necessary but not sufficient to justification'.[69] Again, it is not that particulars are unimportant, but, for MacCormick, it is crucial to see that they are alone not enough. Something more is needed: this something more is what MacCormick refers to as universalist justification, or recognising that 'universalisability is of the essence of *justifying reasons* for decisions and judgments'.[70]

It is, again, crucial to see that the need for, the duty of, universalist justification emerges out of the particular: a particular claim made by a particular person in the course of a particular dispute with other particular persons. Universalist justification is needed because this is what the pragmatic scene of communication demands: both in order to be heard, but also to hear the other, we must translate our particularity into terms that they, and other members of the community, can find intelligible and potentially acceptable. The universal emerges out of the particular and is a process – a difficult, creative process[71] – of translating particulars so as to construct an inter-subjective space in which deliberation, and eventually decision, can proceed.[72]

That MacCormick was sensitive to the pragmatics of this relational scene, within the institutionalised context of legal argumentation, is clear from the outset of his 1978 book. In the first chapter, he sets out to show that 'It is sometimes possible to show conclusively that a given decision is legally justified by means of a purely deductive argument'.[73] This possibility, however, sits within an institutionalised process of justification: it depends on persons, the claimants in a case, selecting, from the endless particular facts, those that they can fit into a pre-existing legal language – of rules, principles, prior decisions – such that, precisely, others (here, the other claimant and the judge(s)) can find them intelligible and potentially acceptable. These pre-existing materials are also pragmatically significant in another way: they tell us who bears the burden of proving what

[69] MacCormick, 'Universalisation' (1987), 91.

[70] Ibid., original emphasis.

[71] See MacCormick, LRLT (1978), 122.

[72] For some great takes on this issue, see also Bańkowski and McLean, *Universal and Particular* (2006), where numerous contributors speak of the reconcilability of the particular and the universal.

[73] MacCormick, LRLT (1978), 18.

and to what standard. Indeed, in many ways, the point of MacCormick's presentation of deductive logic in the first chapter of the 1978 book was to illuminate these pragmatics of proof,[74] structuring the various claims that need to be made, enabling the process of translation of particular facts into a potentially successful universal justification.

This universalist justification, however, must not only be formulated in a way that fits pre-existing legal materials, though potentially transforming those materials in the very process of translation. Any such justification must situate itself not only in the past – as now constructed by the proposed justification – but also into the hypothetical future. This was an element that MacCormick emphasised from early on, and prior to the 1978 book. In part inspired by the work of Chaïm Perelman, one book of whose he attempted in the 1970s to translate from the French into the English,[75] MacCormick emphasised the sense in which universalist justification – as an embodiment of formal justice – has both a backward-looking as a well as a forward-looking element:

> Too often, it seems to me, we assume that the idea of formal justice, of treating like cases alike, has only a backward looking application. Certainly, formal justice supplies a reason which is always good if never indefeasible in favour of following relevant precedents when one is making decisions. For a court, faced with deciding a case, the existence of relevant precedent decisions of the same court constitutes a strong reason for deciding the instant case in the manner determined by the precedent, for to do otherwise is to decide today's case in a manner unlike the manner of one's decision of yesterday's like case. To that extent indeed, the principle of formal justice has a backward looking, indeed a conservative principle… But as I say, and think it important to acknowledge, the principle of formal justice has a forward looking as well as a backward looking and conservative application. After all, if cases decided this year ought to be justifiable by the same reasons as those applied to similar cases decided last year, that ought to have been a factor in the court's mind when it decided the relevantly similar case last year. At any given point in time, a court ought to satisfy itself that its decision is based upon reasons which will be acceptable as reasons for giving the same decision at a later point in time if a similar case should subsequently arise for decision.[76]

[74] Ibid., 47.

[75] The translation was conducted at some point together with Peter Goodrich; this project appears to have been abandoned, though a good chunk of it was completed (and is available in the archives); see Perelman, *Justice* (1967), cited in MacCormick, 'Formal Justice' (1976), 109.

[76] MacCormick, 'Formal Justice' (1976), 109–10.

Thus, the pragmatics of the scene of communication, of the relational scene that is a case in court, require the parties to translate their particulars into terms that both comply with the requirements of proof, including their burdens and standards, but also, in ways that are intelligible and potentially acceptable to both past law-makers as well as future law-makers.

Again, although MacCormick often speaks of the duties of the court, the duties of the decision-makers in a particular case, who, as above, are under the duty to give a ruling that is universal, treating like cases alike, including both actual past cases and potential future cases, it is clear that he sees this operating in a pragmatic situation where it is the parties that first translate their particular claims into the kinds of terms that the judges might agree with.[77] The point, once more, is that the whole process is designed to enable the construction of an inter-subjective space in which persons can come together, hear each other's claims, and for the dispute to be resolved in a way that is acceptable to the community – a community that has a past as well as a future.

In keeping with various legal theorists – in particular, Julius Stone, whose works MacCormick read and reviewed early on[78] – MacCormick was well aware that any such universalist justification could come in various levels of generality. As MacCormick said:

> The 'facts' of any case being unique and particular there is no end to the possible labels at possible levels of generality which can be stuck on them. What principles you assert as justifying, or entertain as possible justifications of, your decision is then determined by how you choose to classify the facts and so there must be an enormously large if not indeed an infinite range of possible principles to be considered.[79]

Thus, in his 1978 book, MacCormick duly cited Stone's famous exposition of the many possible levels of generality at which one might classify the facts in *Donoghue* v *Stevenson*: one might, for instance, describe them as relating to 'the presence of dead snails or any snails or any unpleasant foreign body, or any foreign body or any unexpected quality', or 'The Plaintiff being a) a Scots Widow, or a Scotswoman, or a woman, or any adult or any human being or any legal person who b) received the objective directly from a purchaser for value from a retailer who ought directly from the defendant, or from a purchaser for value from such', and so on.[80]

[77] See MacCormick, LRLT (1978), 119–22.
[78] See MacCormick's two reviews of Stone's books in 1966.
[79] MacCormick, 'Formal Justice' (1976), 113.
[80] Stone, *Province and Function of Law* (1946), 187–8, cited in MacCormick, LRLT (1978), 117.

There is a real, difficult, and creative choice to make here, and that is what the parties – as well as, ultimately, the judge – must do when translating the particulars of the claim into a potential ruling. As creative as it is, the process is not wholly indeterminate though, because, again, it must fit into the pre-existing materials as well as project into the future; it must comply with formal justice, i.e., treating like cases alike. The point is that, although any such potential justification can vary at the level of generality – can vary, in other words, in the ways in which the facts are classified, described, and thus translated – all such potential justifications must be in logically universal form, i.e., they must be stated as applying to a certain class of persons in a certain set of circumstances.[81] MacCormick, then, was very sensitive to – even if he never really focused on, and only later was more explicit about – problems of fact classification, description, and translation, including problems of proof and what he called 'narrative' (as distinct from 'normative') coherence.[82]

Let me repeat again, for it is crucial to MacCormick's theory of practical reason, that the justification we may be called upon to give in a certain pragmatic scene – as claimants in a case, or as judges deciding it – must be in universal form, and that this involves translating particular claims into a logically universalist language. Thus, for instance, in his 'Artificial Reason and Judgement of Law' (1981), MacCormick briefly discusses Dworkin's famous example of *Riggs* v *Palmer* (1889), a case in which, as is well known, a nephew murders their uncle, going on to claim under the uncle's will. Here is what MacCormick says:

> Whatever a court decides in such a case, it seems plain that the deciding court must be ready to make some ruling on the matter in hand. A purely *ad hoc* decision against (or for) *this* beneficiary would be unsatisfactory. The question, properly, is whether a beneficiary, any beneficiary, may or may not succeed to a bequest under the will of a person he has murdered. That question must be answered. A *ruling* must be given. Justifying the particular decision involves universalising it… Each side has to show that it seeks not some act of particular grace, but instead seeks what is right in the circumstances. But what is right in the circumstances is right in any such circumstances. What one propounds as a *justified* claim one propounds as calling for satisfaction whoever makes it whenever the circumstances are materially similar given the description one has put upon them.[83]

[81] See, e.g., MacCormick, LRLT (1978), 78.

[82] See MacCormick, 'Universalisation' (1987), which was later transformed into chapter 5 of RRL (2005); see also 'Time, Narrative' (1994), which was transformed into chapter 11 of RRL (2005). MacCormick was in conversation with a number of theorists here, e.g., Bernard Jackson and William Twining.

[83] MacCormick, 'Artificial Reason and Judgement of Law' (1981), 110; original emphasis.

Doing this, as also stated above, is a matter of formal justice. As MacCormick adds: 'One who has to do *justice* among other persons, and one who seeks this or that as a matter of *justice*, is committed at least to the principle that like case are to be treated alike and differences of treatment to be grounded in difference of relevant factors in a situation'.[84]

One cannot even attempt to do justice in this way if one does not universalise – if one does not employ universalist justification. It is easy to see how this applies to the judge making a decision, but it is important to remember that it also applies to the parties in the case: the parties must, to participate in this scheme of justice, first translate their particular claims into universalistic language. It is in this way that a debate can begin. The first requirement of the exercise of practical reason is this process of translation, and thus the generation of potential, rival universalistic justifications (or rulings).

The question, however, is why MacCormick thinks this is so significant. Why does MacCormick insist on – and return to, throughout his over five-decade-long reflections – the duty of universalist justification?

To answer this question we need to turn to the roots of MacCormick's interest in justification, including universalist justification. Whereas, arguably, MacCormick's perspectivalism about value, as I have tried to reconstruct it above, emerged in large part in the course of a life-long conversation with Hume, MacCormick's interest in universalist justification is formed in an equally life-long conversation, this time, with Kant. Here, however, it is crucial to place MacCormick's interest in Kant in the context in which he first encountered it and thereafter explored it. As we will see, this will be fundamental to understanding what attracted MacCormick to Kant, and thus also why universalist justification mattered so much to him.

MacCormick's interest in Kant begins early on, in the late 1950s, when he is studying philosophy. However, MacCormick was not studying philosophy in a placeless and timeless vacuum: he was studying philosophy in Glasgow. Within that context, it is true, Kant loomed large. However, the task, as his teachers saw it, and as he came to adopt too, was to restate Kant – and thus to reformulate his insights – in the light of the Scottish tradition of moral philosophy. Without wishing to simplify unduly, the Scottish tradition that MacCormick was exposed to in Glasgow was, as we have seen in previous chapters, a tradition that situated morals in the rough ground of communal practices that developed over time. Kant

[84] Ibid.

enriched this tradition enormously – there is no doubt about that, and it will be important to consider why. However, what is vital to see is that the Scots, including MacCormick's teachers at the time he was in Glasgow, did not see Kant as necessarily opposed to Scottish moral philosophy; rather, they were invested in seeing how Kant and the Scots could be reconciled.

To recall, briefly, for Lamont, perhaps MacCormick's most influential philosophy teacher in Glasgow, it was not necessary to accept any 'extreme "rationalist" interpretation sometimes placed upon' Kant's philosophy.[85] Lamont added that he thought it was significant that Kant asked his students to attend his lectures in anthropology before those of ethics.[86] Lamont took Kant's often quite abstract account of the moral reasoner, seemingly distanced from the practice of everyday life, and sought to situate that reasoner precisely in certain concrete circumstances, making decisions about how to act in a social environment, where what one was training oneself to see, as a moral reasoner, was the impact of the basis upon which one acts on others.

Lamont was already articulating this view early on in his books in the 1940s and 1950s, but he also returned to it, explicitly, in the late 1970s in a book that – as we have seen from Chapter 2 – MacCormick was himself deeply involved in: *Law and the Moral Order* (1981). In that book, Lamont returns to the question of how to read Kant and, as he did when teaching MacCormick, urges his readers to see that it is possible to read Kant as, in fact, very much a grounded, practical, realistic moral philosopher. Kant's moral reasoner, he says, is situated within 'a down-to-earth desire for some end in certain circumstances', and what Kant is encouraging that reasoner to do is to both 'make explicit the maxim he proposes to follow – I shall pursue this end x by these means y in these circumstances z', as well as to test that maxim by imagining what would happen if 'every person everywhere [were] to pursue such an end by such means in such circumstances'.[87] Would that reasoner really wish that to happen?

Moral reasoning here is not some abstractly autonomous act of legislating norms for oneself. To understand Kant in this way, according to Lamont, is to misunderstand him. Moral reasoning, for Kant, properly understood, is a deeply social process. It is also both an act of imagination (one has to imagine what life would be like if everyone adopted such-and-such a basis for their actions) as well as a very concrete exploration

[85] Lamont, *Principles of Moral Judgement* (1947), 22, fn. 1.

[86] See also Hildebrand, 'Feeling, Cognition' (2023).

[87] Lamont, *Law and the Moral Order* (1981), 113.

of the circumstances one is in. Understood this way, it may even be said to involve emotions in a certain sense: emotions may, for instance, be involved in helping us understand the situation or circumstances in which another is in, and thus how they are experiencing it. Emotions may accompany moral reasoning, though, for Kant, moral reasoning is not, strictly speaking, dependent on feeling certain emotions in the course of reasoning. Again, for Kant, moral reasoning may not be bereft of emotion, nor indeed of imagination – it may just harness imagination and emotion, and their evaluating-enabling power, within a certain kind of reasoning process, giving those powers a certain structure and disciplining them.

What is important, arguably, for this understanding of Kant is that the process is a practical one and that it involves the moral agent checking themselves, testing their proclivities to act in a certain way, thereby precisely becoming more aware of those around them, both now and in the future. Self-legislation need not be at odds with realistic, other-oriented, future-projected judgement in social circumstances: it may, instead, be a means of doing so. Kant's moral philosophy is not reducible to some naïve, rationalistic decision-procedure for monadic persons. At the same time, Kant realises that any moral philosophy must address persons as selves, including as agents that are prone to self-deception and self-favour. Once again, the key is to find a balanced and nuanced reading of Kant.

Lamont's approach to Kant is, in the end, not that dissimilar to Hare's reading of Kant's process of universalisation,[88] which, as we know from previous chapters, was also a vital source for MacCormick's reflections on Kantian moral reasoning. Hare's Kantian-inspired account of moral reasoning – his 'prescriptivism', as he called it – which involves a process of acting only on universalizable principles, was also very practically situated, and grounded in an imaginative projection of possible and likely consequences of acting on the basis of a certain reason.

As we saw in Chapter 3, Hare was an early champion of applied philosophy; he was also deeply interested in the significance of cultural diversity for a theory of moral reasoning. His 'prescriptivism' carefully avoided positing moral realities – or some other metaphysical entities – precisely out of respect for the sheer cultural diversity that Hare himself experienced, most profoundly, when he became a prisoner of war, held by the Japanese after the Battle for Singapore in 1942. Much depended here on the

[88] See Hare, *Freedom and Reason* (1963); Hare, 'Principles' (1973); and Hare, *Moral Thinking* (1981).

prospects for reason being practical: in the absence of metaphysical moral certainties, and without a theory of reason, one would end up in hopeless relativism, if not nihilism. Fear of relativism or nihilism, however, should not push one – Hare thought – into questionable moral metaphysics. The middle path was a theory of practical reason, which was a situated process of reflecting on the basis of one's own actions by imagining their implications when universalised, i.e., applying to anyone in the same or similar situation. Universalisation, understood in this way, was no blind acting out of duty; it was a world-oriented, other-oriented, practical, grounded, realistic process of disciplining one's inclinations to act by imagining their real-world consequences.

Needless to say, these are but inadequate summaries of complex philosophical theories – both at the time, and still now, Kant's approach to moral reasoning is the subject of enormously subtle and nuanced debates.[89] The point here, however, is not the detailed exegesis of Kant's moral philosophy, but that MacCormick's own references to Kant, and his consistent interest in related concepts and processes, such as universalisation, need to be understood in this context of teaching and theorising about Kant as part of a particular tradition of moral philosophy.

In this tradition, to reiterate, every effort is made to show that Kant, properly understood, was not at odds with a grounded, realistic, and applied approach to moral philosophy, which acknowledged the role of social change and the presence of cultural diversity. Further, Kant's process of moral reasoning was not so demanding as to be only actionable by exceptional persons of high nobility – a certain elite class that was trained in Kantian methods; instead, it was exercisable, and exercised, at least sometimes, by ordinary persons in the course of everyday life – something

[89] Amongst sources in the 1950s, where this debate, around the practicality and exemplarity of Kant's notion of universalisation, was aired, see Jonathan Harris, 'Kant's Examples of the First Formulation of the Categorical Imperative' (1957), and the response from Jonathan Kemp, 'Kant's Examples of the Categorical Imperative' (1958). An important figure in this debate, familiar also to MacCormick, was Paton, and especially his *Categorical Imperative* (1971) [1947]. In addition, there was a lively debate around Hare's account of universalizability, including by Alasdair McIntyre, Don Locke, and Peter Singer (part of which MacCormick was clearly aware of). See also the work of Barbara Herman, 'The Practice of Moral Judgement' (1985) and her later work, which offers a nuanced, practice-oriented interpretation of Kant. More recently, see Hildebrand, 'Feeling, Cognition' (2023), and references therein. What this, and other work in this vein, shows is that Kant's picture of moral agency, and associated processes of reasoning, are not necessarily at odds with an acknowledgement of cultural diversity, and of the role of imagination and emotion in moral reasoning. There may be a future yet for a Scottish Kant.

Lamont, in particular, emphasised. Within these approaches, Kant was indeed brought down to earth – situated in historical developments, anthropologised, and democratised – but with the claim being that that's where he was all along. In a way, Kant was always more of a Scot than he was often portrayed to be.

It is in light of this context that we need to understand MacCormick's invocation of universalisation as a key part of practical reason, both in morality and in law – indeed, in this respect, again with a nod to Lamont, universalist justification was one crucial bridge between law and morality, for it was common to the reasoning processes for both, despite other differences between them. Thus, very significantly, when MacCormick came to publish *Legal Reasoning and Legal Theory* (1978), this built on already by then over two decades of reflection by MacCormick on the process of, first, moral reasoning, and then, second, legal reasoning. We know that much of this book was written already when MacCormick was a tutor in Oxford (from 1967 to 1972), but that its publication was delayed when MacCormick took on the duties of being Dean in Edinburgh (from 1973 to 1976) – a delay undoubtedly further exacerbated by his involvement in Scottish politics in the 1970s. We also know that the ideas for the book were being aired already in Dundee, when he started to teach law and logic, as a young lecturer in his first job in a law school (1965–67). This was, then, a project that was linked closely to, following hot on the heels of, MacCormick's formation as a Glaswegian moral philosopher in the late 1950s and early 1960s.

As we have seen above, in the first part of the introductory (first) chapter of the 1978 book, MacCormick frames the issues he will go on to discuss in his book with a Scottish debate over the practicality of reason – beginning with Stair, followed by a (moderately) sceptical response from Hume, to which, in turn, Reid and Kant reply. Kant is thus positioned as an interlocutor in a Scottish debate about the practice of moral reasoning, and in particular, the extent to which it may or may not be, in part, a matter of reason. Again, as we have seen above, MacCormick is not interested in opposing, say, Hume and Kant, and then choosing between them. Instead, he opens up an inclusive intellectual space in which he can theorise with both: Hume is right to a degree, for desire and affect surely matter, but, Reid and Kant, too, are also right to a degree, for it is also true that persons, as moral agents, can act for reasons, and thus their actions can also be manifestations of their rationality. Or, put the other way round: Reid and Kant are surely right that reason is a vital ingredient in our normative life, but Hume is also surely right that reason alone cannot do the job and that it also has its limits. The practicality of reason consists in recognising *both* reason's value *and* reason's limits.

There is no doubt that part of what attracts MacCormick to Kant is his defence of a free and active moral agent – or autonomy. MacCormick sometimes emphasised this Kantian centrality of autonomy to moral reasoning as key to what made morality distinctive. As MacCormick put it in his last book:

> The idea of human practical reason cannot make sense unless we postulate a human capability for self-command or self-government in dealing with dilemmas and decisions and in making plans about what to do. 'Autonomy', in Kantian terms, is a transcendental presupposition of our capacity to be active selves in the world. So far as we somehow can make or find law for ourselves and mould our conduct to it, we are truly acting subjects. Otherwise, we do not 'act' at all, but are acted upon.[90]

The alternative to Kantian autonomy would be that we would be nothing but 'tides which are pulled by gravity'.[91] For MacCormick, as arguably for other Scots, there was a political context to this being an unacceptable way of conceptualising the human condition: there was something deeply valuable about autonomy, and hence freedom – something that at least made it possible, under the right conditions, for human beings to exercise agency and make and plan their own lives in their own way. Kant, perhaps more than anyone, illuminated the possibility and the value of autonomy, freedom, and thus self-determination. In doing so, he also inspired a critical tradition: 'I', MacCormick said, 'like many people … find this line of thought an inspiring ideal as the basis for a critique of actual moral practices and social institutions',[92] especially if those practices and institutions were imposed by a distant power, some allegedly sovereign norm-giver, rather than emerging, democratically, from within a community of norm-users.

However, and this is crucial to seeing why universalist justification was so important for MacCormick, it is not really autonomy that MacCormick finds most important about Kant's insight. Autonomy, in any event, did not operate in a vacuum. Indeed, MacCormick often indicated that autonomy's centrality to morality could be taken too far – as it was when it obscured the sense in which 'our moral, like our legal, life has a necessary social setting, which provides us with a basis of rules and principles in the context of which we can frame and test new principles of action in new or

[90] MacCormick, PRLM (2008), 3.
[91] Ibid.
[92] Ibid., 56.

difficult circumstances'.[93] 'Autonomy', MacCormick added, 'is real, but only against a backcloth of heteronomy'.[94] As he then continued, in the last paragraphs of the 1978 book:

> If autonomy is supposed to involve the experience of inventing a moral universe from scratch it is non-existent, just as much as if scientific originality were to be ascribed only to those who develop a whole branch of science where previously nothing was known. [Instead] … the development of autonomy means the gradual taking of responsibility for a 'moral code' which one already has and uses in a sub-moral heteronomous way. But then the judging and deciding one does as an autonomous moral agent presumably involves testing and modifying and extrapolating from an already established moral position.[95]

One can put the point here in a variety of ways. One can say that the space that interests MacCormick lies between a fully fledged autonomy and a fully fledged heteronomy.[96] Kant, to the extent he emphasises autonomy, still matters, but this is placed in generative tension with heteronomy, thereby creating a kind of inter-subjective space where a person, in their particularity, can, with autonomy, but as set against a backcloth of heteronomy, articulate their claim in ways that others can find intelligible and go on to debate.

Or, one could argue that the very concept of autonomy is understood by MacCormick in a specific way – a way that was compatible with the way Kant was read by many Scots, including MacCormick's teachers. Within this reading, autonomy was not about being a self-legislating agent: it was never so inward-looking. Kantian autonomy was, in Scottish eyes, always a social phenomenon: it was a matter of responsibility. The point lay in how one exercised one's autonomy: when reasoning morally, what one needed to do was discipline oneself and one's proclivities to act in one's own favour. To do that, one had to imagine the implications, for others (as much as oneself), if everyone in the community were to act on a certain maxim: such is the ethical – in the sense of social – value of the Categorical Imperative. 'Act only', Kant says in the *Groundwork*, 'in accordance with that maxim through which you can at the same time will that it become a universal law'.[97] For Kant, one could argue, generating this maxim – from

[93] MacCormick, LRLT (1978), 124.
[94] Ibid.
[95] Ibid., 273.
[96] See also MacCormick, 'The Concept of Law' (1993); and 'The Heteronomy of Law' (1996).
[97] Kant, *Groundwork* (1997) [1785], 4:421–2.

within one's own particular circumstances, and that is important – is a process of self-appraisal, of self-discipline, such that we give ourselves a chance to distance ourselves from our own self-love, to which we are so easily prone, and give due consideration, as is our moral duty, to others, including not only immediate others in our vicinity, but to the members of the community in the future.

Of course, this chapter is not the moment to argue over how Kant might be interpreted. Neither was Kantian exegesis MacCormick's primary concern. Whether MacCormick really interpreted Kant in line with his teachers – Lamont especially – is not the key question. What is significant is that, in part by drawing on Kant, albeit always in the context of reading and being an active member himself of the Scottish moral philosophical tradition, MacCormick reflected deeply on practical reason and its value.

As we have seen, a key aspect of practical reason and its value was this first step, i.e., the initial construction of an inter-subjective space via the process of translating particulars into candidate universalist justifications (or rulings). Read with character, as I am trying to read it, this process is not a matter of some kind of monadic, autonomous fantasy, in which a person departs from concrete circumstances and from the messiness of social practices, to legislate; to the contrary, universalistic justification is a relational act, i.e., an act of respect shown to others, a process of reflecting on one's self in order to translate it into terms that others can find intelligible and possibly accept. Universalist justification is a fundamentally other-regarding act: an act of civility.

That this is so can also be gleaned from how, from early on his reflections on practical reason, and then again at the end of his life in his last book, MacCormick looked for ways in which to connect Kant to Smith. MacCormick's engagement with Smith deserves extended treatment, which I cannot provide here. But it was certainly crucial for MacCormick: it was with genuine excitement that MacCormick read Smith's newly discovered and newly published (in 1978) *Lectures on Jurisprudence*.[98] Although Smith is only mentioned once in MacCormick's 1978 book, already by 1981, MacCormick is referring to, and emphasising the importance of, Smith's impartial-spectator-based account of natural rights.[99]

In a paper 'On Reasonableness', delivered first in 1981, and then published in 1984 in another collection edited by Perelman, and in part responding to Perelman and to Stone, MacCormick drew even more explicitly on

[98] See MacCormick, 'Review of Smith' (1978); 'Smith' (1981).

[99] MacCormick, 'Smith' (1981), 247.

Smith's impartial spectator. Recognising that Smith drew his ideas, in part, from Hume – it is a pity, indeed, that MacCormick never developed this, for there was much to be said for the similarities not only with Smith, but also with Kant, in Hume's 'general point of view' – MacCormick characterised Smith's impartial spectator in the following way:

> He [the impartial spectator] is for each of us an imaginary or fictitious being whom we figure to ourselves as the impartial judge or critic of our actings and other persons' actings in the social milieu. He represents our permanent and never successful attempt to find a common point of intersubjective agreement through reference to which we can harmonise our initially different and always potentially conflicting subjective and affective evaluations of acts and goals and constraints upon action. He provides the measure by which we can correct for mere subjectivity our reactive feelings toward our own and others' acts and omissions. Such an appeal to an ideal impartial spectator or reasonable man represents our common desire to find common criteria of moral and practical judgement which have at least inter-subjective, if not absolutely objective, validity within a given social milieu.[100]

This passage is an important one: it shows how MacCormick was endeavouring to read Smith's impartial spectator as akin to the process of Kantian universalist justification, thereby also placing the latter in a certain relational light. The point of both is to construct an inter-subjective space, stepping back from our own subjective view, so that we can reason together about matters of value, giving ourselves a chance to find some common ground, no matter how fragile or provisional this may be. As MacCormick was to say later, in 1987, in an essay on universalisability, thereby explicitly connecting universalist justification to Smith's impartial spectator procedure:

> This [universalising] is not unlike the resort in Adam Smith to the ideal impartial spectator. By abstracting from one's particular involvement and confronting an issue either in universalised terms or as it would appear to an ideal impartial spectator, one objectifies the issue. One poses it as anyone's question, open to anyone's answer. Exactly what made Smith the most persuasive of the particularists turns out to be in truth a surrogate for universalisation in his theory.[101]

'Objectifying' here is meant precisely as a process of creating an inter-subjective space. As MacCormick puts it, a few lines later, 'If we seek a commonly tenable inter-subjective view, we must temper our reactions to

[100] MacCormick, 'Reasonableness' (1984), 153.
[101] MacCormick, 'Universalisation' (1987), 104.

what we think it possible for others to go along with' – this being a 'quasi-objective test'.[102] This is a process – something that takes time and is difficult. It is a kind of reflexive adjustment of our own perspective, correcting it, moving between perspectives, in the search for some potential common ground. It is, further, all the better for enabling reflection on our 'private emotional response' by comparing it, and against adjusting it to, the emotional responses of others.[103] Here, MacCormick goes a long way with Smith. A long way, but perhaps not the whole way. As he puts it, in this 1987 paper: 'Smith has finally for me the most complete and almost convincing view, because his device of the ideal impartial spectator supplies for us a common intersubjective yardstick against which to adjust and objectify our particular passionate responses to cases'.[104]

'Almost convincing'.[105] Why not fully so? Here, again, we must see what MacCormick is trying to do: MacCormick is less in the business of offering an authoritative interpretation of Smith (or Hume or Kant, for that matter). Further, he is less interested in showing that any of them was right, especially such that the other was wrong. This is in keeping with his character, i.e., his manner or style of relating with others. MacCormick is inclusive – he seeks to create an intellectual space in which he can combine, and continue to learn from, both Smith and Kant. MacCormick's intellectual style, at once creativity, here is to formulate concepts and languages that create an inclusive middle in which insights can be combined, fused, and synthesised, though without losing their own distinctive identities.

It is in light of this inclusive disposition that we need to read MacCormick's invocation, in *Practical Reason in Law and Morality* (2008), building on earlier hints,[106] of the 'Smithian Categorical Imperative'.[107] The formulation of this is as follows: 'Enter as fully as you can into the feelings of everyone directly involved in or affected by an incident or relationship, and impartially form a maxim of judgement about what is right that all could accept if they were committed to maintaining mutual beliefs setting a common standard of approval and disapproval among themselves'.[108]

[102] Ibid.

[103] Ibid.

[104] Ibid., 94.

[105] See also MacCormick, 'Reasonableness and Objectivity' (1999), as well as 'Particulars and Universals' (2006). It is, indeed, a pity that MacCormick did not pursue his plan to publish a book on Smith's jurisprudence in the 1980s.

[106] E.g., see MacCormick, 'Attempted Response' (2006), in particular by reference to Bańkowski's arguments: 257–8.

[107] MacCormick, PRLM (2008), chapter 3.

[108] Ibid., 64.

Having so done, one is then enjoined to 'Act in accordance with that impartial judgement of what it is right to do in respect of the given incident or relationship'.[109]

This is, in many respects, classic MacCormick. He relates not only Smith and Kant, but also, as he himself says, 'feeling, judgement, decision, and action'.[110] He creates an inclusive intellectual space in which one can combine aspects of insights from both Smith and Kant. From Kant, MacCormick takes the self-disciplining duty to be other-regarding – that responsible exercise of autonomy – which is assisted by having a formula, i.e., the formalised and dutiful language of the Categorical Imperative. There is a seriousness about this that clearly appeals to MacCormick. Perhaps one could find something like this in Smith too – after all, Smith emphasises the virtue of self-command:

> Being properly in command of oneself involves restraining oneself from hasty or impulsive responses to the unfolding drama of daily life. It involves a capacity to stand back and consult 'the man within the breast', the ideal spectator, before rushing to judgement. It involves a firm determination to respond as severely or as leniently to events as sound judgement dictates, not as the cry of the mob or the surge of fellow-feeling may prompt in the heat of a heated moment. The fully mature moral person starts from sympathy with all fellow-humans, but refines judgement by attempting rigorous impartiality and maximal self-knowledge, together with attention to whatever can be found out of the facts of any matter coming under moral scrutiny.[111]

There is, in Smith, emphasis, as in Kant, on rigour, determination, discipline, and restraint. Perhaps, in the end, the insistence on Kant being present in the discussion helps us to remember these aspects of Smith and see that he was not some simplistic sentimentalist. In any event, what is important is not who is right, as if only one had to be, or who owns any one idea.

As the above passage also indicates, however, it is clear that Kant's insight, at least if read in a certain way – and MacCormick acknowledges how controversial it is to read Kant too rationalistically[112] – is not sufficient on its own, and something of Smith's sensibility is needed. There is, in Smith, real and sustained attention to the emotions of others and the particular circumstances in which they occur. Just as Smith is no

109 Ibid.
110 Ibid.
111 Ibid., 60.
112 Ibid., 63.

simple sentimentalist, so he is no straightforward particularist; nevertheless, there is in the texture of Smith's very writing, in *The Theory of Moral Sentiments*, patient and careful attention to the emotions of those affected. It may well have been this explicit and sustained other-regarding disposition in Smith that attracted MacCormick to him.

Further, there is in Smith an interactionist and developmental account of the acquisition of moral knowledge by persons:[113] knowledge of norms and values, then, comes from interaction over periods of time – an approach that, as we saw in Chapter 9, MacCormick found drawn to in his institutional reflections on law. As MacCormick put it in an earlier paper, 'Our sense of right and wrong emerges from our actual interactions with others, but of course becomes principled awareness only through thought, reflection and universalisation.[114] There is no blueprint, no rule book, to start with: there is no 'foundation' in that sense; instead, there is an ongoing, practical, incremental, working out, in the course of interaction over time, of how best to live together, with none of us having a bird's eye-view, and thus with all of us being necessarily partial and limited, dependent on learning from the particular kinds of relations we have with others.

None of this is to say that we could not offer a reading of Kant, too, along these lines – for instance, there are many emotionally informed, other-regarding examples in Kant's lectures in ethics and anthropology – but that is not the point. In a way, MacCormick's fusing of Kant and Smith performs the very value of practical reason he urges us to see: its deeply mutually regarding nature, and thus its difficult and never-ending endeavour to find inclusive spaces in which we can learn from each other. For MacCormick, what matters is that we make this effort to construct an inter-subjective space in which we begin to converse and think together.

Of course, making this space cannot be the effort of any one person. A lot depends on the social structures in place in a particular community. The pragmatics here really matter: it matters, in other words, what structures of proof we set up, who is allocated the burden of proving what, and to what standard, and all the procedural safeguards we introduce as part of the process of law-making. All this requires balancing the values of predictability, stability, and relative certainty, including the articulation of law in the form of rules that are well publicised, available in advance, and not impossible to understand, with the values of contestability, responsiveness, and change. I will return to aspects of this in the following

[113] See MacCormick, PRLM (2008), 59–61.

[114] MacCormick, 'Ideal and Actual' (1997), 17.

section – for it relates to the status we attribute to any decision that is ultimately reached – but it also has implications for the importance of constructing an inter-subjective space to begin with.

Thus, in his 2005 book, *Rhetoric and the Rule of Law*, it is no accident that MacCormick articulates a conception of the rule of law that incorporates what he refers to as its 'dynamic aspect': namely, 'the rights of the defence, and the importance of letting everything that is arguable be argued'.[115] Understood as an inter-subjective space, the rule of law is precisely that space of inclusion – of making room for the particular to speak, for everyone to be given the chance to articulate how they see things.[116] In that respect, particularistic persuasion – the practice of rhetoric, the arguable character of law – is not at odds with law; it is not a danger to law or the absence of law. Instead, properly understood, 'the arguable character of law' is one of the 'components' of the rule of law. However, law is also not a realm of pure particulars: it is, instead, an inter-subjective space that is made by the pragmatic efforts we all need to make to translate particulars into universals. This is not a process that ever ends, but that does not make it any less valuable – in fact, it may be valuable because it never ends.

Deliberation and Decision I: Testing

Once an inter-subjective space has been created, precisely via the process of translating particulars into universals, and thus generating candidate, rival universals (or rulings), the process of deliberation – of testing and debate – begins and continues until a decision is reached. There are two aspects here that are important: first, the very process of testing, which MacCormick theorises by considering the role and complex interplay of arguments concerning consistency, coherence, and consequences; and second, the status of the decision reached – especially, in this context, the question of how to conceive of precedent – which MacCormick was careful to qualify by emphasising the defeasibility and revisability of decisions, thereby also reiterating one of the frequent themes of his thought, i.e., an ethic of gradualism, of only ever relative stability, of a normative order always on the move, and thus a concept of law that is never reducible to the domination of persons by an arbitrary will. Let me consider these two aspects in turn.

115 MacCormick, RRL (2005), 31.

116 See also MacCormick, 'Formal Justice' (1976), 16.

Any reader of the 1978 book will soon discover two features of MacCormick's treatment of the process of testing within this inter-subjective space, and thus at the level of non-deductive, second-order justification: first, that it is packed with cases; and second, that the definition, as well as interrelation, of the three tests – consistency, coherence, and consequences – is not systematic and not always clear. With respect to the second point, one need only observe that, the order in which these tests are discussed in the book – consequences first, then coherence, and then consistency last – does not match the relative significance MacCormick accords these different tests, or the order in which he sometimes suggests they proceed, e.g., consistency as a basic first test, then coherence, and finally consequences.

In what follows, to keep the discussion manageable, I shall focus on the relations between coherence and consequences, putting consistency aside. This is not to suggest that consistency does not matter. As MacCormick says, 'however desirable on consequentialist grounds a given ruling might be, it may not be adopted if it is contradictory of some valid and binding rule of the system'.[117] Arguments from consistency are especially relevant when one is justifying a decision in the context of statutory provisions: one cannot simply propose a ruling, as a party, or choose one as a judge, that can be argued to be in contradiction with existing statutory provisions.[118] Testing for possible contradictions, or indeed if challenged upon this score, one must at least construct an argument to show how the statutory provision(s) in question can be interpreted so that there is no inconsistency – one must engage in the process of 'reconciliation'.[119] Of course, within MacCormick's theory, such reconciliation, and thus arguments over interpretation of the meaning of statutory provisions, will ultimately call upon the assistance of arguments of coherence and consequences. Thus, consistency – even if it is important as a stand-alone test (and one that MacCormick treats in a separate chapter of the 1978 book: Chapter 8) – arguably ultimately rests on the argumentative resources of coherence and consequences.

When it comes to the relative significance and order of coherence and consequences, throughout the 1978 book, even though he treats consequences first (in Chapter 6), MacCormick insists that it is the appeal to consequences that is the last port of call, the final determinant of the choice

117 MacCormick, LRLT (1978), 106.

118 See also MacCormick, LRLT (1978), 106.

119 Ibid.

between rival rulings. Whereas, as often happens in hard cases, both parties can provide a ruling that is equally consistent and coherent, the justification – the choice amongst the candidate, universalised rulings – finally depends on the matter of consequences. Here, however, we cannot force one of the sides to accept, on rational grounds, the superiority of one or the other: as MacCormick says, with respect to consequences, we 'find ourselves beyond that which can be reasoned out, although we go there for reasons'.[120]

Consequences, then, are crucial, both because they are the 'clinching point of the justification', and thus a resource that 'moves us from the eminently justifiable to the fully justified decision',[121] but also because they mark the limits of rationality: at the level of consequences there can be 'pure practical disagreement',[122] with the choice being a matter of preference for one 'pattern of human conduct in society'[123] over another. Again, this preference is not arbitrary – it can be reached by reason – but it is, at the same time, not something that can be shown to be objectively correct or right; it is, instead, something over which persons – reasoning persons of goodwill and honesty – can disagree.

It is important – crucially important in light of the perspectivalism about value discussed above – that MacCormick's theory of legal reasoning seeks to leave room for this 'pure practical disagreement', while at the same time, respecting the choice made for one over another ruling (on this basis of consequences) as still rational, to an extent. For MacCormick, the inter-subjective space we create by generating universalised rulings is a space of genuine contestation, genuine debate, and potentially irresolvable disagreement. At the same time, of course, decisions must be reached.

So the argument from consequences has this dual facing role: it is the final place or moment of choice, and it is important for MacCormick that the basis of the choice is made explicit – that a reason still be given for going one way or another – but it is also the marker of an irreducibly social exercise, of this being a space where multiple voices can reach the 'bedrock of the value of preferences which inform our reasoning but which are not demonstrable by it'.[124] Again, for MacCormick, it is vital to make room for

120 Ibid., 254.
121 Ibid., 252.
122 Ibid., 254.
123 Ibid., 104.
124 Ibid., 105.

such 'irresoluble differences of opinion between people of goodwill and reason',[125] while not undermining or characterising as unjustifiable the choice that such persons make – indeed, quite the contrary, treating it, as above, as that which moves us into a fully justified decision. Like so much of his thought, this is a difficult, delicate place, but one which ultimately conveys a thorough respect for persons.

For all its importance, however, it is also the case that MacCormick is not always clear about the differences between coherence-based and consequence-based arguments. The discussion of coherence in the 1978 book is marked by the debate over the relative importance of principles and rules in legal justification – a debate that was intensified, no doubt, by Dworkin's criticisms of Hart, but that MacCormick had already been exposed to and contributed to (e.g., in his paper on 'Stare Decisis' in 1966) by way of a comparison between Scottish and English approaches to precedent, a point to which I return below. For MacCormick, as he explained it in 1978, a coherence-based argument involves appeal to – including potentially the construction or reconstruction of – a principle that makes sense of a series or group of instances, where such instances can either be rules (as found in statutes, for instance) or cases, especially if, in order to facilitate a coherence-based argument, we approach each case as yielding a particular rule (a certain *ratio*).

The sense in question here is a normative sense, i.e., one gathers into a group a certain set of instances on the basis of a claim that, when taken together, can be understood to be in pursuit of a certain value. This is exactly what a 'principle' is: a kind of justification for grouping a set of instances into one group, where the group is said to 'make sense' precisely because it collectively aims to realise a certain value. Principles, then, are not free-floating or detached justifications; they are ways of making sense of the legal materials we are working with, whether these be statutory rules or particular cases (or indeed both together). As MacCormick put it, 'the principles of a legal system are the conceptualised general norms whereby its functionaries rationalise the rules which belong to the system in virtue of criteria internally observed'.[126]

The process of articulating these 'conceptualised general norms' involves attributing to a group of rules 'some end conceived as valuable, or some general mode of conduct conceived to be desirable'.[127] It is also

[125] Ibid., 106.
[126] Ibid., 155.
[127] Ibid., 156.

important to add that more than one principle may be constructed with respect to any one grouping of rules, and that these principles can also come into conflict. Here is an example:

> Thus, it is a rule of law in the UK that vehicles must be driven on the left-hand side of the road: there is no special reason why we should choose the left rather than the right, but there is a compelling reason, safety, why we should fix on one or the other. The principle is that safety on the roads ought to be secured by specifying codes of conduct for drivers, or that people ought to drive in a way which will minimise danger to other road users. These principles (or, the principle alternatively stated) are the underlying reason for, the whole body of Road Traffic laws, not merely of the 'keep left' rule. There may of course be other principles, such as that the free and speedy movement of traffic on the roads ought to be fostered, which laws imposing parking restrictions and prohibiting obstruction are seen as embodying. So even in this simple, and almost banal case, we can identify at least two principles underlying the rules of one branch of law, which principles are obviously capable of coming into conflict with each other.[128]

The value of this process – of making a set of instances (rules or cases) cohere by seeing them as 'directed at securing general ends' – is that it helps us to 'create the possibility of perceiving the Road Traffic Acts' as 'not just a congeries of arbitrary commands, prohibitions and permissions',[129] but as something that makes normative sense to us as members of a community. Again, multiple principles may make a certain set of rules cohere, and thus there may be multiple ends that any such set can be said to aim at.

This process of constructing and reconstructing principles is undoubtedly a creative process,[130] and one which can be especially complicated when it comes to grouping together cases. With respect to cases, which, at least in certain legal traditions, include extensive descriptions of facts, this process includes analogy. However, for MacCormick, it is crucial to see that analogical processes, although they may involve comparisons of factual similarity or difference, cannot be reduced to that. Sometimes, indeed, advocates and judges do find it helpful to compare factual similarities and differences, e.g., as between rescuer cases and 'salvor' cases (where a person acts not to save another person, but to protect property);[131] indeed, it is a virtue of common law adjudication, with its generous descriptions of the facts of cases, including potentially differences in such descriptions amongst judges

128 Ibid.

129 Ibid., 157.

130 See, e.g., MacCormick, LRLT (1978), 122.

131 See Ibid.

in multi-judge panels, that it enables such a process of exploring factual similarities and differences, thereby deferring for a moment appeal to value.

However, ultimately, any such process of examining and comparing similarities and differences at the level of facts must be driven by a judgement of not factual, but normative, similarities and differences, i.e., precisely by considering whether both cases can be understood as pursuing the same normative end. What MacCormick sometimes calls 'visual similarity'[132] or 'cognitive closeness' between cases,[133] while it may be heuristically helpful, is never sufficient on its own: what is needed is 'evaluative closeness',[134] i.e., precisely the possibility of grouping together the cases as serving a common normative end. Nevertheless, just as with traffic rules, so also with groups of cases: multiple principles may be said to support the grouping of cases, and these principles can conflict.

Sometimes, when discussing coherence, MacCormick stops there – at the mere possibility of a principled grouping – again, as above, the argument that a certain set of instances (statutory rules or cases, or indeed both together) can be so grouped on the basis that they have a tendency, direction, or orientating towards the protection or realisation of a certain value.[135] The boundary, then, of coherence would be the mere possibility of the articulation of such principles. Acknowledging that there are multiple such principles that can be generated, what comes next is something else: a choice between principles. Indeed, throughout his chapter on coherence in the 1978 book, MacCormick keeps returning to the necessity of this further choice, characterising it as based on consequences. Here, then, would be the marker – the border – between coherence and consequences: we first generate, via coherence, potential principles, and then we choose between them. On this view, what a consequential argument involves is a reason given for preferring one principle to another, i.e., one coherence-based grouping of instances over another.

I will turn to consequential arguments in a moment, but it is important to see here that one could articulate coherence-based arguments more robustly – and in a way that effectively includes the further alleged consequential choice or evaluation between principles, thereby rendering consequential arguments unnecessary. Thus, one could argue that

132 Ibid., 186.

133 Ibid., 191.

134 Ibid., 191.

135 It is interesting that MacCormick uses this language of 'tendency', e.g., he speaks of groups of rules 'conceived of as tending to secure, or being aimed at securing, some end conceived as valuable': MacCormick, LRLT (1978), 156.

when it comes to grouping instances, when one formulates a principle, one already does so on the basis that this is not only a possible, but the most desirable, basis for the grouping. Arguably, this is precisely the more robust process of coherence that Dworkin includes as part of his integrity-based account of common law adjudication. In his subsequent discussions of coherence – alongside his return to Dworkin's theory over the years – MacCormick clearly wrestled with this issue, i.e., how to conceive of coherence, and whether a more robust theory of coherence effectively pulls the carpet from beneath MacCormick's insistence on consequences being the decisive factor in legal reasoning.

There is no doubt that MacCormick realised there was this option of stating a more robust theory of coherence. But there is also no doubt, especially through the 1980s and 1990s, that he was reluctant to go there. In his 1984 paper on 'Coherence in Legal Justification', MacCormick was certainly defending the value of coherence-based arguments – they were essential to the process of justification and explained a good part of what it is that judges do, and should do, when deciding cases. However, there was a limit to coherence – for MacCormick, a judgement of coherence remained a 'formal' judgement, whereas a 'consequential' argument was an argument of 'substance'.[136] As he put it, somewhat enigmatically – and here one thus feels MacCormick's difficulty – 'The issue is: what is the best principle on which to decide the case in hand? It is not: what is the principle which best explains the law as heretofore established by those responsible for establishing it?'.[137]

For MacCormick, for all the attractiveness of arguments of coherence, it was important to see they were limited in their reach. Similarly, in 1985, when discussing 'The Limits of Rationality', MacCormick insisted that, as important as it was for us, as rational agents, to actively construct a set of ends that we can understand ourselves as pursuing, and thus formulate a kind of rational system for ourselves, i.e., a coherent set of principles with which we act, this still 'leaves open the possibility that there may be a plurality of equally rational systems … different in their practical substance though not in their rational form'.[138] Choosing between such 'equally rational possibilities', however, was not a matter of 'reason itself' or reason on its own – it necessitated other virtues, such as 'wisdom, far-sightedness, justice, humanity or compassion, courage'.[139] As he put it,

[136] 'Coherence in Legal Justification' (1984), 244.
[137] Ibid.
[138] MacCormick, 'The Limits of Rationality' (1985), 199.
[139] Ibid.

at the level of choice between two equally coherent – equally formally valuable – rational systems … we have come to that which is pre-rational or extra-rational rather than a deliverance of practical (rational) discourse itself. As with general practical rationality, we come to the point at which it is values or virtues other than rationality itself which furnish with rational but not conclusive grounds of choice.[140]

Over the course of the 1990s, even when he finds himself moving further and further towards admiration and even 'substantial agreement' on many points with Dworkin,[141] MacCormick still insisted that there are limits: one will still reach, no matter how good one's coherence-based arguments, no matter how persuasive one's formulation of principle, a kind of bedrock of choice, which 'remains a matter of opinion', which in turn will necessitate, if there is such disagreement in a panel of judges, for example, a kind of institutional resolution via 'hierarchies of authority and then by voting'.[142] Of course, one can find later statements, especially in the 2000s, when MacCormick expresses, characteristically generously, if not overgenerously, admiration for fellow colleagues, including Dworkin, where MacCormick says that, in his view, Dworkin was right after all. 'Dworkin', MacCormick says, 'has over the years, cumulatively persuaded me that this [his view that there was no right answer] is a mistake':[143] 'There is no reason to suppose that there is not, in the last resort, a more reasonable answer to any given problem, and a less reasonable one, even if both of them are fairly reasonable, and even if you take full account of the law. I am now an acceptor of a version of the right answer thesis'.

Even here, however, in one of the last pieces he wrote before he died, MacCormick was not entirely sure, saying only that he accepted 'a version of the right answer thesis'. Indeed, it is instructive that, for all his generosity to Dworkin, MacCormick was still reluctant to endorse Dworkin's style of thought: 'My dear friend', Dworkin, he said, 'always surveys the world from a single position: his own'.[144] MacCormick then continued:

> My own style has tended towards the other direction. I enjoy a good argument as much as anybody else. I like the dialectical-critical bit of the work. But I notice, when I review a book, for example, that I always tend to start by trying to see it from the author's point of view. It takes me a long time

[140] Ibid., 205.
[141] See, e.g., MacCormick, 'Donoghue v Stevenson' (1991), 211–2.
[142] Ibid., 212.
[143] MacCormick, 'MacCormick on MacCormick' (2008), 21.
[144] Ibid., 17.

> to discover if I agree with a book, because if you try to understand it, you should read it sympathetically, with willing suspension of disbelief. Once you master the ideas, you think, 'hmm, that is rather persuasive', even if it says what you do not think; or what you did not use to think. The upshot of this is, of course, that people who have this attitude tend to shift their position. If you read with sympathy and interest (there is something in that, better take that on board) you will be willing, from time to time, to acknowledge a change, a shift in position, because you have felt that some other argument which you had not thought about, was a strong one, and you needed to acknowledge and adapt or adopt.[145]

This is no self-indulgent form of self-congratulation: MacCormick quickly adds that this is not entirely desirable, for it makes him 'a moving target' and someone who risks 'inconsistency and, perhaps, worst of all … mere eclecticism'.[146] Perhaps, then, he reflected, one had to find a middle path between 'the critical-dialectical and the constructive-collaborative'.[147]

MacCormick indeed never sits still: he continues to think, forming thesis and antithesis, and then a synthesis, only to find himself doubting the synthesis, and starting all over again. How it could be otherwise? For MacCormick, these were live, difficult issues of philosophy – one could not help but mulling them over, turning once this way, once that. Was that not what it meant to think? Nevertheless, taken as a whole, despite such statements as the above, which are in any event qualified, it is clear that MacCormick stopped short of endorsing a fully blown, fully robust, account of coherence: there was something of value worth preserving – arguably, precisely the kind of respect to the views of others he discusses above when reviewing another's book – that meant that one had to hold back, and restrain oneself from such an account.

This, of course, still leaves the question: if coherence-based processes do not capture the whole of legal reasoning, then what else is left? Well, as above, we have precisely the realm of consequences. But in what sense exactly is consequential reasoning a matter of *reasoning* at all? Is it not just a choice – ultimately, an arbitrary preference – between two equally possible – as in formally equivalent – candidate rulings? This is precisely where MacCormick encountered another difficulty.

For what we find in MacCormick's account of the test of consequences is an effort to make the process as rational as possible, i.e., to show that it is not mere arbitrary preference, but still, a preference that one reaches for

145 Ibid., 17.
146 Ibid.
147 Ibid., 18.

reasons. In doing so, in articulating the test or argument for consequences in this way, MacCormick finds himself reaching further and further into what is, in effect, the realm of coherence. In other words, and especially after the 1978 book, when MacCormick returned to consequentialist-based reasoning, he brought this ever closer to a process in which one both formulated and evaluated, at the same time, a principle that, for one, ultimately justified the case.

One can see this as a contradiction in his theory, but I do not think that one must read it this way: instead, in accordance with perspectivalism about value, as articulated above, we can see this as an expression of respect for persons, but just from the other direction. Thus, whereas with respect to coherence, MacCormick did not want to push this so far that it will iron out the inter-subjective space to such an extent that there is no disagreement, and thus where one view ends up being the only correct one, so also with his articulation of consequences: MacCormick did not want this to be characterised as mere arbitrary preference, which may thereby be undermined and de-legitimised, effectively once again de-relationalising that inter-subjective space.

Ultimately, what mattered was maintaining relations: one had to, at bottom, be respectful and considerate towards others. This included showing that persons were, even in these ultimate choices that were at some level not rational – and marked, as we saw, the limit of rationality – nevertheless manifestations of reason, and thus deserving of respect. The point was never to destroy the inter-subjective, which would in turn mean downgrading relations to those of domination, thereby disrespecting persons. The danger of doing so could come from two different directions: first, from insisting on some right answer, as one would do if adopting a fully robust theory of coherentist justification, or, second, from having too thin a theory of consequences, which would end up de-legitimising, treating as merely arbitrary, the preference for one ruling over another. For MacCormick, more important than any systematicity of a theory was a matter of character: that one kept up relations, that one respected others.

It is in light of this that we need to see MacCormick pushing, as he does in the 1978 book, but even more so after, consequential reasoning further and further into the realm of coherence. It should be emphasised here that by no means was consequentialism a new idea for MacCormick in 1978. Already in 1966, when discussing precedent, including differences in attitude to past cases as between English and Scottish courts, MacCormick pointed to the presence of disagreements between judges as to the 'desirability' of a certain ruling, which was tested by 'the hypothetical consequences of the adoption of the rule'.[148] MacCormick's example was from *Donoghue* v *Stevenson*[149] where:

> Lords Buckmaster and Tomlin argued that a decision in favour of the appellant … would imply so far-reaching a rule that there would arise an infinity of trivial and unjustified actions; while on the other side Lord MacMillan refused to believe that the law could contain a rule whereby a negligent baker who let quantities of arsenic get into his bread would have no civil liability to the consumers, but would suffer criminal sanctions alone.[150]

Characterising this type of argument in 1966, MacCormick referred to it as 'utilitarian' or as resting 'upon considerations of general utility',[151] and there is no doubt that debates over utilitarianism – in particular, over the prospects of 'rule utilitarianism', in which what one evaluates is the desirability of a rule, rather than some kind of all out utility – was an important philosophical context for MacCormick's interest in, and the emphasis he placed on, consequential reasoning.[152] Equally important, however, and certainly present in MacCormick's reflections on legal reasoning in the mid 1970s, was the rhetorical tradition, as it was being revived by Perelman.[153] Significantly, just as with the 1966 paper where what was

148 MacCormick, 'Stare Decisis' (1966), 211.

149 *Donoghue* v *Stevenson* [1932] AC 562 – an example he would often return to, e.g., MacCormick, LRLT (1978), chapter 5.

150 MacCormick, 'Stare Decisis' (1966), 211–2.

151 Ibid., 212.

152 See MacCormick, LRLT (1978), 105–6, where MacCormick refers to Lyons, *Forms and Limits of Utilitarianism* (1965); Hodgson, *Consequences of Utilitarianism* (1967); an important source of MacCormick, which also employed the language of first-order and second-order levels of justification, was Wasserstrom, *The Judicial Decision* (1963); another source was the work of Julius Stone, which MacCormick was familiar with in the 1960s, see, e.g., LRLT (1978), 117; later, in 1983, MacCormick also referred to Anscombe's 'Modern Moral Philosophy' (1958), as an early source for him of the language of 'consequentialism': see 'Dewey' (1983), 241, fn. 3. Amongst these sources, there is no doubt that Wasserstrom was of particular and direct relevance: as MacCormick wrote in a letter to L. B. Schwartz on 25 March 1975: 'Actually, I am still fiddling away with the manuscript of a book the main part of which (rather along the lines of Richard Wasserstrom's 'The Judicial Decision') looks at the way in which consequences are treated as relevant in justifying rulings handed down by judges in actual cases. One way or another, what is essential is that students (and all of us) should be genuinely aware of the processes involved, not merely of the black letter results'.

153 MacCormick first met Perelman at a Scots Philosophical Club conference in Stirling 1976, where, MacCormick said, Perelman 'befriended me … and encouraged me to develop thoughts on legal reasoning of a kind generally inspired by his "new rhetoric"': RRL (2005), vii. He visited Perelman's Centre in Brussels several times, as well as corresponding with him during the mid 1970s. For instance, in a letter dated 5 August 1976, MacCormick described the changes he had made to his 'Motivation of Judgements in the

being compared were different attitudes to precedent as between English and Scottish courts, so in these papers in the mid 1970s, at least some of MacCormick's insights emerged from encounters with scholars working on legal reasoning in the civilian tradition, e.g., in his 'The Motivation of Judgements in the Common Law' (published in 1978, but presented in Brussels, in Perelman's Centre, in 1976), MacCormick contrasted the common and civilian law practice of judgement by emphasising the explicitness of appeals to consequentialism in the former, unlike in the latter:

> The latter practice [i.e., that of the Civilian judiciary] may tend to conceal what the former makes plain, that many questions of law are in their essence disputable and are therefore not susceptible of scientifically correct answers. Judging involves choosing, and the factors which are material to justifying choices are in some measure subjective. Different views may be taken about the desirability of the consequences of alternative choices; a system which permits plurality of judicial opinions opens the door to a candid admission of, and indeed reliance upon, the consequentialist considerations which one or another judge regards as significant in justifying the decision which he favours.[154]

Comparative considerations were, then, significant for MacCormick in coming both to notice and to emphasise the significance of consequential reasoning. Equally important, as noted above, was the fact that MacCormick was eager to relate his account of legal reasoning to Perelman's. Judges, MacCormick argued in this piece, presented in Brussels, regularly ask: 'what will be the consequences if one rather than another of alternative available rulings is chosen?'.[155] The very form of this question was influenced by Perelman and his and other rhetoricians' sensitivity to the 'acceptability' of decisions to a certain audience.[156]

Although it may seem, at first blush, that Perelman and the rhetorical tradition is far away from Kantianism and the Kantian Categorical Imperative, in fact, when looked at closely, the two share the basic

Common Law', as well as accepting an invitation to translate, from the French, Perelman's text, 'Logique Juridique', a task which he in the end did not complete. Interestingly, at this point, the title of the 1978 book was to be 'Justification of Legal Decisions'. The book clearly went through many titles, including also the straightforward 'Legal Argument': the final title was reached only in the summer of 1977: see Letter to L. A. Blizzard, an Editor at Oxford University Press (16 August 1977).

154 MacCormick, 'The Motivation of Judgement' (1978), 169.

155 Ibid., 180.

156 MacCormick, LRLT (1978), 104; MacCormick also regularly cited the work of Esser, Viehweg, and Toulmin in this context: see, e.g., 'Legal Reasoning and Interpretation' (1998), 257.

orientation to testing one's proclivity to decide or act on the basis of a certain reason by reference to its implications for a wider community. The scope of the two communities may differ – with the rhetoricians' arguably concerned with a more immediate community of other legal officials reading the judgement (though it is also significant that Perelman referred to a 'universal audience'), but in whichever form, the underlying idea is similar: out of respect for those affected by such an act or decision in the future, one must take into account its consequences. In other words, although there are elements of pragmatism and realism at work in MacCormick's appeal to consequences, and their significance in legal reasoning, including the value of making explicit such consequential considerations, lying deep within this appeal is the respect one needs to show, if one is to act reasonably now, for those one might affect in the future.

Indeed, what happens to the consequential argument, as MacCormick reflects on it further, both in the 1978 book, but especially later, is that it is brought ever closer to a more formal, coherence-like judgement. Thus, when asking the above question – as to the consequences of one choosing one ruling over another – the issue is immediately raised as to what are and what ought to be the criteria according to which one will evaluate the desirability of such consequences. There are two points that are important here: one is that in his discussions, especially in 1978, of such criteria, MacCormick insists on their plurality, i.e., that judges referred to considerations such as 'justice', 'common sense', 'public policy', and 'convenience' or 'expediency' in 'weighing the case for and against rival rulings';[157] the second is that, as his view developed, and in particular in answer to certain objections, perhaps the most important of which was by Bernard Rudden,[158] MacCormick came to emphasise the criterion of 'justice'.

In his 1982 Dewey Lecture in Jurisprudence, published in 1983, MacCormick distinguished between various uses of consequences, e.g., acts versus their results, or consequences and outcomes, and he argued that what he really meant by 'consequences' were neither the effects of a certain ruling on the parties in the case, nor even mainly the 'behavioural consequences' of a certain ruling (on behaviour in the community in general), but more the 'implications' (what Rudden called 'the juridical consequences') of a certain ruling. Thus, when, in *Dudley* v *Stevens*, Lord

[157] Ibid., 105; here, an important source of MacCormick was Lord Reid's lecture, 'The Judge as Law Maker' (1972).

[158] Rudden, 'Juridical Consequences' (1979).

Chief Justice Coleridge expressed 'the awful danger' of adopting, in the law, a principle according to which 'necessity' would be a 'justification for killing order to save one's life', worrying that such a principle 'might be made the legal cloak for unbridled passion and atrocious crime,[159] then what the judge was doing was evaluating consequences-as-implications, i.e., in particular the consequences for the law in adopting a certain ruling for the future. Of particular use to this process of evaluation, it should be added, were hypothetical future cases: indeed, judges often employed such hypotheticals precisely in order to test the implications of choosing one ruling over another.

The process, however, needed to end in a judgement, i.e., that such-and-such consequences – as implications, as juridical consequences – were unacceptable. Whereas, as noted above, in the 1978 book, MacCormick emphasised the plurality of possible criteria, here, although still acknowledging such plurality, MacCormick instead emphasised justice.[160] In extrapolating this notion of justice he said:

> Established bodies of law focus on given values or complexes of value. It is against those very values that we test and eliminate rival rulings in hard cases. In considering the juridical consequences of a ruling by way of its implications for hypothetical cases we discover whether a ruling commits us to universally treating as right deeds that subvert or fail of sufficient respect for the values at stake, or to treating as wrong forms of conduct which include no such subversion or failure. Either consequence is unacceptable because it wreaks injustice, that is, fails of the proper virtue of legal institutions.[161]

In other words, in this version of consequential argumentation, what MacCormick ends up with, arguably, is a form of consequentialism that comes to look very much like coherence. The only difference might lie in the temporal orientation: whereas 'coherence' looks to already existing, past legal materials, drawing upon them to construct principles and then testing proposed rival rulings against such principles, 'consequences' look to the future, testing such proposed rival rulings against the principles one might formulate on the basis of hypothetical cases. Certainly, if what is emphasised is the criterion of justice, and that criterion is explained, as above, by reference to the principles against which one evaluates the

[159] MacCormick, 'Dewey' (1983), 250.
[160] Ibid., 255, fn. 39.
[161] Ibid., 256–7.

desirability of consequences, it is difficult to avoid the conclusion that there is a considerable overlap between coherence and consequences.

Of course, MacCormick was not unaware of this; indeed, in answer to some points made by Robert Summers,[162] MacCormick said 'I confess to a certain conflation' of what Summers called 'rightness reasons and goal reasons', adding that he thought 'rightness and goal orientation are two sides of the same coin'.[163] There may be different ways to read this turn, if that is what it is, after 1978, to an emphasis on consequences-as-implications, where consequential reasoning comes to look very much like a form of coherentist justification, albeit a future-oriented one. One is to say MacCormick was simply confused and his theory is contradictory. But I do not think that is a helpful reading. For it is clear that what animated MacCormick most here – as indeed throughout his work – was the importance of paying one's respect to one's fellow reasoners.

MacCormick was clearly worried about the potential for de-legitimising the reasonableness of judicial decision-making if it was said to rely on a somewhat arbitrary preference for some behavioural outcome – this ventured, it seems, too far from the practice of reason, especially within a certain community of value (such as the law). In focusing on consequential acceptability via the criterion of justice, MacCormick was indeed trying to hold on to the reasonableness, the reasonable acceptability, of judicial decision-making. More deeply than this, there is a sense in which it mattered to MacCormick that a judge, in making such evaluations, was not striking too far out on her own: that they made judgements, still, within the evaluative resources that mattered to that community. Either way, it is clear that for MacCormick the deep value of consequential reasoning – why it really mattered – was relational, i.e., as he put it in his 1982 lecture, if one had a view of legal reasoning that ignored consequences, this would put in peril respect for one's fellows:

> It [a view that does not take into account consequences] ignores both the extent to which the nature and quality of decisions and acts is itself constituted by the consequences the decider intends, foresees, or hopes to bring about, and also, more seriously, the extent to which both prudence and responsibility to one's fellows require that one give serious thought to the foreseeable outcomes of one's acts and decisions before finally acting or deciding, the more so the more momentous the act or decision in view.[164]

[162] See Summers, 'Two Types of Substantive Reasons' (1978).
[163] MacCormick, 'Dewey' (1983), 257.
[164] Ibid., 239–40.

What mattered most, then, was this ultimate respect for one's fellows – this civility, this considerateness, for others. MacCormick's various characterisations of consequences, on their own but also in relation to coherence, including the limits he placed on coherence itself – as we have seen, not extending it too far – stem from this basic relational orientation.

I noted above that a feature of MacCormick's 1978 version of consequential argument was that he was more willing to acknowledge the many different criteria judges used when evaluating the acceptability of one ruling over another. And, indeed, for all of MacCormick's concern with overstretching the concept of consequences, there is no doubt that this acknowledgement did attract him. In particular, as I have suggested one sees in his work on legal reasoning in general, MacCormick always returned, with ever-new enthusiasm and energy, to the richness of practices themselves. The 1978 book is packed with cases – indeed, it is significant that, much like his teacher, Lamont, when he came to give examples of the various types of arguments, including consequential, he did so, or so he said, 'at random'.[165]

Thus, another way of reading MacCormick's equivocation over the limits of coherence and consequences, is that it mattered to him that his account was responsive to the messiness of practice – to its rough ground. One sees examples of this throughout his writings, e.g., perhaps especially clearly, in 1991, of the 'structured pluralism' of justificatory resources employed by courts, where MacCormick discussed how judges draw on 'precedent, principle, logic, analogy, policy and pragmatism'[166] – indeed, almost whatever they can get their hands on – to make their justification as cumulatively persuasive as they can. It is a striking feature, and a really important one, of MacCormick's work on legal reasoning that he dives, again and again, into the riches of practice, not in order to prove his theory right, but genuinely in order to test it, and thus acknowledge the limits of his own conceptual framework. Philosophy was never finished: it was a work in progress, which always needed the sustenance – the genuine challenge – of practice, which it could never quite capture.

It is also very possible – indeed likely – that an important context for this frequent return to the messiness of practice was his involvement in the Bielefelder Kreis. I have already noted, above, how comparison across systems and traditions was significant for MacCormick's reflections on legal reasoning in the UK (which, in turn, was itself marked by differences,

[165] MacCormick, LRLT (1978), 140.
[166] MacCormick, '*Donoghue* v *Stevenson*' (1991), 196.

especially between England and Scotland). This comparative context was brought very much to the explicit surface in the Bielefelder Kreis. This was a group that, as recalled by MacCormick, was formed, informally, in 1982, following discussions between Enrico Pattaro and Aleksander Peczenik, and which came together, formally, for the first time, at the IVR World Congress in 1983.[167] The group was called the Bielefelder Kreis because, as MacCormick explained, 'its work has been sponsored off and on over many years by the Centre for Interdisciplinary Studies at the University of Bielefeld in Germany'.[168] The Group, which involved many continental legal philosophers,[169] and which MacCormick often led in collaboration with numerous colleagues, especially Robert Summers and Zenon Bańkowski, was clearly important to MacCormick, resulting in two large co-edited projects, one a comparative study of statutory interpretation and the other on precedential reasoning.[170]

The story of this two-decade-long collaboration remains to be told, but there is no doubt that it informed MacCormick's recognition, mentioned above, as to the complexity of the practice of legal reasoning. Indeed, MacCormick, in reflecting on his involvement in the Kreis, often said how it showed him that 'argumentation', whether statutory or precedential, is 'highly complex and involves many types of potentially cumulating or conflicting arguments'.[171] It was in the context of his own contributions to those collective projects that MacCormick often returned to the complex, overlapping, dynamic relations between these various types of argument, including coherence and consequences.[172]

Deliberation and Decision II: Status

It is also, significantly, in the context of the Bielefelder project that MacCormick reflected on the status of any decision reached, especially

167 MacCormick and Summers, 'Comparative Precedent Project' (1998), 147.

168 Ibid.

169 Including: Aulius Aarnio, Robert Alexy, Zenon Bańkowski, Ralf Dreier, Sven Eng, Christophe Grzegorczyk, Francisco Laporta, Massimo La Torre, Geoffrey Marshall, Lech Morawski, Enrico Pattaro, Aleksander Peczenik, Michele Taruffo, Michel Troper, Jerzy Wróblewski, and Marek Zirk-Sadowski: MacCormick and Summers, 'Comparative Precedent Project' (1998), 148.

170 *Interpreting Statutes* (1991); and *Interpreting Precedents* (1997).

171 MacCormick, 'Notes on Narrativity' (1991), 173.

172 See, e.g., MacCormick and Summers, 'Interpretation and Justification' in *Interpreting Statutes* (1991); for more on how the group worked, see MacCormick and Summers, 'Comparative Precedent Project' (1998).

by a court in the context of the practice of precedent. As mentioned at the outset of this section, when a decision is finally reached – and thus a choice is made, by a court, amongst the various candidate rulings – then there arises a question as to the attitudes one ought to adopt to the status of such decisions. In his various articulations about the significance of the Bielefelder collaboration, MacCormick regularly emphasised its 'major implications for what one may call voluntaristic theories of law', whether in positivist or natural law varieties.[173] In other words, what MacCormick, along with his fellow collaborators and sometime-co-authors, emphasised as emerging from the comparison they engaged in was that it was untenable, especially in the context of a theory of precedent, to think that judicial law-making could be described or justified as a matter of 'discrete acts of will on the part of officials occurring at particular moments of time'.[174] As MacCormick, writing with Summers, put it:

> Decisions can be precedents only to the extent that they are conceived to rest upon justifying grounds; for these justifying grounds, according to a model of rational and discursive justification, cannot be confined to the single case… So even with the single case, it is those features of decision-making other than the particularly volitional, namely the rationally deliberative and discursive features, that account for the exemplary character of the case qua precedent. All the plainer is this when several precedents accumulate… Thus the law becomes something that takes on a force of its own, and over time becomes something that is not so much 'laid down' from above as something that 'grows up'. Indeed, it emerges from a great patchwork of choices articulated through many deliberations and discourses, and at each time of its application has to be rethought, in however a partial way.[175]

The view expressed in the above passage is key to understanding MacCormick's overall theory of precedent, and thus more broadly, his theory of the attitudes one ought to take to the status of decisions, especially those of courts, reached following the process of universalisation and then testing. It is clear, from the above passage that precedential law-making must be studied as a cross-temporal phenomenon: it is not a matter of one rule after another, corresponding to one case's ratio after another; it is, instead, a process that evolves, taking on further momentum as time expands and further cases accumulate, though even then not in a linear way, but more as a kind of 'patchwork' or network of cases,

[173] MacCormick and Summers, 'Comparative Precedent Project' (1998), 151.
[174] Ibid.
[175] Ibid.

containing various kinds of 'deliberations and discourses', and thus constituted by discursive thickness, which was not reducible, once again, to any one rule. Precedents, MacCormick and Summers continued to say, 'do not have validity in the all-or-nothing way characteristic of acts performed under requirements of procedural formality'; instead, one could perhaps speak of the 'soundness' of precedent; even if one were to speak of its 'bindingness', then one should think of this 'as a continuum rather than as a dichotomy'.[176] Indeed, seeing precedent in this way might 'cast doubt on the concept of a source of law' or at least that it 'needs to be rethought'.[177]

This emphasis on evolution – of a work in progress, of something that 'grows up' rather than something 'laid down' – is a consistent feature of MacCormick's theory of precedent, though also, more broadly, his theory of authority. We have seen this already at work throughout this book: authority matters, but it cannot result in arbitrary domination of one will over many others. One could, and should, acknowledge the authority of past decisions, but one could not take that acknowledgement so far as to entirely exclude past decisions from a certain kind of judgement as to their soundness or reasonableness. 'In any legal order with institutionalised adjudication', MacCormick said in 1998, 'precedent would carry weight' but, 'having regard to the decisions of others' was 'not the same thing as being slavishly obedient' to them.[178]

Amongst all the various 'rationales' one might propose for precedent – something that the members of the Bielefelder Kreis investigated intensely – the ones that MacCormick thought were most promising were those that travelled a middle path between too much and too little authority, often precisely by way of recognising the cross-temporality of precedential reasoning. One such candidate, for instance, was what MacCormick, this time writing with Bańkowski and Marshall, called the 'determinative theory' of precedent, according to which: 'Legal rules and judicial rulings on points of law are … understood as "determinations" (in the Thomistic sense) of background principles – neither simple deductions from them nor arbitrarily discretionary decisions about them, but partly discretionary decisions as to the best way of making the law determinate for a given (type of) case'.[179]

176 Ibid., 151–2.
177 Ibid., 152.
178 MacCormick, 'Precedent as a Source' (1998), 179.
179 MacCormick, Bańkowski, and Marshall, 'Precedent in the UK' (1998), 332.

To think of precedent in this way was to think of its authority as 'defeasible', but also, within any account of its evolution, as partial, i.e., any one decision was only ever of partial legal significance, its legal worth constantly reconstructed and re-evaluated as time went on, sometimes shrinking and sometimes expanding, being caught up in this 'holistic' and 'customary' development of an area of law, itself comprised of many decisions as well as other legal materials (such as cases and academic opinions).[180] As MacCormick put it, a little earlier, in 1993:

> The omnipresence of authority reasons in legal argumentation is not, however, independent of substantive reasons... Ultimately, to make intelligible (not to say acceptable) any claim of authority, is to enter into either deontological reasoning or teleological reasoning, or both. Authority has to be grounded in some way on the rightness of observing norms posed or evolved in a certain way, or on the values (peace and good order, perhaps) secured by such recognition.[181]

Authority mattered, no doubt, and that included attributing some authoritative significance even to individual past decisions, but this was always, for MacCormick, to be seen as part of a kind of holistic, customary, reason, a sort of moving whole, thought of better as a group of cases travelling in time. Again, yes, there is an important, if not 'central',[182] place for authority in any institutionalised system, such as law, but this was always 'grounded in' 'some sense of values to be realised by action or by principles to be observed in it', including importantly, in the 'interpersonal disputability of the values and principles that should guide us'.[183]

Typically, just as soon as MacCormick emphasised one aspect – say, reasonableness – he found himself articulating the other face of it, institutionalism. Thus, just as it was important to temper institutionalised authority by (practical, customary, holistic, contestable) reason, so it was important not to take reason too far, detaching it entirely from institutional convention and thus from the authority of the past. This was even so in political contexts where a new political regime was replacing an old one: sure, in such contexts – such as South Africa, where MacCormick was speaking in 1997, or Poland, Germany, Spain, and Italy, dealing with their various problematic pasts – it was understandable that the new order 'will involve a critical interrogation of the inherited case law', but even

[180] Ibid., 334.

[181] MacCormick, 'Argumentation and Interpretation' (1993), 19.

[182] Ibid.

[183] Ibid., 28.

then, MacCormick argued, 'this does not amount to an abandonment of aspiration to legal coherence as a value', which necessitated proceeding slowly and carefully, and therefore with some deference to the past.[184]

There is one final context that is important to mention for this conception of precedential authority as a kind of holistic, customary, and contestable reason – where authority was attached not to any one decision, but instead to the moving whole, e.g., a group of cases. This was a context that itself emerged very clearly, and naturally, from MacCormick's involvement in the Bielefelder Kreis, but which was, of course, much more deeply rooted in MacCormick, both prior to and after his involvement in that group. That context is Scots law, including its theorisation by certain Scottish thinkers.

That this tradition was represented in the Bielefelder Kreis, by MacCormick, is clear from his various contributions. For example, in the above-quoted piece, written with Bańkowski and Marshall, MacCormick considered the affinities between the 'determinative theory' and T. B. Smith's view that, in Scots law, there was a 'broader conception of the ratio decidendi', with a 'less strict view of the binding quality of individual precedents'.[185] Indeed, MacCormick said, 'historically in Scotland Stair and his contemporaries attached authority primarily to lines of concordant decisions rather than to particular cases'.[186]

All this was very much in keeping with MacCormick's fascination with what might be thought of as a Scottish tradition of practical reason – whether in the form of a 'Humean critical rationalism', and its moderately and generatively sceptical view of a customary accumulation of (imagined) probabilities, which were to some extent artificial and to some extent natural,[187] or in the form of Smith's model of learning morally from a life-time of interactions with others and their emotional reactions, or indeed from Stair, and his particular 'awareness of a the time-bound and developmental character of positive law'.[188]

For Stair, law was indeed a 'rational discipline', but this was not God's reason, for human beings, after the Fall, did not have that kind of divine insight; instead, the rational discipline of humans was always partial, always in development, never perfect, and thus best situated in the

[184] MacCormick, 'Significance of Precedent' (1998), 177.
[185] MacCormick, Bańkowski, and Marshall, 'Precedent in the UK' (1998), 336.
[186] Ibid., 340.
[187] MacCormick, 'Smashing Two Way Mirror' (1982), 15.
[188] MacCormick, 'Rational Discipline' (1981), 156.

incremental, case-based customary reason of the courts. As MacCormick put it, summarising Stair's view of practical reason:

> The role of reason in human affairs is to provide a continuous critique of inherited and established ways of doing and thinking with a view to rationalising and improving the inherited social and scientific order, testing it out for its inconsistencies and incoherences, amending it in the light of the practical or theoretical consequences to which it gives rise.[189]

This was very much a collective task, of many hands over an ongoing period of time, which never ends, even if it is punctuated with moments of authoritative decision. This was no place for heroes who, unlike the rest of us, could see right answers. It was, instead, an intersubjective space of genuine contestation, in which multiple voices could be heard, though also one that required the practical necessity of making decisions that resolved particular disputes.

It is in this light – with this emphasis on evolution, on custom, on a gradualist ethic of change – that it also makes sense to see MacCormick's statements about the *ratio decidendi* of a case. It is true that MacCormick considered it both possible and desirable to articulate the ruling of a case. Thus, for instance, he defined the ratio decidendi of a case in the following way: 'A ratio decidendi is a ruling expressly or impliedly given by a judge which is sufficient to settle a point of law put in issue by the parties' arguments in a case, being a point on which a ruling was necessary to his justification (or one of his alternative justifications) of the decisions in the case'.[190]

However, for MacCormick, the point – the value – of this practice is one which he variously captured under such concepts as universalist justification, or formal justice, or the ethics of legalism: there was value, in the name of the knowability of law, and the importance of this for making official power transparent and accountable and for citizens planning their lives, in making the effort to articulate a ruling in a logically universal form. Articulating such a ruling was especially important when one looked forward, and thus in light of the respect one ought to show to persons who will come after one.

However, once articulated, one should not make too much of any one such pronouncement – any one such articulation. Thus, when looking back, this time as a decision-maker in the present case (with one of one's eyes always on the future of one's own decision), one had to approach past

[189] Ibid., 149.
[190] MacCormick, 'Why Cases' (1987), 170.

cases more dynamically: not so much one at a time, but more holistically, and thus with attention to their soundness and reasonableness. Of course, this attention was itself embedded in a world of principles, which were being dynamically reconstructed on the basis of existing materials, as well as future hypotheticals. There was never a sense in which one was striking out on one's own – one's acts were always made in the company of others, past, present, and future.

The point, within the context of a theory of precedent, was to 'combine' a 'strict theory about the definition and identification of the ratio' with a 'weaker theory of precedent'.[191] It was the combination that mattered: there was an ethics involved in stating rulings, and thus in seeing individual cases as settling rules, but only when this was set within an overall practice of holistic, customary, and contestable reason. This was really the only way to secure what really mattered: civility shown to all, including both past members of the community reasoning their way to certain decisions, present members asking their case to be heard by the community, and future reasoners. Once again, both at the level of testing and at the level of the status of decisions reached, what mattered to MacCormick was protecting the quality of relations between persons.

[191] Ibid., 171.

Epilogue

Death and Character

If we understand, as I tried to suggest we could in Chapter 10, the question of reason's practicality as also a question about the role and value of philosophy, then we can see MacCormick's life-long reflection as not only a matter of grappling with a difficult philosophical puzzle, but also as a matter of reflecting on the practice of philosophy and what we could hope from it. In this sense, it is telling that, writing his very last book, at a time when he knew he did not have long to live,[1] MacCormick returned to the question of reason's practicality. In the final chapter of *Practical Reason in Law and Morality*, and in the final pages of that chapter, MacCormick explicitly tied the question of reason's practicality to what we may expect from philosophy. He said:

> This book makes a contribution to moral as well as legal philosophy. It may have disappointed readers who think philosophers should tell them how to live. This would manifest a longing for the rule-book conception of morality and a hope for some philosophical insight into its content. Alas, the philosopher's rule book, like the philosopher's stone, does not exist.[2]

There was no philosophical eternal truth about how to live; there were no such 'recipes'.[3] A philosopher was no superior being who could somehow

[1] MacCormick became ill on 1 February 2008 – the day he retired. He was diagnosed soon after with an inoperable cancer. In September 2008 a celebration was held in Bute House and hosted by Alex Salmond to commemorate the anniversary of his father's *The Flag in the Wind*. MacCormick could not attend as he was too ill, but he was visited by a journalist from the *Herald*. He was asked about his illness, but, typically, rather than focusing on his own fate, his thoughts were instead with Flora, his wife: 'Death comes to us all and it is not in itself something to be afraid of. It's something not to be in a hurry about. I'm not in a hurry but it's in a hurry with me. And also my other deep conviction is that death is hellish for the survivors, Flora in particular. She looks after me heroically. Flora and I have a joint life and we looked forward to a joint retirement. If somebody's cheated, she's cheated, and I didn't cheat her': MacCormick, quoted in 'An Independent Spirit', *The Herald* (27 September 2008).

[2] MacCormick, PRLM (2008), 205.

[3] Ibid.

see more about what there is to see and instruct the rest of us, the blind and the ignorant, about what to do. Just as there were limits to reason's practicality – marked by the messiness and difficulty of practice itself – so there were limits to philosophy:

> ...the philosopher has no business to pretend to superior wisdom in practice over the non-philosophical polemicist. People with real moral problems to solve should go to wise counsellors with much experience in matters of the kind causing the problem. They should be guided by them, but not directed, far less commanded. And they should put the philosophy books aside till a quieter day.[4]

Was this a cause for depression – a kind of cry of self-pity, of a sense of failure, having devoted one's life to philosophy? Far from it. The practical value of both reason and philosophy could be celebrated without this becoming an argument for superiority and thus of domination of one class of persons over another. One had to see oneself as a member, and only ever a member, of a community, which itself existed in time, and thus whose members came and went. This approach might even be extended to the value of life: 'life alone hardly justifies itself' MacCormick wrote.[5] He then added:

> There are other worthwhile things to do apart from securing survival, and if there were not, life itself would lose its savour. Life is of value as a keystone in an arch which requires other stones for its sustenance. The metaphor needs a cautionary rider – most of these stones are non-material and intangible. Thus qualified, it is a valid metaphor.[6]

Valid, and indeed very moving, given these were some of the final published words of a man with death in sight. Even in death, when others might have found themselves lamenting their demise, the projects left undone, the people left behind, so many dreams and visions unarticulated, MacCormick only ever saw himself as one traveller amongst many, as but one 'keystone in an arch which requires other stones for its sustenance'.

It is, then, perhaps in this, his final book, where we could look to better grasp the gift that MacCormick left for us. It is as if, knowing that this was the end, MacCormick reached far back, into all the various corners of this thought, where they were at their deepest and most resonant, and brought them into one succinct articulation. As a result, given what I have

[4] Ibid., 207.
[5] Ibid.
[6] Ibid.

been arguing about MacCormick's character, *Practical Reason in Law and Morality* is replete with the terminology of good relations: mutuality, reciprocity, civility, trust, reliance, sincerity, co-operation, connection, communication, consideration, engagement, inclusiveness, inter-subjectivity, sympathy, and the search for a common ground, are all terms that pervade the book.

What MacCormick probes throughout – to pick out just a few of the recurring threads – includes: the vital significance of 'other-regarding reasons' in deliberation;[7] the social powers of the mind, especially as evidenced by language;[8] the ethics of not disappointing others, of not letting others down;[9] the practice of extensive sympathy, of feeling with others;[10] the task of projecting, when deliberating, an 'imagined common point of view', always working to generate that which 'everyone can go along with',[11] and always realising that 'we think best when we test our thoughts out with other people';[12] co-ordinating with each other, orienting ourselves 'towards each other',[13] via mutual deference and mutual expectations;[14] having discourses that are mutually respectful and non-coercive;[15] and 'encountering others as peaceful fellow-users of social space', thereby maintaining the 'civility of civil society'.[16]

As he writes, MacCormick is always looking over his own shoulder; 'selfishness is always a risk',[17] he says; 'is this too self-centred a picture?',[18] he asks. Have I, in reasoning, been sufficiently respectful of the emotional worlds of others? Have I worked hard enough to find common ground, to include others, to 'build into my whole set of activities elements that are beneficial to you'?[19] Have I monitored and moderated myself, spectated as it were on myself,[20] and thus tried hard enough to help bring about relations of trust, of mutual reliance, of civic peace?

7 MacCormick, PRLM (2008), 11.
8 Ibid., 28–9.
9 Ibid., 5.
10 Ibid., 33.
11 Ibid., 62–3.
12 Ibid., 11.
13 Ibid., 51.
14 Ibid., 53.
15 Ibid., 93.
16 Ibid., 124.
17 Ibid., 43.
18 Ibid., 15.
19 Ibid., 119.
20 Ibid., 58.

Have I been sufficiently considerate, sufficiently respectful, sufficiently concerned for you?

I leave the last words to MacCormick and to his challenge to us, to think of law, of reason, of philosophy, of the very kernel of ourselves, as resting on the ability to hear others, to listen to their call:

> Practical reasoning in morality certainly concerns my plans for myself, but it even more saliently raises the issue of the calls other people have to make on me. What about my children, my spouse, my friends, my colleagues, my employer, my fellow citizens, and indeed all my fellow human beings with all their sufferings? How do they figure in my plans? More urgently, how should they? Isn't that the very essence of every moral problem? What do we owe to others? How do we respond to them?[21]

[21] Ibid., 15.

NEIL MACCORMICK: A BIBLIOGRAPHY

This bibliography focuses on the academic and published works referenced in this book. Some periodical/newspaper articles and some speeches are listed, but not all. Some reprinting is listed, and some occasions on which the relevant publications were presented, are also listed, but this too is not exhaustive. This bibliography also does not list translations of MacCormick's works but see here: www.qmul.ac.uk/law/maccormick/bibliography/.

1965

- 'Glasgow Style and Oxford Manners', *The Glasgow Herald*, 13 February 1965, 10.

1966

- 'Can Stare Decisis Be Abolished?', *Juridical Review (New Series)*, 11, 197–213.
- 'Review of *Legal Systems and Lawyers' Reasonings* by J. Stone', *Juridical Review (New Series)*, 11, 187–191.
- 'Review of *Sovereignty within the Law* by A. Larson, C. W. Jenks and Others', *Juridical Review (New Series)*, 11, 283–286.
- 'Review of *Human Law and Human Justice* by J. Stone', *Scots Law Times (News)*, 7–8.

1967

- 'Seabathing, Sunbathing and Sea Coal', *Scots Law Times (News)*, 69–71.
- '*The Misrepresentation Act* 1967', *Scots Law Times (News)*, 190–192.
- 'Review of *Other People's Law* by Lord Kilbrandon', *Journal of the Law Society of Scotland*, 12(2), 77–79.

1969

- 'Balliol's Experimental Summer School', *Oxford Magazine* 4 (Michaelmas), 44–46.

1970

- *The Scottish Debate*, (ed.) (London: Oxford University Press).
- 'Introduction', in N. MacCormick (ed.), *The Scottish Debate* (London: Oxford University Press), 1-3.
- 'Independence and Constitutional Change', in N. MacCormick (ed.), *The Scottish Debate* (London: Oxford University Press), 52–64.
- 'Delegated Legislation and Civil Liberty', *Law Quarterly Review*, 86, 171–180.
- 'Ius Quaesitum Tertio: Stair v. Dunedin', *Juridical Review*, 15, 228–246.
- 'Review of *Morality and the Law* by S.E. Stumpf', *The Philosophical Quarterly*, 20(80), 300–301.
- 'Review of *The Ethics of Punishment* by W. Moberly', *The Philosophical Quarterly*, 20(80), 301–302.

1971

- 'Social Services and Controls', in H. W. R. Wade (ed.), *Annual Survey of Commonwealth Law* (London: Butterworths), 666–685.
- 'Review of *The Concept of a Legal System: An Introduction to the Theory of Legal System* by J. Raz', *The Philosophical Quarterly*, 21(85), 380–381.
- 'Review of The *Constitutional Decisions* of John Marshall (ed.) by J.P. Cotton', *Notes and Queries*, 18(10), 394–395.

1972

- 'Voluntary Obligations and Normative Powers', *Aristotelian Society (Supplementary Volume)*, 46, 59–78 (symposium with J. Raz) (also published with modification as chapter 10 in *Legal Right and Social Democracy*, 1982).
- 'Review of *Constitutional and Administrative Law* by S.A. de Smith', Summer, *Public Law*, 174–179.

1973

- 'Legal Obligation and the Imperative Fallacy', in A. W. B. Simpson (ed.), *Oxford Essays in Jurisprudence, 2nd Series* (Oxford: Clarendon Press), 100–130.
- *Law as Institutional Fact*, Edinburgh University Inaugural Lecture, No. 52 (Edinburgh: Edinburgh University Press) (also published in the *Law Quarterly Review* in 1974, and as chapter 2 of *An Institutional Theory of Law* in 1986).
- 'Introductory Lecture to Students', Jurisprudence course at Edinburgh Law School, September 1973 (Edinburgh University Archives).
- 'A Note upon Privacy', *Law Quarterly Review*, 89, 23–27.

- 'Justice According to Rawls', *Law Quarterly Review*, 89, 393–417.
- 'Review of James Kellas, *The Scottish Political System*', *Scottish International Review*, 6(4), 27–28.

1974

- 'Law as Institutional Fact', *Law Quarterly Review*, 90, 102–129 (also published by Edinburgh University Press in 1973, and as chapter 2 of *An Institutional Theory of Law* in 1986).
- 'Privacy: A Question of Definition', *British Journal of Law and Society*, 1(1), 75–78.
- 'Principles of Law', *Juridical Review (New Series)*, 19, 217–226.
- 'The Rise of Scottish Nationalism: A Case of Too Little Too Late?', *The Round Table*, 64(256), 425–438.
- 'Jurisprudence in the Law Course: A Footnote', *Journal of the Society of Public Teachers of Law (New Supplement)*, 13(1974–1975), 359–362.
- 'A Filial Look at Home Rule's Founding Father', *The Scotsman*, 20 November 1974, 13.

1975

- *Independence and Federalism after the Referendum*, presented to the Andrew Fletcher Society in June 1975, Dundee: Andrew Fletcher Society, 10 pages.
- 'Rapports Introductifs de la Responsabilité considérée comme un droit', *Revue de Sciences Criminelle et Droit Pénal Comparé*, 2, 484–497 (translated into French by D. Chast) (presented at 21 Journées de défense sociales: Journées Franco-Ecossaises, Edinburgh, 25–27 September 1974).
- 'We Need a New Politics', *Life and Work*, February, 12–18.

1976

- *Lawyers in their Social Setting* (ed.) (Edinburgh: W. Green & Son).
- 'Editor's Foreword', in N. MacCormick (ed.), *Lawyers in Their Social Setting* (Edinburgh: W. Green & Son), vii–ix.
- 'Accountability, Professionalism and the Scottish Judiciary', in M. G. Clarke and H. M. Drucker (eds.), *Our Changing Scotland* (Edinburgh: Polygon Press), 79–86.
- 'Minority Report', with I. Aitken, T. Brinton and J. Haviland, *Report of the Committee on Financial Aid to Political Parties*, Cmnd. 6601, 75–81.
- 'Justice: An Un-Original Position', *Dalhousie Law Journal*, 3, 367–384 (presented as a lecture at the Institut für Rechts- und Sozialphilosophie der Universität des Saarlandes, 1 June 1975) (also published with modification as chapter 5 in *Legal Right and Social Democracy*, 1982).

- 'Children's Rights: A Test Case for Theories of Right', *Archiv für Rechts- und Sozialphilosophie*, 52(3), 305–316 (also published with modification as chapter 8 in *Legal Right and Social Democracy*, 1982).
- 'Formal Justice and the Form of Legal Arguments', *Etudes de Logique Juridique*, 6, 103–118.
- 'The Mandate Question', *Question*, 12, 8–9.
- 'Review of *How to Do Things with Rules* by W. Twining and D. Miers', *British Journal of Law and Society*, 3(2), 279–282.
- 'Review of *Independence and Devolution: The Legal Implications for Scotland* by J.P. Grant (ed.)', *Scots Law Times (News)*, 303–304.
- 'Two-Stranded Support for Legislative Devolution', *The Scotsman*, 5–6 February 1976, 7.

1977

- *Civil Liberties and the Law*, presented at Heriot-Watt University on 25 October 1977, Edinburgh: Heriot-Watt University Special Lecture Series, 20 pages (also published with modification as chapter 3 in *Legal Right and Social Democracy*, 1982).
- 'Rights in Legislation', in P. M. S. Hacker and J. Raz (eds.), *Law, Morality and Society* (Oxford: Clarendon Press), 189–209.
- 'Challenging Sociological Definitions', *British Journal of Law and Society*, 4(1), 87–94.
- 'Iudex qui Litem Suam Fecit', *Acta Juridica* 149–165.
- 'Provincialism and the Scottish Universities', *Question*, 18 March 1977, 3.
- 'Liberty and Law', Letter to the Editor, *The Scotsman*, 27 October 1977.
- 'Westminster Must Beware of Pushing the SNP into an All-out Battle', *The Times*, 17 May 1977, page 14.
- 'The Referendum: Historical Parallels?', *The Scotsman*, 6 December 1977.

1978

- *Legal Reasoning and Legal Theory* (Oxford: Clarendon Press) (reprinted with a new foreword in 1994).
- 'The Motivation of Judgement in the Common Law', in Ch. Perelman and P. Foriers (eds.), *La Motivation des Décisions de Justice* (Brussels: Bruylant), 167–194 (presented as a lecture at the Centre National de Recherches de Logique, Brussels, 18 May 1976).
- 'Privacy and Obscenity', in R. Dhavan and C. Davies (eds.), *Censorship and Obscenity* (Oxford: Martin Robertson & Co), 76–97 (also published with modification as chapter 9 in *Legal Right and Social Democracy*, 1982).

- 'The Obligation of Reparation', *Proceedings of the Aristotelian Society (New Series)*, 78, 175–193 (presented at a Meeting of the Aristotelian Society, London, 20 March 1978) (also published with modification as chapter 11 in *Legal Right and Social Democracy*, 1982).
- 'Does the United Kingdom Have a Constitution? Reflections on MacCormick v. Lord Advocate', *Northern Ireland Legal Quarterly*, 29(1–2), 1–20.
- 'Dworkin as Pre-Benthamite', *Philosophical Review*, 87(4), 585–607 (extended review essay of R. Dworkin, *Taking Rights Seriously*) (also published with modification as chapter 7 in *Legal Right and Social Democracy*, 1982).
- 'Review of *Lectures on Jurisprudence* by A. Smith', in R. L. Meek, D. D. Raphael, P. G. Stein (eds.), *The Economic Journal*, 88(352), 837–839.
- 'What Assembly? Why?', *The Patriot for Scotland, Referendum Special*, December 1978–March 1979, 2.

1979

- 'Constitutional Points', in D. I. Mackay (ed.), *Scotland: The Framework for Change* (Edinburgh: Paul Harris), 47–67.
- 'Nation and Nationalism', in C. MacLean (ed.), *The Crown and the Thistle* (Edinburgh: Scottish Academic Press), 97–111 (also published with modification as chapter 13 in *Legal Right and Social Democracy*, 1982).
- 'Constitution', in C. MacLean (ed.), *The Crown and the Thistle* (Edinburgh: Scottish Academic Press), 149–155 (also published in a modified version, by SUNY Press, in 1999).
- 'Law, Obligation and Consent: Reflections on Stair and Locke', *Archiv für Rechts- und Sozialphilosophie*, 65(3), 387–411 (presented as the Austin Lecture, UK Association for Legal and Social Philosophy in 1978) (also published with modification as chapter 4 in *Legal Right and Social Democracy*, 1982).
- 'Review of *Law and Society: Crisis in Legal Ideals*, by E. Kamenka, R. Brown and E. R. S. Tay', *Political Studies*, 27(3), 525.

1980

- 'The Coherence of a Case and the Reasonableness of Doubt', *Liverpool Law Review*, 2, 45–50.
- 'Wie ernst soll man Rechte Nehmen?', *Rechtstheorie*, 11(1), 1–7 (review essay of R. Dworkin, *Taking Rights Seriously*, 1978).
- 'Review of *Natural Law and Natural Rights*, by J. Finnis', *Political Studies*, 28(4), 651.

1981

- *H.L.A. Hart* (London: Edward Arnold) (2nd edition, with substantive revisions, in 2008 with Stanford University Press).
- 'Stair as Analytical Jurist', in D. M. Walker (ed.), *Stair Tercentenary Studies* (Edinburgh: Stair Society), 276–288.
- 'The Artificial Reason and Judgement of Law', in A. Aarnio, I. Niiniluoto and J. Uusitalo (eds.), *Methodologie und Erkenntnistheorie der Juristischen Argumentation, Rechtstheorie Beiheft* [Supplement] 2 (Berlin: Duncker & Humblot), 105–120.
- 'Adam Smith on Law', *Valparaiso University Law Review*, 15(2), 243–263 (also published with modification as chapter 6 in *Legal Right and Social Democracy*, 1982).
- 'Natural Law Reconsidered', *Oxford Journal of Legal Studies*, 1(1), 99–109.
- 'Law, Morality and Positivism', *Legal Studies*, 1(2), 131–145 (also published as chapter 6 of *An Institutional Theory of Law* in 1986).
- 'The Limits of Reason: A Reply to Dr. Knud Haakonssen', *Archiv für Rechts- und Sozialphilosophie*, 67, 504–509 (also published with modification as part of chapters 6 and 13 in *Rhetoric and the Rule of Law*, 2005).
- 'The Rational Discipline of Law', *Juridical Review (New Series)*, 26, 146–160 (presented at the Stair Tercentenary Conference, University of Glasgow, 28 March 1981).
- 'A Political Frontier of Jurisprudence: John Chipman Gray on the State', *Cornell Law Review*, 66(5), 973–985.
- 'Review of *Justice and Liberty* by D.D. Raphael', *Archiv für Rechts- und Sozialphilosophie*, 67(4), 557–558.
- 'Review of *Judging Justice: An Introduction to Political Philosophy* by P. Pettit, and *Justice* by E. Kamenka and A. Erh-Soon Tay' (ed.), *Legal Studies*, 1(2), 213–216.

1982

- *Legal Right and Social Democracy: Essays in Legal and Political Philosophy* (Oxford: Oxford University Press).
- 'Law and Enlightenment', in R. H. Campbell and A. S. Skinner (eds.), *The Origins and Nature of the Scottish Enlightenment* (Edinburgh: John Donald), 150–166.
- 'On Analytical Jurisprudence', in P. Trappe (ed.), *Conceptions Contemporaires du Droit*, Vol. I (Wiesbaden: Archiv für Rechts- und Sozialphilosophie Supplementa), 29–41 (also published as chapter 4 of *An Institutional Theory of Law* in 1986).
- 'Coercion and Law', in P. Trappe (ed.), *Conceptions Contemporaires du Droit*, Vol. II (Wiesbaden: Archiv für Rechts- und Sozialphilosophie Supplementa),

259–271 (also published with modification as chapter 12 in *Legal Right and Social Democracy*, 1982).

- 'Legal Reasoning and Practical Reason', in P. A. French, T. E. Uehling Jr and H. K. Wettstein (eds.), *Midwest Studies in Philosophy*, Vol. 7 (Minneapolis: University of Minnesota Press), 271–286.
- 'Rights, Claims and Remedies', in M. A. Stewart (ed.), *Law, Morality and Rights* (Dordrecht: D. Reidel), 161–181 (also published in *Law and Philosophy*, 1982).
- 'Rights, Claims and Remedies', *Law and Philosophy*, 1(2), 337–357 (also published by Reidel in 1982).
- 'Legal Right and Social Democracy', *Queen's Quarterly*, 89(2), 209–304 (presented as the Corry Lecture at Queen's University, 19 March 1981) (also published with modification as chapter 1 in *Legal Right and Social Democracy*, 1982).
- 'The Nature of Legal Reasoning: A Brief Reply to Dr. Wilson', *Legal Studies*, 2(3), 286–290.
- 'The Polity and Values: The Question of Moral Disestablishment', *International Social Science Review*, 57(1), 32.
- 'Review of *Social Order and the Limits of Law: A Theoretical Essay*, by I. Jenkins', *Political Studies*, 30(1), 153–154.
- 'Review of *The Science of a Legislator*, by K. Haakonssen', *Political Studies*, 30(2), 328–329.
- 'Dr. W.D. Lamont', *The Times*, 20 November 1982.
- 'Boldness on the Bench. Review of *What Next in the Law*, by Lord Denning', *Times Literary Supplement*, 4148, 1 October 1982, 1076.

1983

- 'Contemporary Legal Philosophy: The Rediscovery of Practical Reason', *Journal of Law and Society*, 10(1), 1–18 (also published by Dartmouth in 1996).
- 'Jurisprudence and the Constitution', *Current Legal Problems*, 36, 13–30 (also published as chapter 8 of *An Institutional Theory of Law* in 1986).
- 'Legal Decisions and Their Consequences: From Dewey to Dworkin', *New York University Law Review*, 58, 239–258 (presented as the Dewey Lecture in Jurisprudence, School of Law, New York University, 5 October 1982) (also published with modification as chapter 6 of Rhetoric and the *Rule of Law*, 2005).
- 'What Is Wrong with Deceit?', *Sydney Law Review*, 10(1), 5–19 (presented as a public lecture at the School of Law, University of Sydney, 22 July 1981).
- 'Reply to Mr Tur', *Philosophical Books*, 24(4), 205–208.
- 'Gewirth's Fallacy', *Queen's Law Journal*, 9(2), 345–351 (1983–1984) (review of A. Gewirth, *Human Rights*).
- 'At the Side of the Accused. Review of *Not Without Prejudice*, by D. Napley', 4164 *Times Literary Supplement*, 21 January 1983, 66.

1984

- 'The Idea of Liberty: Some Reflections on Lorimer's Institutes', in V. Hope (ed.), *Philosophers of the Scottish Enlightenment* (Edinburgh: Edinburgh University Press), 233–248 (Festschrift for George Davie).
- 'On Reasonableness', in C. Perelman and R. Vander Elst (eds.), *Les Notions à Contenu Variable en Droit* (Brussels: Bruylant), 233–248 (also published with modification by *Notre Dame Law Review* in 1999, and as chapter 9 of *Rhetoric and the Rule of Law*, 2005).
- 'Coherence in Legal Justification', in W. Krawietz, H. Schelsky, H. Winkler and A. Schramm (eds.), *Theorie der Normen: Festgabe für Ota Weinberger zum* 65. (Geburtstag, Berlin: Duncker & Humblot), 37–53 (also published by Reidel in 1984 and Jurisdiska Fakulteten i Uppsala in 1992).
- 'Coherence in Legal Justification', in A. Peczenik, L. Lindahl and B. van Roermund (eds.), *Theory of Legal Science: Proceedings of the Conference on Legal Theory and Philosophy of Science, Lund, Sweden*, 11–14 December 1983 (Dordrecht: D. Reidel), 235–251 (also published by Duncker & Humblot in 1984 and Jurisdiska Fakulteten i Uppsala in 1992).
- 'Der Rechtsstaat und die Rule of Law', *Juristenzeitung*, 39, 65–70.
- 'Analytical Jurisprudence and the Possibility of Legal Knowledge', *Saskatchewan Law Review*, 49, 1–13 (1984–1985).
- 'Review of *Max Weber*, by A.T. Kronman', *Political Studies*, 32(3), 512–513.
- 'Review of *Ethics and the Rule of Law*, by D. Lyons', *Political Studies*, 32(4), 695–696.
- 'Between the One and the Many. Review of *Public and Private in Social Life*, by S. I. Benn and G.F. Gaus', 4216 *Times Literary Supplement*, 20 January 1984, 58.
- 'Education for Judges', *The Times*, Letter, 18 January 1984, 11.

1985

- *Grundlagen des Institutionalistischen Rechtspositivismus*, with O. Weinberger (Berlin: Duncker & Humblot) (Schriften zur Rechtstheorie, Heft 113) (published in English in 1986 by Reidel).
- *Conditions of Validity and Cognition in Modern Legal Thought* [*Geltungs- und Erkenntnisbedingungen im modernen Rechtsdenken*], with S. Panou and L. Lombardi Vallauri (eds.) (Stuttgart: Franz Steiner Verlag) (*Archiv für Rechts- und Sozialphilosophie, Beiheft* [Supplement], 25).
- 'Alcuni problemi circa l'ordine spontaneo', in S. Ricossa and E. Robilant (eds.), *Libertà giustizia e persona nella società tecnologica* (Milan: Dott A. Giuffré), 51–68 (presented in Turin in April 1984) (also published, with

modifications, under the title 'Spontaneous Order and the Rule of Law: Some Problems', in 1986 (*Jahrbuch des Öffentlichen Rechts der Gegenwart*) and 1989 (*Ratio Juris*)).

- 'The Limits of Rationality in Legal Reasoning', in A-J. Arnaud, R. Hilpinen and J. Wróblewski (eds.), *Juristic Logic, Rationality and Irrationality in Law* (*Rechtstheorie, Beiheft* [Supplement], 8) (Berlin: Duncker & Humblot), 161–177 (also published as chapter 9 of *An Institutional Theory of Law* in 1986).
- '*The Idea of a Free Government*', *Occasional Paper of the Wilson Center* (Washington, DC: The Wilson Center), 7–17 (presented at Johns Hopkins University, 12 September 1985).
- 'The Democratic Intellect and the Law', *Legal Studies*, 5(2), 177–183 (Presidential Address to the Society of Public Teachers of Law, 19 September 1984).
- 'A Moralistic Case for A-Moralistic Law?', *Valparaiso University Law Review*, 20(1), 1–41 (presented as the Seegers Lectures at the Valparaiso School of Law, 26 and 27 March 1985).
- 'A Too Brief Reply to D'Amato, Boyle, Cullison and Stith', *Valparaiso University Law Review*, 20(1), 77–82.
- 'Review of *Good Law: Towards a Rational Lawmaking Process*, by H.J.M. Boukema', *Rechtstheorie*, 16, 503–504.
- Translator of 'The Digest of Justinian: Book One', in T. Mommsen and P. J. Krueger (eds.) (English translation edited by A. Watson), *The Digest of Justinian* (Philadelphia: University of Pennsylvania Press), 1–39.

1986

- *An Institutional Theory of Law: New Approaches to Legal Positivism*, with O. Weinberger (Dordrecht: D. Reidel) (originally published in German in 1985 by Duncker & Humblot).
- *The Legal Mind: Essays for Tony Honoré*, with P. Birks (eds.) (Oxford: Oxford University Press).
- 'Editors' Preface', with P. Birks, in P. Birks and N. MacCormick (eds.), *The Legal Mind: Essays for Tony Honoré* (Oxford: Oxford University Press), v–vi.
- 'Speech Acts, Legal Institutions and Real Laws', with Z. Bańkowski, in P. Birks and N. MacCormick (eds.), *The Legal Mind: Essays for Tony Honoré*, with P. Birks (eds.) (Oxford: Oxford University Press), 121–134.
- 'The Interest of the State and the Rule of Law', in P. Wallington and R. Merkin (eds.) *Essays in Memory of Professor F.H. Lawson* (London: Butterworths), 169–187 (originally presented as the 5th Annual Lawson Lecture, Lancaster University, 12 March 1985) (also published with modification as chapter 3 in *Questioning Sovereignty*, 1999).
- 'Theory in the Law Curriculum', with W. Twining, in W. Twining (ed.), *Legal Theory and Common Law* (Oxford: Oxford University Press), 238–254.

- 'Spontaneous Order and the Rule of Law: Some Problems', *Jahrbuch des Öffentlichen Rechts der Gegenwart*, 35, 1–13 (presented at Liberty Fund conference at Gleneagles, Scotland, July 1986) (also published in *Ratio Juris* in 1989; earlier version in Italian published by Dott A. Giuffrè in 1985).

1987

- 'Comment on G. Postema's "The Normativity of Law"', in R. Gavison (ed.), *Issues in Contemporary Legal Philosophy* (Oxford: Clarendon Press), 105–113.
- 'Universalisation and Induction in Law', in C. Faralli and E. Pattaro (eds.), *Reason in Law* (Milan: Seminario Giuridico dell Università di Bologna), 91–106 (also published with modification as part of chapter 5 of *Rhetoric and the Rule of Law*, 2005).
- 'Smashing the Two-Way Mirror', in E. Simpson (ed.), *Anti-Foundationalism and Practical Reasoning: Conversations between Hermeneutics and Analysis* (Edmonton, Alberta: Academic Printing and Publishing), 201–216.
- 'Why Cases have Rationes and What These Are', in L. Goldstein (ed.), *Precedent in Law* (Oxford: Clarendon Press), 155–182 (also published with modification as chapter 8 of *Rhetoric and the Rule of Law*, 2005).
- 'Law', in D. Miller (ed.), *The Blackwell Encyclopaedia of Political Thought* (Oxford: Basil Blackwell), 274–294.
- 'John Austin', in D. Miller (ed.), *The Blackwell Encyclopaedia of Political Thought* (Oxford: Basil Blackwell), 27–28.
- 'William Blackstone', in D. Miller (ed.), *The Blackwell Encyclopaedia of Political Thought* (Oxford: Basil Blackwell), 47.
- 'Hans Kelsen', in V. Bogdanor (ed.), *The Blackwell Encyclopaedia of Political Institutions* (Oxford: Basil Blackwell), 309–310.
- 'Law', in V. Bogdanor (ed.), *The Blackwell Encyclopaedia of Political Institutions* (Oxford: Basil Blackwell), 319–321.
- 'Sovereignty', in V. Bogdanor (ed.), *The Blackwell Encyclopaedia of Political Institutions* (Oxford: Basil Blackwell), 583–584.
- 'Review of *The Ivory Tower: Essays in Philosophy and Public Policy*, by A. Kenny', *Political Studies*, 35(4), 702.
- 'Review of *A Matter of Principle*, by R. Dworkin', *Political Studies*, 35(3), 533.
- 'Review of *Essays on Kelsen*, by R. Tur and W. Twining (eds.)', *Philosophical Books*, 28(3), 183–186.
- 'Review of *Philosophy and the Criminal Law* by A. Duff and N.E. Simmonds' (ed.), *Canadian Philosophical Reviews*, 7(5), 190–192.
- 'Review of *Precedent and Law: Dynamics of Common Law Growth*, by J. Stone', *Summer Public Law*, 297–299.
- 'Foreword', in O. Weinberger, *Law, Institution, and Legal Politics: Fundamental Problems of Legal Theory and Social Philosophy* (Dordrecht: Kluwer Academic Publishers), ix–xi.

- 'Access to the Goods. Review of *The Morality of Freedom*, by J. Raz', 4392 *Times Literary Supplement*, 5 June 1987, 599.

1988

- *Constitutionalism and Democracy*, presented as the 3rd Lecture at the Scottish National Party Annual National Conference, Inverness, September 1988 (Edinburgh: SNP Publications Department), 16 pages.
- 'Persons as Institutional Facts', in E. Weinberger and W. Krawietz (eds.), *Reine Rechtslehre im Spiegel Ihrer Fortsetzer und Kritiker* (Vienna and New York: Springer-Verlag), 371–393 (also published with modification as chapter 5 in *Institutions of Law*, 2007).
- 'The Ethics of International Intervention: Reply to Mr. McMahan', in A. Ellis (ed.), *Ethics and International Relations* (Manchester: Manchester University Press), 82–85.
- 'On the Interpretation and Understanding of Case Law', in S. Panou, G. Bozonis, D. Georgas and P. Trappe (eds.), *Theory and Systems of Legal Philosophy*, Vol. III (Stuttgart: Archiv für Rechts- und Sozialphilosophie Supplementa), 134–144.
- 'The Determinacy of Selves', in W. J. A. Macartney (ed.), *Self-Determination in the Commonwealth* (Aberdeen: Aberdeen University Press), 112–118.
- 'Institutions, Arrangements and Practical Reason', *Ratio Juris*, 1(1), 73–82.
- 'Le Raisonnement juridique', *Archives de Philosophie du Droit*, 33, 99–112.
- 'Law, Morality and Discursive Rationality: Foreword', with Jerzy Wróblewski, in A. Aarnio and K. Tuori (eds.), *Law, Morality, and Discursive Rationality* (Helsinki: Publications of the University of Helsinki), 1–7 (proceedings from the Law and Legitimacy symposium in Murikka Centre, Finland, August 1988).
- 'Courage in Costume. Review of *A "Life is too Short" – Autobiography, Vol 1*, by N. Fairbairn', 4426 *Times Literary Supplement*, 29 January 1988, 107.
- 'How the Tories Raised the Stakes', *The Scotsman*, 17.

1989

- *Enlightenment, Rights and Revolution: Essays in Legal and Social Philosophy*, with Z. Bańkowski (eds.) (Aberdeen: Aberdeen University Press).
- 'Editors' Preface', with Z. Bańkowski, in Z. Bańkowski and N. MacCormick (eds.), *Enlightenment, Rights and Revolution: Essays in Legal and Social Philosophy* (Aberdeen: Aberdeen University Press), ix–xii.
- 'La Texture Ouverte des Règles Juridiques', in P. Amselek (ed.), *Controverses autour de l'Ontologie Juridique* (Paris: P.U.F.), 109–126 (also published in English by Edinburgh University Press in 1991).
- 'Law, Morality and Discursive Rationality: Foreword', with J. Wróblewski, in A. Aarnio and K. Tuori (eds.), *Law, Morality and Discursive Rationality* (Helsinki: Department of Public Law, University of Helsinki), 1–7.

- 'Some Principles of Statutory Interpretation', with Z. Bańkowski, in J. van Dunné (ed.), *Legal Reasoning and Statutory Interpretation* (Arnhem: Youda Quint), 41–53 (presented as one of the Rotterdam Lectures in Jurisprudence, 1 June 1988).
- 'Unrepentant Gradualism', in O. D. Edwards (ed.), *A Claim of Right for Scotland* (Edinburgh: Polygon Press), 99–109.
- 'Constitutionalism and Constitutions', in D. McCrone (ed.), *What Scotland Wants: Ten Years On*, Proceedings of a One Day Conference on 25 February 1989 (Edinburgh: Unit for the Study of Government in Scotland), 3–8.
- 'Constitutionalism and Democracy', in O. Weinberger (ed.), *Aktuelle Probleme Der Demokratie* [Actual Problems of Democracy], *Internationales Jahrbuch für Rechtsphilosophie und Gesetzgebung* (Vienna: Manzsche Verlags- und Universitätsbuchhandlung), 17–28.
- 'Discretion and Rights', *Law and Philosophy*, 8(1), 23–36.
- 'Spontaneous Order and Rule of Law: Some Problems', *Ratio Juris*, 2(1), 41–54 (also published in *Jahrbuch des Öffentlichen Rechts der Gegenwart* in 1986; translation into Spanish referred to under 1986; earlier version in Italian published by Dott A. Giuffré in 1985).
- 'Preface', *Southern California Law Review*, 62, 743–745 (Symposium: The Works of Joseph Raz).
- 'The Ethics of Legalism', *Ratio Juris*, 2, 184–193.
- Translator, with R. Alder, of R. Alexy, *A Theory of Legal Argumentation* (Oxford: Clarendon Press).

1990

- 'Universalisation and Induction in Law', in South Korean IVR (eds.), *Philosophy of Law and Social Philosophy East and West: Festschrift for Dr. Ton-Kak Suh's 70th Birthday* (Seoul), 105–118.
- 'General Legal Concepts', in T. B. Smith and R. Black (eds.), *The Laws of Scotland: Stair Memorial Encyclopaedia*, Vol. 11 (Edinburgh: The Law Society of Scotland and Butterworths), 359–419 (also published with modification as chapters 5–9 in *Institutions of Law*, 2007).
- 'Reconstruction after Deconstruction: A Response to CLS', *Oxford Journal of Legal Studies*, 10, 539–558 (also published, in a shorter version, by Edinburgh University Press in 1993).
- 'Of Self-Determination and Other Things', 15 *Bulletin of the Australian Society of Legal Philosophy*, 1–20.
- 'Commentary on "The Future of Legal Systems" by T. Koopmans' (Edinburgh: David Hume Institute) (response to the Presidential Address to the David Hume Institute delivered at Royal Society of Edinburgh, November 1989), 13–18.

1991

- *Interpreting Statutes: A Comparative Study*, with R. S. Summers (eds.) (Aldershot: Dartmouth).
- *Controversies About Law's Ontology*, with P. Amselek (eds.) (Edinburgh: Edinburgh University Press).
- 'On Method and Methodology', with Z. Bańkowski, R. S. Summers and J. Wróblewski, in N. MacCormick and R. S. Summers (eds.), *Interpreting Statutes: A Comparative Study* (Aldershot: Dartmouth), 9–28.
- 'Statutory Interpretation in the United Kingdom', with Z. Bańkowski, in N. MacCormick and R.S. Summers (eds.), *Interpreting Statutes: A Comparative Study* (Aldershot: Dartmouth), 359–406.
- 'Interpretation and Justification', with R. S. Summers, in N. MacCormick and R. S. Summers (eds.), *Interpreting Statutes: A Comparative Study* (Aldershot: Dartmouth), 511–544.
- 'On "Open Texture" in Law', in P. Amselek and N. MacCormick (eds.), *Controversies About Law's Ontology* (Edinburgh: Edinburgh University Press), 72–83 (also published in French by P.U.F. in 1989).
- 'Foreword to English Edition', in P. Amselek and N. MacCormick (eds.), *Controversies About Law's Ontology* (Edinburgh: Edinburgh University Press), vii–x.
- 'An Idea for a Scottish Constitution', in W. Finnie, C. Himsworth and N. Walker (eds.), *Edinburgh Essays in Public Law* (Edinburgh: Edinburgh University Press), 159–181.
- 'Moral Disestablishment and Rational Discourse', in H. Jung, H. Müller-Dietz and U. Neumann (eds.), *Recht und Moral* (Baden-Baden: Nomos Verlag), 219–234.
- 'Preface', with W. Twining, in W. Twining (ed.), *Issues of Self-Determination* (Aberdeen: Aberdeen University Press), xi–xvii.
- 'Is Nationalism Philosophically Credible?', in W. Twining (ed.), *Issues of Self-Determination* (Aberdeen: Aberdeen University Press), 8–19 (also published with modification as chapter 10 in *Questioning Sovereignty*, 1999.
- '*Donoghue v. Stevenson* and Legal Reasoning', in P. T. Burns and S. J. Lyons (eds.), *Donoghue v. Stevenson and the Modern Law of Negligence* (Vancouver, B.C.: Continuing Legal Education of British Columbia), 191–214.
- 'Philosophy in Legal Education', *Scots Philosophical Newsletter*, March, 5–9.
- 'Notes on Narrativity and the Normative Syllogism', *International Journal for the Semiotics of Law*, 4(2), 163–174 (also published with modification as part of chapter 4 of *Rhetoric and the Rule of Law*, 2005).
- 'Citizens' Legal Reasoning and its Importance for Jurisprudence', *Archiv für Rechts- und Sozialphilosophie (Beiheft* [Supplement], 40), 15–21 (ed. by E. Dais, S. Jorgensen and A. Erh-Soon Tay).
- 'Neil Gunn and Nationalism: A Memoir', *Chapman*, 67 (Winter), 63–64 (Reprinted in A. McCleery (ed.), *Nation and Nationalism* (2013) (Dunbeath: Whittles Publishing), 39–42.

- 'Law, State and Feminism: MacKinnon's Theses Considered. Review of C. MacKinnon, *Toward a Feminist Theory of the State*, *Law and Philosophy*, 10(4), 447–452.
- 'Llewellyn Revisited. Review of *The Case Law System in America*, by K. Llewellyn', with Z. Wiseman, *Texas Law Review*, 70, 771–779 (1991–1992).
- 'Review of D. Lieberman: *The Province of Legislation Determined*', *Utilitas*, 3(2), 313–317.
- 'Doing and Discussing. Review of *General Theory of Norms*, by H. Kelsen', 4607 *Times Literary Supplement*, 19 July 1991, 22.

1992

- *Legal Reasoning*, Vols. I and II, with A. Aarnio (eds.) (Aldershot: Dartmouth).
- *The Judicial Application of Law* by J. Wróblewski, with Z. Bańkowski (eds.) (Dordrecht: Kluwer Publishing).
- 'Introduction', with A. Aarnio, in A. Aarnio and N. MacCormick (eds.), *Legal Reasoning*, Vol. I (Aldershot: Dartmouth), ix–xvii.
- 'Introduction', with A. Aarnio, in A. Aarnio and N. MacCormick (eds.), *Legal Reasoning*, Vol. II (Aldershot: Dartmouth), xi–xvii.
- 'Republicanism and Enlightenment Thought: Observations from Scotland', in A. E. Dick Howard (ed.), *The United States Constitution: Roots, Rights and Responsibilities* (Washington, DC and London: Smithsonian Inst. Press), 97–114.
- 'Coherence in Legal Justification', in *De Lege: Skrifter av Fakultetens Hedersdoktorer*, Jurisdiska Fakulteten i Uppsala, Yearbook 2, 311–330 (also published by D. Reidel in 1984).
- 'La Raisonnement Juridique en Common Law: La Motivation Comme Justification', in P. Legrand (ed.), *Common Law: d'un siècle à l'autre* (Cowansville, Québec: Editions Yvonne Blais), 309–332 (also published in *Archives de philosophie du droit* in 1988).
- 'Natural Law and the Separation of Law and Morals', in R. P. George (ed.), *Natural Law Theory* (Oxford: Clarendon Press), 105–133.
- 'Further Thoughts on Institutional Facts', *International Journal for the Semiotics of Law*, 5(1), 3–15.
- 'Legal Deduction, Legal Predicates and Expert Systems', *International Journal for the Semiotics of Law*, 5(2), 181–202 (also published with modification as part of chapter 4 of *Rhetoric and the Rule of Law*, 2005).
- 'A Deductivist Rejoinder to a Semiotic Critique', *International Journal for the Semiotics of Law*, 5(2), 215–224 (also published with modification as part of chapter 4 of *Rhetoric and the Rule of Law*, 2005).
- 'The North Star: Scotland in Europe', 1 *Edit: University of Edinburgh Magazine*, 26–27.
- 'Time to Tear Ourselves Away', Thursday, 6 February 1992, *The Scotsman*.
- 'Responsibility', *The Scotsman*, Letter, 8 February 1992.
- 'H. L. A. Hart', *The Guardian*, 23 December 1992.

1993

- 'Law', in P. H. Scott (ed.), *Scotland: A Concise Cultural History* (Edinburgh: Mainstream Publishing), 343–355.
- 'Reconstruction after Deconstruction: Closing in on Critique', in A. Norrie (ed.), *Closure or Critique: New Directions in Legal Theory* (Edinburgh: Edinburgh University Press), 142–156 (also published, in a longer version, in *Oxford Journal of Legal Studies* in 1990).
- 'Constitutionalism and Democracy', in R. Bellamy (ed.), *Theories and Concepts of Politics* (Manchester: Manchester University Press), 124–147.
- 'Beyond the Sovereign State', *Modern Law Review,* 56(1), 1–18 (delivered as the Chorley Lecture at LSE on 3 June 1992).
- 'Argumentation and Interpretation in Law', *Ratio Juris,* 6(1), 16–29 (also published in *Argumentation* in 1995, and with modification as chapter 7 of *Rhetoric and the Rule of Law*, 2005).
- 'H.L.A. Hart: In Memoriam', *Ratio Juris,* 6(3), 337–338.
- 'Can a Law Be Bad? Review of *Norm and Nature*, by R. Shiner', 4696 *Times Literary Supplement*, 28 April 1993, 23.
- 'With Due Respect: Ties of Sentiment and the Vindication of Rights. Review of *What's Wrong with Rights?* by E.F. Kingdom, and *Toward a Feminist Theory of the State*, by C. MacKinnon', 4686 *Times Literary Supplement*, 22 January 1993, 3–4.

1994

- *Legal Reasoning and Legal Theory*, 2nd ed. (Oxford: Oxford University Press) (includes new 'Foreword', ix–xvi).
- *Prescriptive Formality and Normative Rationality in Modern Legal Systems*, with W. Krawietz and G. H. von Wright (eds.) (Berlin: Duncker and Humblot).
- 'Four Quadrants of Jurisprudence', in W. Krawietz, N. MacCormick and G. H. von Wright (eds.), *Prescriptive Formality and Normative Rationality in Modern Legal Systems* (Berlin: Duncker and Humblot), 53–70.
- 'Legal Concepts', in R. Asher (ed.) and J. W. Simpson (exec. ed.), *Encyclopaedia of Language and Linguistics* (Oxford: Pergamon Press), 2069–2074.
- 'Diritto, "Rule of Law", e democrazia', translated into Italian by E. Diciotti and R. Guastini, in P. Comanducci and R. Guastini (eds.), *Analisi e Diritto* (Torino: Giappichelli), 189–209.
- 'What Place for Nationalism in the Modern World?', in H. McQueen (ed.), *In Search of New Constitutions, Hume Papers in Public Policy*, 2 (Edinburgh: The David Hume Institute), 79–95 (presented as Stevenson Lecture in Citizenship, University of Glasgow, 18 June 1994; also published by Westview Press in 1996, and with modification as part of chapter 11 in *Questioning Sovereignty*, 1999).

- 'Constitutionalism, Democracy and Welfare', in M. Adler (ed.), *Democracy and Social Security*, Proceedings of the 5th Annual Erasmus/Tempus Course on 'Social Security in Europe' (Edinburgh: University of Edinburgh), 5–8.
- 'Legal Reasoning and the Institutional Theory of Law', in P. Koller, W. Krawietz and P. Strasser (eds.), *Institution und Recht* (Berlin: Duncker & Humblot) (*Rechtstheorie Beiheft [Supplement]*, 14), 117–139 (also published with modification as chapter 4 of *Rhetoric and the Rule of Law*, 2005).
- 'The Concept of Law and the Concept of Law', *Oxford Journal of Legal Studies*, 14(1), 1–23 (also published by Clarendon Press in 1996) (presented as the Hart Lecture, University of Oxford, 11 May 1993).
- 'Sovereignty, Democracy and Subsidiarity', *Juridisk Tidskrift vid Stockholms Universitet*, 2, 290–297 (also published by Lothian Foundation Press in 1995; by Sakkoulas Publications in 1994; by Schäffer-Poeschel in 1997; and in *Rechtstheorie* in 1994) (presented as a Lecture on the occasion of receiving a Doctor Juris honorary degree at the University of Saarland).
- 'Sovereignty, Democracy and Subsidiarity', in L. Kotsiris (ed.), *Law at the Turn of the 20th Century* (Thessaloniki: Sakkoulas Publications), 1994, 185–197 (also published by Lothian Foundation Press in 1995; by Schäffer-Poeschel in 1997; in *Juridisk Tidskrift vid Stockholms Universitet* in 1994; and in *Rechtstheorie* in 1994).
- 'Sovereignty, Democracy and Subsidiarity', *Rechtstheorie*, 25, 281–290 (also published by Lothian Foundation Press in 1995; by Sakkoulas Publications in 1994; by Schäffer-Poeschel in 1997; and in *Juridisk Tidskrift vid Stockholms Universitet* in 1994).
- 'On Justification and Interpretation', with J. Wróblewski, *Archiv für Rechts- und Sozialphilosophie*, 53, 255–268.
- 'John Smith: An Appreciation', *Scottish Affairs*, 8, 5–8.
- 'In Memoriam: Eugene Kamenka', *IVR Newsletter*, 17, 1–2.
- 'Review of *Interpretation and Legal Theory* by A. Marmor', *Ethics*, 105(1), 195–196.
- 'Names Can Hurt People: Should "Shameless Indecency" Be an Exception to Free Speech? Review of *Only Words* by C.A. MacKinnon', *Times Literary Supplement*, 4757, 3 June 1994, 3–4.
- 'Free Under the Law. Review of *Ethics in the Public Domain*, by J. Raz', 4787 *Times Literary Supplement*, 30 December 1994, 11.
- 'Rights of a Sovereign Nation', *The Scotsman*, 20 December 1994, page 6.
- 'Legal Training', *The Scotsman*, Letter, 21 June 1994.
- *Contemporary Questions in Legal Theory: Intensive Course*, Course Reader for the Faculty of Law, University of Toronto, 202 pages.

1995

- 'Defeasibility in Law and Logic', in Z. Bańkowski, I. White and U. Hahn (eds.), *Informatics and the Foundations of Legal Reasoning* (Dordrecht: Kluwer

Academic Publishers), 99–117 (also published with modification as chapter 12 in *Rhetoric and the Rule of Law*, 2005).

- 'Argumentation und Interpretation im Recht: "Rule Consequentialism" und rationale Rekonstruktion', in G. Teubner (ed.), *Entscheidungsfolgen als Rechtsgrund* (Baden-Baden: Nomos Verlagsgesellschaft), 39–53 (draws on passages from 'On Method and Methodology' in *Interpreting Statutes*, 1991) (translated into German with the assistance H. Jung).
- 'Sovereignty, Democracy and Subsidiarity', in R. Bellamy, V. Bufacchi and D. Castliglione (eds.), *Democracy and Constitutional Culture in Europe* (London: Lothian Foundation Press), 95–106 (also published in *Juridisk Tidskrift vid Stockholms Universitet* in 1994, and in *Rechtstheorie* in 1994, both in slightly different versions).
- 'Time, Narratives and Law', in J. Bjarup and M. Blegvad (eds.), *Time, Law and Society, Archiv für Rechts- und Sozialphilosophie, Beiheft* (Stuttgart: Franz Steiner Verlag), [Supplement], 64, 111–125 (also published with modification as chapter 11 in *Rhetoric and the Rule of Law*, 2005).
- 'Sovereignty: Myth and Reality', in *De Lege: Uppsala University Law Faculty Yearbook* (Special Issue ed. by N. Jareborg, 'Towards Universal Law: Trends in National, European and International Lawmaking') (Uppsala: Iustus Förlag), 227–248 (also published with modification in *Scottish Affairs* in 1995, and as chapter 8 in *Questioning Sovereignty*, 1999).
- 'Sovereignty: Myth and Reality', *Scottish Affairs*, 11, 1–13 (also published with modifications by Iustus Förlag in 1995, and as chapter 8 in *Questioning Sovereignty*, 1999).
- 'The Maastricht-Urteil: Sovereignty Now', *European Law Journal*, 1(3), 259–266.
- 'The Relative Heteronomy of Law', *European Journal of Philosophy*, 3(1), 69–85 (presented at the Legal Theory Workshops Series, Faculty of Law, University of Toronto, 23 September 1994) (also published with modification as chapter 14 in *Institutions of Law*, 2007).
- 'Argumentation and Interpretation in Law', *Argumentation*, 9(3), 467–480 (also published in *Ratio Juris* in 1993).
- 'Eugene Kamenka 1928–1994', *Bulletin of the Australian Society of Legal Philosophy*, 20, 1–3.
- 'The European Union?', with Z. Bańkowski and A. Scott, RUSEL Working paper No. 22, Department of Politics, University of Exeter, 10 pages.
- 'Professor Barrie Wilson: A Tribute by the Provost of Law and Social Sciences', in 5 *Bulletin: The University of Edinburgh News*, 1 and 24.
- 'Review of H. Kelsen, *General Theory of Norms*. Trans. by M. Hartney', *Political Studies*, 43(4), 784.
- 'Evils that Mann Did. Review of *Crossing Over the Line, Legislating Morality and the Mann Act*, by D.J. Langum', 4800 *Times Literary Supplement*, 31 March 1995, 10.

1996

- 'What Place for Nationalism in the Modern World?', in S. Caney, D. George and P. Jones (eds.), *National Rights, International Obligations* (Boulder: Westview Press), 34–52 (also published by The David Hume Institute in 1994, and with modification as part of chapter 11 in *Questioning Sovereignty*, 1999).
- 'The Concept of Law and *The Concept of Law*', in R. P. George (ed.), *The Autonomy of Law: Essays on Legal Positivism* (Oxford: Clarendon Press), 163–194 (also published in the *Oxford Journal of Legal Studies* in 1994).
- 'Law and Philosophy: The Rediscovery of Practical Reason', in P. A. Thomas (ed.), *Legal Frontiers, Aldershot: Dartmouth*, 41–65 (also published in the *Journal of Law and Society* in 1983.
- 'The Maastricht-Urteil: Sovereignty Now', in F. Fleerackers, E. van Leeuwen, and B. van Roermund (eds.), *Law, Life and the Image of Man: Modes of Thought in Modern Legal Theory, Festschrift for Jan. M. Broekman* (Berlin: Duncker & Humblot), 1996, 447–453.
- 'Liberalism, Nationalism and the Post-sovereign State', *Political Studies,* 44(3), 553–567 (special issue ed. by R. Bellamy and D. Castiglione) (also published with modification as part of chapter 11 in *Questioning Sovereignty*, 1999).
- 'Libertad, Igualdad y Nacionalismo', *Sistema: Revista de ciencas sociales,* 130, 31–49 (translated into Spanish by L. R. Abascal).
- 'Institutional Normative Order: A Conception of Law', *Cornell Law Review,* 82, 1051–1070 (also published with modification as chapter 1 in *Questioning Sovereignty*, 1999).
- 'Justice as Impartiality: Assenting with Anti-contractualist Reservations. Comment on *Justice as Impartiality* by B. Barry', *Political Studies,* 44(2), 305–310.
- 'Preface' to Japanese translation of *H. L. A. Hart* (1981), translated into Japanese by T. Tsunoda, as *Hāto Hórigaku no zenizō, Kōyō: Shobō*, 1996.
- 'The Law Is a Mongrel: How a Separate Legal Tradition Underpins Scottish Nationhood. Review of *A Legal History of Scotland, Vol. 2*, by D.M. Walker', 4845 *Times Literary Supplement*, 9 February 1996, 3–4.
- 'Whither Scotland's Flower?', *The Times Higher Education Supplement*, 13 December 1996 (1258), 16.

1997

- *Interpreting Precedents: A Comparative Study*, with R. S. Summers (eds.) (Aldershot: Dartmouth).
- *Constructing Legal Systems: 'European Union' in Legal Theory*, (ed.) (Dordrecht: Kluwer Academic Publishing).

- 'Democracy, Subsidiarity and Citizenship in the "European Commonwealth"', in N. MacCormick (ed.), *Constructing Legal Systems: 'European Union' in Legal Theory* (Dordrecht: Kluwer Academic Publishing), 1–26 (also published in *Law and Philosophy* in 1997).
- 'Introduction', with R. S. Summers, in N. MacCormick, R. S. Summers and A. L. Goodhart (eds.), *Interpreting Precedents: A Comparative Study* (Aldershot: Dartmouth), 1–15.
- 'Precedent in the United Kingdom', with Z. Bańkowski and G. Marshall, in N. MacCormick, R. S. Summers and A. L. Goodhart (eds.), *Interpreting Precedents: A Comparative Study* (Aldershot: Dartmouth), 315–354.
- 'Further General Reflections and Conclusions', with R. S. Summers, in N. MacCormick, R. S. Summers and A. L. Goodhart (eds.), *Interpreting Precedents: A Comparative Study* (Aldershot: Dartmouth), 531–550.
- 'The Ideal and the Actual of Law and Society', in J. Tasioulas (ed.), *Law, Values and Social Practices* (Aldershot: Dartmouth), 15–37.
- 'Universal and Particular: The Problem with Precedent', in A. Aarnio, R. Alexy and G. Bergholtz (eds.), *Justice, Morality and Law: A Tribute to Aleksander Peczenik on the Occasion of his 60th Birthday*, 16 November 1997 (Lund: Juristförklaget i Lund), 261–271.
- 'On Institutional Normative Order: An Idea About Law', in E. G. Valdés, W. Krawietz, G. H. von Wright and R. Zimmerling (eds.), *Normative Systems in Legal and Moral Theory: Festschrift for Carlos E. Alchourrón and Eugenio Bulygin* (Berlin: Duncker & Humblot), 1997, 411–425.
- 'Sovereignty, Democracy and Subsidiarity', in M. Herberger, A.-W. Scheer and J. Zentes, *Entwicklungslinien in Recht und Wirtschaft* (Stuttgart: Schäffer-Poeschel), 247–254 (also published by Lothian Foundation Press in 1995; by Sakkoulas Publications in 1994; by Schäffer-Poeschel in 1997; in *Juridisk Tidskrift vid Stockholms Universitet* in 1994; and in *Rechtstheorie* in 1994).
- 'Estado de derecho y rule of law', in J. Thesing (ed.), *Estado de Derecho y Democracia* (Buenos Aires: Konrad Adenauer Stiftung), 101–117.
- 'Democracy, Subsidiarity and Citizenship in the "European Commonwealth"', *Law and Philosophy*, 16(4), 331–356 (also published by Kluwer Academic Publishing in 1997, in *Diritto Pubblico* in 1999, and with modification as chapter 9 in *Questioning Sovereignty*, 1999; delivered as the Annual European Lecture at Queen Mary and Westfield College, 11 November 1996).
- 'Law as Institutional Normative Order', *Rechtstheorie*, 28, 219–234 (contribution to special issue, ed. by A. Aarnio and W. Krawietz, 'New Approaches and Ways of Legal Thinking: The Otto Brusiin Lectures 1982–1997') (also published with modification as chapter 1 in *Questioning Sovereignty*, 1999).
- 'The Memory of Sir Walter Scott', *Bulletin of the Edinburgh Walter Scott Society*, 6–14.

- 'Speaking Volumes: J.M. MacCormick's *The Flag in the Wind*', *The Times Higher Education Supplement*, 26 December 1997, Issue 1312, 22.
- 'Scottish National Party', *Round&About*, April 6.
- 'Stop Grousing and Play Rugby', *Daily Record*, January 9.

1998

- *Laws, Institutions and Facts*, with H. de Jong (eds.), *Law and Philosophy*, 17(3), 213–345 (Special Issue).
- 'Sovereignty or Subsidiarity? Some Comments on Scottish Devolution', in A. Tomkins (ed.), *Devolution and the British Constitution* (London: Key Haven Publications), 1–18.
- 'Sovereign States and Vengeful Victims: The Problem of the Right to Punish', with D. Garland, in A. Ashworth and M. Wasik (eds.), *Fundamentals of Sentencing Theory: Essays in Honour of Andrew von Hirsch* (Oxford: Oxford University Press), 11–30.
- 'Weinberger, O', in E. Craig (ed.), *Routledge Encyclopaedia of Philosophy* (London: Routledge), 701–702.
- 'Villey, M', in E. Craig (ed.), *Routledge Encyclopaedia of Philosophy* (London: Routledge), 614–615.
- 'Savigny, F. K. von', in E. Craig (ed.), *Routledge Encyclopaedia of Philosophy* (London: Routledge), 482–483.
- 'Renner, K', in E. Craig (ed.), *Routledge Encyclopaedia of Philosophy* (London: Routledge), 267–268.
- 'Pound, R', in E. Craig (ed.), *Routledge Encyclopaedia of Philosophy* (London: Routledge), 609–610.
- 'Pothier, R. J.', in E. Craig (ed.), *Routledge Encyclopaedia of Philosophy* (London: Routledge), 608–609.
- 'Llewellyn, K. N.', in E. Craig (ed.), *Routledge Encyclopaedia of Philosophy* (London: Routledge), 661–662.
- 'Hohfeld, W. N.', in E. Craig (ed.), *Routledge Encyclopaedia of Philosophy* (London: Routledge), 476–477.
- 'Hart, H. L. A.', in E. Craig (ed.), *Routledge Encyclopaedia of Philosophy* (London: Routledge), 234–236.
- 'Frank, J', in E. Craig (ed.), *Routledge Encyclopaedia of Philosophy* (London: Routledge), 725–726.
- 'Legal Reasoning and Argumentation', in E. Craig (ed.), *Routledge Encyclopaedia of Philosophy* (London: Routledge), 525–531.
- 'Law, Philosophy of', with B. Brown, in E. Craig (ed.), *Routledge Encyclopaedia of Philosophy* (London: Routledge), 464–468.
- 'The English Constitution, the British State, and the Scottish Anomaly', *Scottish Affairs* (Special Issue: 'Understanding Constitutional Change' (delivered as

The British Academy Lecture 1997), 129–146 (also published in *Proceedings of the British Academy* in 1999, and with modification as chapter 4 in *Questioning Sovereignty*, 1999).

- 'The Dialectic of Might and Right: Legal Positivisms and Constitutional Change', *Current Legal Problems,* 51, 37–63 (special issue, ed. by M. D. A Freedman, 'Legal Theory at the End of the Millennium', Oxford: Oxford University Press) (also published with modification as chapter 5 in *Questioning Sovereignty*, 1999).
- 'Raimo Siltala, *A Theory of Precedent: From Analytical Positivism to A Post-Analytical Philosophy of Law*, Opponent's Review', *Oikeus,* 4, 424–432.
- 'Norms, Institutions and Institutional Facts', *Law and Philosophy,* 17(3), 301–345 (also published with modification as chapters 1 and 2 in *Institutions of Law*, 2007).
- 'After Sovereignty: Understanding Constitutional Change', *The King's College Law Journal,* 9, 20–38 (also published with modification as chapter 6 in *Questioning Sovereignty*, 1999).
- 'Precedent as a Source of Law', *Archiv für Rechts- und Sozialphilosophie,* 60, 177–185 (special issue ed. by E. Attwooll and P. Comanducci).
- 'The Significance of Precedent', *Acta Juridica* 174–187.
- 'Reasonableness and Objectivity', *Notre Dame Law Review,* 74(5), 1575–1603 (1998–1999) (also published with modification by Bruylant in 1984, and as chapter 9 of *Rhetoric and the Rule of Law*, 2005).
- 'The Scottish Parliament as Law-Maker: Laws for an Information Age?', *Law Librarian,* 29(3), 152–156 (presented as the Annual Lecture of the Scottish Group of the Society for Computers and Law, Edinburgh, 18 June 1998).
- 'Preface', with H. de Jong, *Law and Philosophy*, 17(3), 213.
- 'A Parliament Once Again?', *Times Literary Supplement*, 4976, 14 August 1998, 11–12.
- 'The Comparative Precedent Project of the Bielefelder Kreis. 1992–97', with Robert Summers, *Archiv für Rechts- und Sozialphilosophie/Archives for Philosophy of Law and Social Philosophy,* 84(1), 147–152.
- 'Risking Constitutional Collision in Europe?', *Oxford Journal of Legal Studies,* 18(3), 517–532 (review of D. Rossa Phelan, *Revolt or Revolution: The Constitutional Boundaries of the European Community*) (also published with modification as chapter 7 in *Questioning Sovereignty*, 1999).
- 'Jurisprudence, Democracy, and the Death of the Weimar Republic. Review of *Popular Sovereignty and the Crisis of German Constitutional Law* by P.C. Caldwell and *Legality & Legitimacy* by D. Dyzenhaus', *Texas Law Review,* 77(4), 1095–1106 (1998–1999).
- 'To "Ought" from "Is". Review of *The Disintegration of Natural Law: Aquinas to Finnis*, by P.C. Westerman', 4980 *Times Literary Supplement*, 11 September 1998, 26.
- 'Introduction', in A. Artosi, M. Atienza and H. Yoshino (eds.), *From Practical Reason to Legal Computer Science*. IVR 17th World Congress Bologna, 16–21 June, 1995, Proceedings (Bologna: CLUEB), 7–12.
- 'Time for a Rethink about Ferries', *Herald Scotland*, 10 July 1998.

- 'Independence has to be Transformed from Abstract Ideal to Concrete Proposal', *Herald Scotland*, 14 November 1998.
- 'Obituary: Allan Macartney', *The Independent*, 27 August 1998.
- 'Right of Reply: The SNP's constitutional affairs spokesman counters David Aaronovitch's attack on the Scots', *The Independent*, 4 September 1998.

1999

- *Questioning Sovereignty: Law, State and Nation in the European Commonwealth* (Oxford: Oxford University Press).
- 'Subsidiarity and Academic Governance', Speech delivered at the University of Iceland, 1 March 1999 (Edinburgh University Archives).
- 'Laws, Facts and Values' (ed.), *Law and Philosophy*, 18(5), 443–577 (Special Issue).
- 'My Philosophy of Law', in L. Wintgens (ed.), *The Law in Philosophical Perspective: My Philosophy of Law* (Dordrecht: Kluwer Academic Publishers), 121–145 (also published with modification as part of chapter 1 in *Questioning Sovereignty*, 1999).
- 'Nation and Nationalism', in R. Beiner (ed.), *Theorizing Nationalism* (Albany: SUNY Press), 189–204 (also published, in an earlier version, by the Scottish Academic Press, in 1979, and with modification as chapter 13 in *Legal Right and Social Democracy*, 1982).
- 'Does a Nation Need a State? Reflections on Liberal Nationalism', in E. Mortimer and R. Fine (eds.), *People, Nation and State: The Meaning of Ethnicity and Nationalism* (London: I.B. Tauris), 125–137.
- 'Rhetoric and the Rule of Law', in D. Dyzenhaus (ed.), *Recrafting the Rule of Law: the Limits of Legal Order* (Oxford: Hart Publishing), 163–177 (also published by the Philosophy Documentation Center in 2001, and with modification as chapter 2 of *Rhetoric and the Rule of Law*, 2005) (presented at the Perelman Symposium, 20th World Congress of Philosophy, Boston, 1998).
- 'Can Judges Make Mistakes?', in H. Jung and E. Neumann (eds.), *Rechtsbegründung–Rechtsbegründungen* (Baden-Baden: Nomos Verlaggeselsschaft), 76–89 (presented as the Annual Lecture of the Centre for Law and Society, University of Edinburgh, 1986) (also published with modification as chapter 13 in *Rhetoric and the Rule of Law*, 2005).
- 'Powers and Power-Conferring Norms', in S. Paulson (ed.), *Normativity and Norms: Critical Perspectives on Kelsenian Themes* (Oxford: Oxford University Press), 493–506 (an earlier and narrower version was presented at the 5th Siena Kelsen Symposium, June 1993) (also published with modification as chapter 9 in *Institutions of Law*, 2007).
- 'Decentralisation, Devolution and Confederal Independence', in E. Bort and R. Keat (eds.), *The Boundaries of Understanding* (Edinburgh: Edinburgh University Press), 197–208.

- 'The Impact of Information Technology on Legal Scholarship: Commentary' (comment on paper by R. Susskind), in T. Coppock (ed.), *Information Technology and Scholarship: Applications in the Humanities and Social Sciences* (Oxford: Oxford University Press), 186–188.
- 'The English Constitution, the British State, and the Scottish Anomaly', *Proceedings of the British Academy,* 101, 289–306 (also published in *Scottish Affairs* in 1998, and with modification as chapter 4 in *Questioning Sovereignty,* 1999).
- 'Institutions and Laws Again', *Texas Law Review,* 77(6), 1429–1441.
- 'Democracy and Subsidiarity', *Diritto Pubblico,* 1, 49–60 (also published by *Law and Philosophy* in 1997, by Kluwer Academic Publishing in 1997, and with modification as chapter 9 in *Questioning Sovereignty,* 1999).
- 'Editor's Preface', *Law and Philosophy,* 18(5), 443–445 (Special Issue on 'Laws, Facts and Values').
- 'Untitled [describing Adam Smith and John MacCormick]', *The Scottish Review,* 20, 62–64 (A contribution to a symposium on 'The Greatest Scot of the 20th Century and the Greatest Scot in History').
- 'Law Is the New World Order. Review of *Crimes Against Humanity,* by G. Robertson', *The Sunday Herald,* 15 August 1999, 9.
- Review of *Institutional Theory of Law* by Peter Morton', *Law Quarterly Review,* 1999, 145–148.
- 'Scotland and Europe Membership Would Continue', *Herald Scotland,* 1 June 1999.
- 'Negotiation on Several Fronts', *Herald Scotland,* 5 June 1999.
- 'Plight of Arran Aromatics', *Herald Scotland,* 17 June 1999.
- 'Action to End the 'Banana War'', *Herald Scotland,* 23 September 1999.

2000

- *Stands Scotland Where She Did? New Unions for Old in these Islands*, presented as the 6th John Maurice Kelly Memorial Lecture, 21 October 1999, Dublin: Faculty of Law, University College Dublin, 27 pages.
- 'Legality Without Legalism', with Z. Bańkowski, in W. Krawietz, R. S. Summers, O. Weinberger, and G. H. von Wright (eds.), *The Reasonable as Rational? On Legal Argumentation and Justification, Festschrift for Aulis Aarnio* (Berlin: Duncker & Humblot), 181–195.
- 'Ethical Positivism and the Practical Force of Legal Rules', in T. Campbell and J. Goldsworthy (eds.), *Judicial Power, Democracy and Legal Positivism* (Aldershot: Ashgate), 37–57.
- 'Wrongs and Duties', in M. Friedman, L. May, K. Parsons and J. Stiff (eds.), *Rights and Reason: Essays in Honour of Carl Wellman* (Dordrecht: Kluwer Academic Publishers), 139–155 (also published with modification as chapter 6 in *Institutions of Law,* 2007).

- 'Devolved Lands: 1. "Independence in Europe": A Liberal Road for the Scottish National Party', in J. Prest (ed.), *Balliol College Annual Record* 2000 (Oxford: Oxuniprint: Oxford University Press), 11–14.
- 'Is There a Constitutional Path to Scottish Independence?', *Parliamentary*, 53(4), *Affairs*, 721–736.
- 'Problems of Democracy and Subsidiarity', *European Public Law*, 6(4), 531–542 (presented as a lecture at the University of Hull on 11 December 1999).
- 'SNP on Europe', *The Sunday Herald*, Letter, 20 August 2000.
- 'SNP Follows Logic of Independence in Europe', *Herald Scotland*, 9 October 2000.
- 'Maximum Benefits of Glasgow's Grand Watercourse', *Herald Scotland*, Letter, 25 September 2000.
- 'The Republic and Religion', *The Guardian*, Letters, 9 December 2000.

2001

- *A Special Conception of Juvenile Justice: Kilbrandon's Legacy*, presented as the 5th Kilbrandon Child Care Lecture, University of Glasgow, 1 November 2001, Publisher unknown, Pamphlet held by Law and Europa Library, School of Law, University of Edinburgh, 27 pages.
- 'Can Europe Be Democratic?', Ledingham Chalmers Lecture, University of Aberdeen, 10 May 2001 (Edinburgh University Archives).
- 'De Iurisprudentia', in J. Cairns and O. Robinson (eds.), *Critical Studies in Ancient Law, Comparative Law and Legal History: Essays in Honour of Alan Watson* (Oxford: Hart Publishing), 79–82.
- 'Integration and Integrity in the Legal Reasoning of the European Court of Justice', with J. Bengotxea and L. Moral Soriano, in G. De Burca and J. H. H. Weiler (eds.), *The European Court of Justice*, Collected Courses of the Academy of European Law (Oxford: Oxford University Press), 43–86.
- 'Rhetoric and the Rule of Law', in D. M. Rasmussen (ed.), *Proceedings of the Twentieth World Congress of Philosophy* (Charlottesville: Philosophy Documentation Center), Vol. 11, 51–67 (also published by Hart Publishing in 1999).
- 'Some Observations about Sovereignty', in European Law Students' Association – International (ed.), *International Law as We Enter the 21st Century* (Berlin: Berlin Verlag Arno Spitz GmbH), 15–23.
- 'Foreword', in J. Moore and K. Munro, *Scottish Official Publications: An Introduction and Guide* (Edinburgh: The Stationary Office), vii–ix.
- 'On the Very Idea of a European Constitution: Jurisprudential Reflections from the European Parliament', *Juridisk Tidskrift vid Stockholms universitet*, 3, 529–541 (2001–2002) (presented as the Cassel lecture at the University of Stockholm on 1 June 2001).
- 'A Comment on the Governance Paper', in C. Joerges, Y. Meny and J. H. H. Weiler (eds.), *Symposium: Mountain or Molehill? A Critical Appraisal of the Commission*

White Paper on Governance, a contribution to the Jean Monnet Working Paper No.6/01.

- 'Inserting Safeguards in European Arrest Warrants', *The Scotsman*, 21 December 2001.

2002

- 'Untitled', in T. Devine and P. Logue (eds.), *Being Scottish: Personal Reflections on Scottish Identity Today* (Edinburgh: Edinburgh University Press), 152–154.
- 'Prólogo', with Z. Bańkowski, in L. Moral Soriano, *El Precedente Judicial* (Madrid: Marcial Pons), 9–10.
- 'On the Very Idea of Intellectual Property: An Essay according to the Institutionalist Theory of Law', *Intellectual Property Quarterly*, 3, 228–239 (presented as the SCRIPT Presidential Lecture, School of Law, University of Edinburgh, 11 February 2002) (also published with modification as parts of chapters 8 and 13 in *Institutions of Law*, 2007).
- 'EU Update on Legal Aid; Trade in Services; Single Market; Employment Law; Company Law; and a Note on the Convention on the Future of Europe', 1 December, *The Journal Online: The Members' Magazine of the Law Society of Scotland.*
- 'The Real Financial Priorities for MEPs', *Herald Scotland*, 16 September 2002.
- 'Scotland and the Future of Europe', *Herald Scotland*, 5 November 2002.
- 'A European Vote on Media Concentration', *Herald Scotland*, 21 November 2002.
- *Scotland in the European Parliament: A View of Scotland's Potential in Europe*, presented with I. Hudghton, 15 minute film, Edinburgh: Picture Perfect Production for the G/EFA Group in the European Parliament.
- *Why a European Parliament: A Guide to European Decision-Making*, presented with I. Hudghton, 15 minute film, Edinburgh: Picture Perfect Production for the G/EFA Group in the European Parliament.

2003

- *The New European Constitution: Legal and Philosophical Perspective* (Warszawa: Biuro Trybunału Konstytucyjnego) (originally presented as the Leon Petrażycki lecture, at the Polish Constitutional Tribunal, 11 June 2003, translated into Polish by W. Mleczko).
- *Law and Legal Interpretation*, with F. Atria (eds.) (Aldershot: Ashgate).
- 'Introduction', with F. Atria, in F. Atria and N. MacCormick (eds.), *Law and Legal Interpretation*, xi–xxxiii.
- 'Republicanism, Fletcher and Ferguson', in P. H. Scott (ed.), *The Saltoun Papers: Reflections on Andrew Fletcher* (Edinburgh: Saltire Society), 31–39.
- 'How to Have a Healthy Constitution? Reviewing Allott's *Health of Nations*', *Common Market Law Review*, 40(6), 1537–1549.
- 'Fishing Industry will be Key Election Issue', *The Scotsman*, 4 January 2003.

- 'SNP's reckoning on benefits of the EU', Letter, *The Scotsman*, 10 January 2003.
- 'SNP Not Behind the New EU Draft', *The Scotsman*, Letter, 14 February 2003.
- 'Open-Door Approach', *The Scotsman*, Letter, 20 February 2003.
- 'A Strengthened Definition of Subsidiarity', *The Scotsman*, 14 March 2003.
- 'Extension of Powers is Implicit in Scotland Act', *The Scotsman*, 25 April 2003.
- 'Europe...The Devil will be in the Detail', *The Scotsman*, 16 May 2013.
- 'First Step on the Road to Ruin for Scotland', *Scotland on Sunday (Supplement)*, 8 June 2003, 8.
- 'EU Constitution and Democracy', *The Times*, 11 July 2003.
- 'We Must Fly our Flag to Keep Funds', *The Scotsman*, 14 July 2003.
- 'Europe's Beleaguered Nations', *The Scotsman*, 12 December 2003 [A Review of C. Booker and R. North, *The Great Deception*.]
- 'Obituary: Archie Turnbull: Publisher whose scholarly press helped launch the Scottish renaissance', *The Guardian*, 8 April 2003.

2004

- *A Union of Its Own Kind? Reflections on the European Convention and the Proposed Constitution of the European Union*. Edinburgh: Neil MacCormick (personal publication), 40 pages.
- 'Questioning Post-Sovereignty', *European Law Review*, 29(6), 852–863.
- 'The European Constitutional Convention and the Stateless Nations', *International Relations*, 18(3), 331–344 (presented as the Inaugural Lecture marking the establishment of the Wales in Regional Europe (WiRE) project at the University of Wales, Aberystwyth, 3 November 2003).
- 'Doubts about the "Supreme Court" and Reflections on MacCormick v. Lord Advocate', *Juridical Review*, 3, 237–250.

2005

- *Rhetoric and the Rule of Law* (Oxford: Oxford University Press).
- *Who's Afraid of a European Constitution?* (Exeter: Imprint Academic).
- 'New Unions for Old', in W. L. Miller (ed.), *Anglo-Scottish Relations from 1900 to Devolution and Beyond*, Proceedings of the British Academy, Vol. 128 (Oxford: Oxford University Press), 249–255.
- 'Legislative Deliberation: Notes from the European Parliament', in L. Wintgens (ed.), *The Theory and Practice of Legislation: Essays on Legisprudence* (Aldershot: Ashgate), 285–296 (originally delivered as the Ledingham Chalmers Lecture, University of Aberdeen, 10 May 2001).
- 'The Sovereignty Issue in the EU Constitution', in M. C. Specchia and S. Suppa (eds.), *Quaderni del Dottorato* 2003 (Torino: Giappichelli Editore), 69–76 (presented at a workshop at Bari, 30 October 2003).

- 'Enduring Foundations', in W. Alexander (ed.), *Donald Dewar: Scotland's First Minister* (Edinburgh: Mainstream Publishing), 139–145.
- 'The European Constitutional Process: A Theoretical View', *Anales de la Cátedra Francisco Suárez*, 39, 289–313 (Special issue, 'Derecho y justicia en una sociedad global', ed. by M. E. Castillo and M.S. L López) (published earlier, in a non-authoritative version for the IVR Congress, in M. Scarmilla and M. Saavedra (eds.), *Law & Justice in a Global Society* (Spain: Anales de la Cátedra Francisco Suárez), 299–319 (and in Spanish at 275–297)).
- 'Adam Ferguson: How Civil Will Future Society Be?', in B. Shimshon (ed.), *Enlightenment Lectures* 2002 (Glasgow: Smith Institute), 17–24 (delivered on 25 February 2002).
- 'The Health of Nations and the Health of Europe', *The Cambridge Yearbook of European Legal Studies*, 7, 1–16 (presented as the Mackenzie Stuart Lecture at the Faculty of Law, University of Cambridge, 11 November 2004).
- 'Taking Responsibility Seriously', *Edinburgh Law Review*, 9(1), 168–175 (review essay of *Responsibility in Law and Morality* by P. Cane) (also published with modification as parts of chapters 6, 12, and 13 in *Institutions of Law*, 2007).
- 'Hohfeld, W. N.', in E. Craig (ed.), *The Shorter Routledge Encyclopaedia of Philosophy* (London: Routledge), 388–389 [Reprint from 1998].
- 'Hart, H. L. A.', in E. Craig (ed.), *The Shorter Routledge Encyclopaedia of Philosophy* (London: Routledge), 333 [Reprint from 1998].
- 'Philosophy of Law', with B. Brown, in E. Craig (ed.), *The Shorter Routledge Encyclopaedia of Philosophy* (London: Routledge), 546–550 [Reprint from 1998].
- 'Review of *A Life of H.L.A. Hart: The Nightmare and the Noble Dream*, by Nicola Lacey', *Social & Legal Studies*, 14(3), 433–435.

2006

- *The European Union and the Idea of a Perfect Commonwealth*, presented as the 2006 Hume Lecture on 1 March 2006, Hume Occasional Paper No. 68, Edinburgh: The David Hume Institute, 29 pages.
- 'Particulars and Universals' in Z. Bańkowski and J. MacLean (eds.), *The Universal and the Particular in Legal Reasoning* (Aldershot: Ashgate), 1–20.
- 'An Attempted Response', in Z. Bańkowski and J. MacLean (eds.), *The Universal and the Particular in Legal Reasoning* (Aldershot: Ashgate), 251–262.
- 'Does Law Really Matter?', in M. Leskiewicz (ed.), *Australian Legal Philosophy Students Association Annual Publication* (Brisbane: U. Q. Vanguard), 5–23 (presented as the Inaugural Lecture of the Australian Legal Philosophy Students Association, Brisbane, 2005) (also published with modification as part of chapter 4 in *Institutions of Law*, 2007).
- 'Review of *John Smith: A Life* by M. Stuart', *Scottish Affairs*, 56, 142–145.

- 'Entrevista a Neil MacCormick', with M. Atienza, translated into Spanish by M. Atienza, *Doxa: Cuadernos de filosofía del derecho*, 29, 479–489.
- 'Founding Principles', *The Scotsman*, Letter, 15 August 2006.

2007

- *Institutions of Law: An Essay in Legal Theory* (Oxford: Oxford University Press).
- 'Why Law Makes No Claims', in G. Pavlakos (ed.), *Law, Rights and Discourse: The Legal Philosophy of Robert Alexy* (Oxford: Hart Publishing), 59–68.
- 'Sir Neil MacCormick', in M. E. J. Nielson (ed.), *Legal Philosophy: 5 Questions* (New York: Automatic/VIP Press), 171–186.
- 'A Common Approach to Crime? Observations on the European Arrest Warrant and the Democratic Deficit' in H. Müller-Dietz, E. Müller, K-L. Kunz, H. Radtke, G. Britz, C. Momsen and H. Koriath (eds.), *Festschrift für Heike Jung zum 65. Geburtstag am 23. April 2007* (Baden-Baden: Nomos), 535–541.
- 'Judicial Independence: Who Cares?', *Proceedings of the British Academy*, 151, 195–212 (presented as the 2006 British Academy Law Lecture).
- 'On Public Law and the Law of Nature and Nations', *Edinburgh Law Review*, 11(2), 149–161.
- 'The Law School of the University of Edinburgh: Tercentenary Address held in the McEwan Hall, February 2007', *University of Edinburgh Journal*, 53(2), 84–87.
- 'Ronald Dworkin: Mr Justice. Review of *Exploring Law's Empire*, by S. Hershovitz (ed.), *Is Democracy Possible Here?*, by R. Dworkin; *Justice in Robes*, by R. Dworkin; and *Ronald Dworkin*, by A. Ripstein (ed.)', *Times Literary Supplement*, 5462, 5 December 2007, 3–5.
- 'SNP Minority', *The Scotsman*, Letter, 5 November 2007.
- 'Legality of a referendum on the future of the Union and the right of the people to decide', *The Herald (Glasgow)*, Letter, 10 May 2007.

2008

- *Practical Reason in Law and Morality* (Oxford: Oxford University Press).
- *H.L.A. Hart*, 2nd ed. (Stanford: Stanford University Press).
- 'MacCormick on MacCormick', in A. J. Menéndez and J. E. Fossum (eds.), *The Post-Sovereign Constellation: Law and Democracy in Neil D.* [sic] *MacCormick's Legal and Political Theory*, Report 04/08 (Oslo: Arena), 11–20 (also published in 2011 by Springer).
- 'The Convention and Its Constitution: All a Great Mistake?', in H. Petersen, A. L. Kjær, H. Krunke and M. R. Madsen (eds.), *Paradoxes of European Legal Integration* (Aldershot: Ashgate), 17–27.
- 'Church of Scotland', in P. Cane and J. Conaghan (eds.), *The New Oxford Companion to Law* (Oxford: Oxford University Press), 128.

- 'Revolution', in P. Cane and J. Conaghan (eds.), *The New Oxford Companion to Law* (Oxford: Oxford University Press), 1020–1021.
- 'Scottish Parliament', in P. Cane and J. Conaghan (eds.), *The New Oxford Companion to Law* (Oxford: Oxford University Press), 1059–1060.
- 'Treaty of Union', in P. Cane and J. Conaghan (eds.), *The New Oxford Companion to Law* (Oxford: Oxford University Press), 1192.
- 'Introduction', in J. MacCormick, *The Flag in the Wind: The Story of the National Movement in Scotland* (Edinburgh: Berlinn), ix–xvii.
- 'A Reply to Comments on *Rhetoric and the Rule of Law*', *Northern Ireland Legal Quarterly*, 59(1), 43–48.
- 'Review of *Our Knowledge of the Law*, by G. Pavlakos and *Law as a Moral Idea*, by N. Simmonds', *Edinburgh Law Review*, 12(1), 150–153.

2009

- 'Stair and the Natural Law Tradition: Still Relevant?', in H. MacQueen (ed.), *Miscellany Six* (Edinburgh: The Stair Society), 1–10 (presented as a lecture at the Annual General Meeting of the Stair Society, Edinburgh, 3 November 2007).
- 'Concluding for Institutionalism', in M. Del Mar and Z. Bańkowski (eds.), *Law as Institutional Normative Order* (Surrey: Ashgate), 187–200.
- '1968 and All That', in *Balliol College Annual Record*, 13–15.

2010

- 'Sovereignty and After', in H. Kalmo and Q. Skinner (eds.), *Sovereignty in Fragments: The Past, Present and Future of a Contested Concept* (Cambridge: Cambridge University Press), 151–168.
- 'Legal Reasoning and Legal Theory', in N. Kuenssberg (ed.), *Argument Amongst Friends: Twenty Five Years of Sceptical Enquiry* (Edinburgh: The David Hume Institute), 28–34 [Republication of Introduction from *Legal Reasoning and Legal Theory*, 1978/1994].

2011

- 'MacCormick on MacCormick', in A. J. Menéndez and J. E. Fossum (eds.), *Law and Democracy in Neil MacCormick's Legal and Political Theory: The Post-Sovereign Constellation* (Dordrecht: Springer), 17–24 (also published by Arena in 2008).
- 'Direito, Interpretação e Razoabilidade', in R. Porto Macedo Jr (ed.), *Direito e Interpretação: Racionalidade e Instituições* (São Paulo: Editora Saraiva), 31–62.

GENERAL BIBLIOGRAPHY

NB. This bibliography focuses on the academic resources used in this book. It does not list all the newspaper or student periodical sources, or other sources available in the archives (such as letters), which are referenced in the footnotes.

Ambar, S. (2016), *Malcolm X at Oxford Union: Racial Politics in a Global Era* (Oxford: Oxford University Press).

Anscombe, G. E. M. (1958), 'Brute Facts', *Analysis*, 18, 69–72.

Anscombe, G. E. M. (1958), 'Modern Moral Philosophy', *Philosophy*, 33(124), 1–19.

Armstrong, K. (2010), *Governing Social Inclusion: Europeanization through Policy Coordination* (Oxford: Oxford University Press).

Arnold, C. (1979), 'Institutional Aspects of Law', *Modern Law Review*, 42(6), 667–682.

Ascherson, N. (2002), *Stone Voices: The Search for Scotland* (London: Granta).

Atria, F. (2002), *On Law and Legal Reasoning* (Oxford: Hart).

Avbelj, M. and J. Komárek (eds.) (2012), *Constitutional Pluralism in the EU and Beyond* (Oxford: Hart).

Baier, A. (1991), *A Progress of Sentiments: Reflections on Hume's Treatise* (Cambridge, MA: Harvard University Press).

Bańkowski, Z. (1999), 'The Journey of the European Ideal', in K. Reid, S. C. J. J. Kortmann, D. J. Hayton, N. E. D. Faber, and J. W. A. Biemans (eds.), *Towards an EU Directive on Protected Funds* (Dordrecht: Kluwer), 149–172.

Bańkowski, Z. and E. Christodoulidis (1998), 'The European Union as an Essentially Contested Project', *European Law Journal*, 4(4), 341–355.

Bańkowski, Z. and J. MacLean (eds.) (2006), *The Universal and the Particular in Legal Reasoning* (Surrey: Ashgate).

Bańkowski, Z., I. White, and U. Hahn (eds.) (1995), *Informatics and the Foundations of Legal Reasoning* (Dordrecht: Kluwer Academic Publishers).

Barrow, G. W. S. (1965), *Robert Bruce and the Community of the Realm of Scotland* (Berkeley: University of California Press).

Bengoetxea, J. (1993), *The Legal Reasoning of the European Court of Justice: Towards a European Jurisprudence* (Oxford: Clarendon Press).

Bengoetxea, J. (2020), 'Legal Theory and Sociology of Law', in J. Přibáň (ed.), *Research Handbook on the Sociology of Law* (Cheltenham: Edward Elgar), 7–18.

Bentham, J. (1996), *An Introduction to the Principles of Morals and Legislation*, J. H. Burns and H. L. A. Hart (eds.) (Oxford: Clarendon Press).

Bogle, S. (2023), 'Morality before the Enlightenment: An Interpretation of Viscount Stair's Natural Law Theory, c. 1681', *Journal of Scottish Philosophy*, 21(2), 189–209.

Bohlin, H. (2014), 'Effects on the Mind as Objects of Reasoning: A Perspectivist Reading of the Reason-Passion Relation in Hume's Ethics', *Hume Studies*, 40(1), 29–51.

Boucher, D. (2015), 'The Scottish Contribution to British Idealism and the Reception of Hegel', in G. Graham (ed.), *Scottish Philosophy in the 19th and 20th Centuries* (Oxford: Oxford University Press), 154–181.

Bourne, A. K. (2006), 'Bringing Europe Closer to the Citizen? Regions, Stateless Nations and the European Convention', *Regional and Federal Studies*, 16(1), 1–19.

Bryson, G. (1945), *Man and Society: The Scottish Inquiry of the Eighteenth Century* (Princeton: Princeton University Press).

Bulmer, W. E. (2011), *A Model Constitution for Scotland: Making Democracy Work in an Independent State* (Edinburgh: Luath Press).

Bulmer, W. E. (2011), 'An Analysis of the Scottish National Party's Draft Constitution for Scotland', *Parliamentary Affairs*, 64(4), 674–693.

Bulmer, W. E. (2018), *Constituting Scotland: The Scottish National Movement and the Westminster Model* (Edinburgh: Edinburgh University Press).

Burazin, L., K. E. Himma, and C. Roversi (eds.) (2018), *Law as an Artifact* (Oxford: Oxford University Press).

Burns, J. H. (2009), 'Scottish Kantians: An Exploration', *Journal of Scottish Philosophy*, 7(2), 115–131.

Cairns, J. (1984), 'Institutional Writings in Scotland Reconsidered', *Journal of Legal History*, 4(3), 76–117.

Cairns, J. (1991), 'Rhetoric, Language, and Roman Law: Legal Education and Improvement in Eighteenth-Century Scotland', *Law and History Review*, 9(1), 31–58.

Cairns, J. (1996), 'Importing our Lawyers from Holland: Netherlands' Influences on Scots Law and Lawyers in the Eighteenth Century', in G. G. Simpson (ed.), *Scotland and the Low Countries, 1124–1994* (East Linton: Tuckwell Press), 136–153.

Cairns, J. (2001), 'The Moveable Text of Mackenzie: Bibliographical Problems for the Scottish Concept of Institutional Writing', in J. W. Cairns and O. F. Robinson (eds.), *Critical Studies in Ancient Law, Comparative Law and Legal History* (Oxford: Hart), 235–248.

Cairns, J. (2019), 'Legal Theory in the Scottish Enlightenment', in A. Broadie and C. Smith (eds.), *The Cambridge Companion to the Scottish Enlightenment* (Cambridge: Cambridge University Press), 213–233.

Campbell, C. A. (1948), *Moral Intuition and Self-Realisation* (London: British Academy).

Campbell, C. M. (1974), 'Legal Thought and Juristic Values', *British Journal of Law and Society*, 1(1), 13–30.

Campbell, T. D. (1971), *Adam Smith's Science of Morals* (London: Routledge).

Campbell, T. D. (1996), *The Legal Theory of Ethical Positivism* (London: Routledge).

Canihac, H. (2021), 'Law and Virtue in a Post-Sovereign "Commonwealth": Neil MacCormick and the Political Theory of Constitutional Pluralism', *Journal of International Political Theory*, 17(3), 531–552.

Carty, T. and A. McCall Smith (1978), *Power and Manoeuvrability* (Edinburgh: Q Press).

Colvin, E. (1978), 'The Sociology of Secondary Rules', *The University of Toronto Law Journal*, 28(2), 195–214.

Condren, C., S. Gaukroger, and I. Hunter (eds.) (2009), *The Philosopher in Early Modern Europe: The Nature of a Contested Identity* (Cambridge: Cambridge University Press).

Craig, C. (1989), 'Scotland 10 Years On', *Radical Scotland*, 37, 8–11.

Cram, L. (2009), 'Identity and European Integration: Diversity as a Source of Integration', *Nations and Nationalism*, 15(1), 109–128.

Cruz, J. B. (2008), 'The Legacy of the Maastricht-Urteil and the Pluralist Movement', *European Law Journal*, 14(4), 389–422.

Culver, K. and M. Giudice (2010), *Legality's Borders: An Essay in General Jurisprudence* (Oxford: Oxford University Press).

Dardanelli, P. (2003), 'Ideology and Rationality: The Europeanisation of the Scottish National Party', *Österreichische Zeitschrift für Politikwissenschaft*, 32(3), 271–284.

Dauwen, G. and M. Vanhaelewyn (eds.) (2006), *European Free Alliance: Voice of the peoples of Europe, The First 25 Years (1981–2006)* (Antwerp: European Free Alliance).

Davie, G. (2010) [1961], *The Democratic Intellect: Scotland and Her Universities in the Nineteenth Century* (Edinburgh: Edinburgh University Press).

Davies, G. and M. Avbelj (eds.) (2018), *Research Handbook on Legal Pluralism and EU Law* (Cheltenham: Edward Elgar).

De Groot, M. and M. O. Vrielink (1998), 'Legal Theory and Sociological Facts', *Law and Philosophy*, 17(3), 251–270.

Del Mar, M. (2014), 'Learning from W. D. Lamont: Towards a Science of Situated Judgement', in R. Anderson, J. Chalmers, and J. MacLeod (eds.), *Festschrift in Honour of the Tercentenary of the Regius Chair in Law, Glasgow Law School* (Glasgow: Avizandum), 105–124.

Del Mar, M. and Z. Bańkowski (eds.) (2009), *Law as Institutional Normative Order* (Surrey: Ashgate).

Devine, T. (2006), *The Scottish Nation 1707–2000* (London: Penguin).

Dicey, A. V. (1959) [1885], *Introduction to the Study of the Law of the Constitution* (Basingstoke: The Macmillan Press).

Dicey, A. V. and R. Rait (1920), *Thoughts on the Union between England and Scotland* (London: Macmillan and Co.).

Dickson, J. and P. Eleftheriadis (2012), 'Introduction: The Puzzles of European Union Law', in J. Dickson and P. Eleftheriadis (eds.), *Philosophical Foundations of European Union Law* (Oxford: Oxford University Press), 1–22.

Dickson, J. and P. Eleftheriadis (eds.) (2012), *Philosophical Foundations of European Union Law* (Oxford: Oxford University Press).

Douglas, D. (1996), *At the Helm: The Life and Times of Dr. Robert D. McIntyre* (Buckie: NPFI Publications).

Douglas-Scott, S. (2023), *Brexit, Union and Disunion: The Evolution of British Constitutional Unsettlement* (Cambridge: Cambridge University Press).

Downie, R. and E. Telfer (1969), *Respect for Persons* (London: Routledge).

Duclos, N. (2017), 'The 1970s: A "Paradoxical Decade" for the Scottish National Party', *Revue Française de Civilisation Britannique* [Online], 22 (Hors série), available at: http://journals.openedition.org/rfcb/1712 (last accessed 18 September 2024), 1–18.

Dudley Edwards, O. (1989), *A Claim of Right for Scotland* (Edinburgh: Polygon).

Dudziak, M. (2000), *Cold War Civil Rights: Race and the Image of American Democracy* (Princeton: Princeton University Press).

Duff, A. (1980), 'Legal Obligation and the Moral Nature of Law', *Juridical Review*, 25, 61–87.

Dworkin, R. (1984), 'A Reply by Ronald Dworkin', in M. Cohen (eds.), *Ronald Dworkin and Contemporary Jurisprudence* (London: Duckworth), 247–300.

Dworkin, R. (1986), *Law's Empire* (Cambridge, MA: Harvard University Press).

Dyer, M. (2003), 'A Nationalist in the Churchillian Sense: John MacCormick, The Paisley By-Election of 18th February 1948, Home Rule, and the Crisis in Scottish Liberalism', *Parliamentary History*, 22(3), 285–307.

Eden, K. (2022), *Rhetorical Renaissance* (Chicago: Chicago University Press).

Edgeworth, B. (1989), 'H. L. A. Hart, Legal Positivism and Post-War British Labourism', *University of Western Australia Law Review*, 19(2), 275–300.

Edward, D. and J. Bengoetxea (2011), 'The Status and Rights of Sub-state Entities in the Constitutional Order of the European Union', in A. Arnull, C. Barnard, M. Dougan, and E. Spaventa (eds.), *A Constitutional Order of States? Essays in Honour of Alan Dashwood* (Oxford: Hart), 25–38.

Ehrenberg, K. (2016), *The Functions of Law* (Oxford: Oxford University Press).

Eleftheriadis, P. (2010), 'Pluralism and Integrity', *Ratio Juris*, 23(3), 365–389.

Farmer, L. (2001), 'Under the Shadow of Parliamentary House: The Strange Case of Legal Nationalism', in L. Farmer and S. Veitch (eds.), *The State of Scots Law* (London: LexisNexis), 151–164.

Fergusson, D. (2013), 'Scottish Idealism', in N. Boyle, L. Disley, and K. Ameriks (eds.), *The Impact of Idealism: The Legacy of Post-Kantian German Thought* (Cambridge: Cambridge University Press), 270–296.

Finlay, R. (1992), '"For or Against?" Scottish Nationalists and the British Empire 1919–30', *Scottish Historical Review*, 71, 184–206.

Finlay, R. (1994), *Independent and Free: Scottish Politics and the Origins of the Scottish National Party 1918–1945* (Edinburgh: John Donald Publishers Ltd).

Finlay, R. (2020), 'The Declaration of Arbroath and Scottish Constitutionalist Thought in the Twentieth Century', in K. P. Müller (ed.), *Scotland and Arbroath 1320–2020: 700 Years of Fighting for Freedom, Sovereignty, and Independence* (Berlin: Peter Lang), 307–324.

Finlay, R. (2022), *Scottish Nationalism: History, Ideology and the Question of Independence* (London: Bloomsbury).

Flynn, T. (2019), *The Triangular Constitution: Constitutional Pluralism in Ireland, the EU and the ECHR* (Oxford: Hart).

Freeden, M. (1978), *The New Liberalism: An Ideology of Social Reform* (Oxford: Clarendon).

Ghosh, P. (2024), 'Mill Before Liberalism, Parts I and II', *History of European Ideas*, 50(5), 785–836.

Gildea, R. and J. Mark (2013), 'Introduction', in R. Gildea, J. Mark, and A. Warring (eds.), *Europe's 1968: Voices of Revolt* (Oxford: Oxford University Press), 1–18.

Graham, G. (2015), 'Scottish Philosophy after the Enlightenment', in G. Graham (ed.), *Scottish Philosophy in the 19th and 20th Centuries* (Oxford: Oxford University Press), 1–22.

Graham, G. (2015), 'The Integrity of Scottish Philosophy', in G. Graham (ed.), *Scottish Philosophy in the 19th and 20th Centuries* (Oxford: Oxford University Press), 303–322.

Graham, G. (2022), *Scottish Philosophy after the Enlightenment* (Edinburgh: Edinburgh University Press).

Gunn, D. (2013), 'Neil M. Gunn: The Inverness Years' in A. McCleery (ed.), *Nation and Nationalism* (Dunbeath: Whittles Publishing), 33–38.

Guyer, P. (2015), 'The Scottish Reception of Kant: Common Sense and Idealism', in G. Graham (ed.), *Scottish Philosophy in the 19th and 20th Centuries* (Oxford: Oxford University Press), 118–153.

Haakonssen, K. (2008), 'The History of Eighteenth-Century Philosophy: History or Philosophy?' in K. Haakonssen (ed.), *The Cambridge History of Eighteenth-Century Philosophy* (Cambridge: Cambridge University Press), 1–25.

Hailsham, L. (1979), 'The Nation and the Constitution' in C. MacLean (ed.), *The Crown and the Thistle* (Edinburgh: Scottish Academic Press), 71–80.

Halpin, A. and N. Roughan (eds.) (2017), *In Pursuit of Pluralist Jurisprudence* (Cambridge: Cambridge University Press).

Hames, S. (2019), *The Literary Politics of Scottish Devolution: Voice, Class, Nation* (Edinburgh: Edinburgh University Press).

Hamilton, D. (1990), *A Touch of Treason* (Scotland: Neil Wilson Publishing).

Hamilton, D. (1991), *The Taking of the Stone of Destiny* (Moffat: Lochar Publishing).

Hanham, H. J. (1969), *Scottish Nationalism* (London: Faber and Faber).

Happala, T. (2016), *Political Rhetoric in the Oxford and Cambridge Unions, 1830–1870* (Cham: Palgrave).

Hare, R. M. (1952), *The Language of Morals* (Oxford: Oxford University Press).

Hare, R. M. (1955), 'Ethics and Politics', *The Listener*, 54, 593–594; 55, 651–652.

Hare, R. M. (1963), *Freedom and Reason* (Oxford: Clarendon Press).

Hare, R. M. (1973), 'Principles', *Proceedings of the Aristotelian Society*, 73(1), 1–18.

Hare, R. M. (1981), *Moral Thinking* (Oxford: Oxford University Press).

Hare, R. M. (2002), 'A Philosophical Autobiography', *Utilitas*, 14(3), 269–305.

Harris, J. (1957), 'Kant's Examples of the First Formulation of the Categorical Imperative', *The Philosophical Quarterly*, 7(26), 50–62.

Harris, J. (1994), 'The Arts and Social Sciences: 1939–1970', in B. Harrison (ed.), *The History of the University of Oxford: Volume VIII: The Twentieth Century* (Oxford: Oxford University Press), 217–250.

Harrison, B. (1994), 'Government and Administration 1914–1964', in B. Harrison (ed.), *The History of the University of Oxford: Volume VIII: The Twentieth Century* (Oxford: Oxford University Press), 683–719.

Hart, H. L. A. (1949), 'The Ascription of Responsibility and Rights', *Proceedings of the Aristotelian Society*, 49, 171–194.

Hart, H. L. A. (1953), 'Philosophy of Law and Jurisprudence in Britain (1945–1952)', *American Journal of Comparative Law*, 2(3), 355–364.

Hart, H. L. A. (1955), 'Are There Any Natural Rights?', *The Philosophical Review*, 64(2), 175–191.

Hart, H. L. A. (1963), *Law, Liberty, and Morality* (Stanford: Stanford University Press).

Hart, H. L. A. (1967), 'Social Solidarity and the Enforcement of Morality', *University of Chicago Law Review*, 35(1), 1–13.

Hart, H. L. A. (1972), 'Bentham on Legal Powers', *Yale Law Journal*, 81(5), 799–822.

Hart, H. L. A. (1982), *Essays on Bentham: Jurisprudence and Political Philosophy* (Oxford: Oxford University Press).

Hart, H. L. A. (1983) [1970], 'Jhering's Heaven of Concepts and Modern Analytical Jurisprudence', in H. L. A. Hart (ed.), *Essays in Jurisprudence and Philosophy* (Oxford: Clarendon Press), 265–277.

Hart, H. L. A. (2012) [1961], *The Concept of Law* (Oxford: Clarendon Press).

Hart, J. (1998), *Ask Me No More: An Autobiography* (London: Peter Halban).

Hart Committee Report (1969), *Report of the Committee on Relations with Junior Members, Supplement N. 7 to the University Gazette*, 99, May 1969.Hartogh, den G. (2002), *Mutual Expectations: A Conventionalist Theory of Law* (Dordrecht: Kluwer).

Harvie, C. (1976), *The Lights of Liberalism: University Liberals and the Challenge of Democracy 1868–86* (London: Allen Lane).

Harvie, C. (2004), *Scotland and Nationalism: Scottish Society and Politics 1707 to the Present*, 4th ed. (London: Routledge).

Hassan, G. (2009), 'The Making of the Modern SNP: From Protest to Power', in G. Hassan (ed.), *The Modern SNP: From Protest to Power* (Edinburgh: Edinburgh University Press), 1–18.

Hassan, G. (2009), *The Modern SNP: From Protest to Power* (Edinburgh: Edinburgh University Press).

Hawkins, K. (1997), 'Prologue: Donald Harris and the Early Years of the Oxford Centre', in K Hawkins (ed.), *The Human Face of Law: Essays in Honour of Donald Harris* (Oxford: Oxford University Press), 1–17.

Hepburn, E. (2009), 'Degrees of Independence: SNP Thinking in an International Context', in G Hassan (ed.), *The Modern SNP: From Protest to Power* (Edinburgh: Edinburgh University Press), 190–203.

Herman, B. (1985), 'The Practice of Moral Judgement', *The Journal of Philosophy*, 82(8), 414–463.

Hildebrand, C. (2023), 'Feeling, Cognition, and the Eighteenth-Century Context of Kantian Sympathy', *British Journal for the History of Philosophy*, 31(5), 974–1004.

Hochstrasser, T. (2000), *Natural Law Theories in the Early Enlightenment* (Cambridge: Cambridge University Press).

Hodgson, D. H. (1967), *Consequences of Utilitarianism* (Oxford: Clarendon Press).

Hollis, C. (1965), *The Oxford Union* (London: Evans Brothers Limited).

Honoré, T. (1994), 'Herbert Lionel Adolphus Hart 1907–1992', *Proceedings of the British Academy*, 84, 295–321.

Horsburgh, H. J. N. (1962), 'Prudence', *Aristotelian Society Supplementary Volume*, 36(1), 51–76.

Hulsen, P. (1998), 'Back to Basics: A Theory of the Emergence of Institutional Facts', *Law and Philosophy*, 17(3), 271–299.

Hunt, A. (1986), 'Jurisprudence, Philosophy and Legal Education – Against Foundationalism: A Response to Neil MacCormick', *Legal Studies*, 6(3), 292–302.

Hunt, J. (2010), 'Devolution and Differentiation: Regional Variation in EU Law', *Legal Studies*, 30(3), 421–441.

Hutson, L. (2023), *England's Insular Imagining: The Elizabethan Erasure of Scotland* (Oxford: Oxford University Press).

Ichijo, A. (2004), *Scottish Nationalism and the Idea of Europe: Concepts of Europe and the Nation* (London: Routledge).

Jackson, B. (2020), *The Case for Scottish Independence: A History of Nationalist Political Thought in Modern Scotland* (Cambridge: Cambridge University Press).

Jackson, B. (2022), 'From British Labourism to Scottish Nationalism: Jim Sillars's Journey', *Scottish Affairs*, 31(2), 233–239.

Jackson, R. (1942), 'Practical Reason', *Philosophy*, 17(68), 351–367.

Jaklic, K. (2014), *Constitutional Pluralism in the EU* (Oxford: Oxford University Press).

Jay, D. (1963), *Socialism in the New Society* (New York: St Martin's Press).

Jones, J. (2005), *Balliol College: A History* (Oxford: Oxford University Press).

Kant, I. (1997) [1785], *Groundwork of the Metaphysics of Morals*, ed. M. Gregor (Cambridge: Cambridge University Press).

Keane, E. P. H. and P. Robson (eds.) (2023), *The Ian Willock Collection on Law and Justice in the Twenty-First Century* (Vancouver: Fairleigh Dickinson University Press).

Kellas, J. (1973), *The Scottish Political System* (Cambridge: Cambridge University Press).

Kelsen, H. (1967), *Pure Theory of Law*, trans. M. Knight (Berkeley: University of California Press).

Kemp, J. (1958), 'Kant's Examples of the Categorical Imperative', *The Philosophical Quarterly*, 8(30), 63–71.

Kennedy, G. (ed.) (1976), *The Radical Approach: Papers on an Independent Scotland* (Edinburgh: Palingenesis Press).

Kenny, A. (1997), *A Life in Oxford* (London: John Murray).

Kerrigan, J. (2008), *Archipelagic English: Literature, History, and Politics 1603–1707* (Oxford: Oxford University Press).

Kidd, C. (2004), 'Sovereignty and the Scottish Constitution', *Juridical Review*, 3, 225–236.

Kidd, C. (2008), *Union and Unionisms: Political Thought in Scotland, 1500–2000* (Cambridge: Cambridge University Press).

Kidd, C. (2013), *From Jacobitism to the SNP: The Crown, the Union, and the Scottish Question*, The Stenton Lecture, 21 November 2013, University of Reading; From Jacobitism to the SNP, available at: st-andrews.ac.uk (last accessed 18 September 2024).

Kidd, C. (2014), 'The Phillipsonian Enlightenment', *Modern Intellectual History*, 11(1), 175–190.

Kidd, C. (Forthcoming), *Twilight of the Dons* (Princeton: Princeton University Press).

Kidd, C. and M. Petrie (2016), 'The Independence Referendum in Historical and Political Context', in A. McHarg, T. Mullen, A. Page, and N. Walker (eds.), *The Scottish Independence Referendum: Constitutional and Political Implications* (Oxford: Oxford University Press), 29–49.

Krisch, N. (2010), *Beyond Constitutionalism: The Pluralist Structure of Postnational Law* (Oxford: Oxford University Press).

Krisch, N. (2011), 'Who Is Afraid of Radical Pluralism? Legal Order and Political Stability in the Postnational Space', *Ratio Juris*, 24, 386–412.

La Torre, M. (2010), 'A Flag in the Wind: In Memoriam Professor Sir Donald Neil MacCormick (1941–2009)', *Rechtstheorie*, 41(2), 277–284.

La Torre, M. (2010), *Law as Institution* (Dordrecht: Springer).

Lacey, N. (2004), *The Nightmare and the Noble Dream: A Life of H. L. A. Hart* (Oxford: Oxford University Press).

Lagerspetz, E. (1995), *The Opposite Mirrors* (Dordrecht: Kluwer).

Lamont, W. D. (1934), *Introduction to Green's Moral Philosophy* (London: George, Allen and Unwin).

Lamont, W. D. (1935), 'Nationalism and the International Ideal', *Philosophy*, 10(39), 289–299.

Lamont, W. D. (1946), *The Principles of Moral Judgement* (Clarendon: Oxford University Press).

Lamont, W. D. (1955), *The Value Judgement* (Edinburgh: Edinburgh University Press).

Lamont, W. D. (1981), *Law and the Moral Order* (Aberdeen: Aberdeen University Press).

Levitt, I. (1998), 'Britain, the Scottish Covenant Movement and Devolution, 1946–60', *Scottish Affairs*, 22, 33–57.

Little, G. (2014), 'A Flag in the Wind: *MacCormick v Lord Advocate*' in J Grant and E Sutherland (eds.), *Scots Law Tales* (Edinburgh: Edinburgh University Press), 23–44.

Llewellyn, K. (1934), 'The Constitution as Institution', *Columbia Law Review*, 34(1), 1–40.

Loughlin, M. (2003), 'Ten Tenets of Sovereignty', in N Walker (ed.), *Sovereignty in Transition* (Oxford: Hart), 55–86.

Loughlin, M. (2014), 'Constitutional Pluralism: An Oxymoron?', *Global Constitutionalism*, 3(1), 9–30.

Loughlin, M. and S. Tierney (2018), 'The Shibboleth of Sovereignty', *Modern Law Review*, 81(6), 989–1016.

Lynch, P. (1994), *From Versailles to Maastricht: Nationalist and regionalist parties and European integration.* PhD thesis, London School of Economics and Political Science, available at: https://etheses.lse.ac.uk/1314/ (last accessed 19 September 2024).

Lynch, P. (2009), 'From Social Democracy Back to No Ideology: The Scottish National Party and Ideological Change in a Multi-Level Electoral Setting', *Regional and Federal Studies*, 19, 619–637.

Lynch, P. (2013), *SNP: The History of the Scottish National Party* (Cardiff: Welsh Academic Press).

Lyons, D. (1965), *Forms and Limits of Utilitarianism* (Oxford: Oxford University Press).

MacCormick, J. M. (1943), *The Scottish Convention* (Glasgow: The Scottish Convention).

MacCormick, J. M. (2008) [1955], *The Flag in the Wind: The Story of the National Movement in Scotland* (Edinburgh: Birlinn).

Macdonald, C. M. M. (2009), '"To Form Citizens" Scottish Students, Governance and Politics, 1884–1948', *History of Education*, 38(3), 383–402.

Maclagan, W. G. (1960), 'Respect for Persons', *Philosophy*, 35(134), 193–217.

MacNeill, D. H. (1943), *The Scottish Constitution* (Glasgow: The Scottish National Party).

MacNeill, D. H. (1947), *The Scottish Realm: An Approach to the Political and Constitutional History of Scotland* (Glasgow: A. J. Donaldson).

MacQueen, H. (2005), 'Legal Nationalism: Lord Cooper: Legal Nationalism, Legal History and Comparative Law', *Edinburgh Law Review*, 9, 395–406.

MacQueen, H. (2012), 'A Post-Positivist Outlook from the Thistle', in N. Walker (ed.), *MacCormick's Scotland* (Edinburgh: Edinburgh University Press), 3–24.

MacQueen, H. (2013), 'Alan Ferguson Rodger 1944–2011', *Biographical Memoirs of Fellows of the British Academy*, XII, 361–401.

MacQueen, H. (2013), 'Public Law, Private Law, and National Identity', in C. Mac Amhlaigh, C. Michelon, and N. Walker (eds.), *After Public Law* (Oxford: Oxford University Press), 168–198.

Maduro, M., K. Tuori, and S. Sankari (eds.) (2014), *Transnational Law: Rethinking European Law and Legal Thinking* (Cambridge: Cambridge University Press).

Manning, S. (2002), *Fragments of Union: Making Connections in Scottish and American Writing* (Basingstoke: Palgrave).

Marmor, A. (2023), *Foundations of Institutional Reality* (Oxford: Oxford University Press).

Marr, A. (2013), *The Battle for Scotland* (London: Penguin).

Maxwell, S. (2009), 'Social Justice and the SNP', in G. Hassan (ed.), *The Modern SNP: From Protest to Power* (Edinburgh: Edinburgh University Press), 120–134.

McCabe, H. (2021), *John Stuart Mill, Socialist* (Montreal: McGill-Queen's University Press).

McHarg, A. (2020), 'The Declaration of Arbroath and Scots Law', in K. P. Müller (ed.), *Scotland and Arbroath 1320–2020: 700 Years of Fighting for Freedom, Sovereignty, and Independence* (Berlin: Peter Lang), 423–442.

McLean, B. (2005), *Getting It Together: The History of the Campaign for a Scottish Assembly / Parliament 1980–1999* (Edinburgh: Luath Press).

McLean, I. (2020), 'Understanding the Union', in M. Keating (ed.), *The Oxford Handbook of Scottish Politics* (Oxford: Oxford University Press), 118–136.

Mehta, V. (1962), *Fly and the Fly-Bottle, Encounters with British Intellectuals* (Boston: Little Brown & Co).

Mendelson, M. (2002), *Many Sides: A Protagorean Approach to the Theory, Practice and Pedagogy of Argument* (Dordrecht: Springer).

Menéndez, A. J. and E. Fossum (eds.) (2011), *Law and Democracy in Neil MacCormick's Legal and Political Theory: The Post-Sovereign Constellation* (Dordrecht: Springer).

Michell, J., L. Bennie, and R. Johns (2012), *The Scottish National Party: Transition to Power* (Oxford: Oxford University Press).

Mill, J. S. (1985) [1859], *On Liberty* (London: Penguin).

Miller, M., J. Rodger, and O. Dudley Edwards (2010), *Tartan Pimps: Gordon Brown, Margaret Thatcher, and the New Scotland* (Glasgow: Argyll Publishing).

Mitchell, J. (1990), 'Factions, Tendencies and Consensus in the SNP in the 1980's', in *Scottish Government Yearbook* (Edinburgh: Unit for the Study of Government in Scotland, University of Edinburgh), 49–61.

Mitchell, J. (1996), *Strategies for Self-Government: The Campaigns for a Scottish Parliament* (Edinburgh: Polygon).

Mitchell, J. (2000), 'From National Identity to Nationalism, 1945–1999', in H. T. Dickinson and M. Lynch (eds.), *The Challenge to Westminster: Sovereignty, Devolution and Independence* (East Lothian: Tuckwell Press), 154–164.

Mitchell, J. (2009), 'From Breakthrough to Mainstream: The Politics of Potential and Blackmail', in G. Hassan (ed.), *The Modern SNP: From Protest to Power* (Edinburgh: Edinburgh University Press), 31–41.

Mitchell, J. (2015), 'Review of Paula Somerville, *Through the Maelstrom*', *Scottish Affairs*, 24(1), 114–116.

Mitchell, J. D. B. (1964) (2nd edition in 1968), *Constitutional Law* (Edinburgh: Green and Son Ltd).

Moore, J. and M. Silverthorne (1995), 'Protestant Theologies, Limited Sovereignties: Natural Law and Conditions of Union in the German Empire, the Netherlands, and Great Britain', in J. Robertson (ed.), *Union for Empire: Political Thought and the British Union of 1707* (Cambridge: Cambridge University Press), 171–197.

Morton, T. (1998), *An Institutional Theory of Law: Keeping Law in Its Place* (Oxford: Clarendon).

Moyn, S. (2023), *Liberalism against Itself: Cold War Intellectuals and the Making of Our Times* (New Haven: Yale University Press).

Mulcahy, L. (2020), 'Remembering Donald Harris', *Socio-Legal Studies Newsletter*, 92, 9–10.

Munro, C. (2005), *Studies in Constitutional Law* (London: Butterworths).

Page, A. (2020), 'The Scottish Constitution', in M. Keating (ed.), *The Oxford Handbook of Scottish Politics* (Oxford: Oxford University Press), 137–155.

Palonen, K. (2019), *Parliamentary Thinking: Procedure, Rhetoric and Time* (Cham: Palgrave).

Paterson, L. (2015), 'George Davie and the Democratic Intellect', in G. Graham (ed.), *Scottish Philosophy in the 19th and 20th Centuries* (Oxford: Oxford University Press), 236–269.

Paton, H. J. (1968), *The Claim of Scotland* (London: Allen and Unwin).

Paton, H. J. (1971) [1947], *The Categorical Imperative: A Study in Kant's Moral Philosophy* (Philadelphia: University of Pennsylvania Press).

Pennington, D. (2005), 'John Edward Christopher Hill', *Proceedings of the British Academy*, 130, 23–49.

Pentland, G. (2016), 'Douglas Young', in J. Mitchell and G. Hassan (eds.), *Scottish National Party Leaders* (London: Biteback Publishers), 145–164.

Perelman, C. (1963), *The Idea of Justice and the Problem of Argument* (New York: Humanities Press).

Perelman, C. (1967), *Justice* (New York: Random House).

Petrie, M. (2016), 'John MacCormick', in J. Mitchell and G. Hassan (eds.), *Scottish National Party Leaders* (London: Biteback Publishers), 46–63.

Petrie, M. (2018), 'Anti-Socialism, Liberalism, Individualism: Rethinking the Realignment of Scottish Politics 1945–1970', *Transactions of the Royal Historical Society*, 28, 197–217.

Phelan, R. D. (1997), *Revolt or Revolution? The Constitutional Boundaries of the European Community* (London: Round Hall).

Phillips, M. (2023), *The Liberalism Trap: John Stuart Mill and Customs of Interpretation* (Oxford: Oxford University Press).

Phillipson, N. (1976), 'Lawyers, Landowners and the Civic Leadership of Post-Union Scotland', in N. MacCormick (ed.), *Lawyers in Their Social Setting* (Edinburgh: Green and Son), 171–194.

Phillipson, N. (1990), *The Scottish Whigs and the Reform of the Court of Session 1785–1830* (Edinburgh: The Stair Society).

Phillipson, N. and R. Mitchison (1970), *Scotland in the Age of Improvement* (Edinburgh: Edinburgh University Press).

Pittock, M. (2013), *The Road to Independence: Scotland in the Balance* (London: Reaktion).

Pittock, M. (2022), *Scotland: The Global History* (New Haven: Yale University Press).

Porter, L. (2010), 'The Cinematic and Historic Weight of "Stone of Destiny"', *Studies in Popular Culture*, 33(1), 53–77.

Postema, G. (2004), 'Melody and Law's Mindfulness of Time', *Ratio Juris*, 17(2), 203–226.

Power, W. (1943), 'Foreword' to John MacCormick, *The Scottish Convention* (Glasgow: Scottish Convention).

Přibáň, J. (2015), *Sovereignty in a Post-Sovereign Society: A Systems Theory of European Constitutionalism* (London: Routledge).

Price, A. W. (2004), 'R. M. Hare', *Proceedings of the British Academy*, 124, 117–137.

Raphael, D. (1947), *The Moral Sense* (Oxford: Oxford University Press).

Raphael, D. (1956), 'Linguistic Performances and Descriptive Meaning', *Mind*, 65(1), 516–521.

Raphael, D. (1956), 'The Consequences of Actions', *Aristotelian Society Supplementary Volume*, 30(1), 91–119.

Raphael, D. (1970), *Problems of Political Philosophy* (London: Pall Mall Press).

Raphael, D. (1975), 'The Standard of Morals', *Proceedings of the Aristotelian Society*, 75(1), 1–12E.

Rasmussen, D. (2014), *The Pragmatic Enlightenment: Recovering the Liberalism of Hume, Smith, Montesquieu, and Voltaire* (Cambridge: Cambridge University Press).

Rawlings, R. (2013), 'Introduction: Sovereignty in Question', in R. Rawlings, P. Leyland, and A. Young (eds.), *Sovereignty and the Law: Domestic, European, and International Perspectives* (Oxford: Oxford University Press), 1–17.

Rawlings, R., P. Leyland, and A. Young (eds.) (2013), *Sovereignty and the Law: Domestic, European, and International Perspectives* (Oxford: Oxford University Press).

Raz, J. (1980), *The Concept of a Legal System* (Oxford: Clarendon Press).

Reid, L. (1972), 'The Judge as Law Maker', *The Journal of Public Teachers of the Law*, 12, 22–29.

Richter, M. (1964), *The Politics of Conscience: T. H. Green and His Age* (London: Wiedenfeld and Nicholson).

Robertson, J. (1995), 'Elusive Sovereignty: The Course of the Union Debate in Scotland 1698–1707', in J. Robertson (ed.), *Union for Empire: Political Thought and the British Union of 1707* (Cambridge: Cambridge University Press), 198–227.

Rodger, A. F. (1969), 'Molina, Stair and the jus quaesitum tertio', *Juridical Review*, 14, 34–44.

Ross, H. (2001), *Law as a Social Institution* (Oxford: Hart).

Ross, I. S. (1972), *Lord Kames and the Scotland of His Day* (Oxford: Oxford University Press).

Ross, W. D. (1954), *Kant's Ethical Theory: A Commentary on the* Grundlegung zur Metaphysik der Sitten (Oxford: Oxford University Press).

Rudden, B. (1979), 'Juridical Consequences', *Juridical Review*, 24, 193–201.

Ruiter, D. W. P. (1993), *Institutional Legal Facts: Legal Powers and Their Effects* (Dordrecht: Kluwer).

Saunders, R. (2018), *Yes to Europe! The 1975 Referendum and Seventies Britain* (Cambridge: Cambridge University Press).

Scarcello, O. (2023), *Radical Constitutional Pluralism in Europe* (London: Routledge).

Schauer, F. (2009), 'Institutions and the Concept of Law: A Reply to Ronald Dworkin (with some help from Neil MacCormick)', in M. Del Mar and Z. Bańkowski (eds.), *Law as Institutional Normative Order* (Surrey: Ashgate), 35–44.

Schneider, L. (1967), *The Scottish Moralists on Human Nature and Society* (Chicago: Chicago University Press).

Scott, D. (2012), 'Neil MacCormick: Public Intellectual', in N. Walker (ed.), *MacCormick's Scotland* (Edinburgh: Edinburgh University Press), 205–219.

Scott, J. (2012), 'Stateless Nations in the European Union: Two Cheers and Not Three', in N. Walker (ed.), *MacCormick's Scotland* (Edinburgh: Edinburgh University Press), 191–202.

Searle, J. R. (1964), 'How to Derive "Ought" from "Is"', *Philosophical Review*, 73, 43–58.

Searle, J. R. (1969), *Speech Acts* (Cambridge: Cambridge University Press).

Selznick, P. (1976), 'Social Advocacy and the Legal Profession in the USA', in N. MacCormick (ed.), *Lawyers in their Social Setting* (Edinburgh: Green and Son), 63–76.

Simpson, A. W. B. (2011), *Reflections on* The Concept of Law (Oxford: Oxford University Press).

Sloane, T. O. (1993), 'Rhetorical Education', in H. Plett (ed.), *Renaissance Rhetoric* (Berlin: Walter de Gruyter), 163–178.

Smith, T. B. (1957), 'The Union of 1707 as Fundamental Law', *Public Law*, 99–121.

Somerville, P. (2013), *Through the Maelstrom: A History of the Scottish National Party, 1945–1967* (Stirling: Scots Independent).

Squibbs, R. (2014), *Urban Enlightenment and the Eighteenth-Century Periodical Essay: Transatlantic Retrospects* (London: Palgrave).

Stair, V. (1981) [1693], *The Institutions of the Law of Scotland*, ed. D. Walker (Edinburgh: Edinburgh University Press).

Stein, P. (1957), 'Legal Thought in the Eighteenth Century', *Juridical Review*, 1–20.

Stone, J. (1946), *The Province and Function of Law* (Sydney: Maitland Publications).

Stone, J. (1966), *Social Dimensions of Law and Justice* (Stanford: Stanford University Press).

Storrar, W. (2012), 'Scotland's Meridian: A Memoir of Neil MacCormick in the Scottish Public Sphere', in N. Walker (ed.), *MacCormick's Scotland* (Edinburgh: Edinburgh University Press), 220–230.

Summers, R. S. (1963), 'Professor H. L. A. Hart's Concept of Law', *Duke Law Journal* 4, 629–670.

Summers, R. S. (1978), 'Two Types of Substantive Reasons: The Core of a Theory of Common Law Justification', *Cornell Law Review*, 63, 707–788.

Summers, R. S. (1995), 'H. L. A. Hart's "The Concept of Law": Estimations, Reflections, and a Personal Memorial', *Journal of Legal Education*, 45(4), 587–596.

Taylor, W. (1954), *Scot Free: A Book of Gael Warnings* (London: Max Reinhardt Publishing).

Thane, P. (2024), *The Rise and Fall of the British Welfare State: From Poverty in 1900 to Poverty in 2023* (London: Bloomsbury).

Thomas, K. (1994), 'College Life: 1945–1970', in B. Harrison (ed.), *The History of the University of Oxford: Volume VIII: The Twentieth Century* (Oxford: Oxford University Press), 189–215.

Thomson, J. A. K. (1936), 'Winged Words', *The Classical Quarterly*, 30(1), 1–3.

Tierney, S. (2023), 'Scotland in the Union', in P. Cane and H. Kumarasingham (eds.), *The Cambridge Constitutional History of the United Kingdom*, Vol II (Cambridge: Cambridge University Press), 422–442.

Tomkins, A. (2004), 'The Constitutional Law in 'MacCormick v Lord Advocate', *Juridical Review*, 3, 213–224.

Torrance, D. (2020), *'Standing up for Scotland': Nationalist Unionism and Scottish Party Politics, 1884–2014* (Edinburgh: Edinburgh University Press).

Travers, M. (2001), 'Sociology of Law in Britain', *American Sociologist*, 32, 26–40.

Troper, M. (2010), 'The Survival of Sovereignty', in H. Kalmo and Q. Skinner (eds.), *Sovereignty in Fragments: The Past, Present and Future of a Contested Concept* (Cambridge: Cambridge University Press), 132–150.

Tuck, S. (2014), *The Night Malcolm X Spoke at the Oxford Union* (Berkeley: University of California Press).

Tur, R. H. S. (1983), 'Taking Rights Left?', *Philosophical Books*, 24(4), 193–204.

Twining, W. (2012), 'Donald Neil MacCormick 1941–2009', *Biographical Memoirs of Fellows of the British Academy*, 11, 449–471.

Twining, W. (2019), *Jurist in Context: A Memoir* (Cambridge: Cambridge University Press).

Unit for the Study of Government in Scotland (1989), *What Scotland Wants: Ten Years On*, Proceedings of a One Day Conference on 25 February 1989.

Valeria Tarditi, V. (2010), 'The Scottish National Party's Changing Attitude Towards the European Union', *EPERN Working Paper No 22/SEI Working Paper No 112*, 1–48, available at: www.sussex.ac.uk/webteam/gateway/file.php?name=epern-working-paper-22.pdf&site=266 (last accessed 19 September 2024).

Waldow, A. (2020), *Experience Embodied: Early Modern Accounts of the Human Place in Nature* (Oxford: Oxford University Press).

Waldron, J. (2011), 'Legal Judgement and Moral Reservation', in A. J. Menéndez and E. Fossum (eds.), *Law and Democracy in Neil MacCormick's Legal and Political Theory: The Post-Sovereign Constellation* (Dordrecht: Springer), 107–132.

Walker, N. (2002), 'The Idea of Constitutional Pluralism', *Modern Law Review*, 65(3), 317–359.

Walker, N. (2003), 'Late Sovereignty in the European Union', in N. Walker (ed.), *Sovereignty in Transition* (Oxford: Hart), 3–32.

Walker, N. (ed.) (2003), *Sovereignty in Transition* (Oxford: Hart).

Walker, N. (2012), 'Scottish Nationalism for and against the Union State', in N. Walker (ed.), *MacCormick's Scotland* (Edinburgh: Edinburgh University Press), 163–190.

Walker, N. (2016), 'Constitutional Pluralism Revisited', *European Law Journal*, 22(3), 333–355.

Walters, M. D. (2022), *A. V. Dicey and the Common Law Constitutional Tradition* (Cambridge: Cambridge University Press).

Waluchow, W. J. (1994), *Inclusive Legal Positivism* (Oxford: Clarendon Press).

Wasserstrom, R. (1963), *The Judicial Decision: Toward a Theory of Legal Justification* (Stanford: Stanford University Press).

Weiler, J. (1991), 'The Transformation of Europe', *Yale Law Journal*, 100(8), 2403–2483.

Weinberger, O. (1991) [1987], *Law, Institution and Legal Politics: Fundamental Problems of Legal Theory and Social Philosophy* (Dordrecht: Kluwer).

Whately, C. (2007), *The Scots and the Union* (Edinburgh: Edinburgh University Press).

Wheatley, N. (2023), *The Life and Death of States: Central Europe and the Transformation of Modern Sovereignty* (Princeton: Princeton University Press).

White, R. (2018), *Dundee Law 1865–1967: The Development of a Law School in a Time of Change* (Dundee: Book Printers Scotland).

Wilkinson, M. (2019), 'Beyond the Post-Sovereign State? The Past, Present, and Future of Constitutional Pluralism', *Cambridge Yearbook of European Legal Studies*, 21, 6–23.

Williams, S. (1981), *Politics Is for the People* (London: Penguin).

Willock, I. D. (1974), 'Getting on with Sociologists', *British Journal of Law and Society*, 1(1), 3–12.

Wilson, G. (2009), *The SNP: The Turbulent Years 1960–90* (Stirling: Scots Independent).

Wittig, K. (1958) [1978], *The Scottish Tradition in Literature* (Edinburgh: The Mercat Press).

Wolfe, B. (1973), *Scotland Lives: The Quest for Independence* (Edinburgh: Reprographia).

Wright, A. (2009), 'The SNP and UK Relations', in G Hassan (ed.), *The Modern SNP: From Protest to Power* (Edinburgh: Edinburgh University Press), 177–189.

Young, D. (1942), *Free-Minded Scot: The Trial of Douglas C. C. Young in the High Court of Edinburgh* (Glasgow: Scottish Secretariat).

INDEX

For EU product safety concerns, contact us at Calle de José Abascal, 56–1°,
28003 Madrid, Spain or eugpsr@cambridge.org.

www.ingramcontent.com/pod-product-compliance
Ingram Content Group UK Ltd.
Pitfield, Milton Keynes, MK11 3LW, UK
UKHW021413080126
466781UK00018B/344
* 9 7 8 1 0 0 9 6 0 9 8 8 3 *